I0606385

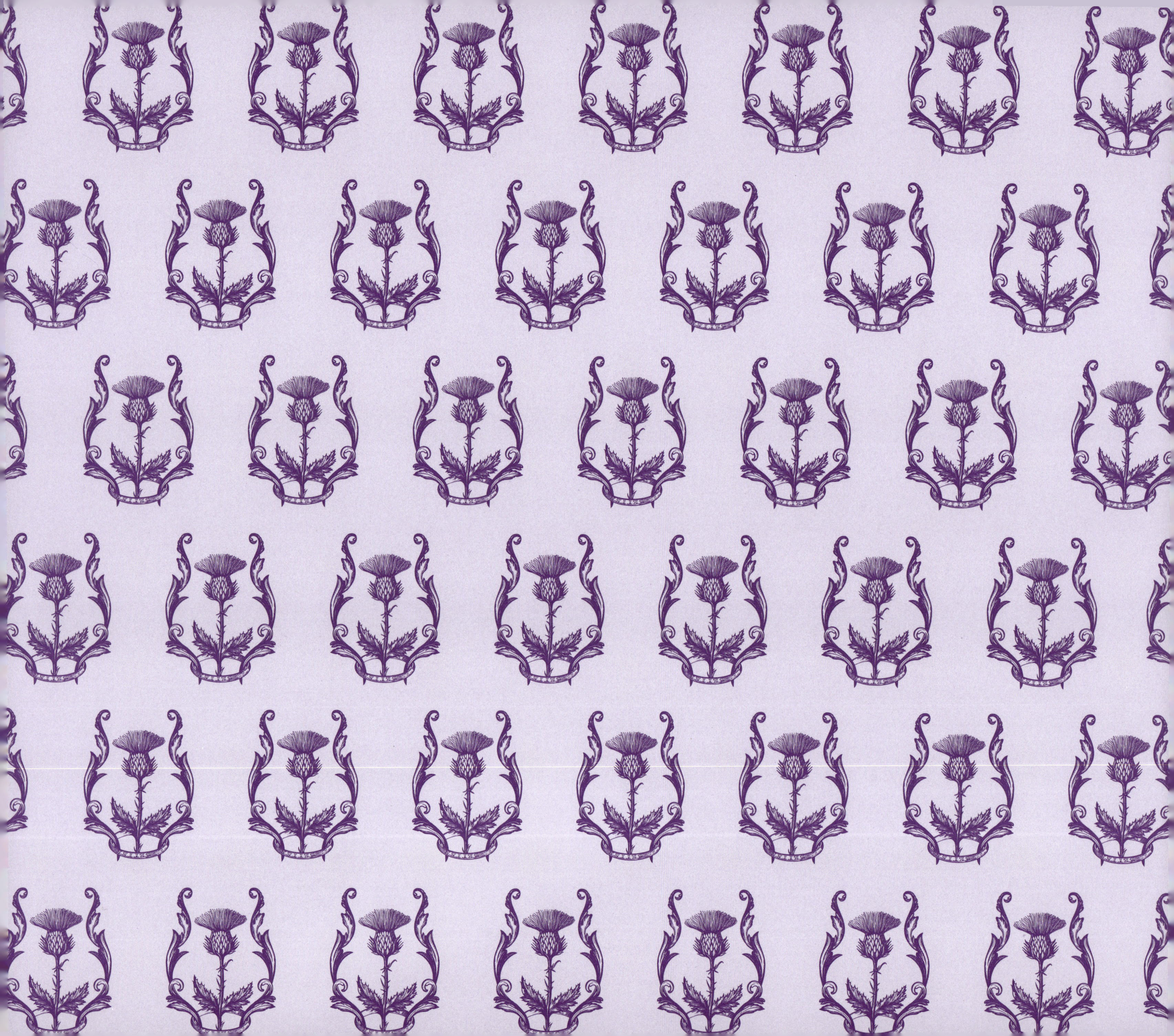

Our *Hearts* Are in SCOTLAND

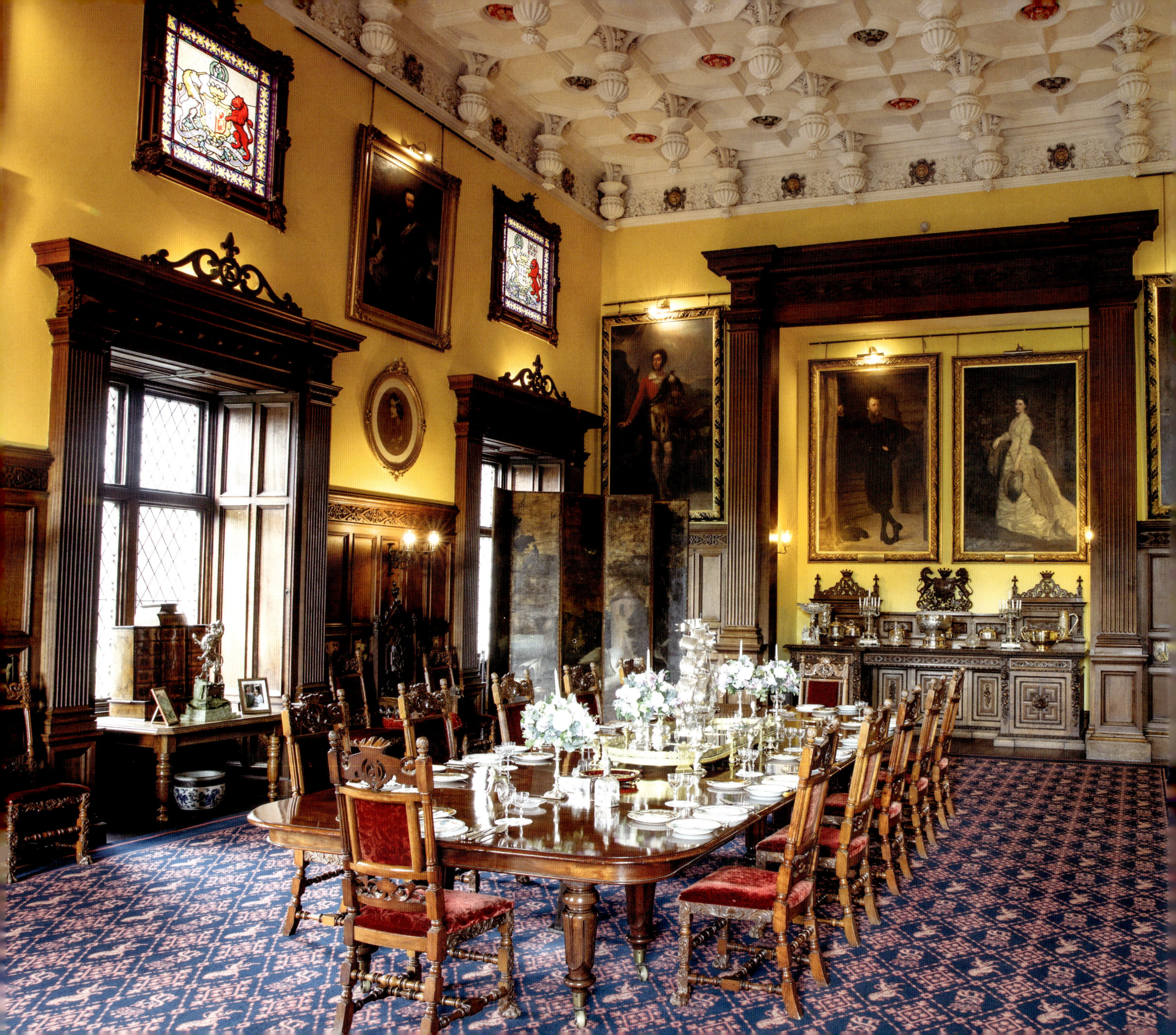

Our *Hearts* Are in SCOTLAND

MELISSA LESTER

83 press

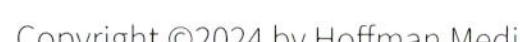

Hoffman Media
2323 2nd Avenue North
Birmingham, AL 35203
hoffmanmedia.com

ISBN # 979-8-9899185-3-9
Printed in China

83 press

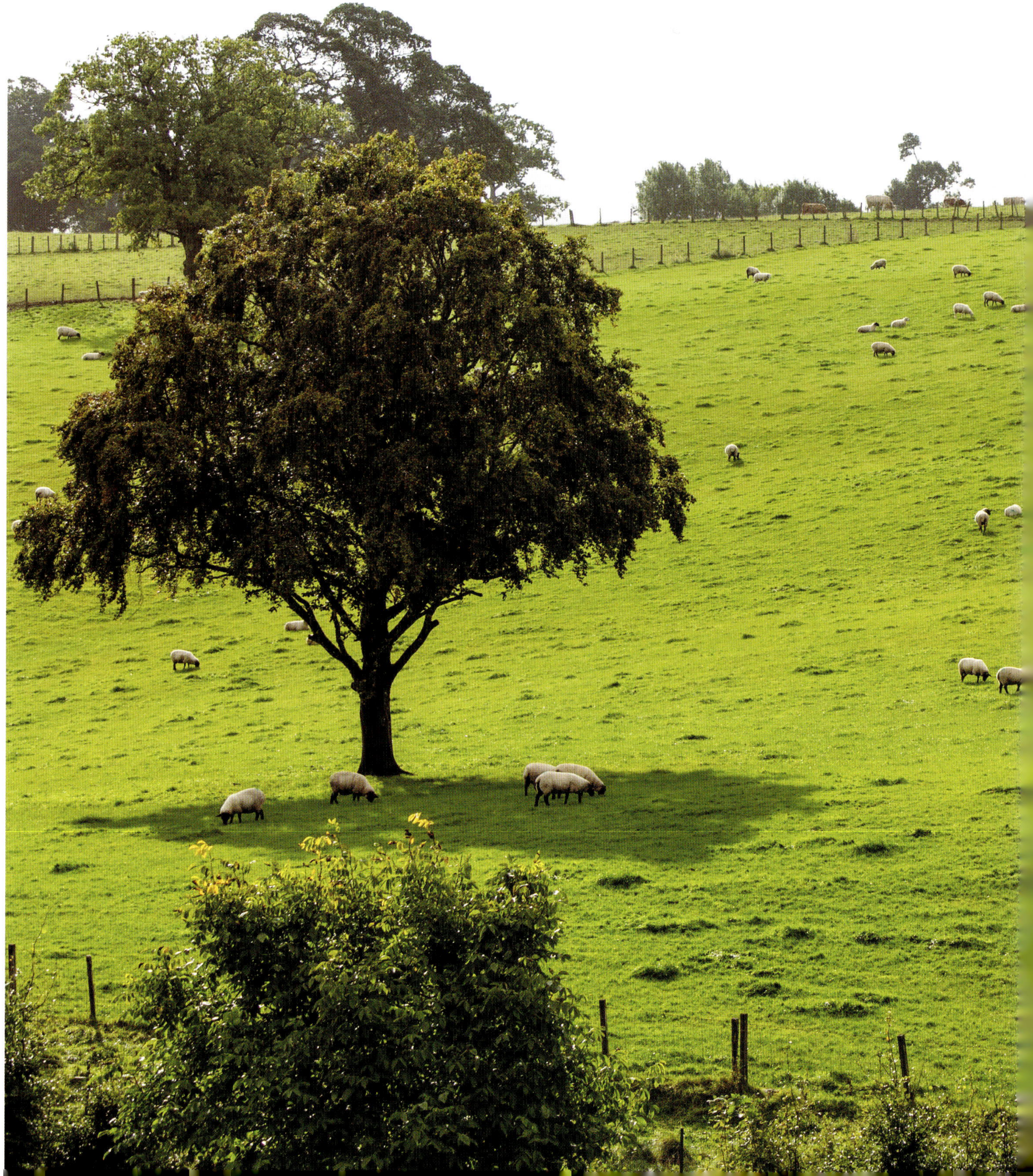

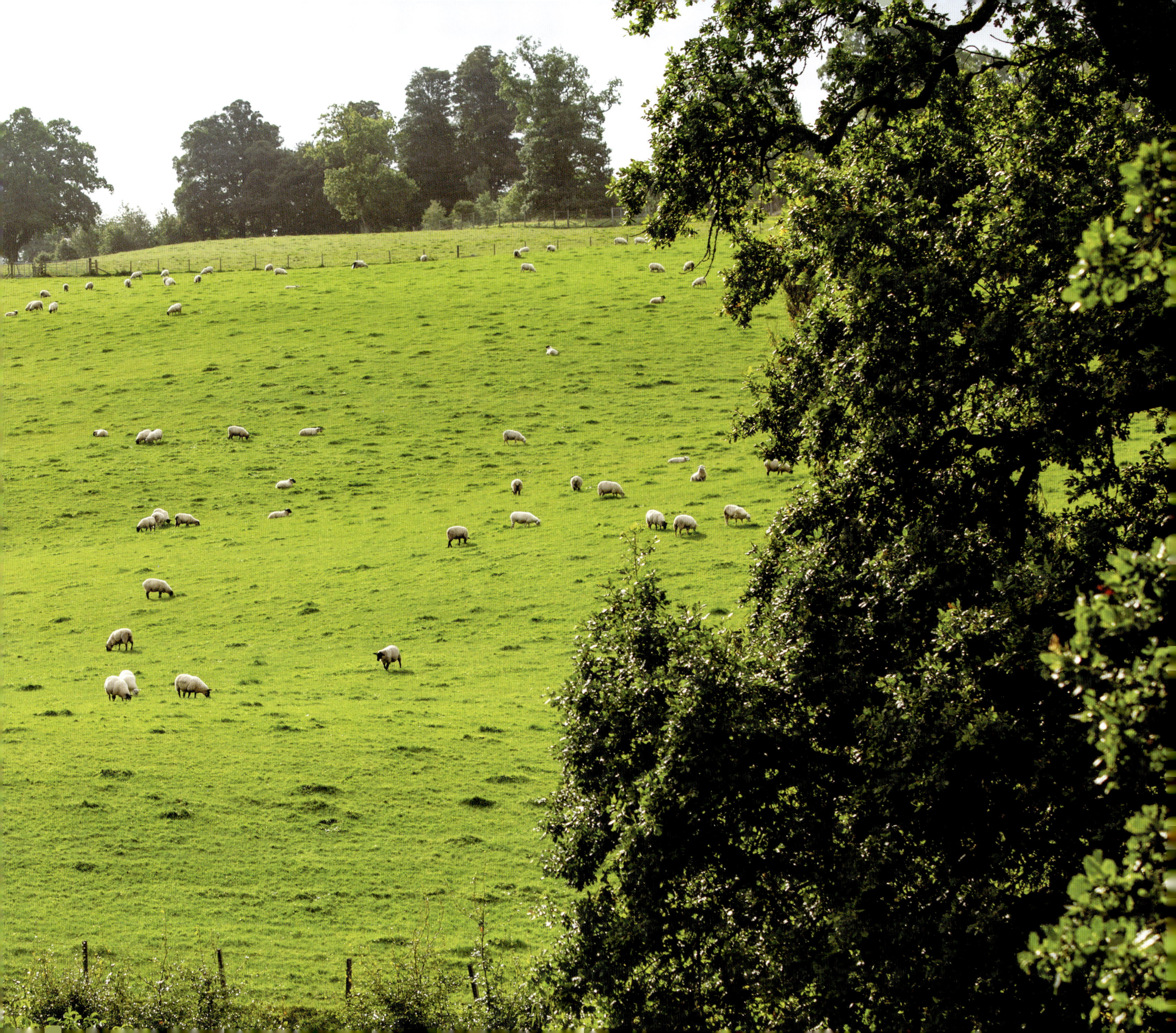

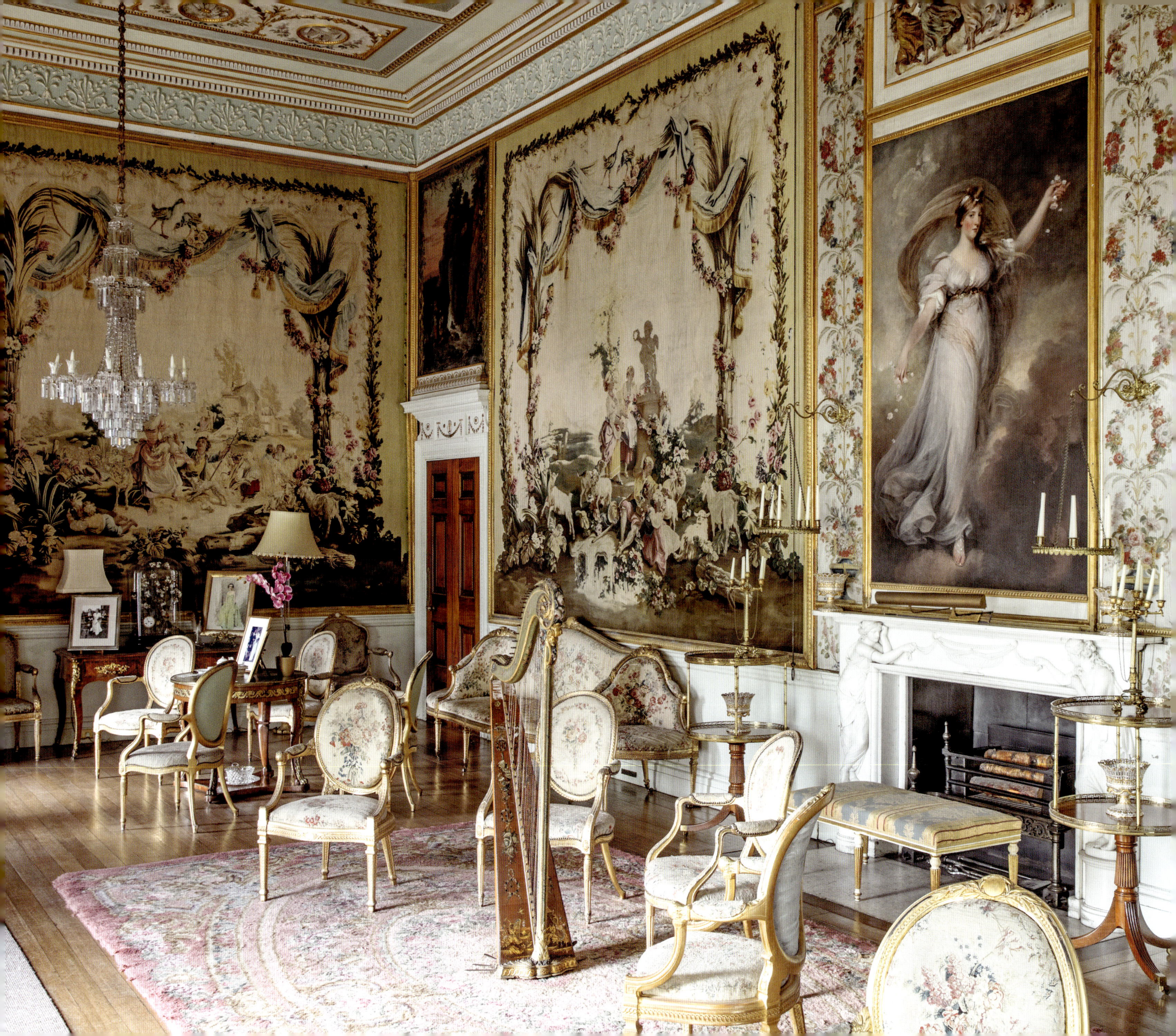

CONTENTS

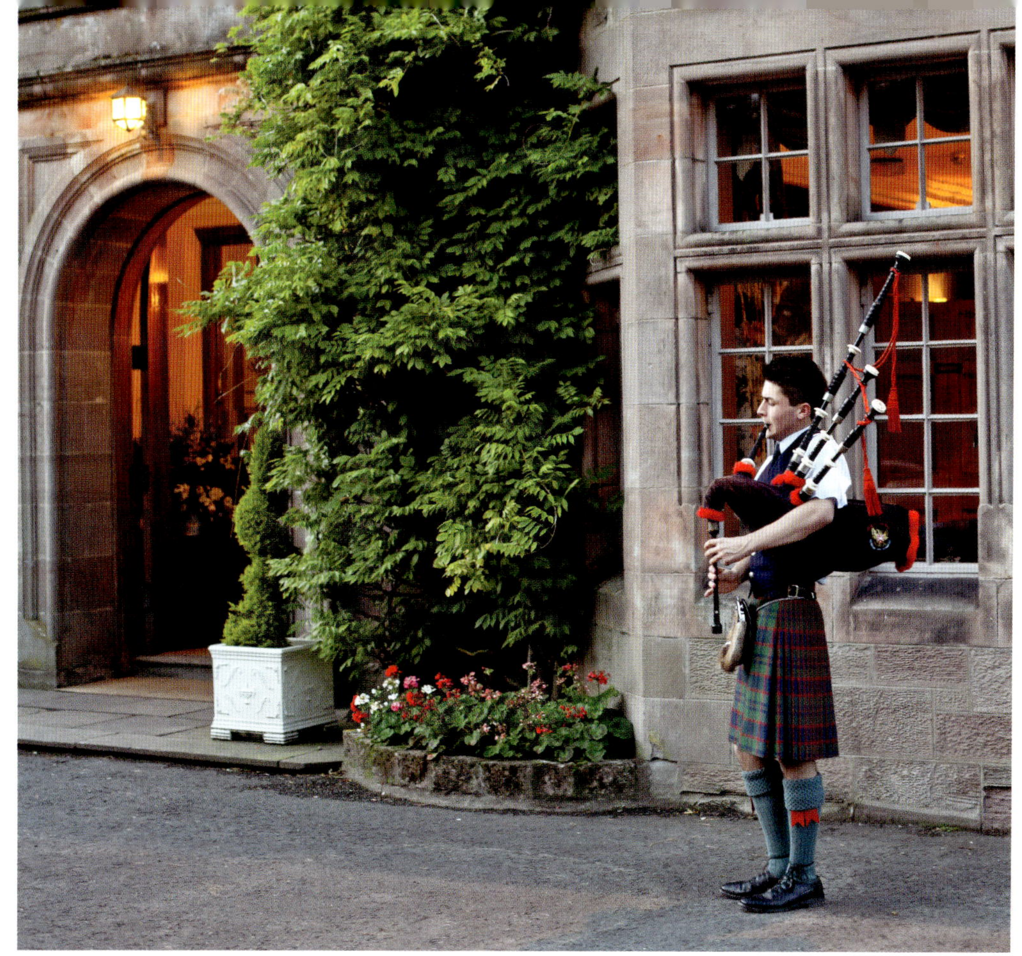

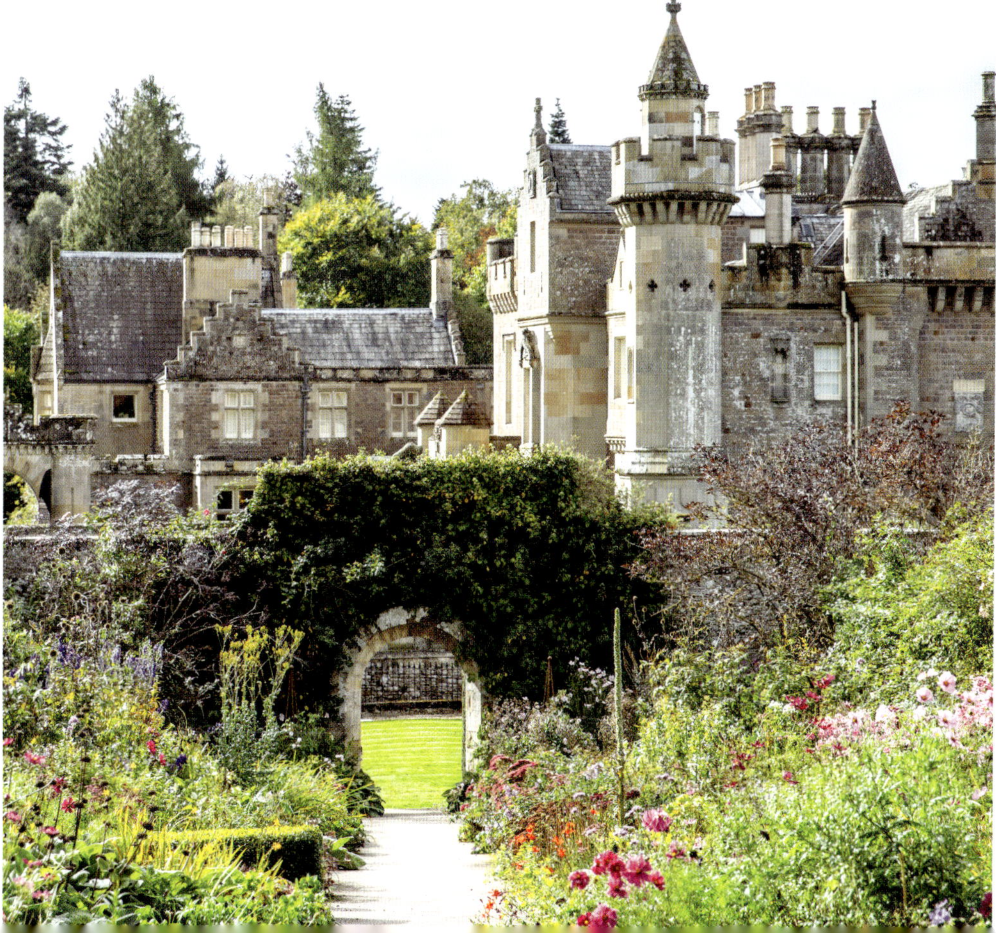

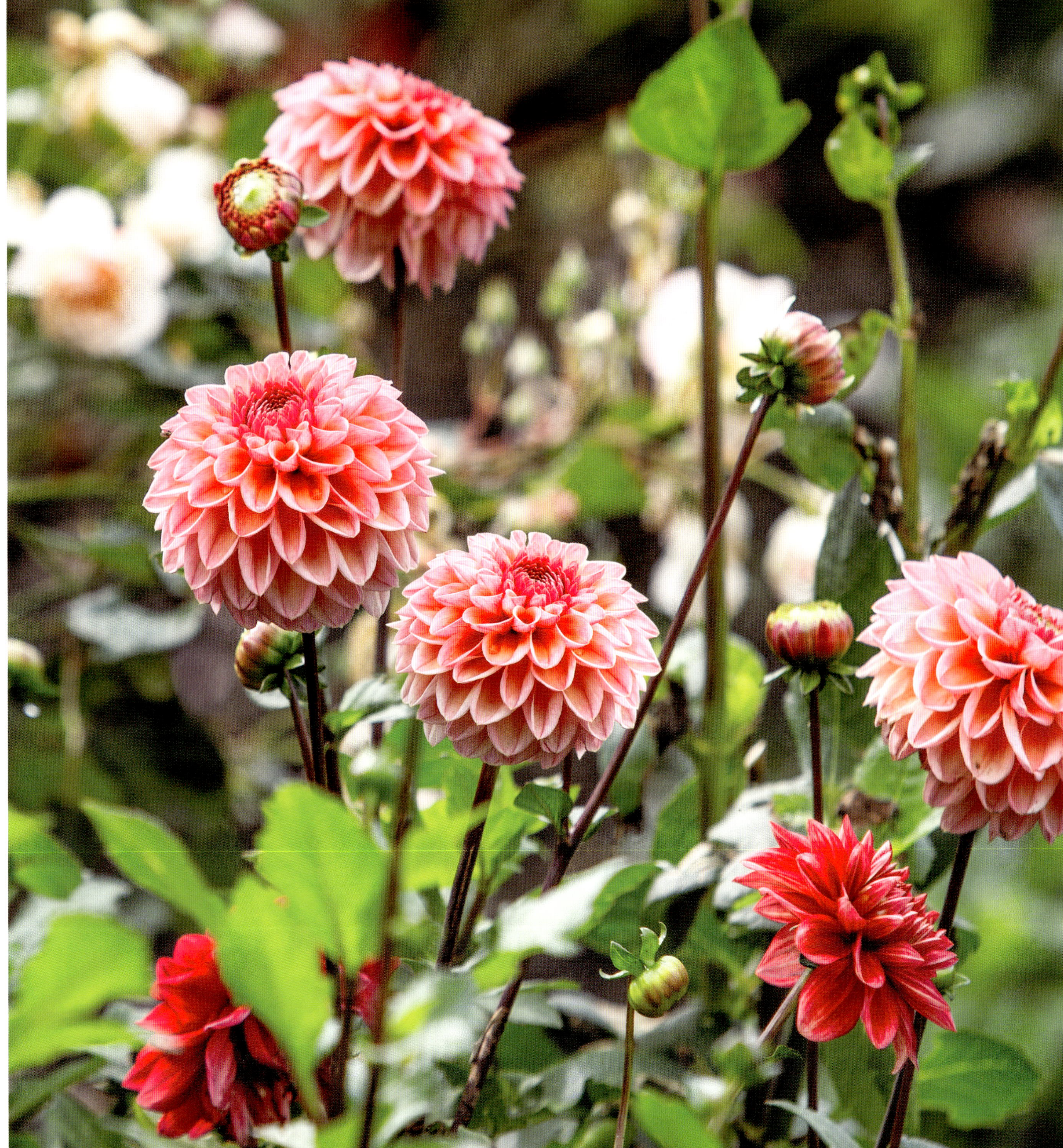

FOREWORD

Delving into the culture of Scotland while planning the themes covered in this volume, I came upon the endearing term *coorie*. "A hug of a word," shares author Gabriella Bennett, who defines it as the "Scottish art of deriving comfort, well-being, and energy from wild landscapes and convivial interiors." She explains the informal usage, which is more personal in nature, as the snug welcome of nestling affectionately with a loved one.

Both senses of the word resonate with me in contemplating *Our Hearts Are in Scotland*. Captivated by the country's immense beauty from the first glimpse of the image that graces our cover—the exterior of Sir Walter Scott's beloved abode, Abbotsford—I am swept away by romantic vistas of sunlight falling on mountains, moors, and meadows. *Victoria*'s editors, the coterie of creatives who have poured their time and talents into this project, draw closer in our pursuit of bliss. In the pages that follow, we also invite you to "coorie in," enveloped by the warmth of generations of Scots who embrace the heritage, traditions, and unique character of the enchanting land they call home.

Melissa Lester

Editor

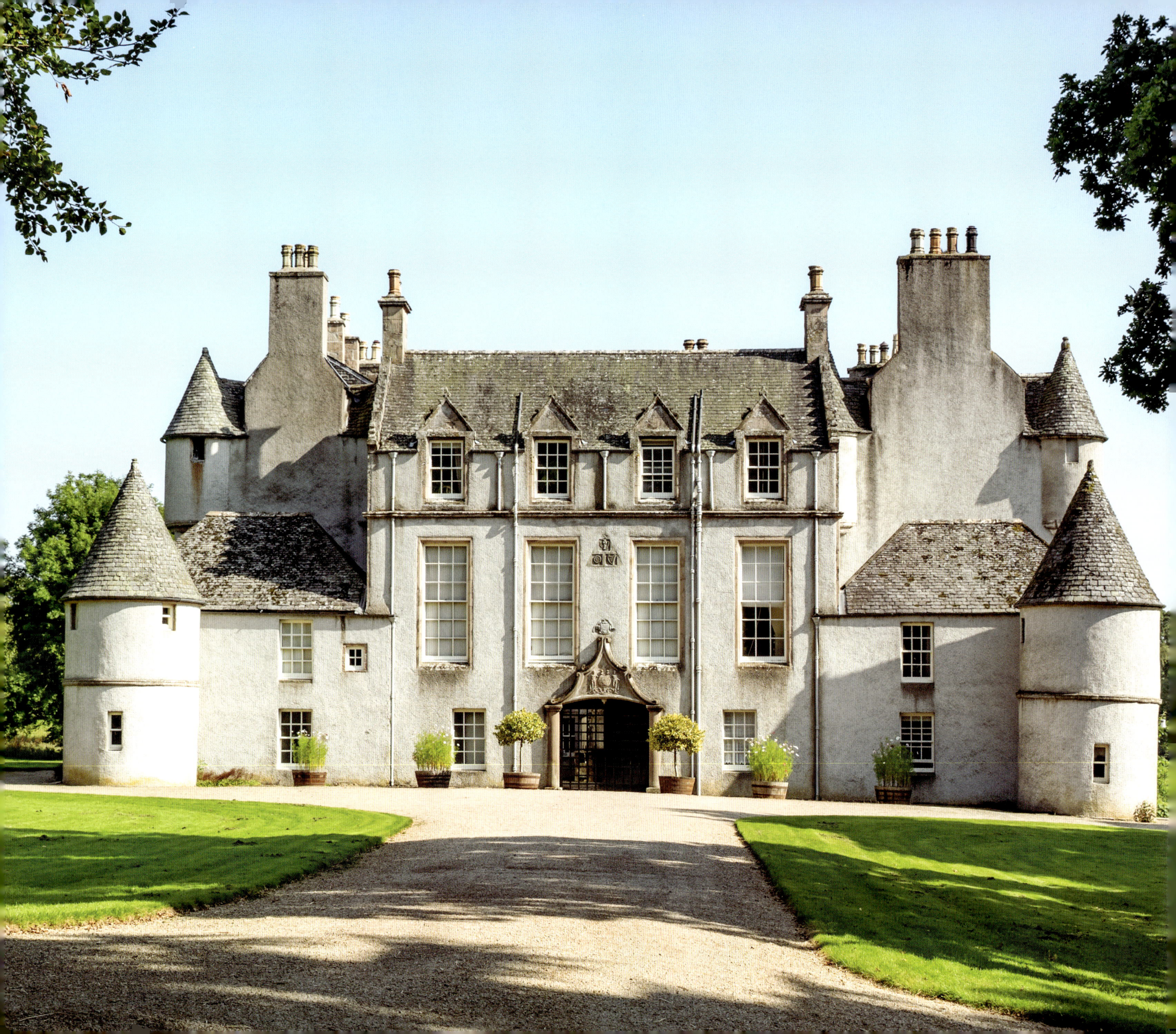

INTRODUCTION

Revered Scottish novelist Sir Walter Scott once penned, "Scotland is a land of mountains, glens, and islands, a land of myths and legends." It is a place where ancient towers rise from the mist like mystical reveries, where shimmering lochs dot the landscape, and rugged peaks stretch toward impossibly blue skies. In these environs, tartans and tweeds grace fashions and furnishings, and the lilt of a Scottish burr can charm the clouds away.

We start our tour of this delightful country with visits to the Borders and the Caledonian countryside before weaving through the Scottish Highlands on the Jacobite steam locomotive. The allure of majestic castles, suffused with history and family lore, draws us to a collection of these grand country mansions. Turn the pages to meet traditional artisans, peruse the finest local shops, and sample delectable regional cuisine. We wrap up our heartfelt tribute with visits to favorite hotels, notable homes, and inspiring houses of worship.

Our Hearts Are in Scotland is *Victoria*'s love letter to the extraordinary land that inspired poet laureate Robert Burns to compose these memorable words: "Wherever I wander, wherever I rove, the hills of the Highlands for ever I love."

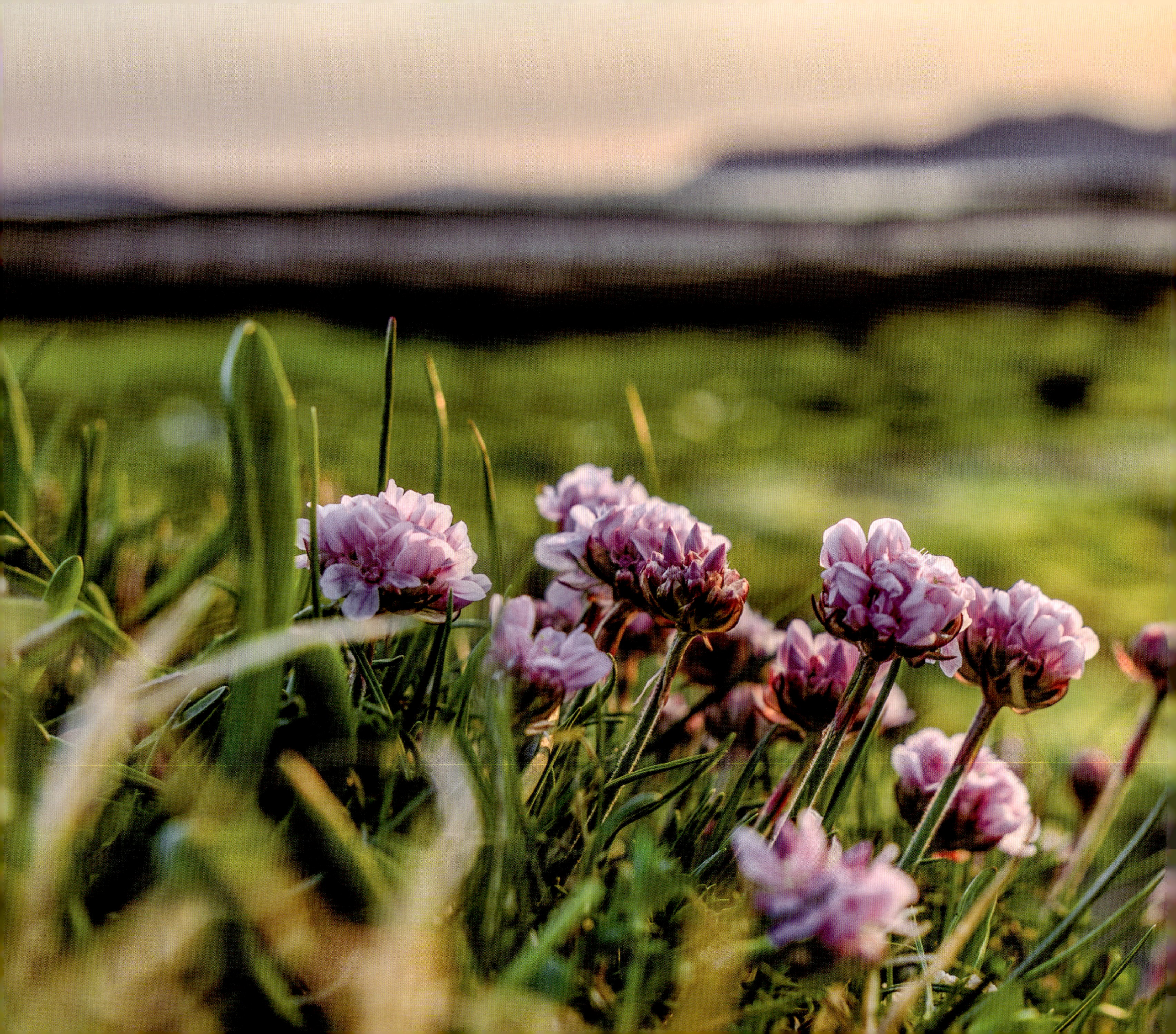

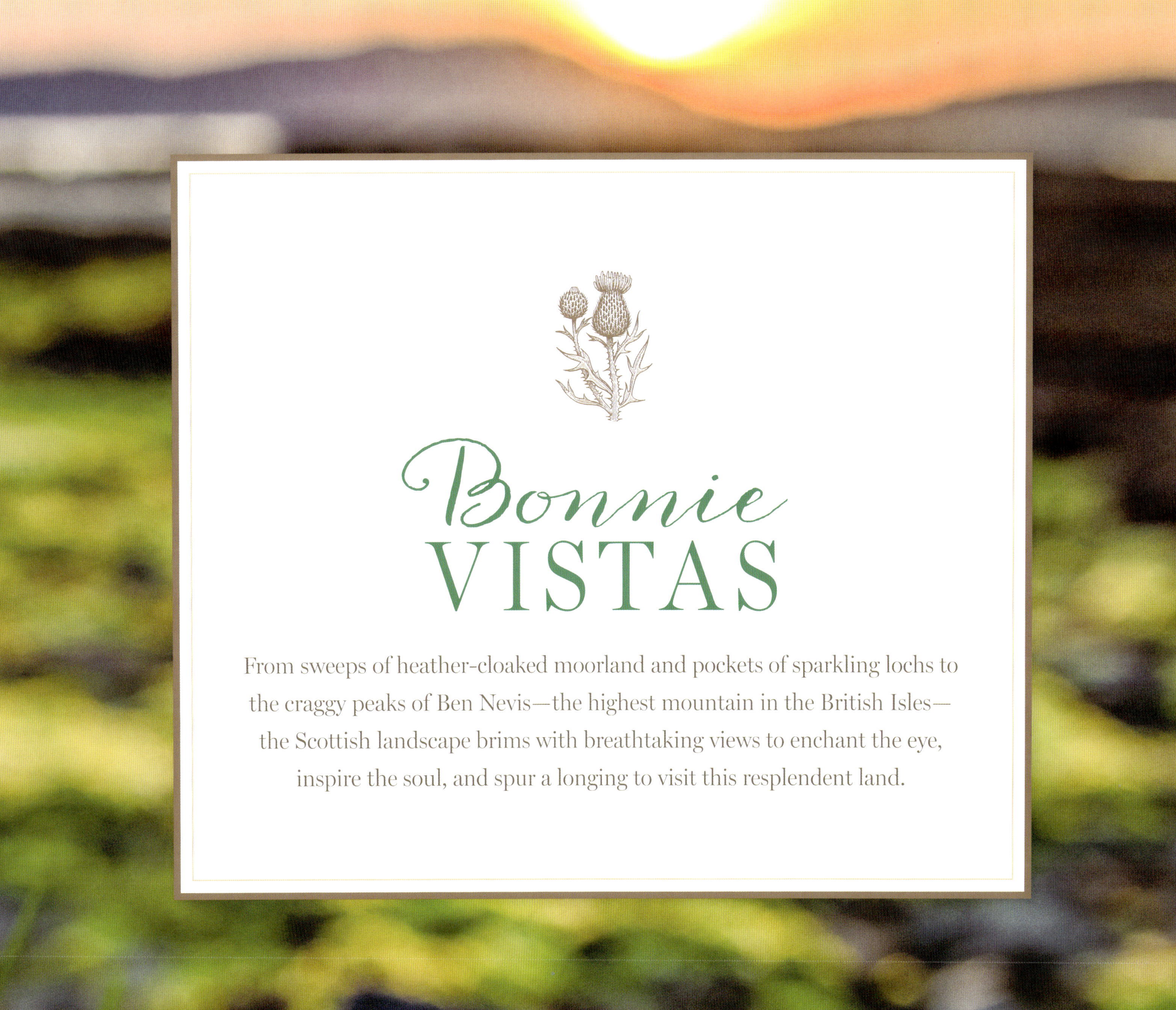

Bonnie VISTAS

From sweeps of heather-cloaked moorland and pockets of sparkling lochs to the craggy peaks of Ben Nevis—the highest mountain in the British Isles—the Scottish landscape brims with breathtaking views to enchant the eye, inspire the soul, and spur a longing to visit this resplendent land.

THE BEAUTY OF THE BORDERS

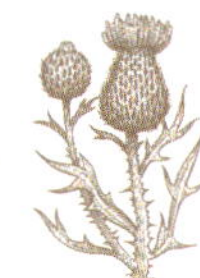

Opening our fantastic tour of Scotland, the picturesque southeastern portion of the country known as the Scottish Borders shares a boundary with England's northernmost counties of Cumbria and Northumberland. The area's fascinating history and rural beauty provided the inspiration behind many of the novels penned by Sir Walter Scott, and this regional bounty continues to draw visitors who are intrigued by the ancient abbeys, stately castles, and awe-inspiring vistas.

At the foot of the triple-peaked Eildon Hills lies the characterful town of Melrose. Its narrow streets are lined with stone-block houses and quaint shops. Burts Hotel on Market Square welcomes patrons to stay in cozy surrounds and to dine at its award-winning restaurant. A three-minute walk from there ends at Melrose Abbey, a former Cistercian monastery dating to the twelfth century.

Designated as a royal burg in 1152, nearby Peebles still retains its ageless charm. An array of merchants and eateries line the High Street, where dozens of quirky alleyways and medieval closes beg further exploration. Just across the street from the venerable Old Parish Church, Coltman's Kitchen, Deli & Bar offers an enticing, seasonally inspired menu of Scottish favorites infused with fresh ingredients procured from local growers.

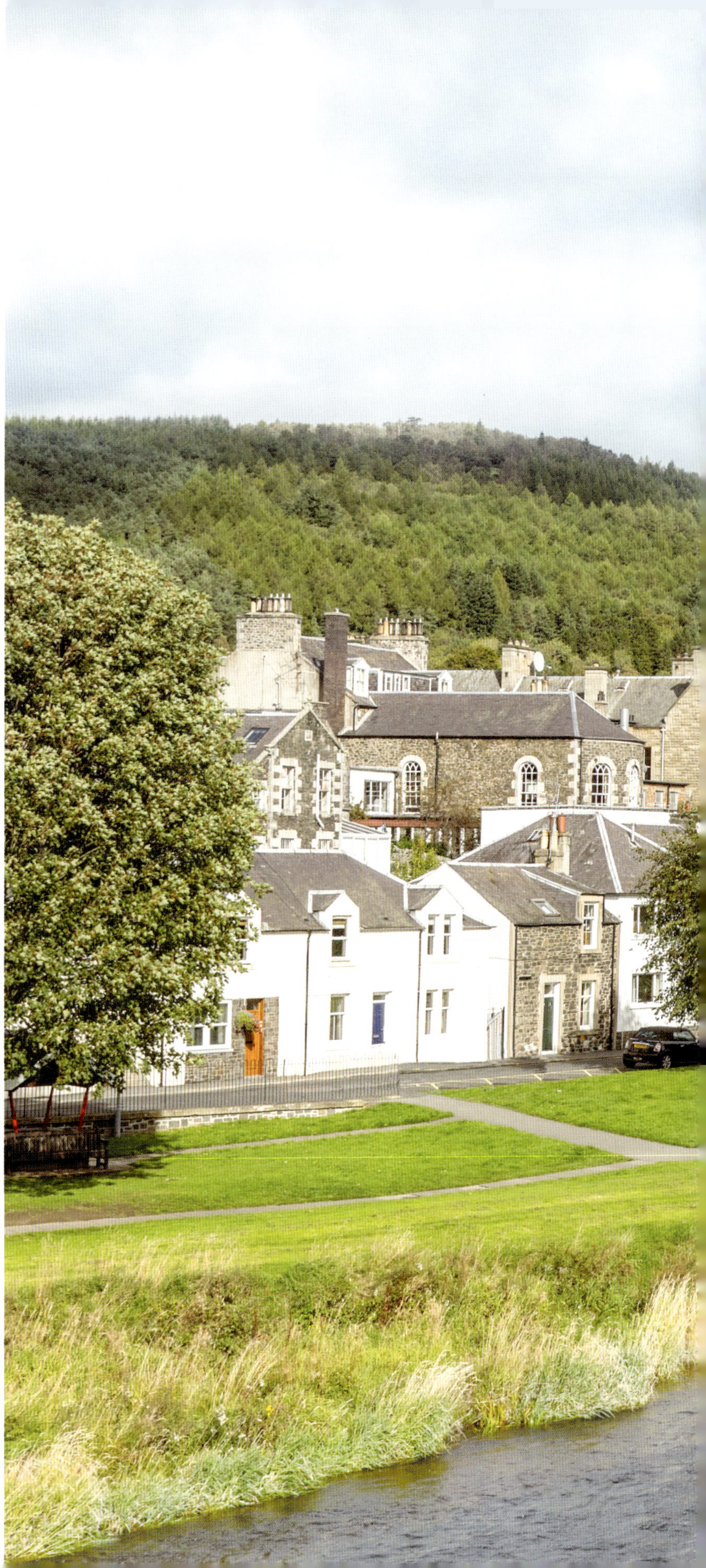

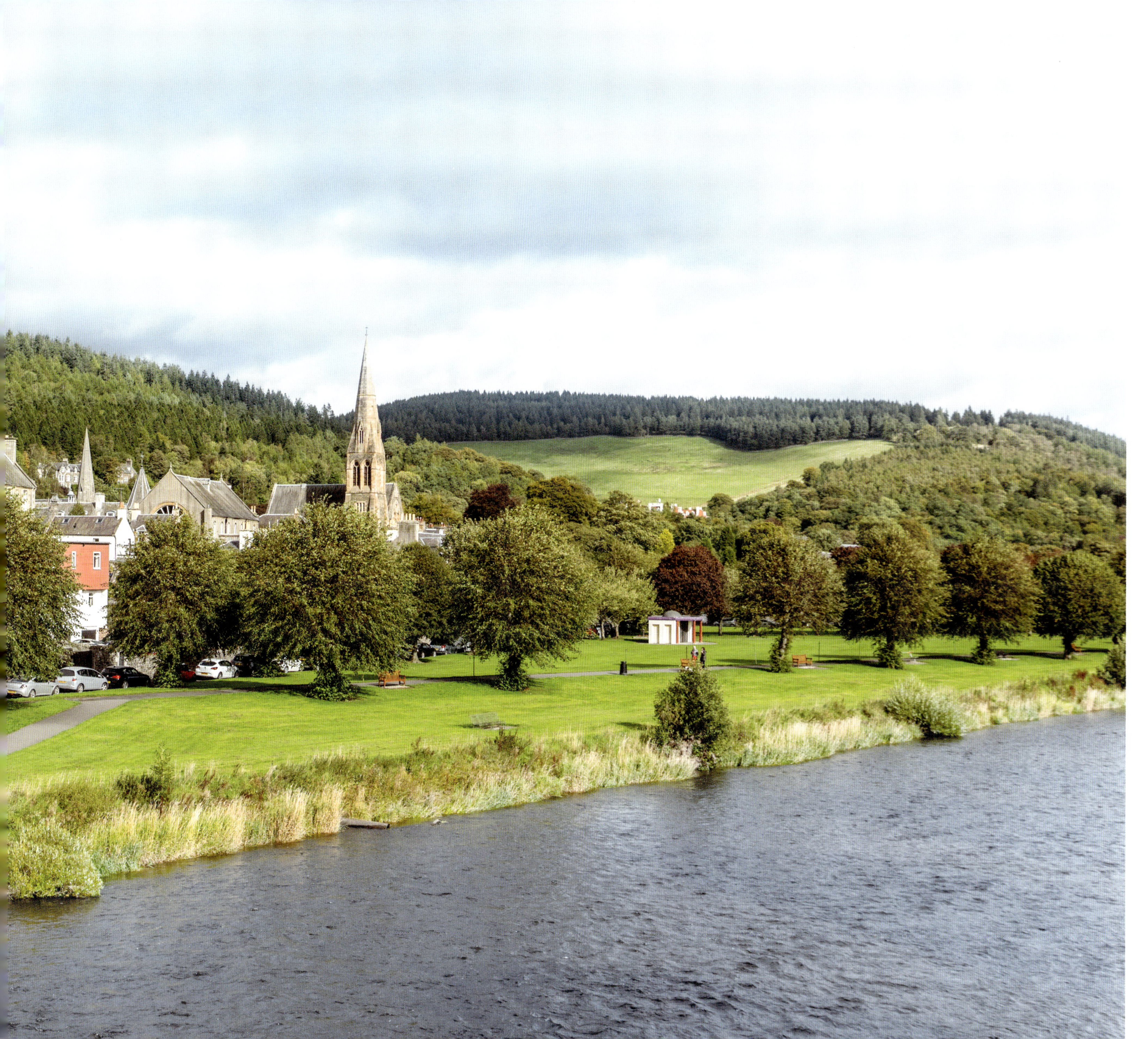

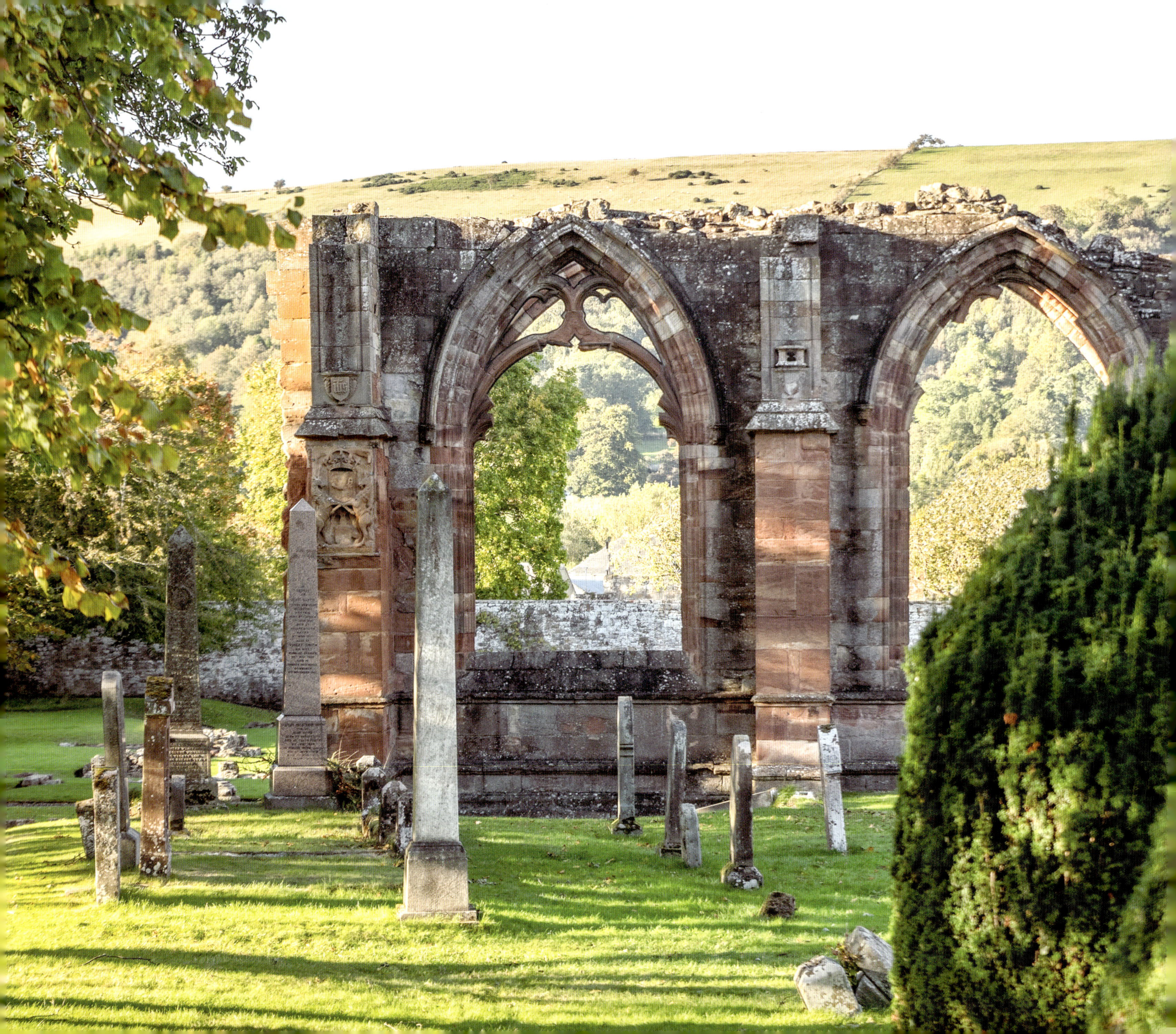

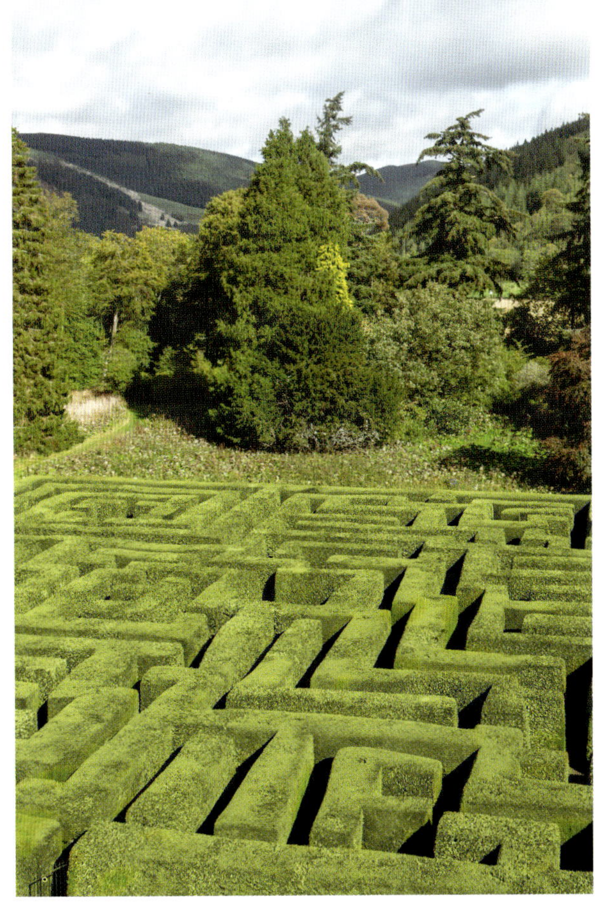

Opposite: Melrose Abbey was founded in 1636 as the first Cistercian monastery in Scotland. Though partially in ruins, the structure still bears decorative details carved by master mason John Morrow. This page, right: The postcard-perfect town of Peebles lies along the banks of the River Tweed. The community itself attracts those interested in the arts, whether it's theatre, dance, or music, and hosts a number of annual festivals and events. Peebles's timeless charm is undeniable, making it an enjoyable destination in any season.

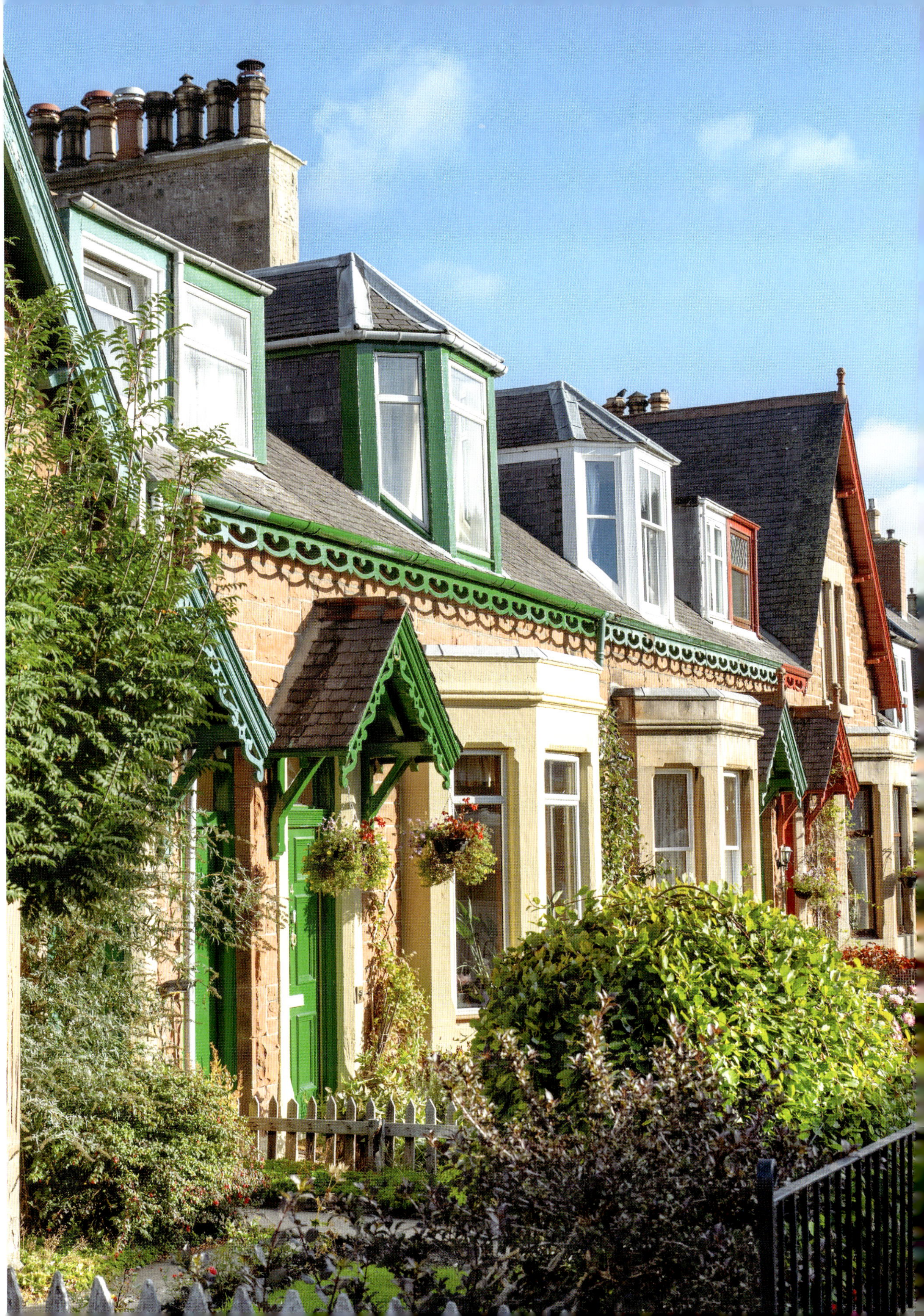

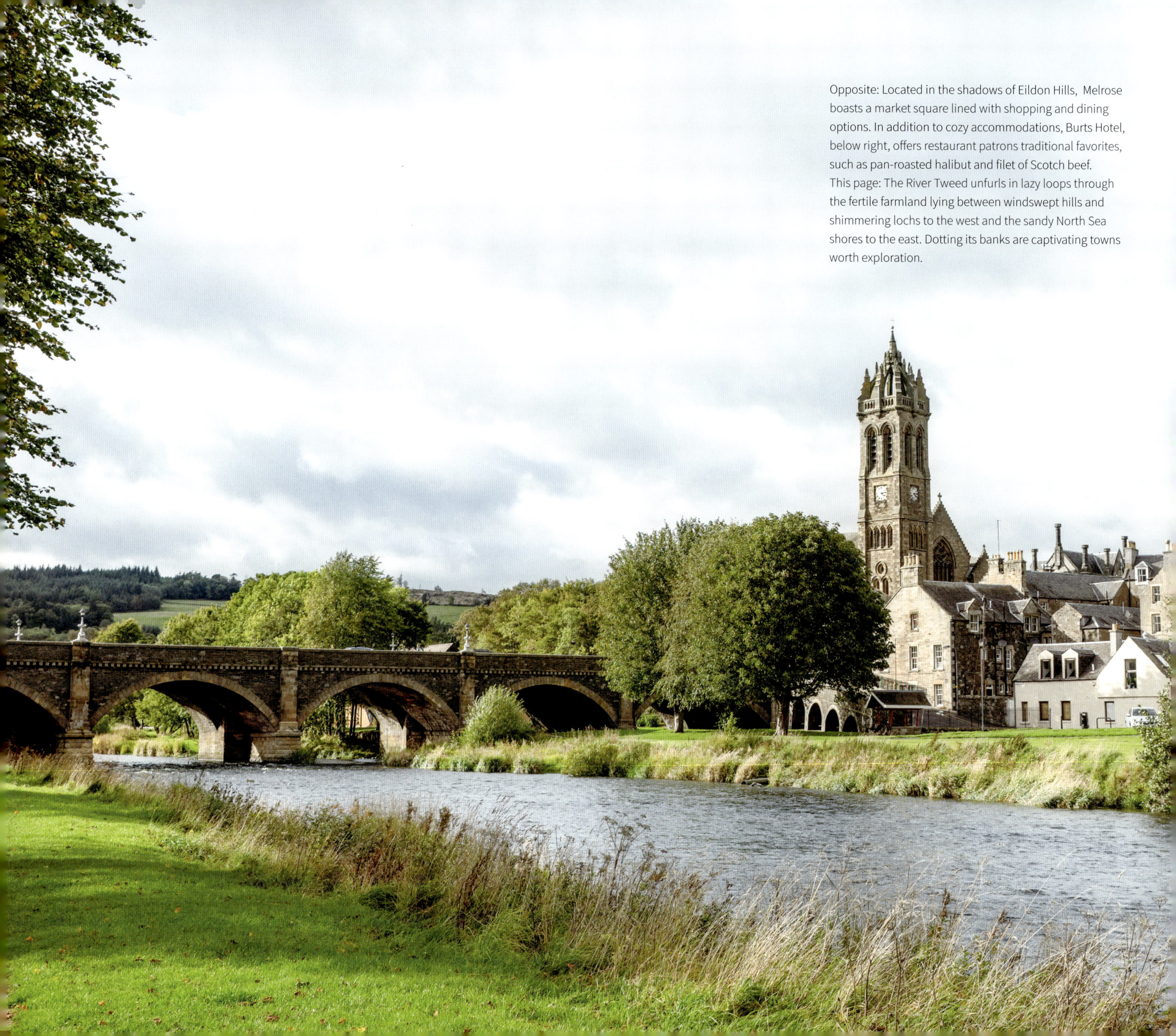

Opposite: Located in the shadows of Eildon Hills, Melrose boasts a market square lined with shopping and dining options. In addition to cozy accommodations, Burts Hotel, below right, offers restaurant patrons traditional favorites, such as pan-roasted halibut and filet of Scotch beef.
This page: The River Tweed unfurls in lazy loops through the fertile farmland lying between windswept hills and shimmering lochs to the west and the sandy North Sea shores to the east. Dotting its banks are captivating towns worth exploration.

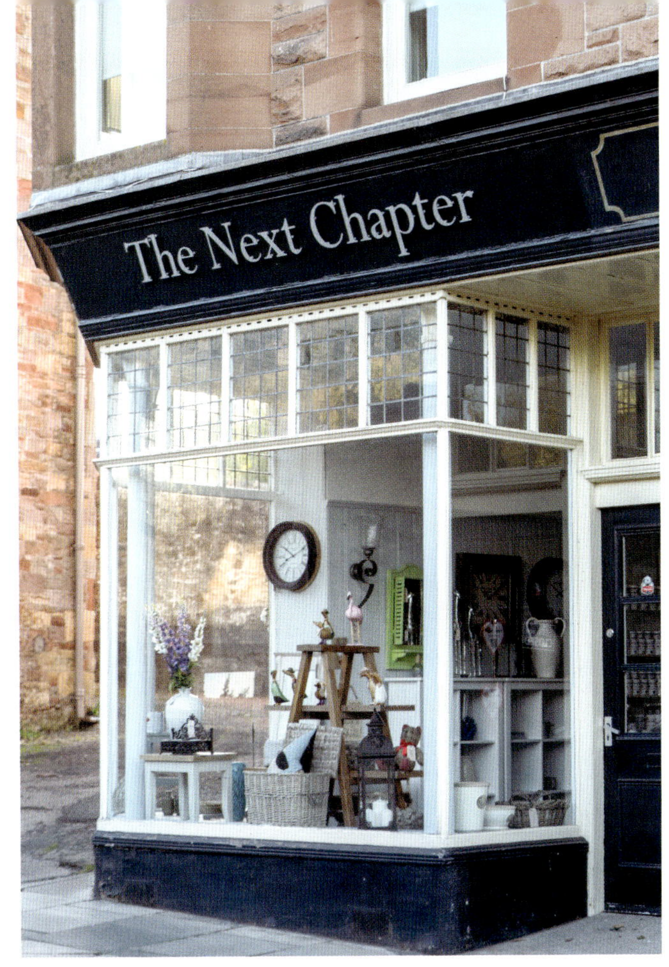
The Next Chapter

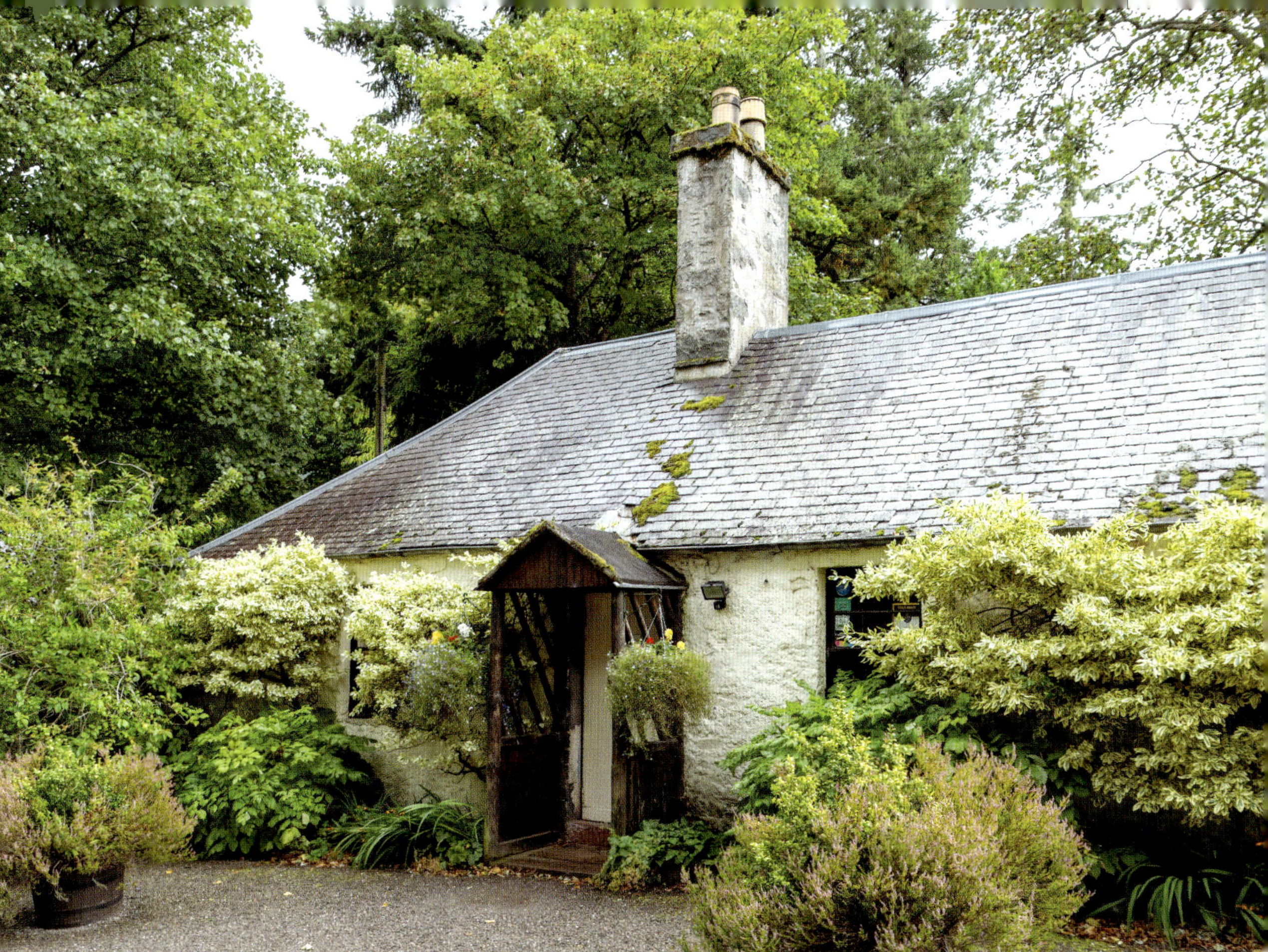

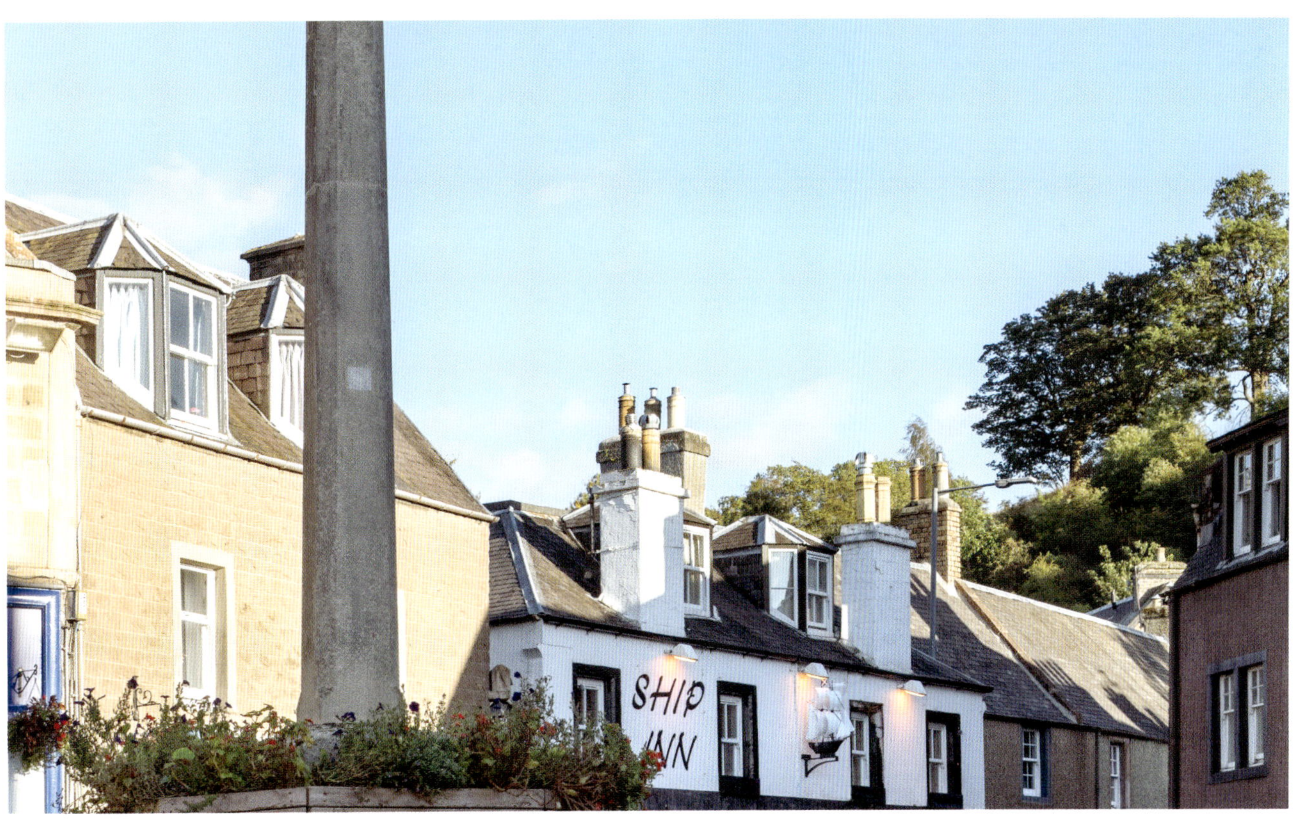
SHIP
INN

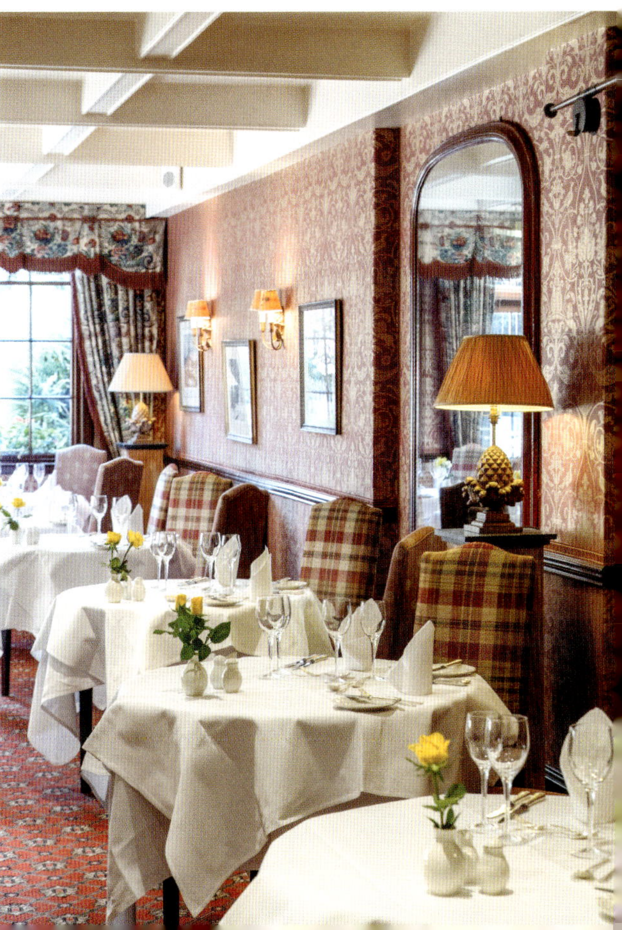

OF KNIGHTS AND NOBILITY

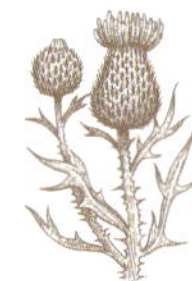

With the arrival of the feudal system in Scotland during the twelfth century, sturdy structures built for administrative purposes eventually evolved into the majestic stone castles we associate with the days of dashing heroes, such as Prince Charles Edward Stuart and William Wallace. Many of these fortresses still stand, forever interwoven with Scottish history, offering visitors the chance to wander about the grounds of these venerable keeps.

Founded by David I as an Augustinian monastery in 1128, the Palace of Holyroodhouse, located in the capital city of Edinburgh, serves as the official residence of the monarchy in Scotland. Its fascinating past includes many notable names, but none as prominent as Mary, Queen of Scots, whose dramatic narrative played out within these walls. Three hours north sits Balmoral Castle, shown right, an impressive example of Scottish baronial architecture. It has been one of the British royal family's favorite pastoral destinations since Prince Albert presented it as a gift to his beloved wife, Queen Victoria, in 1852.

Among the many fortified estates found in the Scottish Highlands is the eponymous Castle Fraser, home to that illustrious family for more than four centuries. A short drive away, near the town of Huntly, stands the grand Leith Hall, known for its bountiful gardens and waymarked trails. Perched above the coastline of the North Sea, the Castle of Mey was the property of Queen Elizabeth The Queen Mother from 1952 until 1996.

With more than a thousand castles dotting this charismatic country, there are endless adventures awaiting sojourners with a penchant for exploring the history-steeped environs of ever-enchanting Scotland.

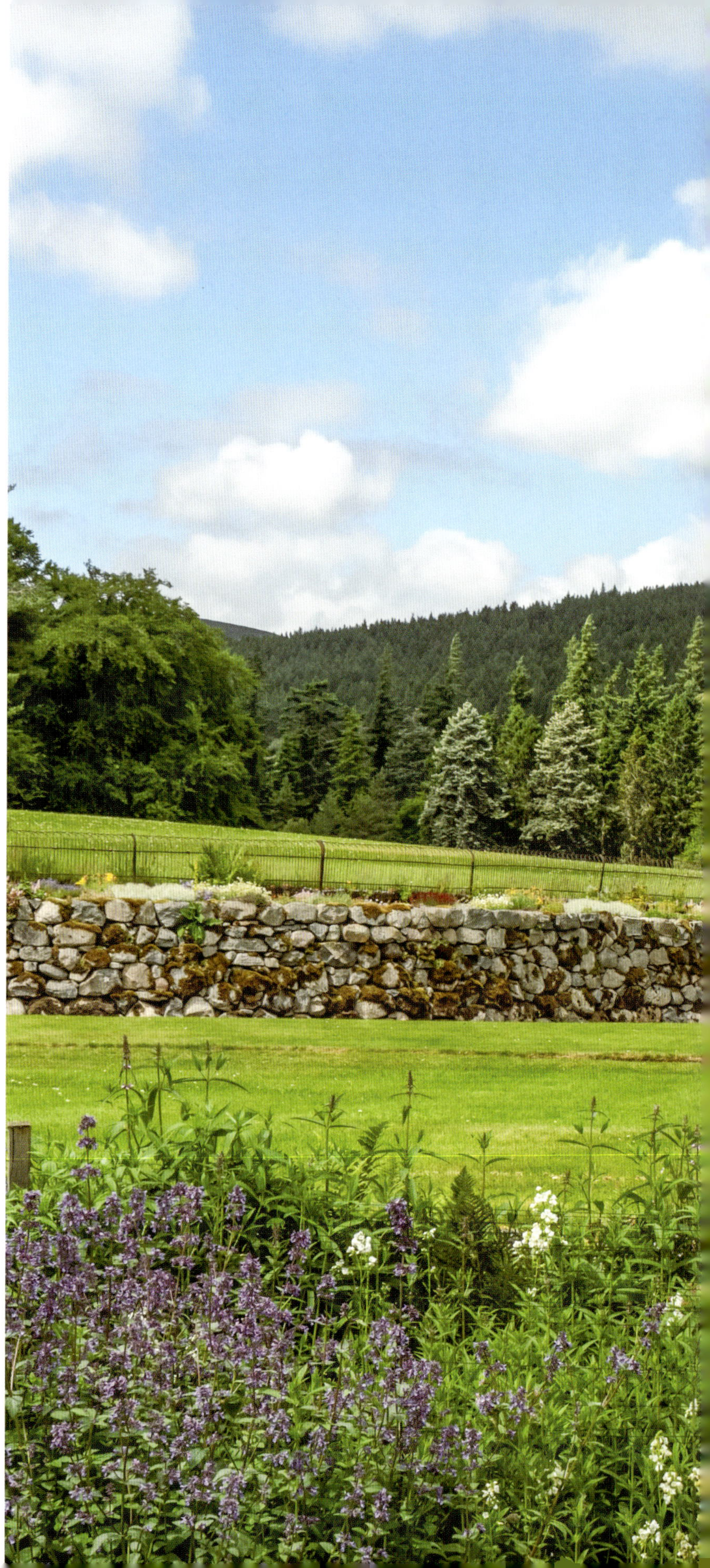

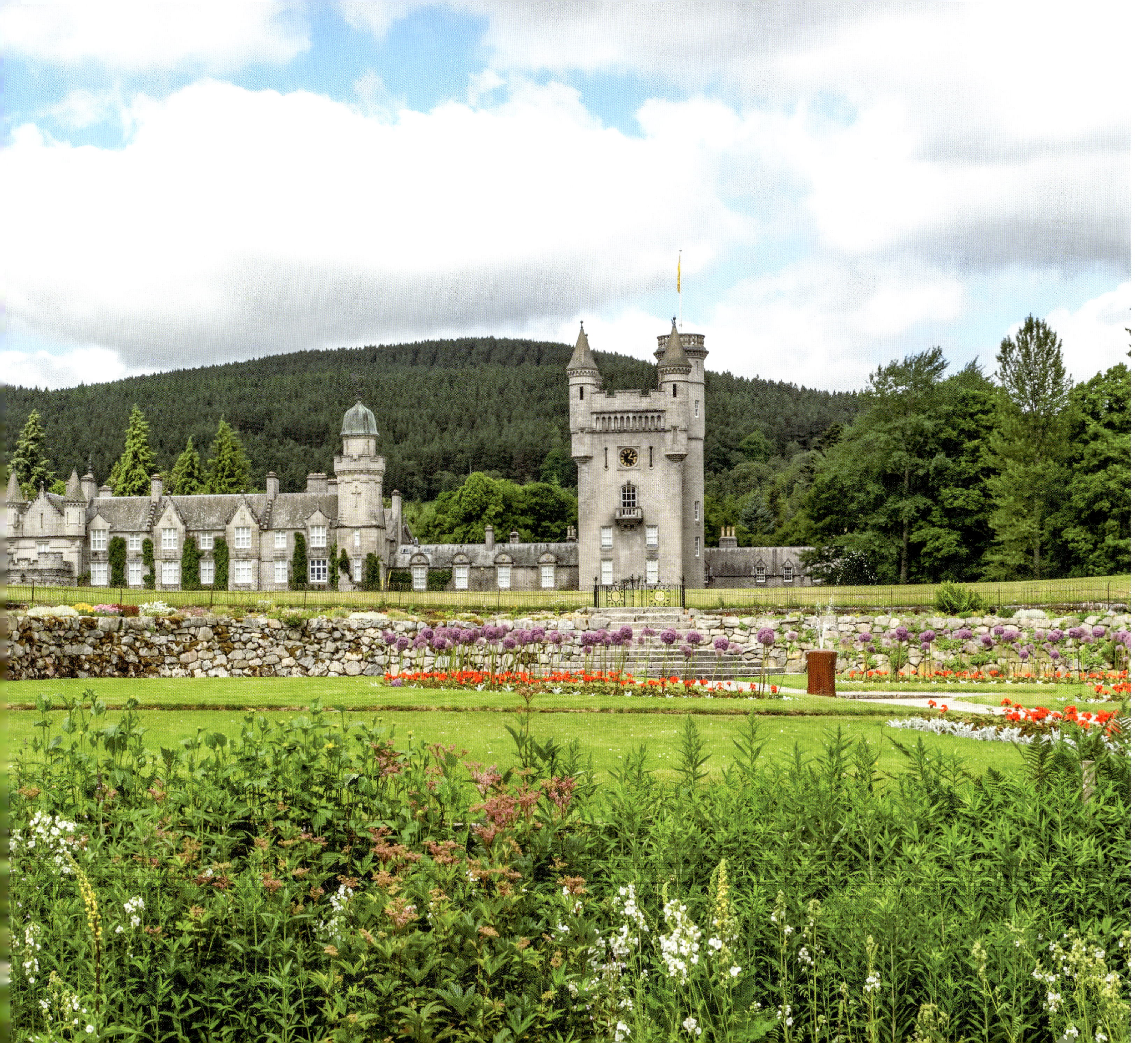

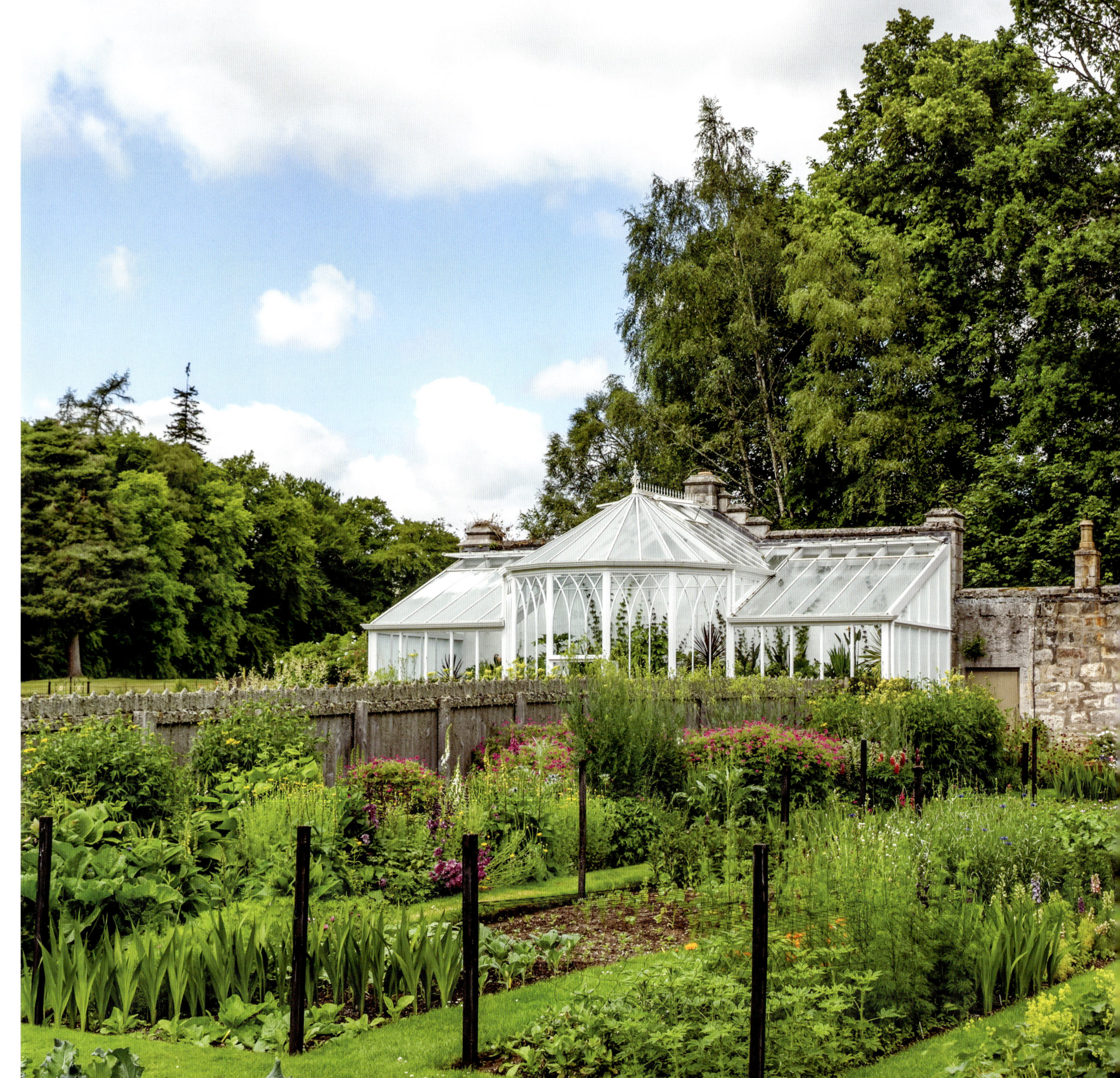

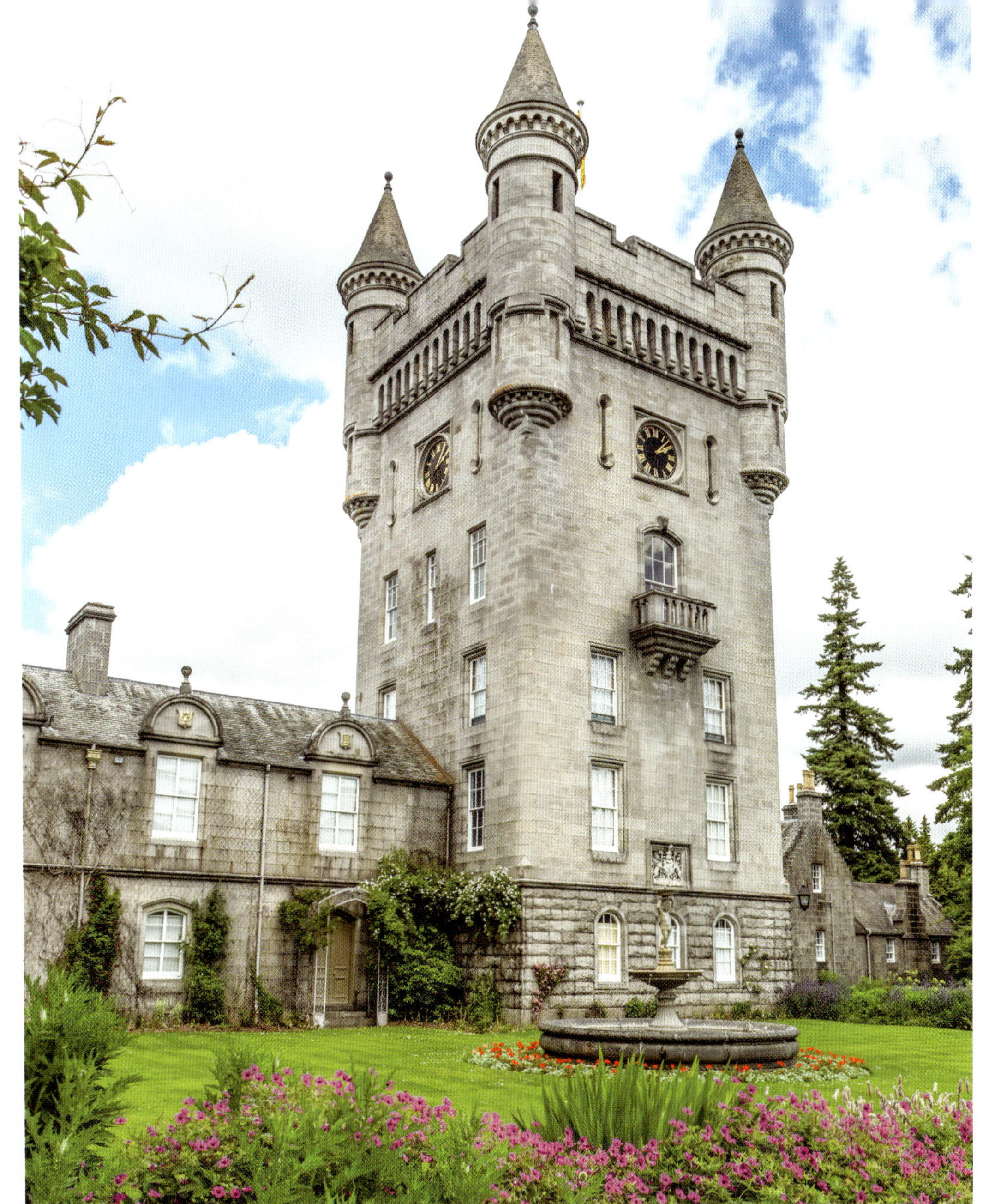

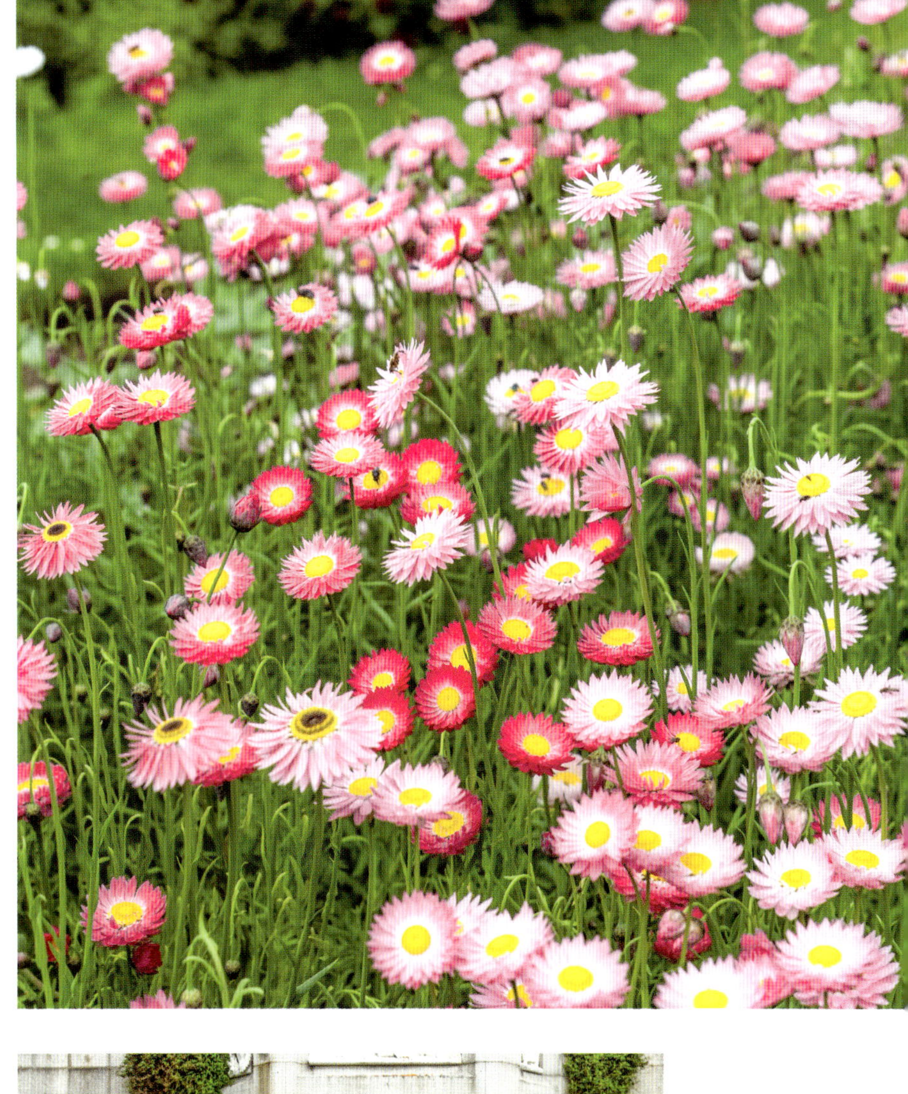

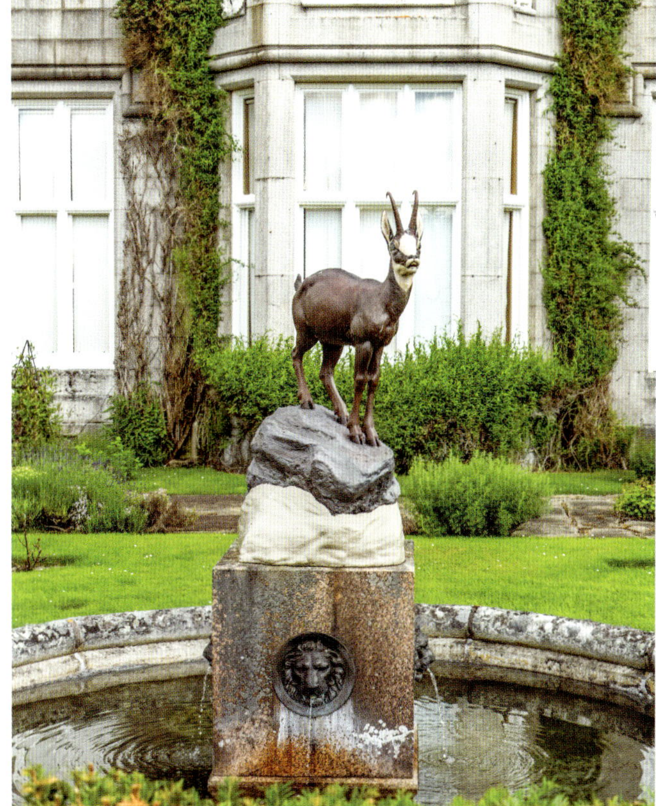

BALMORAL

When Queen Victoria made her inaugural visit to Scotland in 1842, she was immediately captivated by the country's bucolic beauty. Six years later, her husband presented her with the Balmoral property. The original edifice was deemed too small and was replaced with this resplendent castle, completed in 1856. It served as a rustic retreat from their regal duties—a haven that has been enjoyed by succeeding generations of royals.

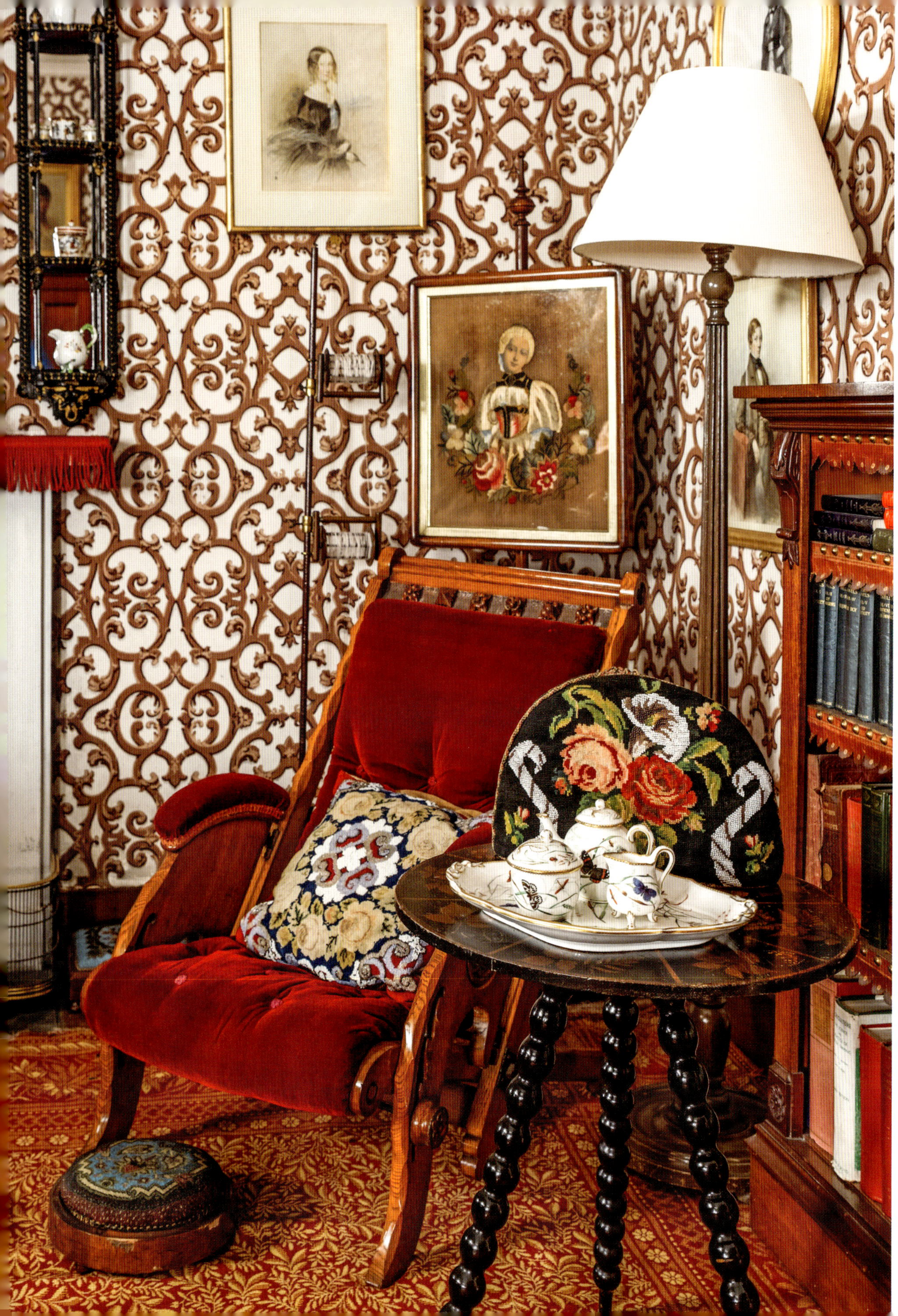

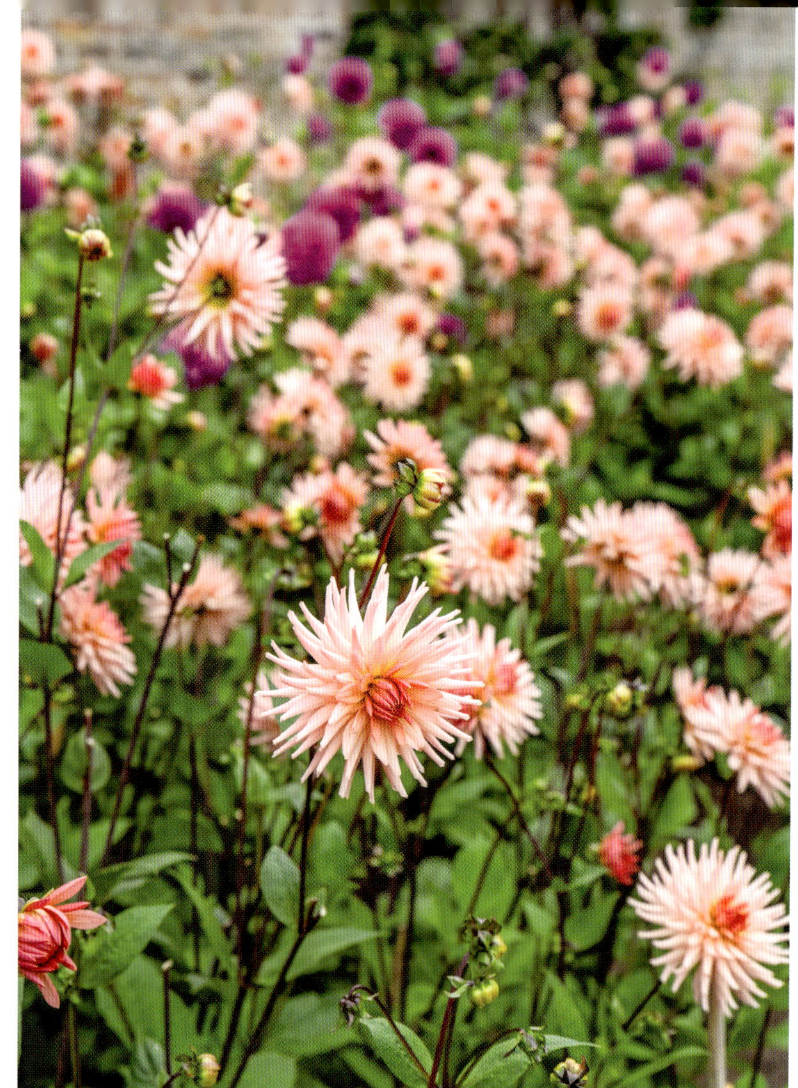

CASTLE FRASER

With its core portion dating to the mid-1450s, Castle Fraser owes its dramatic façade to several renovations that incorporated elements of Regency, Tudor, and Gothic styles. The castle remained in the Fraser lineage until 1921, when it was purchased by the 1st Viscount Cowdray as a project for his son, Clive Pearson, who spent two decades restoring the residence to its former grandeur, complete with Fraser family portraits and memorabilia.

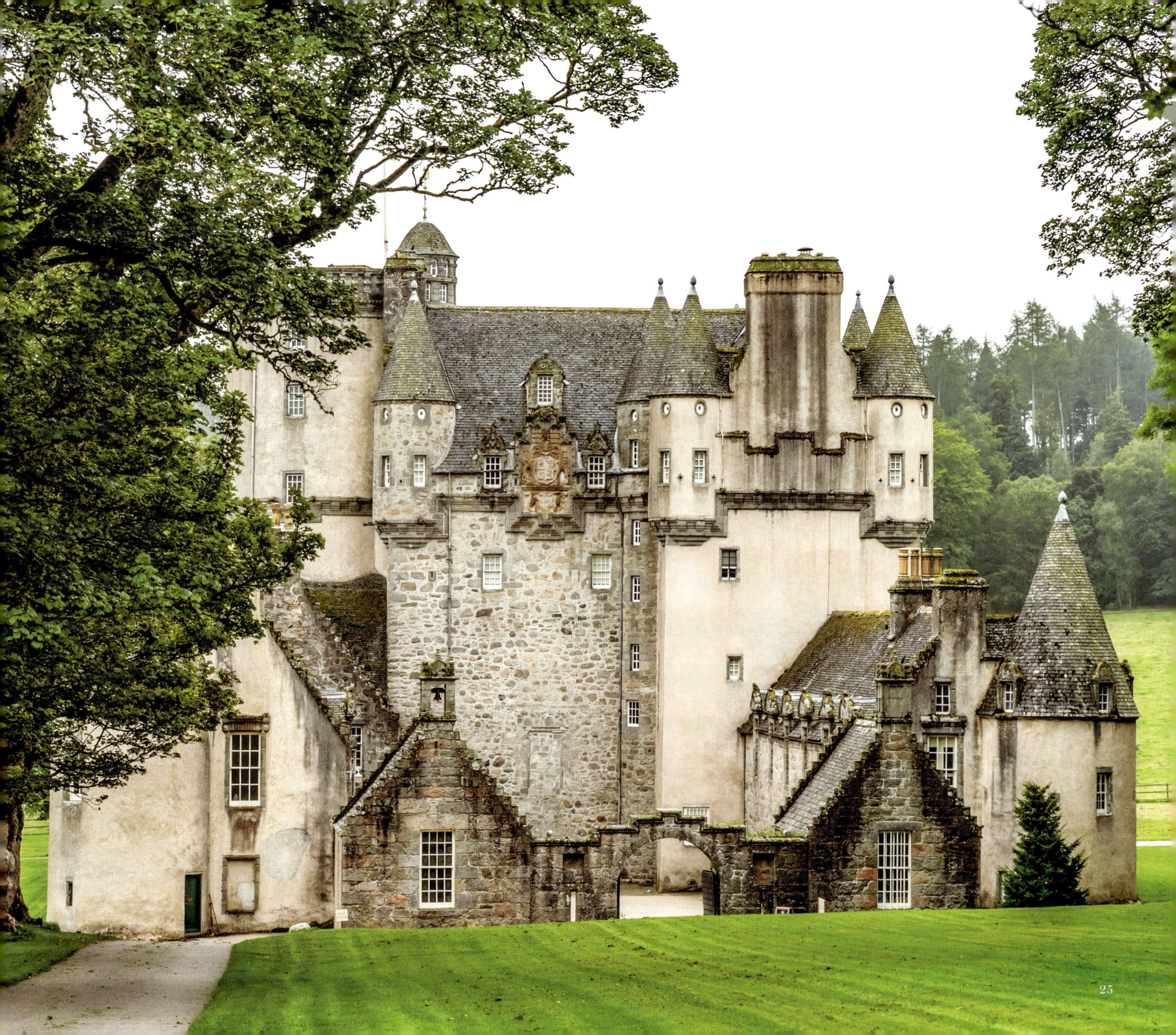

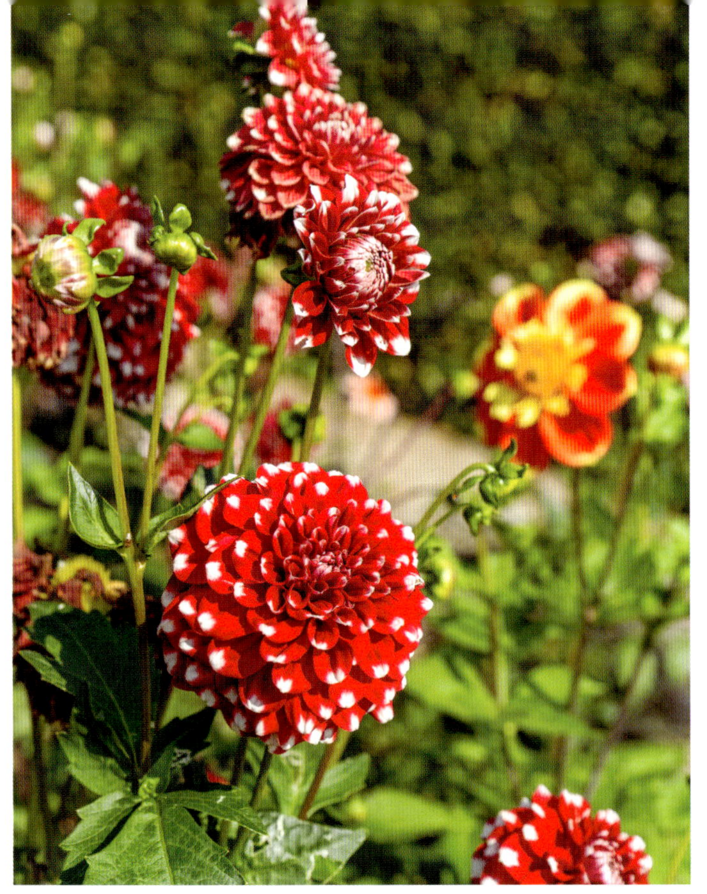

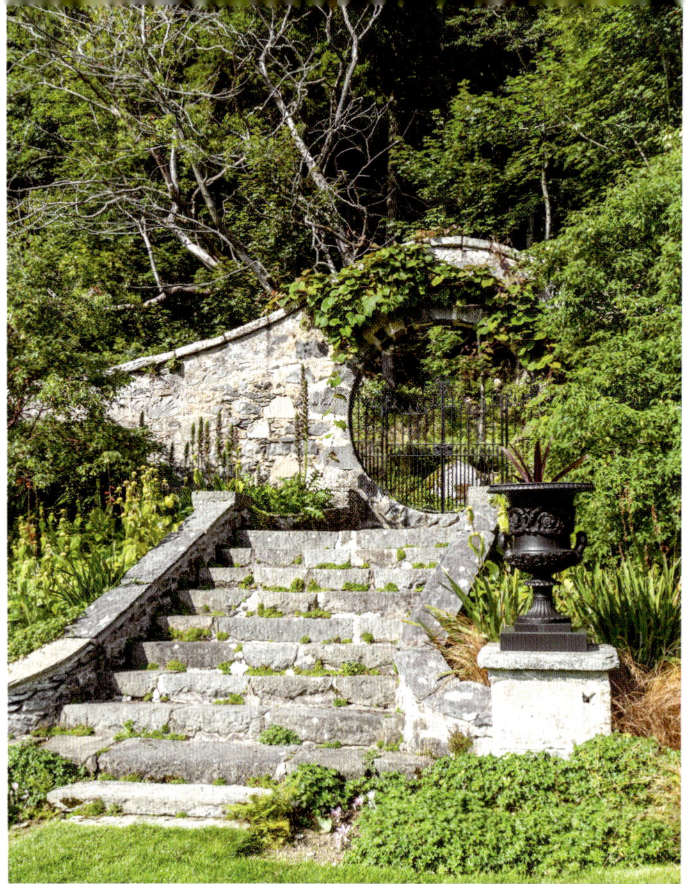

LEITH HALL

Ten generations of the distinguished Leith-Hay family resided in elegant Leith Hall, which dates to 1650. Several wings were added at various points in its storied history, which includes a stint as a Red Cross hospital during World War I. The castle is renowned for its beautiful gardens, with an idyllic stream meandering through all manner of botanical delights.

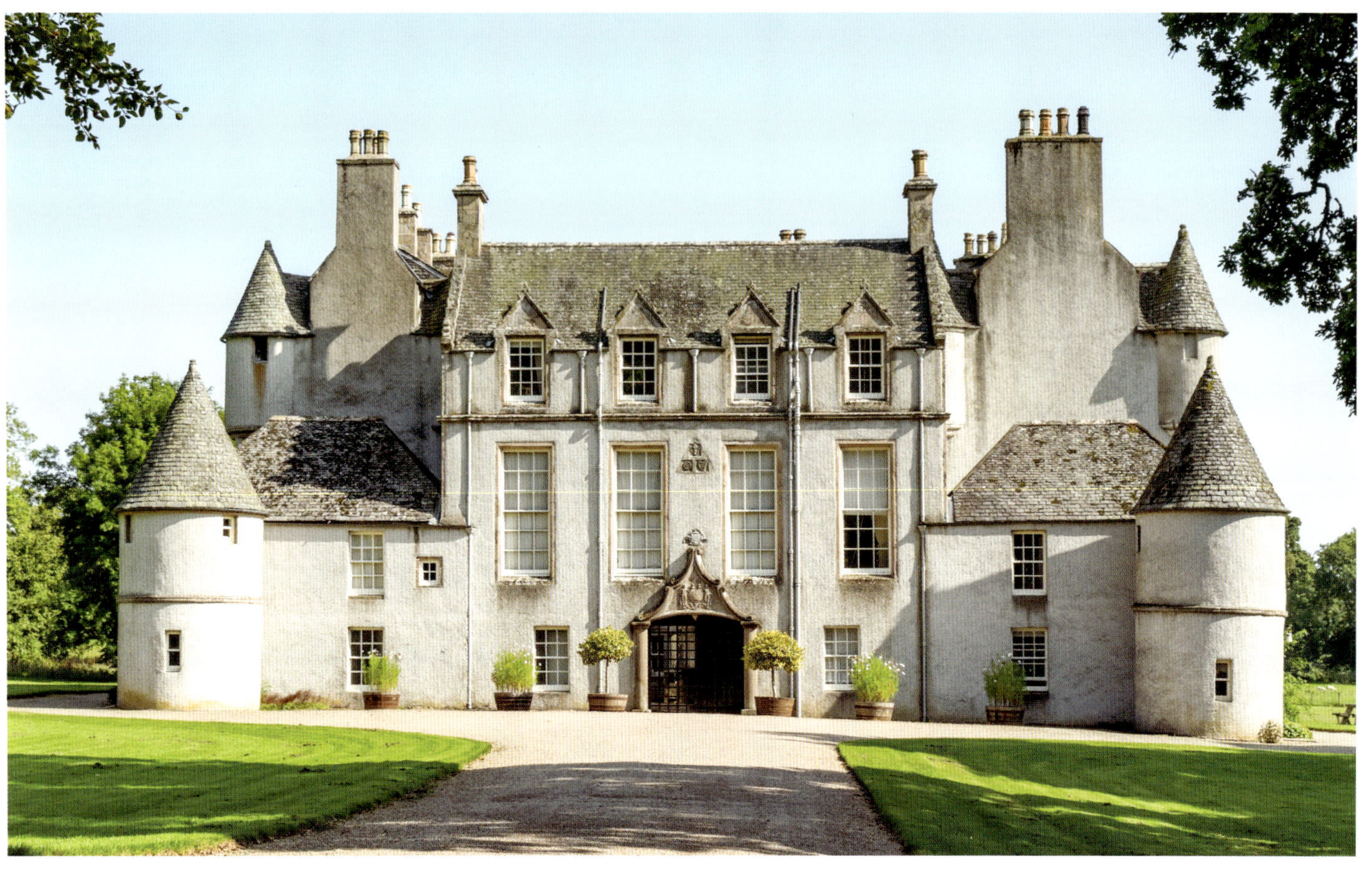

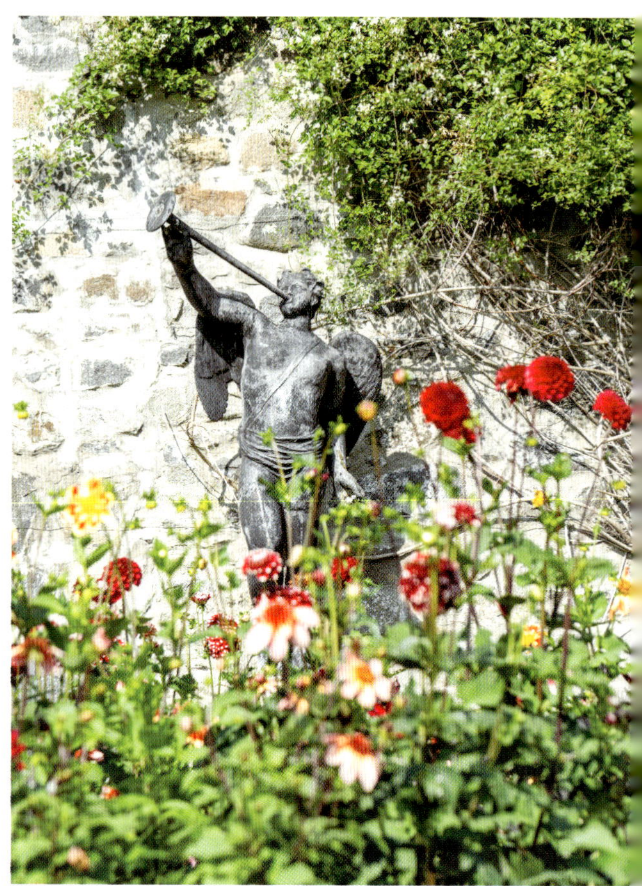

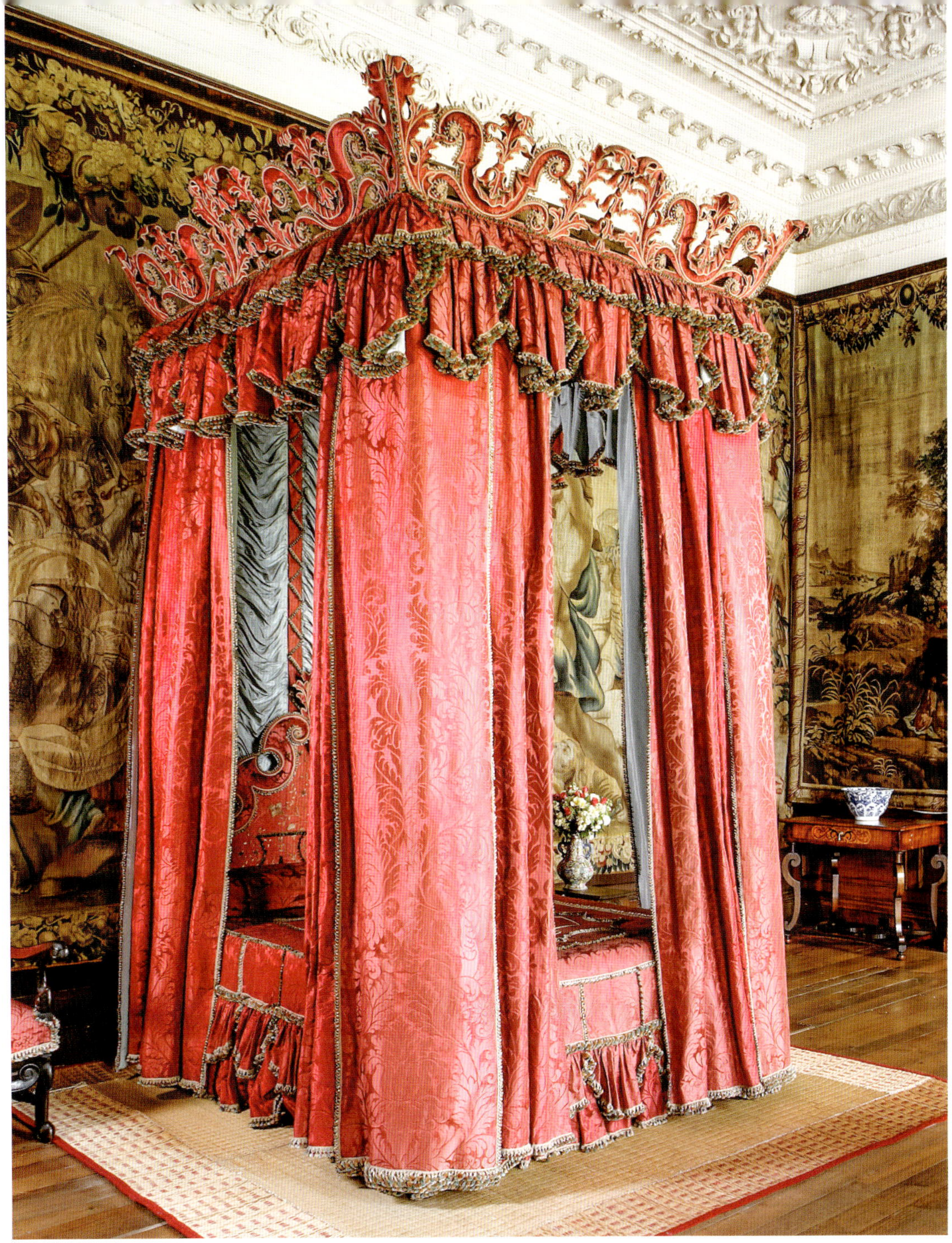

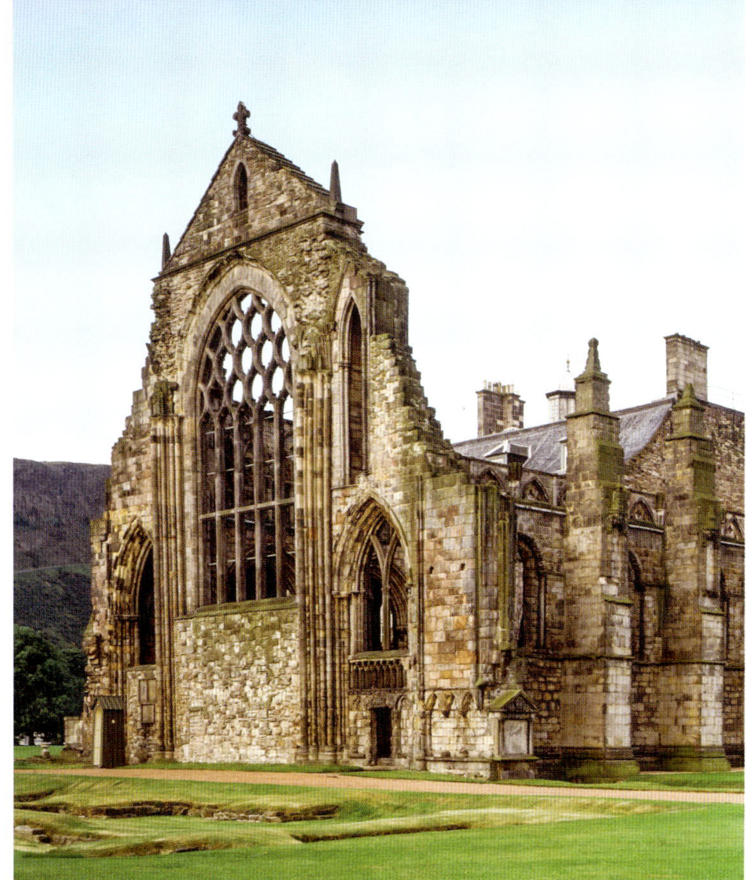

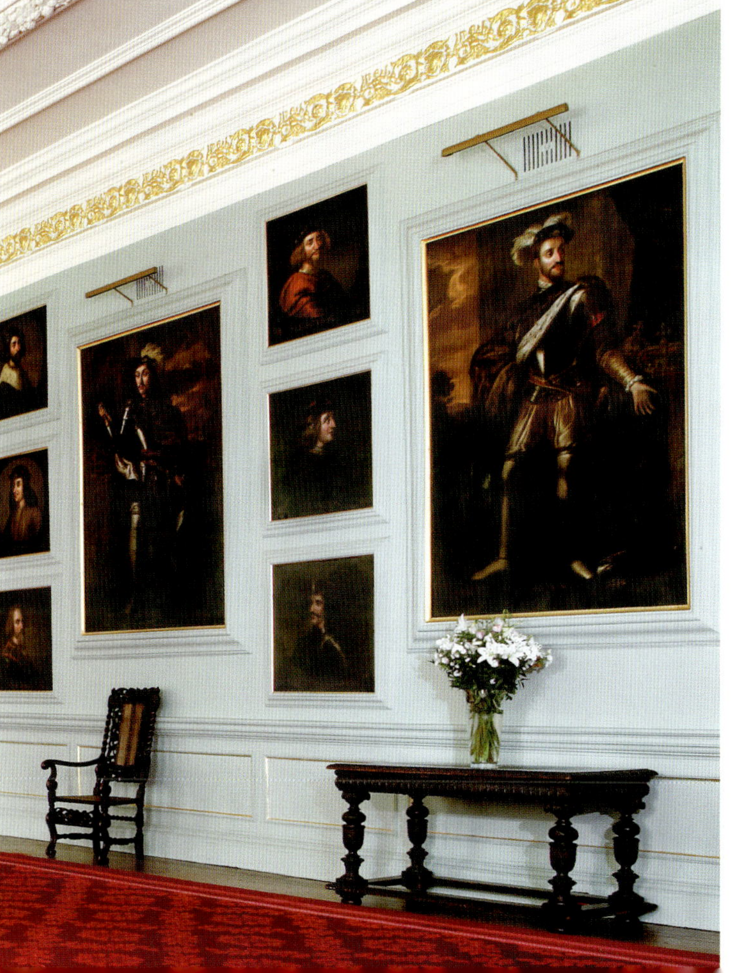

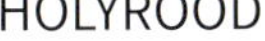

HOLYROOD

The Palace of Holyroodhouse—also called Holyrood Palace—rests at the end of Edinburgh's Royal Mile. The castle has undergone numerous renovations and additions in its long narrative, which includes many prominent names in Scottish history. Mary, Queen of Scots, held two of her weddings at the castle, and Oliver Cromwell's troops once lodged here during the English Civil Wars. When King George V and Queen Mary reigned, they modernized the ancient structure and initiated the tradition of holding garden parties on the verdant grounds.

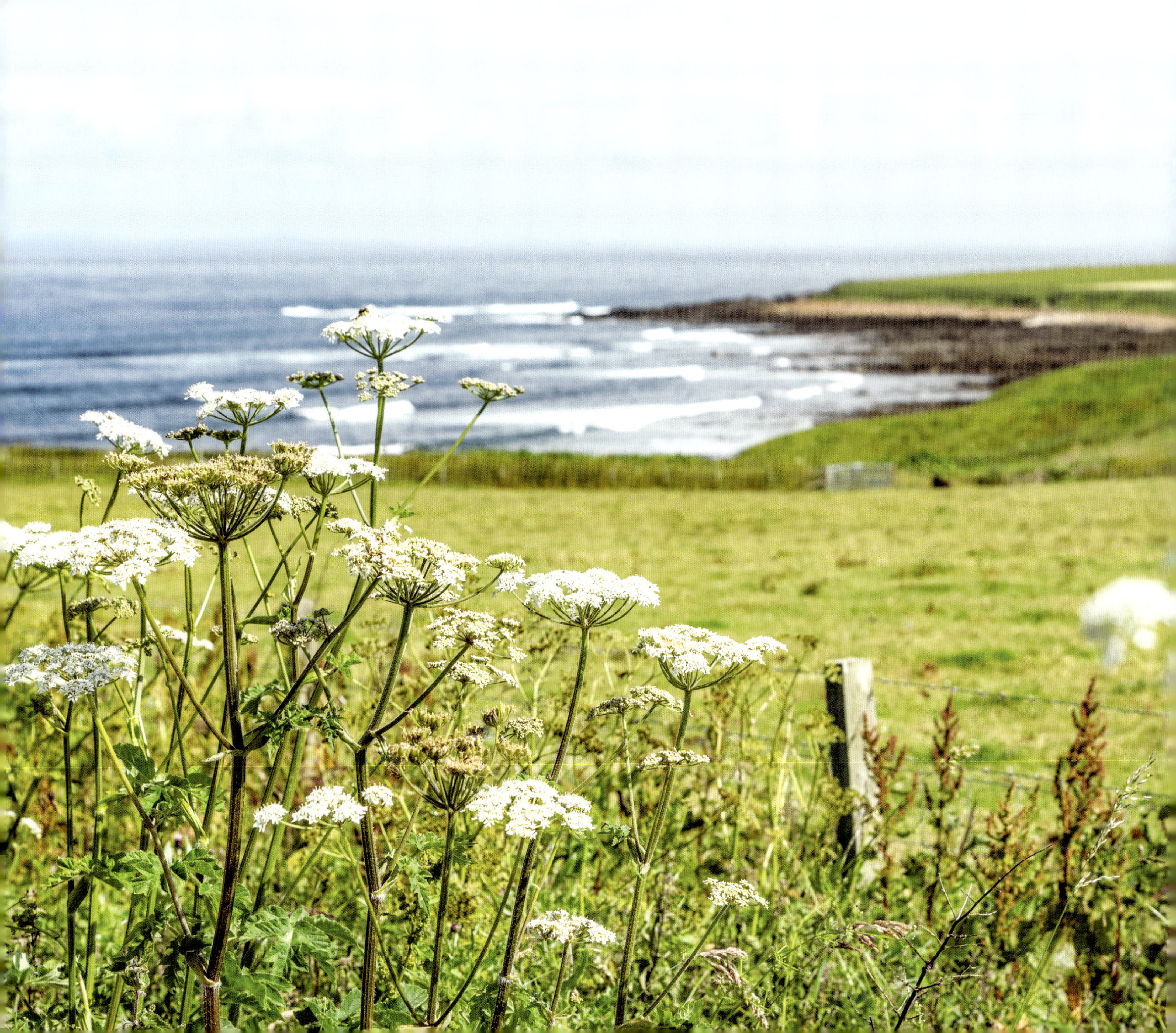

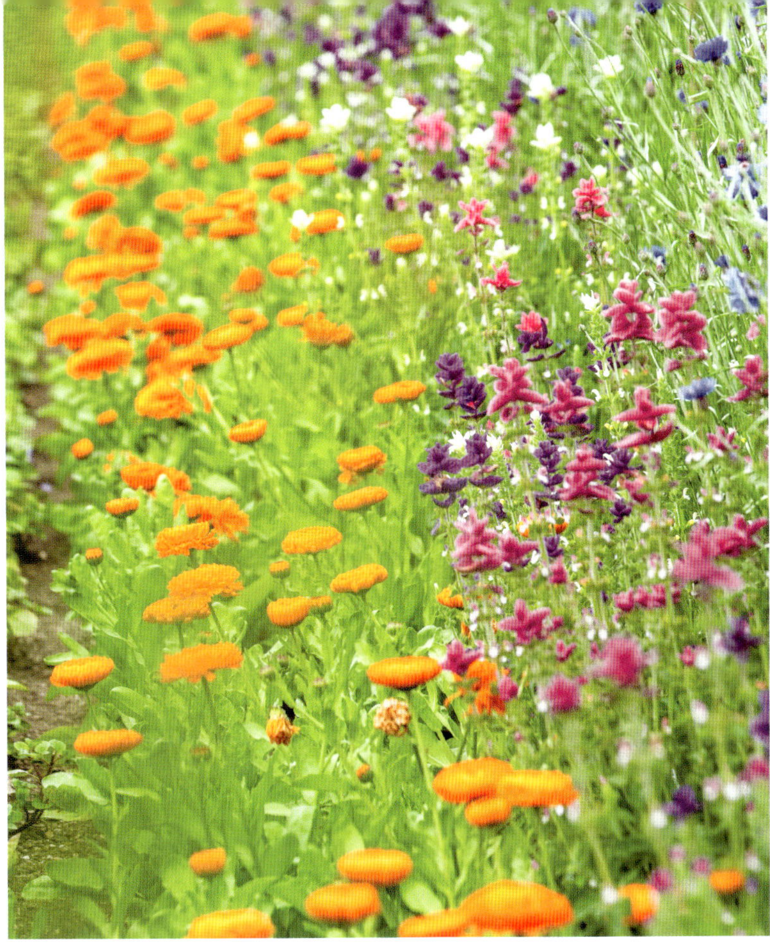

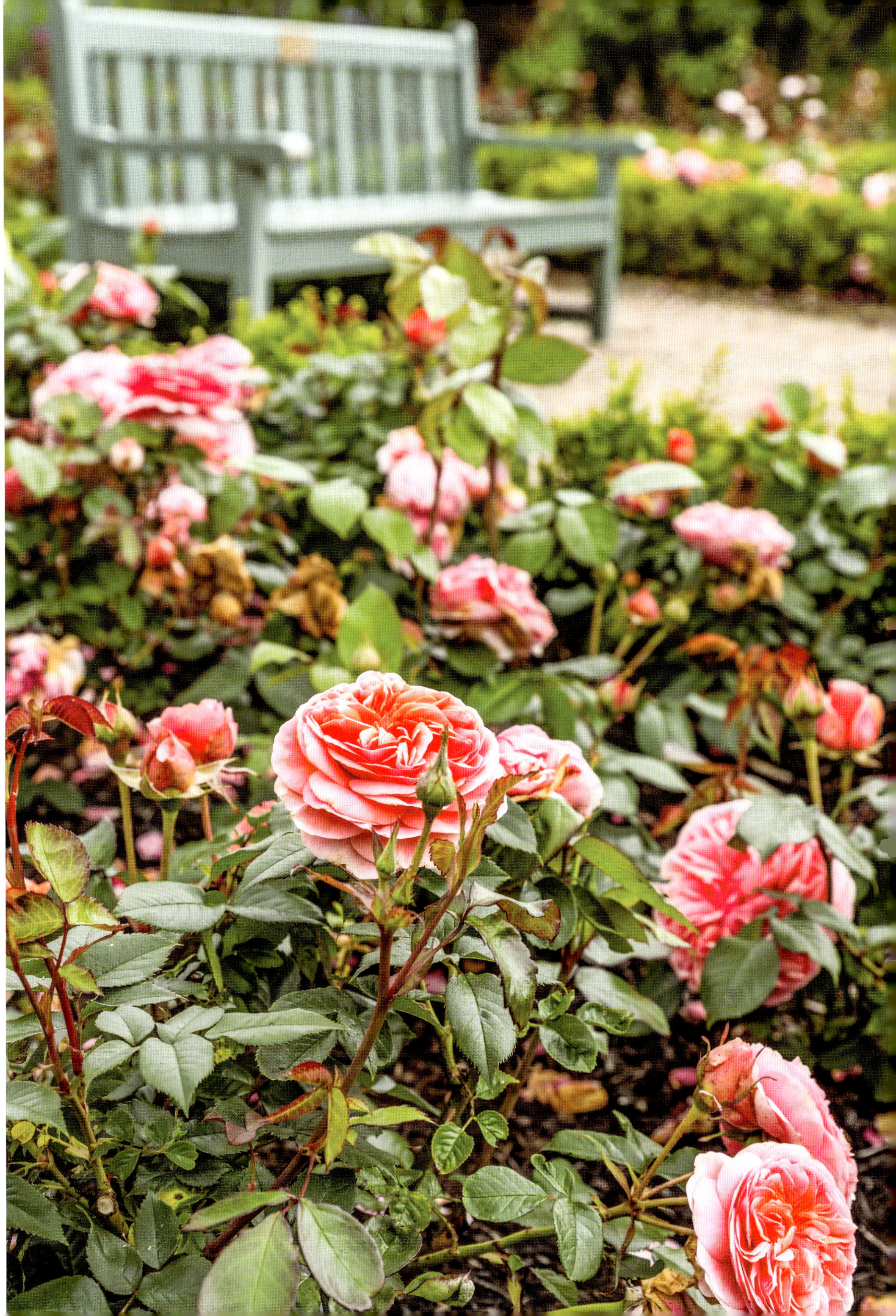

CASTLE OF MEY

The Castle of Mey stands proudly on its breathtaking coastal promontory, with a front-row view to the scenic waters of the North Sea. Built in the second half of the seventeenth century, the edifice incorporates the turrets and towers typical of that time. The gardens benefit from an ongoing rejuvenation, which includes gravel-strewn pathways and sitting areas set amid the colorful floral fanfare.

RIDING THE RAILS

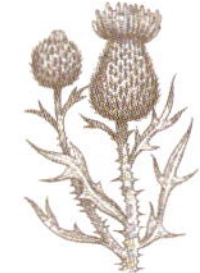

With its sweeps of melancholy moors, rugged rock outcroppings, and sun-dappled lochs, the landscape of Scotland's Highlands region possesses an almost otherworldly beauty that invites exploration. And while many choose to ramble about on foot or take to the motorways to experience these magnificent sights, others are joining in the old-fashioned tradition of traveling by rail.

Since the summer of 1984, thousands of excursionists have boarded the steam-powered train at Fort William, located along the shores of Loch Linnhe, in the shadows of the United Kingdom's tallest mountain, Ben Nevis. With the shrieking of its whistle and a great deal of hissing, the engine pulls out of the station for an eighty-four-mile round trip that crosses the countryside to the town of Mallaig and returns a few hours later.

Leaving a telltale trail of smoke in its wake, the train—named Jacobite for the historic Jacobite political movement, which has ties to the area—chugs merrily along, as heather-covered mile after mile passes by, each one bringing a new sight worth savoring. Sometimes it weaves through tight, steep-banked passages; other times, it skirts along placid lakes that stretch out like sheets of mirrored glass. About an hour from Fort William, the railcars traverse the breathtaking Glenfinnan Viaduct, an impressive, twenty-one-arched structure poised above Loch Shiel, famous for its appearances in the *Harry Potter* movie series.

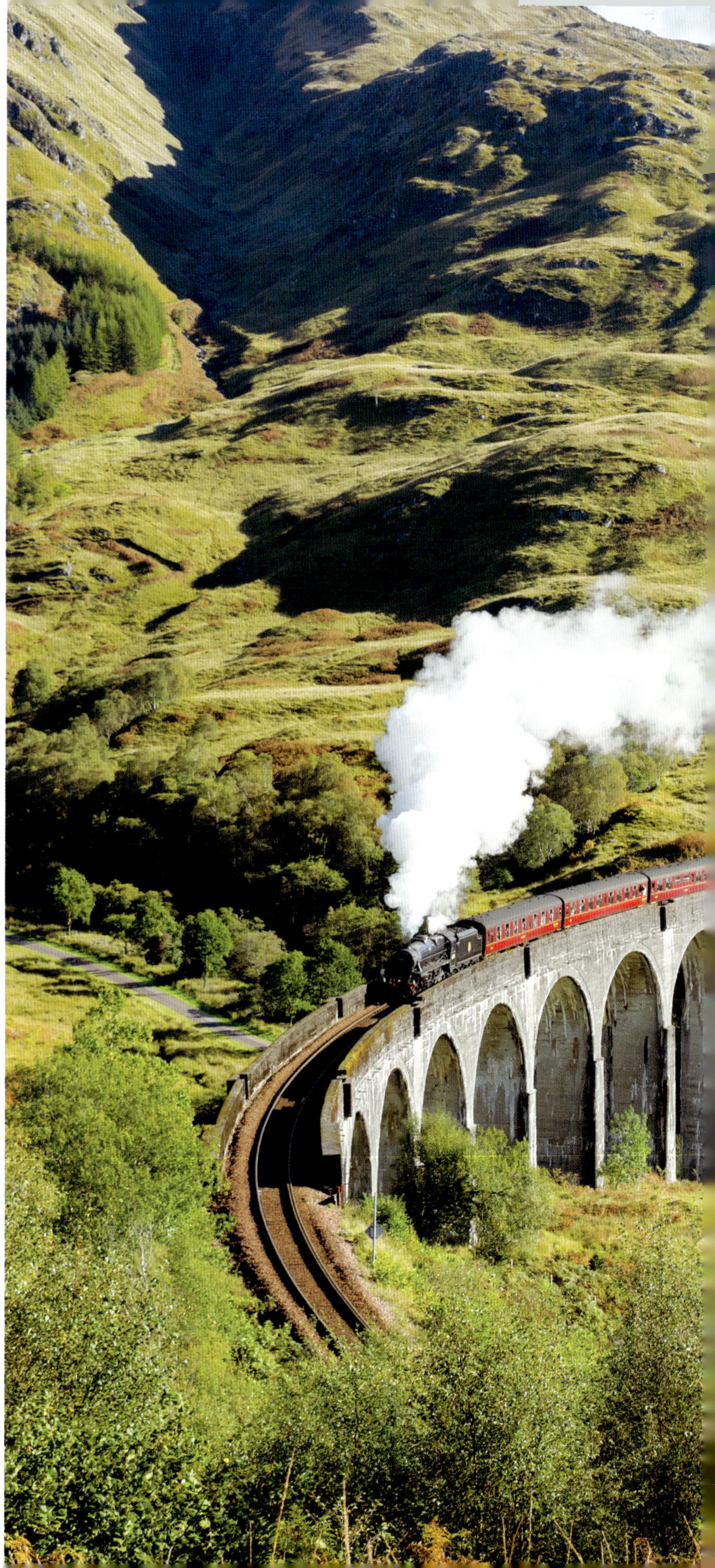

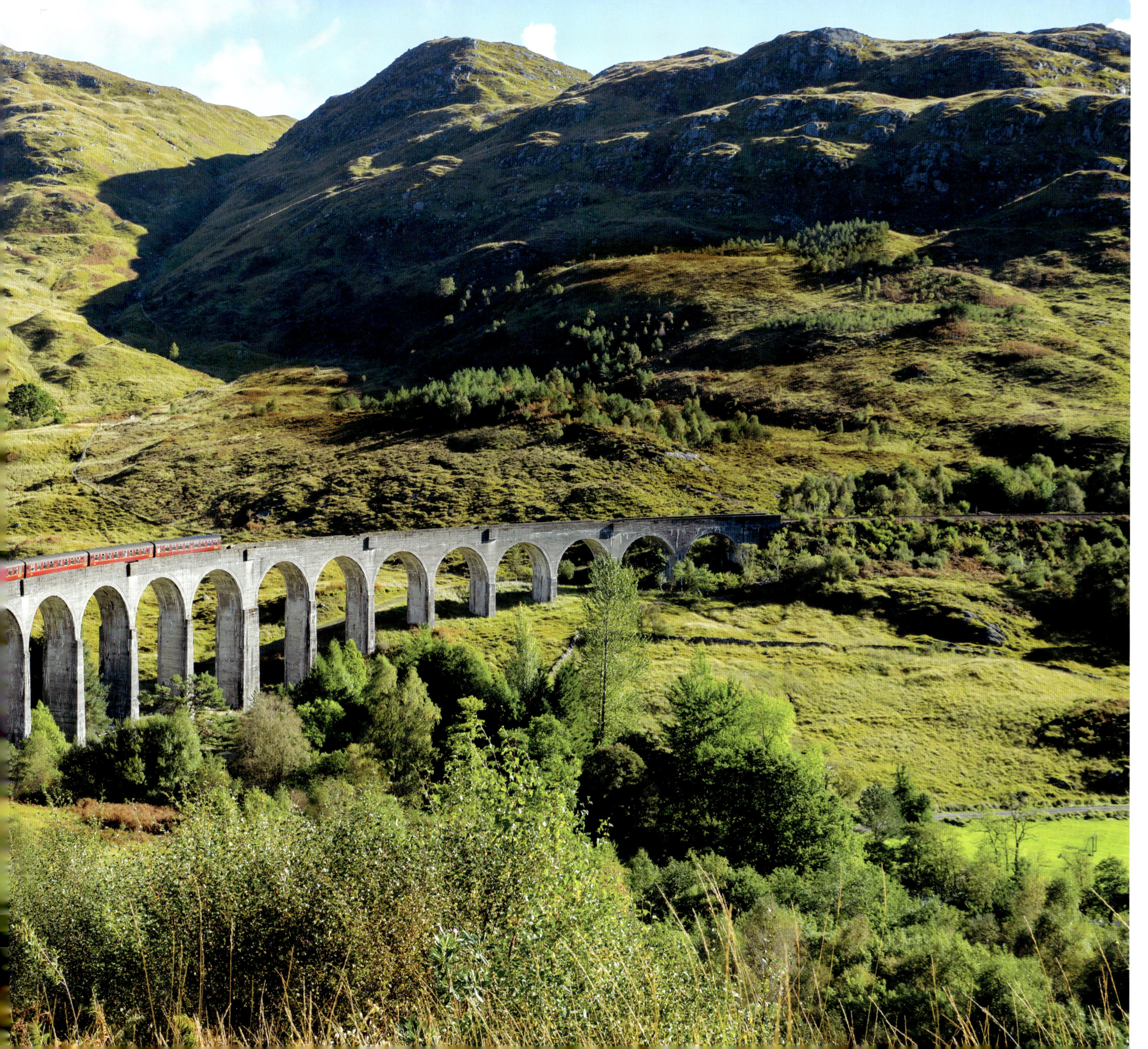

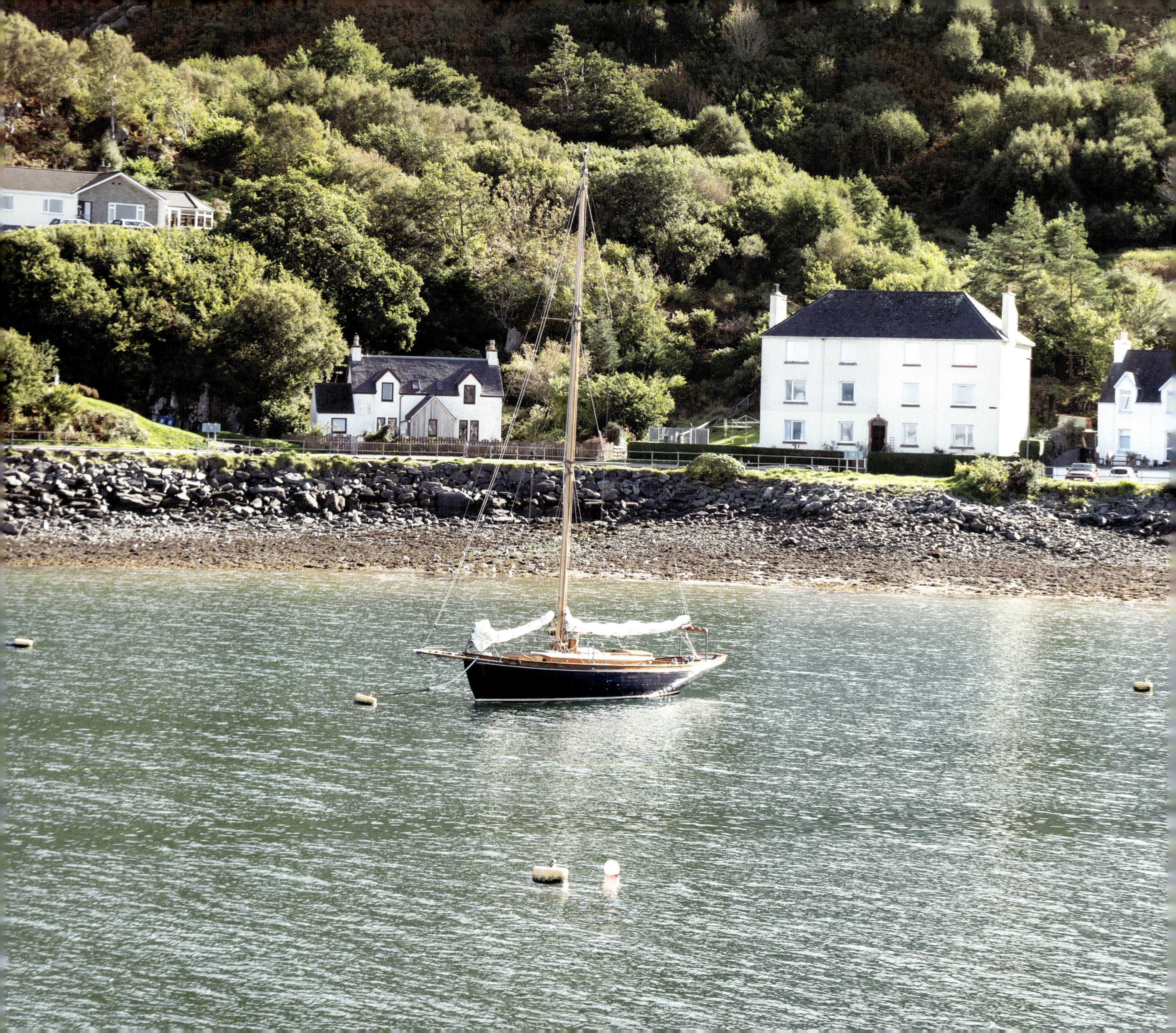

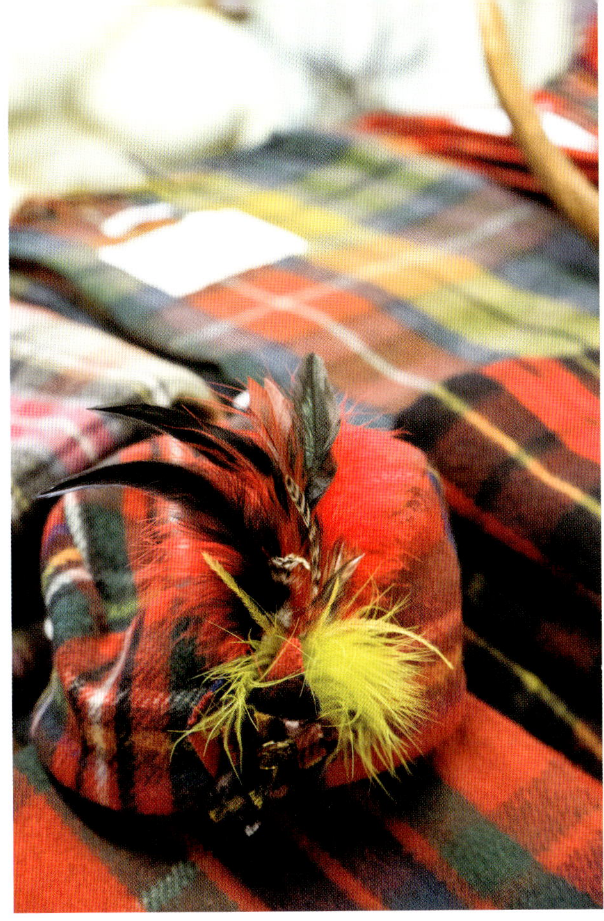

Right: The steam locomotive-hauled Jacobite rests while riders enjoy a lunchtime stopover in Mallaig, a busy fishing port in the Lochaber area. Opposite: Passengers ride in stylish comfort as they take in the waterside views of Mallaig as well as a cavalcade of scenic spots on the return trip to Fort William.

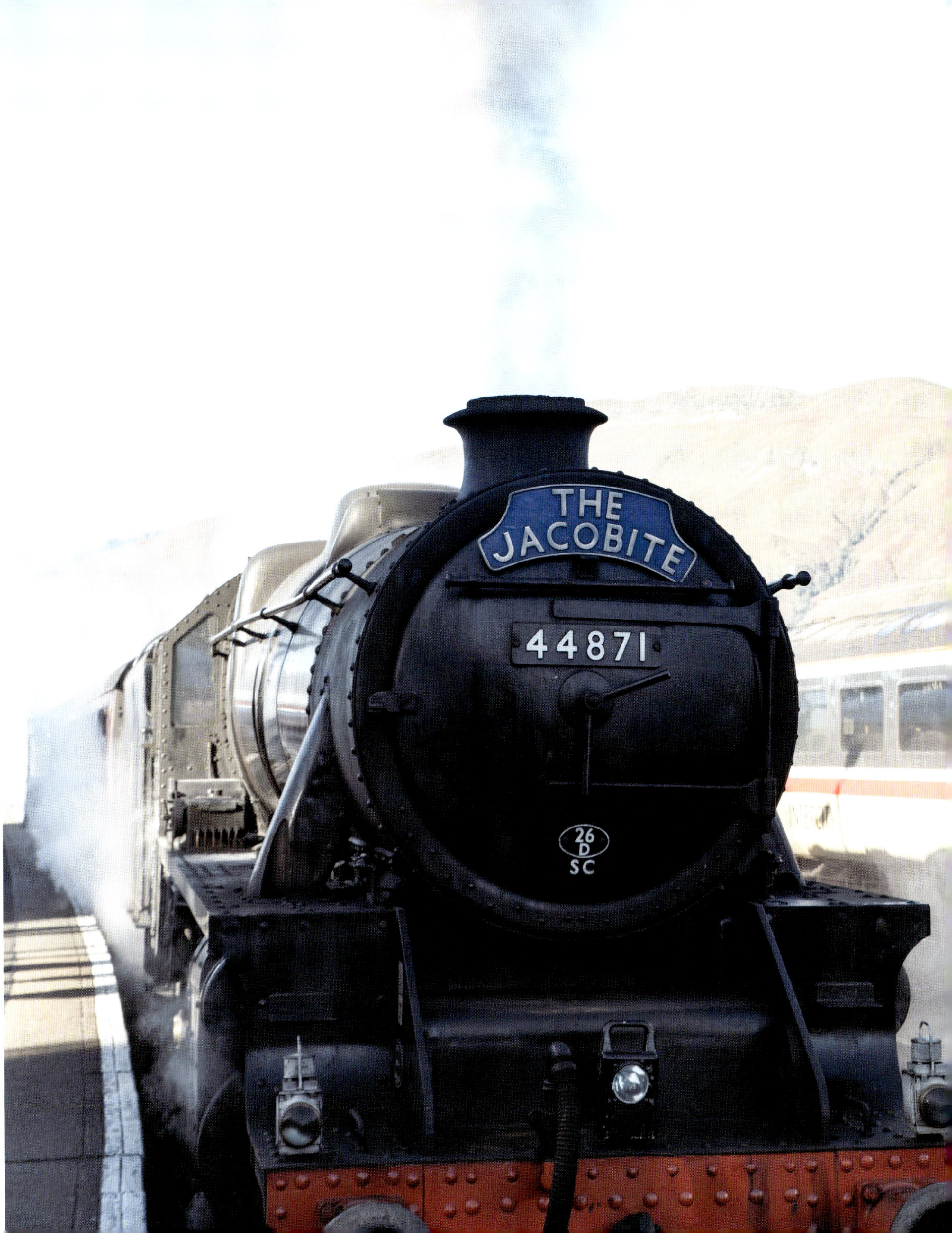

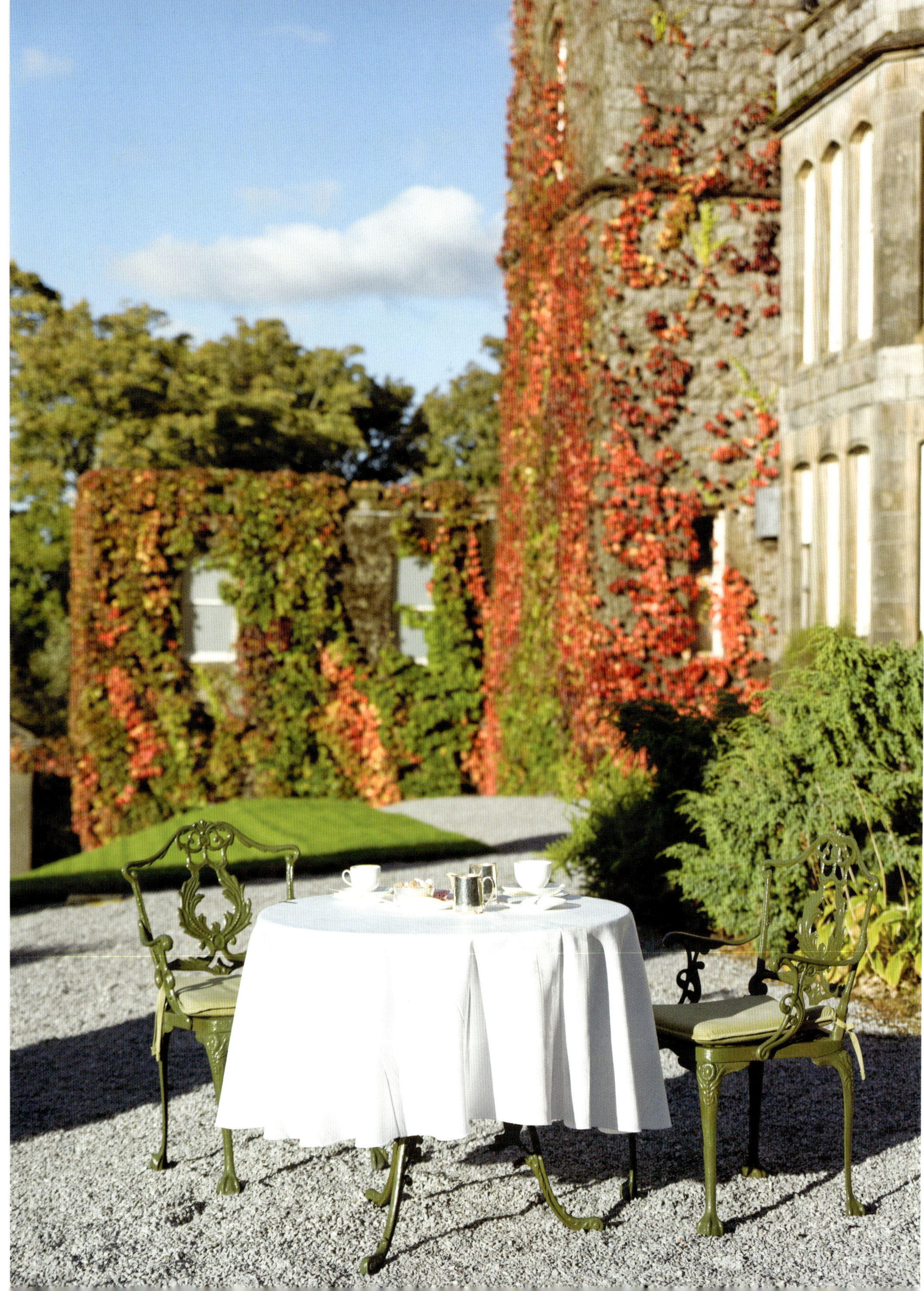

Left: The nineteenth-century Inverlochy Castle Hotel nestles in the countryside outside Fort William. When she visited the five-star luxury auberge in 1873, Queen Victoria penned in her diary, "I never saw a lovelier or more romantic spot." Indeed, some of the prettiest scenery in the Highlands surrounds Inverlochy Castle.

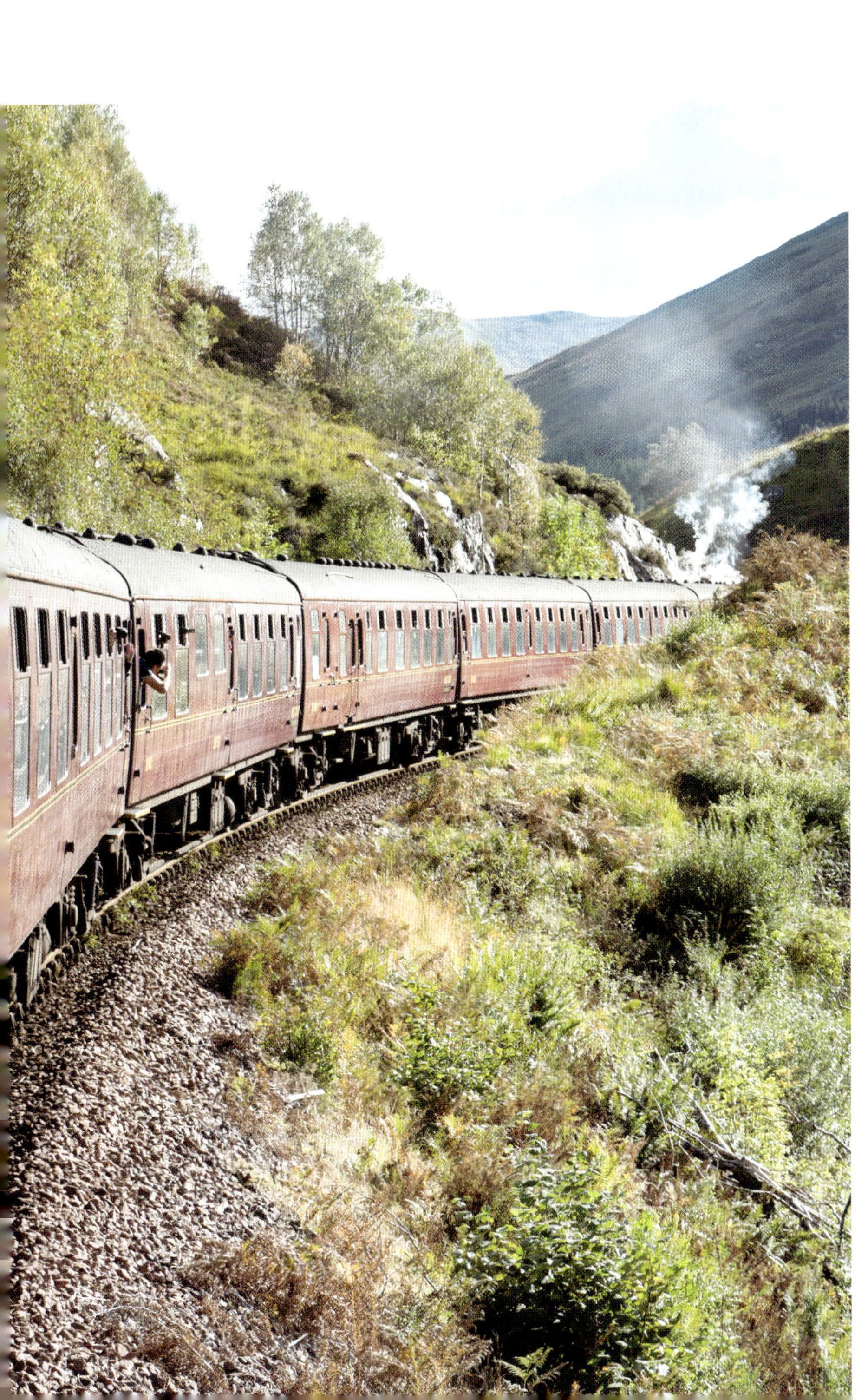

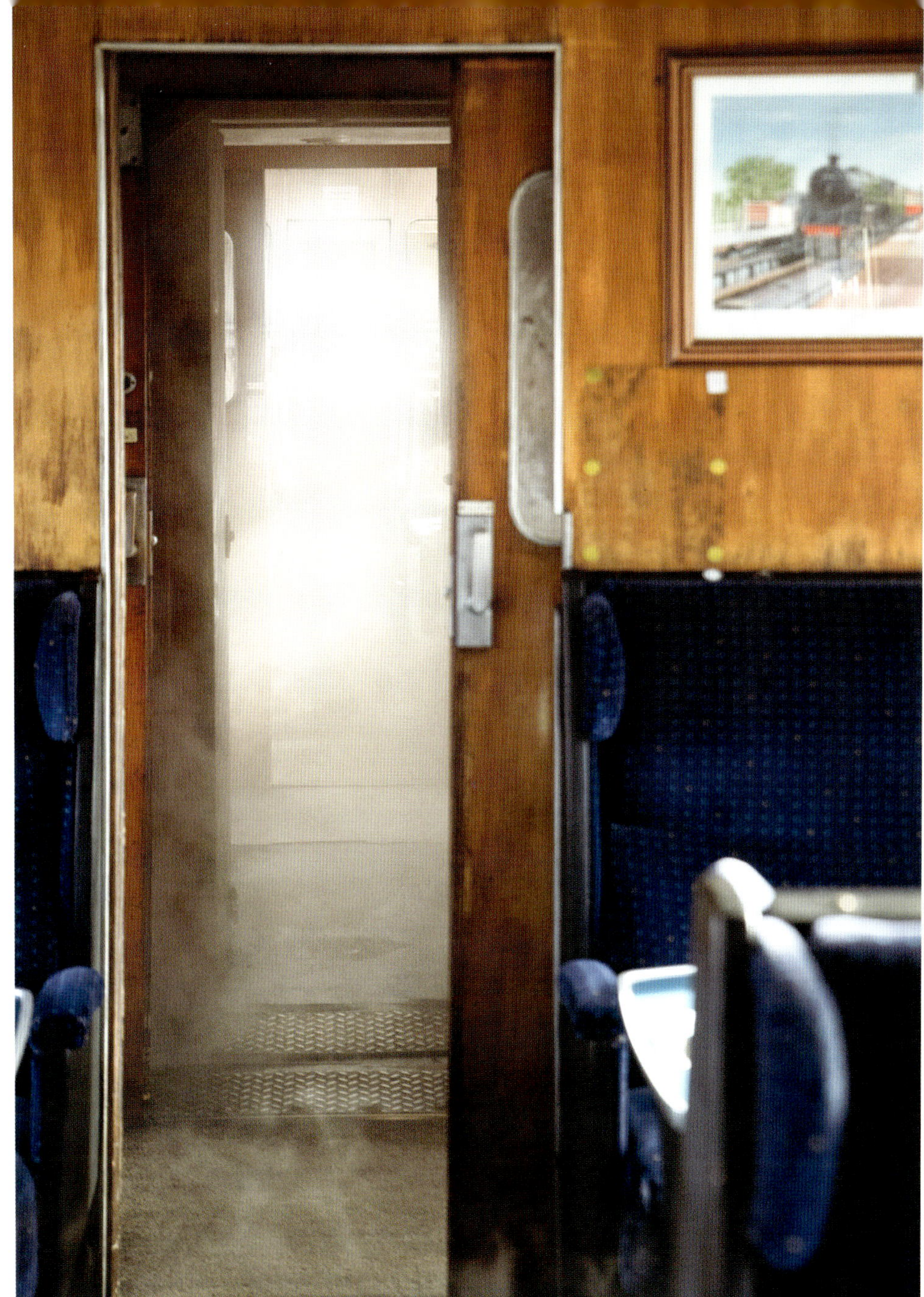

Upon arriving in Mallaig, passengers disembark for an outing that includes a sampling of traditional Scottish fare, such as smoked salmon and Angus beef, and the scouting of wares in local shops. Soon, the whistle sounds, and it's time for the return journey. Windows frame vistas of timeworn castles and windswept scenery as the train heads back, the steady cadence of the wheels a coda to this visual symphony as spellbound travelers make their way home.

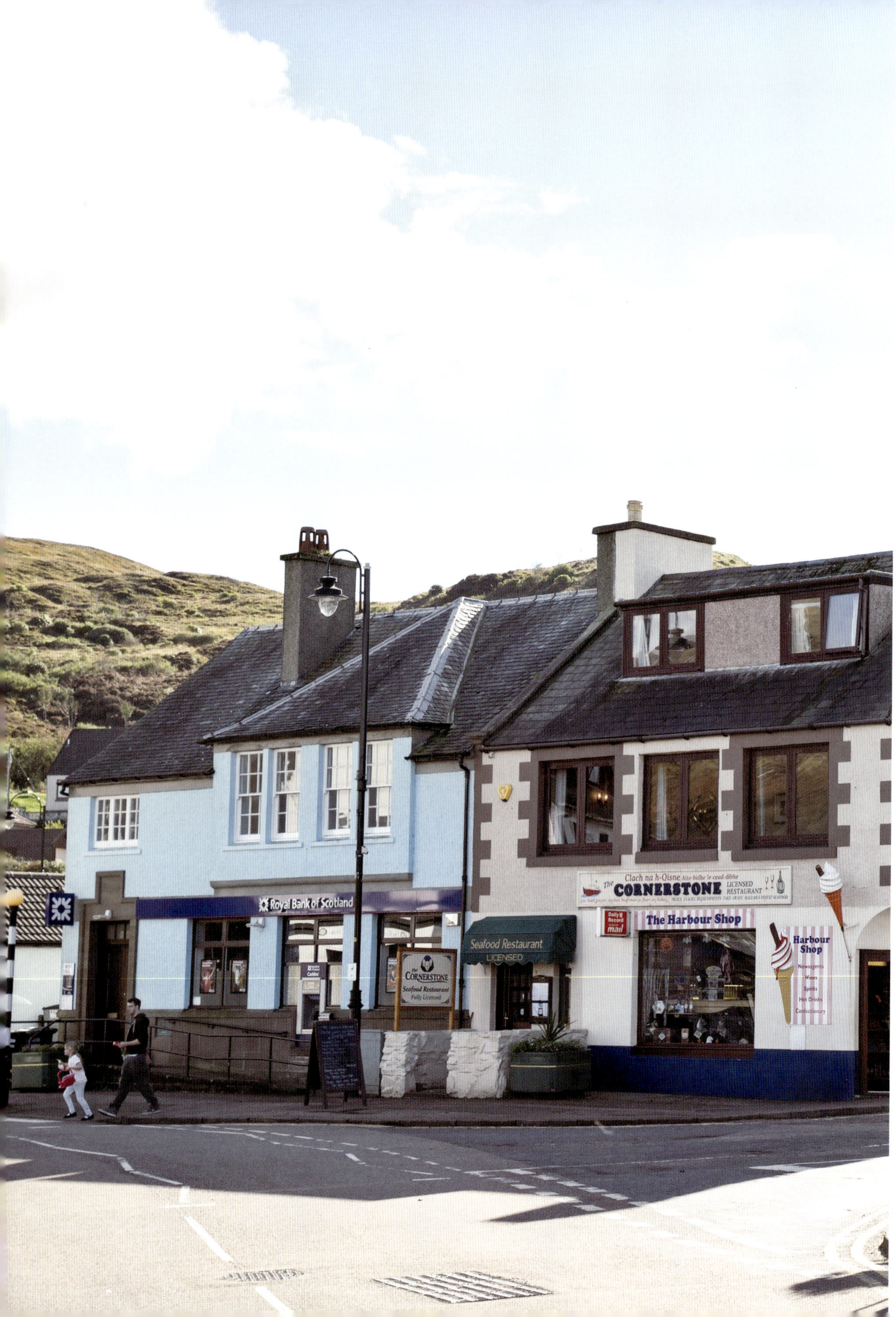

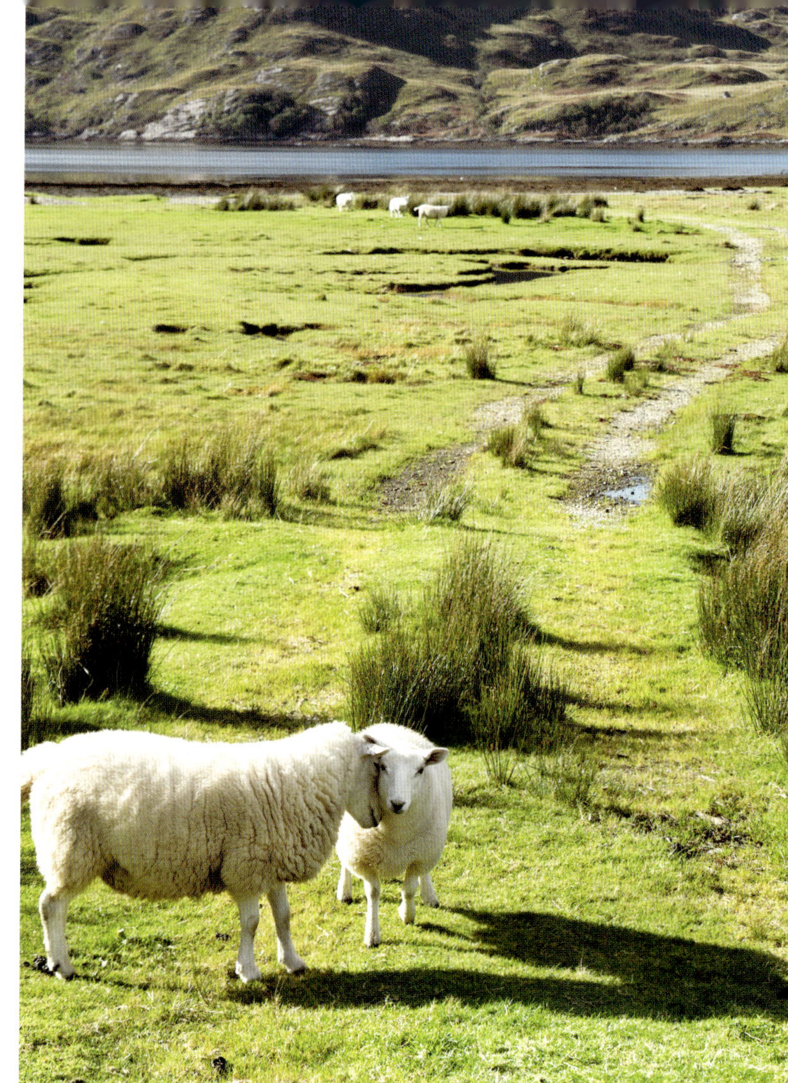

Ordinary cares of the day seem to slip away as moments pass aboard the train, with the locomotive carrying passengers through miles of varied yet beautiful scenery. Quaint villages brimming with shops—such as the town of Mallaig, a fishing port on the northwest coast—bid exploration, left, while pastoral scenes lend serenity to the ride, above. Opposite: Shifting seasons ensure that each ticket promises lovely glimpses of natural beauty.

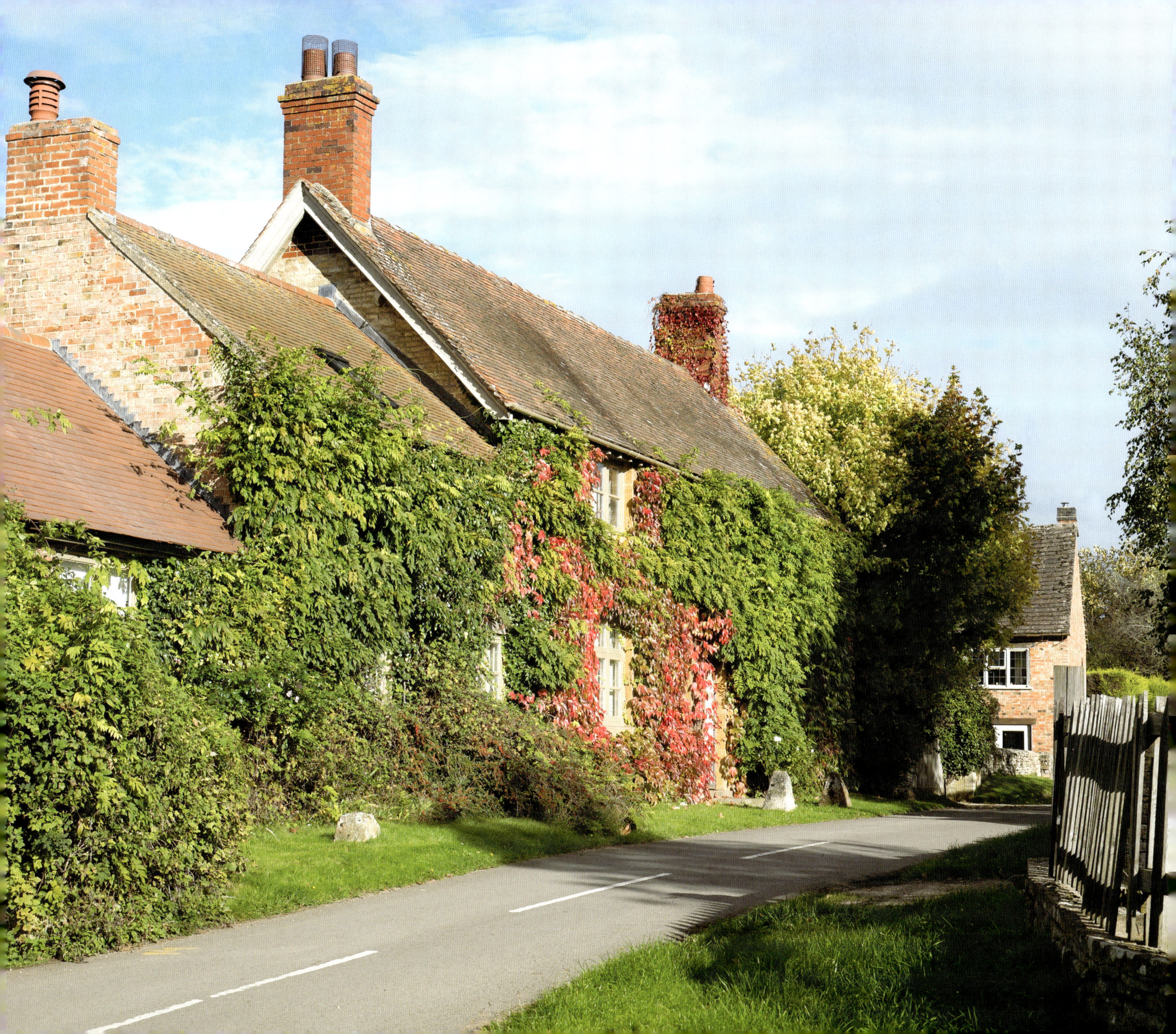

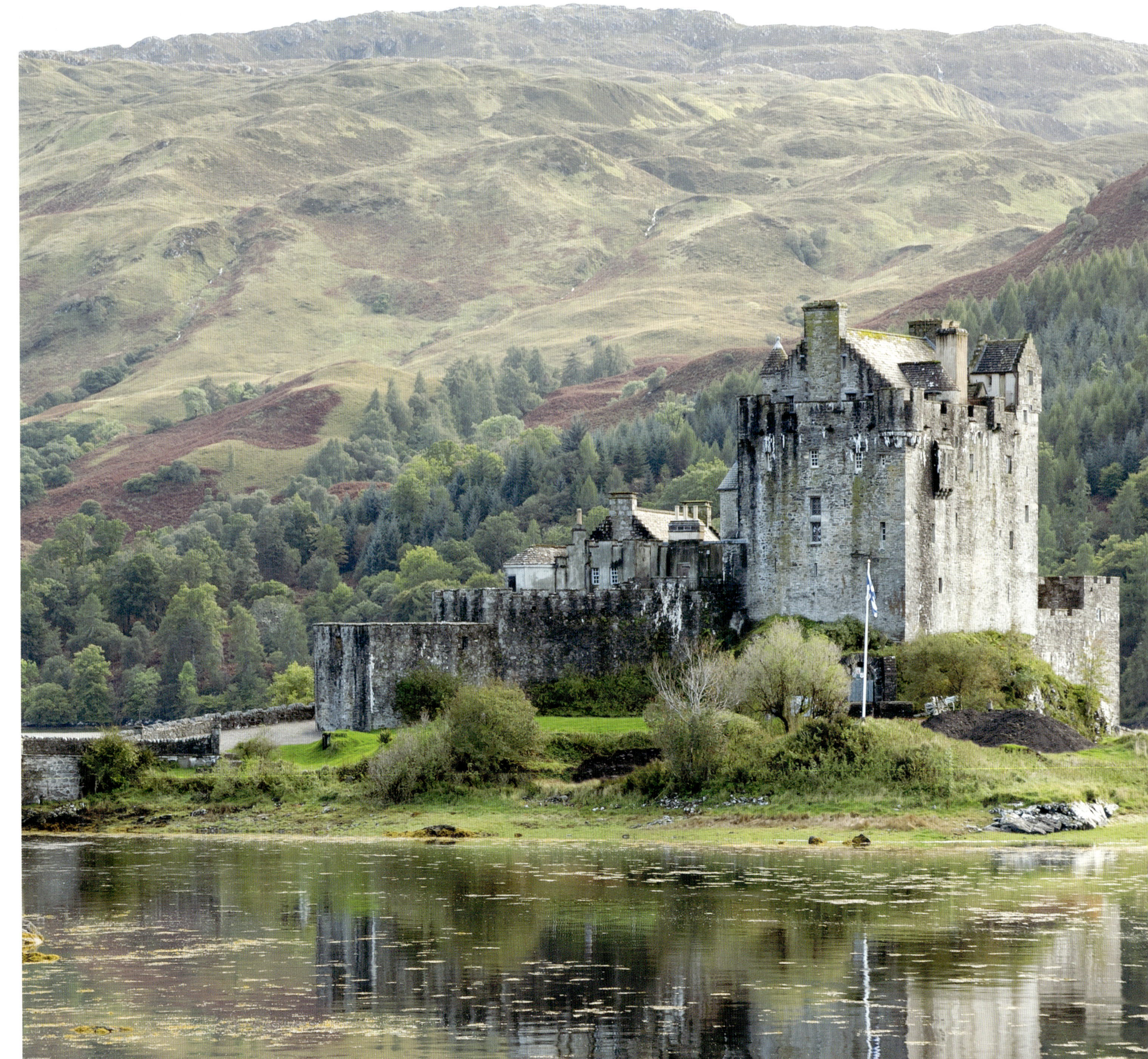

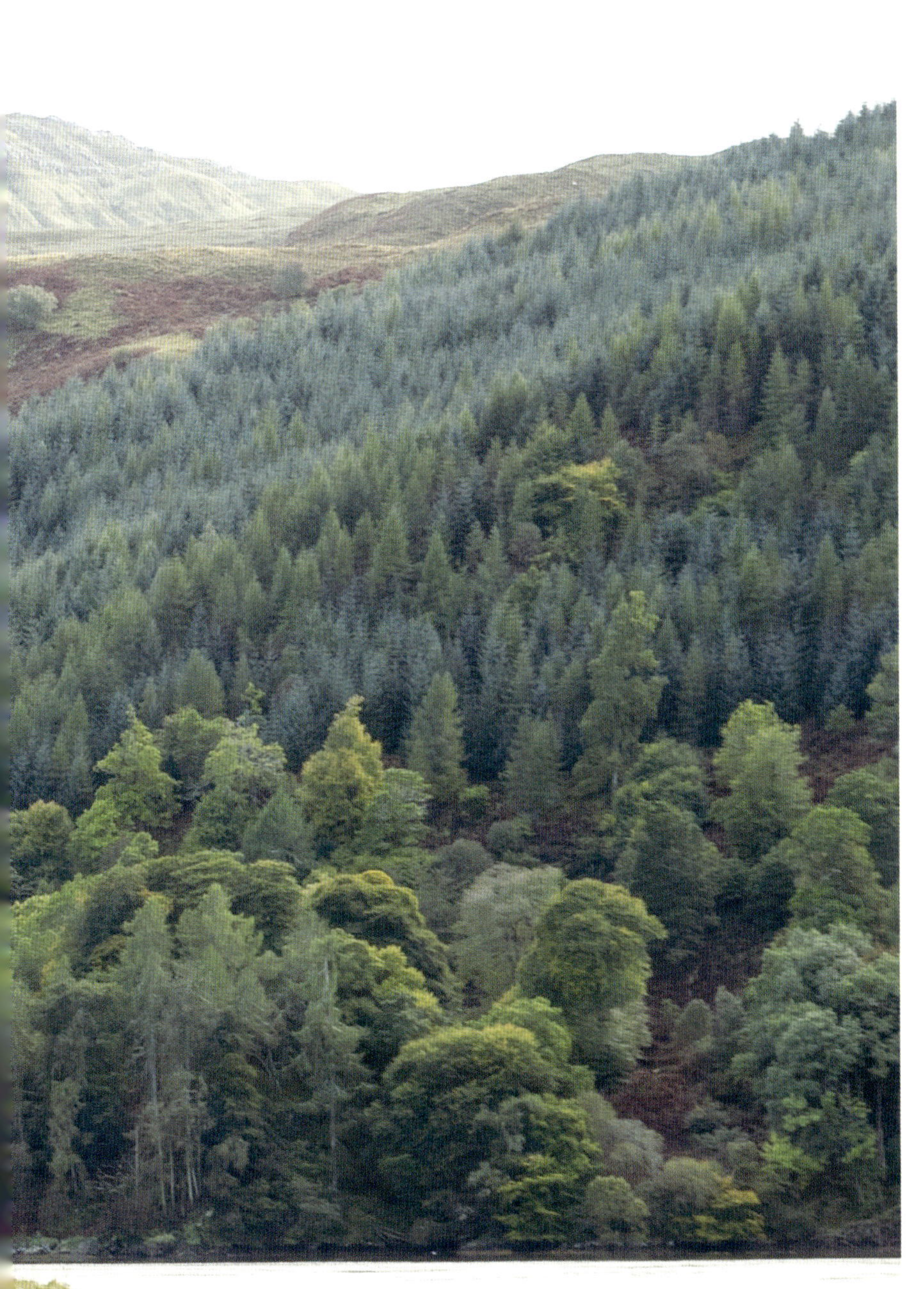

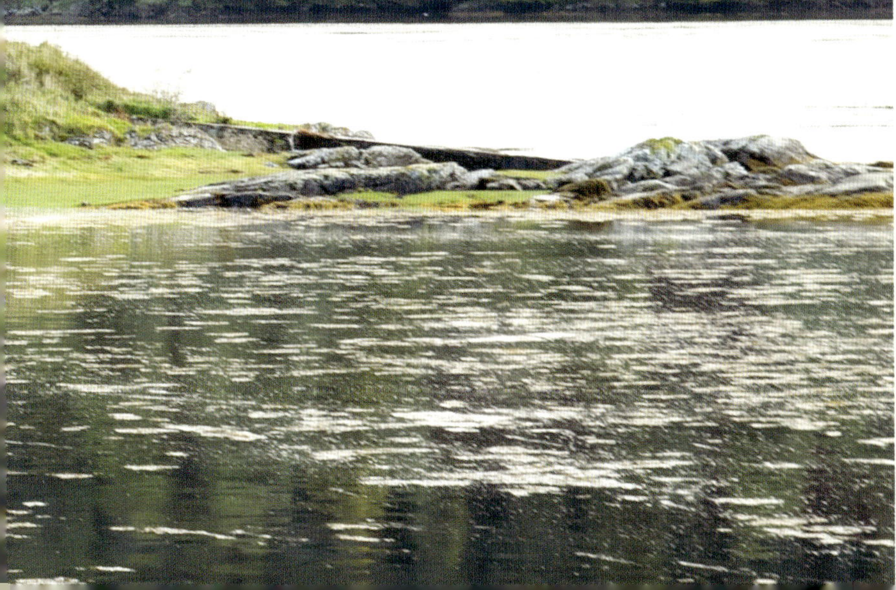

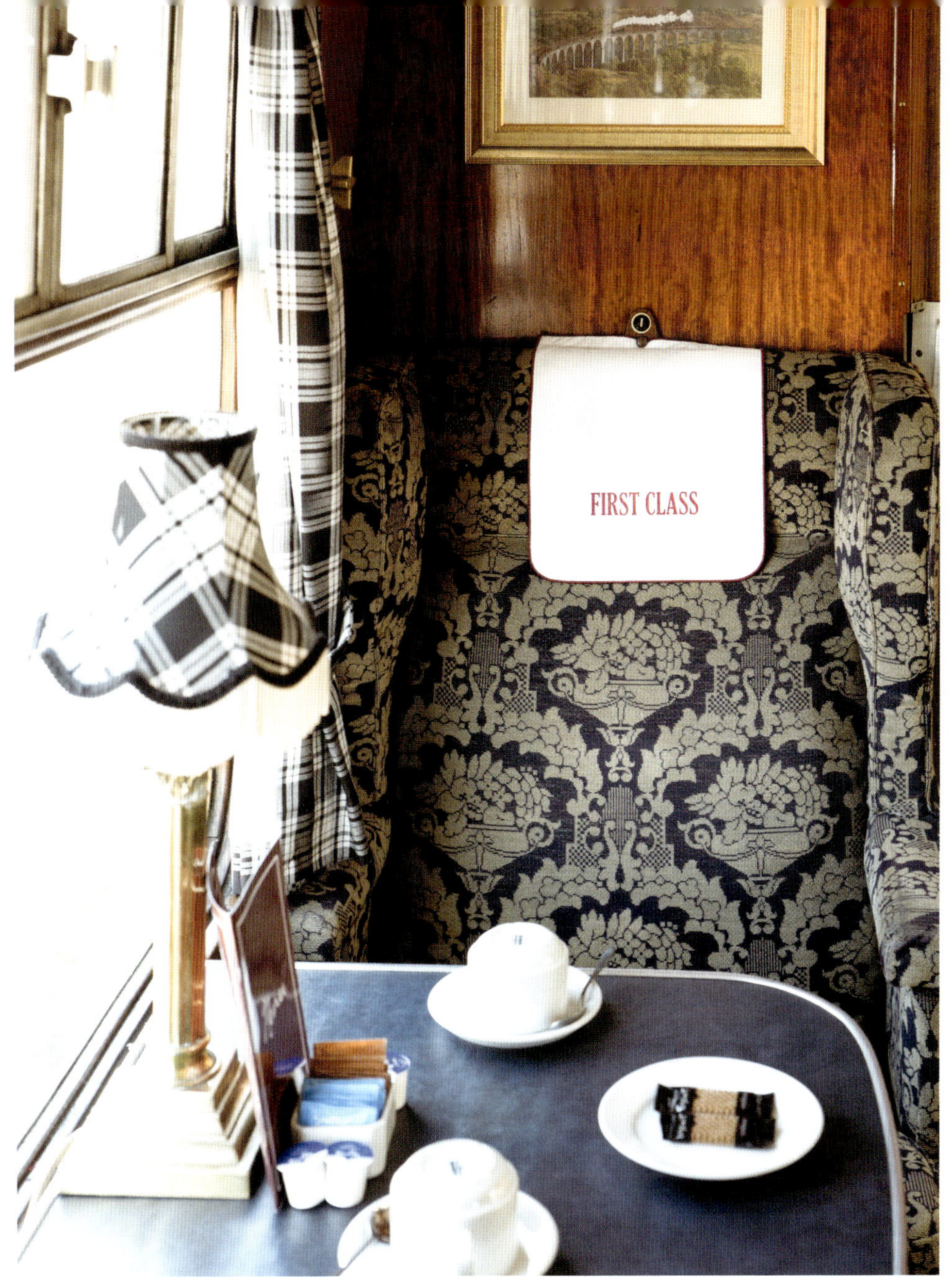

"There's something about the sound of a train that's very romantic and nostalgic and hopeful."

—Paul Simon

ON SCOTLAND'S MOUNTAINS & MOORS

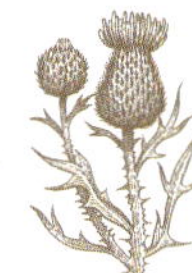

September winds blow across the Scottish moors, stirring spent tufts of cotton grass and a purple haze of heather in its second blooming. In the ageless glens that glaciers chiseled aeons ago, golden oaks, scarlet-berried rowans, and silver-barked birches transform the countryside into a pageantry of color.

The fall season holds sway in the capital city of Edinburgh. At Princes Street Gardens, a public park in the center of town, trees adorned with shawls of colorful leaves encircle monuments to revered Scotsmen, such as author and historian Sir Walter Scott and the poet Allan Ramsay. Nearby, at the Royal Botanic Garden Edinburgh, the brilliant reds and golds of Fothergilla and witch hazel breathe life into the urban cityscape.

Edinburgh is divided into two distinct sections. Old Town, which dates to medieval times, is a maze of cobblestone streets. Its main thoroughfare, the Royal Mile, stretches from Edinburgh Castle to Holyrood Palace, with shops, pubs, and museums interspersed among antiquated structures. In contrast, New Town is laid out in a grid marked by broad streets and green spaces. The Neoclassical and Georgian architecture of the buildings confirm that this quarter was developed in the eighteenth and nineteenth centuries.

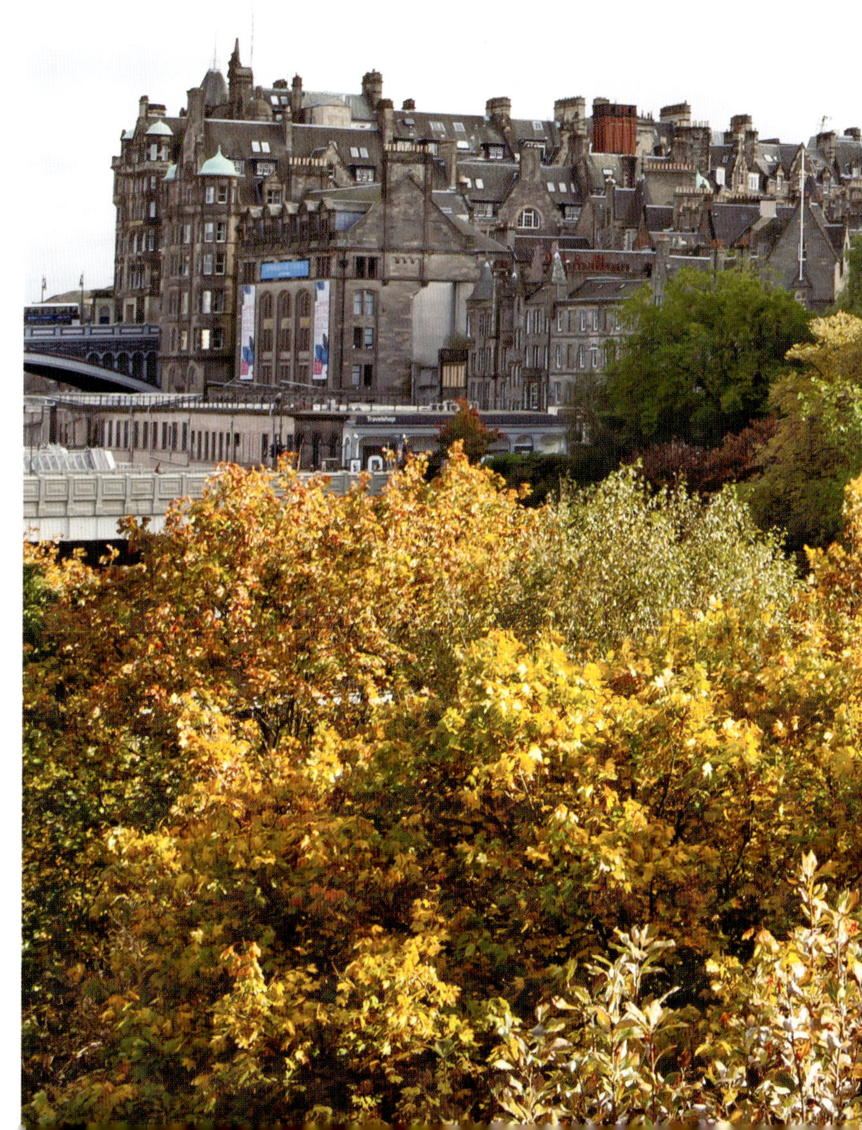

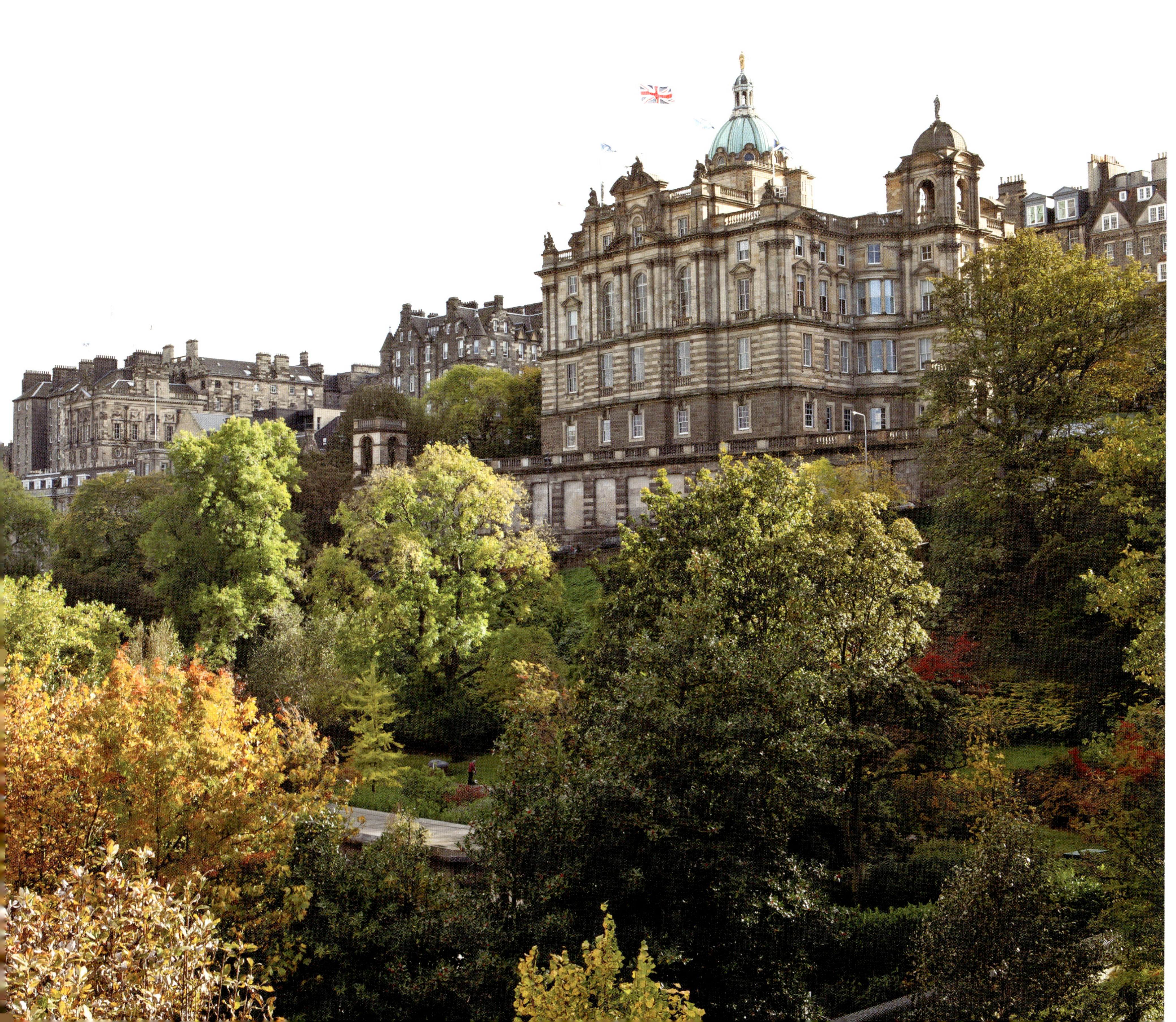

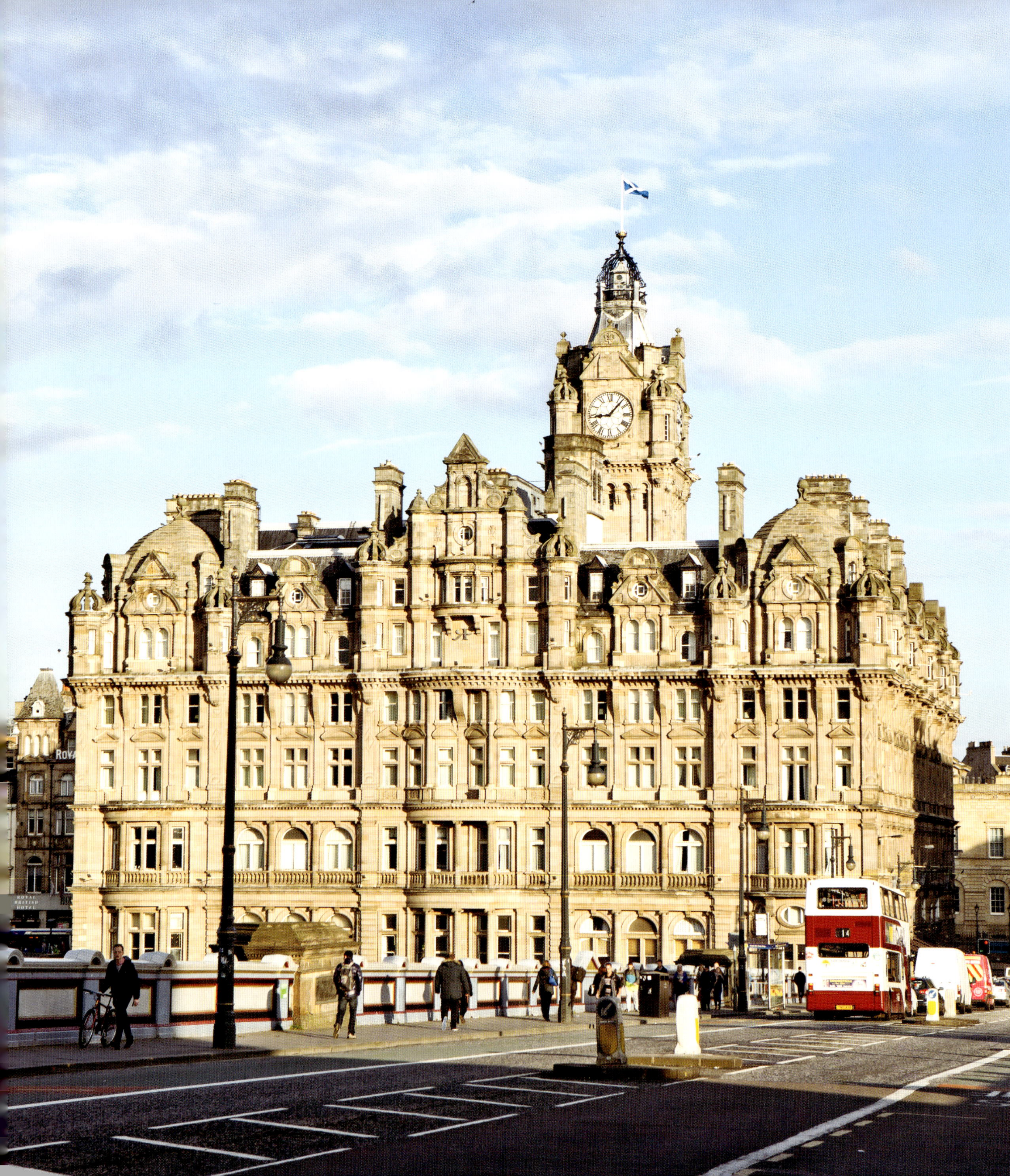

Left: The iconic clock in the tower of The Balmoral Hotel traditionally is set three minutes ahead to ensure rail passengers make their trains on time. Known until the 1980s as the North British Station Hotel (or simply "the N.B."), The Balmoral reflects a mix of Victorian and Scottish baronial-style architecture. Author J.K. Rowling penned the final pages of her *Harry Potter* book series here. Opposite, clockwise from right: In the shadow of Edinburgh Castle, Princes Street Gardens provides a lush botanical retreat within the city's center. A former cotton mill on the River Teith houses the Deanston Distillery, acclaimed for its single-malt Scotch.

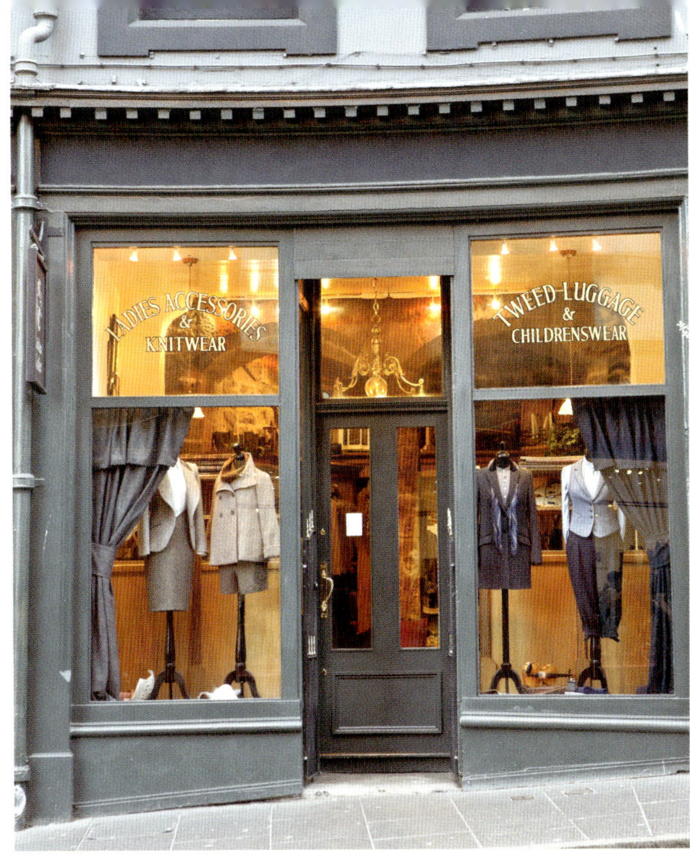
LADIES ACCESSORIES
&
KNITWEAR
TWEED LUGGAGE
&
CHILDRENSWEAR

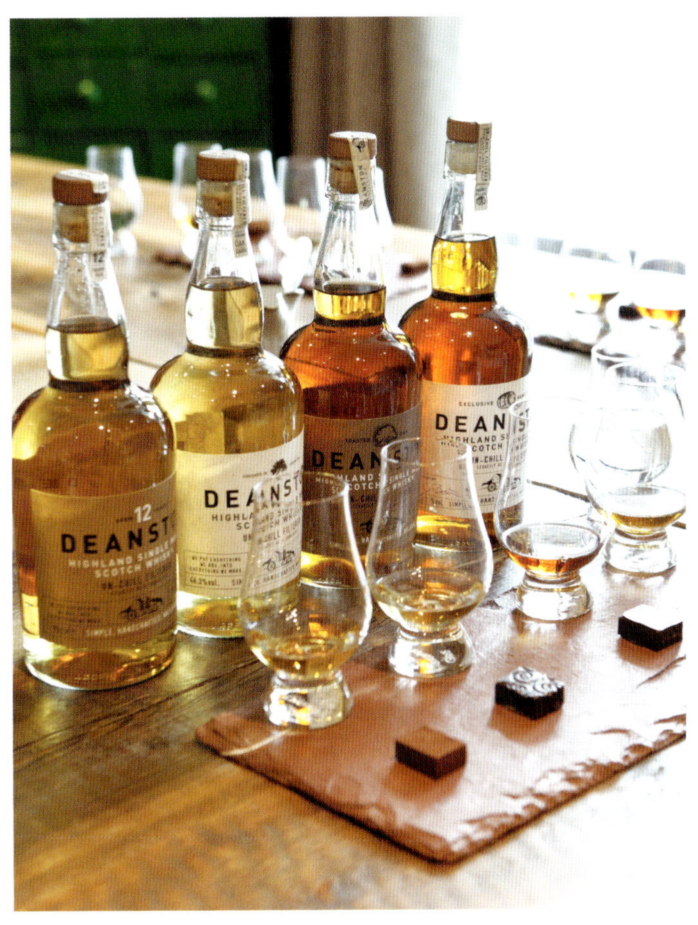

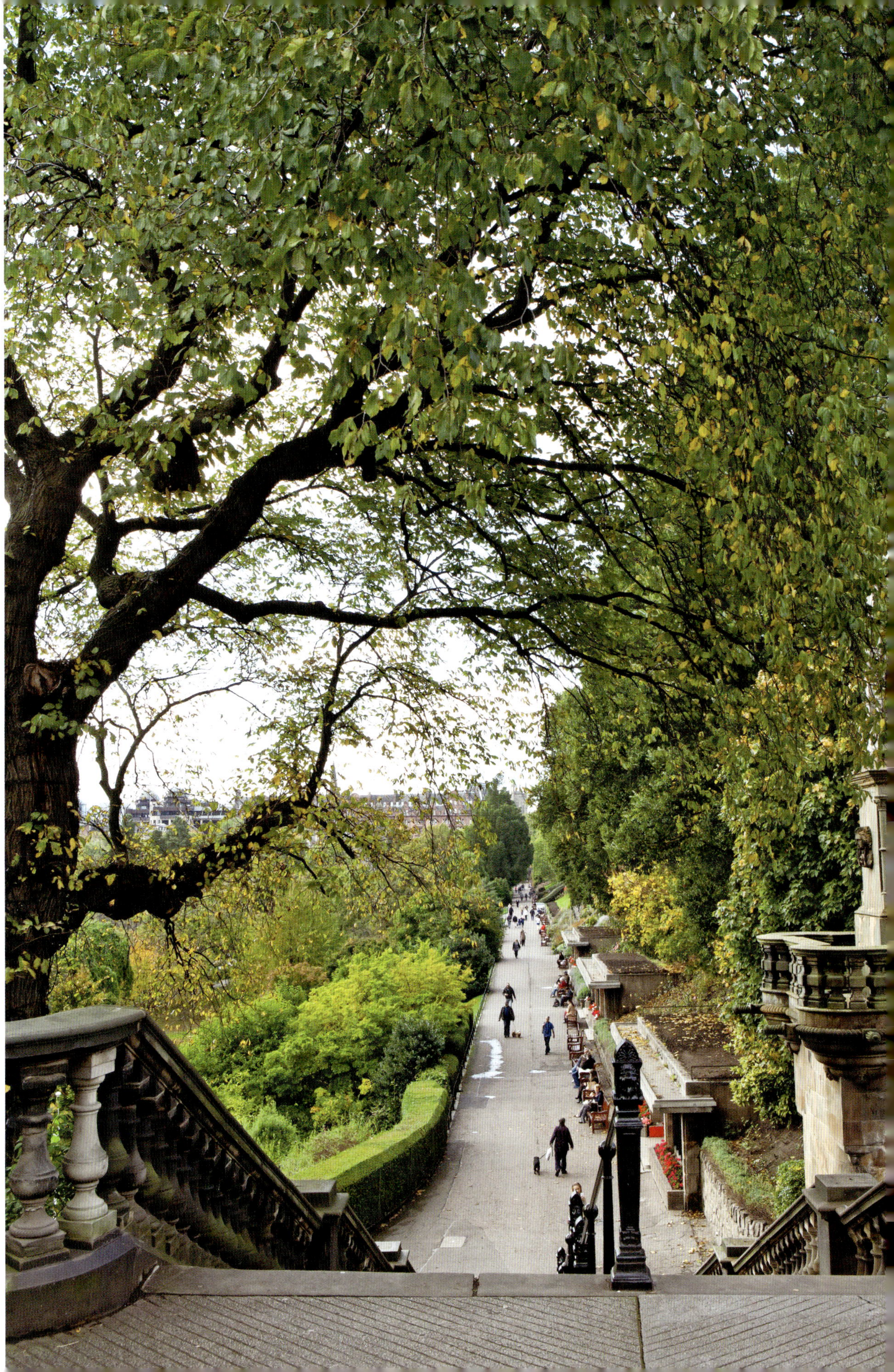

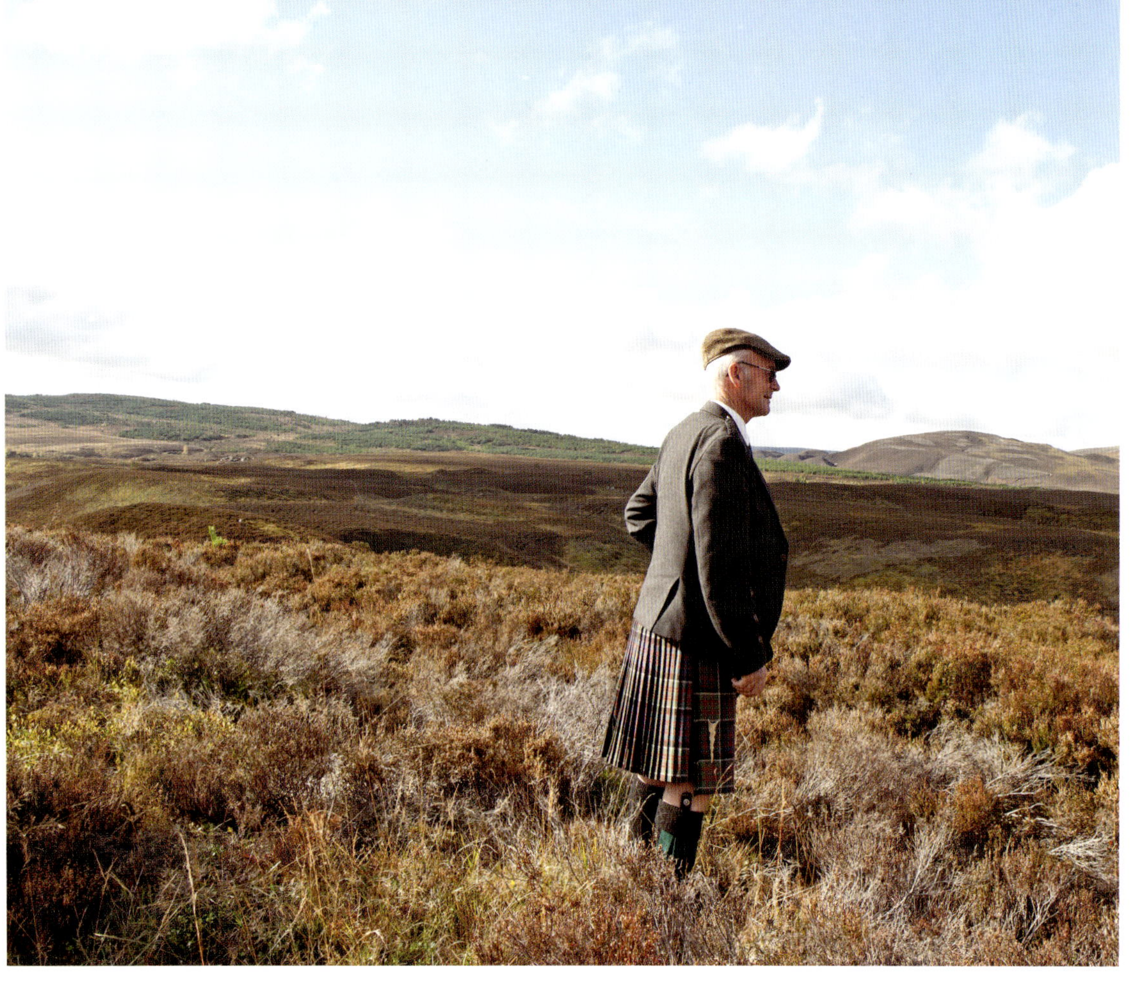

Venturing north from Edinburgh toward the Scottish Highlands, the landscape takes on a different topography. Smooth hills give way to jutting ridges and jagged peaks, with sweeping moors and picturesque lochs providing striking contrast. Perhaps the most notable of these lakes is Loch Ness—famous for its legendary water creature. From this point, the River Ness flows into the Moray Firth, providing the city of Inverness with a breathtaking vantage point. The area is rich in history: The ruins of Urquhart Castle, a fortress dating to the thirteenth century, overlook Loch Ness. Macbeth, the former King of Scotland made immortal in William Shakespeare's play, had a castle here as well.

To the northeast of Edinburgh, the town of St Andrews has graced the shoreline for centuries. Named for Andrew the Apostle, the church has always played an important role here, and the ruins of the largest house of worship ever built in Scotland stand as testament. The area also lays claim as the birthplace of golf. Old Course at St Andrews is still considered the standard by which all other courses are measured.

From the Highlands to the coast and every enchanting mile in between, Scotland beckons travelers to journey through its unforgettable scenery to witness the splendor of autumn in this storied land.

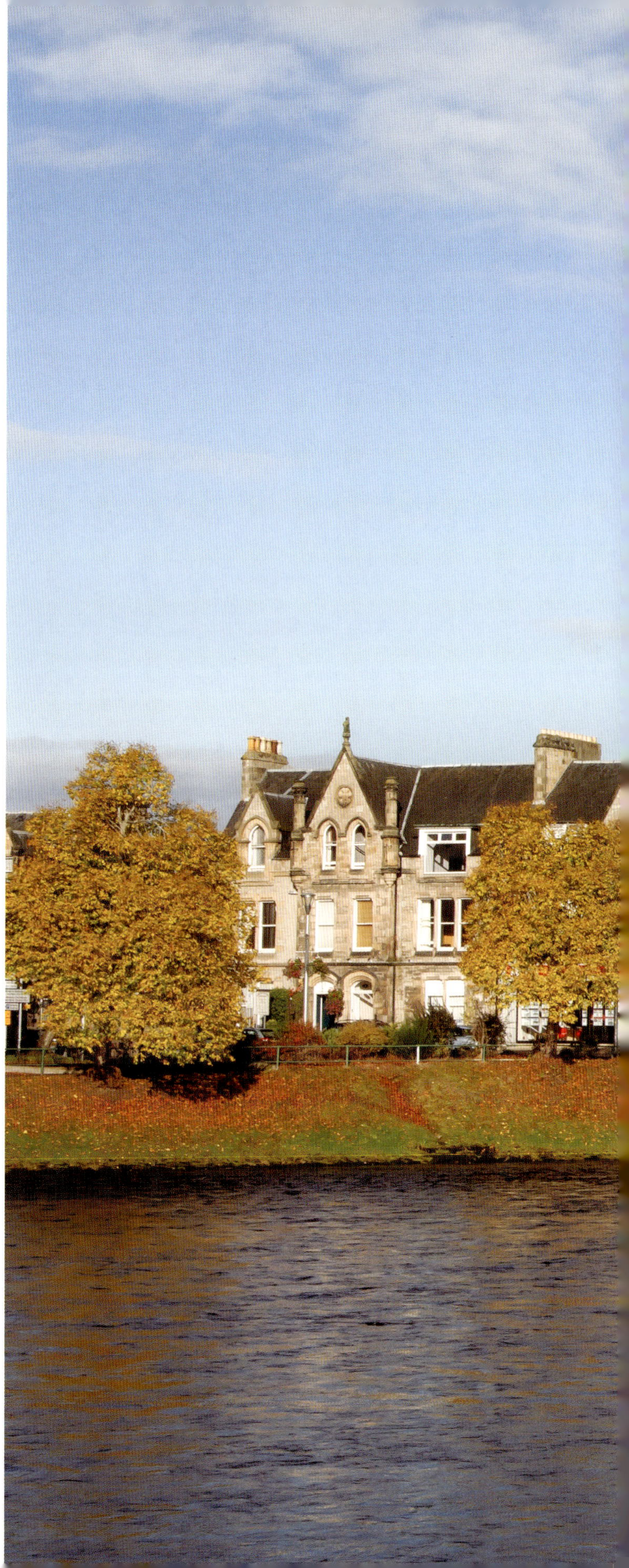

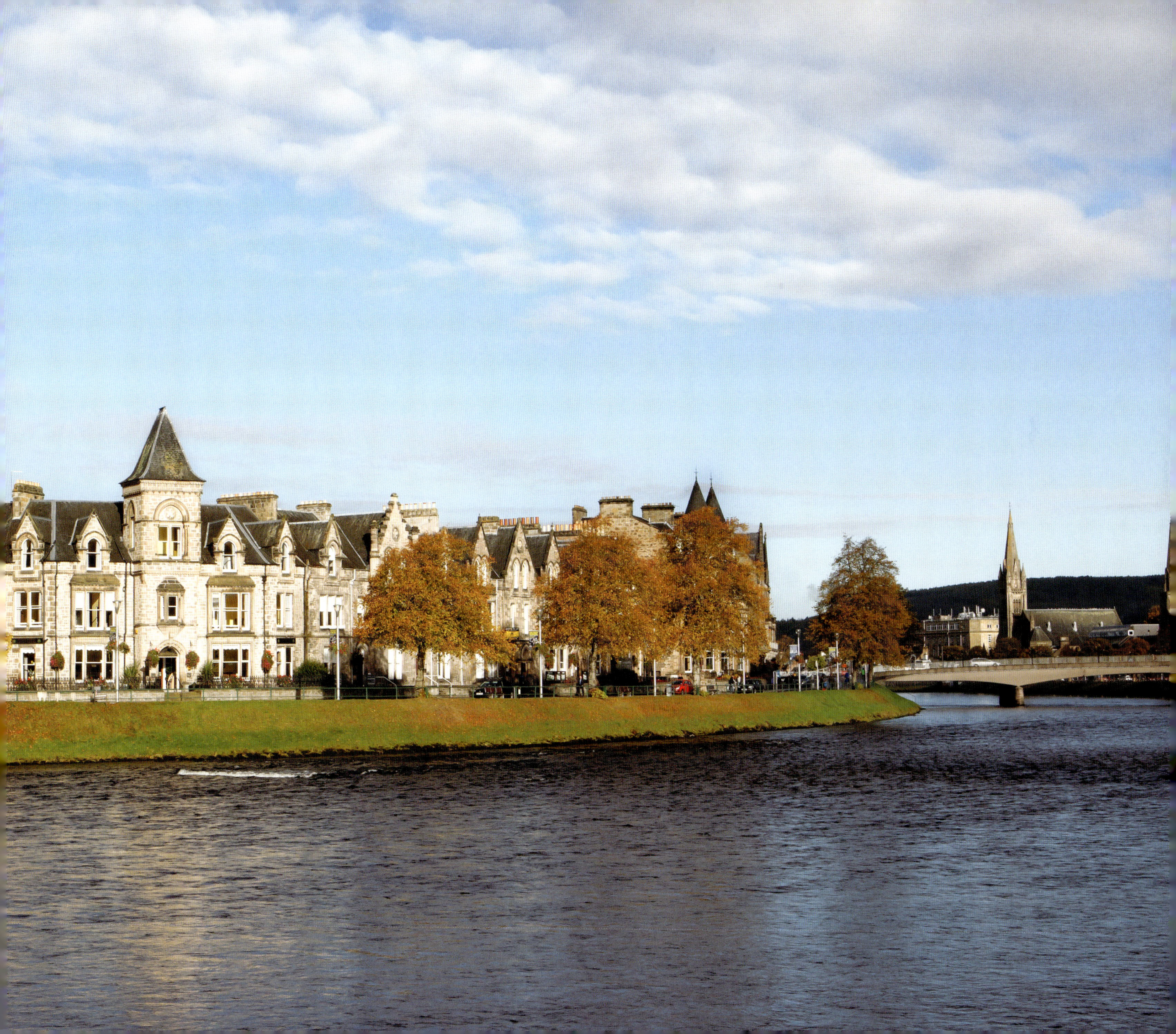

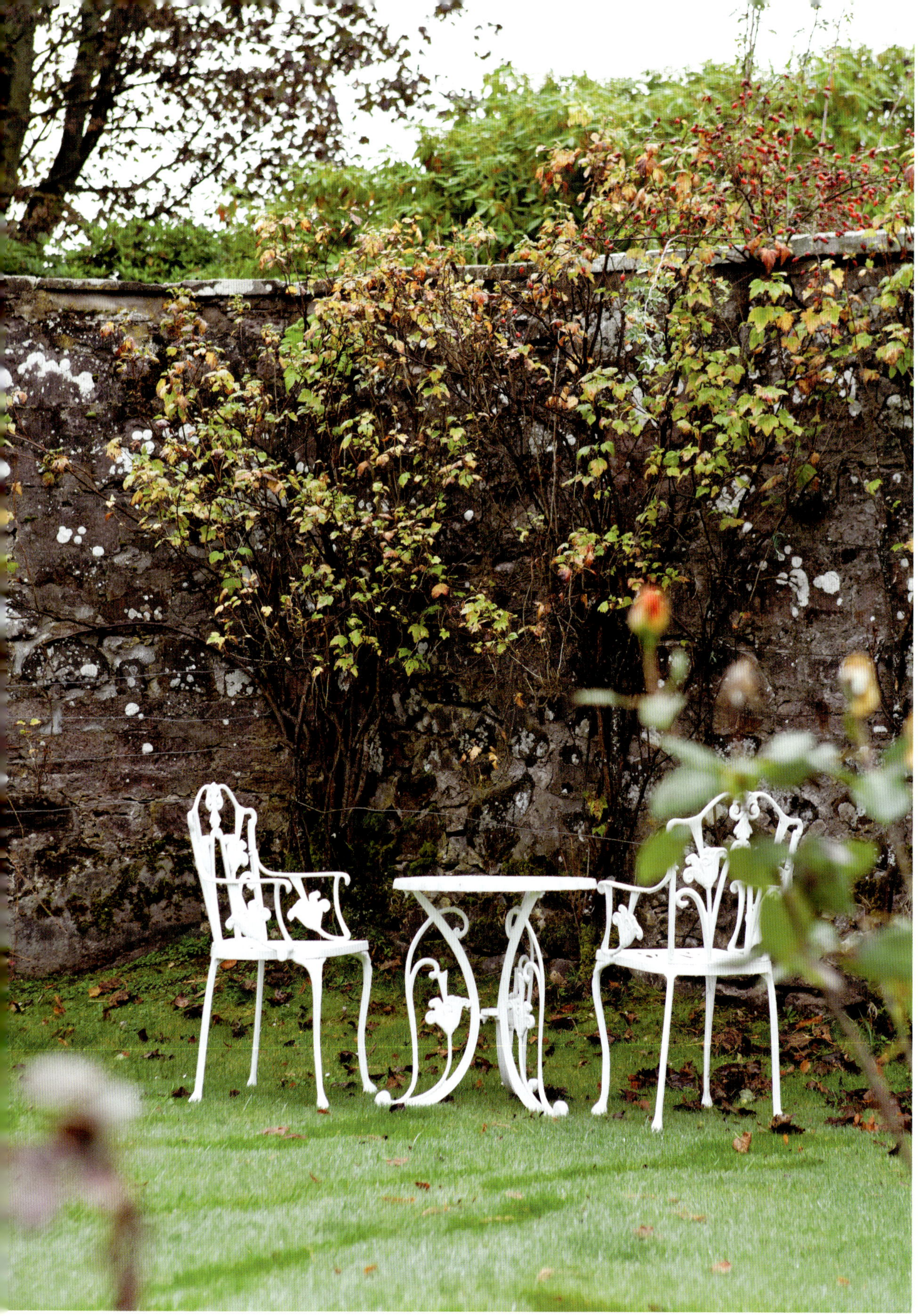

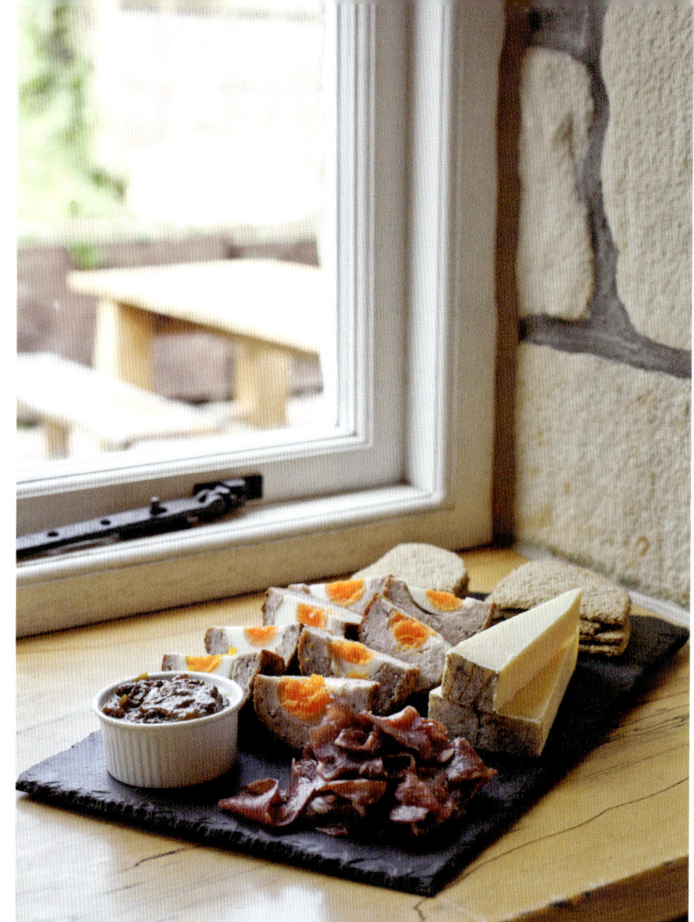

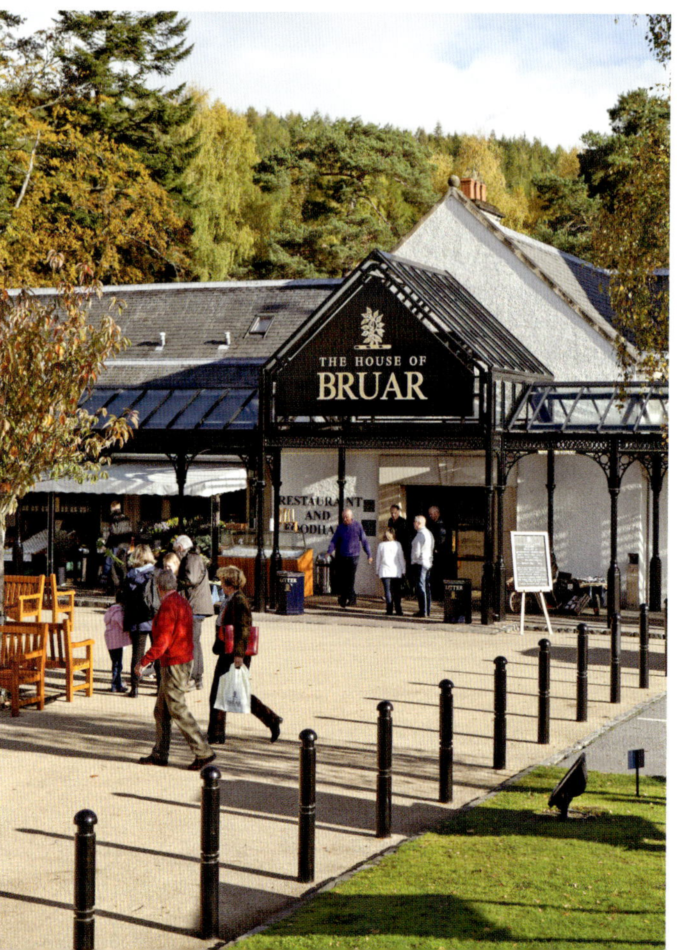
THE HOUSE OF
BRUAR

"Autumn in the Highlands would be brief ... a glorious riot of color blazing across the moors and gleaming every shade of gold in the forests of sheltered glens."

—Elizabeth Stuart

Right and opposite, left: Built by the ancestors of the Earls of Mansfield—the family who dwell in Perthshire's Scone Palace—Murrayshall is a nearby country house hotel sited on an idyllic estate with golf courses. Below right: Renowned Scottish company House of Bruar stocks traditional tweeds. The clothier is known for refined rural style that is appropriate to any weather.

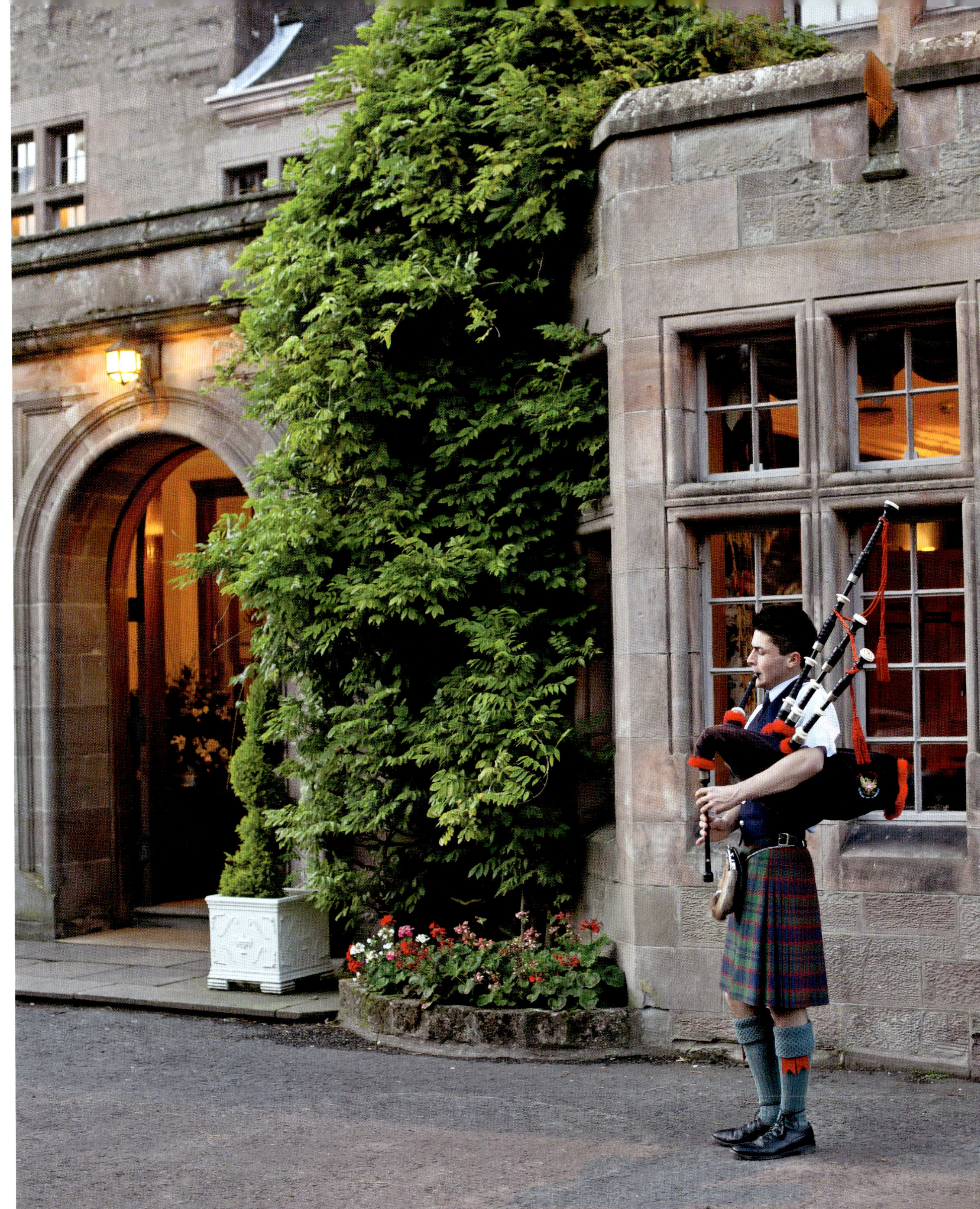

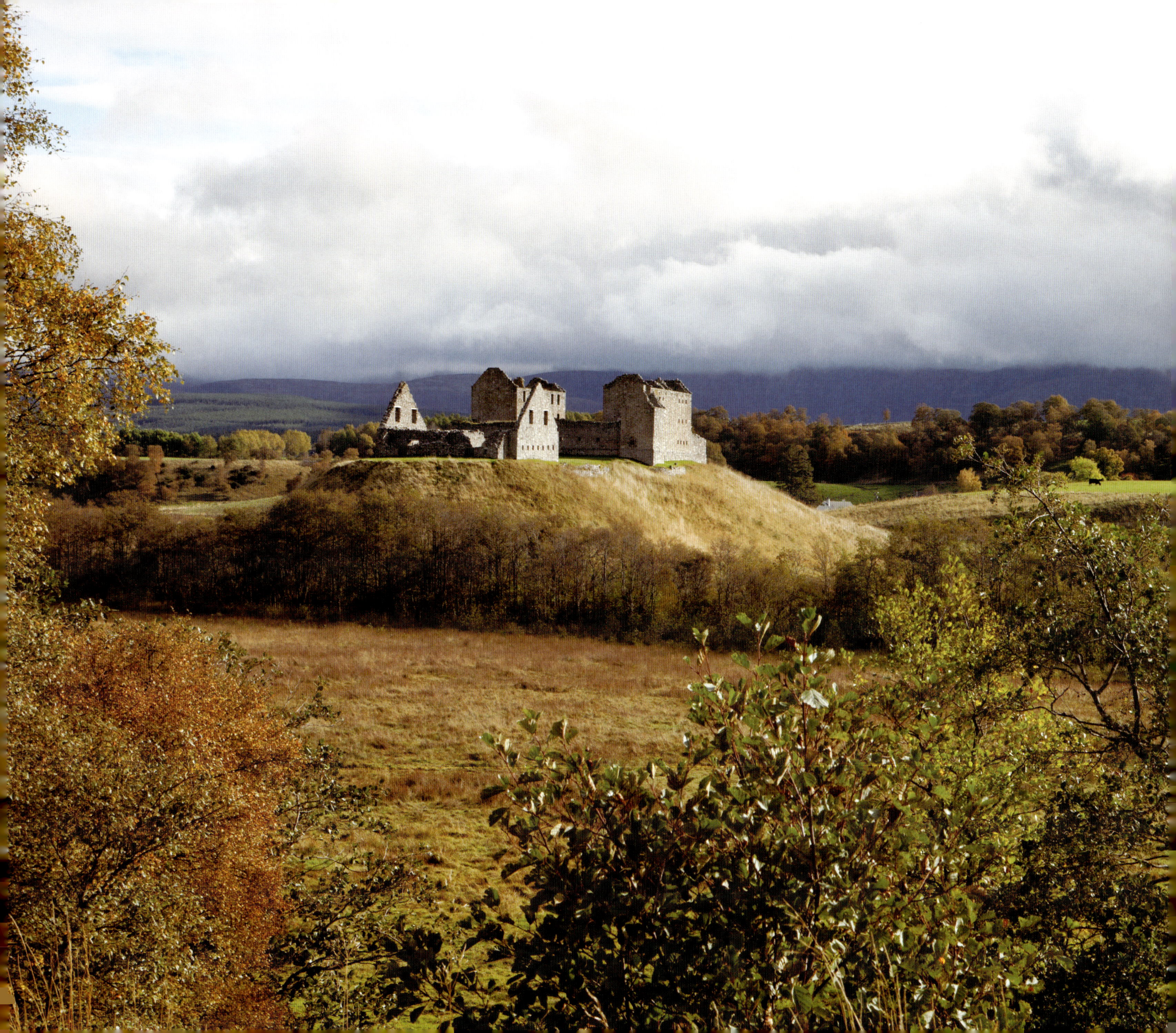

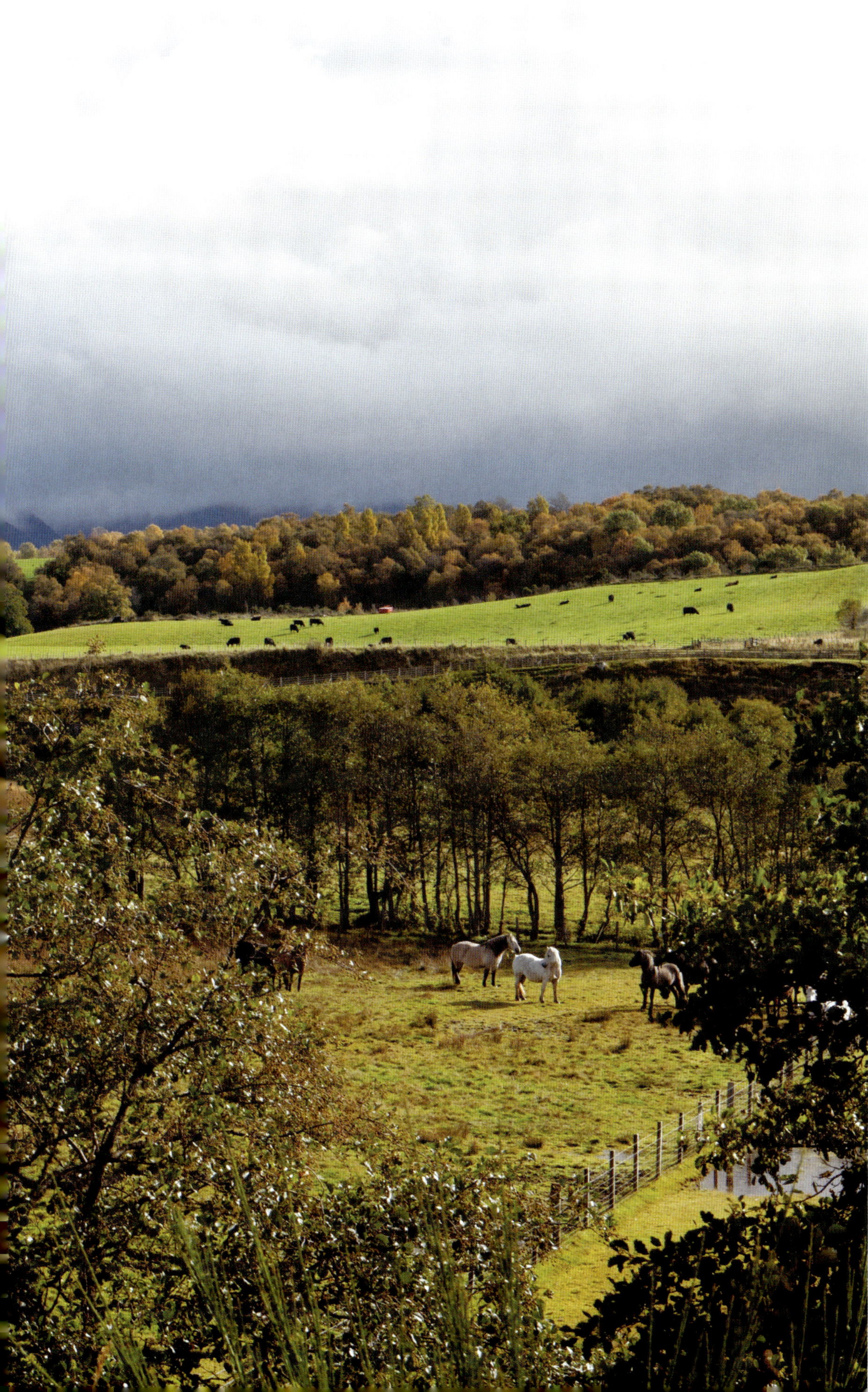

"Give me but one
hour of Scotland,
Let me see it ere I die."

—William Edmondstoune Aytoun

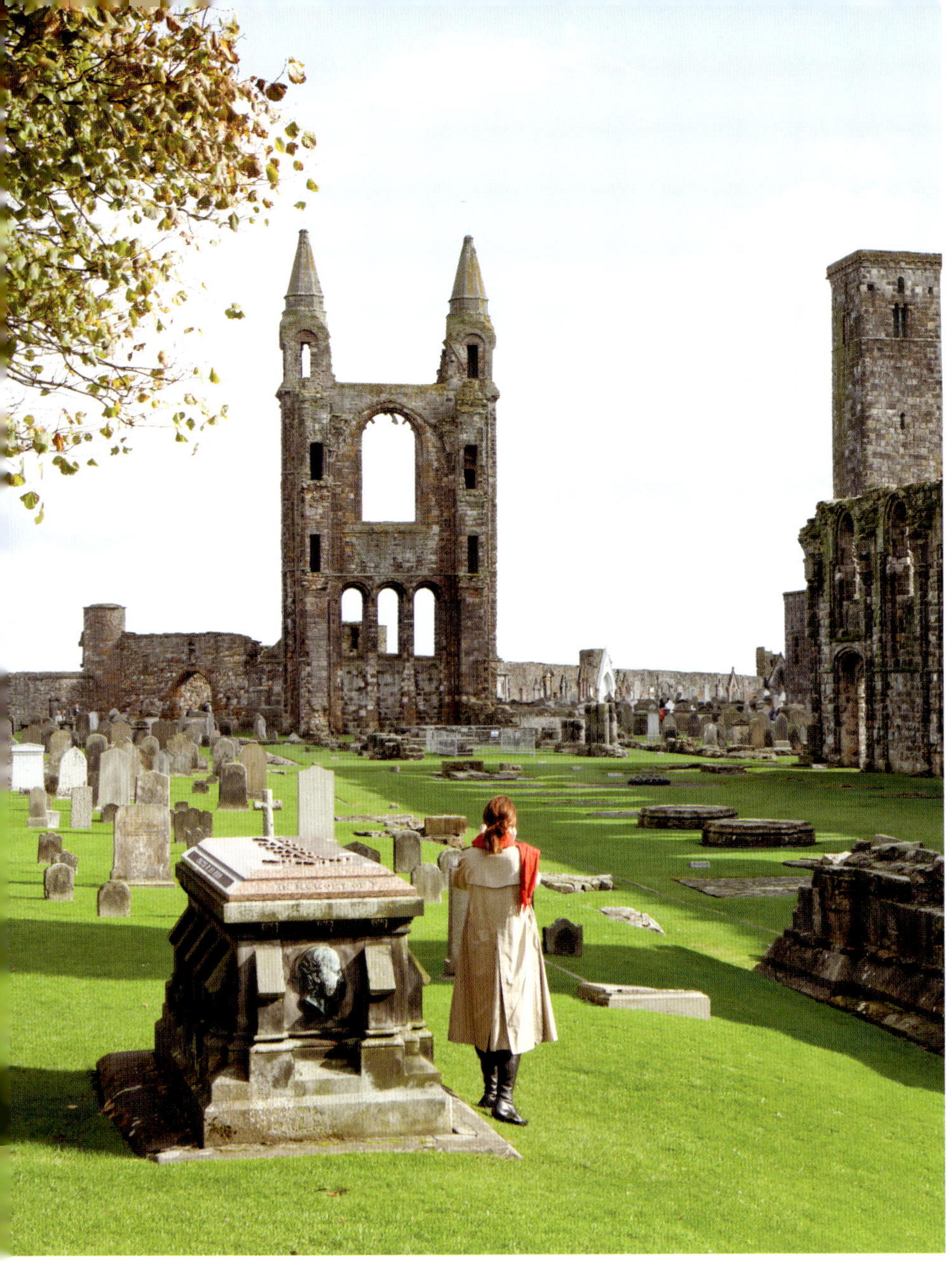

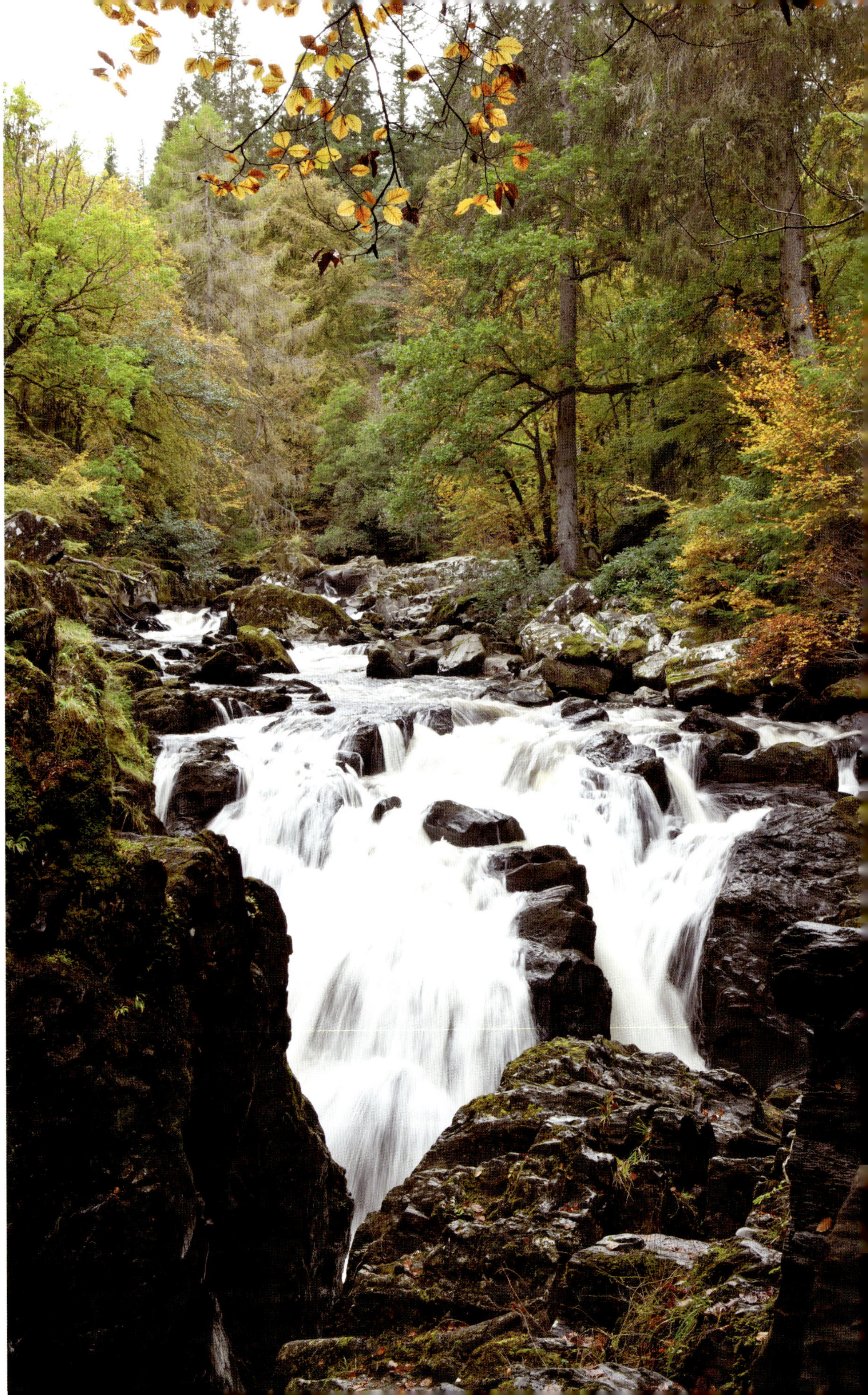

Above: Built in 1158, St Andrews Cathedral was the largest church ever erected in Scotland. The twin-spired ruins are an oft-photographed landmark. Right: The tumbling waters of the Braid Burn meander through the Hermitage of Braid, a 149-acre nature reserve between the Braid Hills and Blackford Hill, near the southwestern edge of Edinburgh. Opposite: Sailboats moor along the seawall of St Andrews Harbour—a protective haven from the swirling waters of the North Sea.

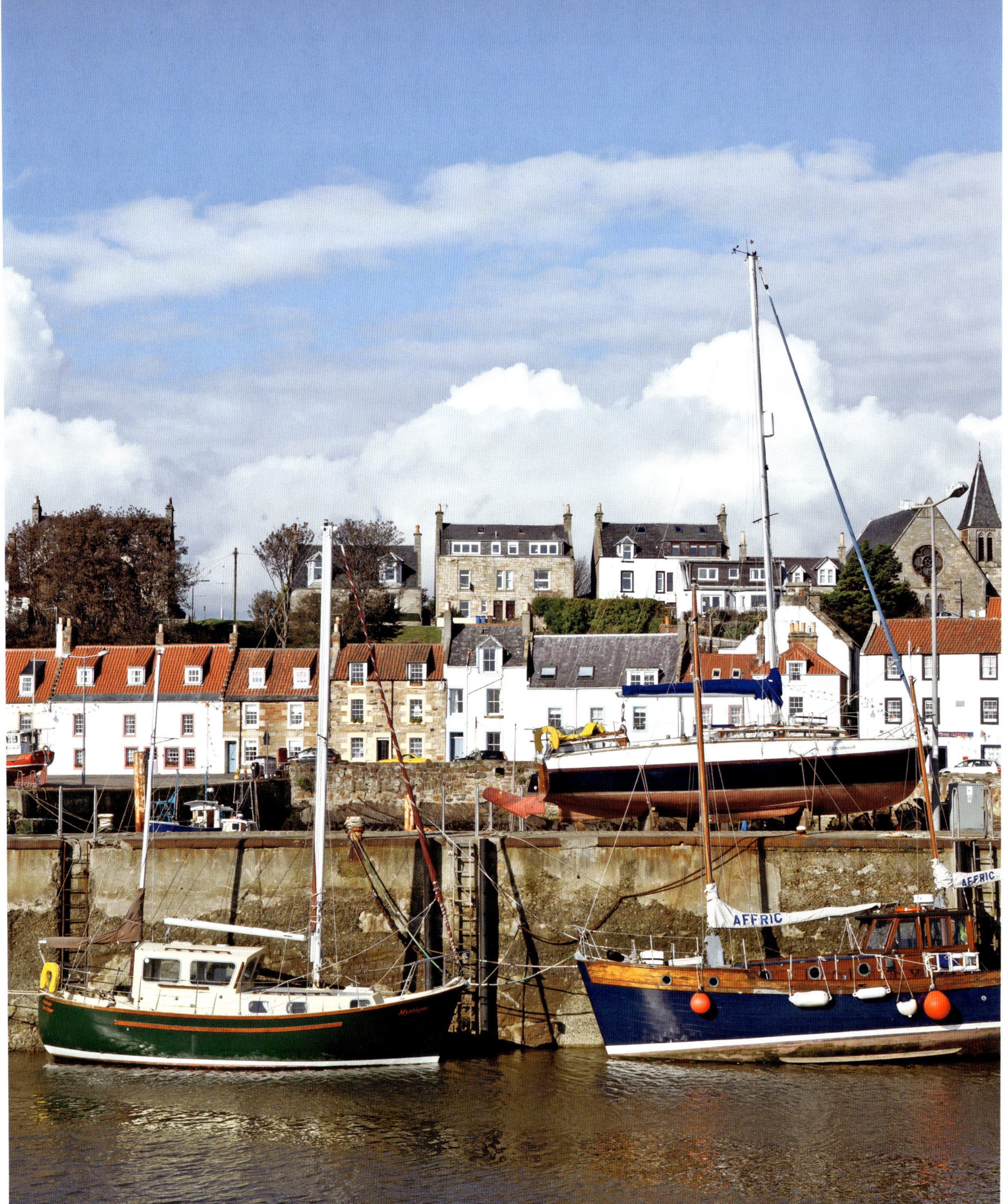
AFFRIC
AFFRIC

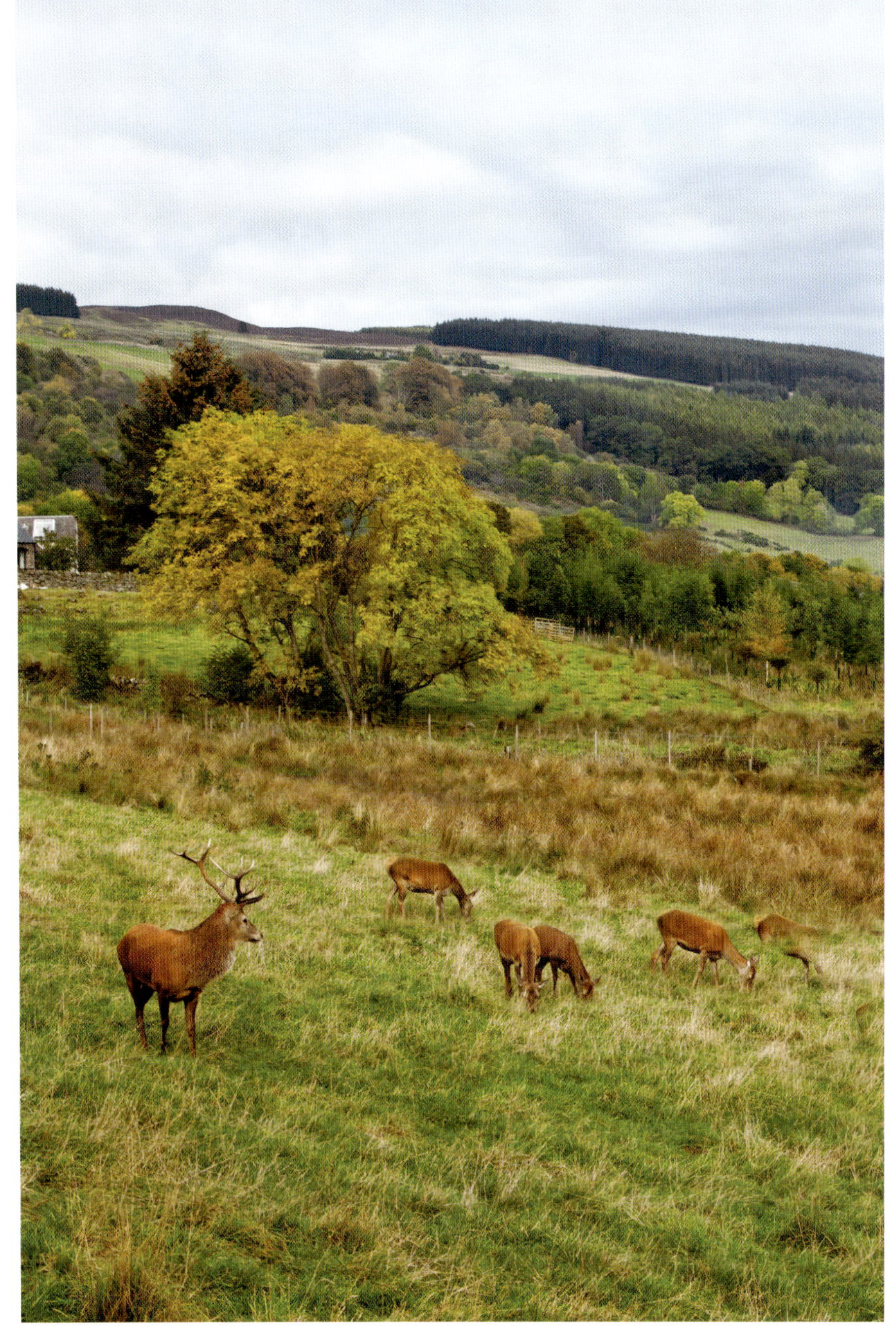

"A-chasing the wild-deer, and following the roe, / My heart's in the Highlands wherever I go."

—Robert Burns

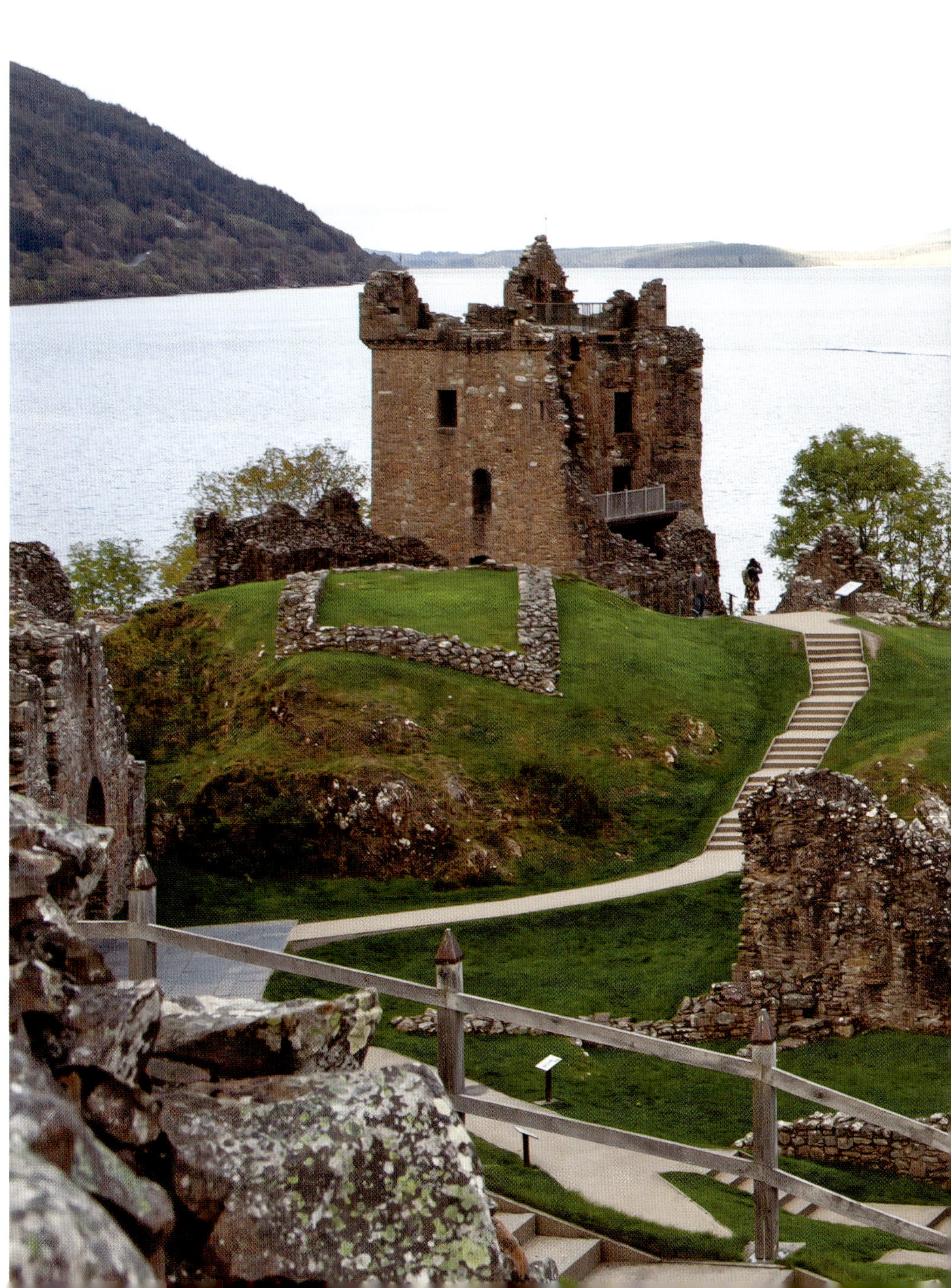

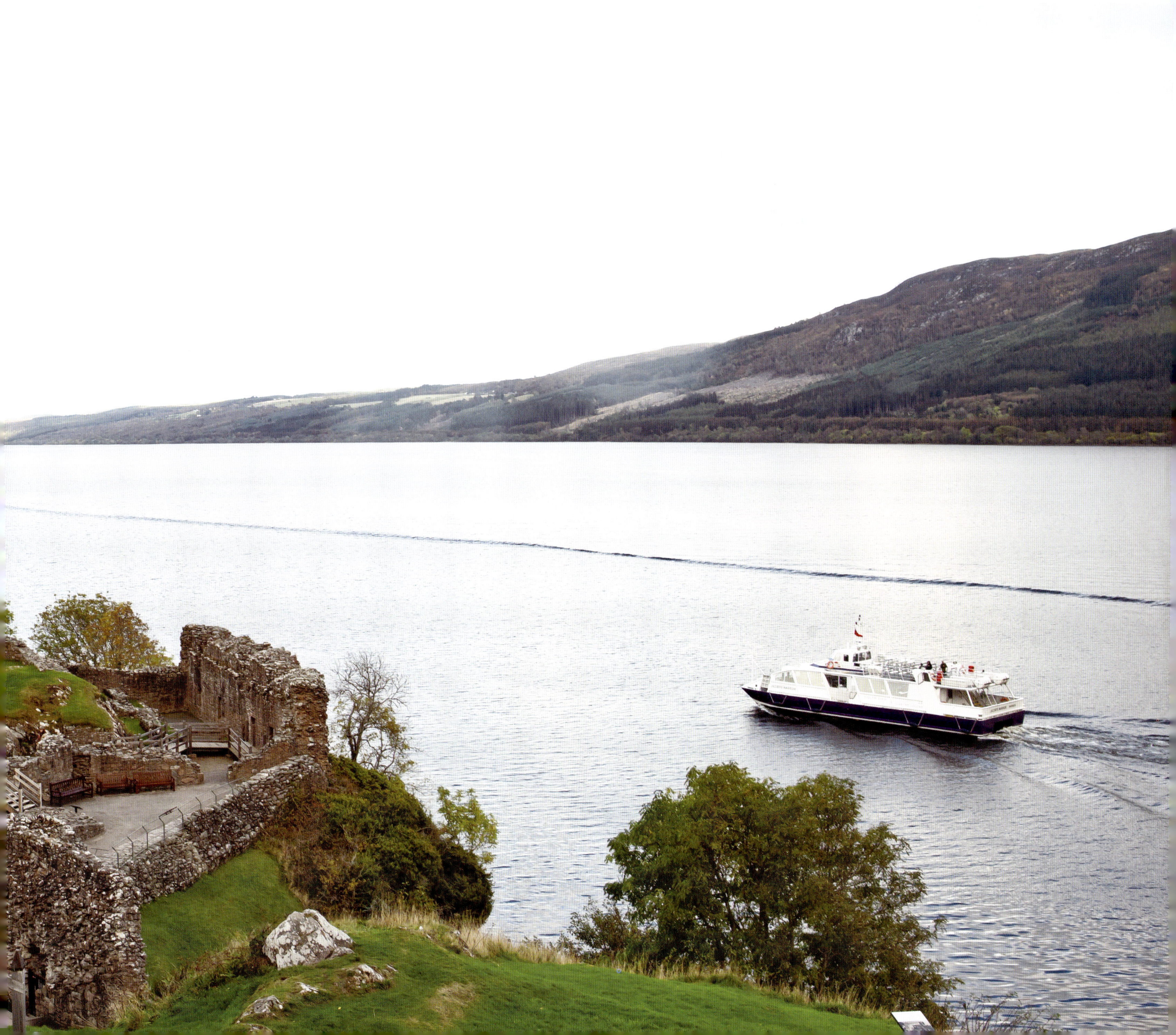

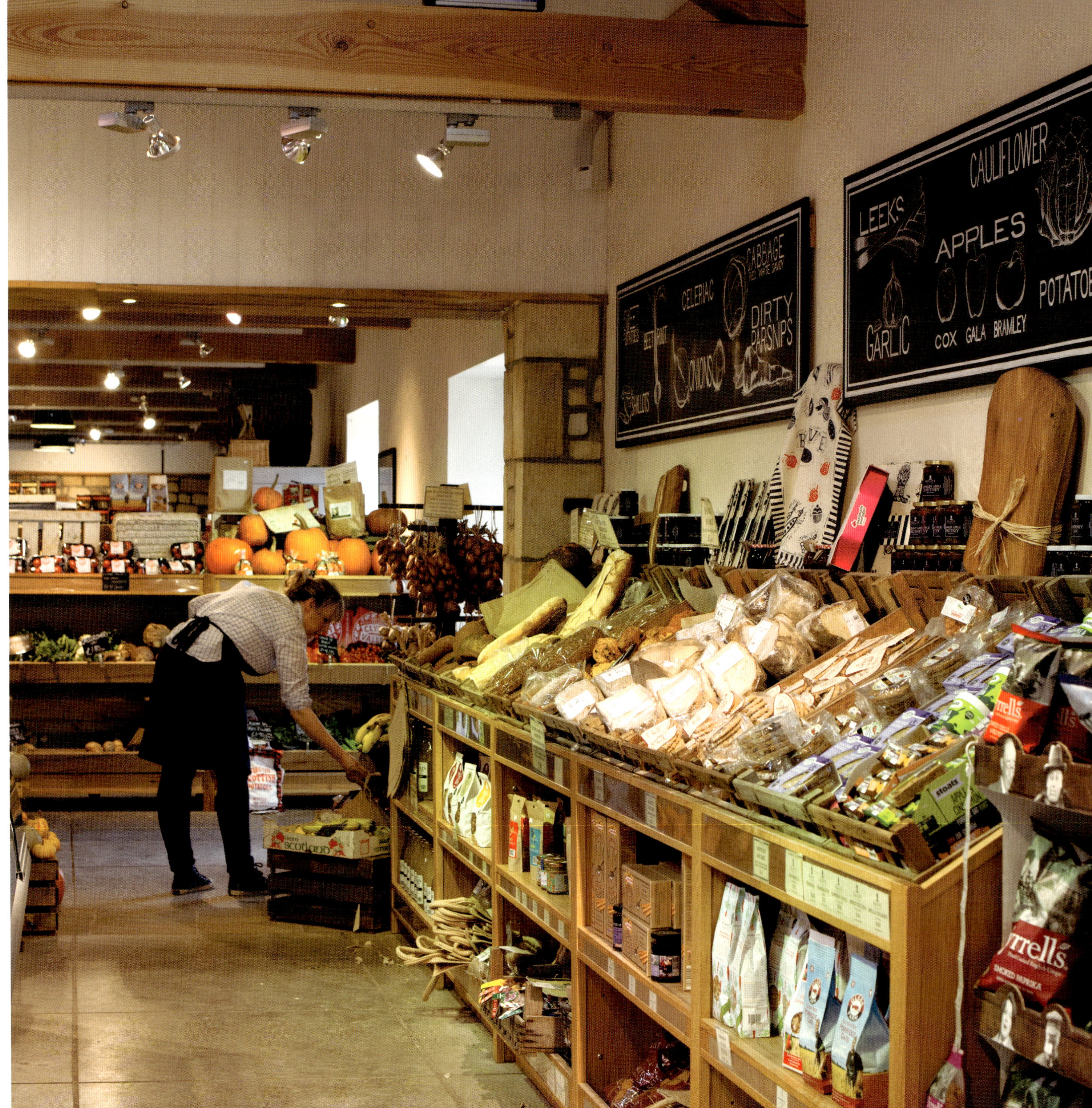

CAULIFLOWER
LEEKS
APPLES
POTATOES
GARLIC
COX
GALA
BRAMLEY
CELERIAC
CABBAGE
DIRTY PARSNIPS
ONIONS
BEETROOT

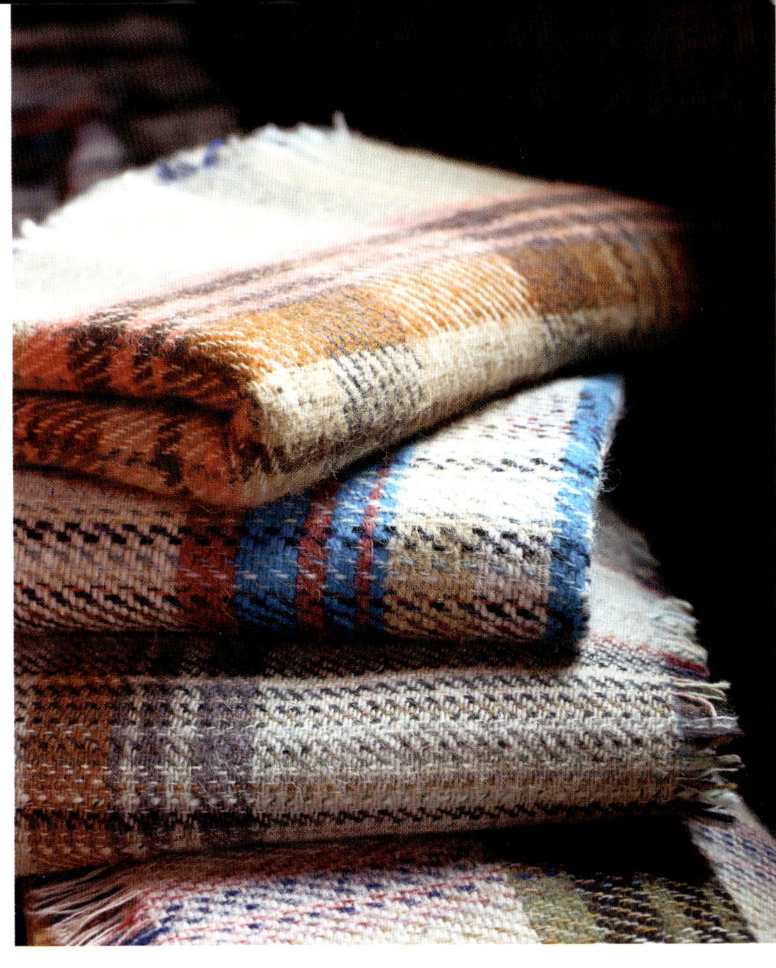

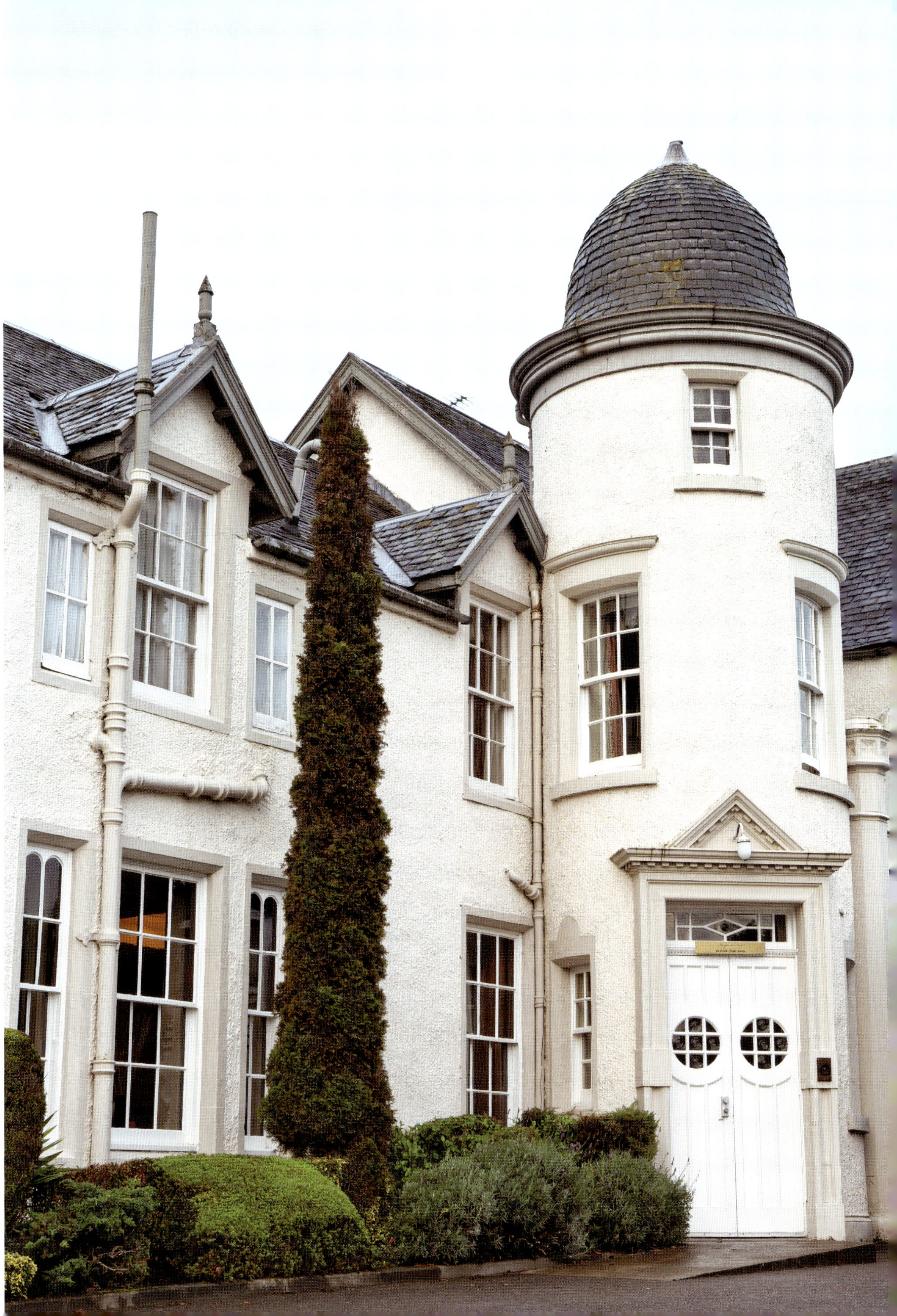

Opposite : At Balgove Larder, a farm shop on the outskirts of St Andrews in Fife, customers are encouraged to take a basket upon entering to stock up on prime Scottish beef and other products. The café is noted for its locally sourced victuals. This page, right: Just a mile from the Inverness city center, Kingsmill Hotel, a gracious eighteenth-century residence, welcomes guests.

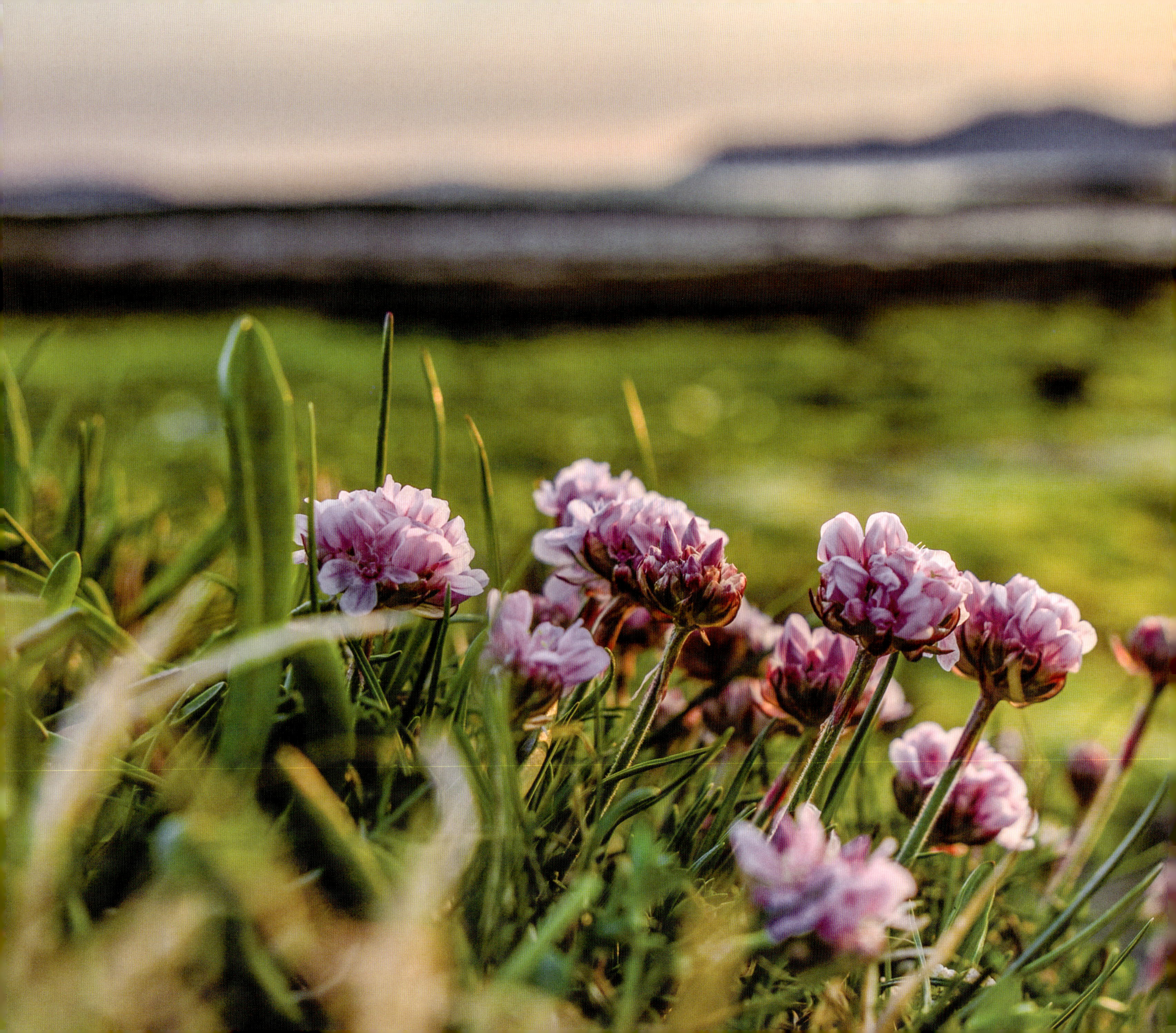

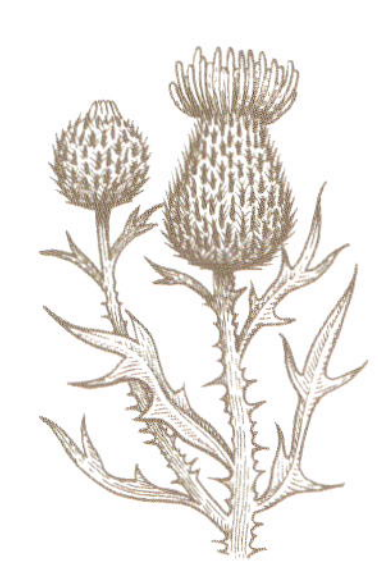

Romantic SPIRES

Though they may seem like something found only in fairy tales, the majestic stone castles of Scotland stand in testament to a time when heraldry and heroics were the order of the day. These remarkable edifices endure, honoring the families that built not only these fortresses but the foundations for Scottish history.

STROLLING THROUGH TIME

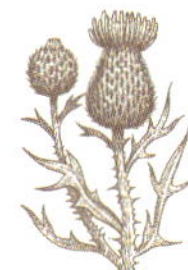

In recognition for outstanding valor at the Battle of Bannockburn in 1314, Sir Malcolm Drummond was awarded an impressive tract of land, which stretches across Perthshire's Gask Ridge—where Roman signal towers and fortifications once stood—before melting into the fertile vale below. Located just a stone's throw from the market town of Crieff, this plot holds the history of subsequent generations of this illustrious family. The first Drummond Castle was built around 1490, but a seventeenth-century extension, along with an eighteenth-century remodel by noted architect George Turnbull Ewing, greatly changed the stone structure's appearance. And while this venerable edifice, incorporating its ancient tower and gatehouse, is impressive to be sure, it is the magnificent gardens to the south of the castle that draw the highest praise.

Though this horticultural masterpiece traces its genesis to 1490, the gardens of today have far exceeded even the loftiest dreams of early planters. The 2nd Earl of Drummond, a Privy Counsellor to both King James VI and King Charles I, is attributed with the most noted transformation, which took place between 1630 and 1636. Later, when many eighteenth-century landscapers bowed to the fashion of the day, the castle gardeners managed to sidestep the trend of replacing formal gardens with great sweeps of parkland, choosing instead to maintain Drummond's classic style.

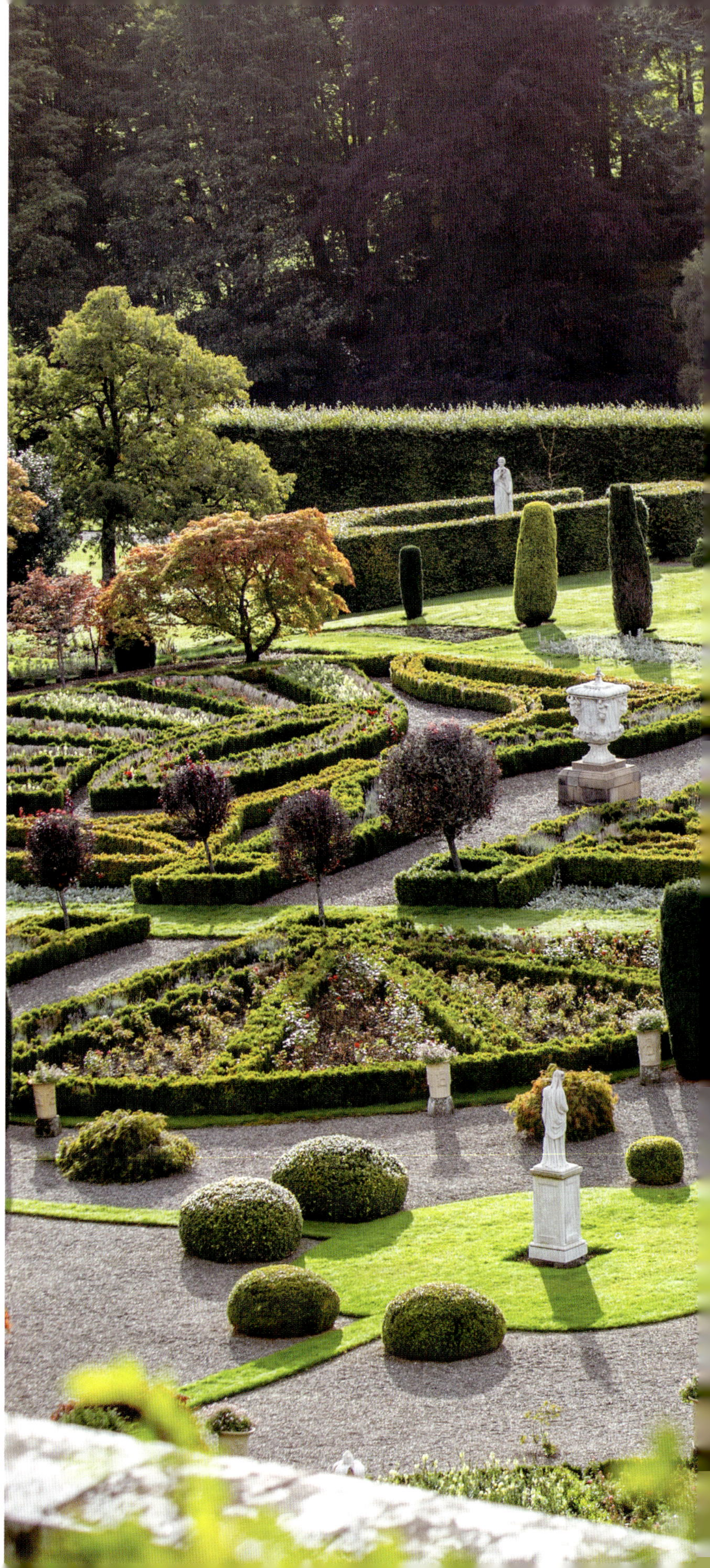

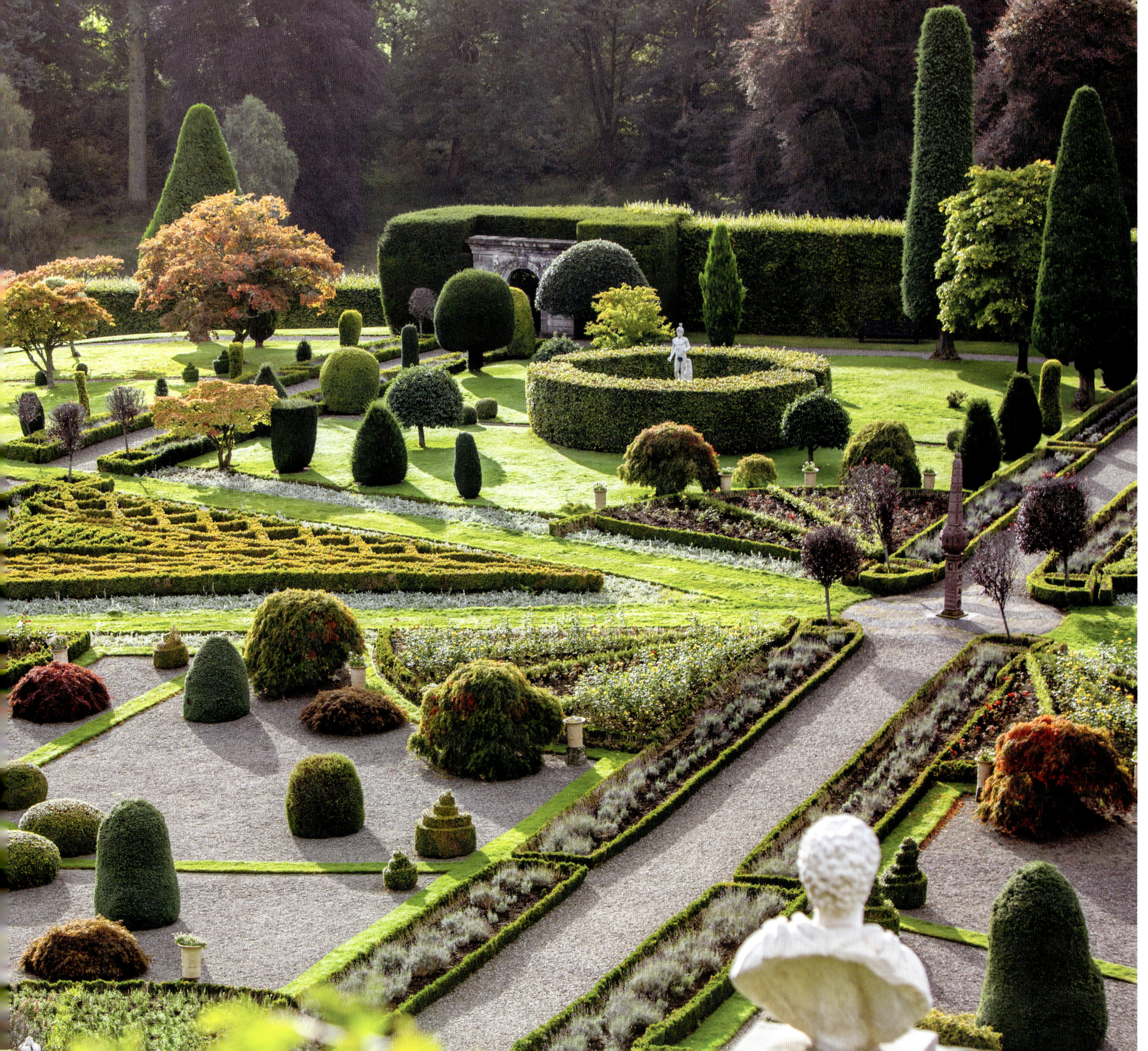

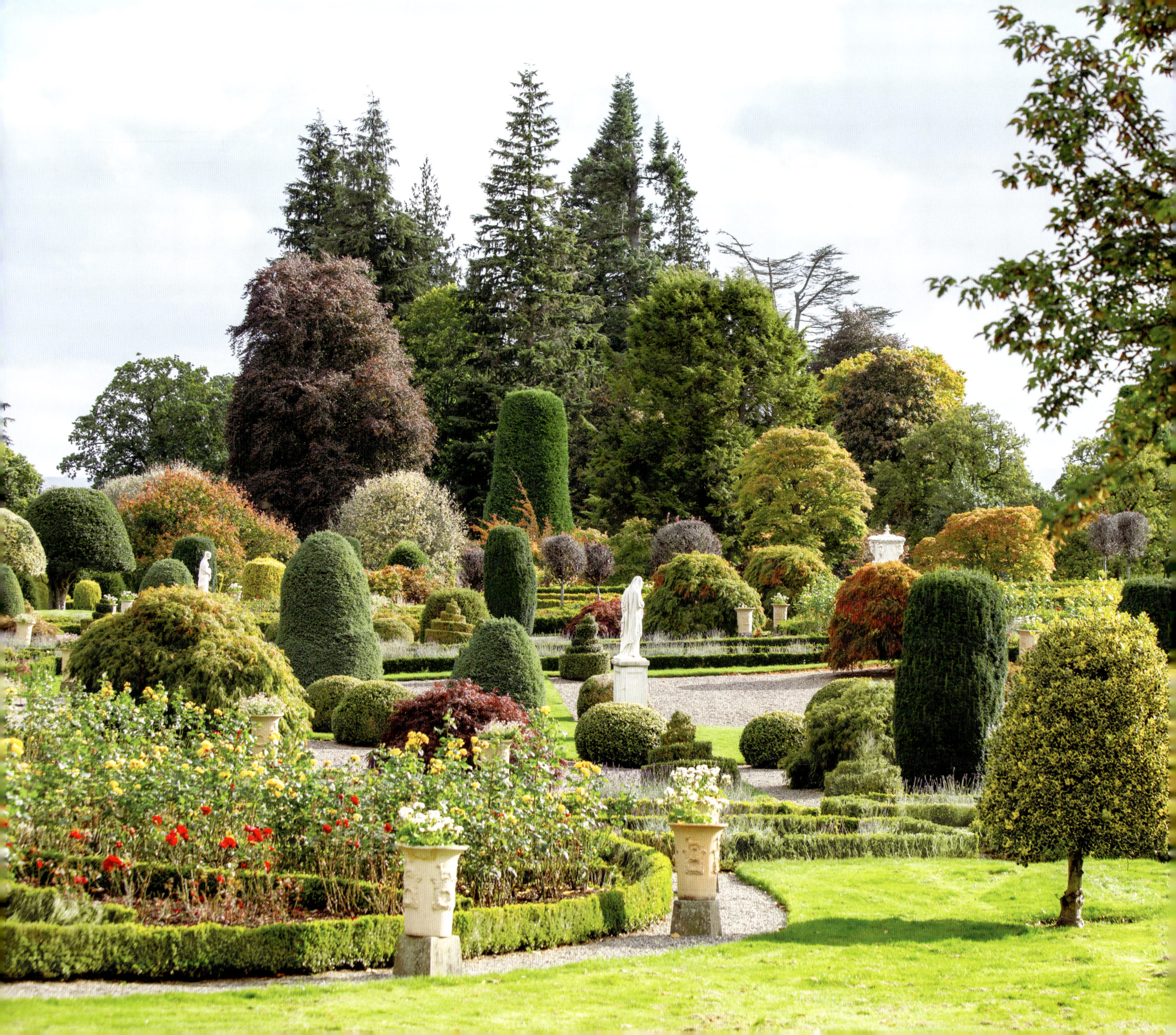

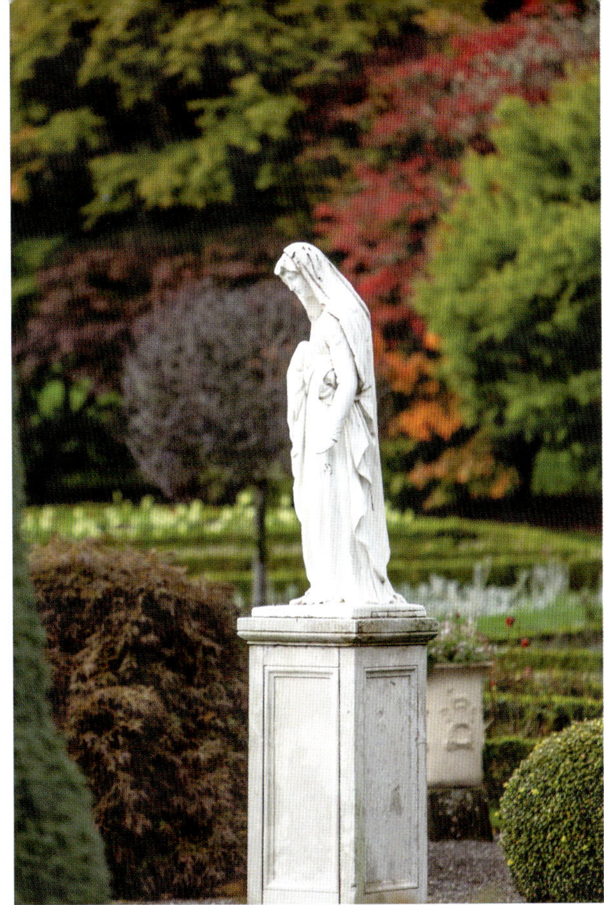

Opposite and this page, above: Timeless marble statues and fountains underscore the classic design of Drummond's parterre garden. The red and yellow roses, seen in the foreground, signify the family's heraldic colors. Right: The current iteration of the castle represents an amalgamation of structures, with the oldest section dating to the late fifteenth century and the last remodel occurring in 1822. The original tower now stands five full stories tall—plus a garret—with a square stair tower jutting from one side. The gatehouse was added in the mid-seventeenth century.

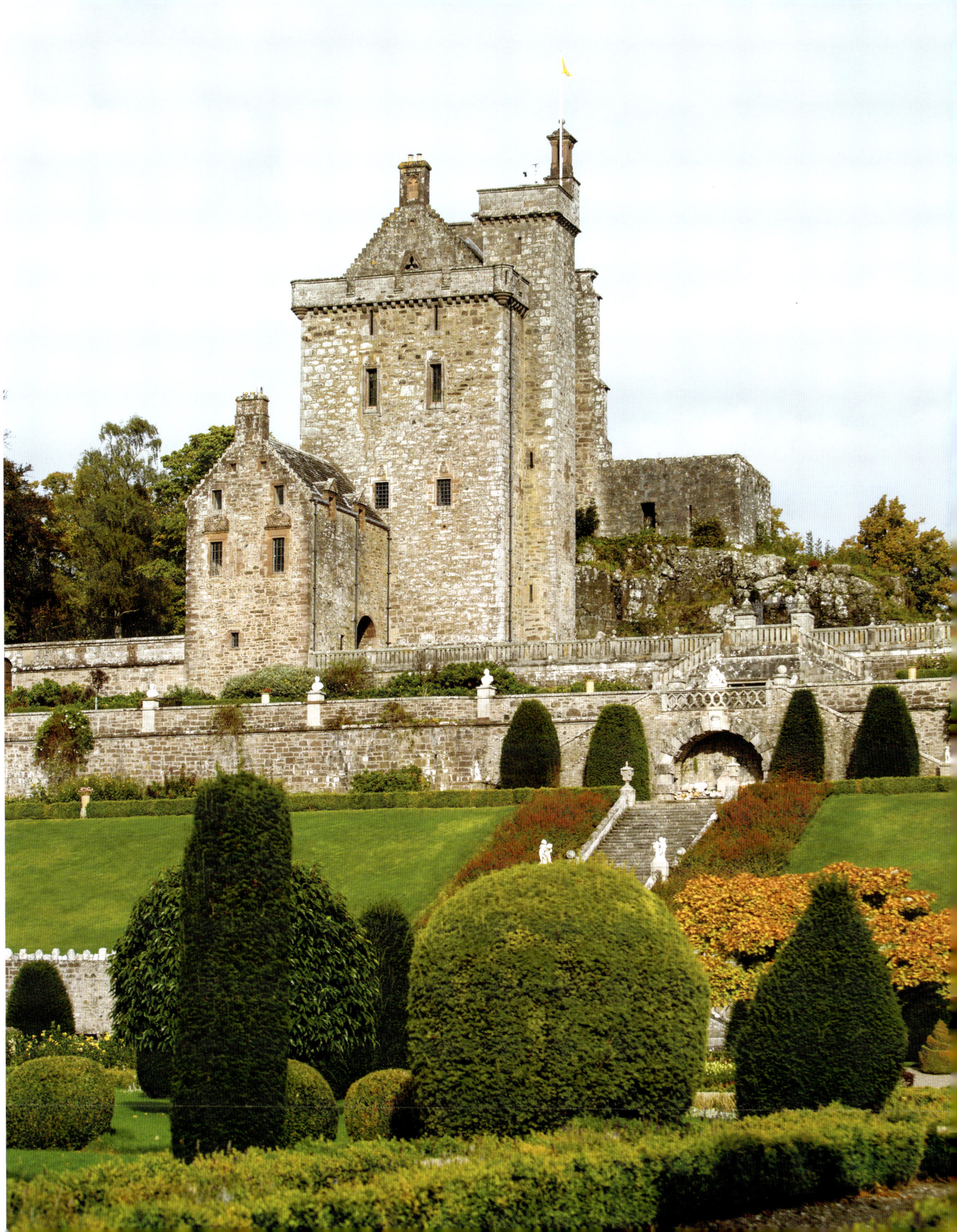

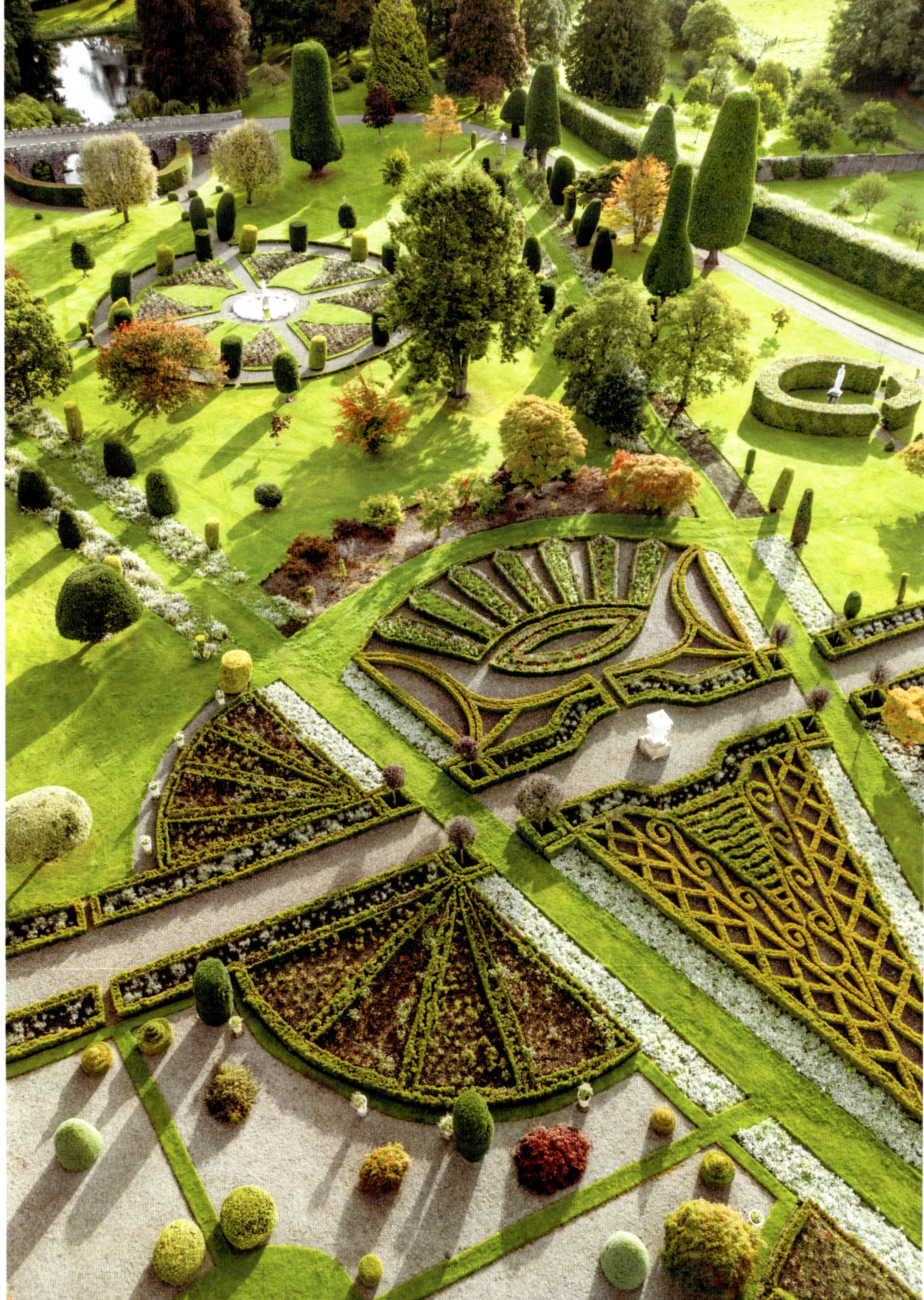

This page: An aerial view of the gardens shows the splendor of the Renaissance-influenced design, with meticulously groomed hedges forming the contours for myriad planting beds, while pathways encourage visitors to amble to their hearts' content. In 1842, when Queen Victoria visited Drummond, she planted two copper beech trees at one end of the garden. Just beyond this formal section lies the kitchen garden, where many varieties of fruits and vegetables take full advantage of the plot's south-facing location. Opposite, left: Statues, such as this stately gentleman sculpted in marble, reflect the gardens' classic roots.

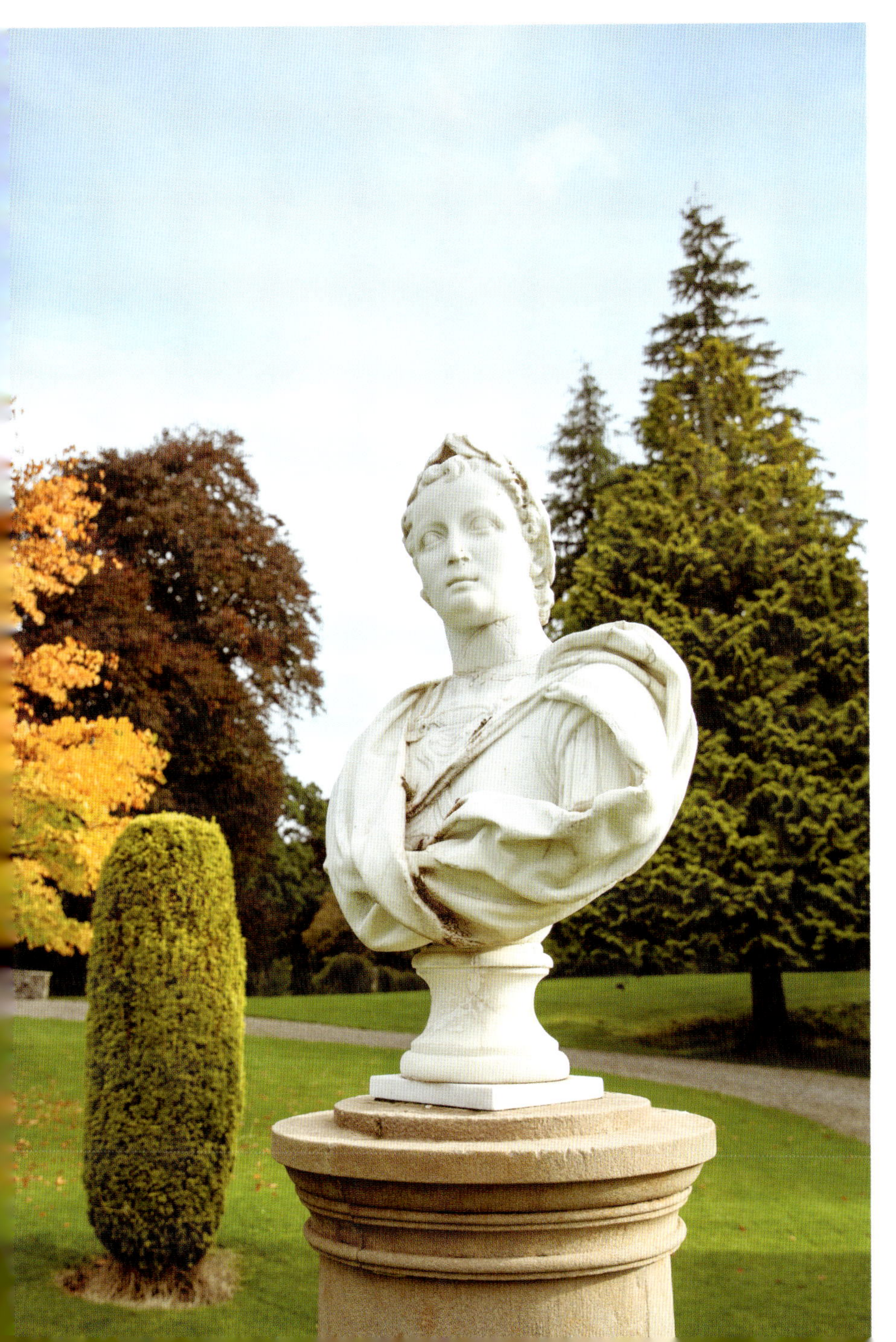

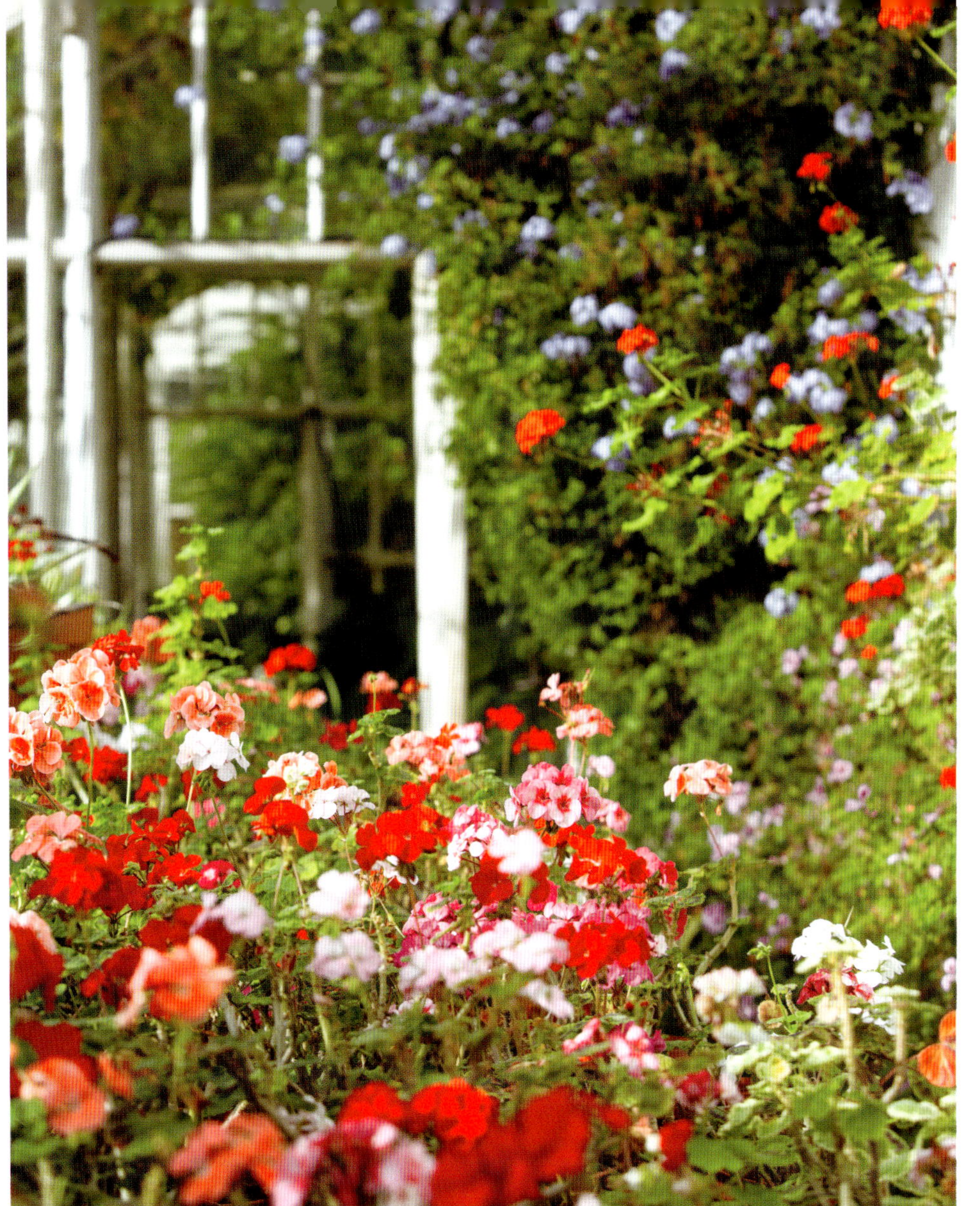

When Clementina Drummond and her husband, Peter Robert Willoughby, assumed ownership of the castle in the early nineteenth century, the couple commissioned a remarkable rejuvenation of the grounds, guided by Lewis Kennedy, who was formerly employed by Empress Josephine at her Malmaison residence in France. The Renaissance-style garden is laid out in a parterre design, comprising formal terraces brimming with classic statuary and fountains. The inner section forms a St. Andrews Cross, where 'Top Rose' and 'Evelyn Fison' roses represent the yellow and red hues of the Drummond heraldic colors. At the center stands a sundial—the work of seventeenth-century master mason John Mylne—which displays the time of day in various world capitals.

Because the precisely clipped hedges alone offer a pleasing visage any time of year, a visit to Drummond Castle Gardens is an enjoyable experience in all seasons. But a summer stroll amid the pathways, with the fragrance of lavender and roses scenting the air, is certain to create the loveliest of memories.

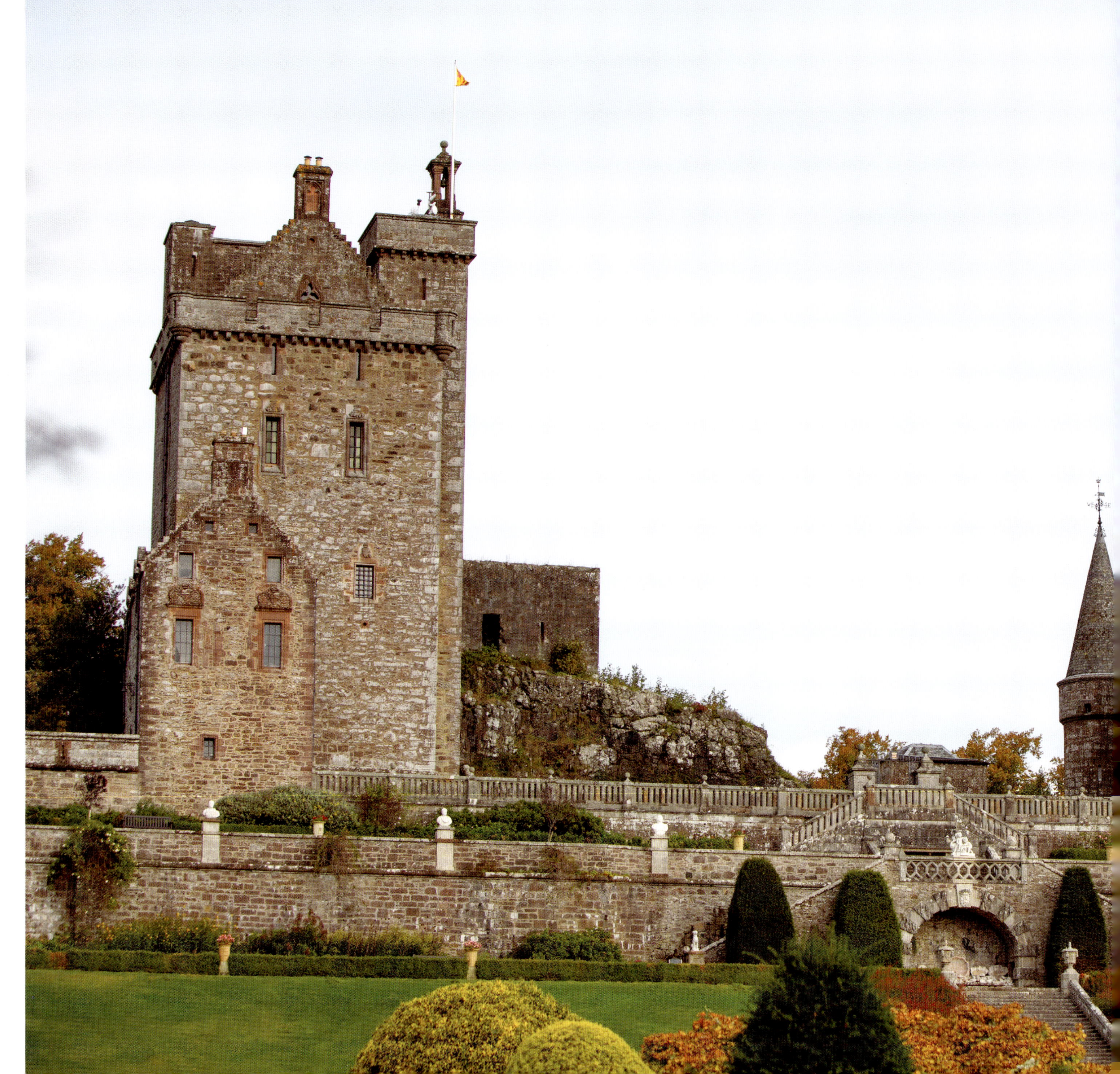

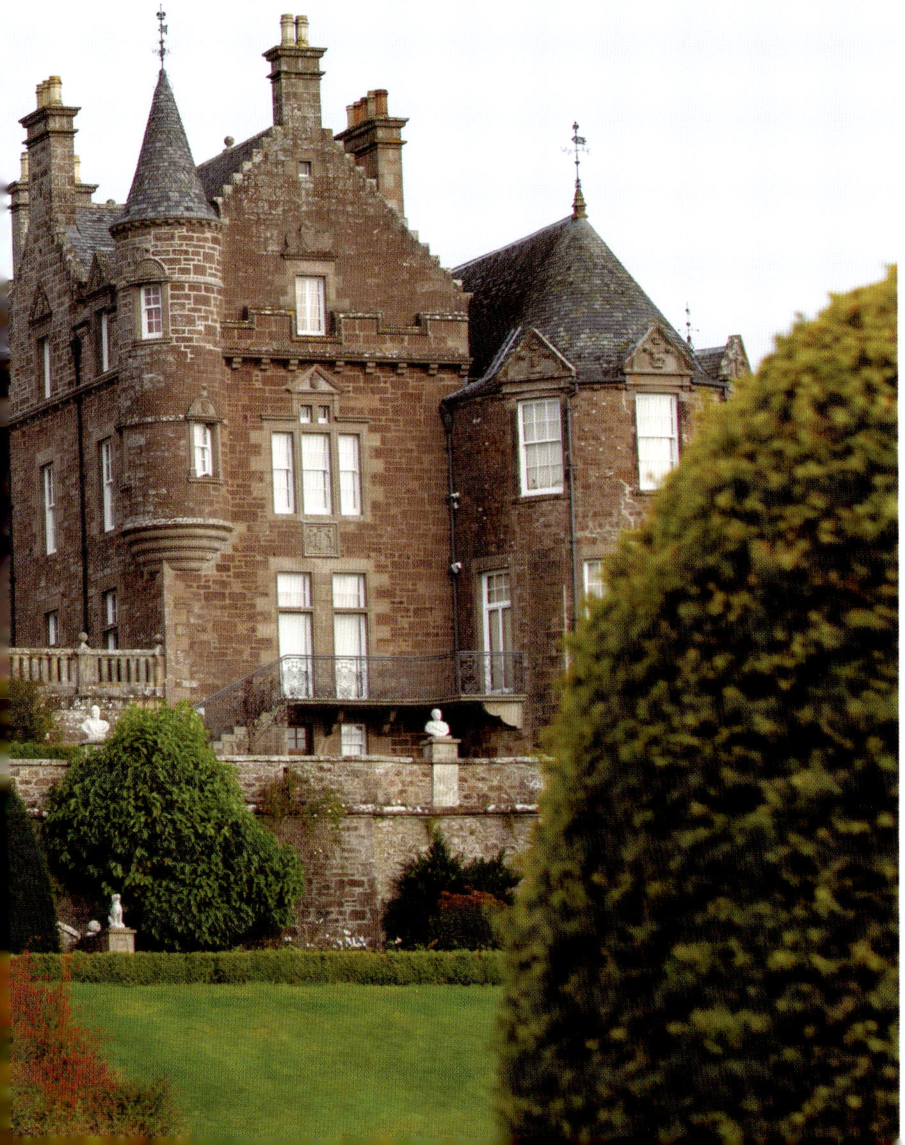

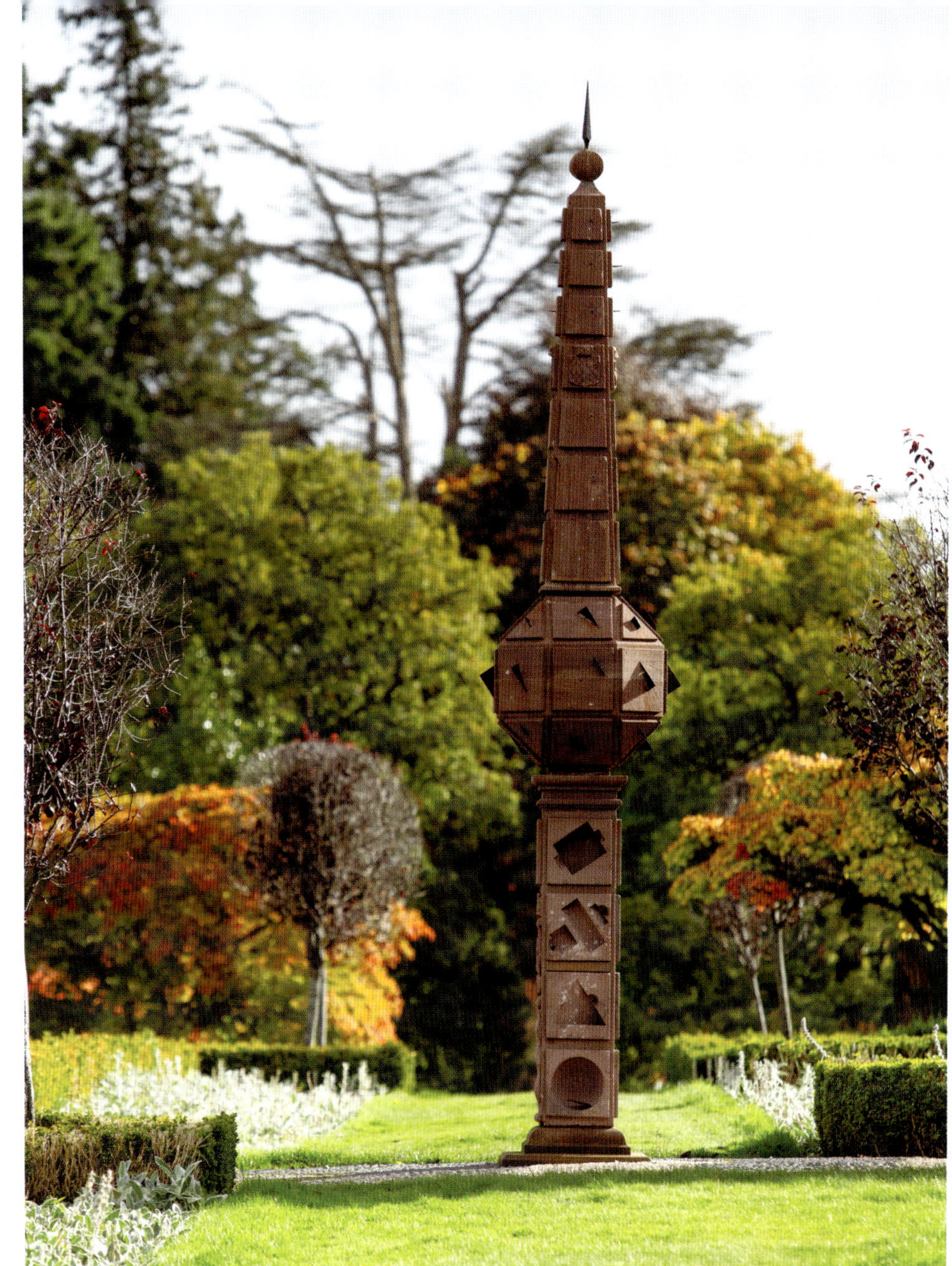

“We walked in the Garden, which is really very fine, with terraces, like an old French garden.”

—Queen Victoria

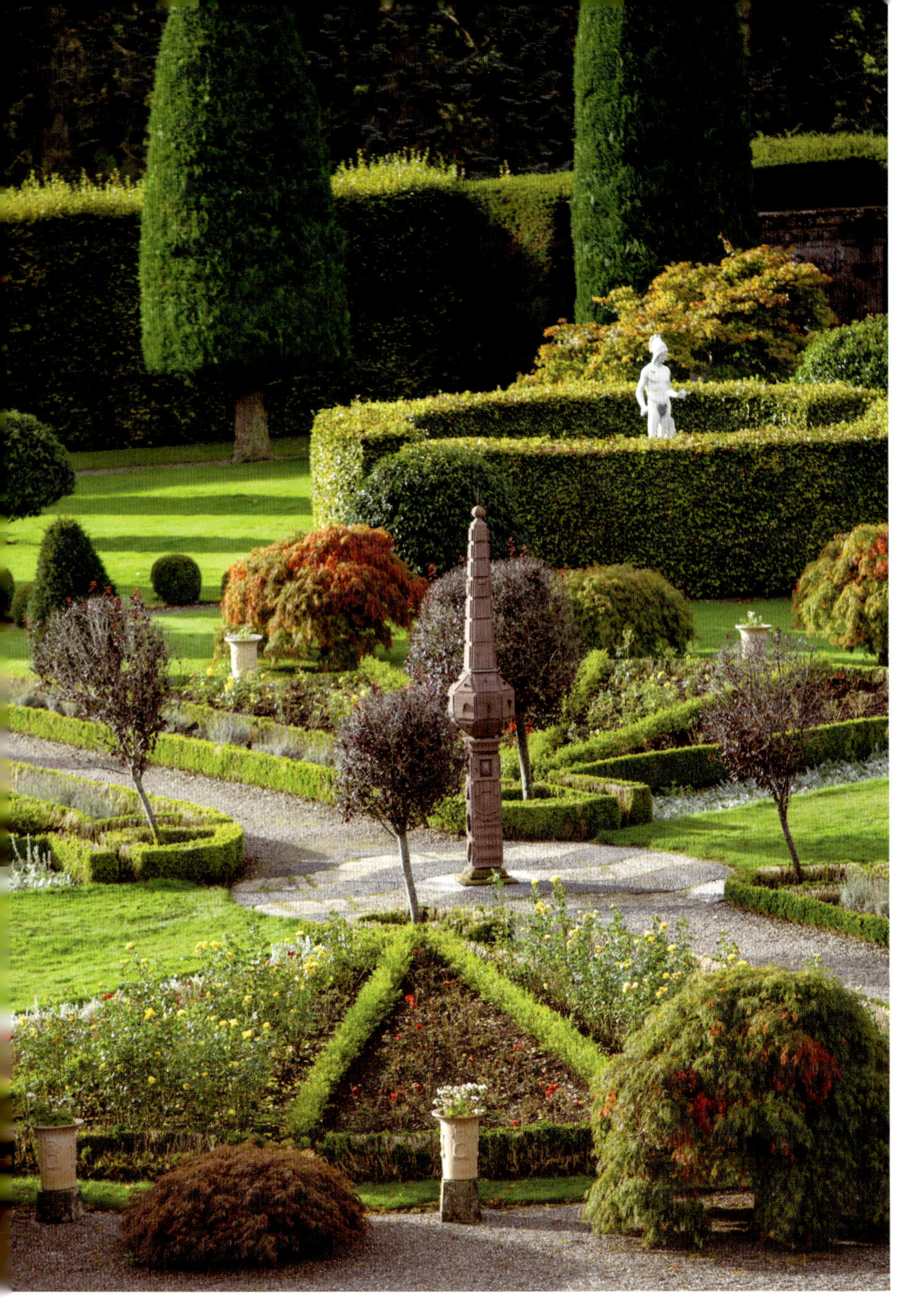

Above: Master mason John Mylne's polyhedral sundial has pride of place in the center of the garden. Black and white pebbles, laid out in wavy lines at the base, echo a design found on the Drummond family coat of arms.

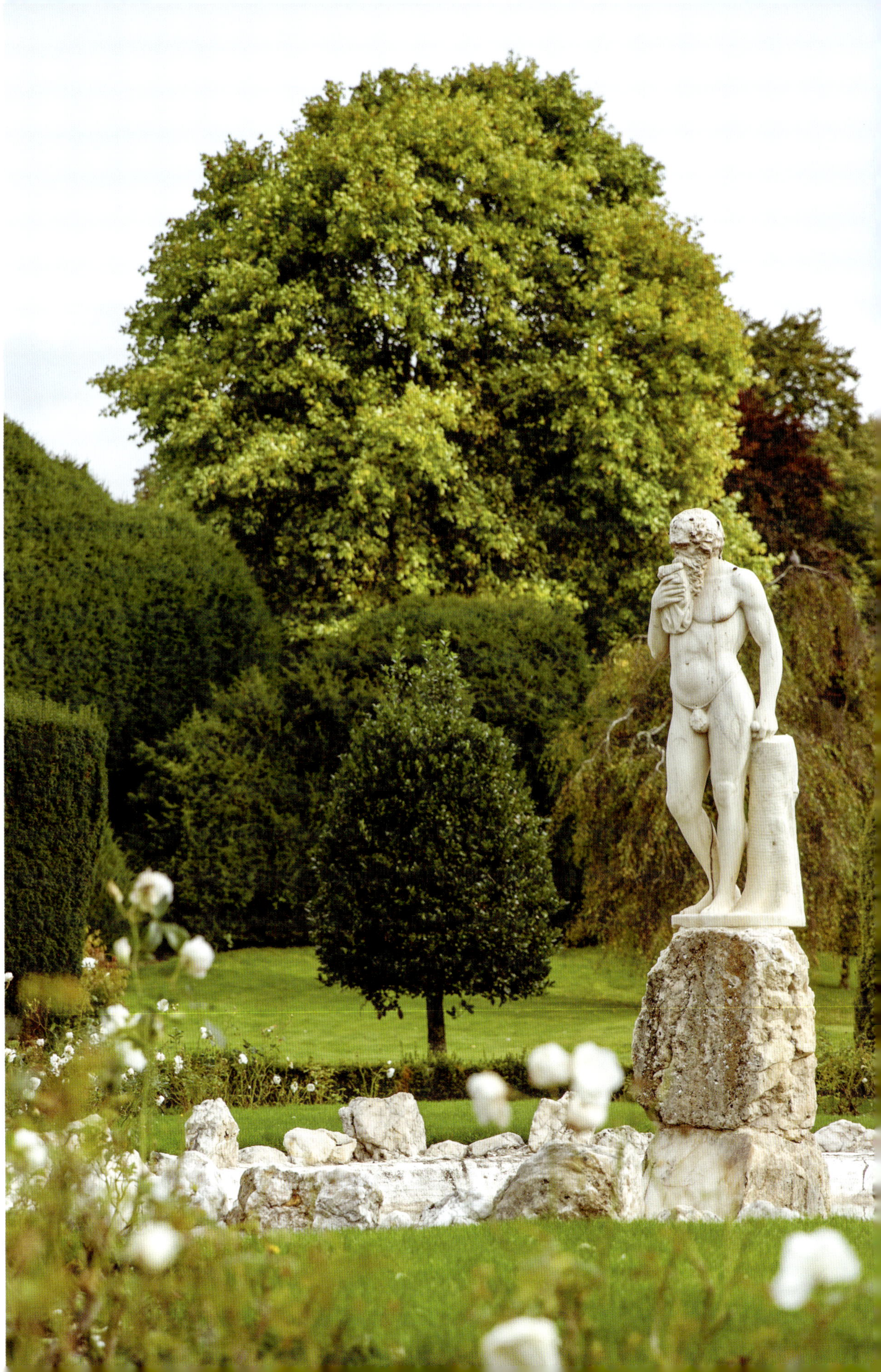

Opposite, right, and this page: The notion of blurring the lines between countryside and formal spaces—a noted characteristic of French horticultural style—lends visual appeal to the property, but garden designers also embraced elements of Italian elegance, as seen in the incorporation of terraces, fountains, urns, and statuary. Visitors to Drummond Castle, with its abounding botanical offerings and inspiring scenery, will immediately understand why filmmakers have been drawn here, choosing these breathtaking surroundings as the perfect backdrop for their period productions.

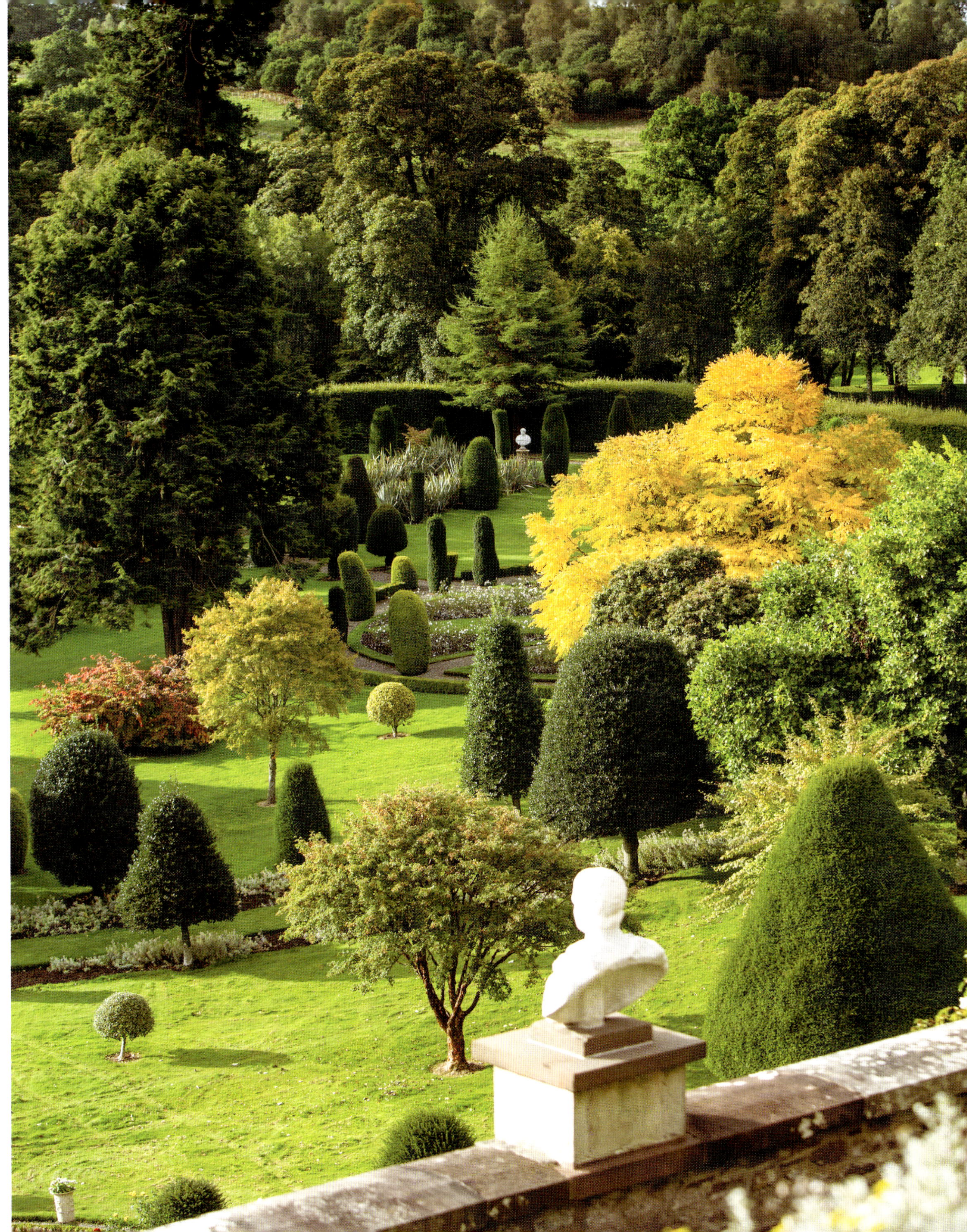

DREAMING IN THE CLOUDS

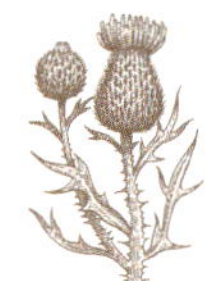

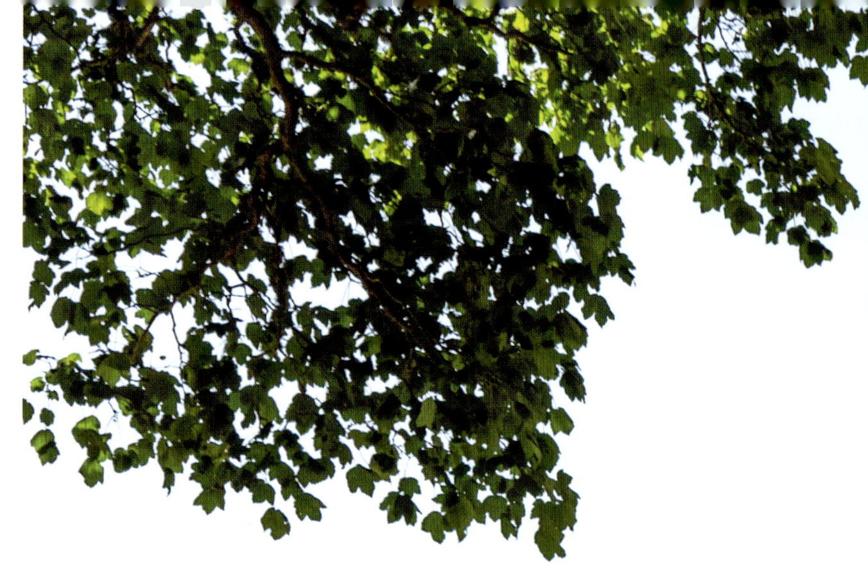

Clans have been an integral part of Scottish life and legends since the early days of the twelfth century, when these kinships lent a sense of identity and loyalty to the people of the Highlands. Taking its name from the area granted to an early ancestor, Clan Sutherland, family seat of the Earls and Dukes of Sutherland, still holds sway in this part of the country, with the magnificent Dunrobin Castle, near the village of Golspie, serving as both the historic and present home of these long-respected nobles.

As one of the oldest continually inhabited houses in Great Britain, the currently configured structure incorporates the earliest portion of the castle: a rectangular keep dating to at least the fourteenth century. Later additions bear the imprints of noted architect Sir Charles Barry, whose projects include London's Houses of Parliament, and Scotland's native son, Sir Robert Lorimer, who spearheaded the restoration and modification of the estate after a fire in 1915.

With its conical towers and tapered spires, Dunrobin evinces the influence of French architectural design, often assimilated in Gothic Revival–style buildings. It comprises an astounding 189 rooms, including the dining hall, with its oak-paneled ceiling and friezes depicting classical Greek scenes, as well as the Green and Gold Bedroom, which holds an ornately carved bed commissioned for an 1872 visit by Queen Victoria.

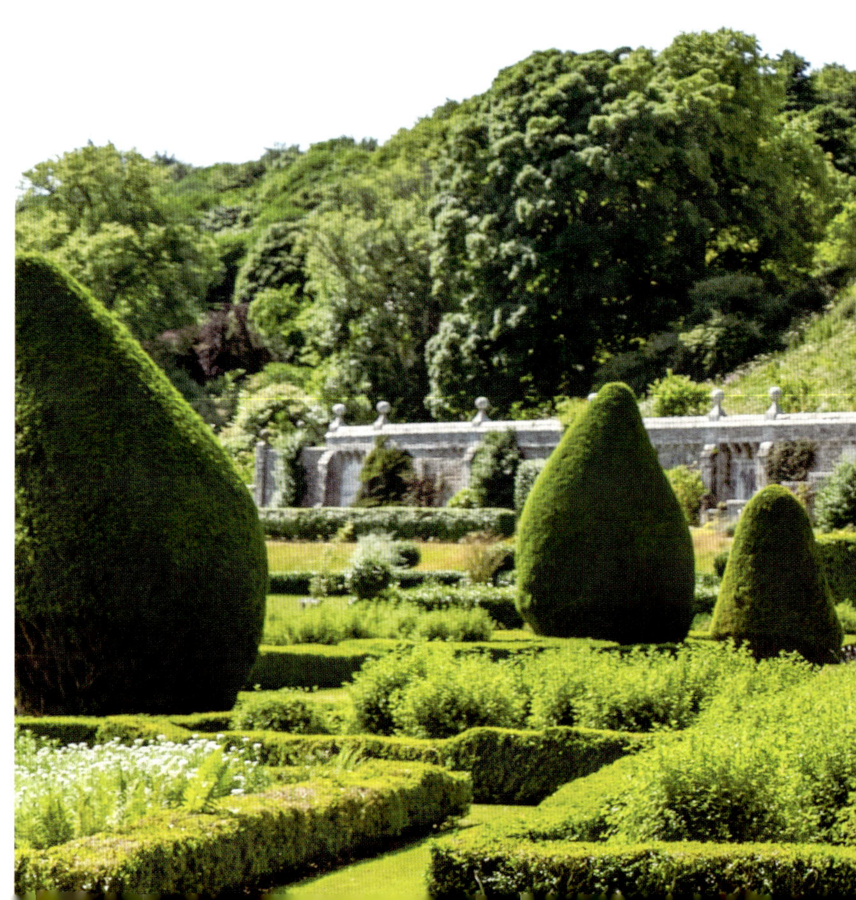

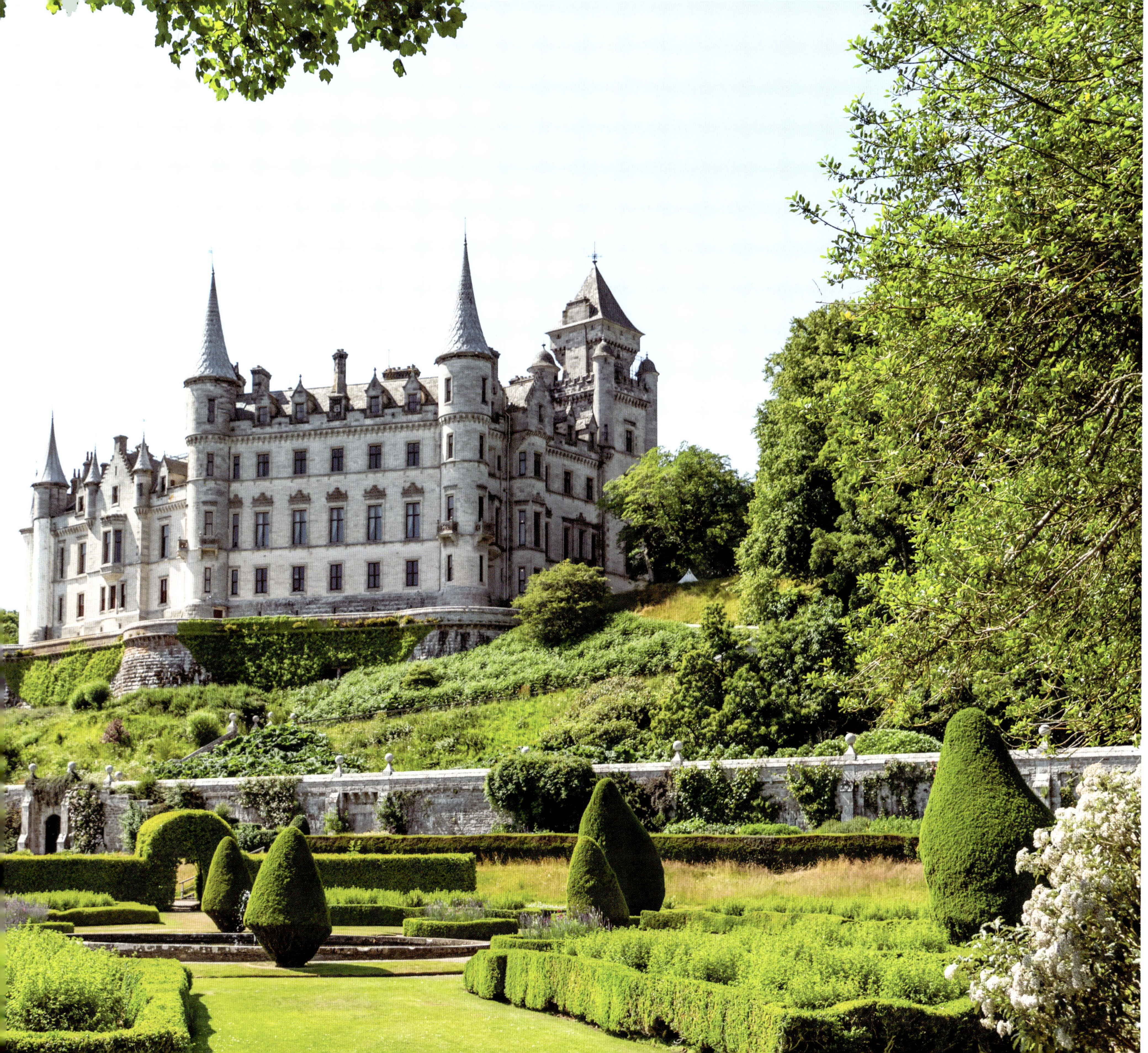

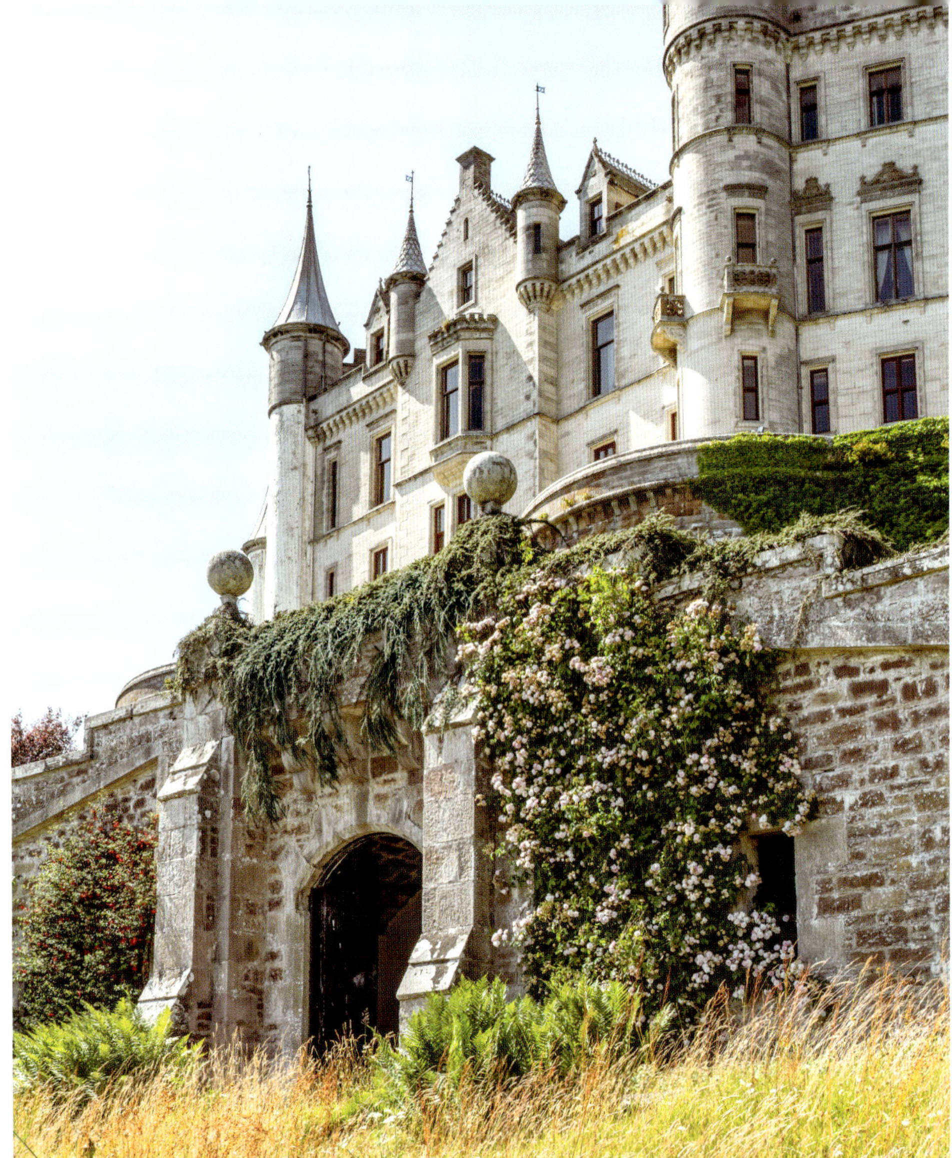

Left: Replete with storybook charm, Dunrobin's façade resembles a French château. Below: Dedicated gardeners ensure that a kaleidoscope of color unfolds throughout the year as different blooms take their turns. Opposite: Dunrobin's grand staircase features a beautifully carved balustrade; the walls are lined with portraits and stag heads.

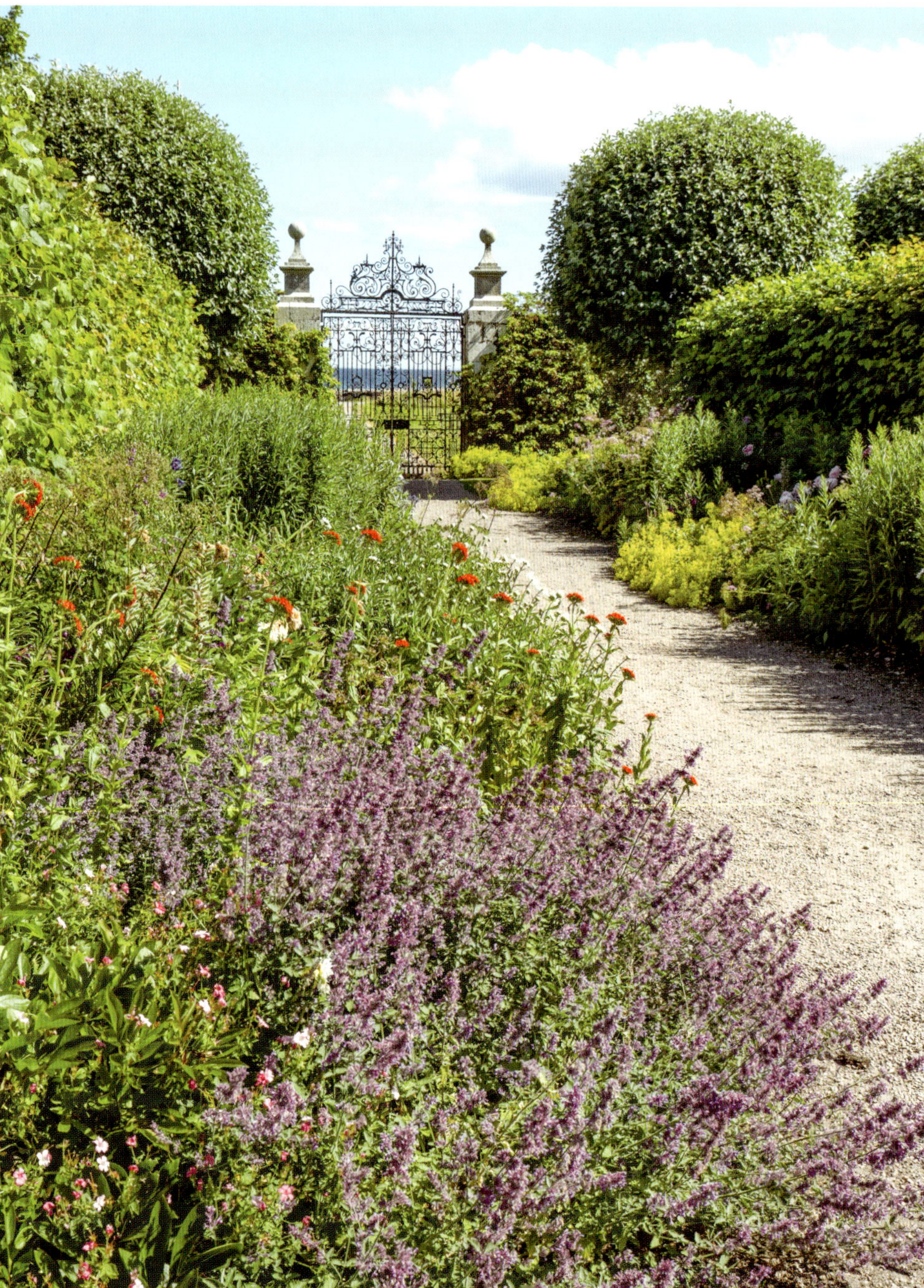

Dunrobin's formal Victorian gardens are another of Sir Charles Barry's contributions. Inspired by the precise parterres at the Palace of Versailles, his designs are virtually unchanged since they were originally laid out in 1850, though present-day gardeners continue to introduce new plants. More recent additions include avenues of whitebeam and 'Tuscan Tower' laurel trees. Visitors to Dunrobin Castle will be delighted to see fresh-clipped flowers from the gardens in the floral arrangements present throughout the great house, adding an extra layer of loveliness to the interiors of this remarkably maintained historical treasure.

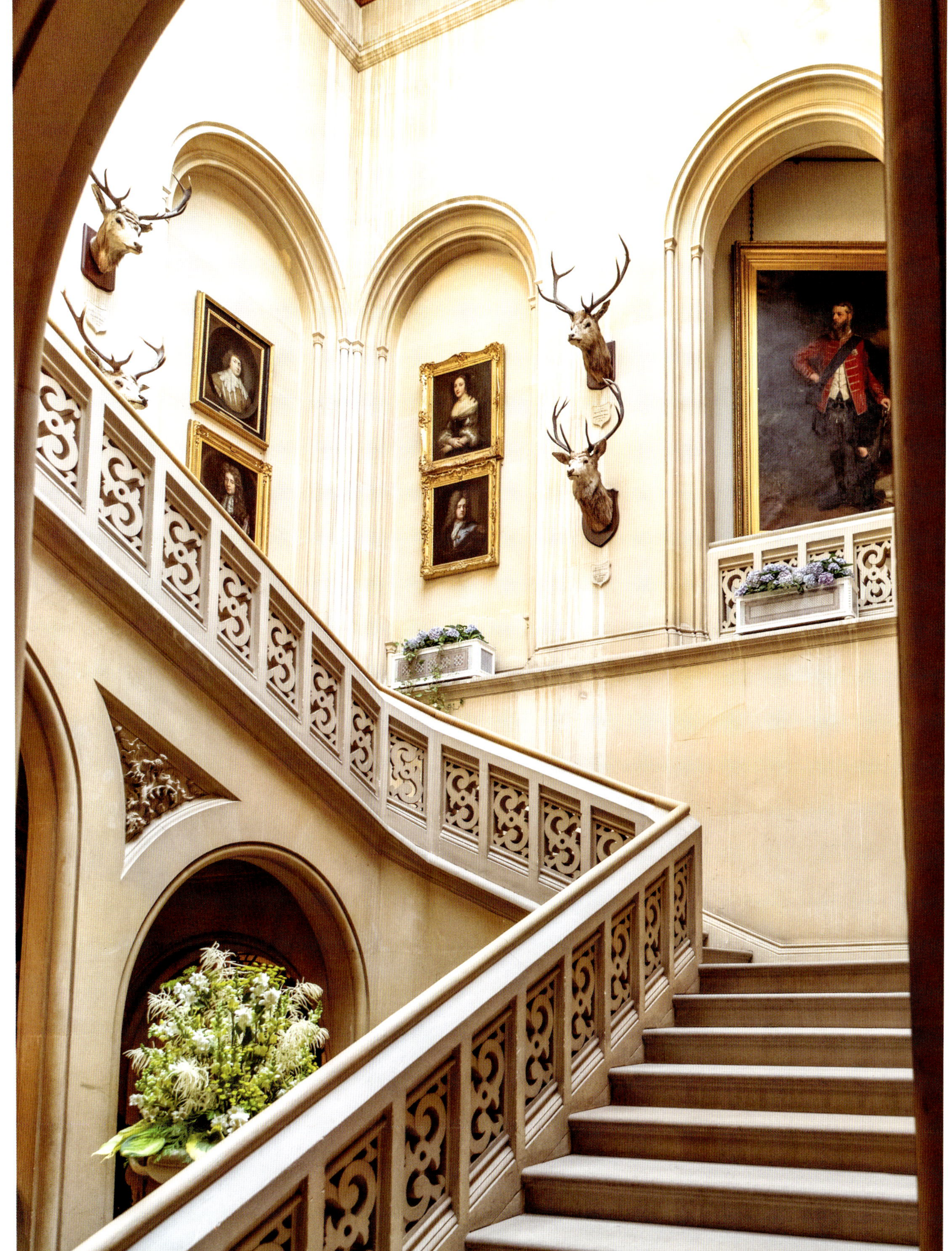

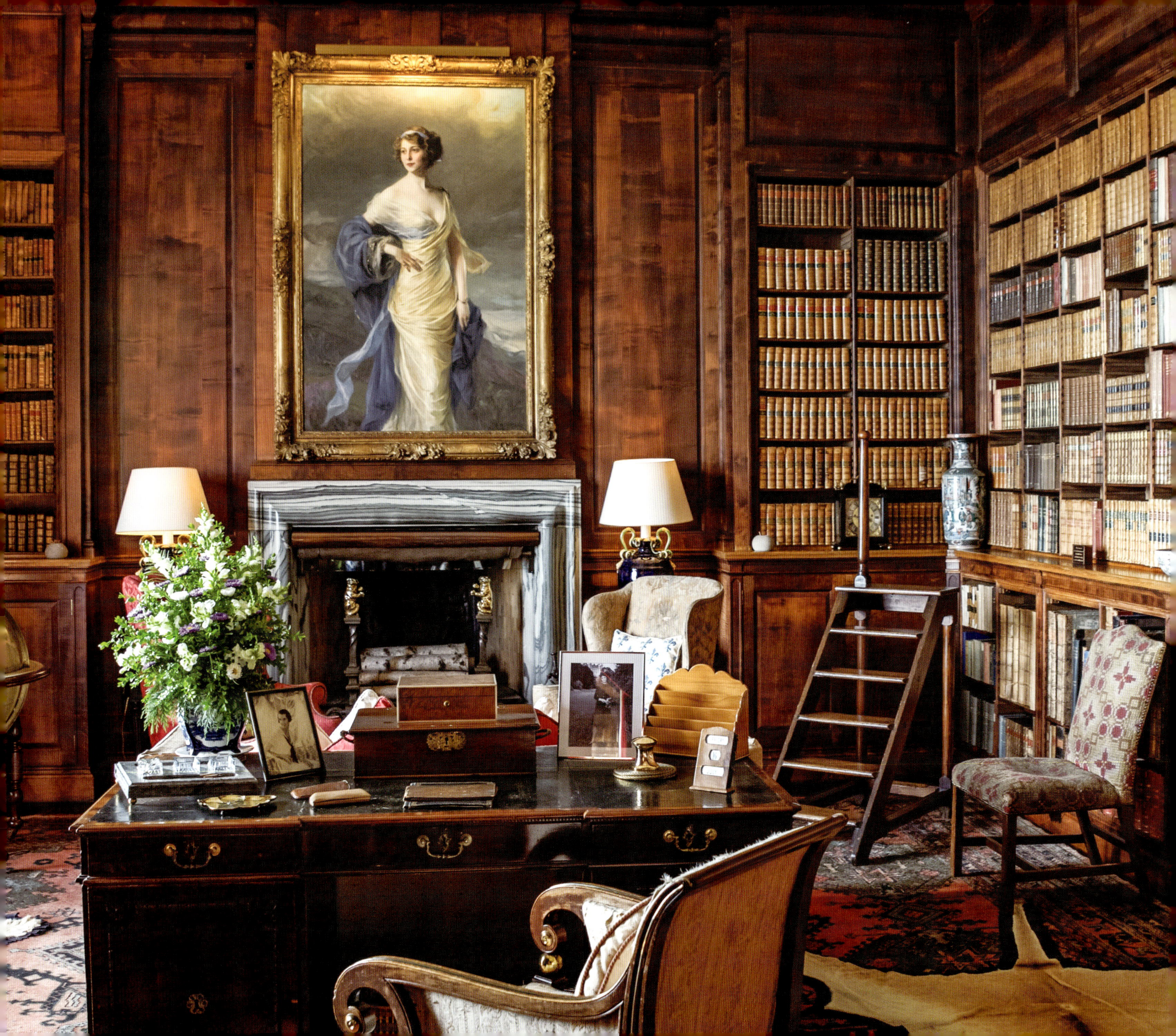

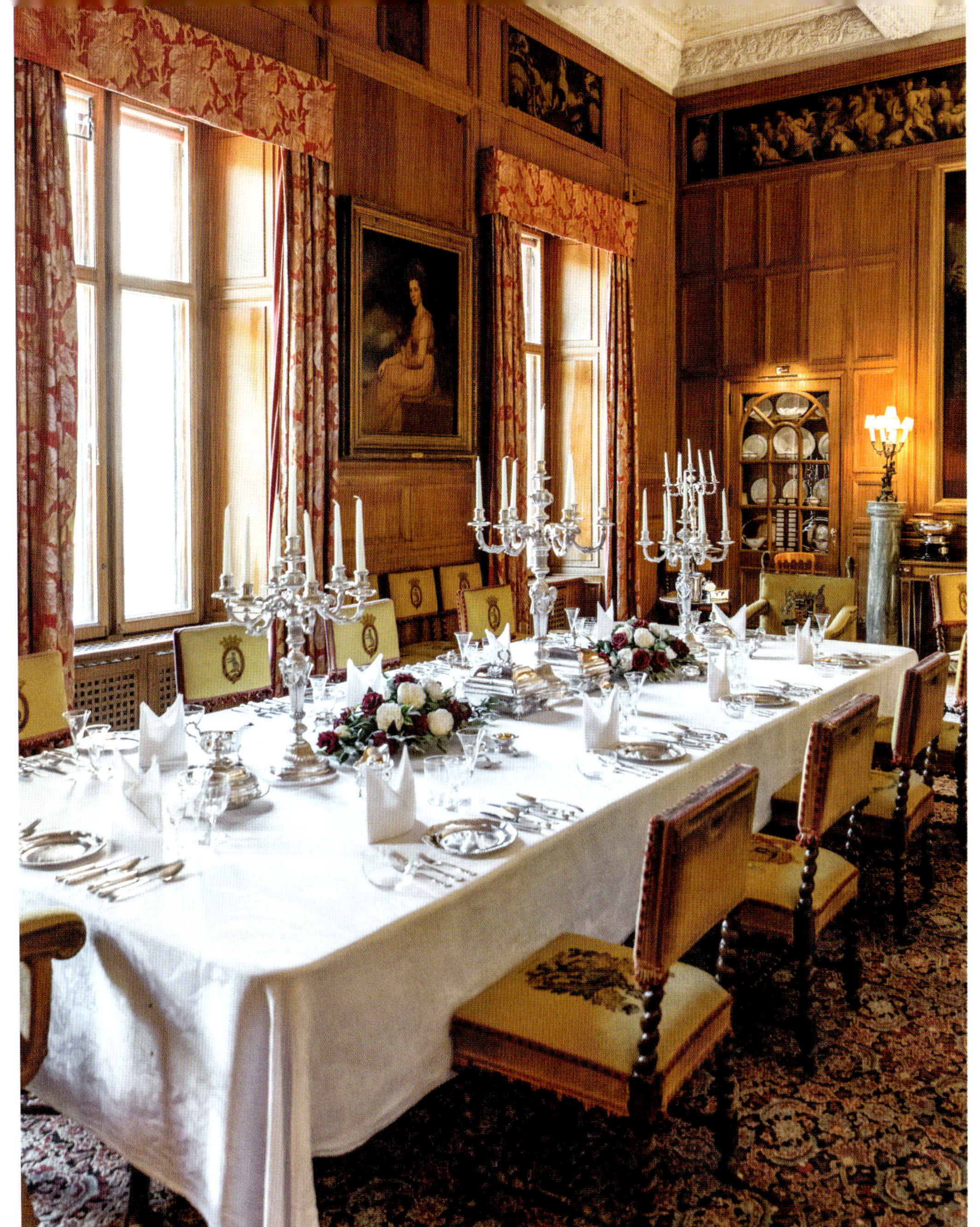

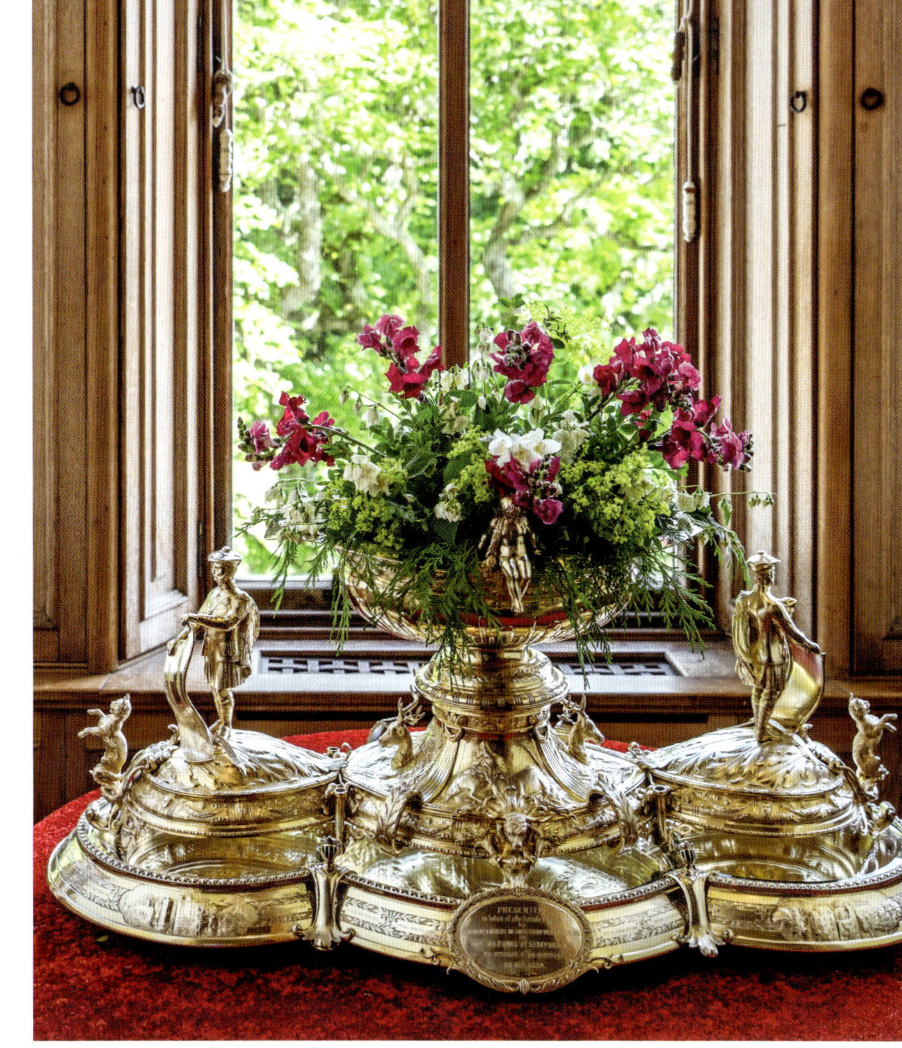

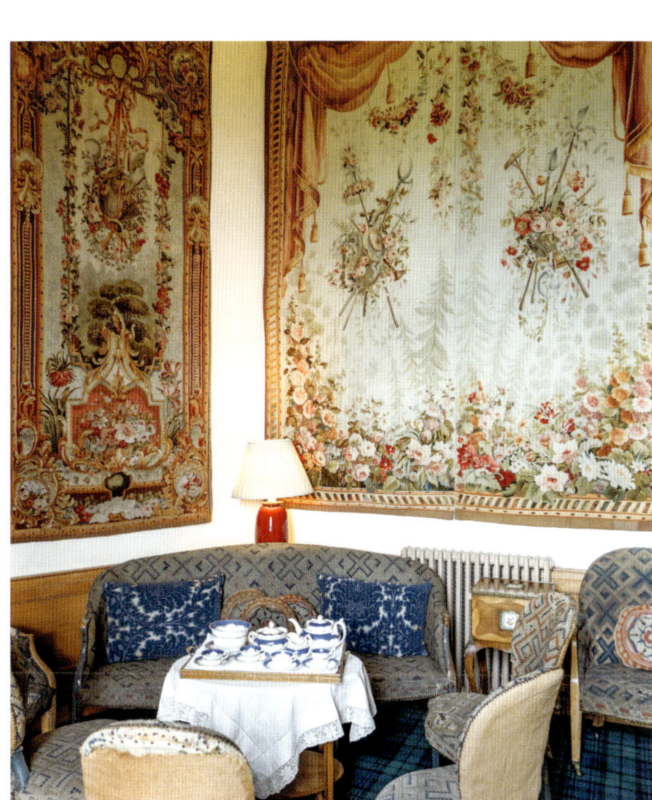

Opposite: The cozy library, which houses more than ten thousand volumes—many of them rare—is delineated by walls made of sycamore wood, per Sir Robert Lorimer's design. This page, above: Drawing interest to the dining hall are a coffered, moulded-plaster ceiling and an Italian classical grisaille frieze. The Jacobean-style chairs are emblazoned with family coats of arms.

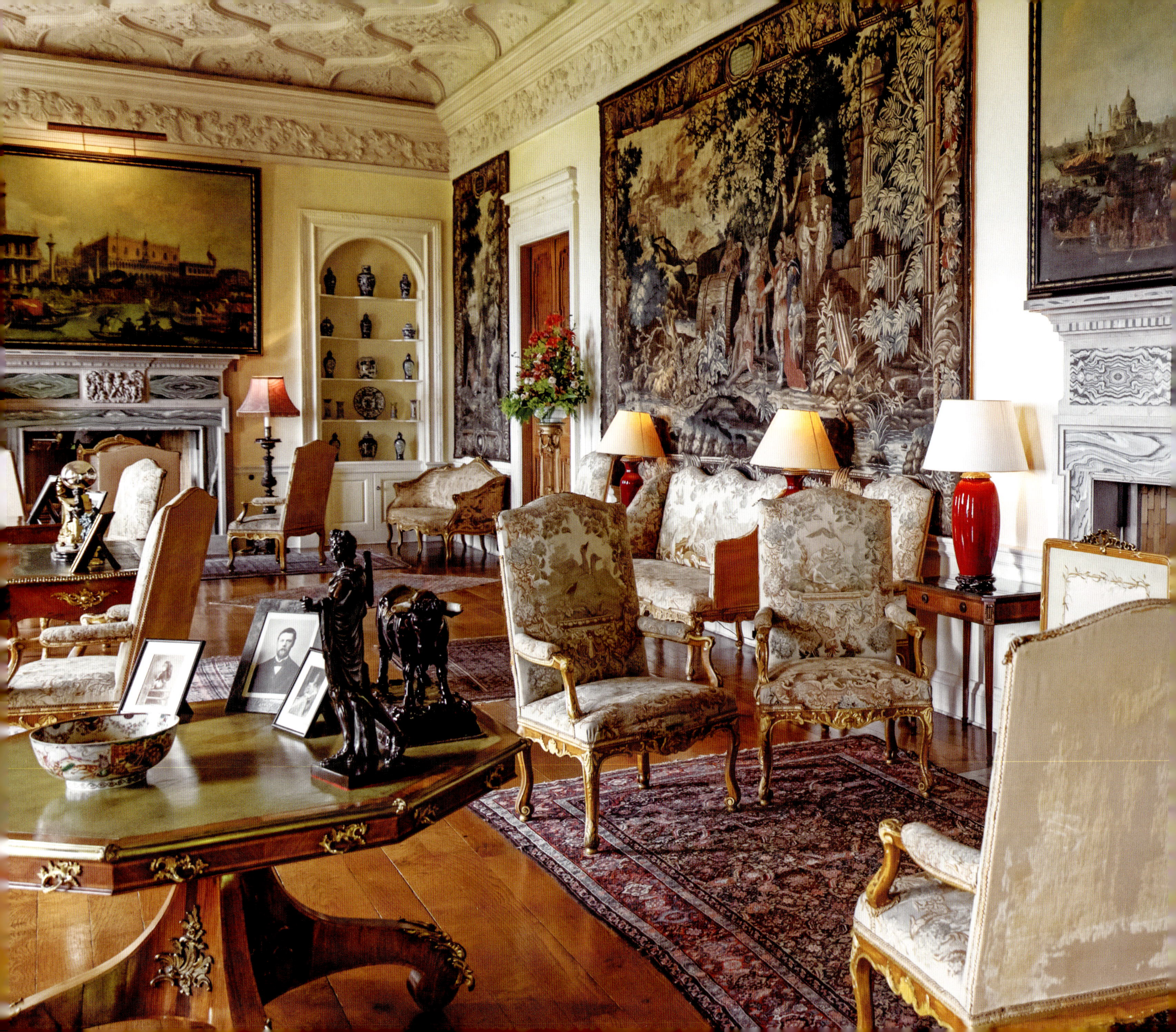

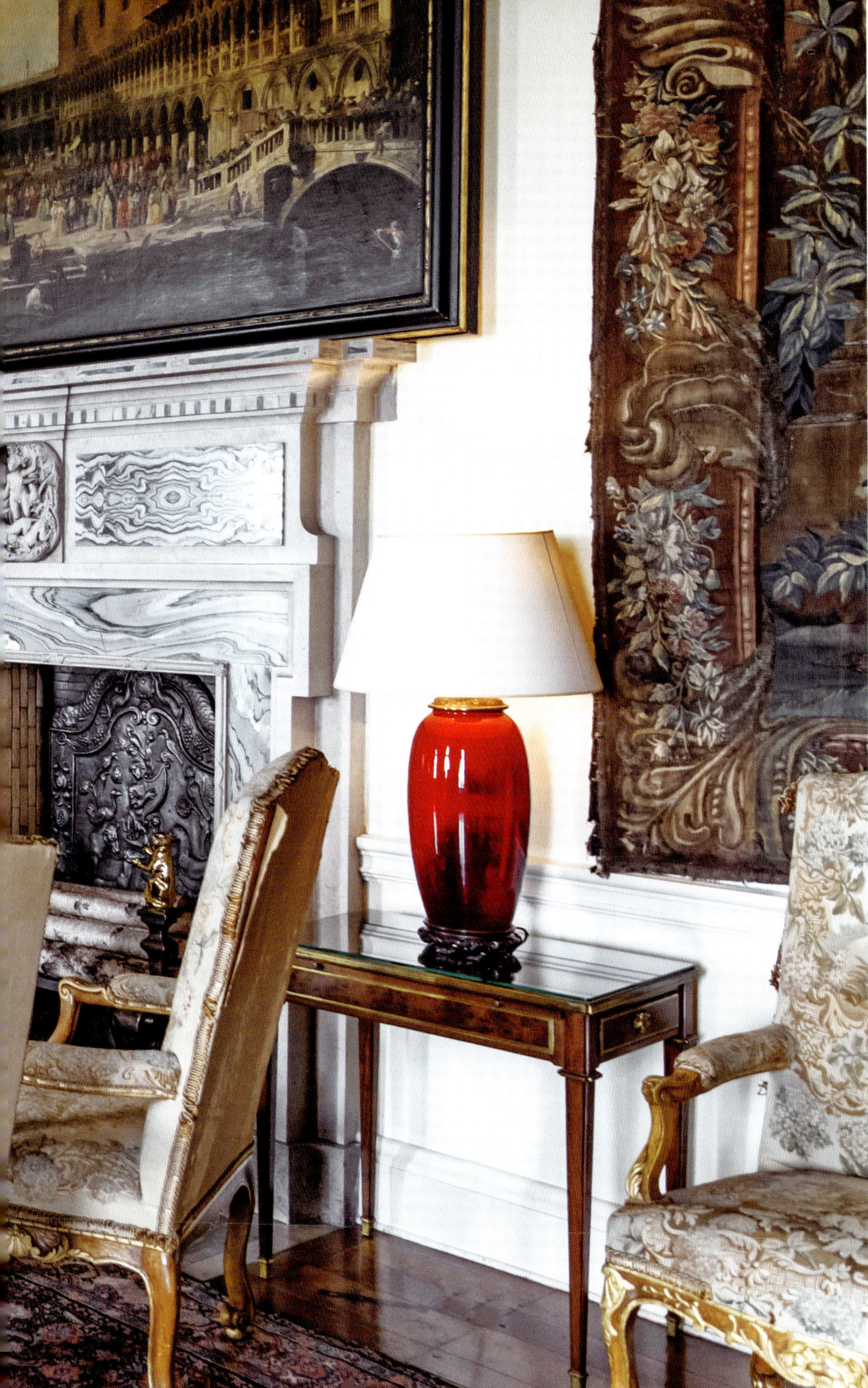

"[Sir Charles] Barry, a master of the Gothic Revival style, was called in to create an example of French elegance on the edge of the North Sea. He succeeded magnificently, creating an ornate fantasy palace decorated with conical turrets."

—David Ross

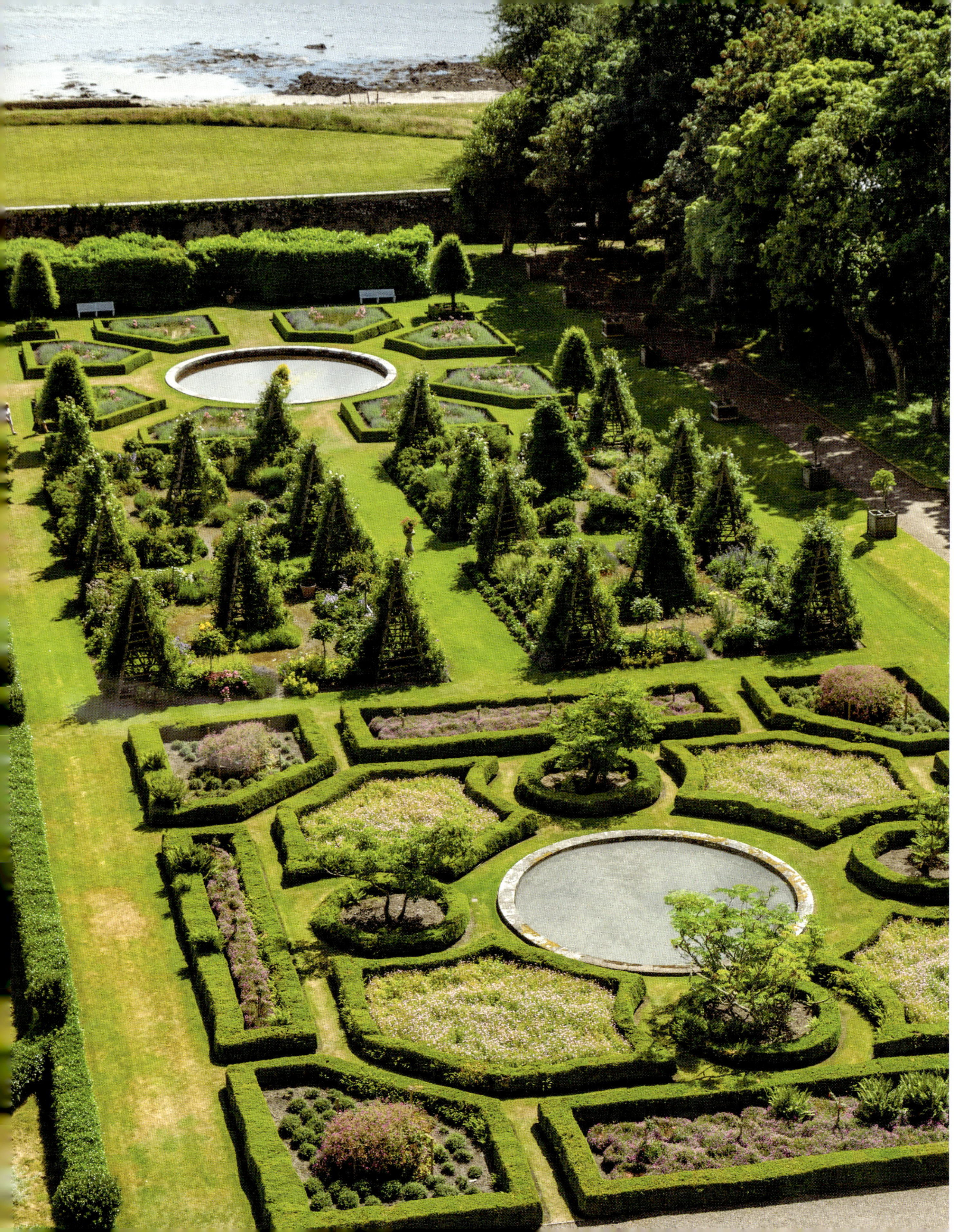

Left: The gardens comprise two elegant parterres, with circular pools at the center of each. Below: With its pyramid-shaped plant supports, this section draws inspiration from French potagers, or kitchen gardens, of the nineteenth century. Opposite: The opulent Green and Gold Bedroom, which holds the bed designed for Queen Victoria's visit, was used by Duchess Eileen.

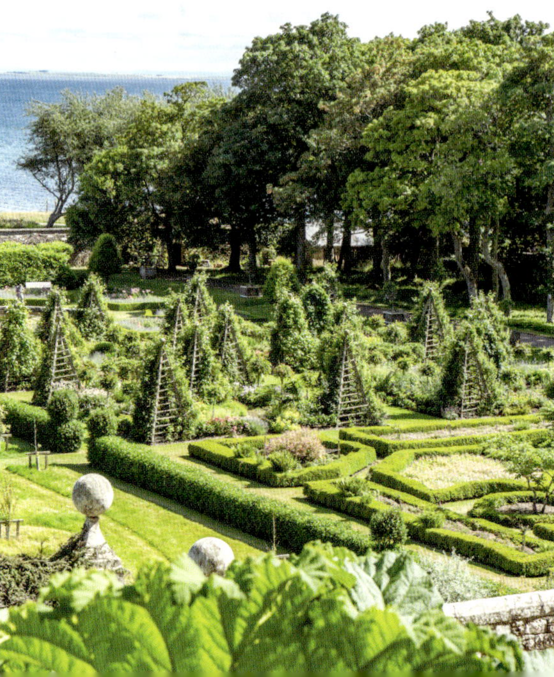

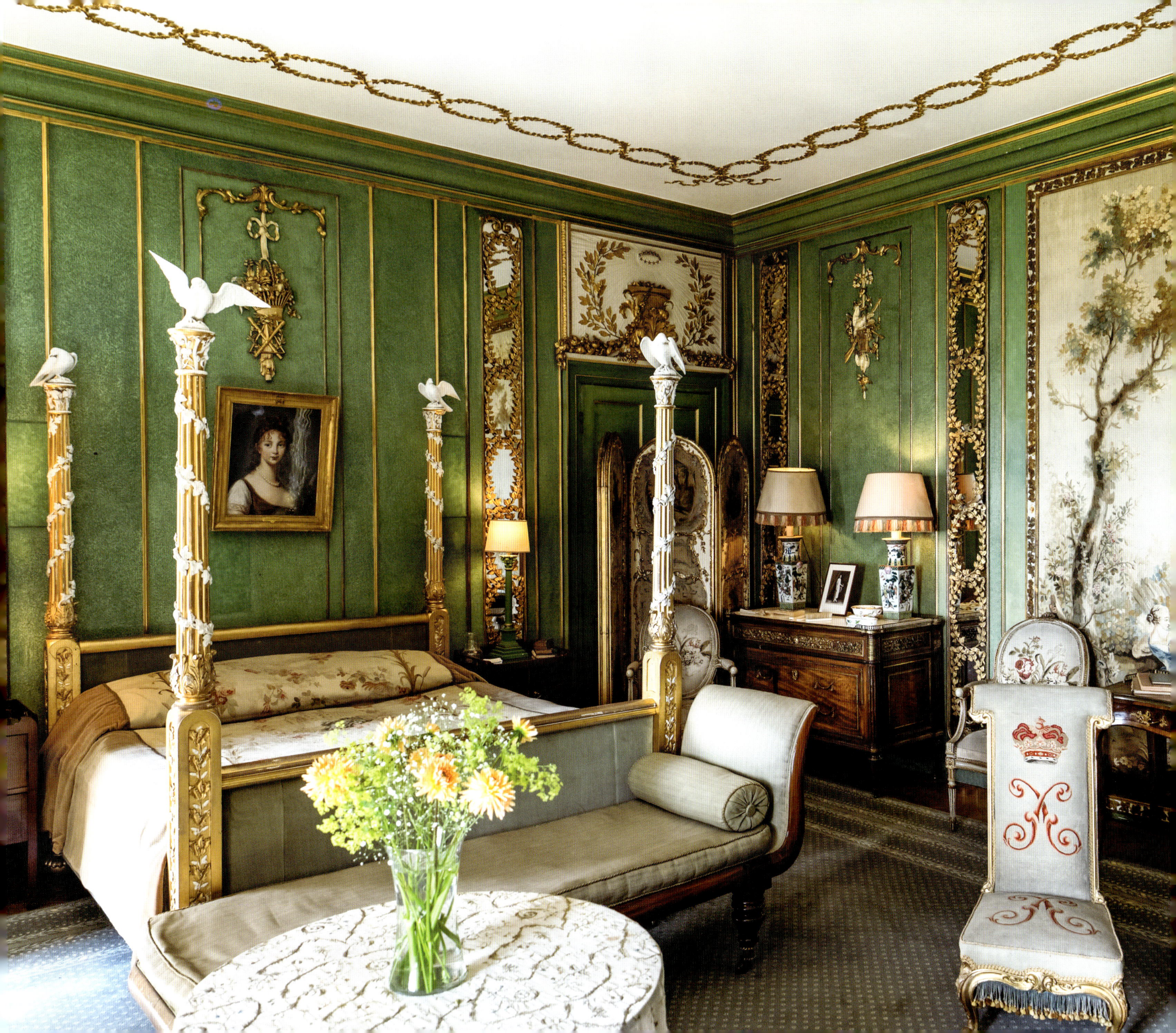

WHERE HISTORY DWELLS

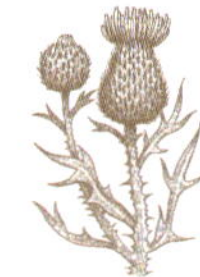

In a country where legends live in the very stones and mortar that make up the ancient fortresses of yore, Glamis Castle has made an indelible mark. Set in the heart of Scotland's Angus region, it boasts a narrative that stretches back six centuries, when King Robert II bestowed the Thane of Glamis to Sir John Lyon in 1372. Henceforth, the property has been the ancestral seat of the Earls of Strathmore and Kinghorne and their Lyon ancestors.

The oldest part of the castle dates to the 1400s, but renovations and additions through the years have seen the edifice grow in breadth and stature, with its turrets reaching closer and closer to the clouds. Many important guests have had the fortune to stay within these storied walls; Mary, Queen of Scots visited briefly while en route to suppress a rebellion. But the family itself has had no shortage of powerful personalities, from the 5th Earl, who fought in the Jacobite Rebellion, to the late Queen Mother, Lady Elizabeth Bowes-Lyon, who grew up here, cared for wounded soldiers brought to Glamis during World War I, and later married the future King George VI of the United Kingdom.

Although it is believed Glamis Castle provided William Shakespeare with the inspiration for the setting of his play *Macbeth*, there is no proof that he ever visited. It is more likely that he crossed paths with the 9th Lord Glamis in London, where the nobleman regaled

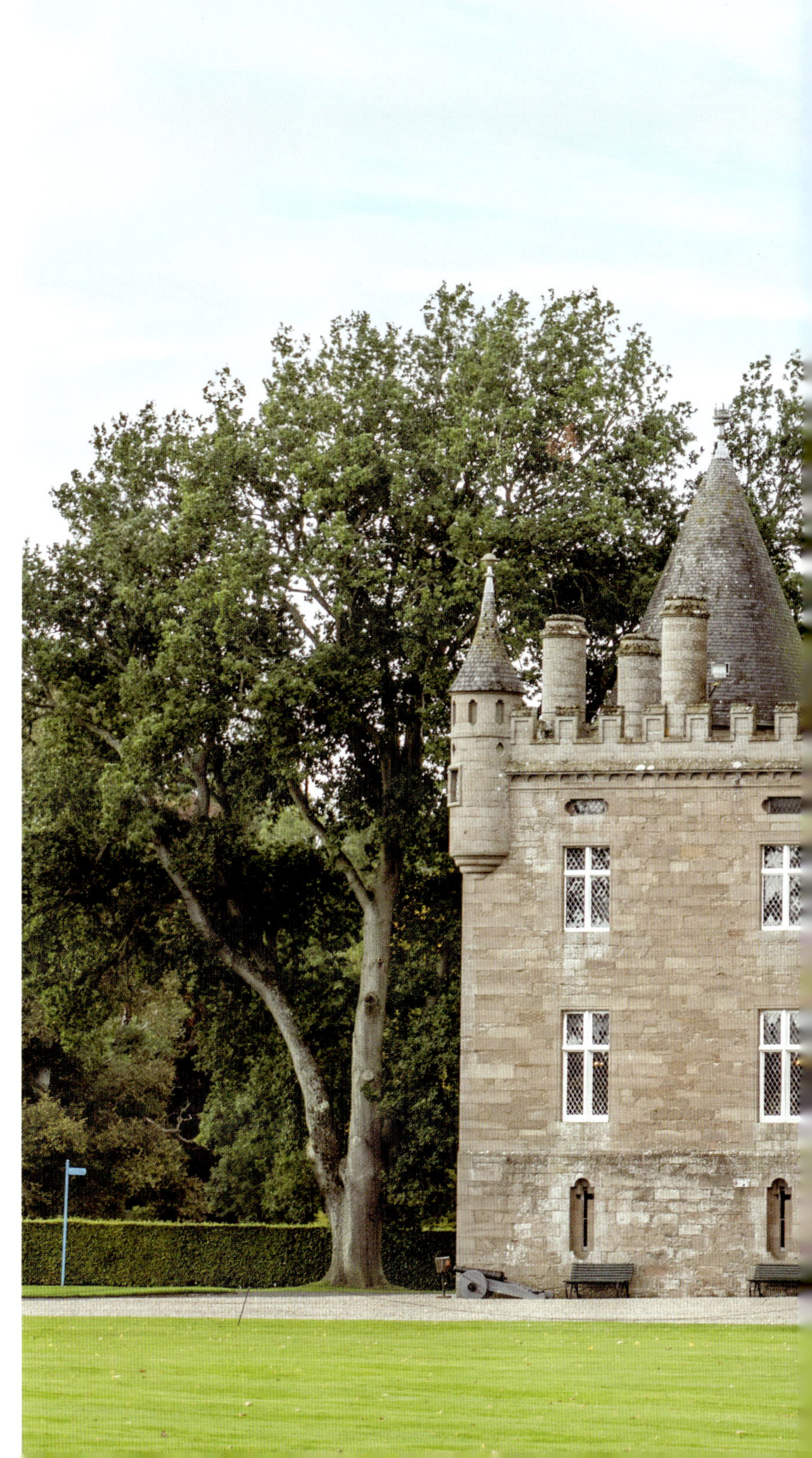

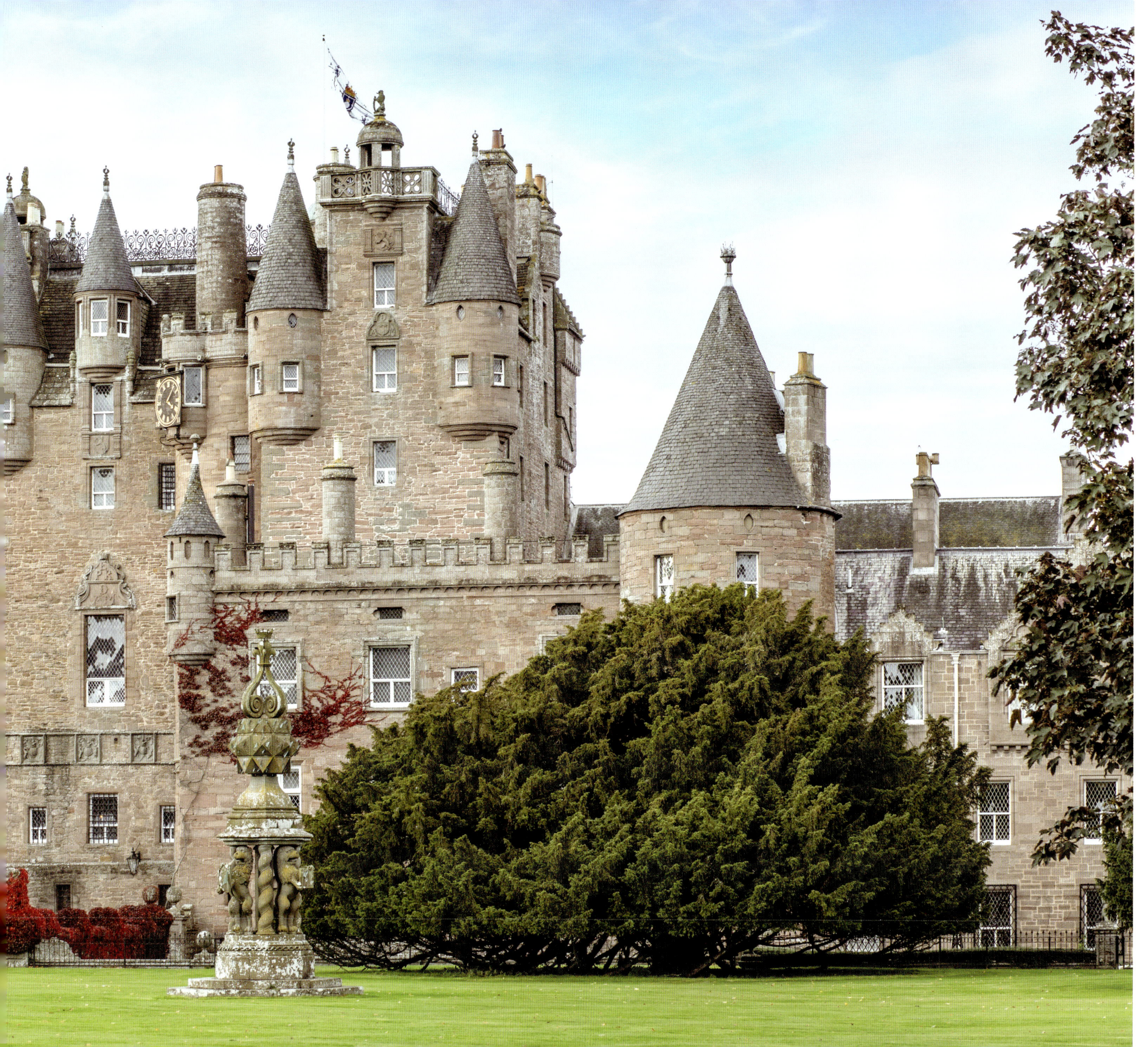

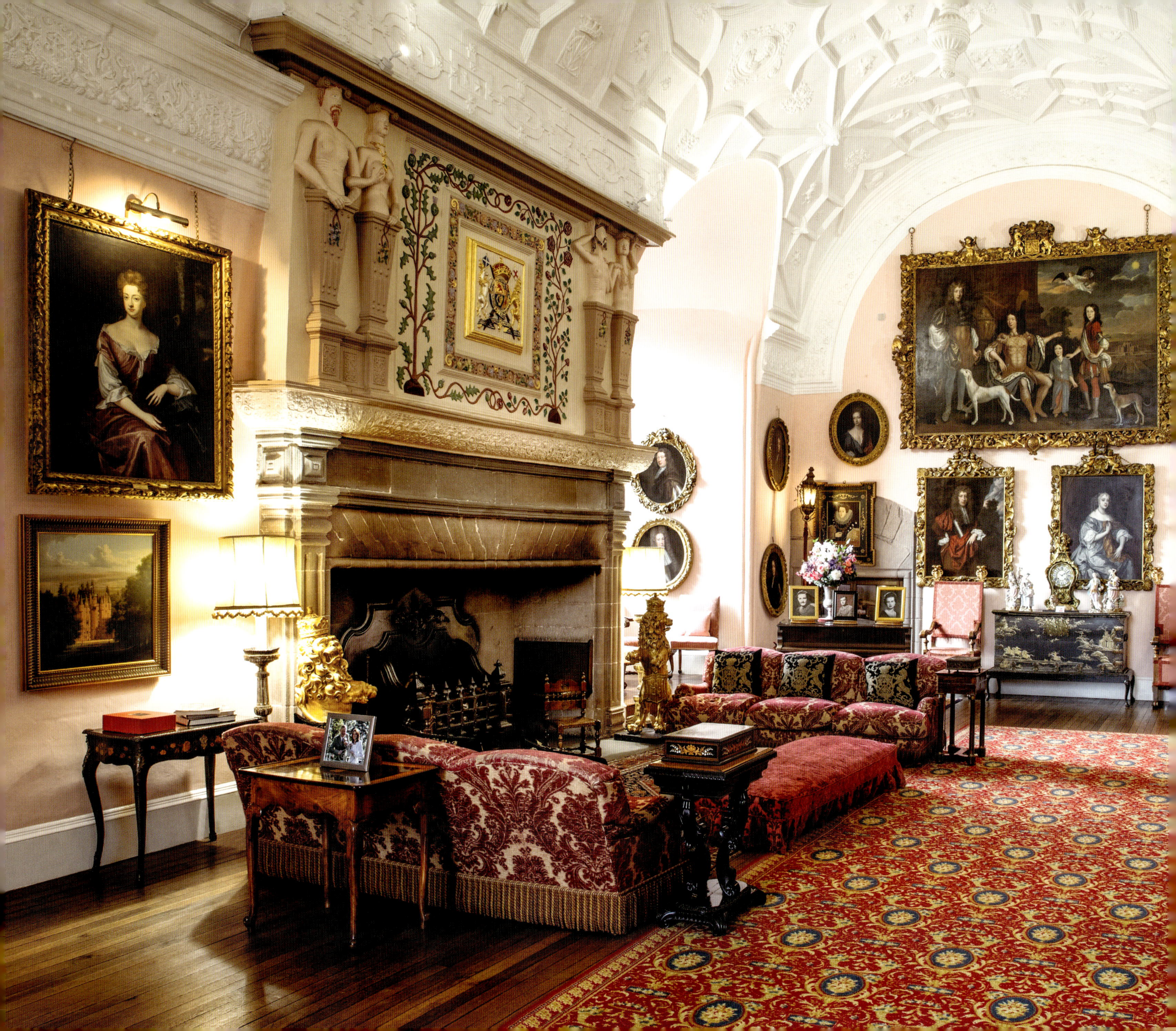

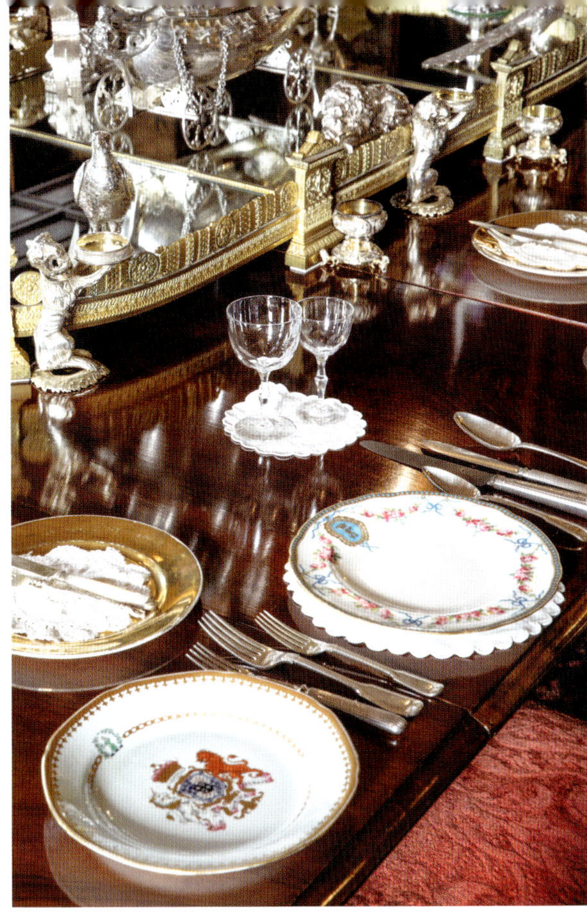

Opposite: A barrel-vaulted plaster ceiling bearing ornate designs arches over the castle's Drawing Room. The capacious fireplace is crowned with an impressive carved overmantel. This page: Beautiful oak paneling embellishes the walls of the Victorian Dining Room, where a William IV mahogany table, paired with velvet-cushioned chairs, can seat up to forty guests. Evocative of the grand table adornments popular during the Middle Ages and the Renaissance period, an elaborate silver nef in the shape of a sailing ship forms the eye-catching centerpiece.

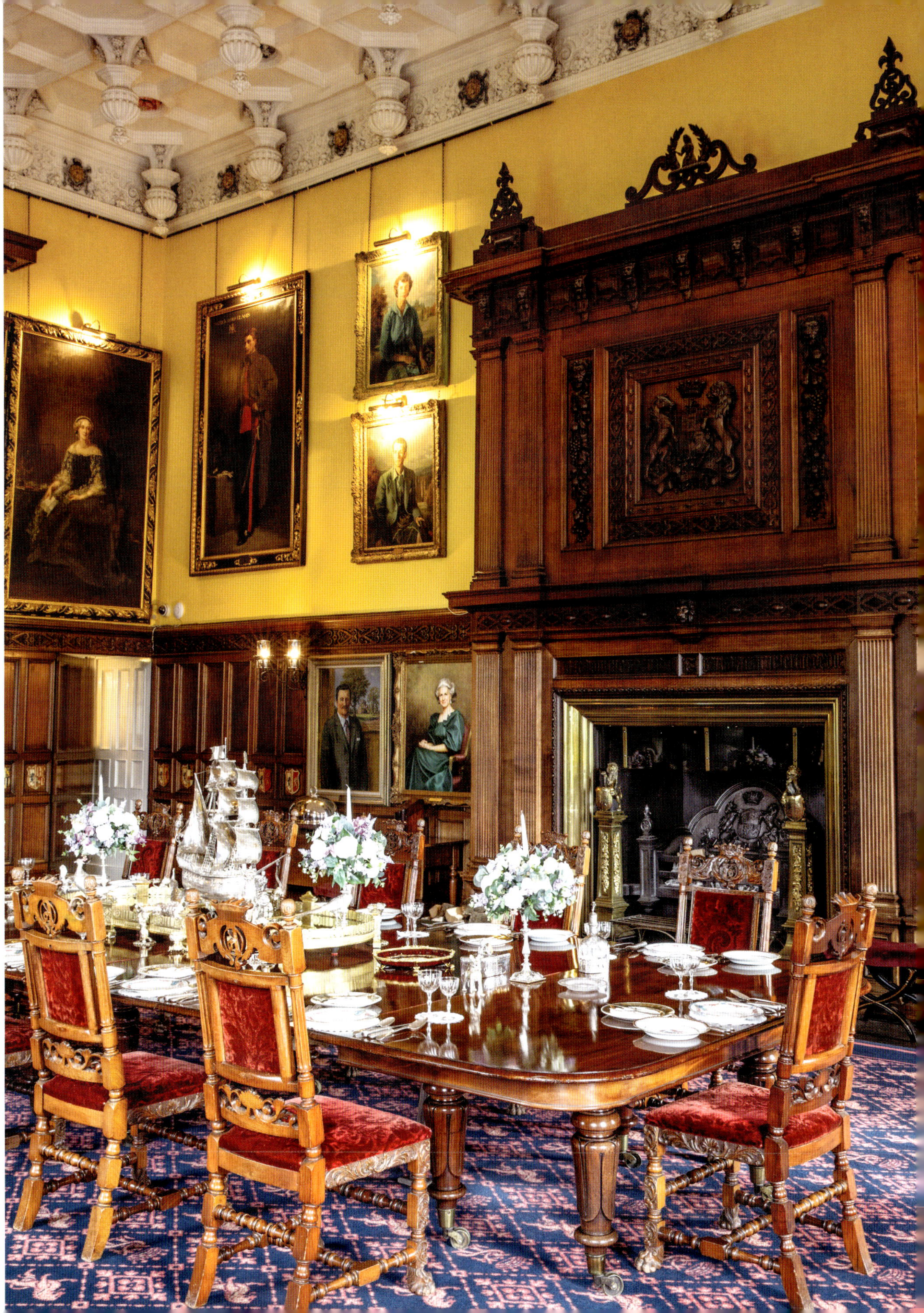

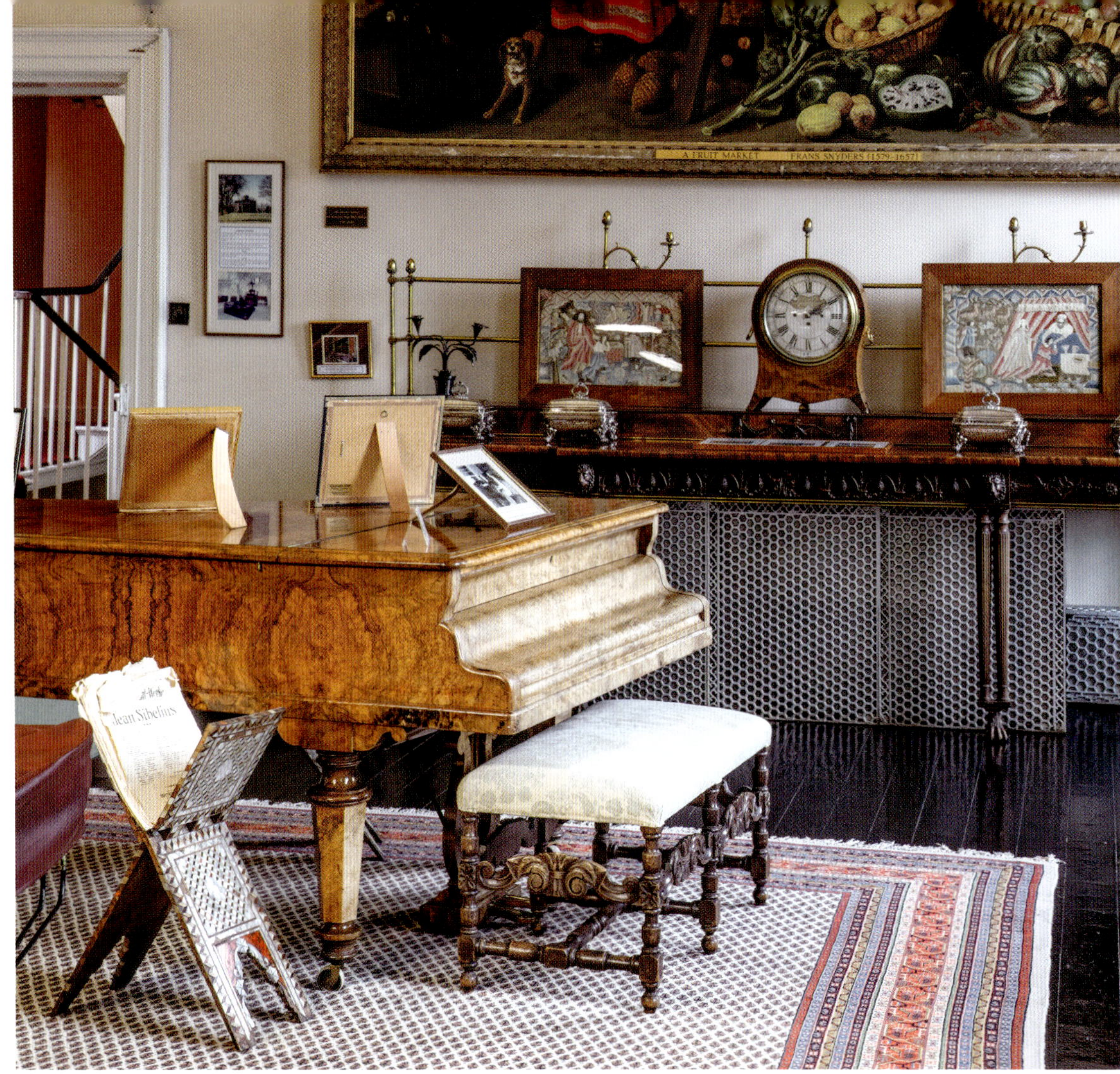

This page, left: Among the furnishings in the Billiard Room—which doubles as the main library—are a piano, tapestries, and a long wall of bookcases. Below: A seventeenth-century Kinghorne bed dominates The King's Room. Opposite: Scottish thistles are woven throughout the shimmering gold décor in the bedroom of the late Queen Mother, Lady Elizabeth Bowes-Lyon. The exquisite headboard was embroidered by her mother, Cecilia.

the bard with adventurous tales of the castle's fascinating history. Regardless of how it came to be, Glamis has enjoyed its association with the drama, and visitors to the property's gardens will be delighted to find a section known as the Macbeth Trail, where seven craggy sculptures depict the play's most memorable scenes.

But this theater-themed path is the just the beginning of Glamis's splendid horticultural plots. The Walled Garden features a plethora of bedding plants as well as espaliered fruit trees, a fountain, and a Monet-inspired bridge. In 1910, Countess Cecilia, mother of the late Queen Mother and a multifaceted designer, created the sumptuous Italian Garden. The formal borders and richly colored blossoms illustrate the vibrancy of the Edwardian era and offer a serene setting for leisurely strolls, especially in summertime, when the verbenas are in full bloom and all of nature seems to celebrate the admirable longevity of this home entwined with centuries of history.

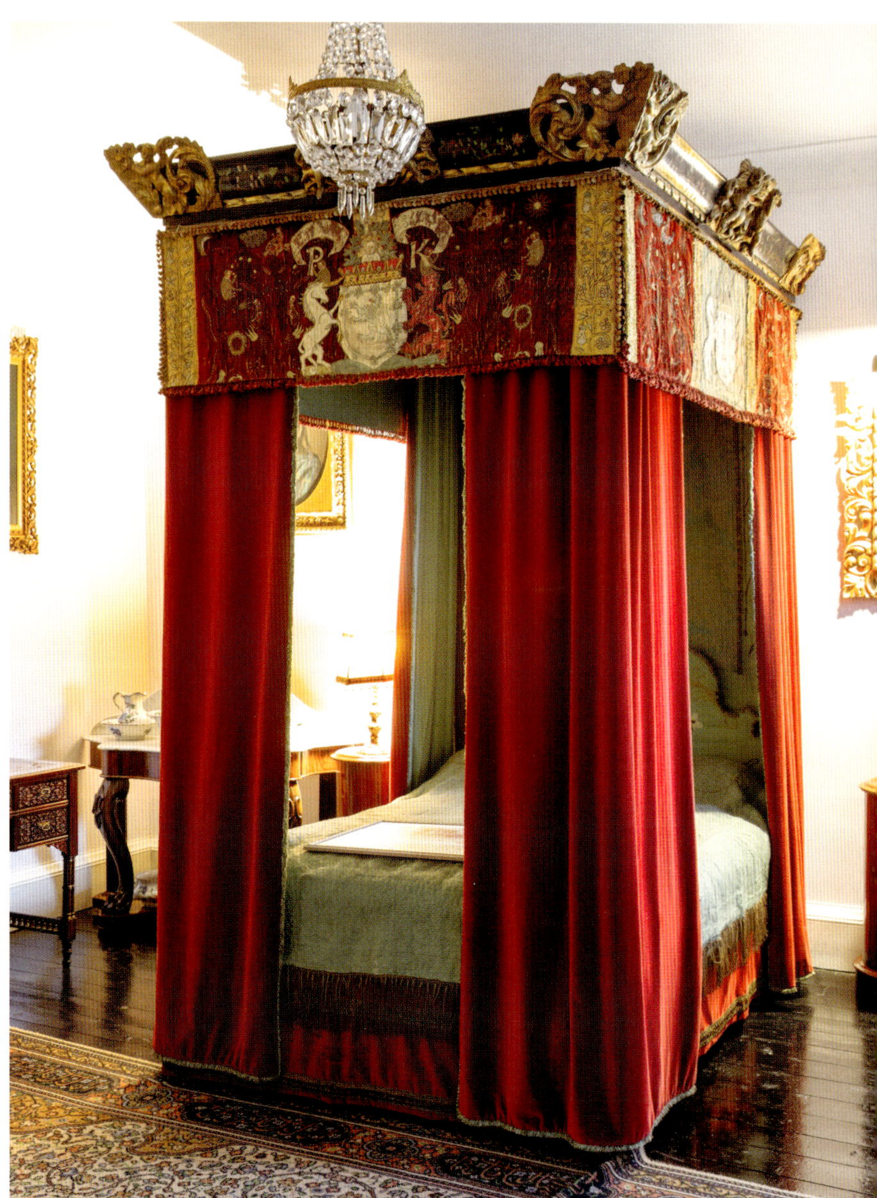

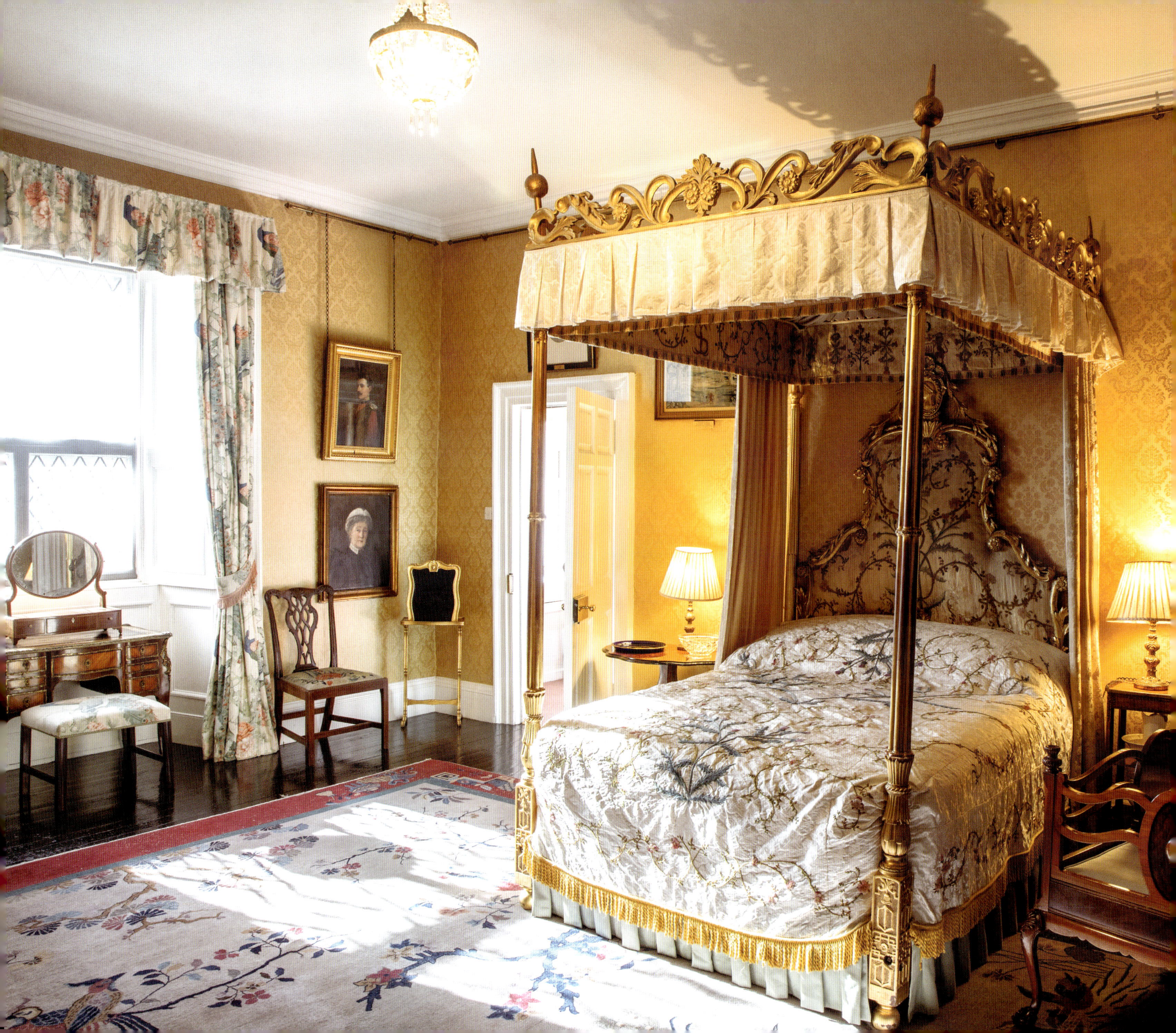

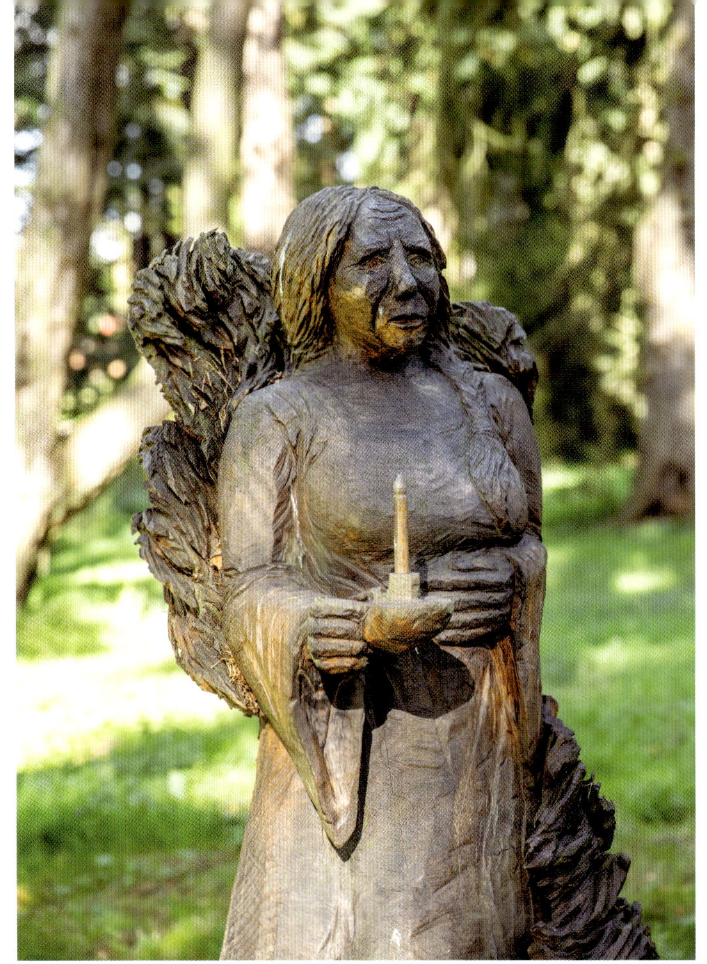

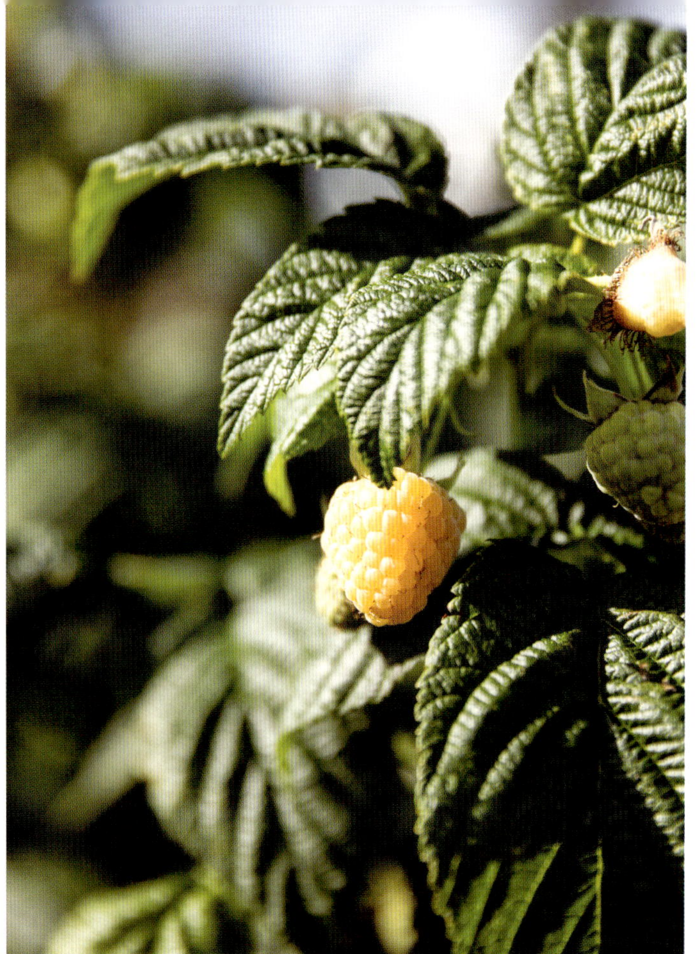

This page: Glamis Castle's literary connection to William Shakespeare's haunting work *Macbeth* is celebrated with the Macbeth Trail. Seven sculptures, including Lady Macbeth, top left, and King Duncan, bottom right, represent scenes from the play, echoing the tenor of this tragic tale. Opposite: Great swaths of purple verbenas burst into bloom each summer in the Italian Garden, which channels the character of Edwardian-era aesthetics and was designed by Countess Cecilia.

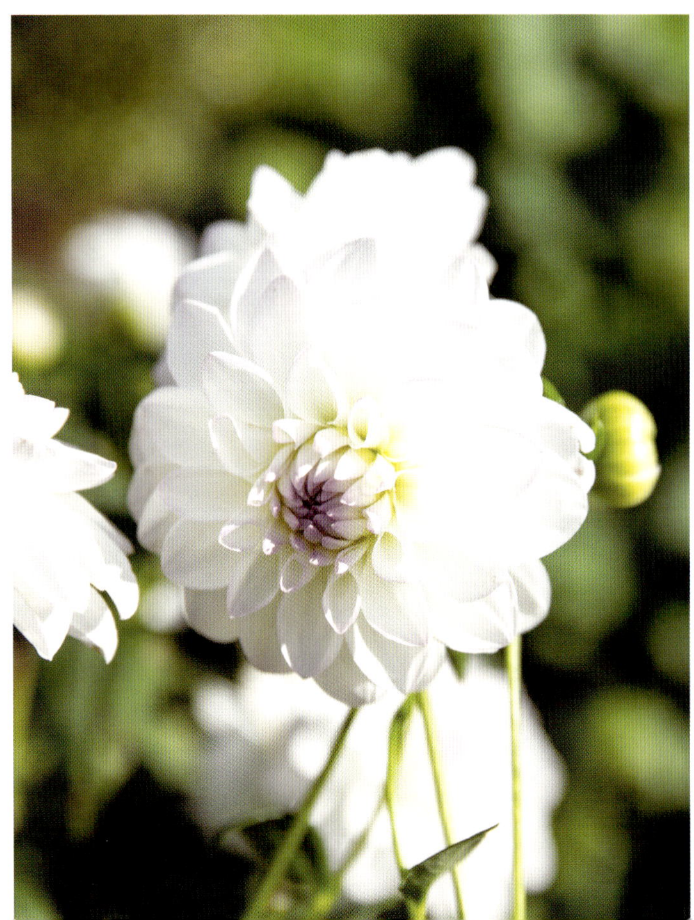

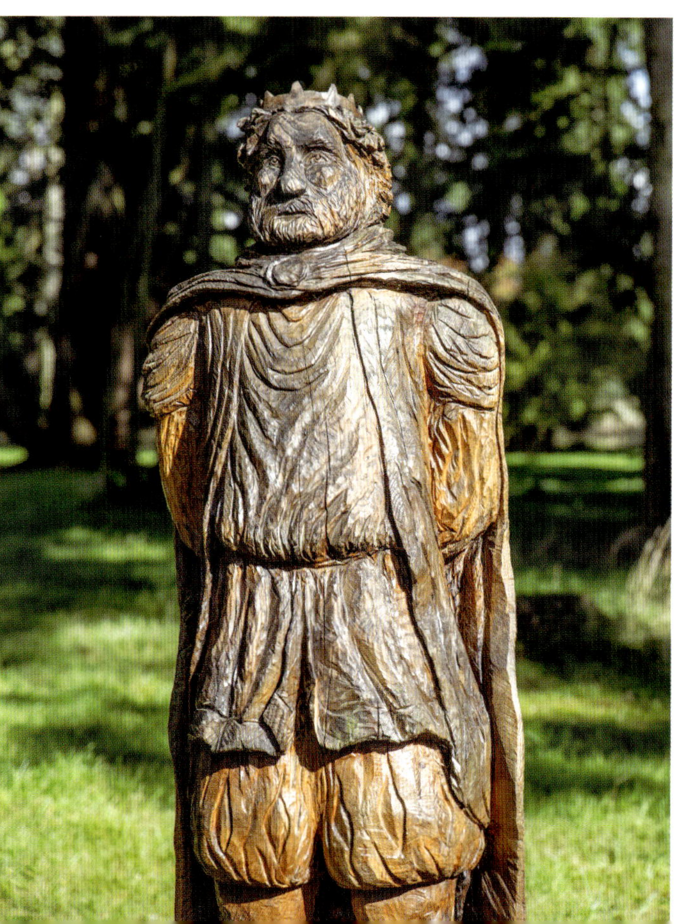

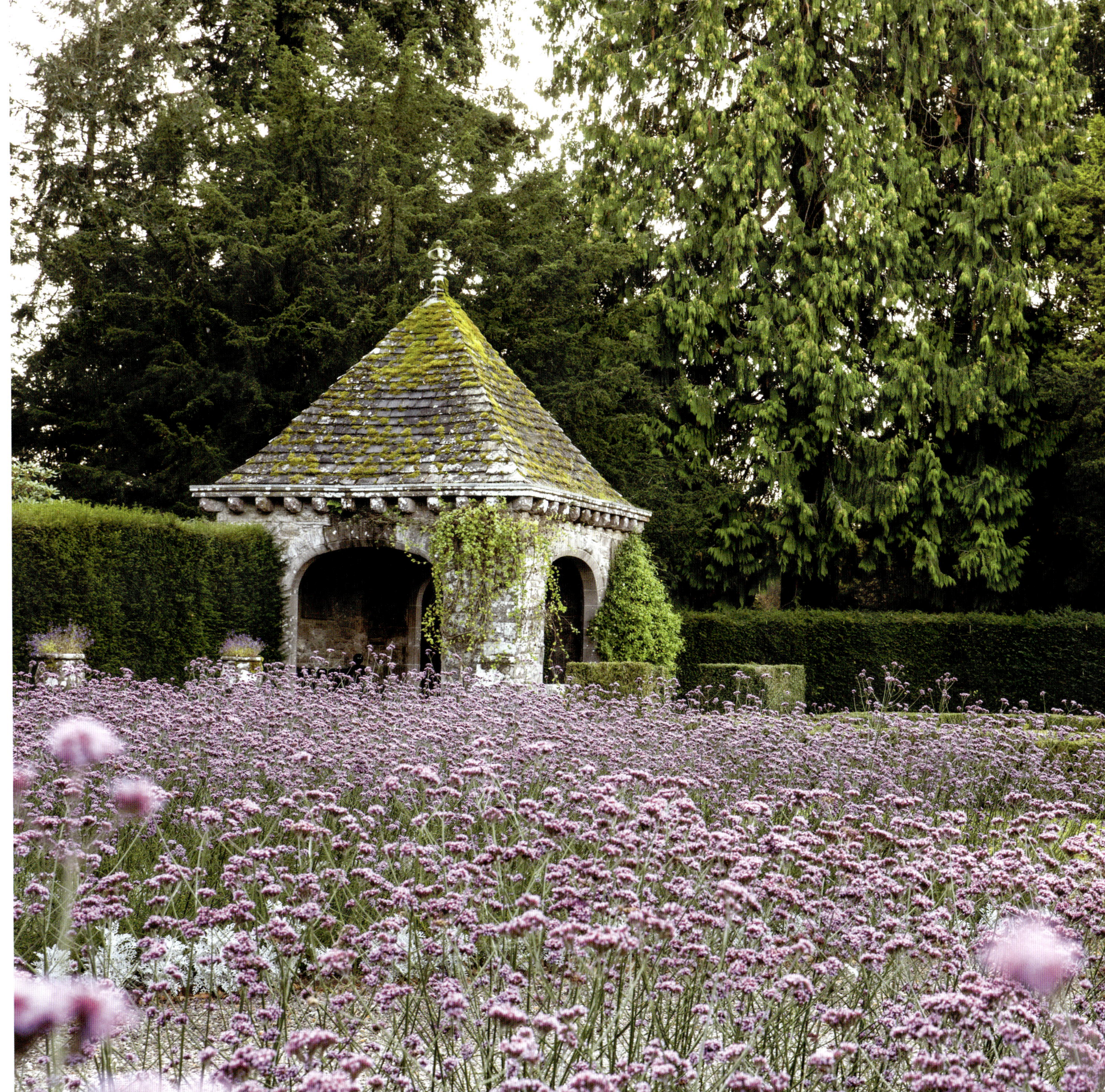

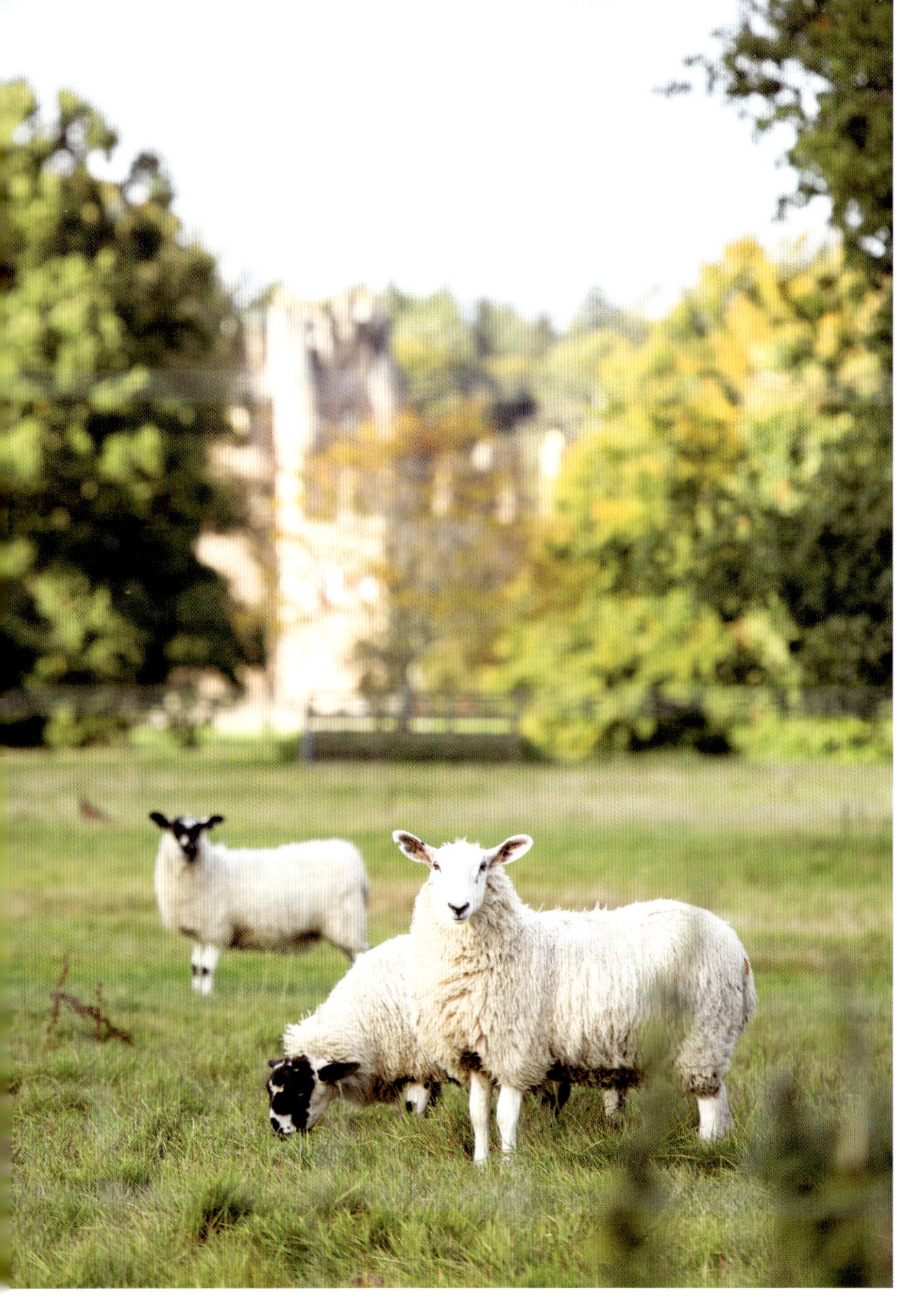

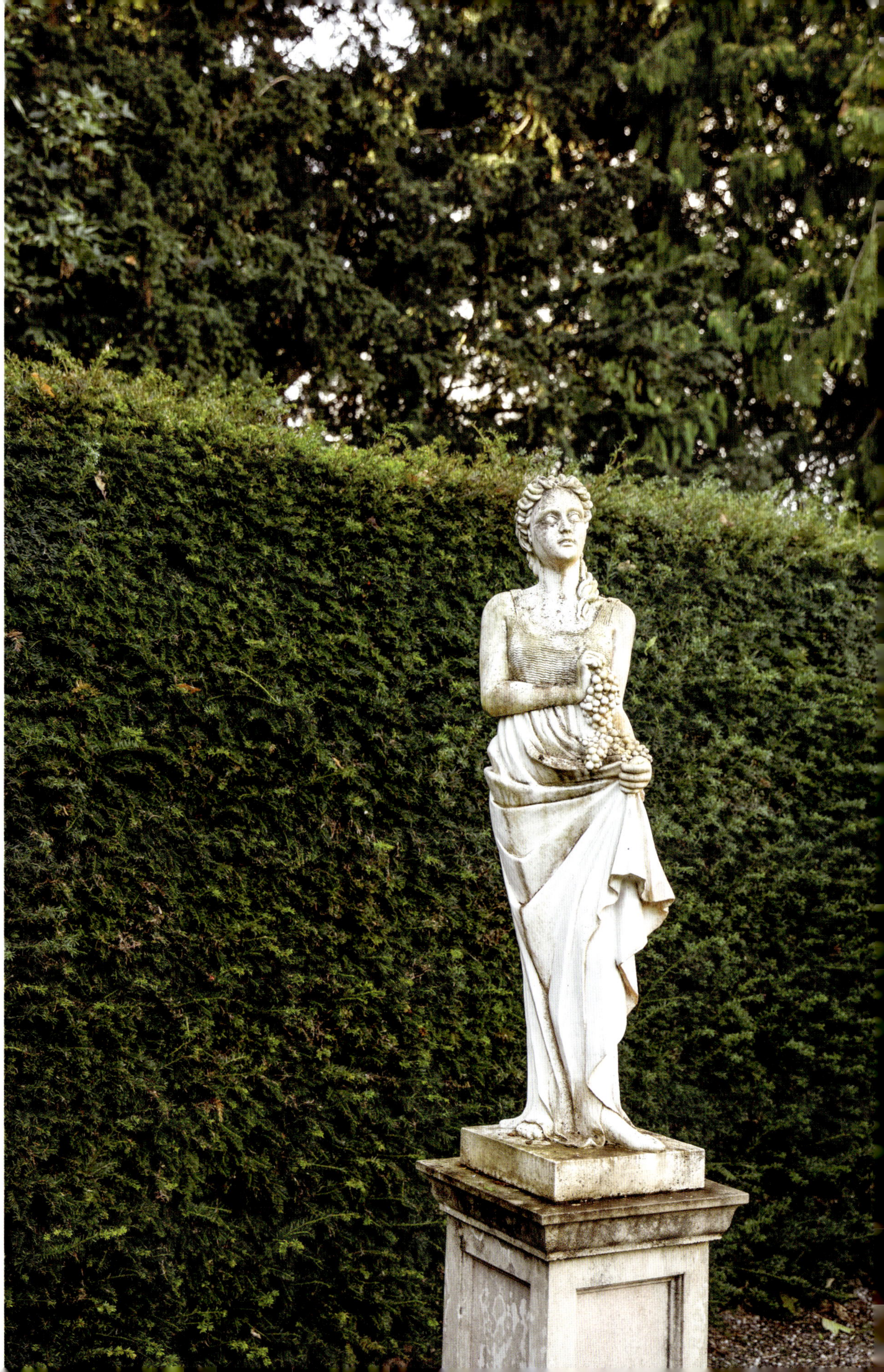

Above: Pastures and woodlands encircle Glamis Castle—verdant playgrounds for the myriad wildlife that call Scotland home. Sheep are often seen grazing alongside the tree-shaded drive leading up to the castle. Right: Stone statuaries offer classic touches to the grounds.

When glimpsed from a distance, the castle's magnificence is on full display. The original tower dates to the fourteenth century, with extensions made in subsequent centuries expanding the structure in both height and girth. Dormers, turrets, and rounded towers lend an almost fairy-tale feel to the façade, with the surrounding countryside offering pastoral charm and the Scottish hills in the distance forming the perfect backdrop.

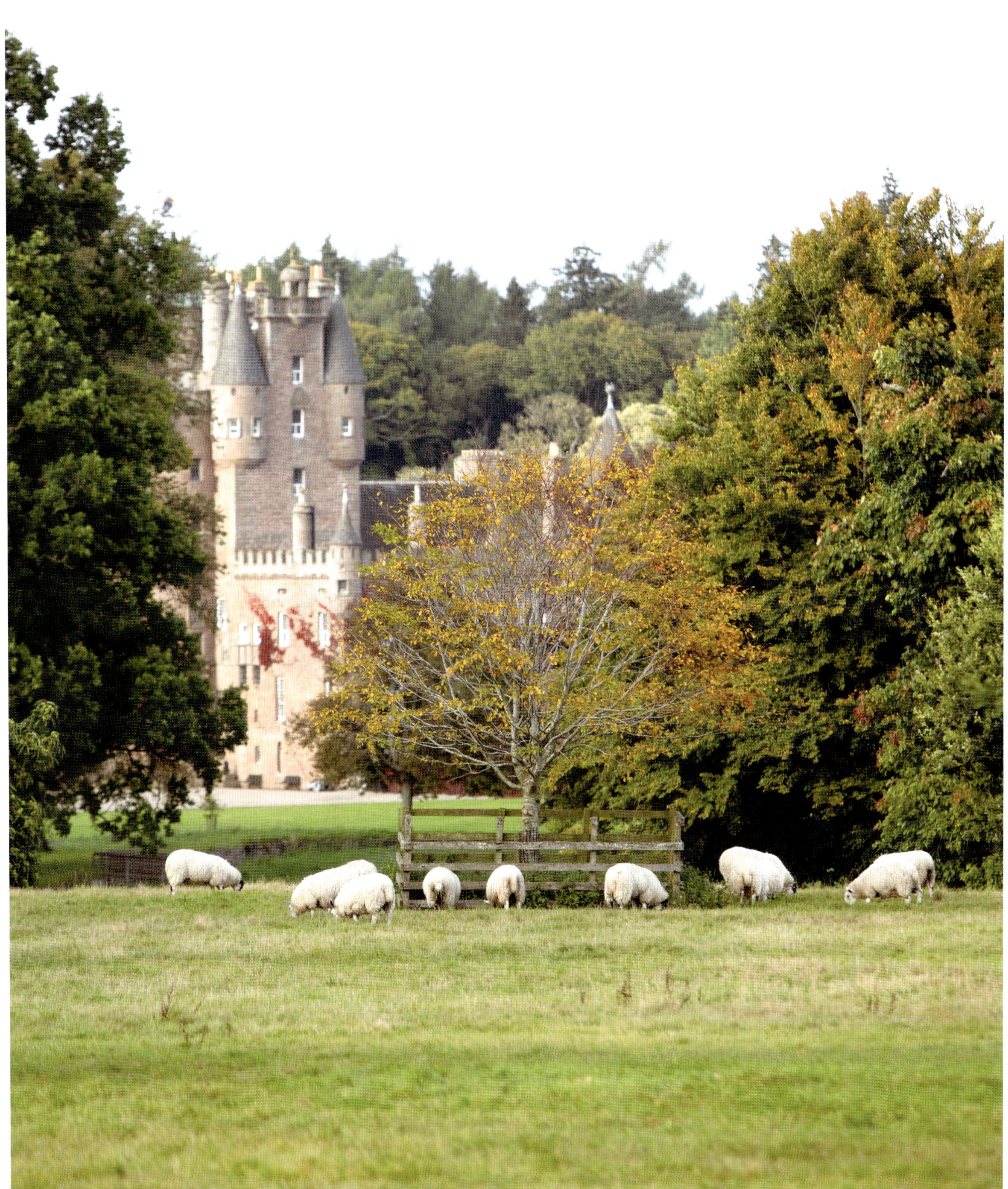

GUARDIAN OF THE HIGHLANDS

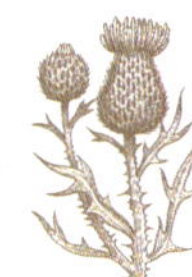

Rising from the site where King of Scots Robert the Bruce once presided over an open-air court, Scotland's Fyvie Castle, like all grand old fortresses of yore, is instilled with the quintessence of Highlands culture and ages of intriguing lore. This impressive stone edifice was built in the early thirteenth century as a simple wooden square enclosing a keep; it served as a royal stronghold until 1390, when it transitioned to a private residence owned by a succession of five families. Numerous transformations through the years increased the castle's size and altered its appearance, with each family adding its own tower to create the distinctive façade.

In 1889, Fyvie was purchased by Alexander Forbes-Leith, who was raised in the area and returned after making his fortune in the American steel industry. With this hard-earned wealth, he amassed an astounding collection of art, furniture, tapestries, and other antiquities that found a perfectly suited setting within the history-bathed walls of the castle. Paintings by Thomas Gainsborough, Sir Henry Raeburn, and Pompeo Batoni keep company with medieval armor and weaponry throughout the home, from the spacious gallery and the characterful library to the cozy sitting rooms. When the National Trust for Scotland purchased the property in 1984, this marvelous assemblage remained.

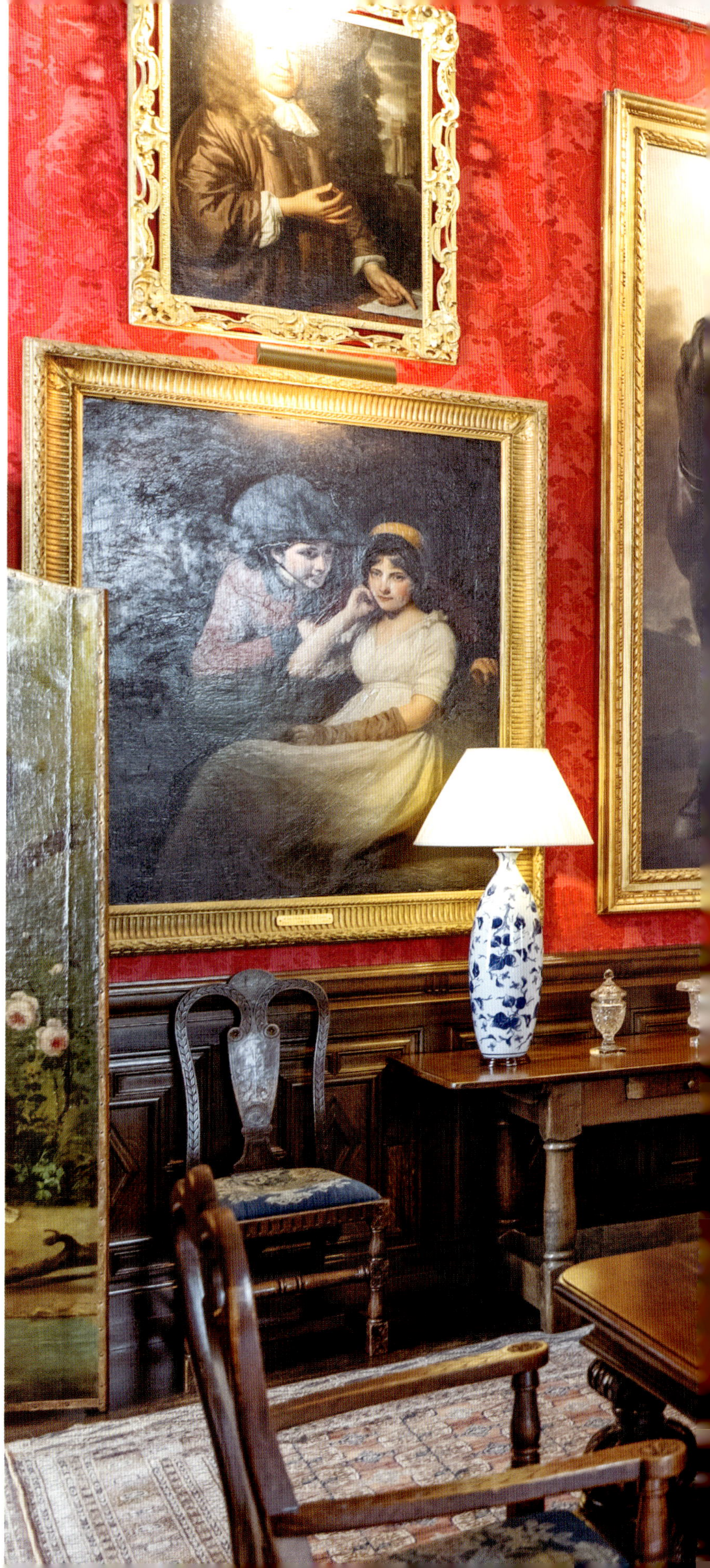

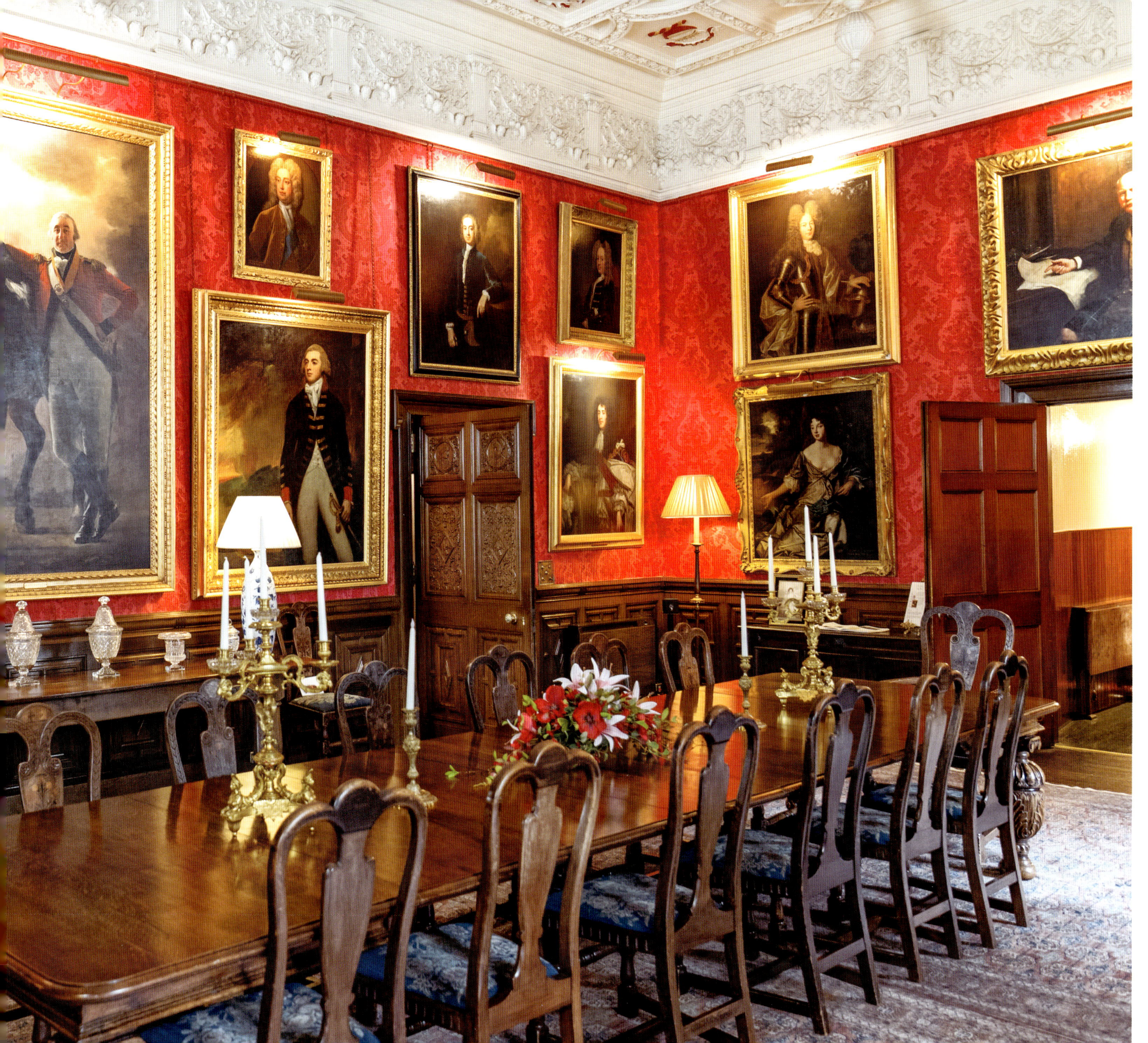

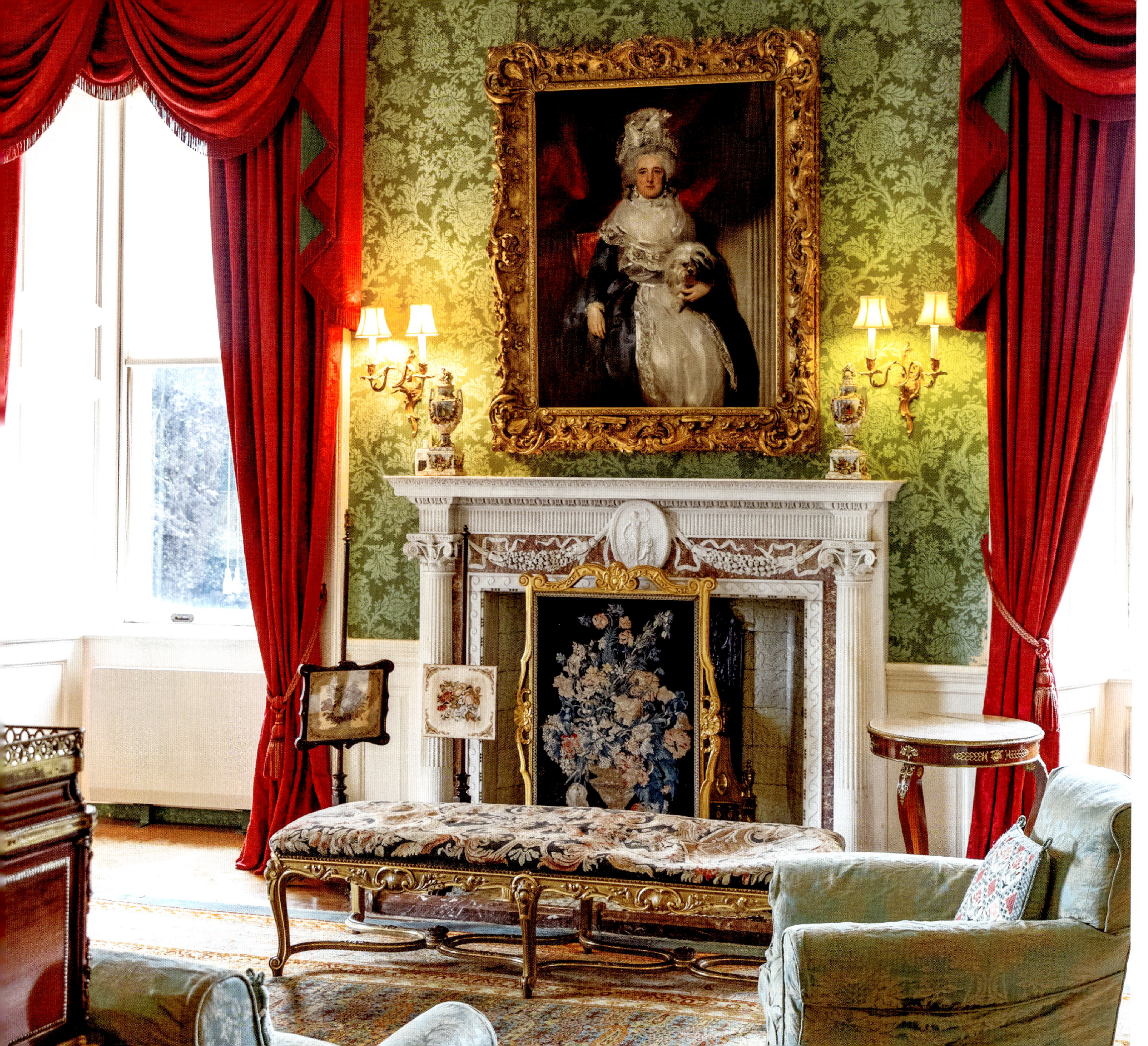

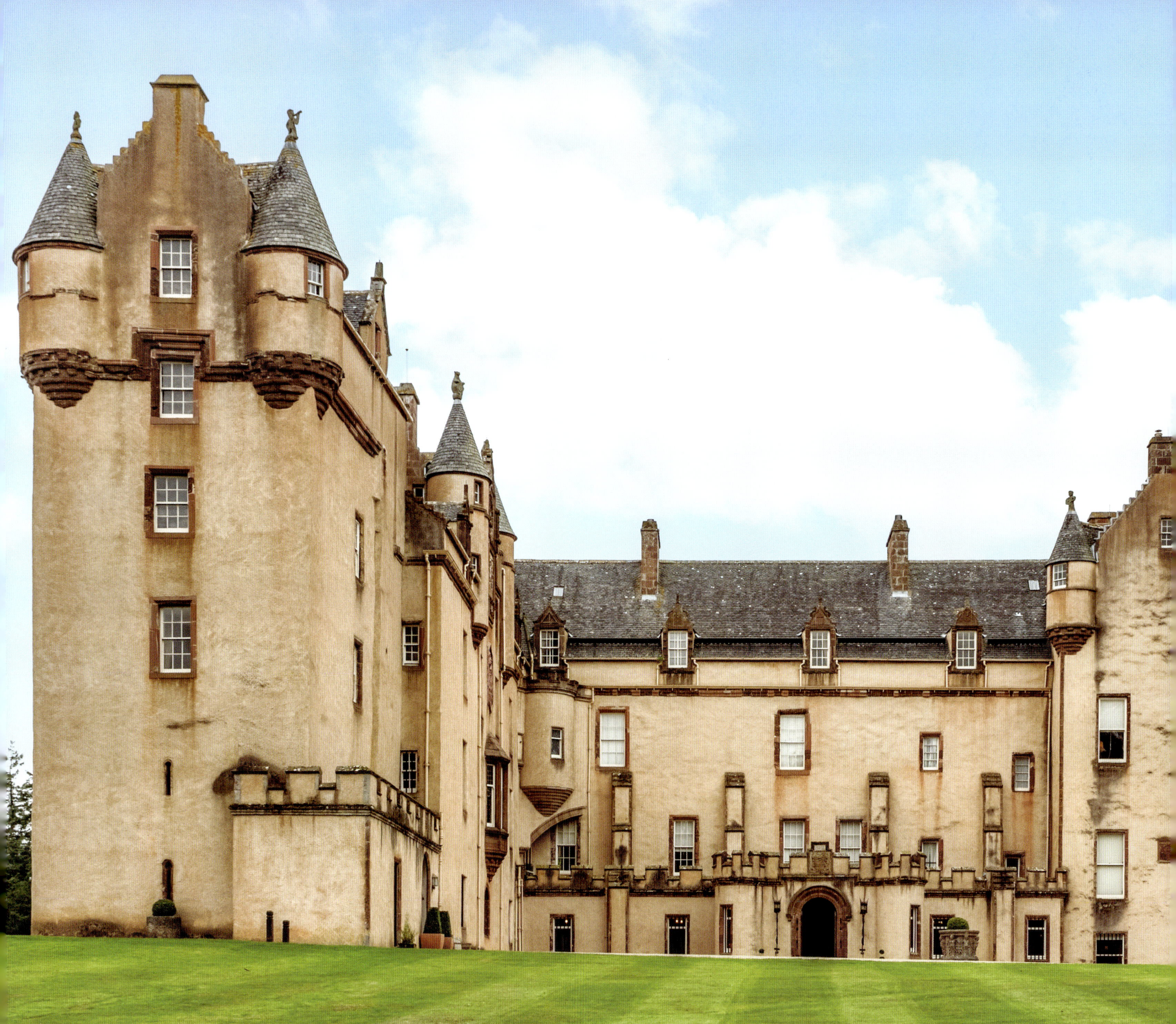

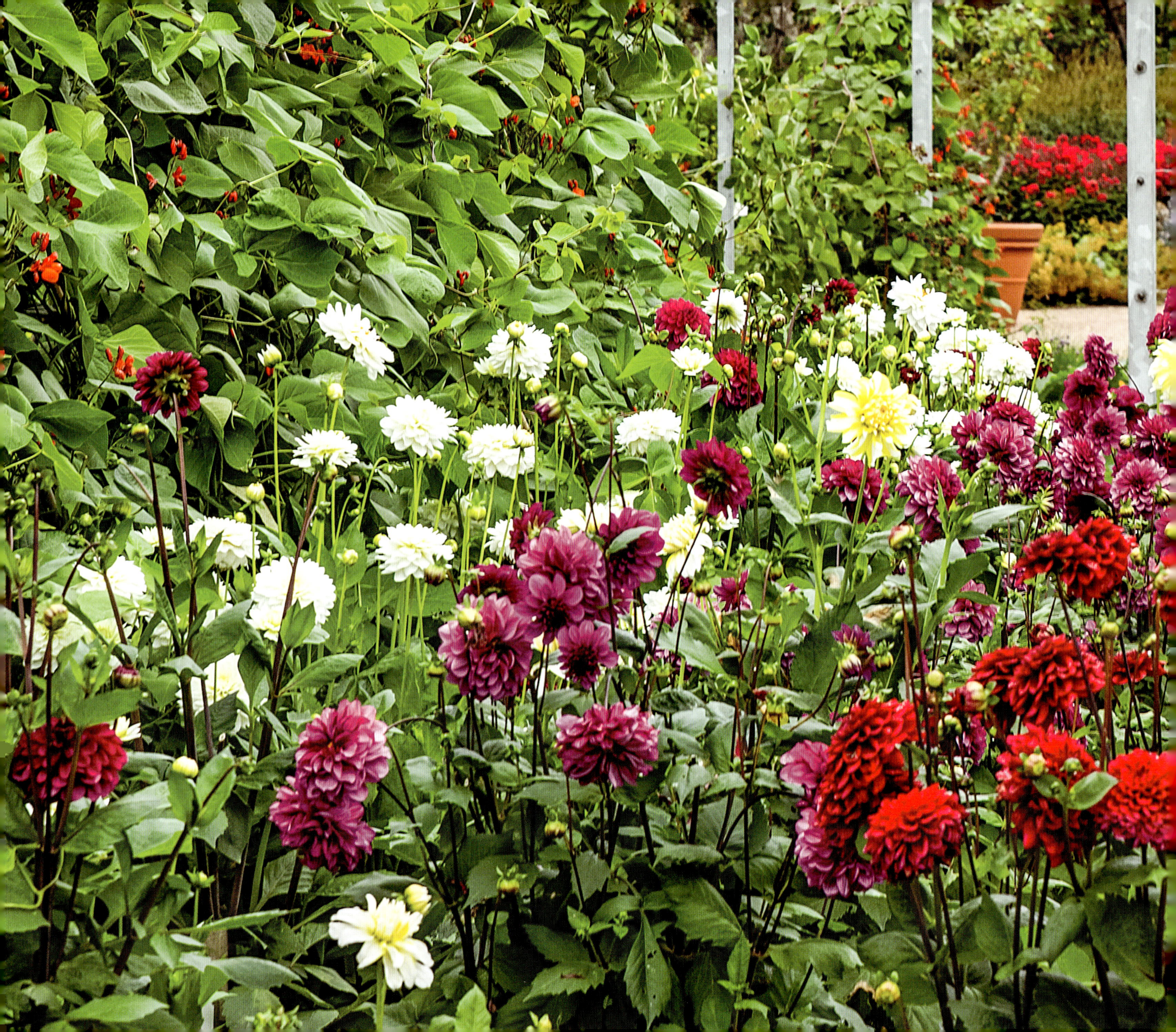

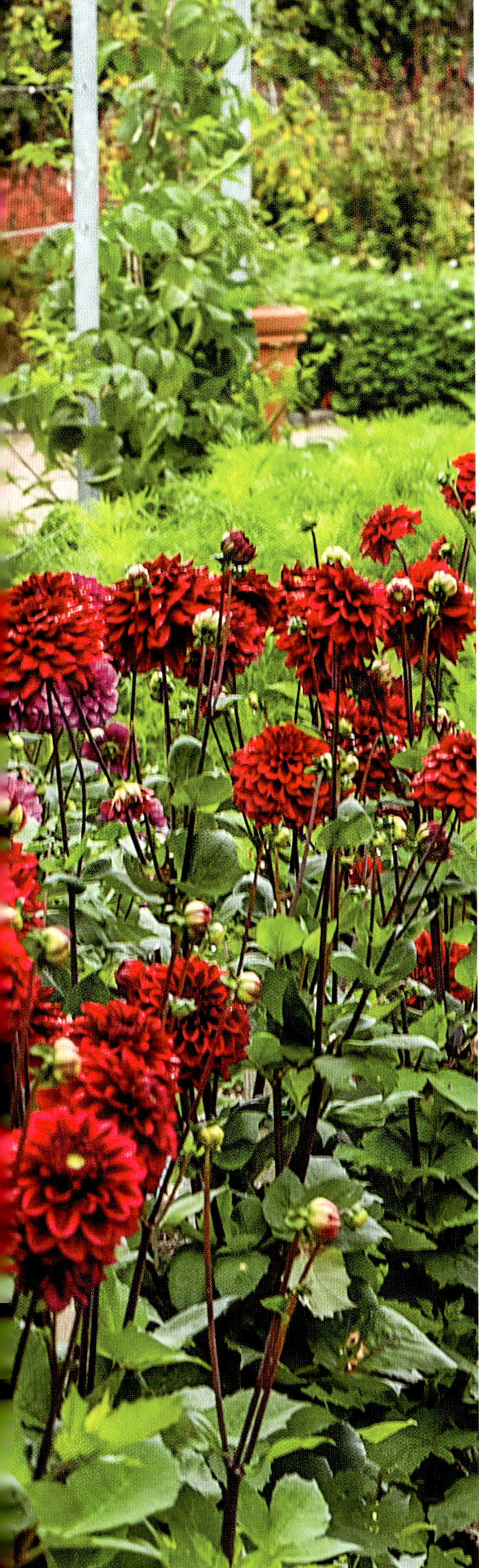

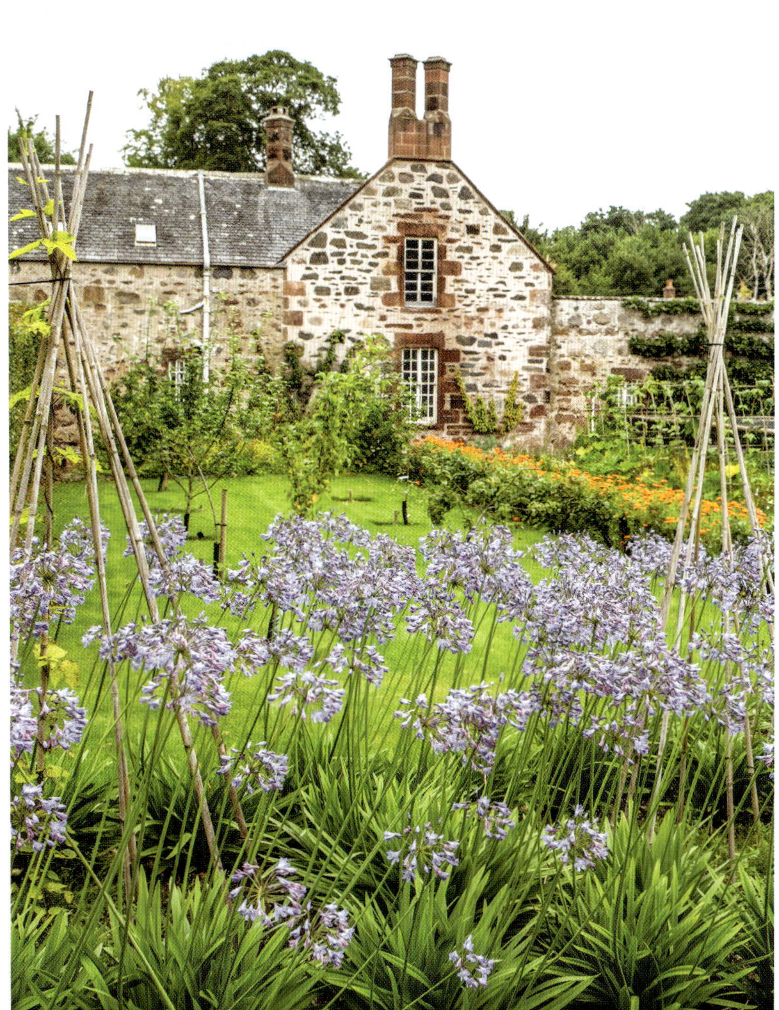

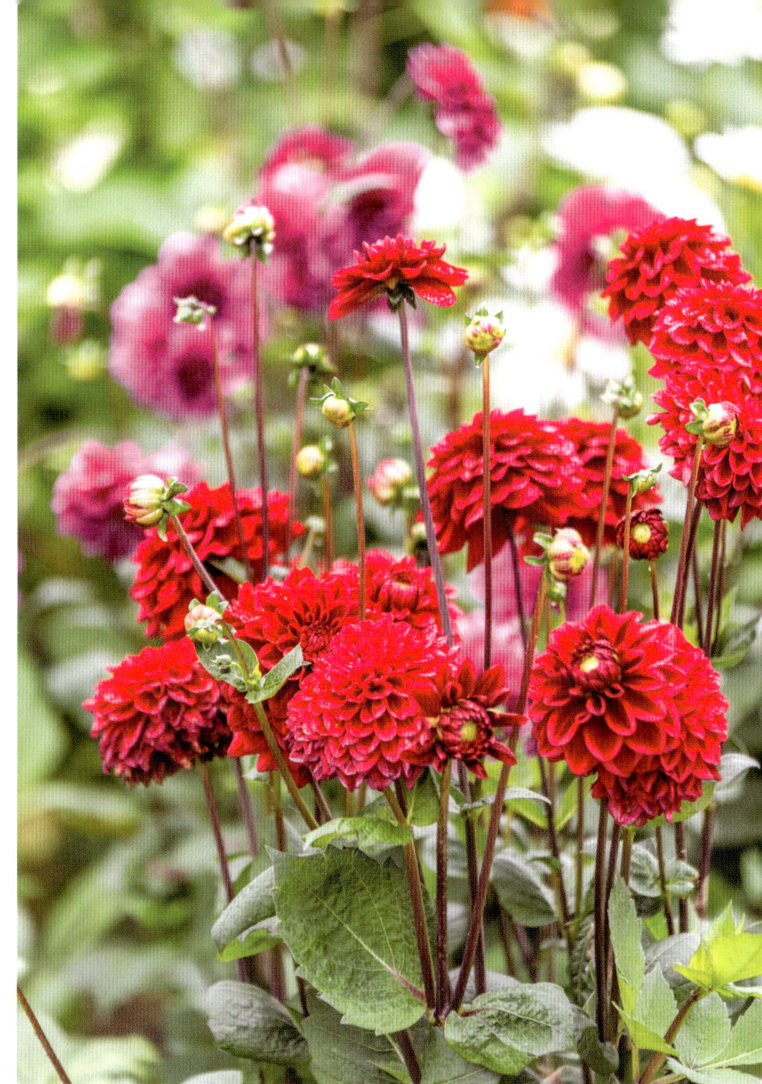

The grounds of Fyvie Castle are equally impressive. Former owner William Gordon is credited with improving the land, planting trees, and establishing the gardens; he also added a lake, which created a haven for the abundance of wildlife that visit daily. The restored Walled Garden, as well as the American Garden commissioned by Lord Leith, brims with botanical beauty—a fitting finish to any tour of this venerable citadel, set amid the splendor of the Scottish Highlands.

In keeping with Fyvie Castle's longtime tradition of growing fruits and vegetables, the Walled Garden was redesigned by National Trust of Scotland advisor Robert Grant in the 1990s to ensure historic Scottish varieties would not be lost to time. The space brims with a kaleidoscope of colorful flowers, including perennials such as dahlias and cosmos, as well as a plethora of annuals.

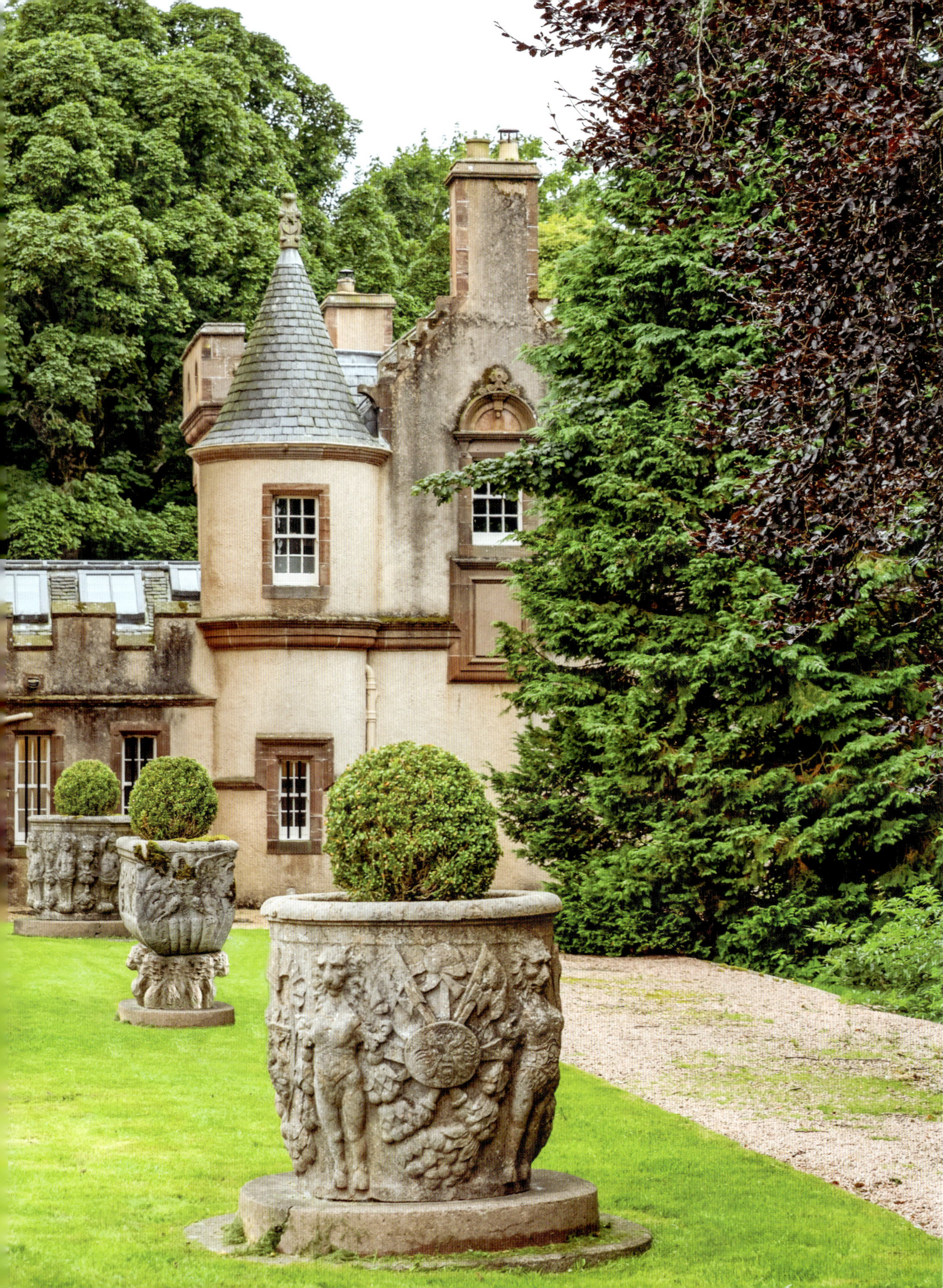

"The Herbert Marshall self-playing organ at Fyvie was one of the first of its type in Britain."

—Vikki Duncan

Left: Etched with the vestiges of time and tasked as the keeper of long-told tales, Fyvie reigns over the Aberdeenshire countryside with an abiding presence that speaks to its prominence in the annals of Scottish history. Opposite: A unique feature of the Drawing Room is its circa 1905 pipe organ, a historic instrument with a self-playing mechanism that has been restored in recent years.

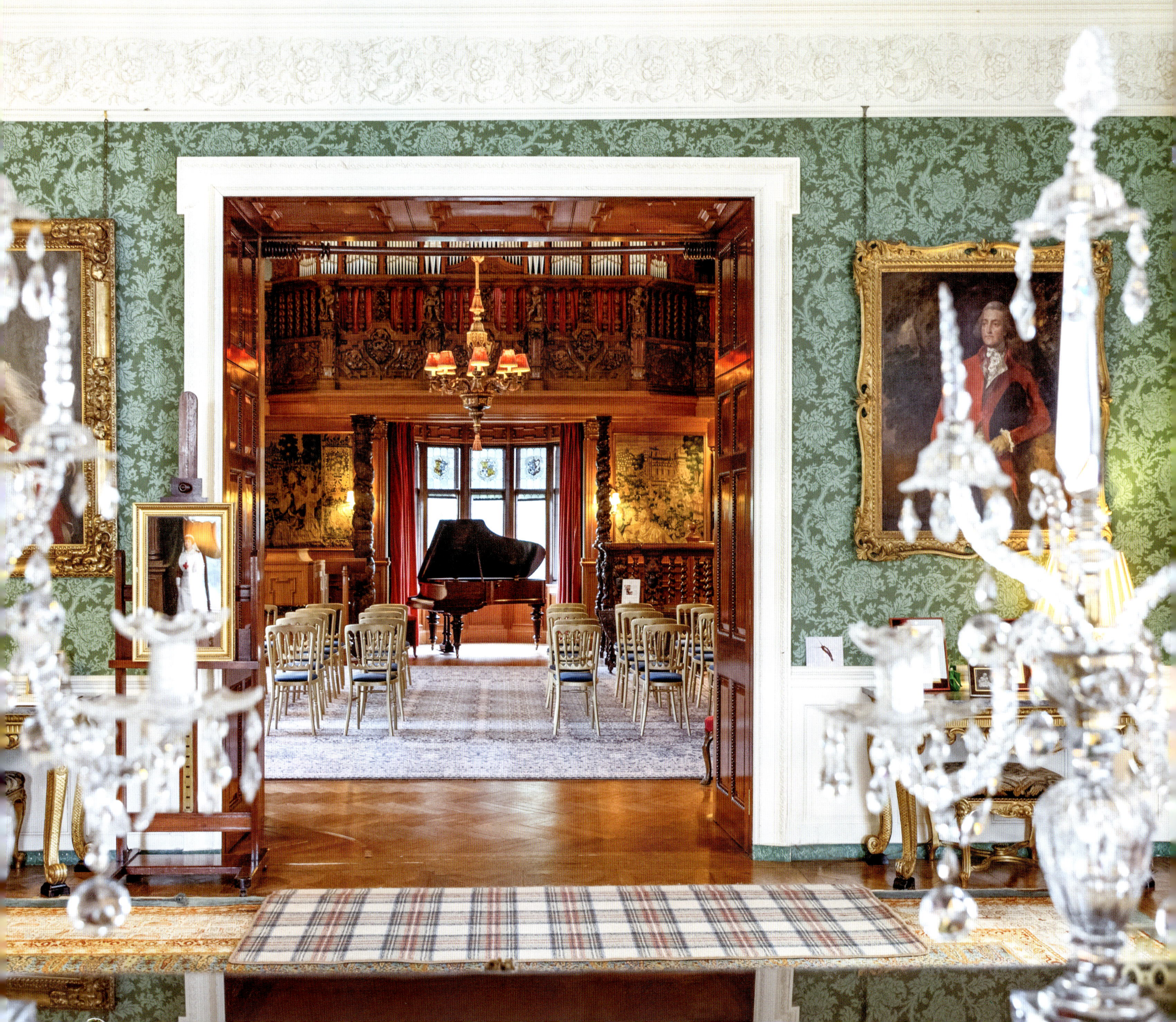

LEGENDS ALONG THE LOCH

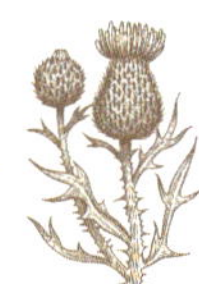

Scottish history is laced with tales of derring-do and adventure involving clans—the kinship groups whose common bonds have endured for centuries as a source of pride and identity. One of these families, Clan Campbell has been an integral part of the Argyll area since they first arrived here as members of a royal exploration party in the early thirteenth century. This land has served as the ancestral seat of the Dukes of Argyll and the Chiefs of Clan Campbell ever since.

Though the Campbells first settled in Loch Aweside, they moved to Inveraray, situated along the banks of beautiful Loch Fyne, in 1450 and erected the first castle on that site. The present edifice was initially inspired by an early eighteenth-century drawing by Sir John Vanbrugh, who designed both Blenheim Palace and Castle Howard in England. When he died shortly thereafter, the project was passed to architects Roger Morris and William Adam, and construction began in 1746.

The castle—built of green chlorite schist, a locally sourced stone—is an amalgam of several styles: a blend of Palladian, Gothic, and Baroque elements that combine to form a unique and majestic fortress. A restoration after a fire in 1877 added a third floor as well as cone-shaped roofs to the corner towers.

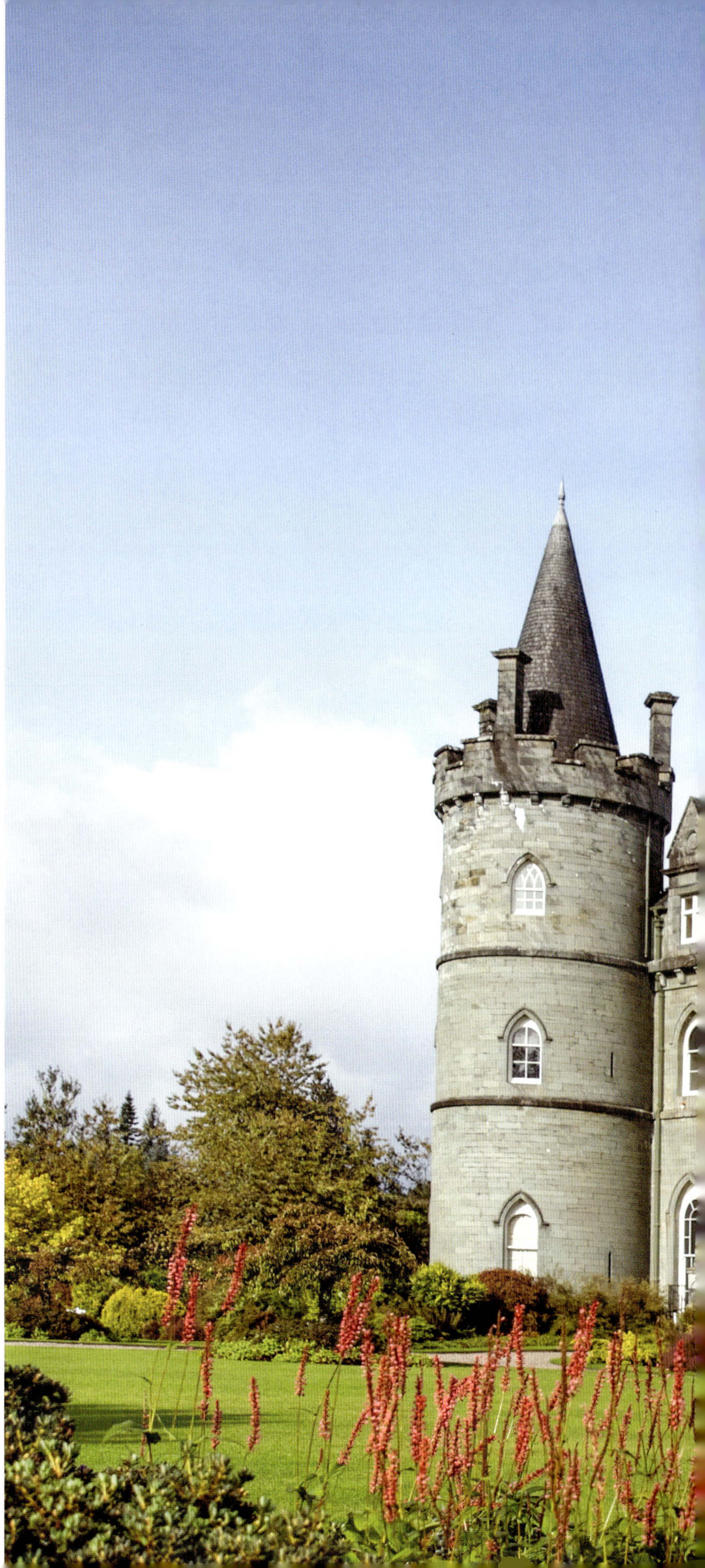

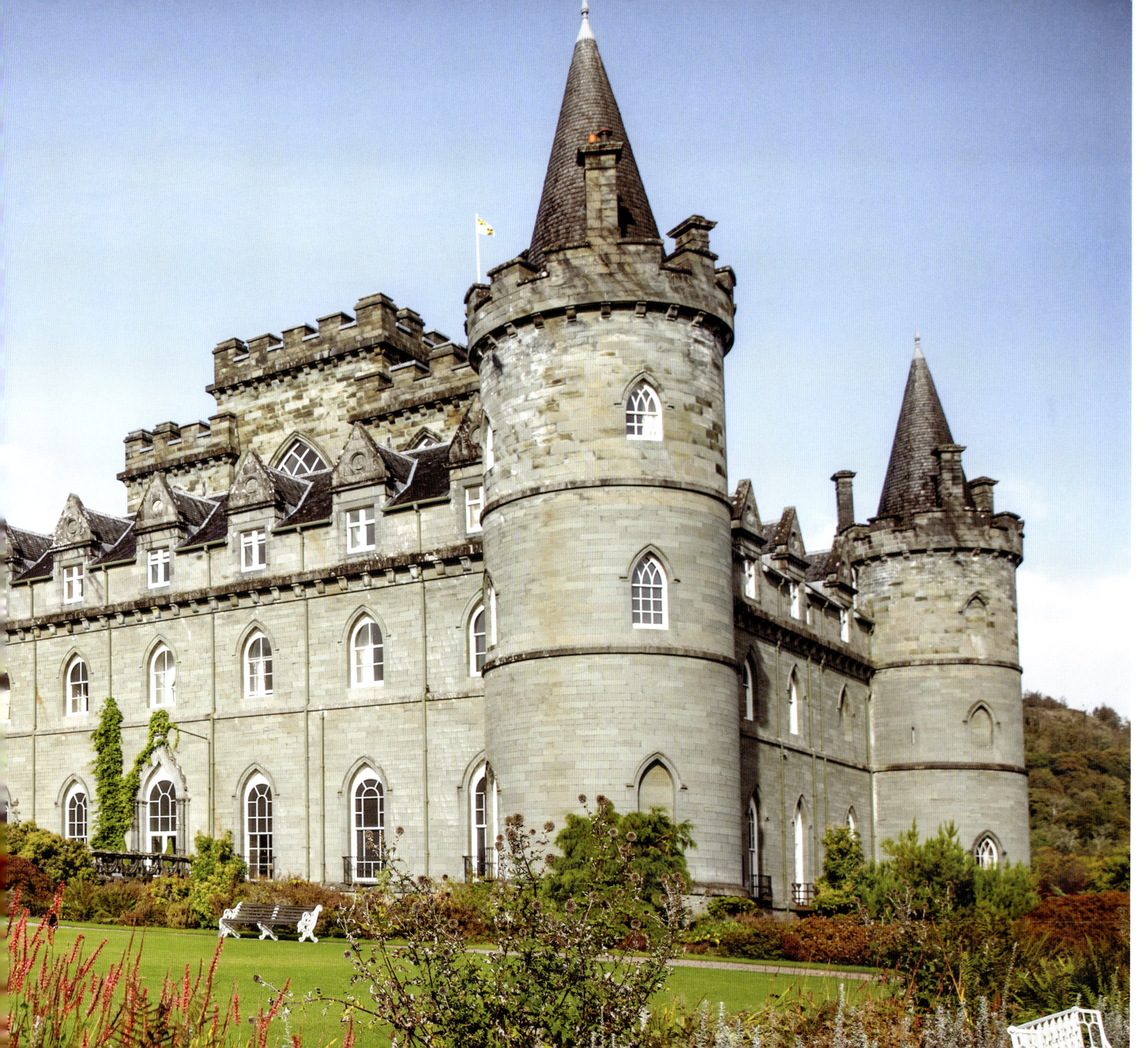

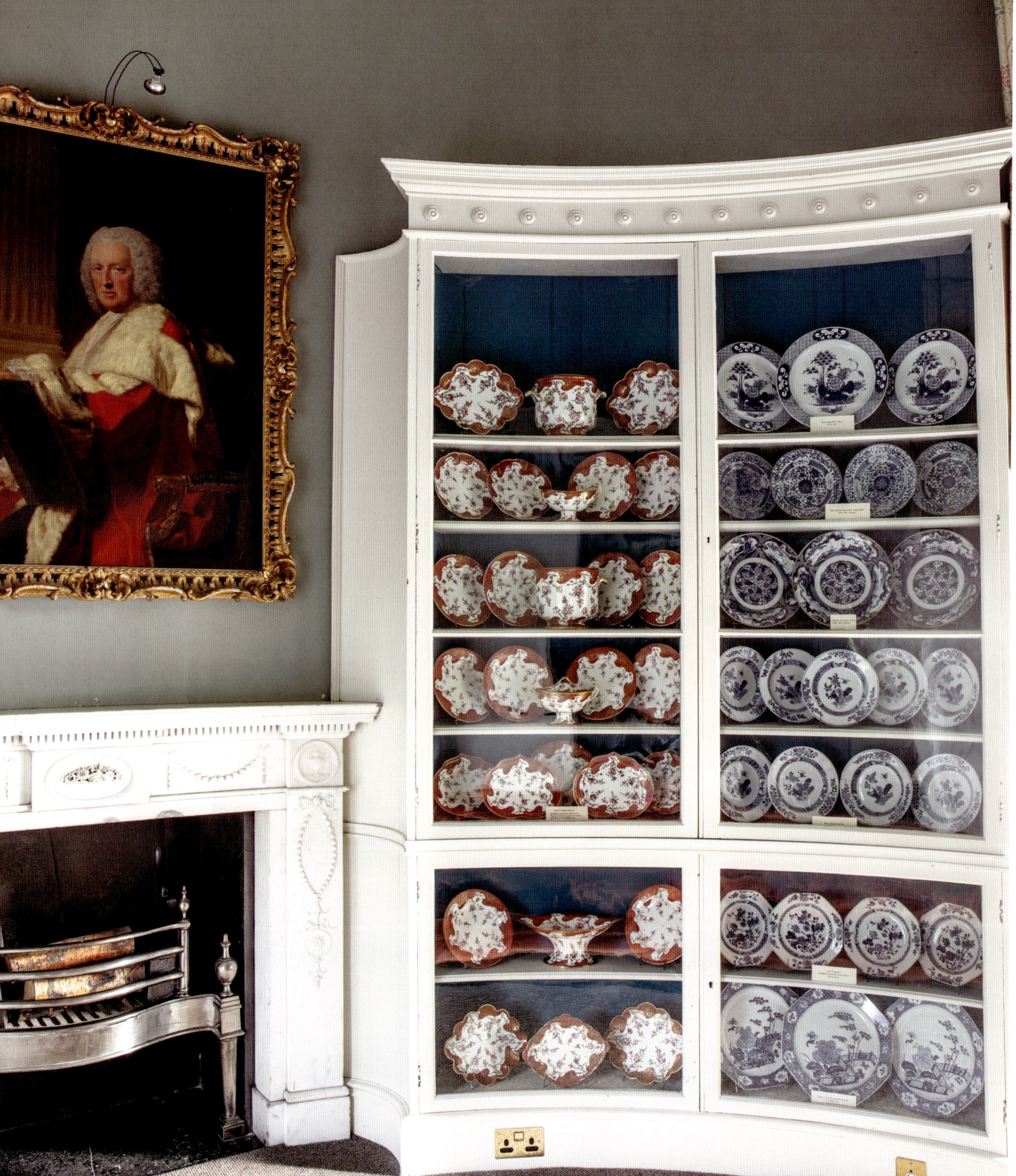

This page: Presided over by a portrait of the 3rd Duke of Argyll, the China Turret houses an enviable collection of European and Oriental porcelain, including early eighteenth-century Japanese Imari-ware and a Meissen dessert service. Opposite, right: Designed in the style of a 1780s Parisian salon, the Tapestry Drawing Room is draped in the beautiful tapestries that give the space its name. Robert Adam designed the ornate ceiling, which was painted by French artist Girard, whose work also appears on the delicately painted shutters.

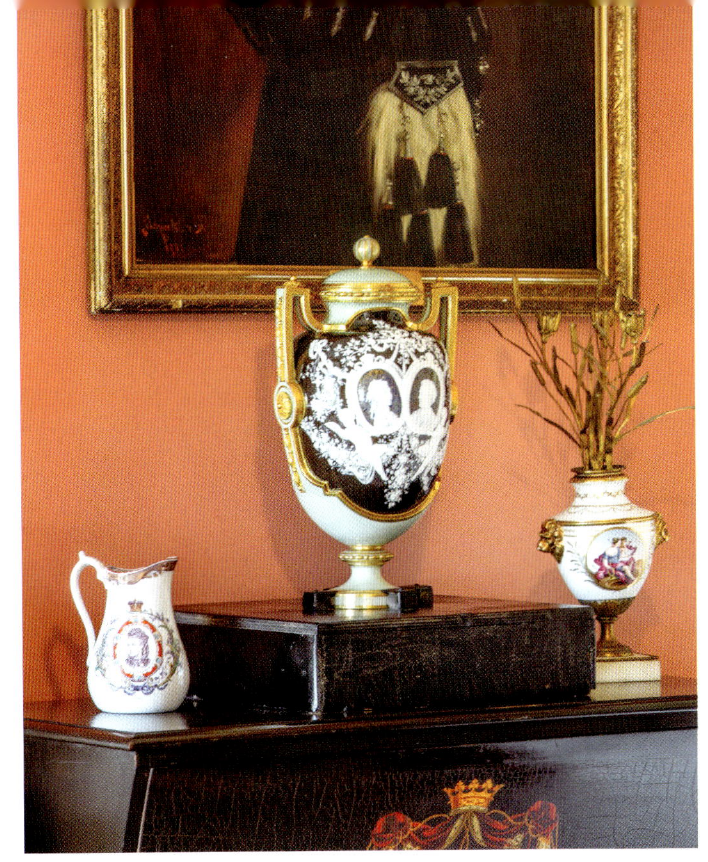

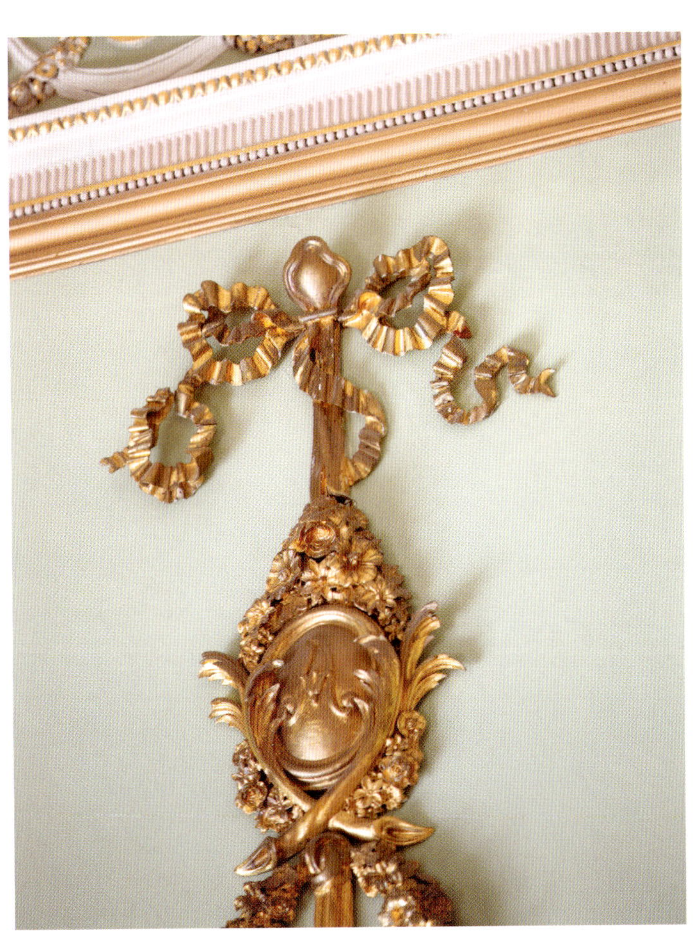

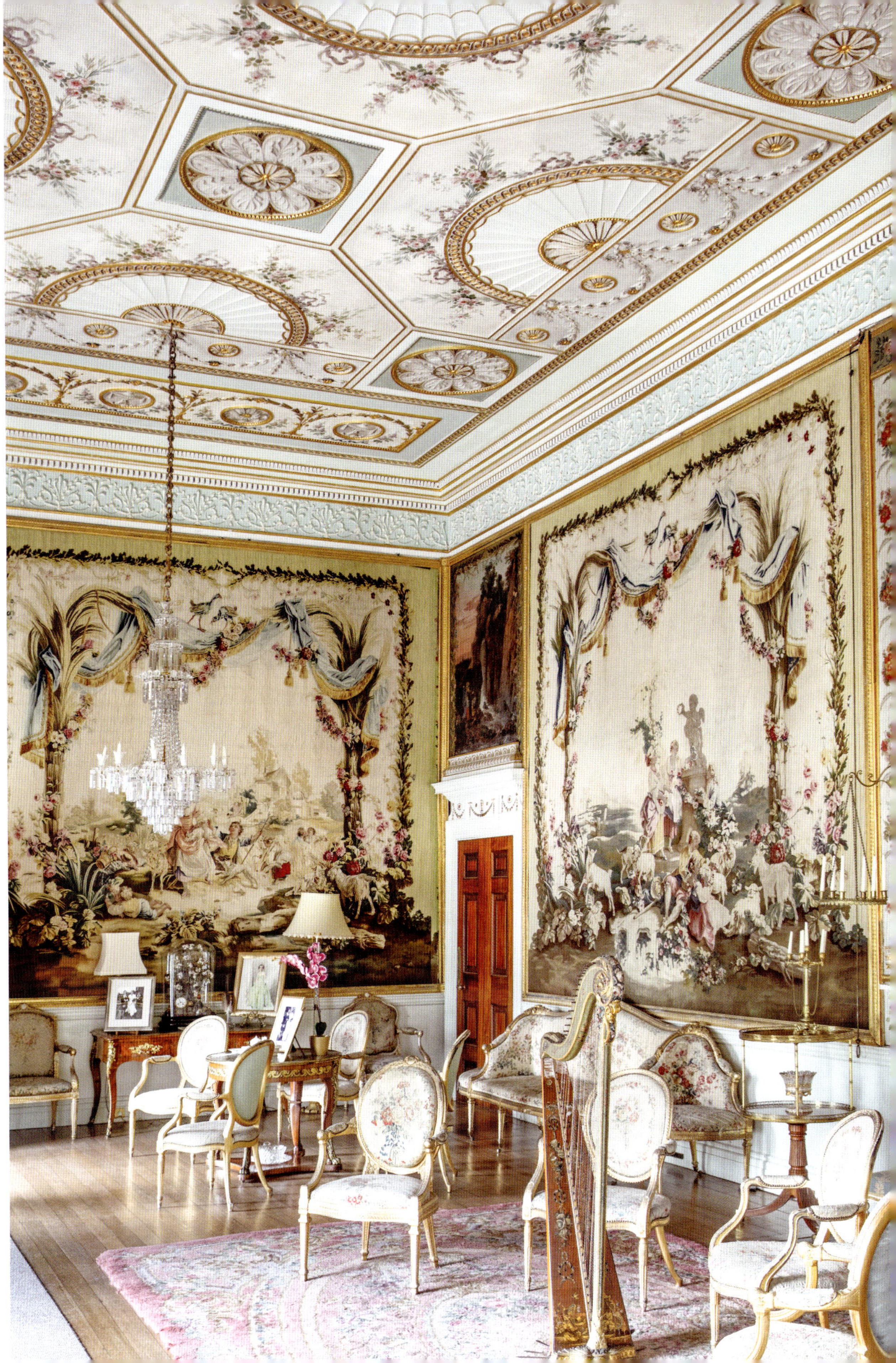

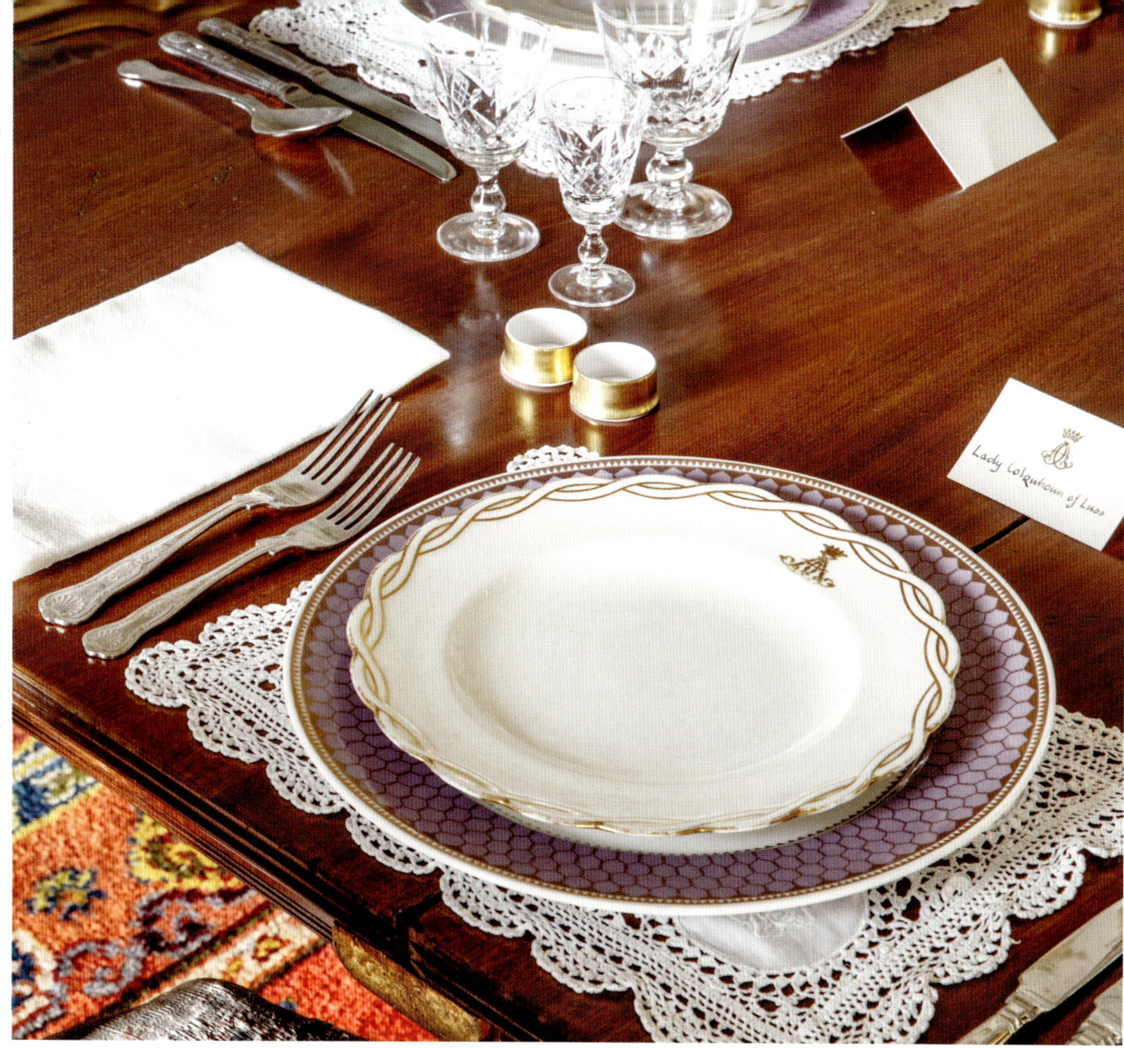

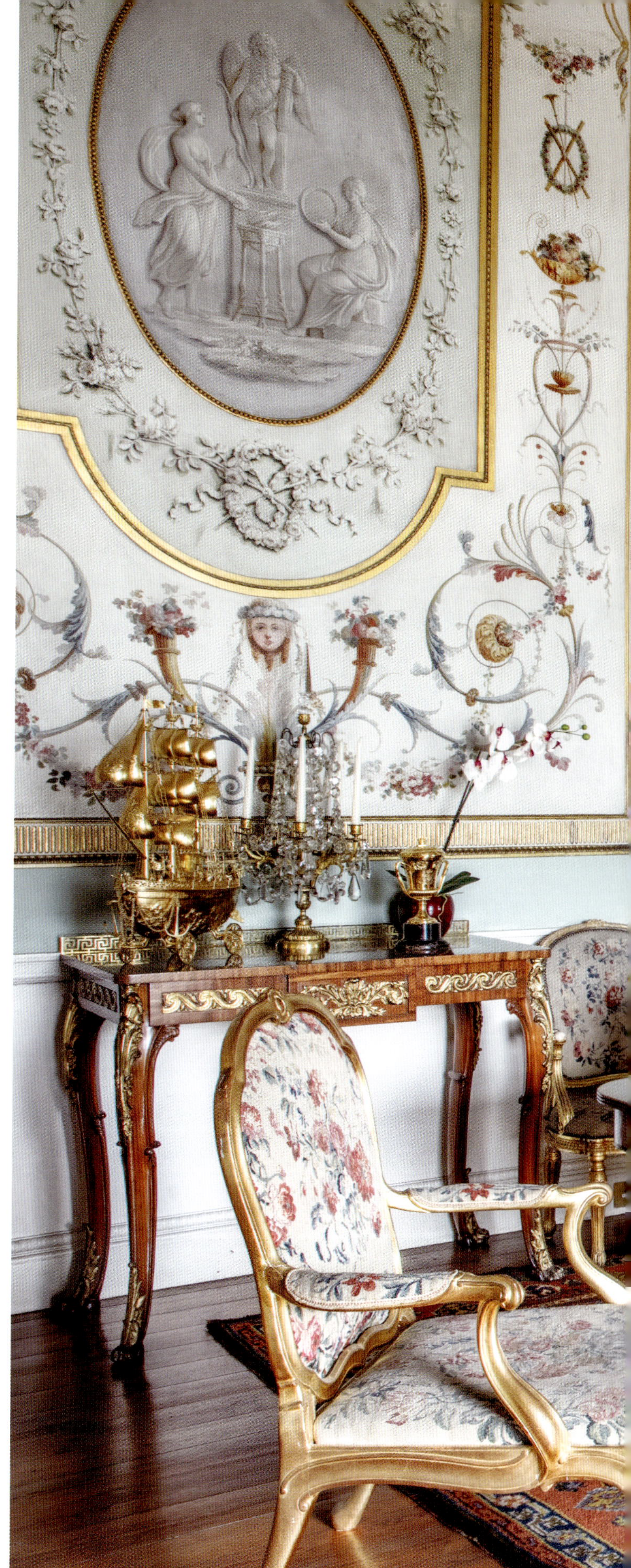

Inveraray serves as the home of the current Duke and Duchess of Argyll, who embrace their roles as both sustainers of the family legacy and stewards of the castle. The interiors brim with opulence, from the gold-embellished State Dining Room, with its elaborate wall paintings, to the Parisian-style Tapestry Drawing Room, adorned with the exquisite Beauvais tapestries that inspired the space. Visitors often stand entranced before the spectacular collection of Oriental and European porcelain displayed in the China Turret. In The Saloon stands a grand piano, where the noted songwriting team of Lerner and Loewe composed some of the songs for their musical *My Fair Lady* while staying at the castle.

Inveraray's sixteen-acre garden is equally enchanting, with two acres devoted to formal lawns and bedding plants. On either side of a central walk, paths known as the Flag Borders are laid out in a St. Andrew's Cross pattern. Azaleas and rhododendrons thrive in the area's rain-rich climate, as do roses, daffodils, and heather. When these elements are paired with the myriad shrubs and trees that permeate the Inveraray property, they perfectly complement this storied castle, nestled amid the splendor of Scotland's West Highlands.

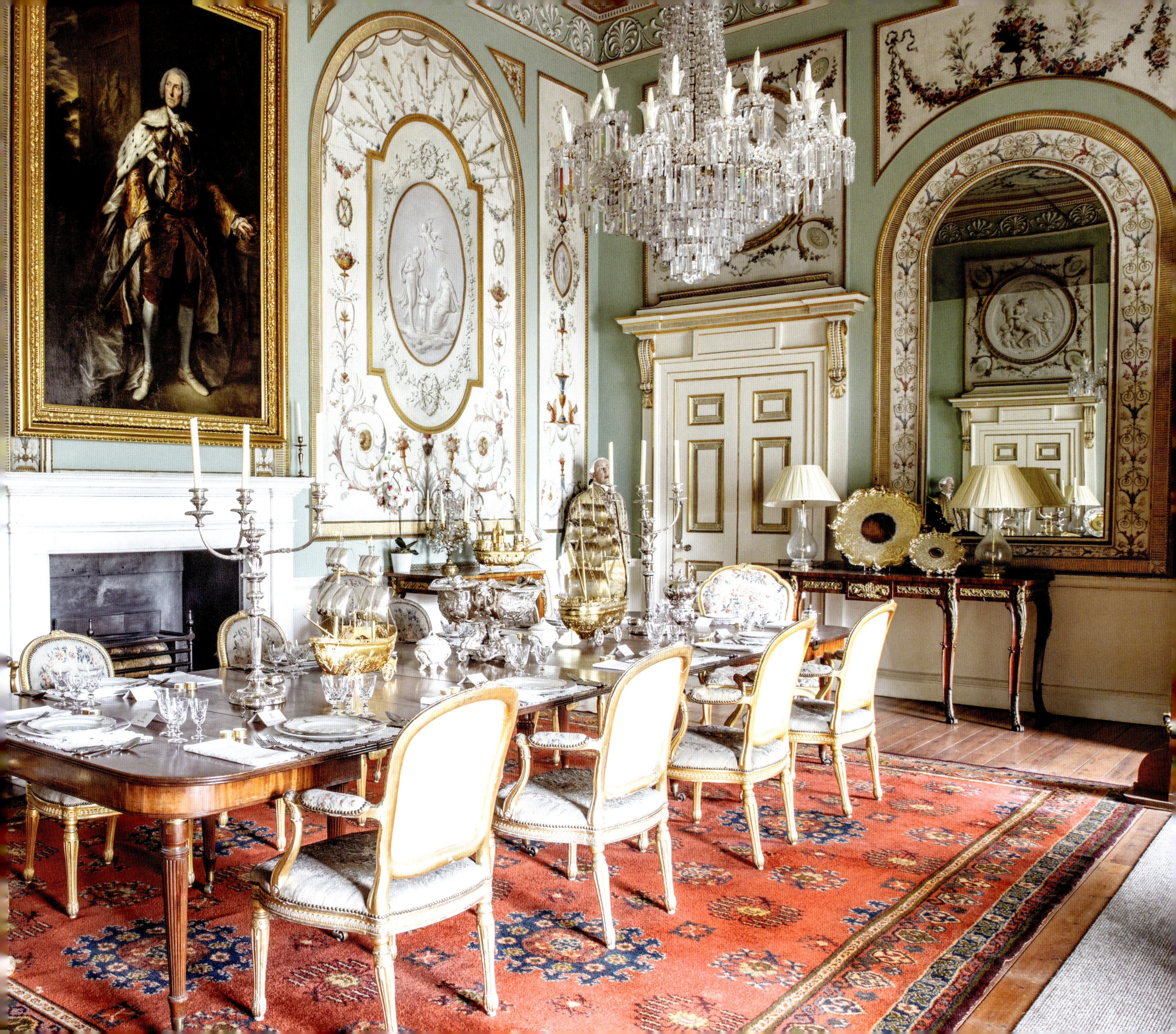

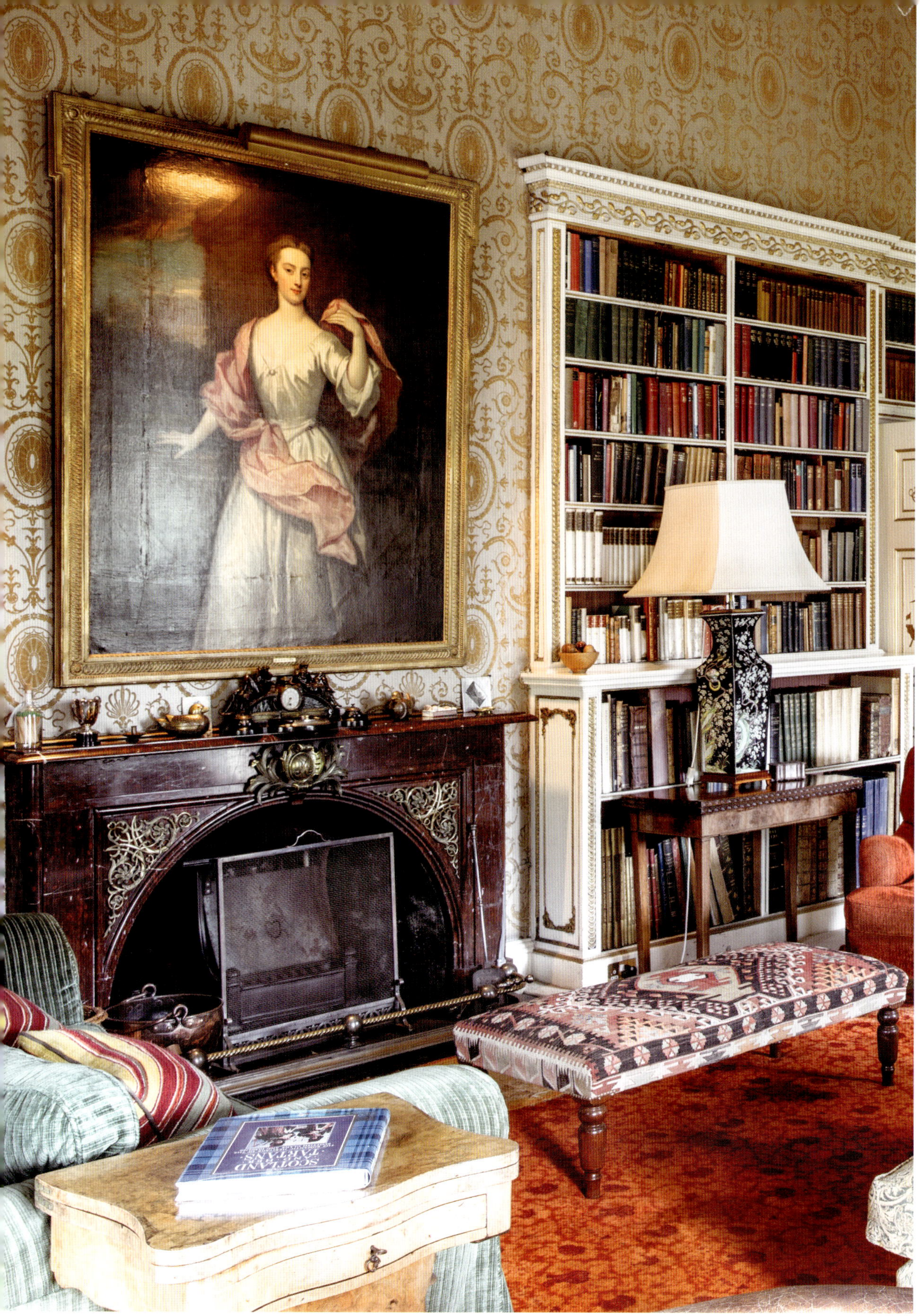

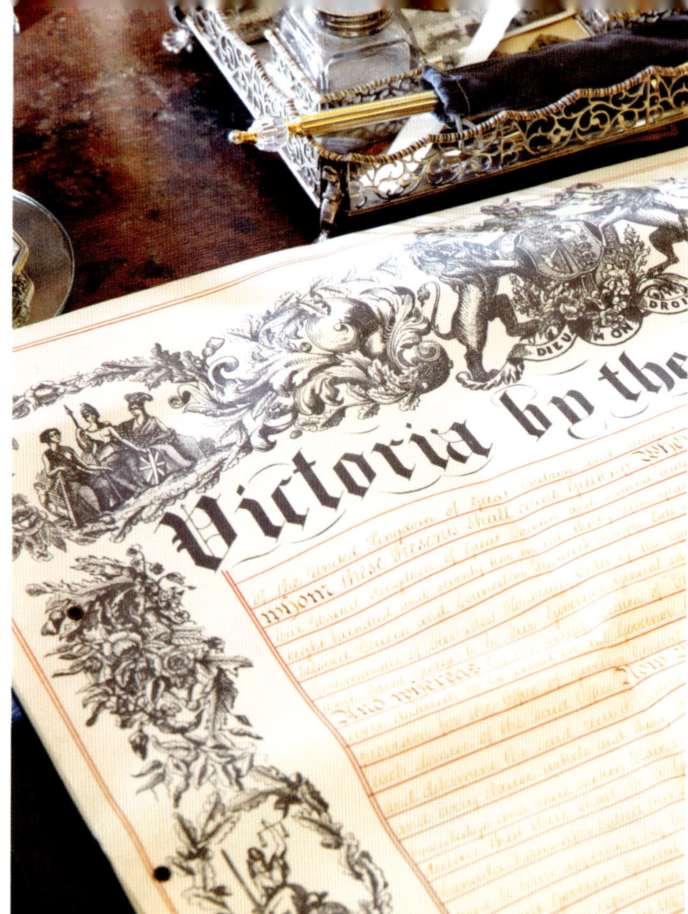
Victoria by the

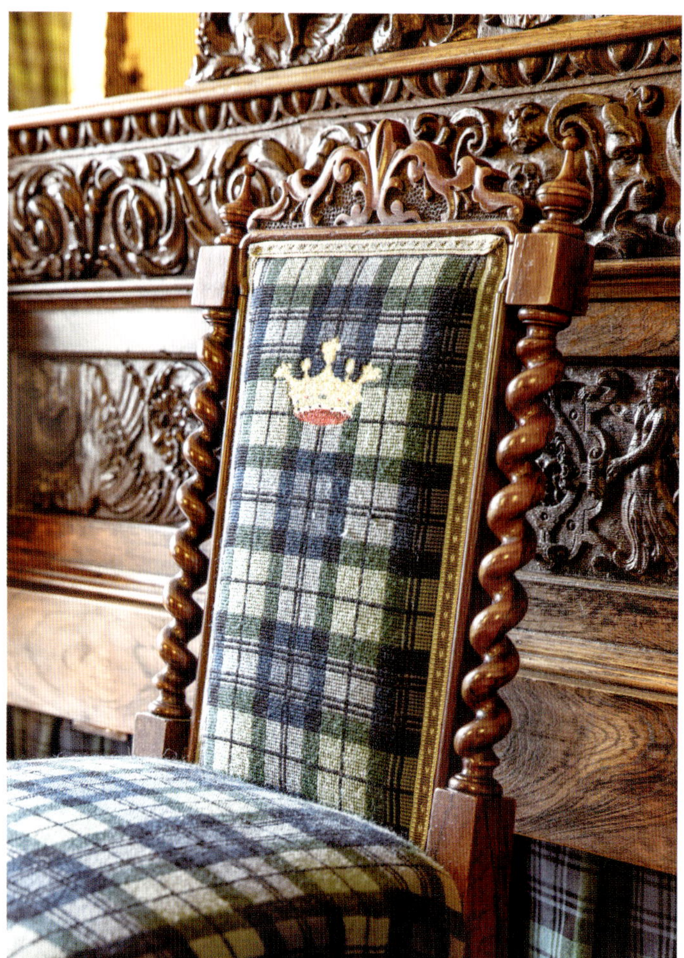

"History is often lost through the years. But here at Inveraray, we have, over the decades, chronicled the past in order to share it with future generations."

—The Duke and Duchess of Argyll

Opposite, left: One of two well-appointed libraries within the castle offers a cozy spot to read in luxurious surroundings. This page: The ornately carved bed in the MacArthur Room is draped in that clan's distinctive tartan plaid fabric. As with most castles of yore, Inveraray has a few ghostly legends imbedded in its history, including one attached to this room. Among the paintings hanging here are Scottish School portraits of Anne Nasmyth and her two children, as well as one of London socialite Elizabeth Gunning.

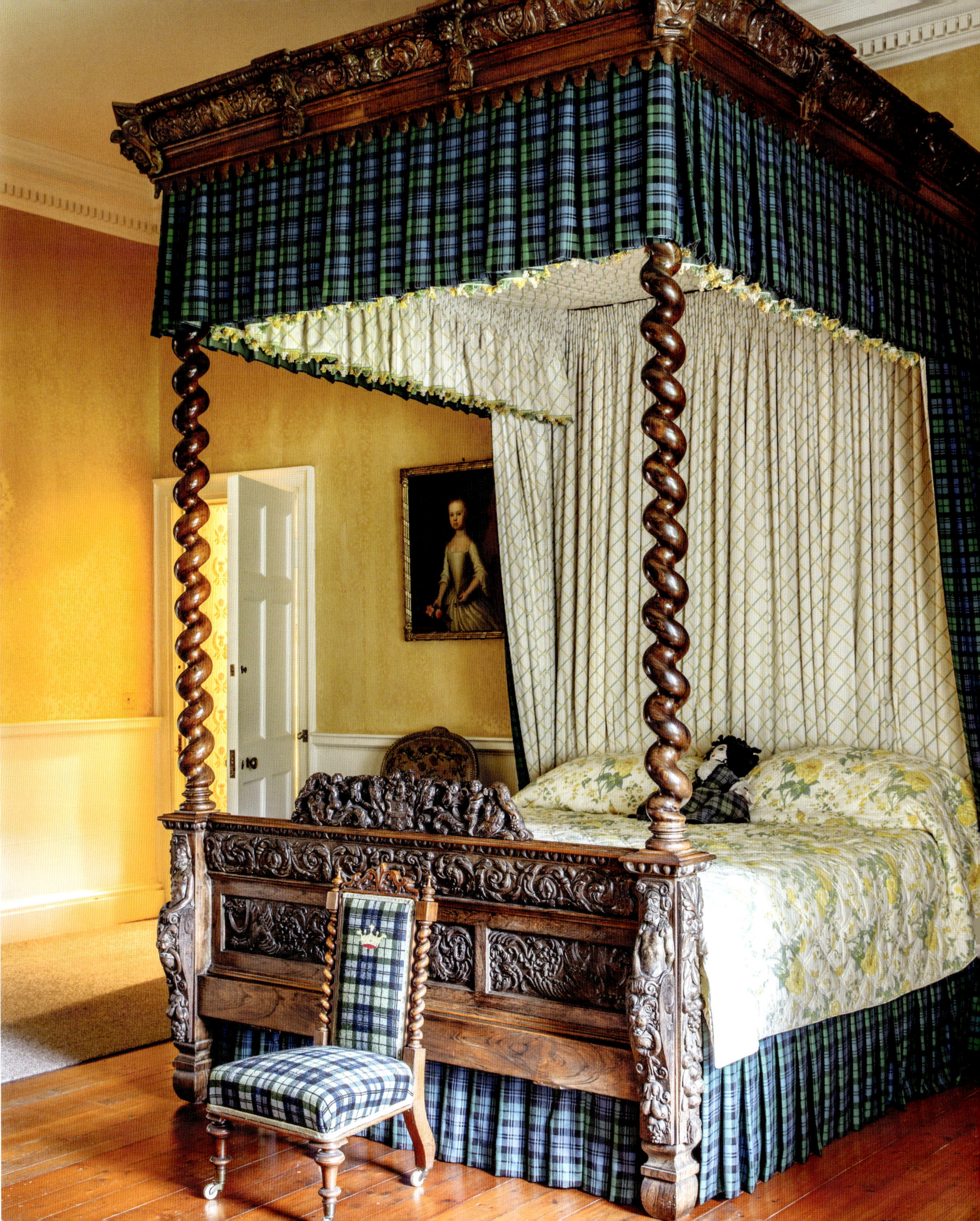

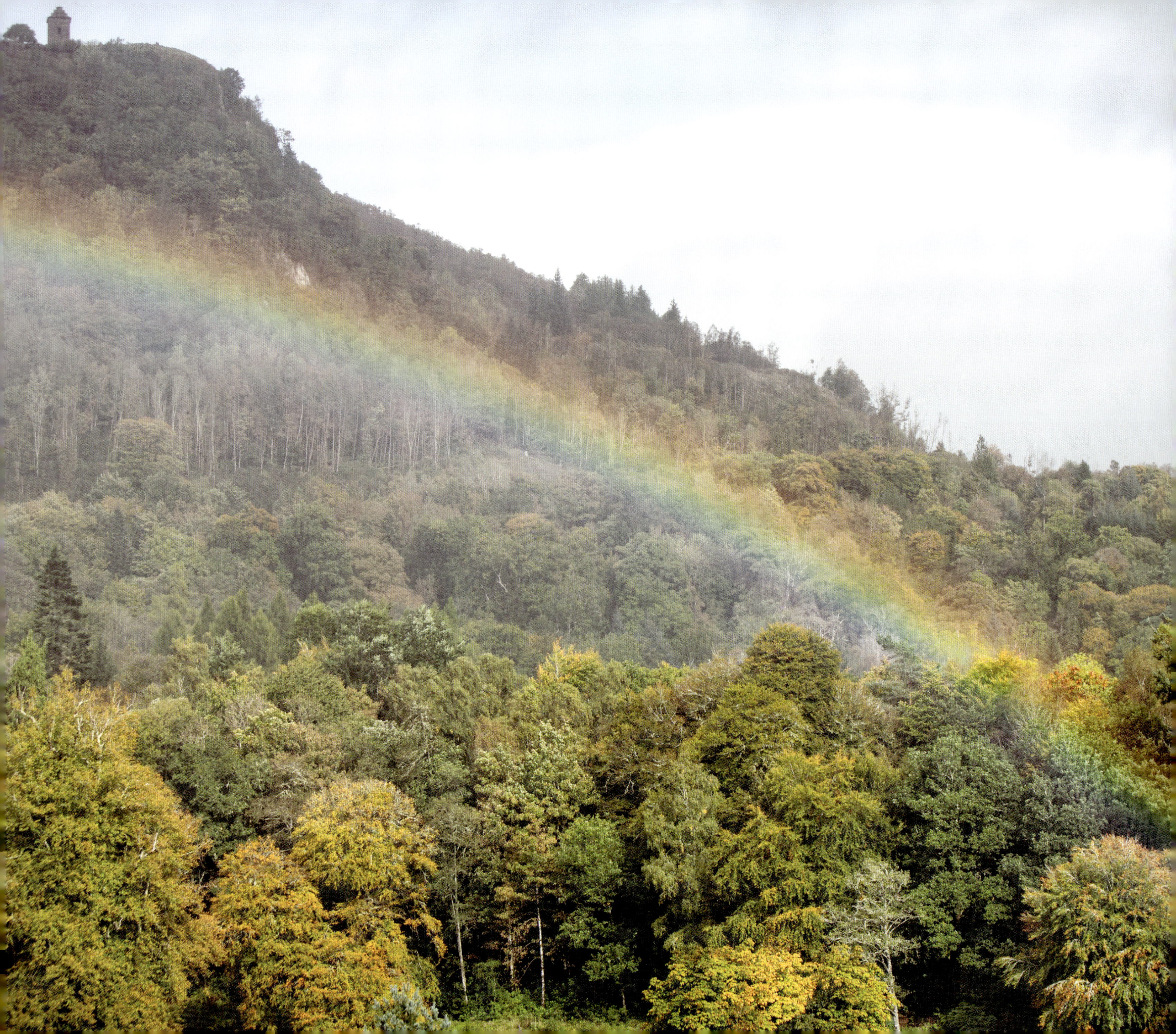

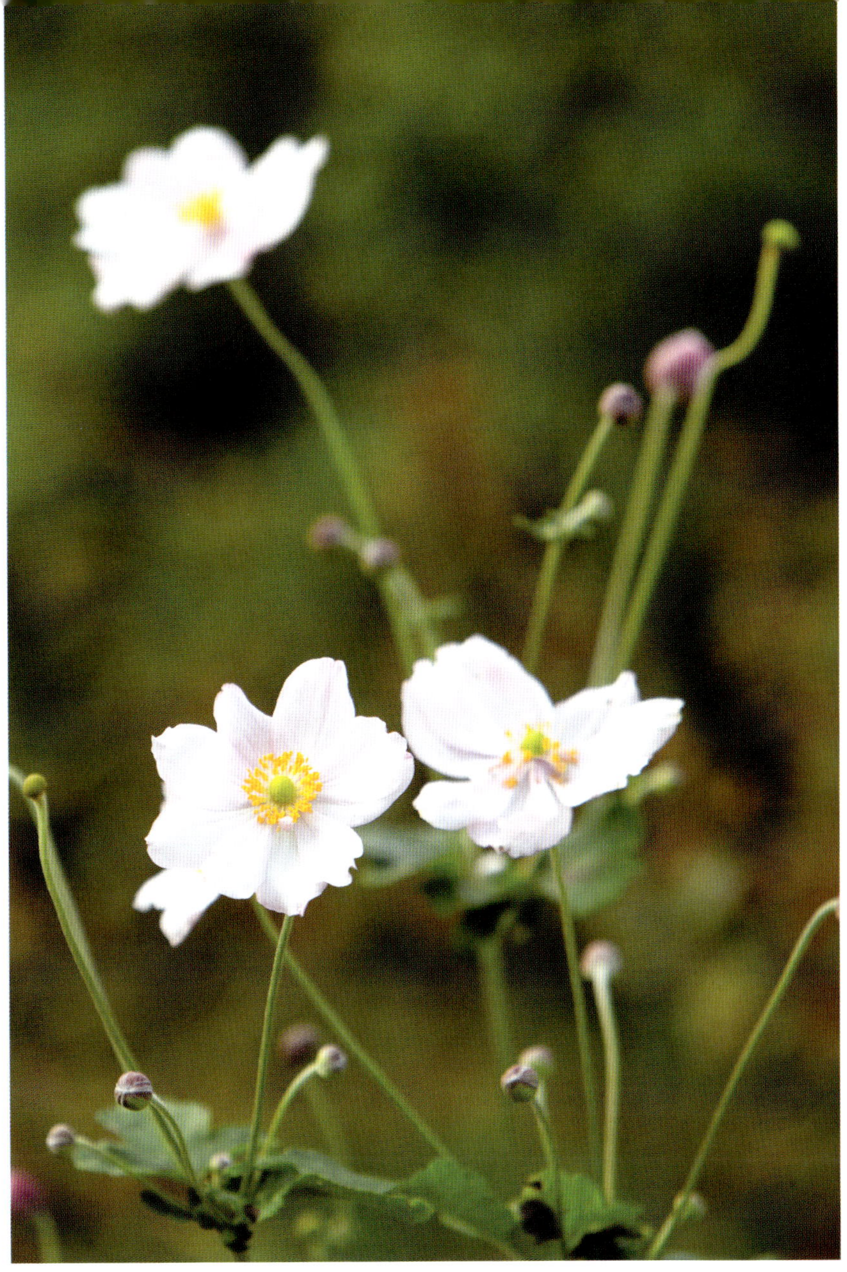

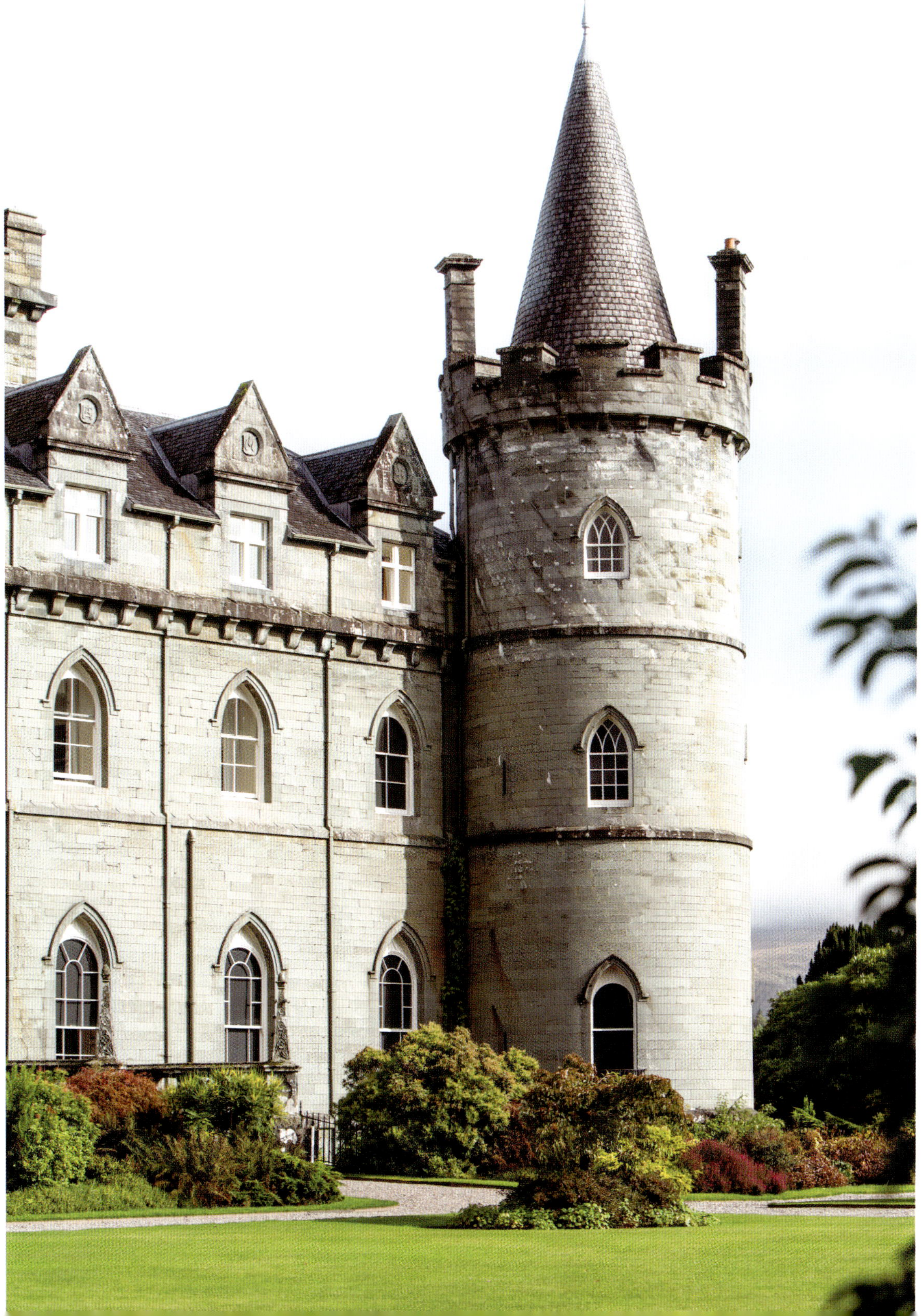

Opposite and this page: Scotland is often blessed with rains that nurture the flower-filled gardens and bequeath prismatic rainbows after the storm has passed. When glimpsed against the stunning backdrop of cloud-kissed sky, Inveraray Castle's distinctive green façade, with its conical towers and neat rows of Gothic windows, is a memorable sight.

CASTLE OF KINGS

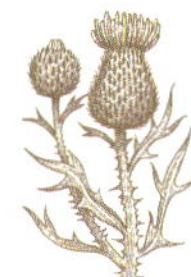

Crimson-hued Virginia creeper vines cascade down the massive gray stone walls of Scone Palace—a spectacular edifice that has endured for nine centuries, bearing witness to the intriguing narrative of Scotland's regal past. The castle was the coronation site for generations of kings, including Robert the Bruce and Charles II, the last monarch to be crowned there. William Shakespeare found the residence worthy of mention in *Macbeth*, and the legendary Stone of Scone (also known as the Stone of Destiny) once stood upon these grounds before it mysteriously disappeared in 1296.

In 1803, a renovation and expansion of the original twelfth-century structure added Georgian touches to the classic Gothic architecture. Today, Scone Palace serves as home to the 9th Earl of Mansfield and his family.

Years of collecting have created a veritable museum of treasures. Among the many fascinating items on display are Marie Antoinette's writing desk, gifted to the 2nd Earl of Mansfield as a token of their friendship, and embroidered bed hangings stitched by Mary Queen of Scots during her imprisonment in Loch Leven Castle. There is also a collection of vernis Martin vases and ornaments, and in the State Dining Room, a table and chairs that were designed and crafted by local village cabinetmakers for Queen Victoria's royal visit in 1852.

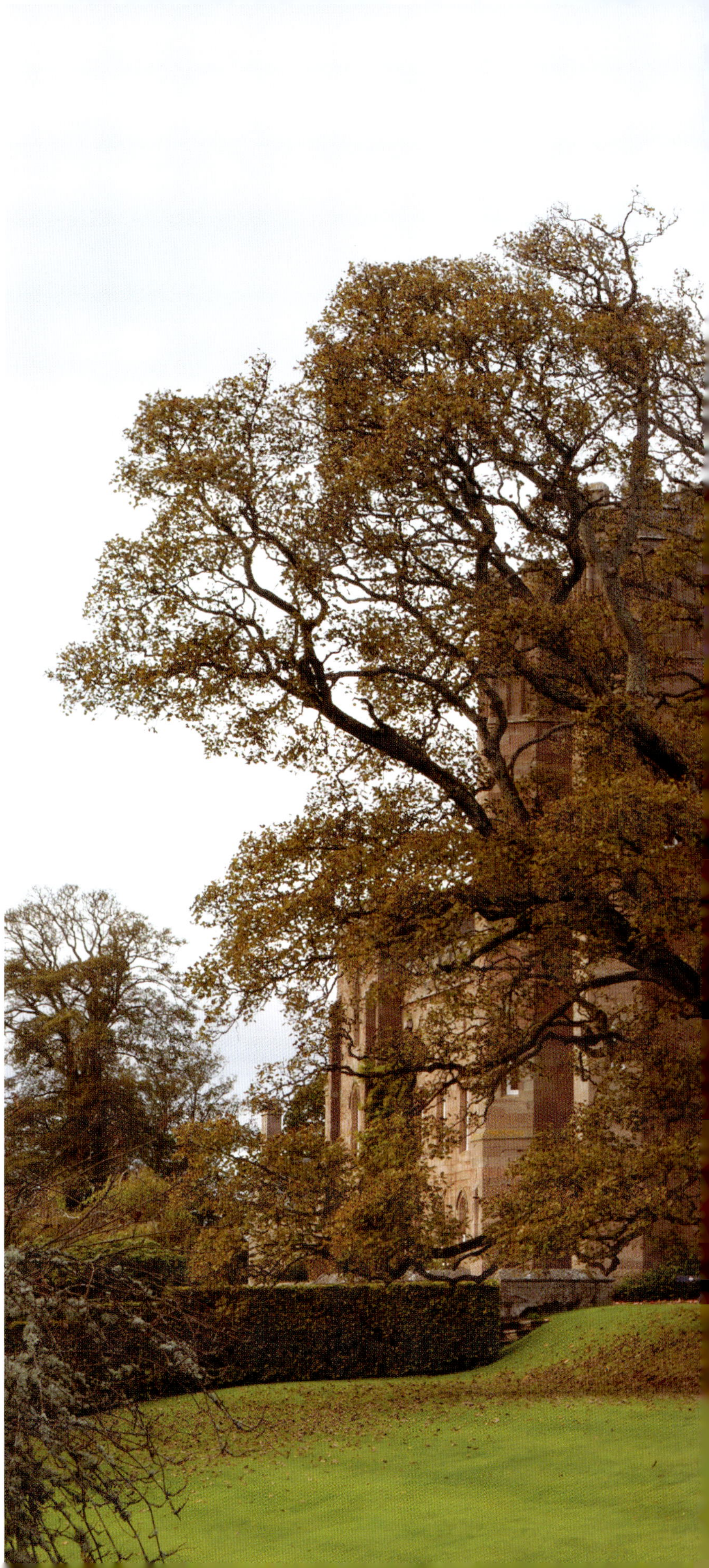

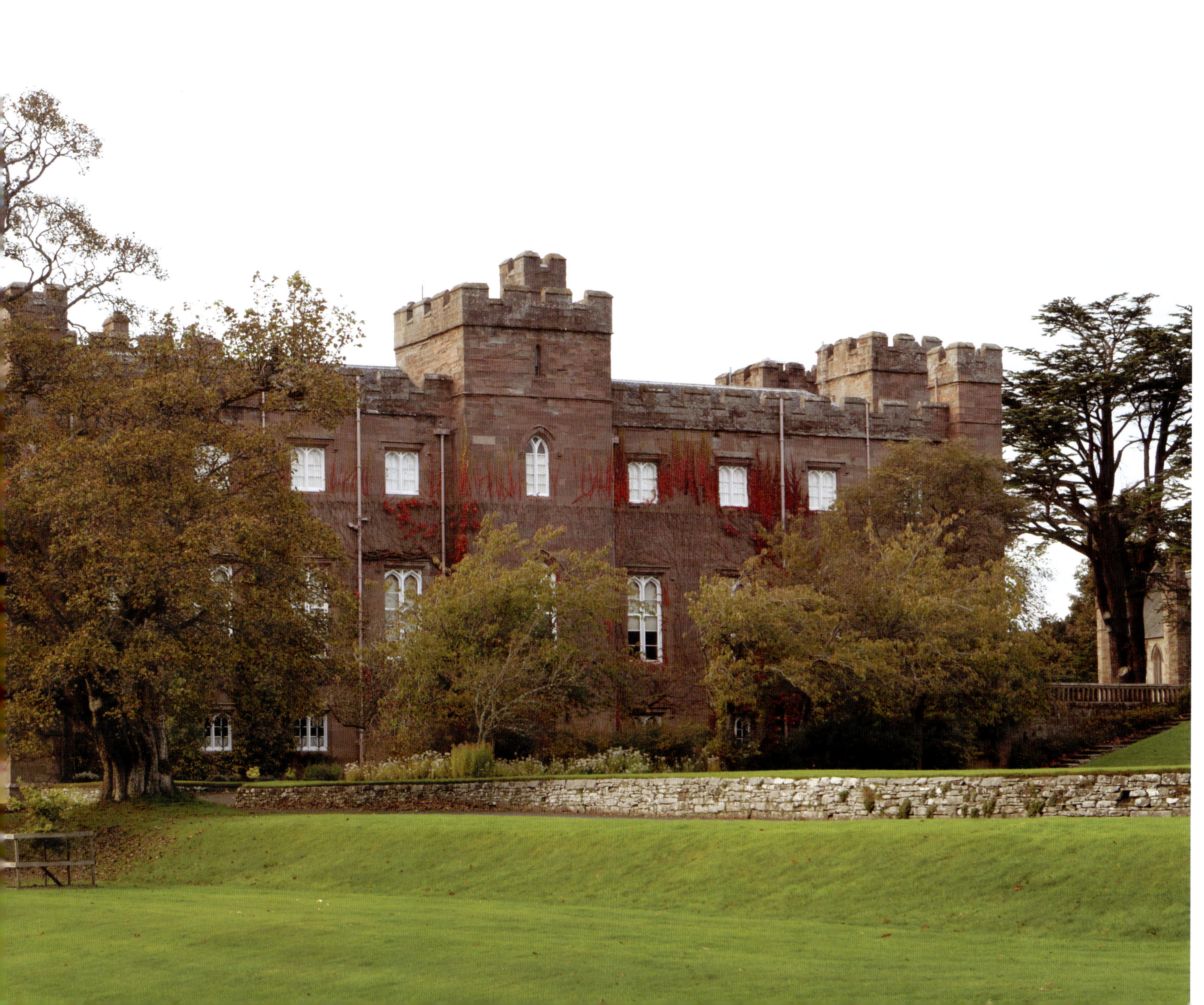

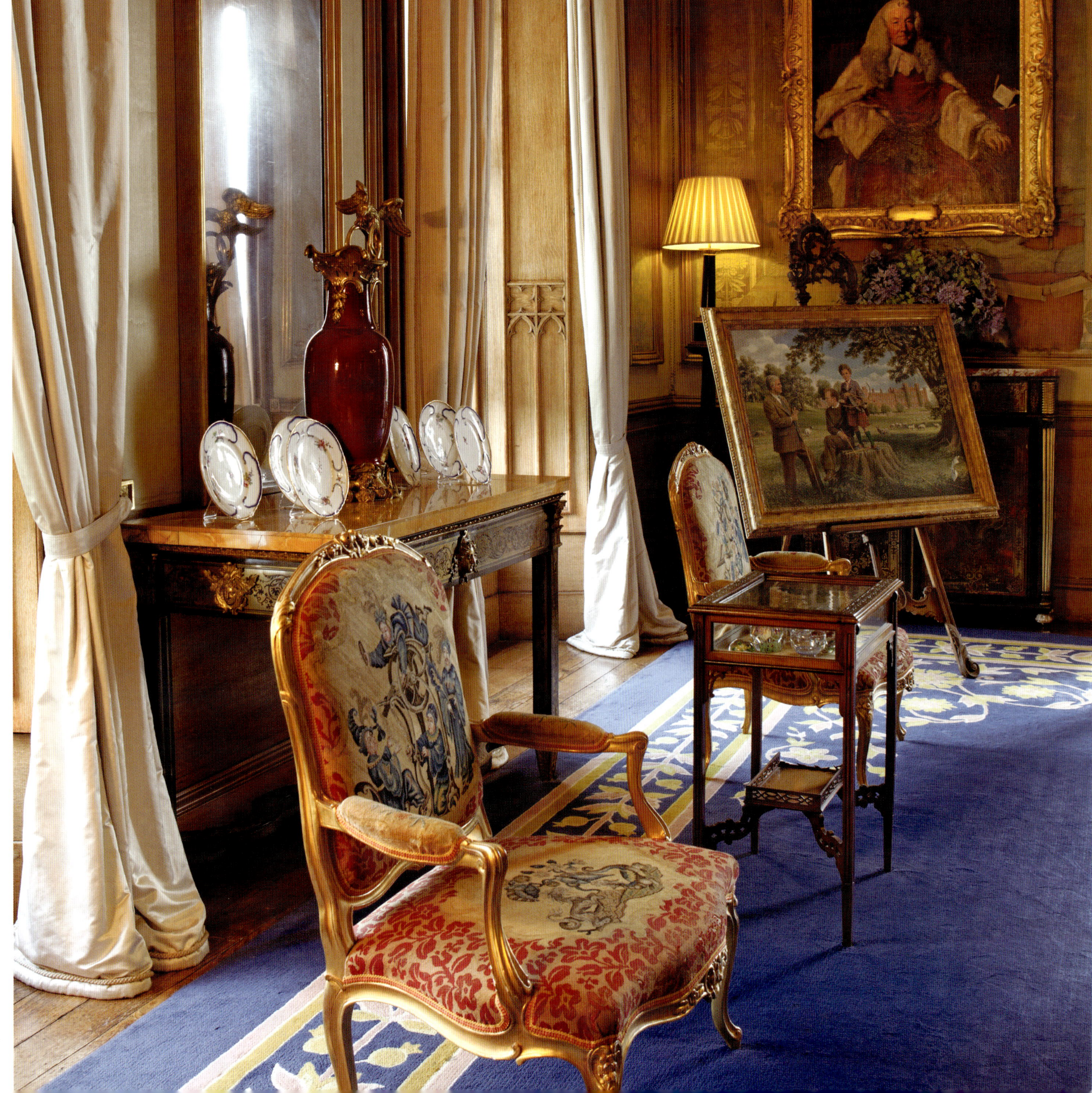

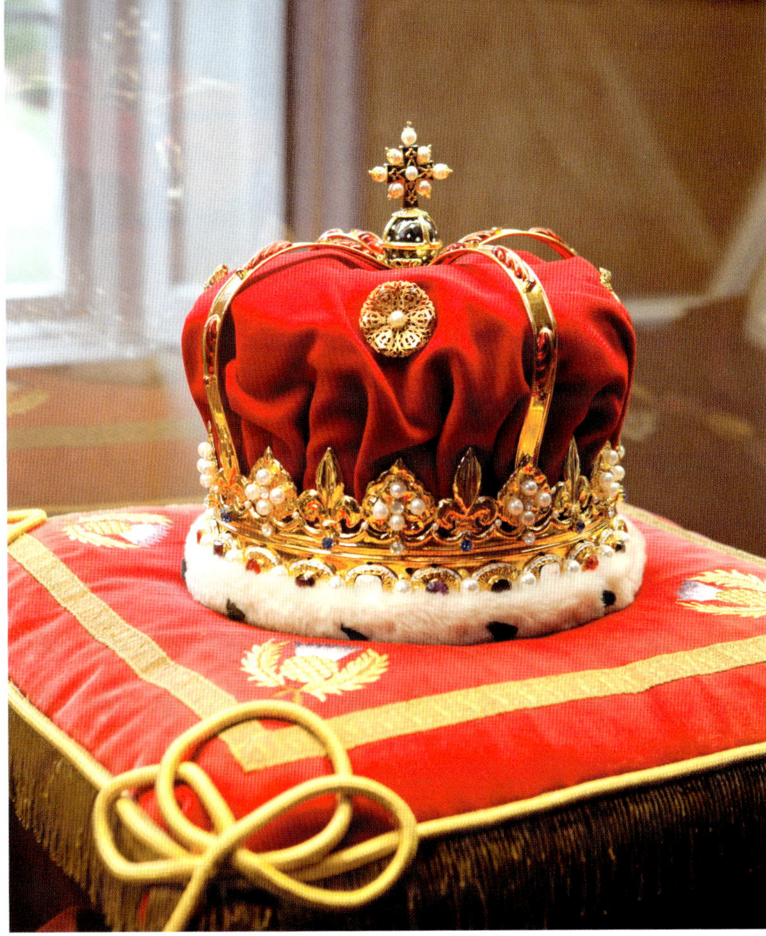

"The walls whispered stories of the past, while the ornate furnishings ... adorned each room with elegance."

—Asif Hossain

This page and opposite: Wrapped in silk-brocade fabric, the Regency-inspired Drawing Room reflects the influence of the 2nd Earl of Mansfield, a diplomat to the court of Versailles. A royal blue–and–gold monogrammed carpet lends a regal touch to this space.

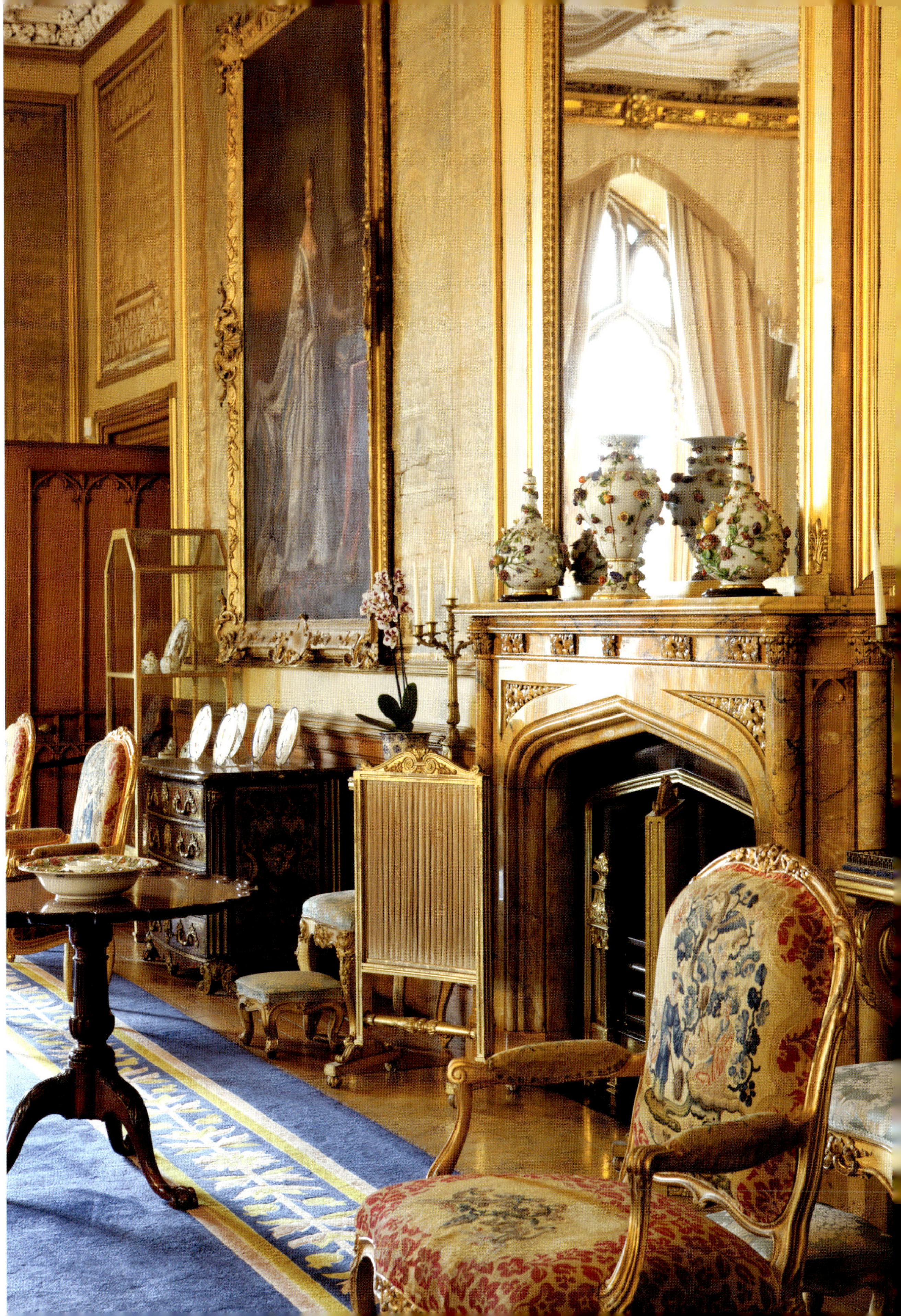

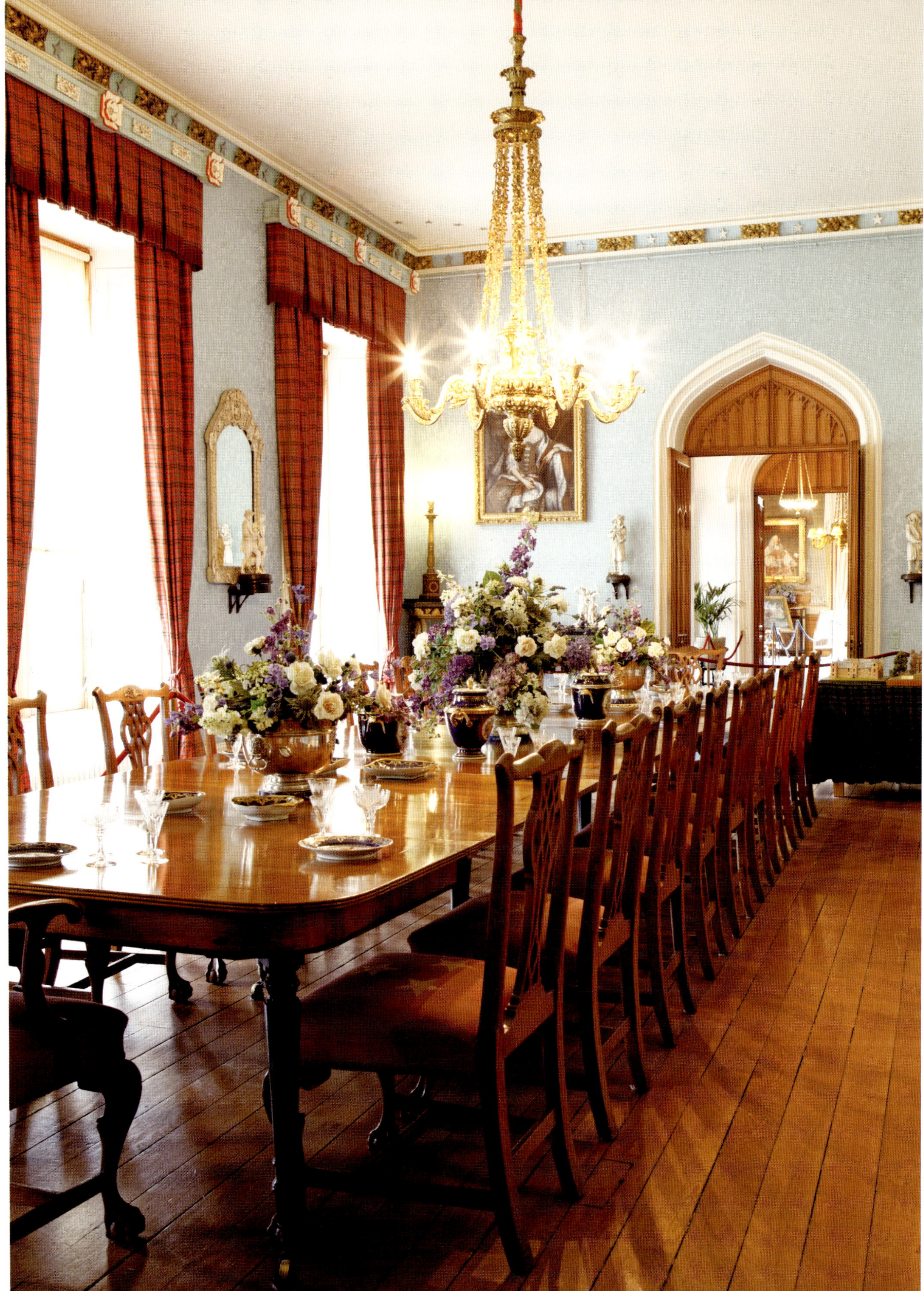

The village of Scone plays a prominent role in Scotland's history, and at the very heart of the story is a beautiful manor—rising majestically along the Tay. Left: The Dining Room played host to Queen Victoria and Prince Albert in 1842, guests of the 4th Earl. The doors, tables, cabinets, and Chippendale-style chairs were constructed of oak grown on the estate. Opposite: Designed to evoke the contemplative ambience of the old abbey, the Ante Room shelters the only Scottish clock displayed in the palace's state rooms—this exquisite timepiece made in 1850 by Burnfield of Perth.

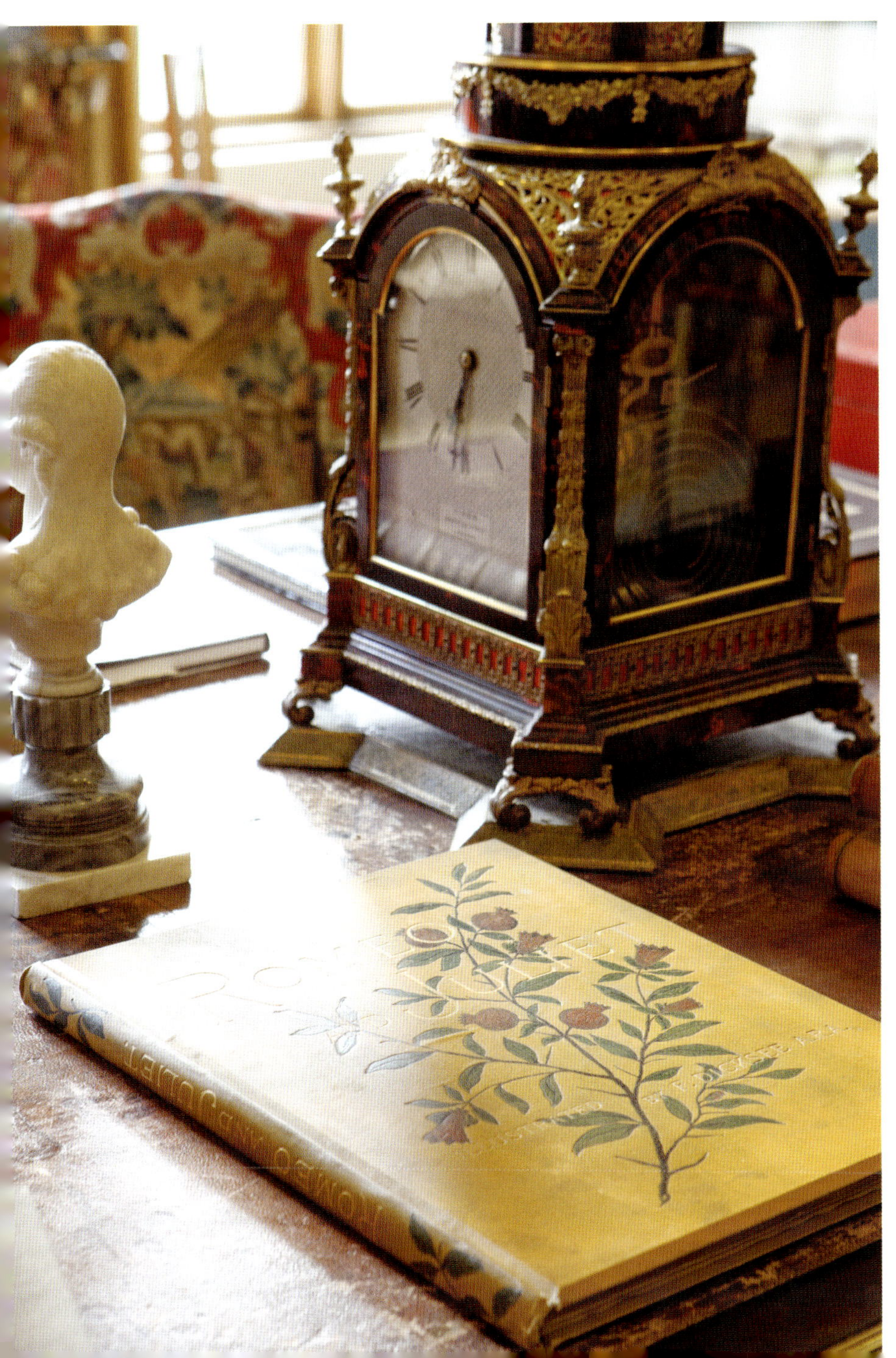

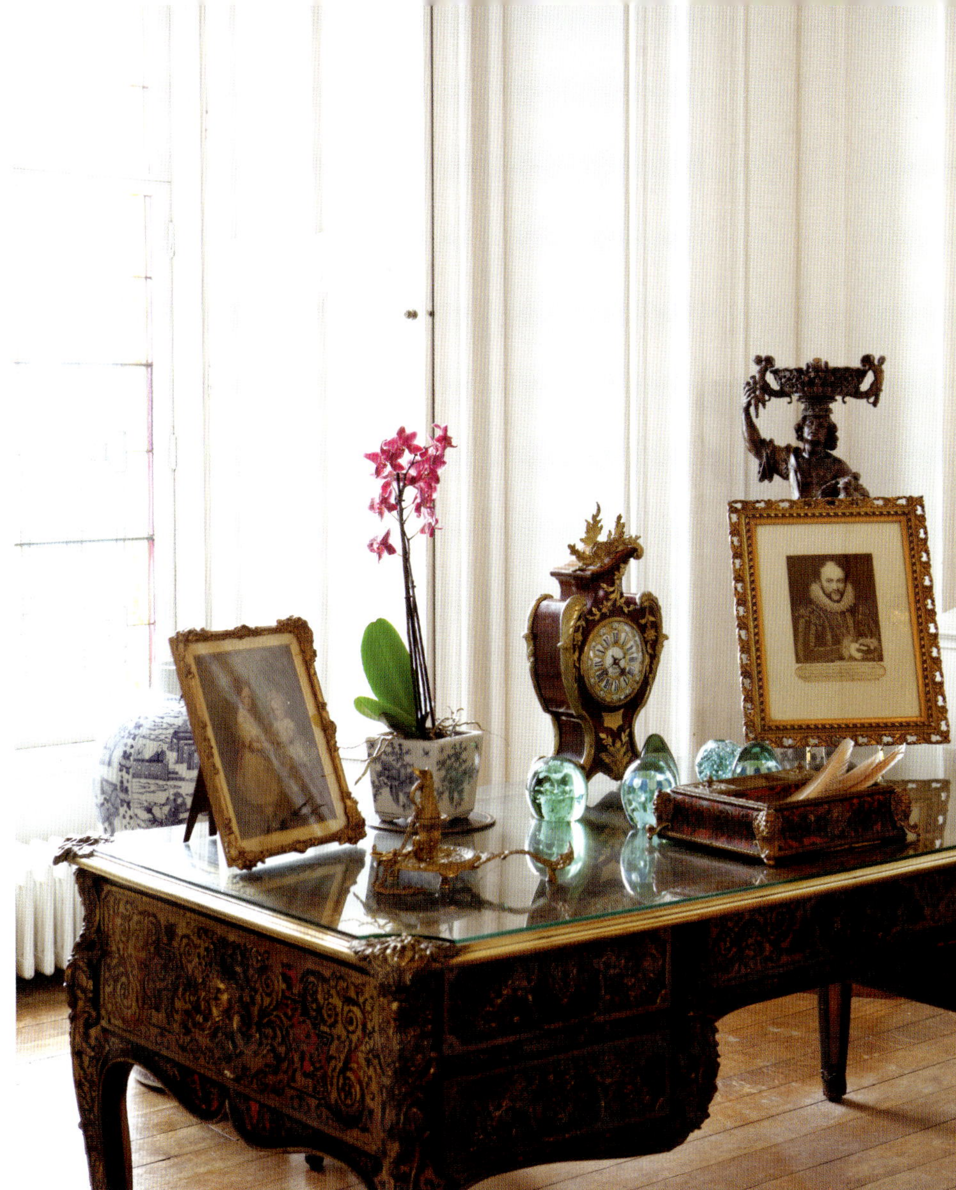

The grounds are a splendor to behold as well. A tiny Gothic chapel, surrounded by stately cedar of Lebanon trees, rises atop Moot Hill—the ancient crowning place of Scottish kings. In lieu of formal gardens, the surrounding woodlands and avenues of flowering trees are equally breathtaking in their natural beauty.

Revered for its historic significance and present-day character, Scone Palace remains a timeless presence in the Perthshire countryside, drawing visitors to experience the magnificence for themselves.

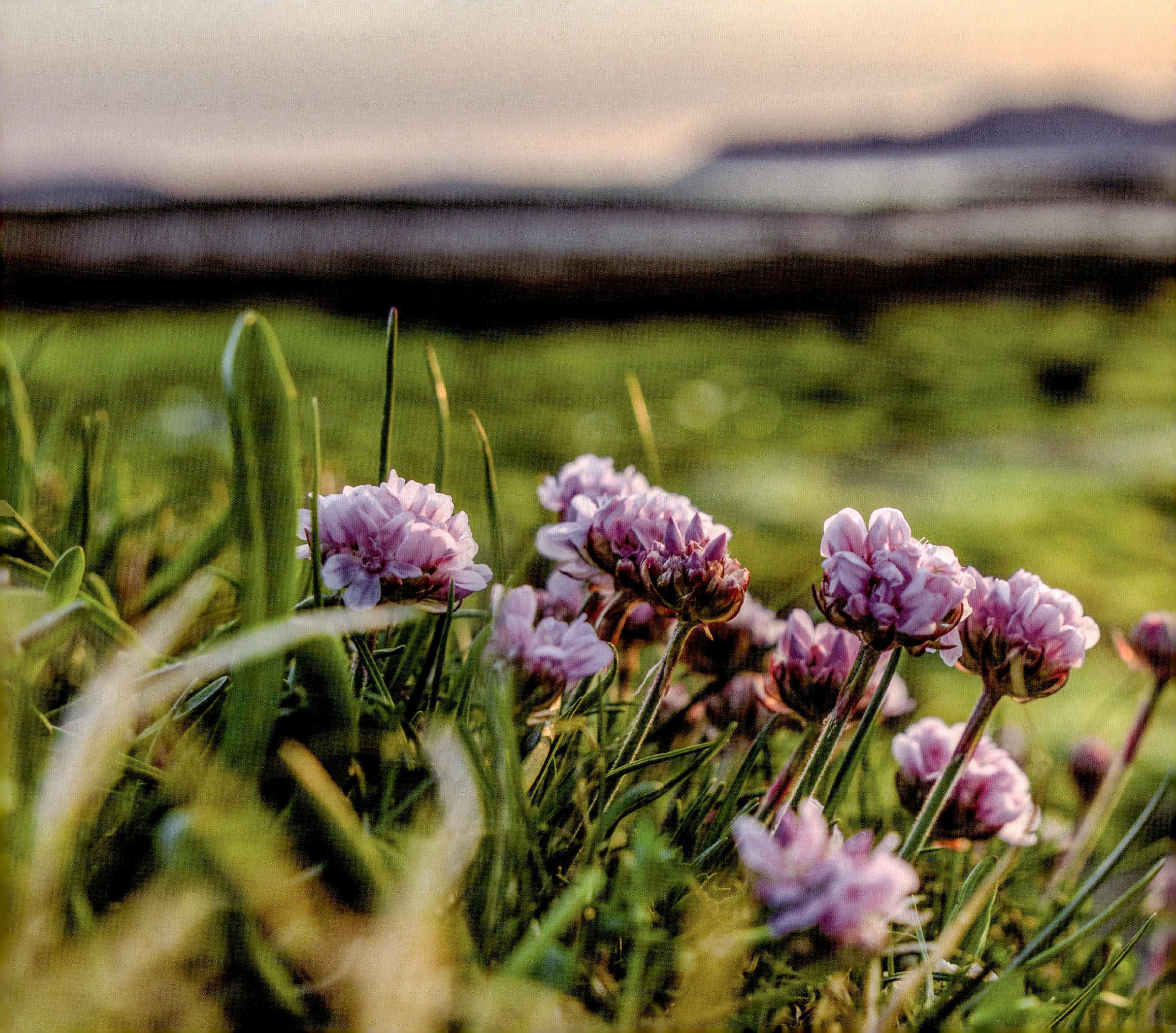

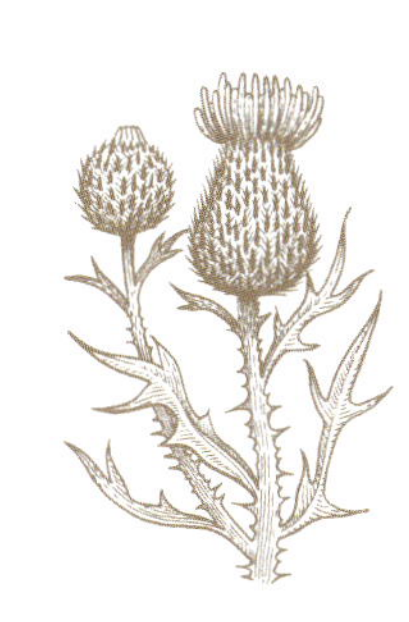

Tradition & CHARM

With inspiration from the heritage, culture, and scenery all around them, Scottish makers and masters bring the infinite charms of their extraordinary country to their crafts, whether it is the beauty woven in traditional tweeds, the creamy flavors of handmade chocolates, or specially blended teas taken in elegant surroundings.

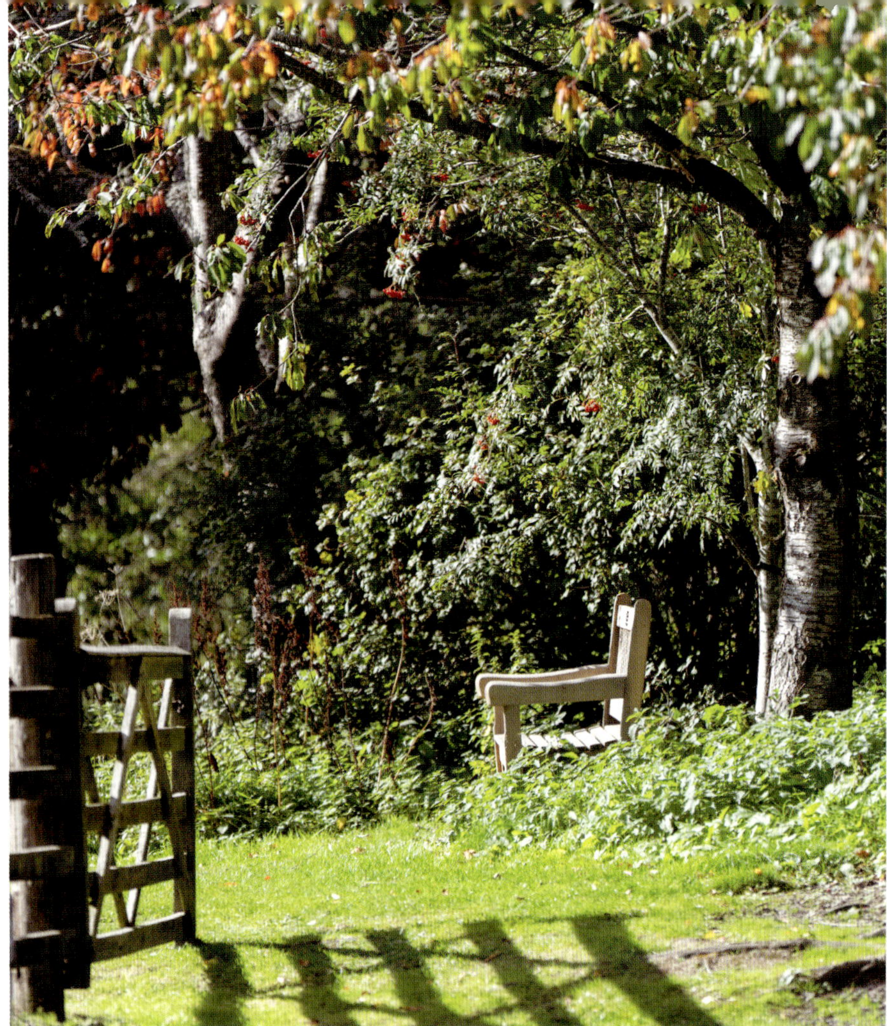

WANDERING HEART

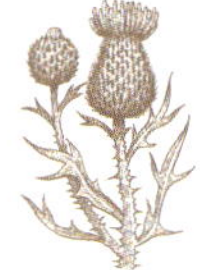

A heart fluttering like a plover's wing, a chilling autumnal breeze tousling the hair, a lingering gaze brimming with wanderlust and anticipation—evoke these dramatic moments through a wardrobe inspired by timeless style and the historic backdrop of a Scottish castle tower overlooking heather and haugh.

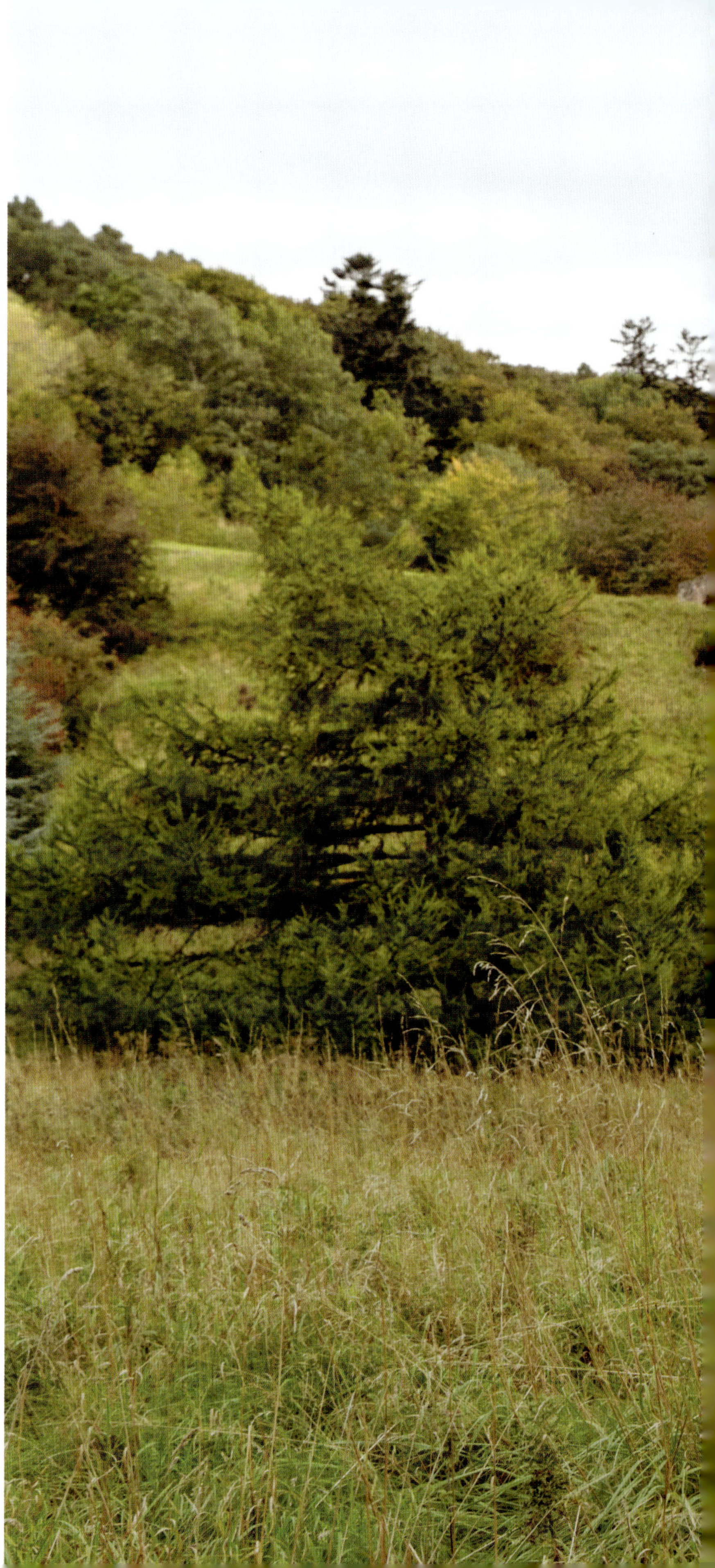

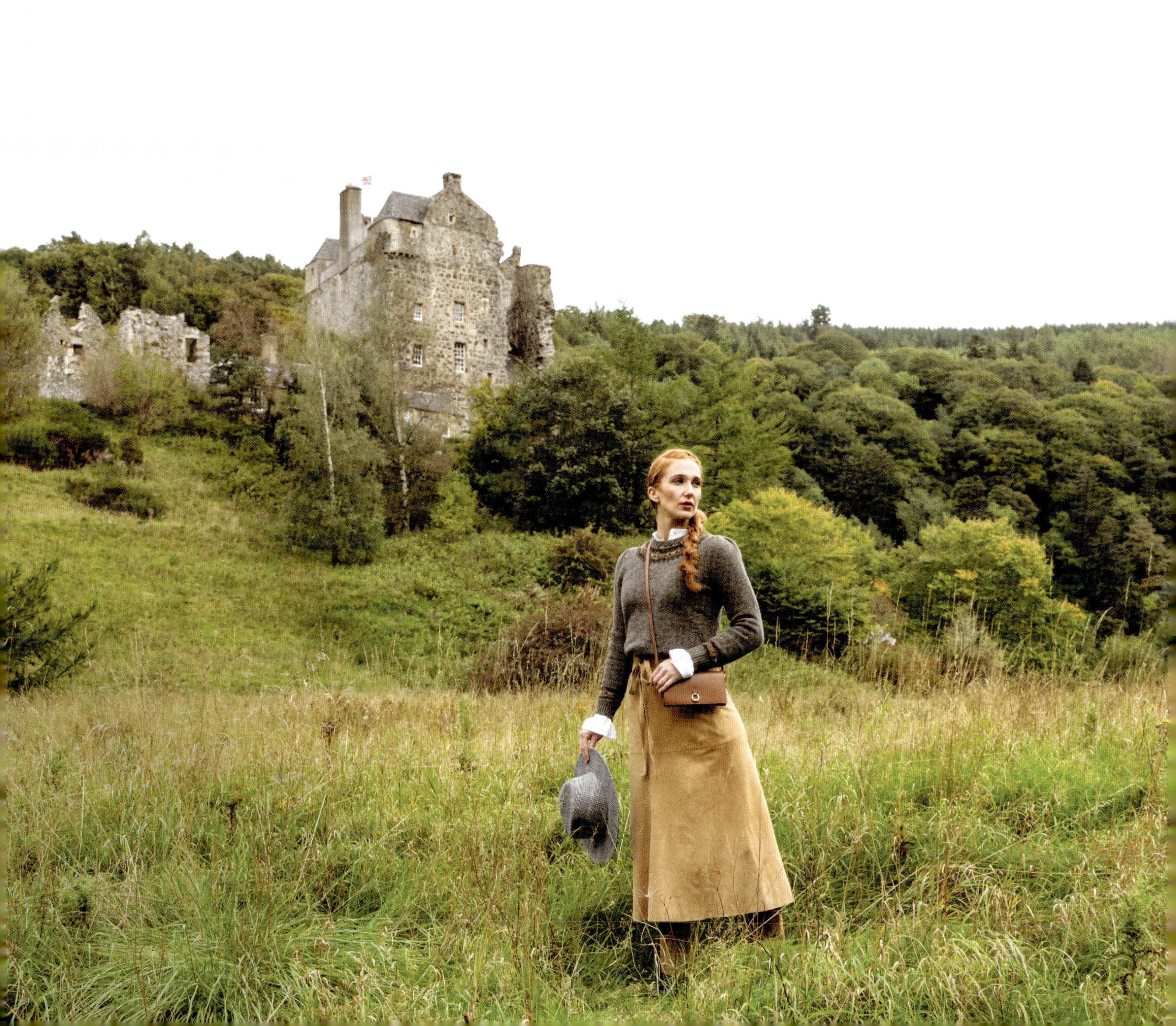

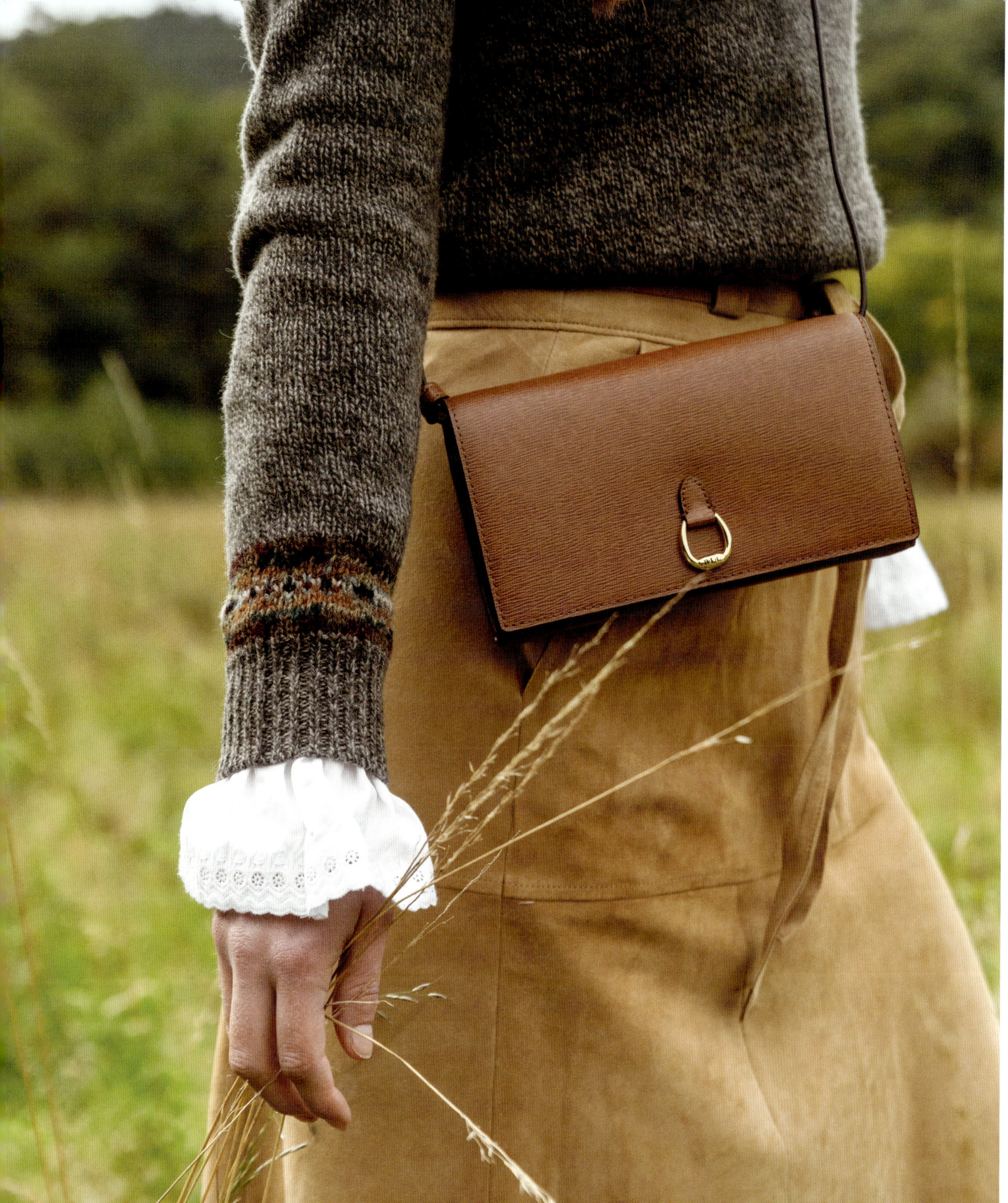

Perched proudly above the River Tweed, Neidpath Castle's current façade was re-erected in 1320. Both Mary Queen of Scots and William Wallace were known to have spent much time here. Left: On the riverside meadow below Neidpath's steady eye, exploration begins with Scottish attire. Our look consists of a Ralph Lauren suede skirt, Fair Isle sweater, cotton broadcloth top, and leather crossbody bag. Opposite, above left and right: Charming mulberry ribbons from a Theory blouse highlight colorful threads in the lambswool Walker Slater Emma Jacket. The Scottish maker's lambswool tweed trousers, worn here over matching navy stockings, lengthen the leg's appearance. Below left: The fruits of rowan trees line the river with brilliant harvest hues.

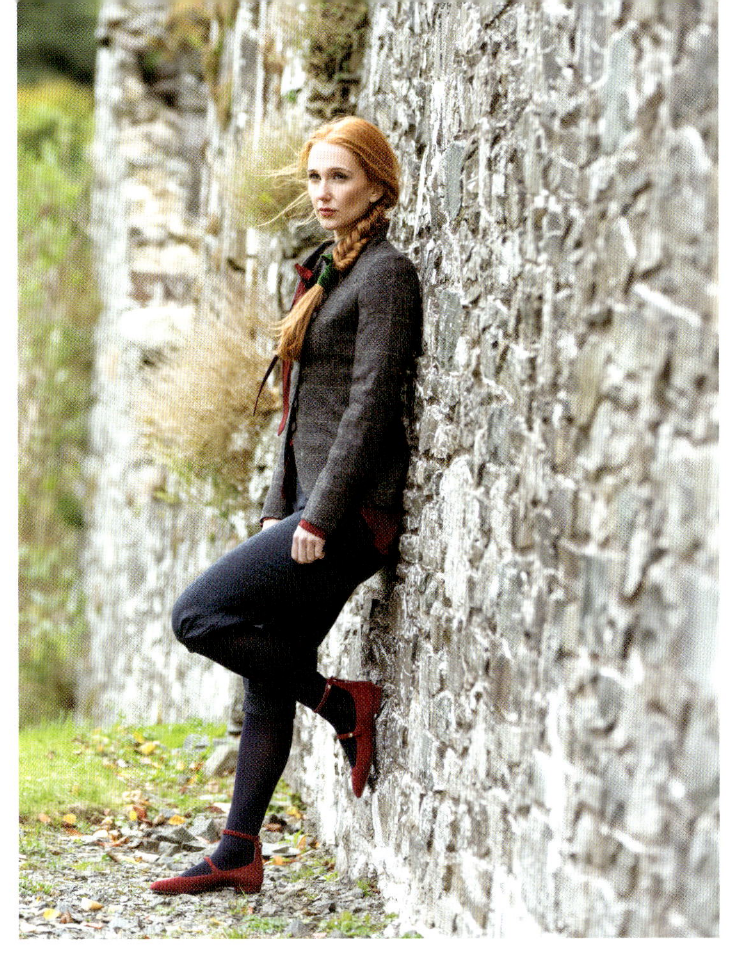

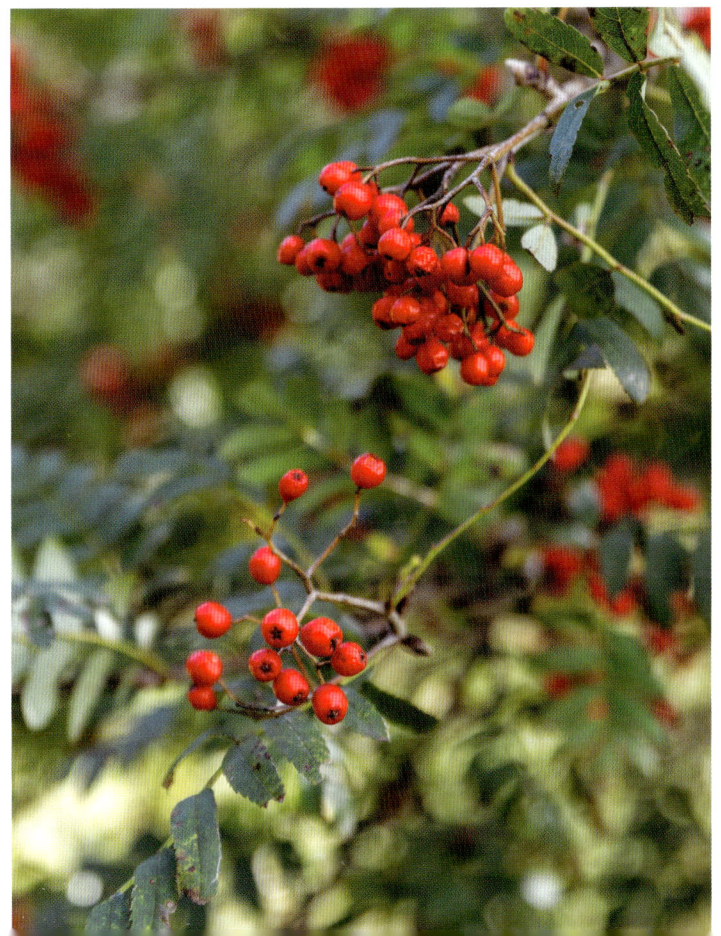

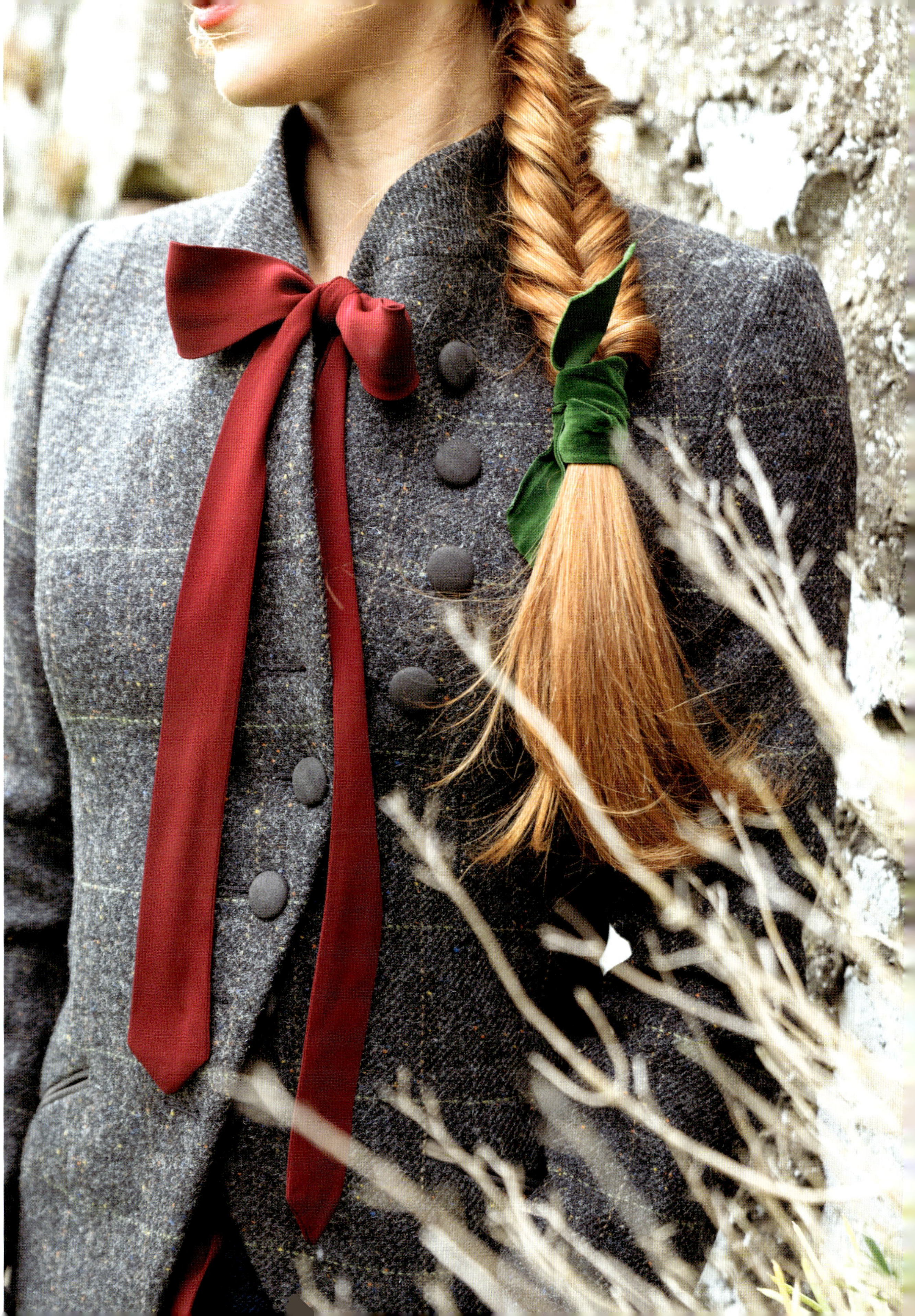

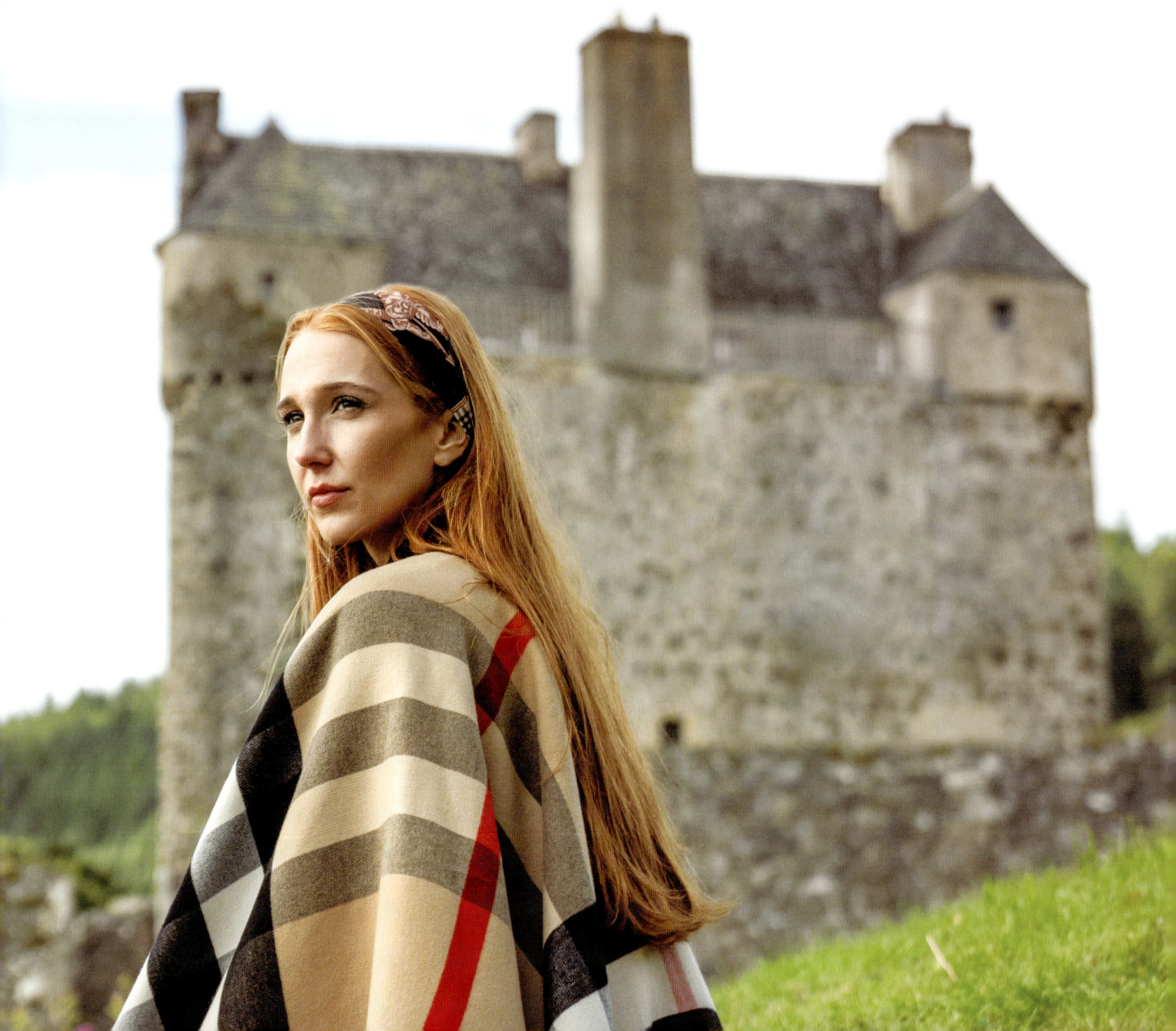

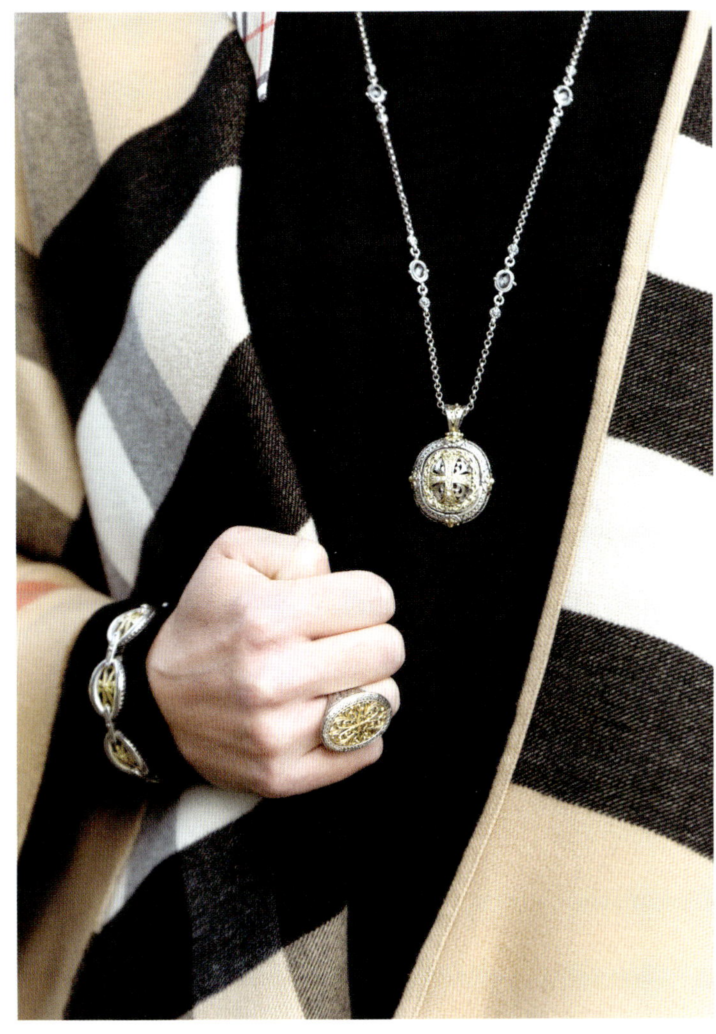

"But to see her was to love her, love but her, and love forever."

—Robert Burns

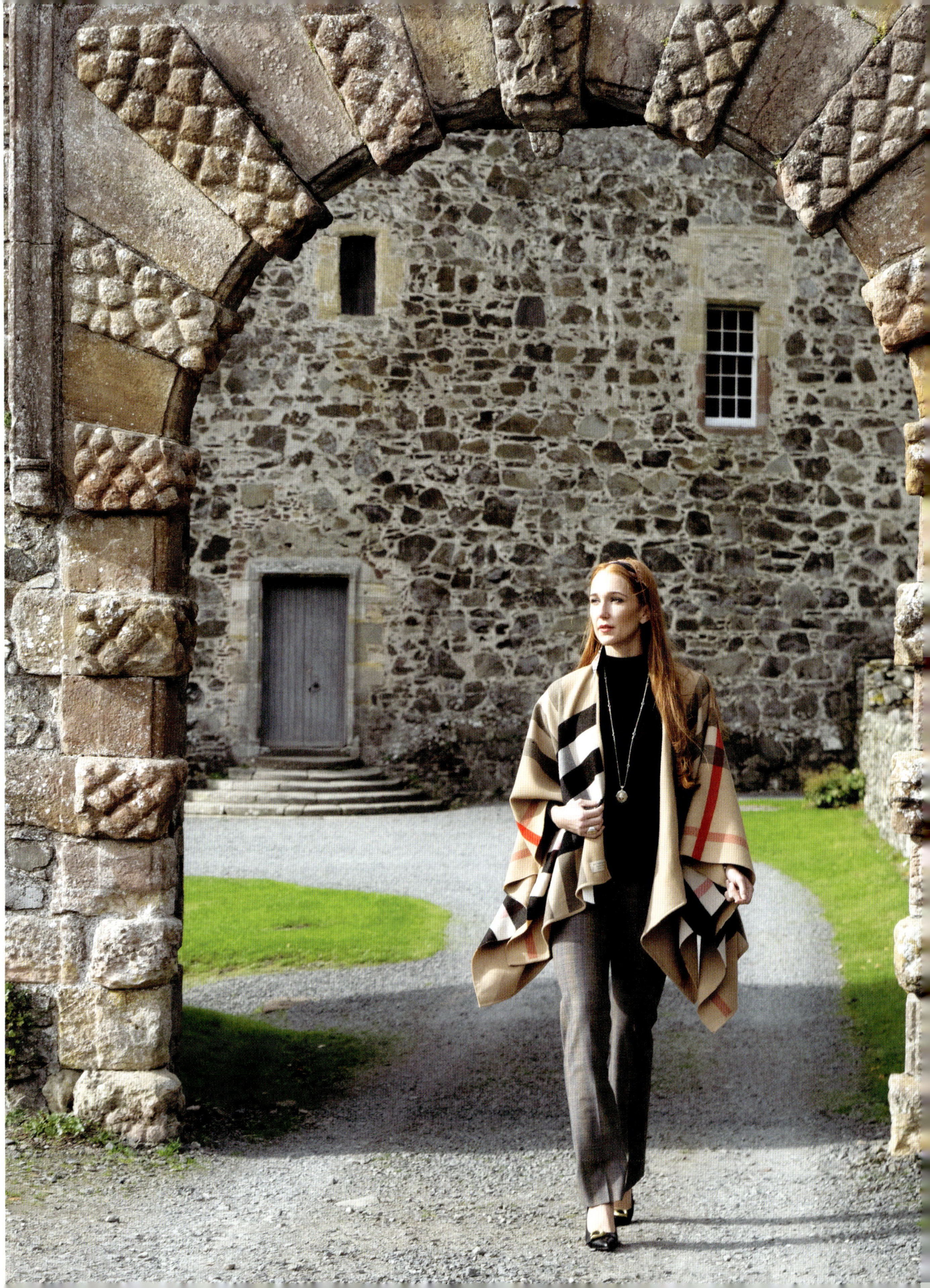

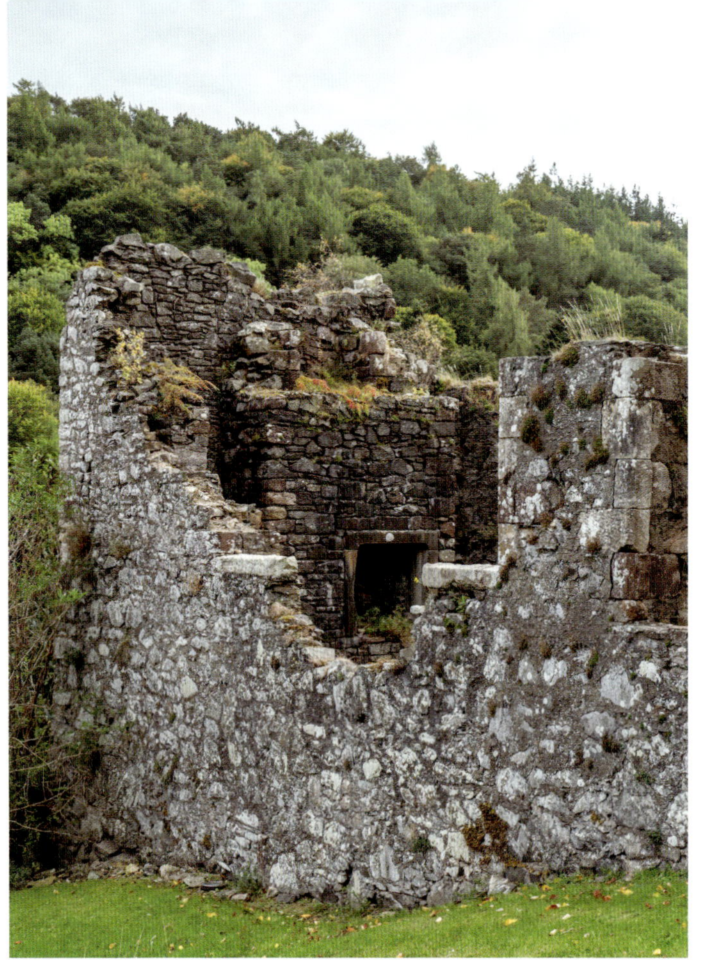

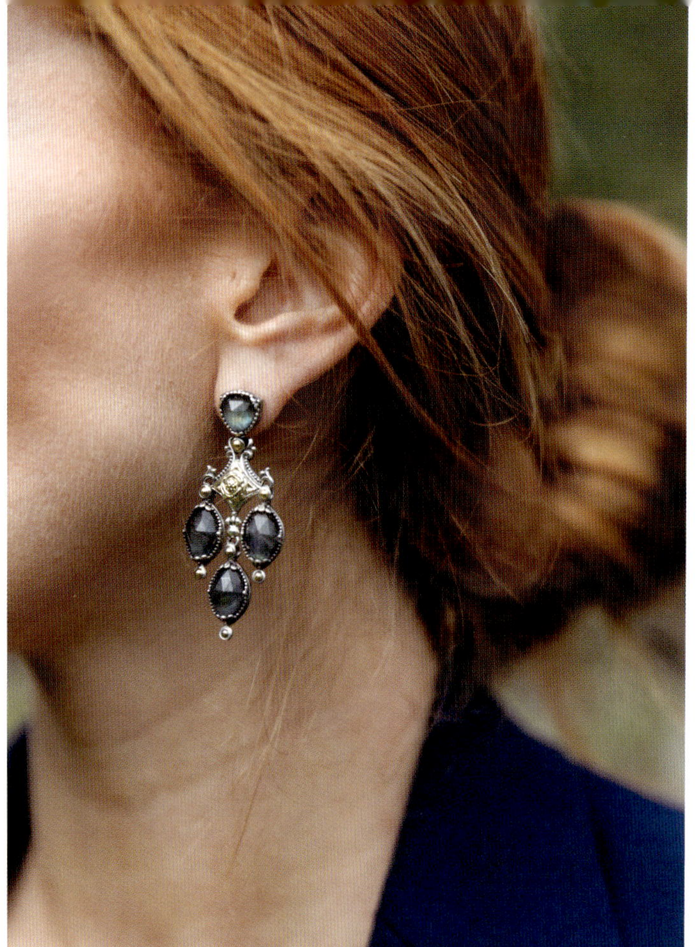

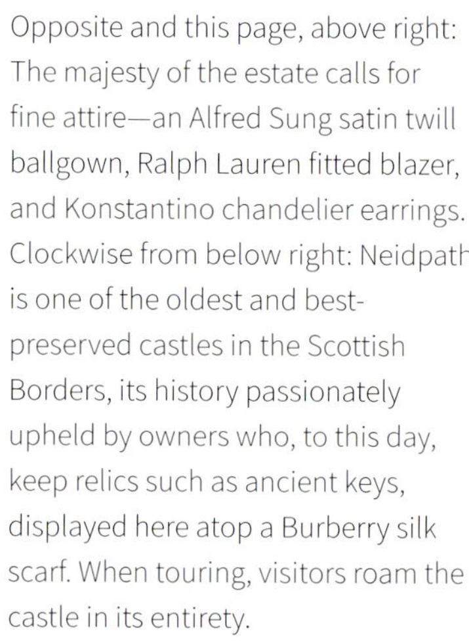

Opposite and this page, above right: The majesty of the estate calls for fine attire—an Alfred Sung satin twill ballgown, Ralph Lauren fitted blazer, and Konstantino chandelier earrings. Clockwise from below right: Neidpath is one of the oldest and best-preserved castles in the Scottish Borders, its history passionately upheld by owners who, to this day, keep relics such as ancient keys, displayed here atop a Burberry silk scarf. When touring, visitors roam the castle in its entirety.

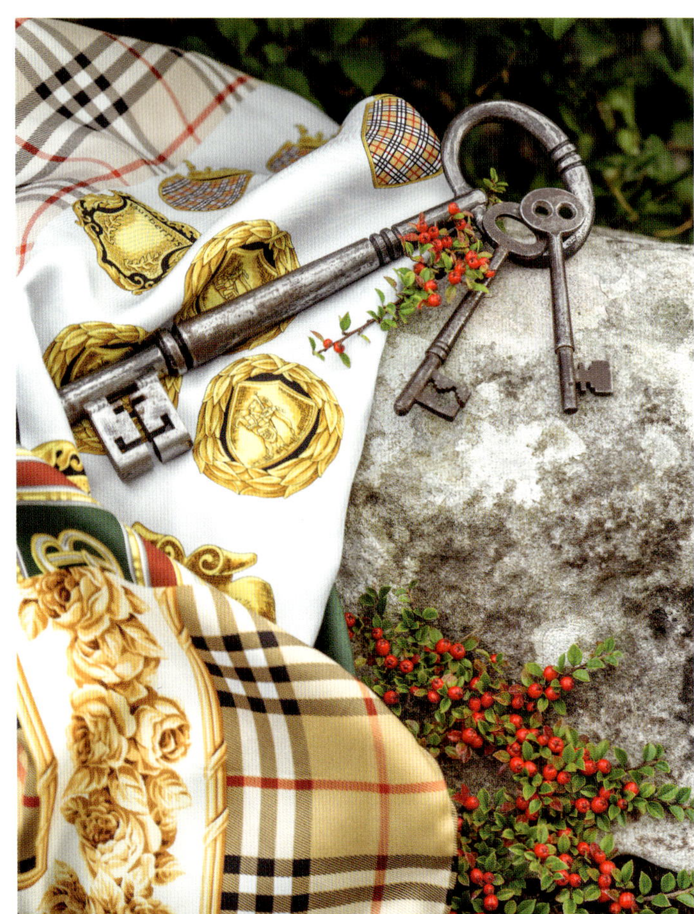

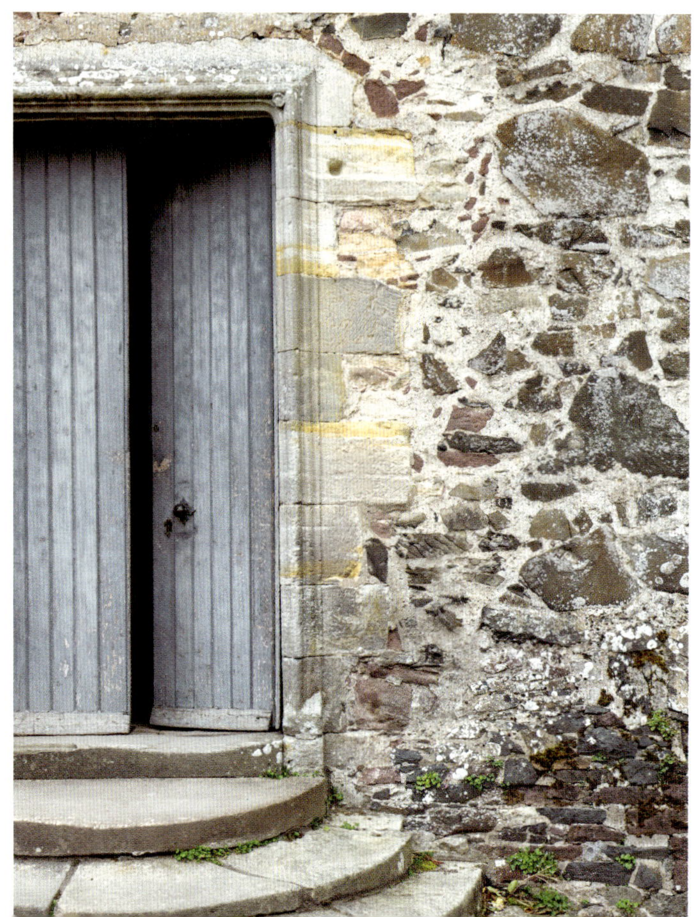

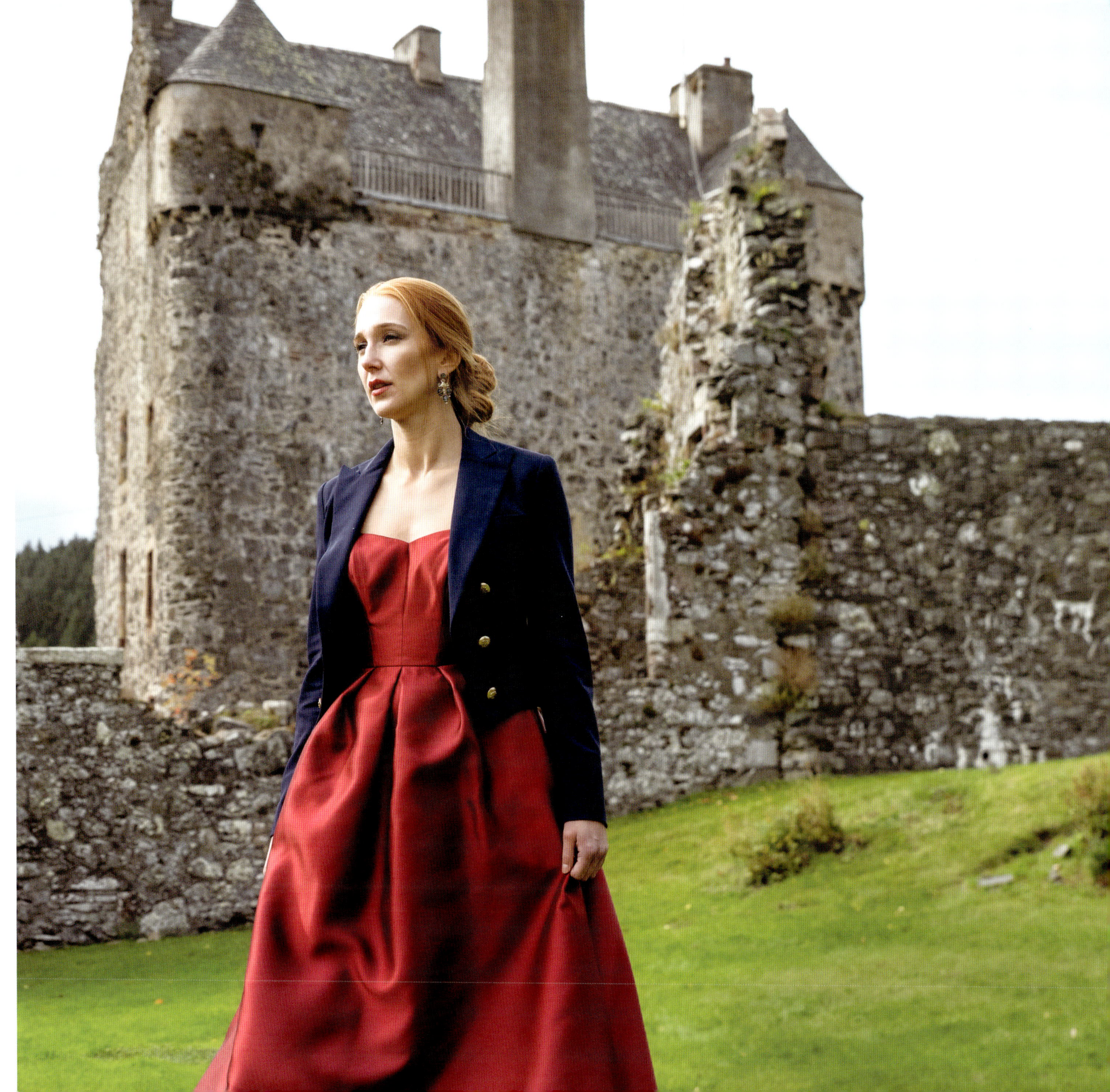

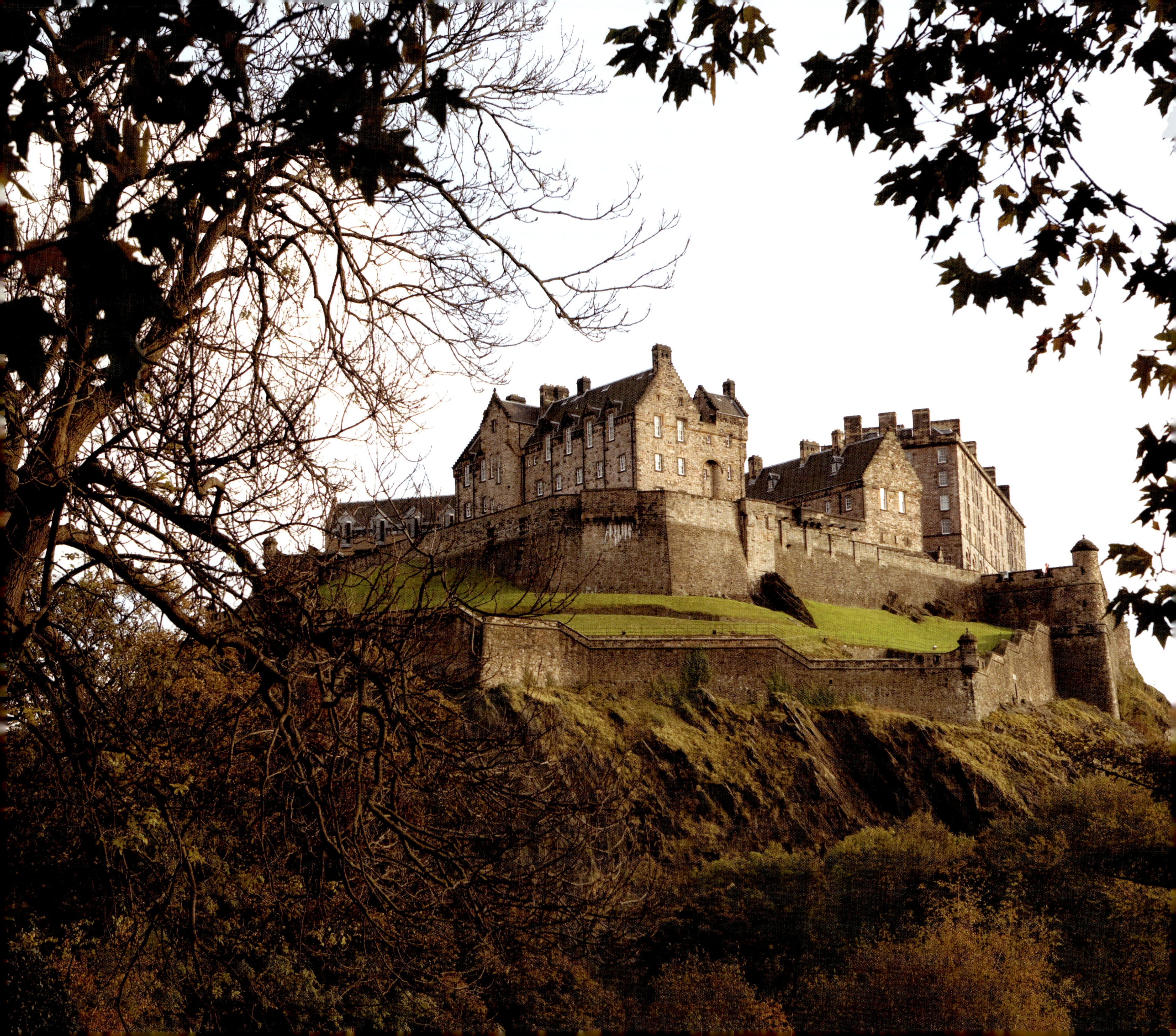

AUTUMN'S REGALIA

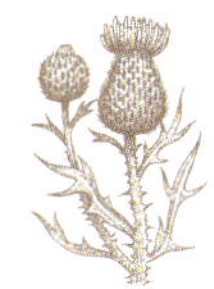

Scotland leaves an imprint on all who experience it. What once brought to mind plaid kilts, misty moors, and brave-hearted Scotsmen has evolved to an entirely new perspective: one of a contemporary land with a rich history, exceptional cuisine, a thriving arts culture, and an abiding respect for its past. In the following pages, discover some of the country's creative treasures and traditions.

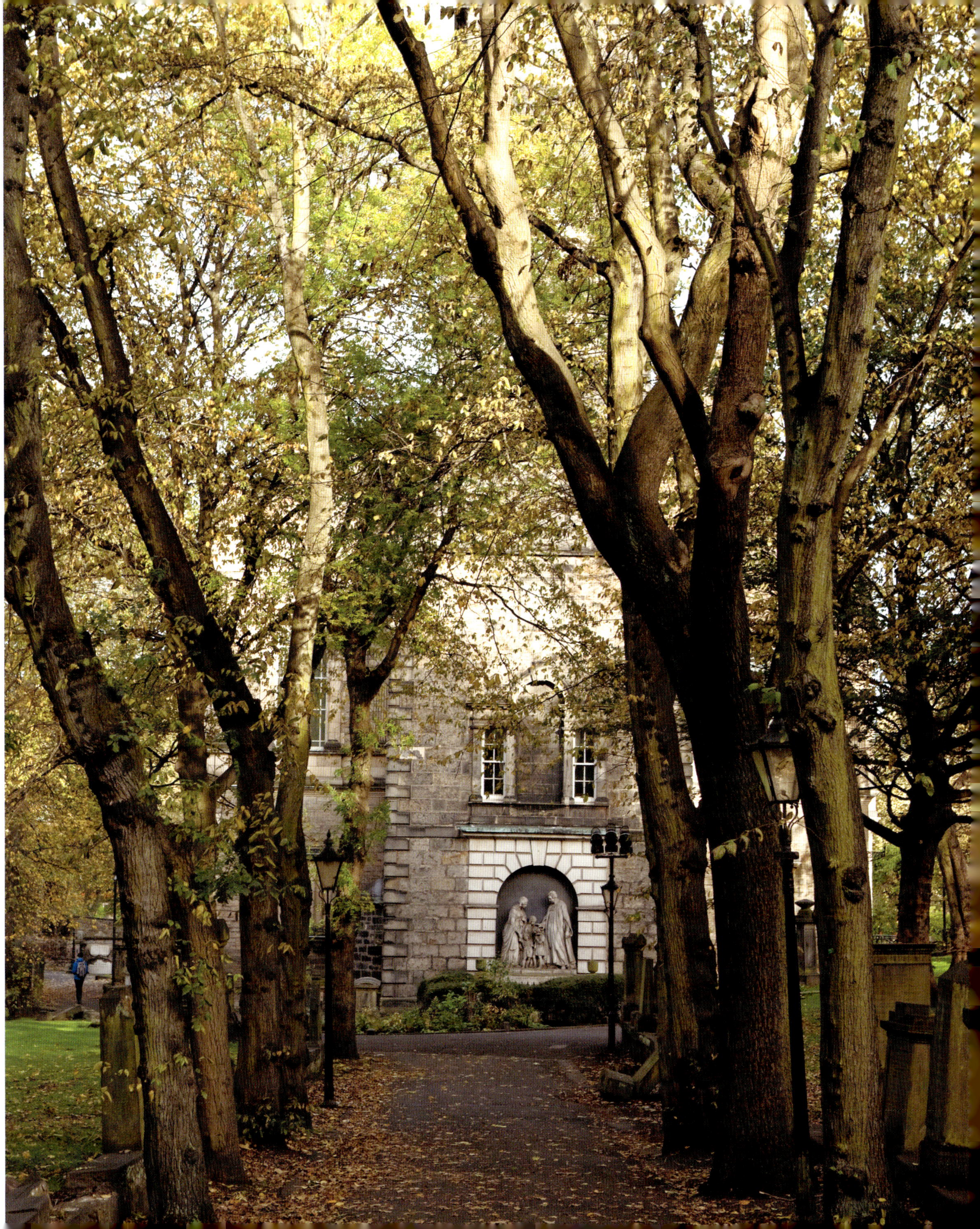

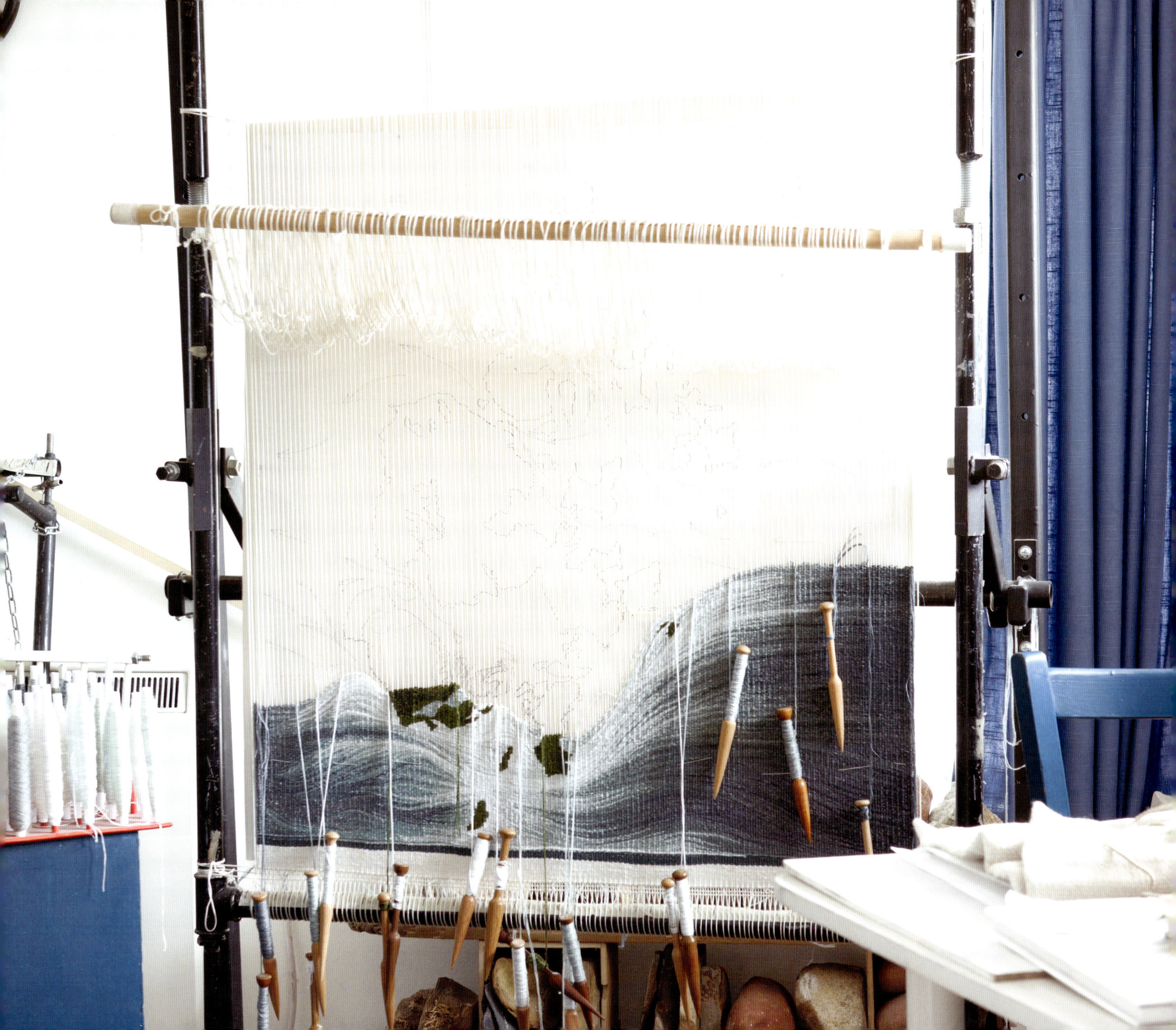

A jewel of the Orkney Islands, the Orkney Craft Trail leads visitors to the workshops, studios, and galleries of talented Scots who display their wares. Hoxa Tapestry Gallery was founded by Leila Thomson, whose legacy of weaving continues on in the hands of family, including her daughter, painter Jo Thomson. Leila's son, Andrew, does the gallery's framing and also creates handmade rugs based on his mother's and sister's drawings.

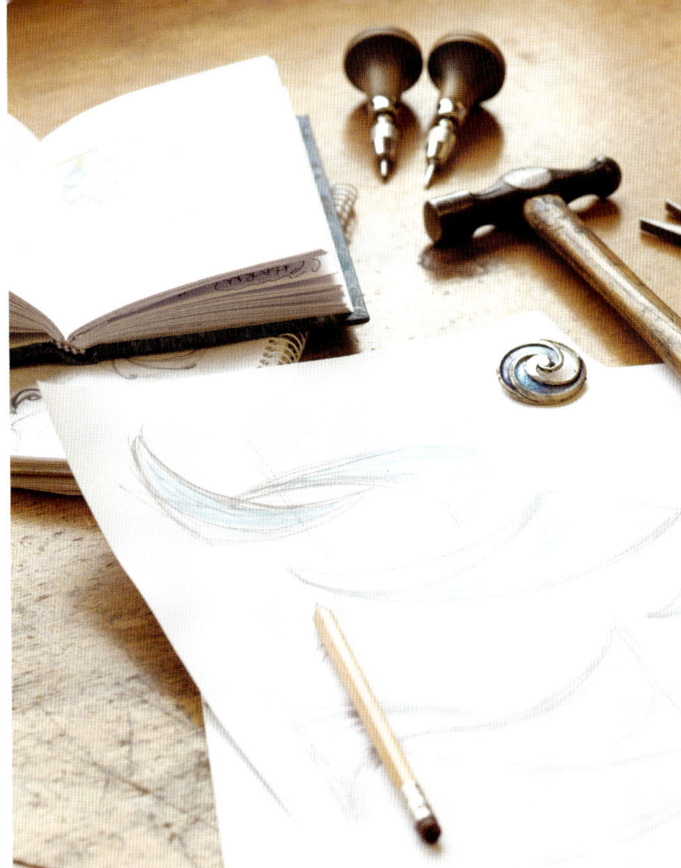

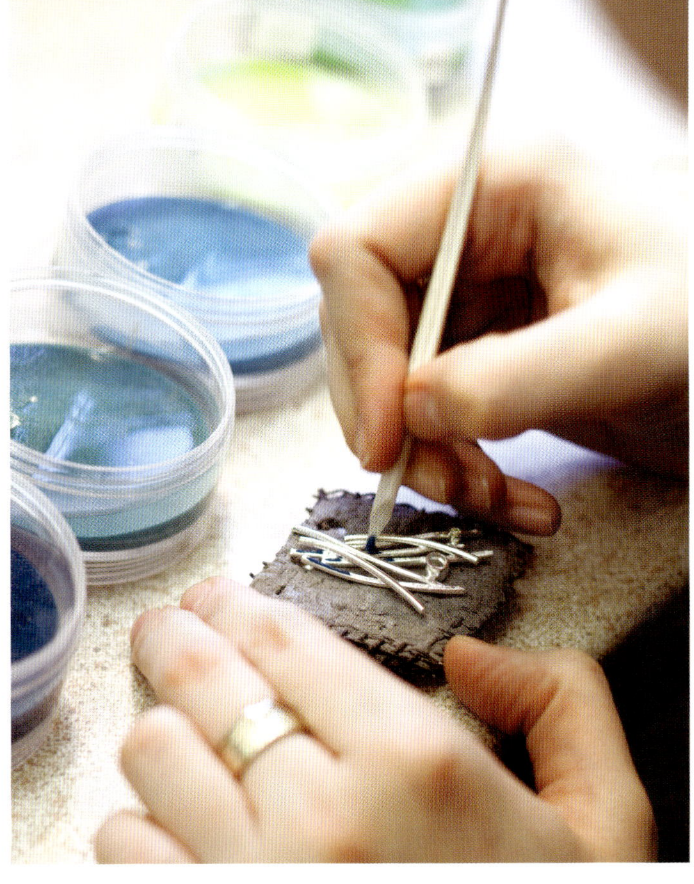

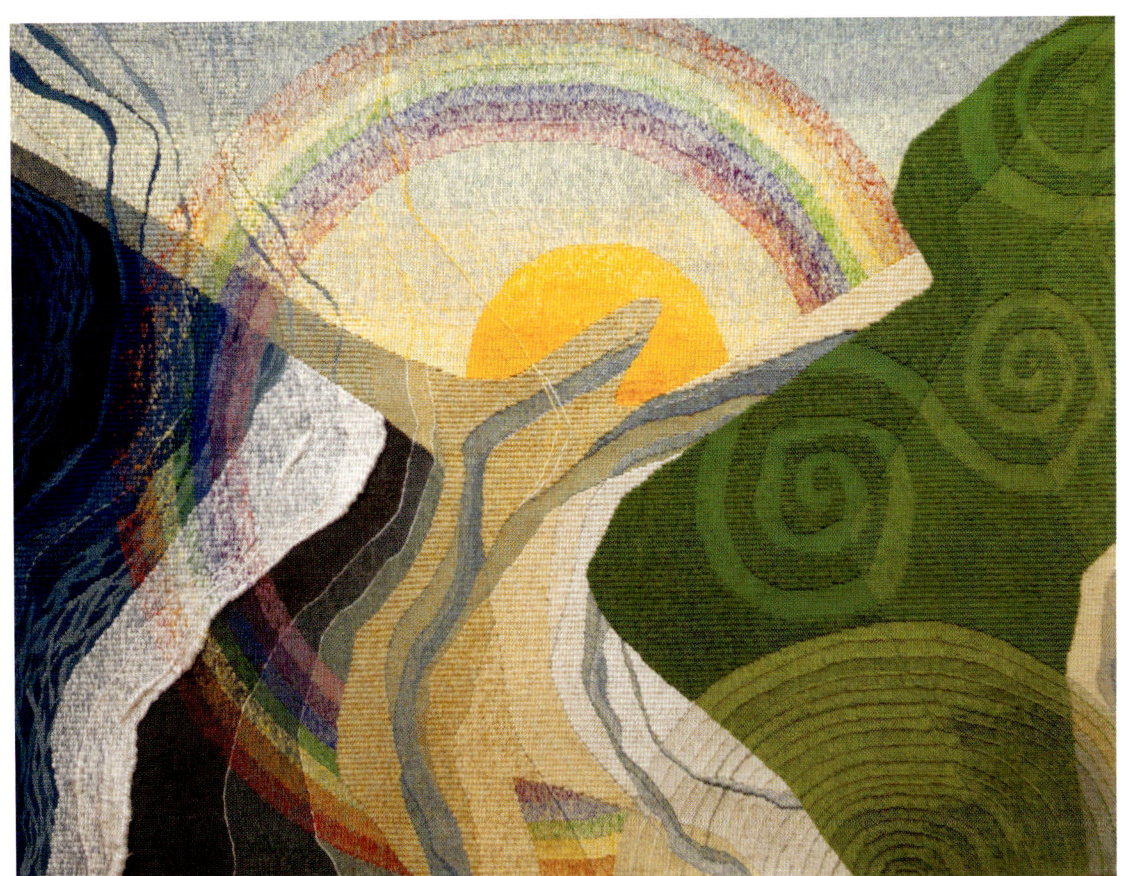

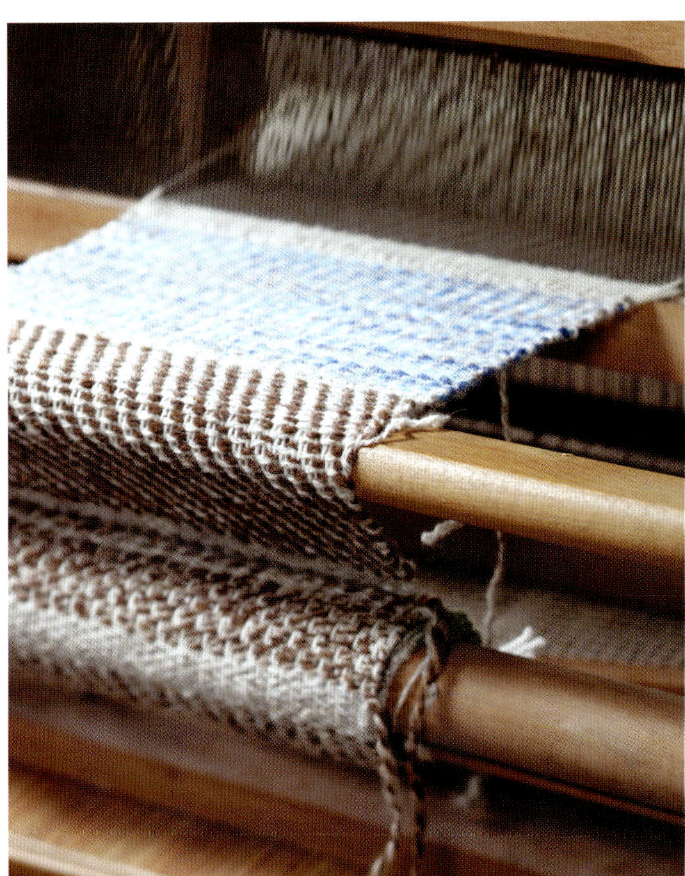

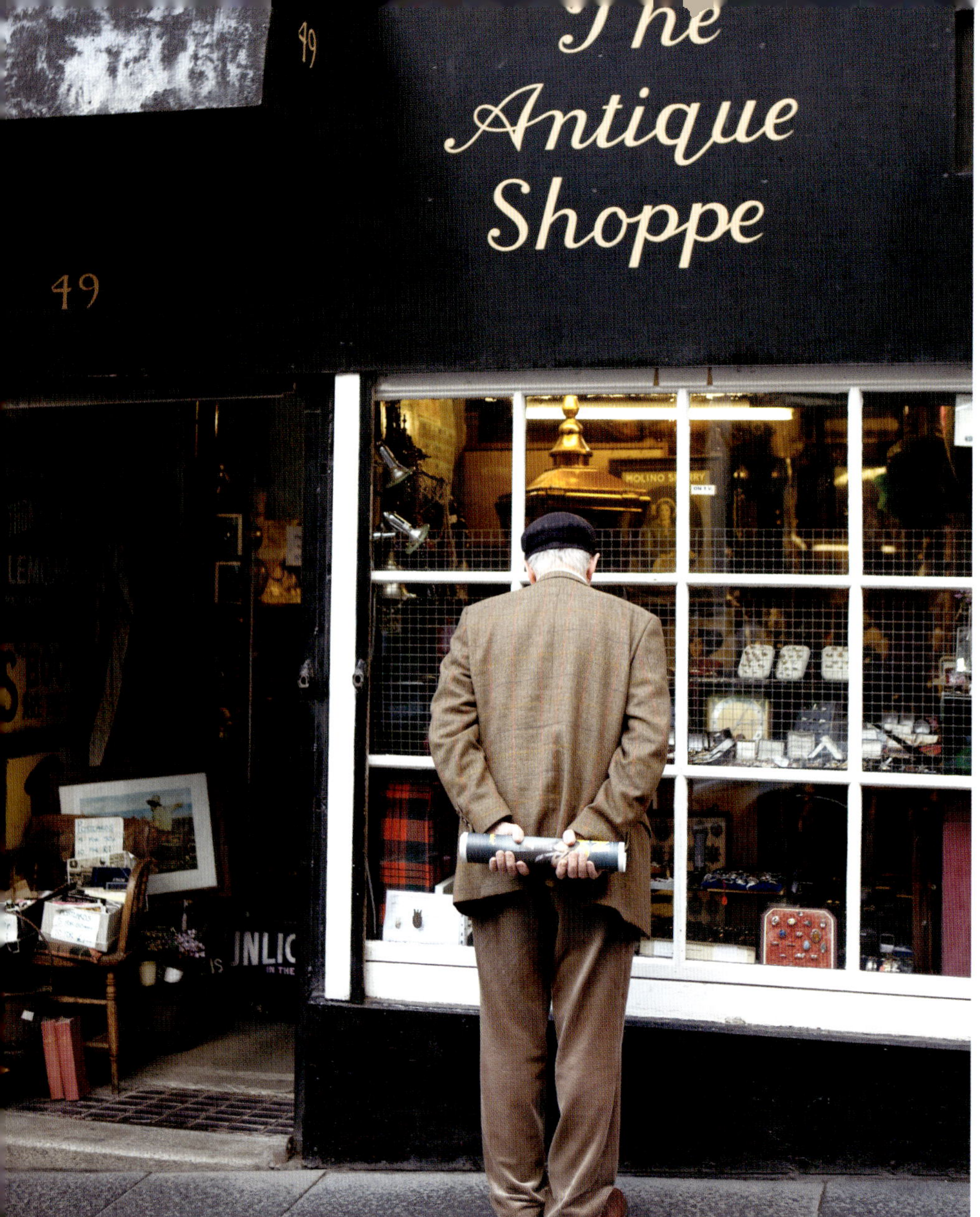

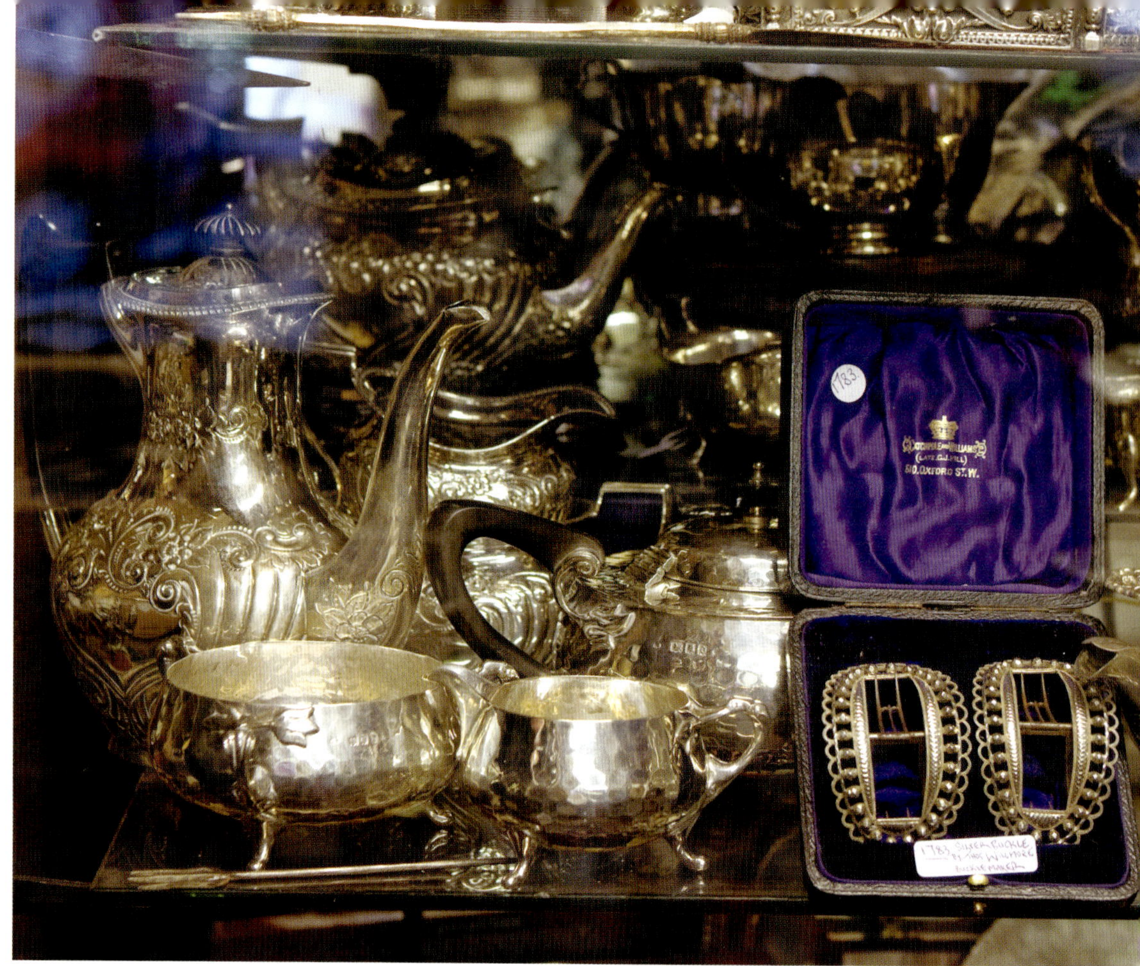

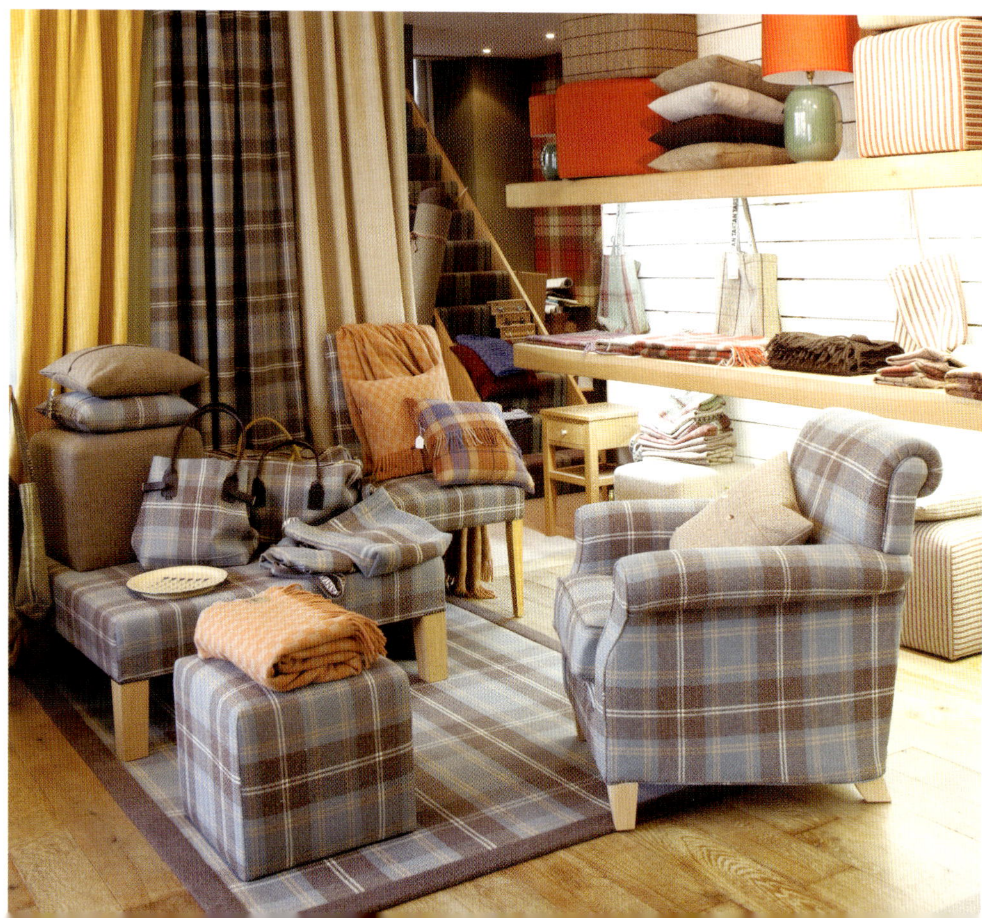

The shops of Edinburgh's Old Town call patrons to the famed Grassmarket district along Victoria Street. Clockwise from above: British silver, cut crystal, and heraldic crests can be purchased at local antiques shops or browsed at leisure by window-shoppers. Tartan remains a classic choice for every room, as evinced by these offerings from ANTA, a maker of home furnishings, textiles, and stoneware based in the Highlands.

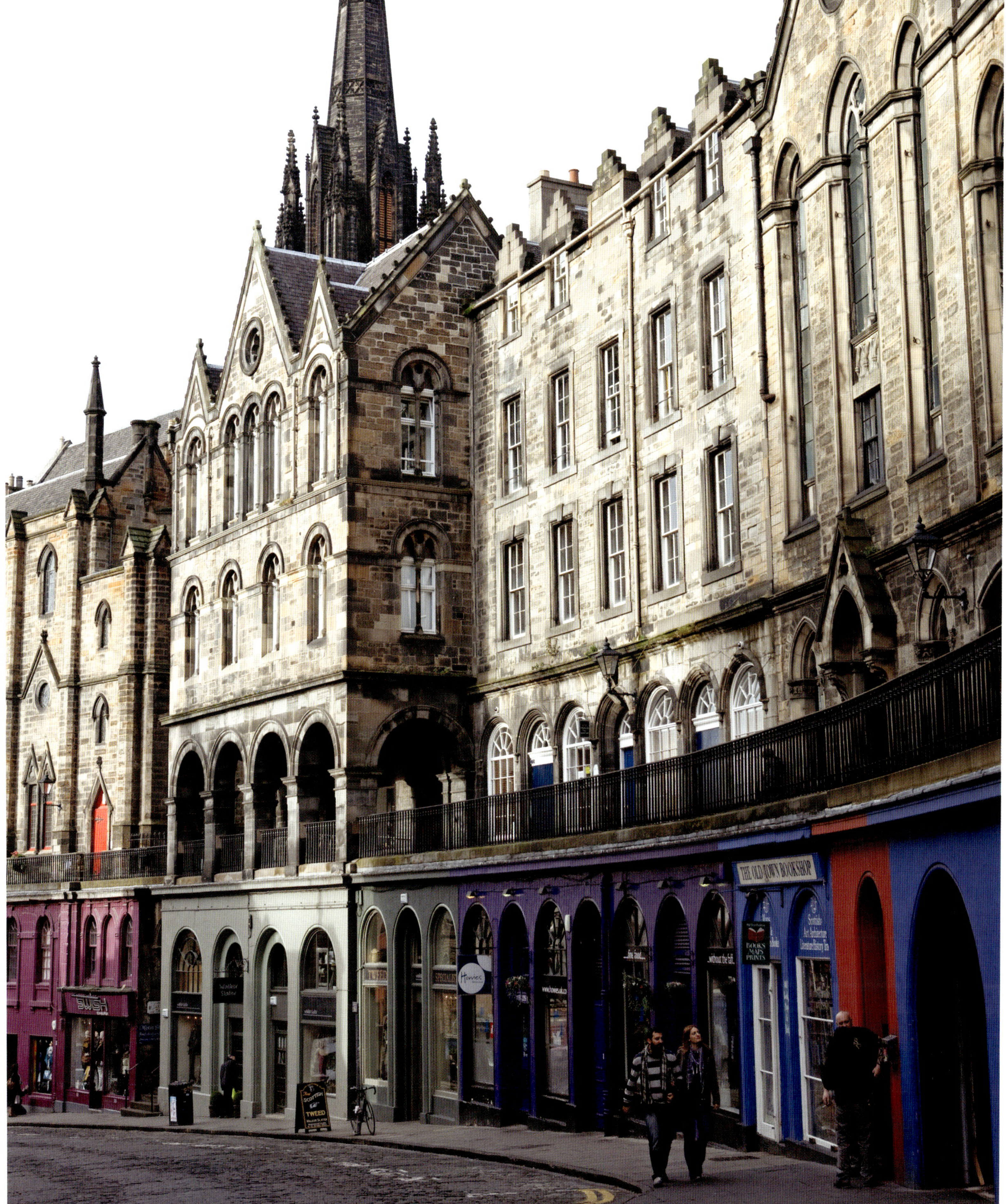
THE OLD TOWN BOOKSHOP
BOOKS
MAPS
PRINTS
TWEED

TEA AND TRANQUILITY

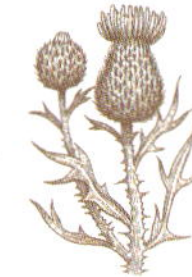

The Royal Mile serves as Edinburgh's main throughfare, where the Edinburgh Castle perches atop Castle Rock at one end and the Palace of Holyroodhouse anchors the other. Tucked within the myriad bustling businesses situated in between lies Colonnades at the Signet Library, a quiet oasis where the cacophony of city life fades away and the taking of tea is a cherished ritual.

Served within the surroundings of the beautifully restored Lower Library, the venue's afternoon tea surpasses simple sustenance to become a truly sublime experience. Fluted Corinthian columns encircling the seating area rise to an upper gallery with Neoclassical-style balustrades, all wearing crowns of gold, while sunlight filters through the windows, embracing the salon with a sense of calm. This halcyon setting is just a preview of the excellent offerings to come.

From the amuse-bouche at the beginning of service to the three tiers of sweetness presented at the end, and through every wonderful delight in between, the menu brims with creativity and culinary perfection. Since the chefs insist on using only the freshest and highest-quality ingredients, they love to lean into the seasons for flavor inspiration and unique combinations, such as Winter Vegetable Pithivier, Chicken Balmoral Pie, and Masala Chai Panna Cotta. No matter the day or the season, a visit to Colonnades at the Signet Library will leave a lasting impression—and prompt a promise to return.

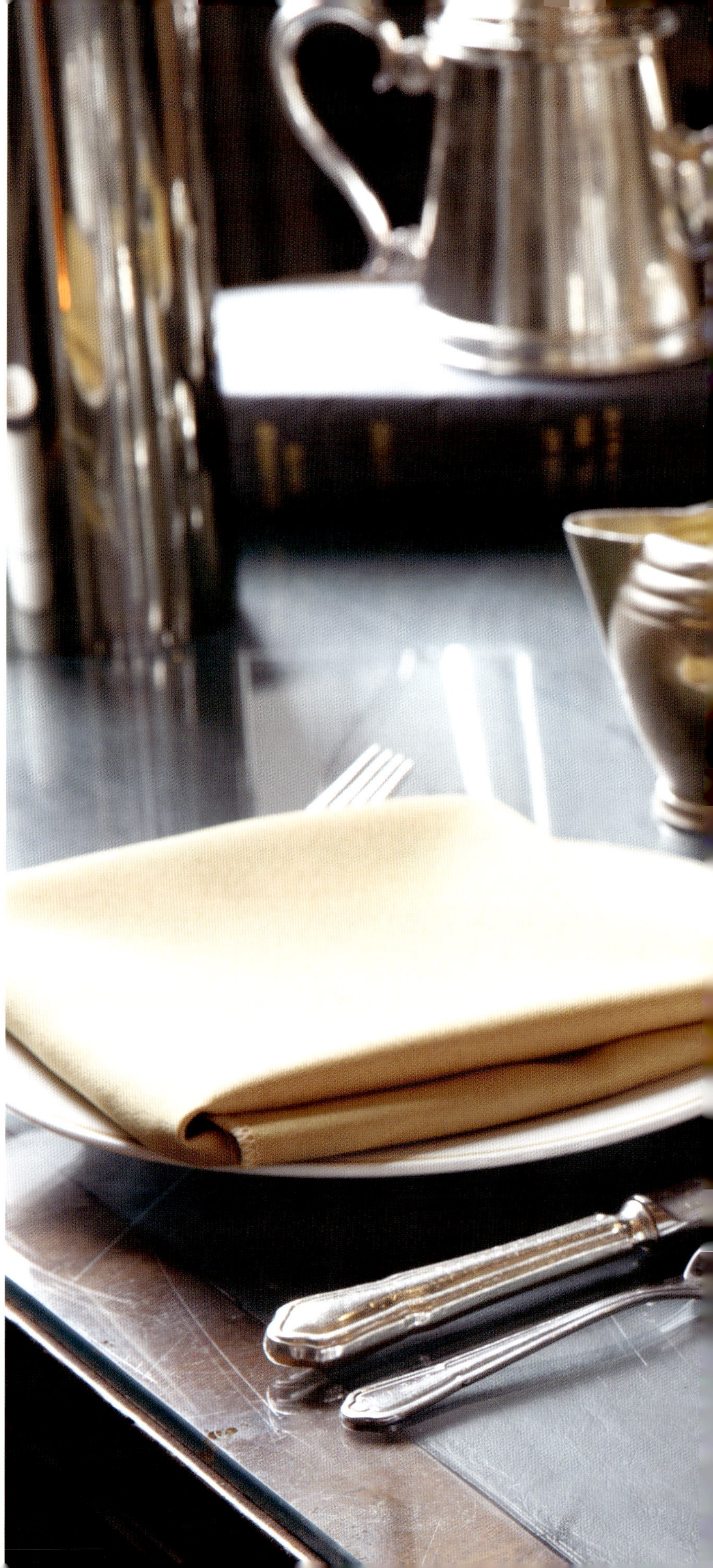

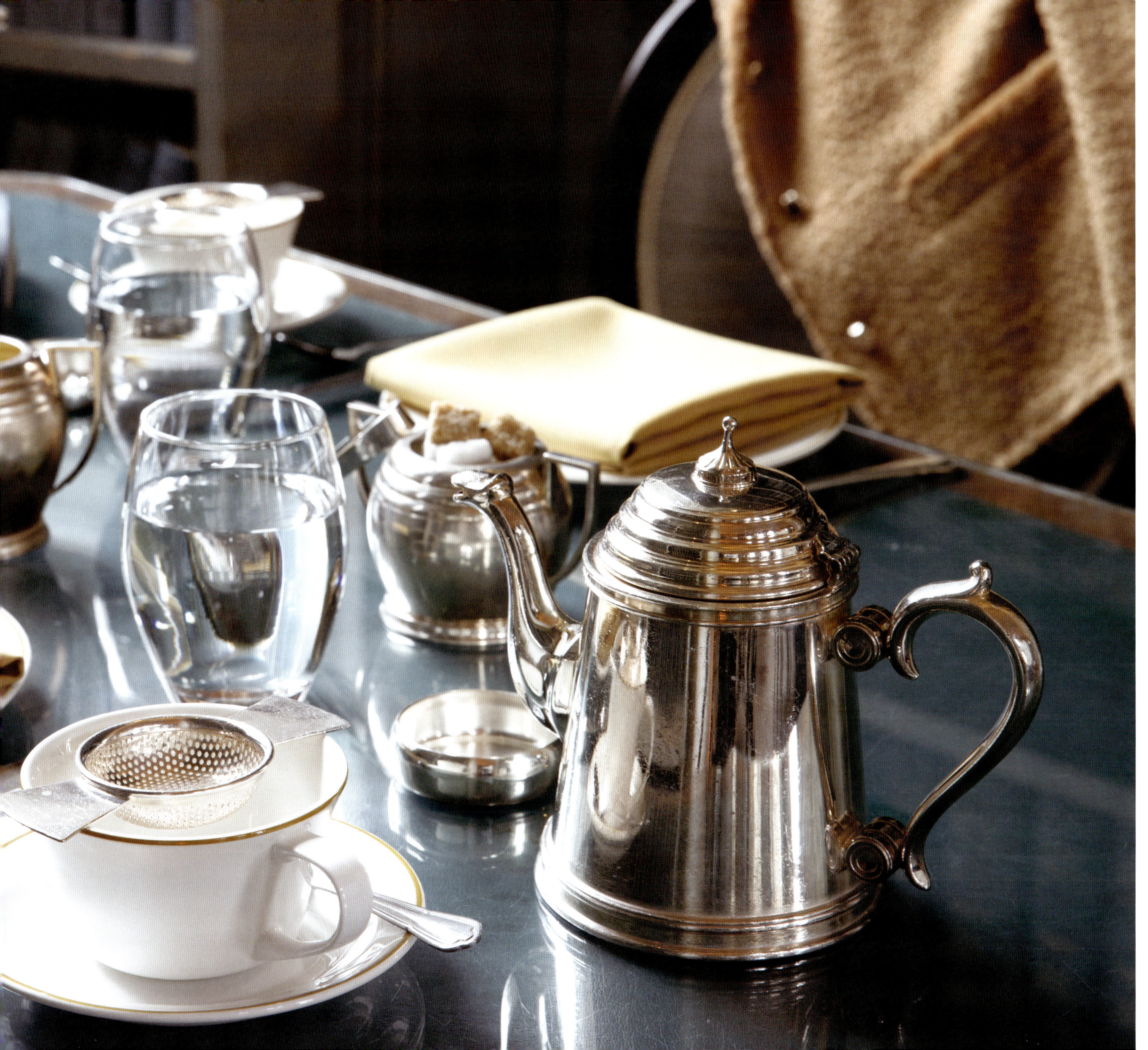

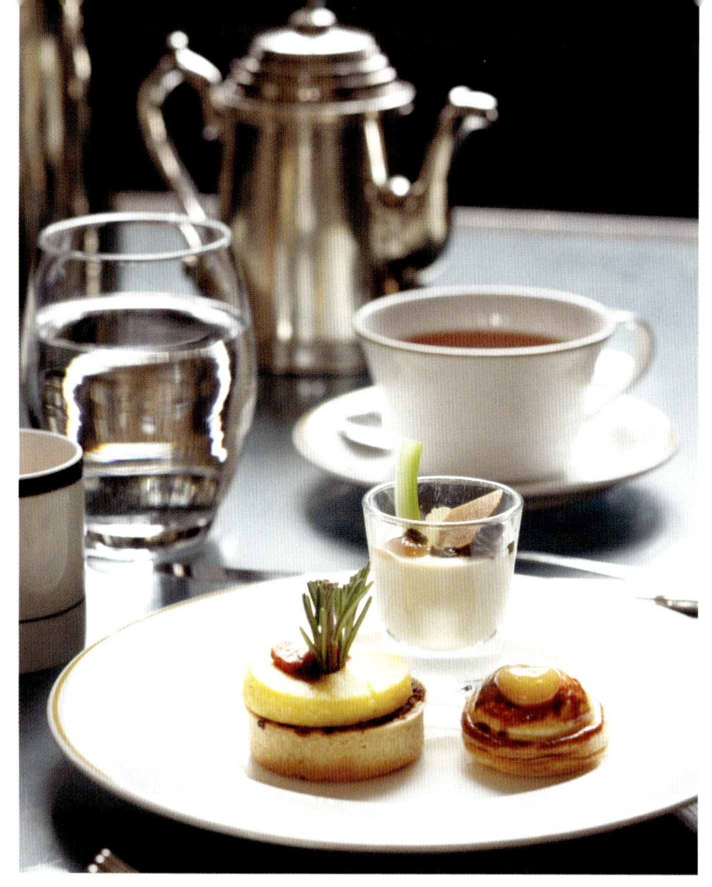
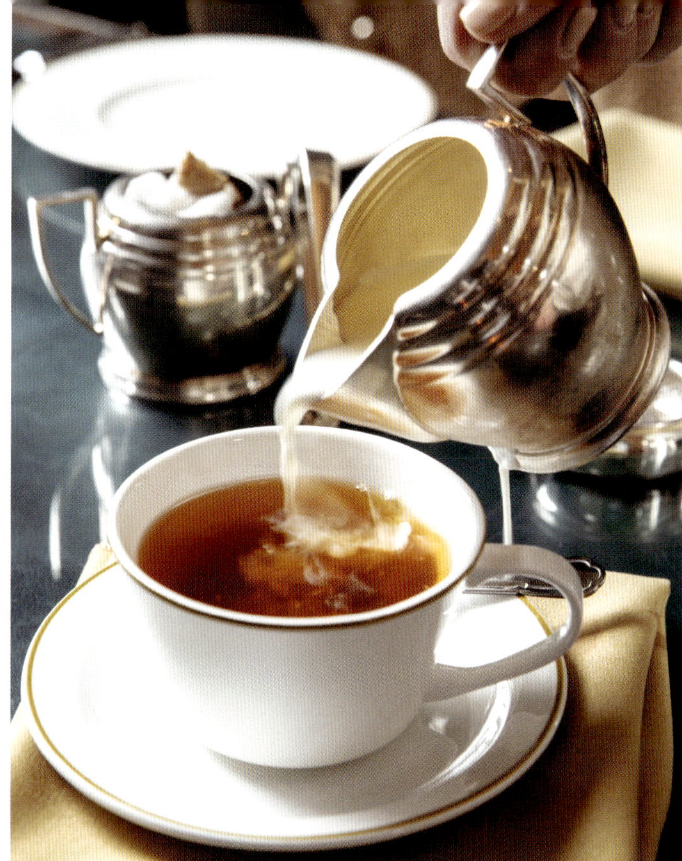
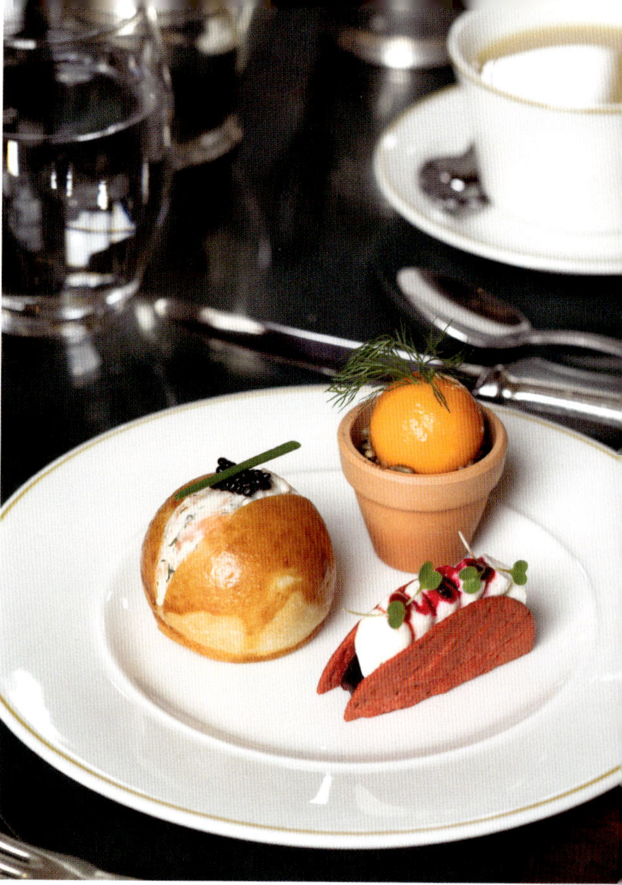
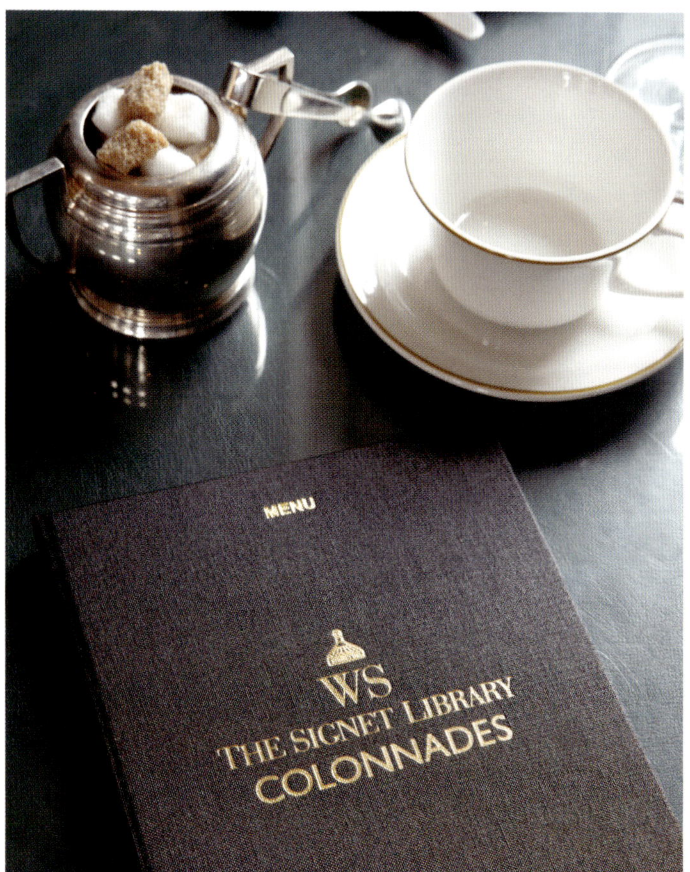
MENU
WS
THE SIGNET LIBRARY
COLONNADES
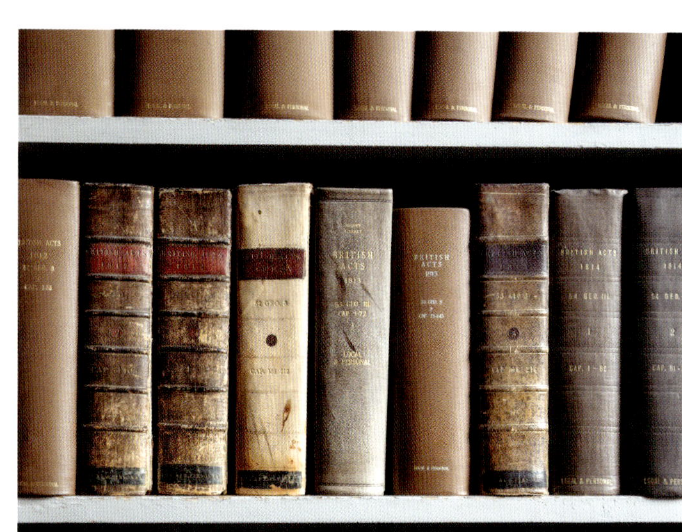
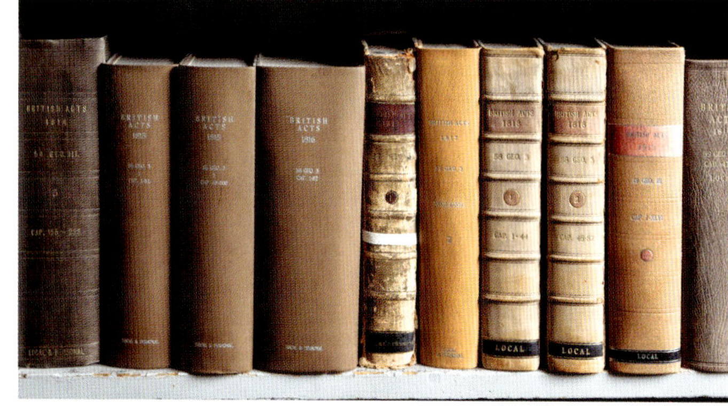
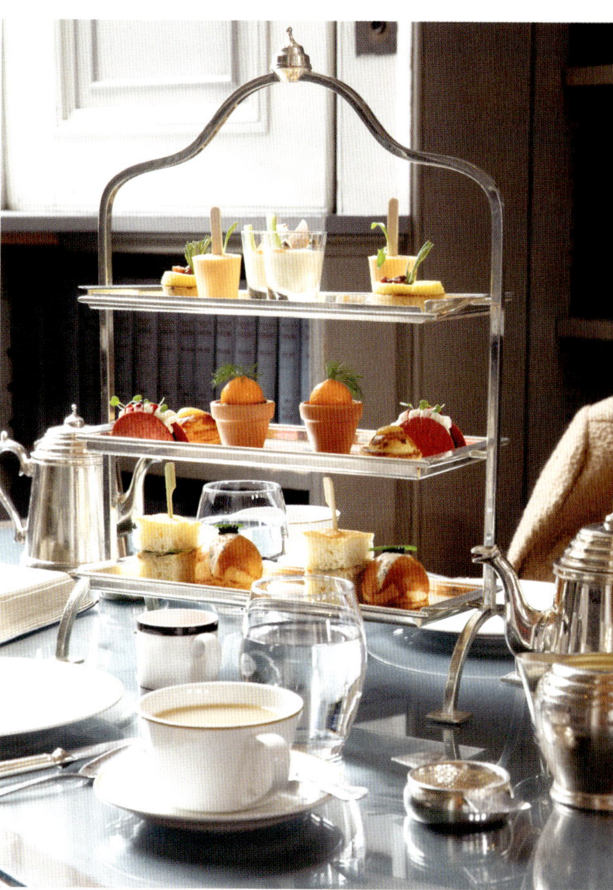

Opposite, clockwise from lower right: Custom-made three-tiered silver tea stands showcase the tearoom's scrumptious offerings, which range from traditional sweets and savories to unexpected flavor pairings that quickly become patrons' new favorites. Vintage volumes related to the law fill bookshelves in this working library. The salon serves a wonderful array of fine teas, including the exclusive Signet Blend, a mix of Assam and Ceylon. This page: The Signet Library is home to The Society of Writers to Her Majesty's Signet, which dates to the fifteenth century. The building itself was completed in 1822; a meticulous restoration returned it to its former glory, creating a splendid atmosphere for sipping and savoring.

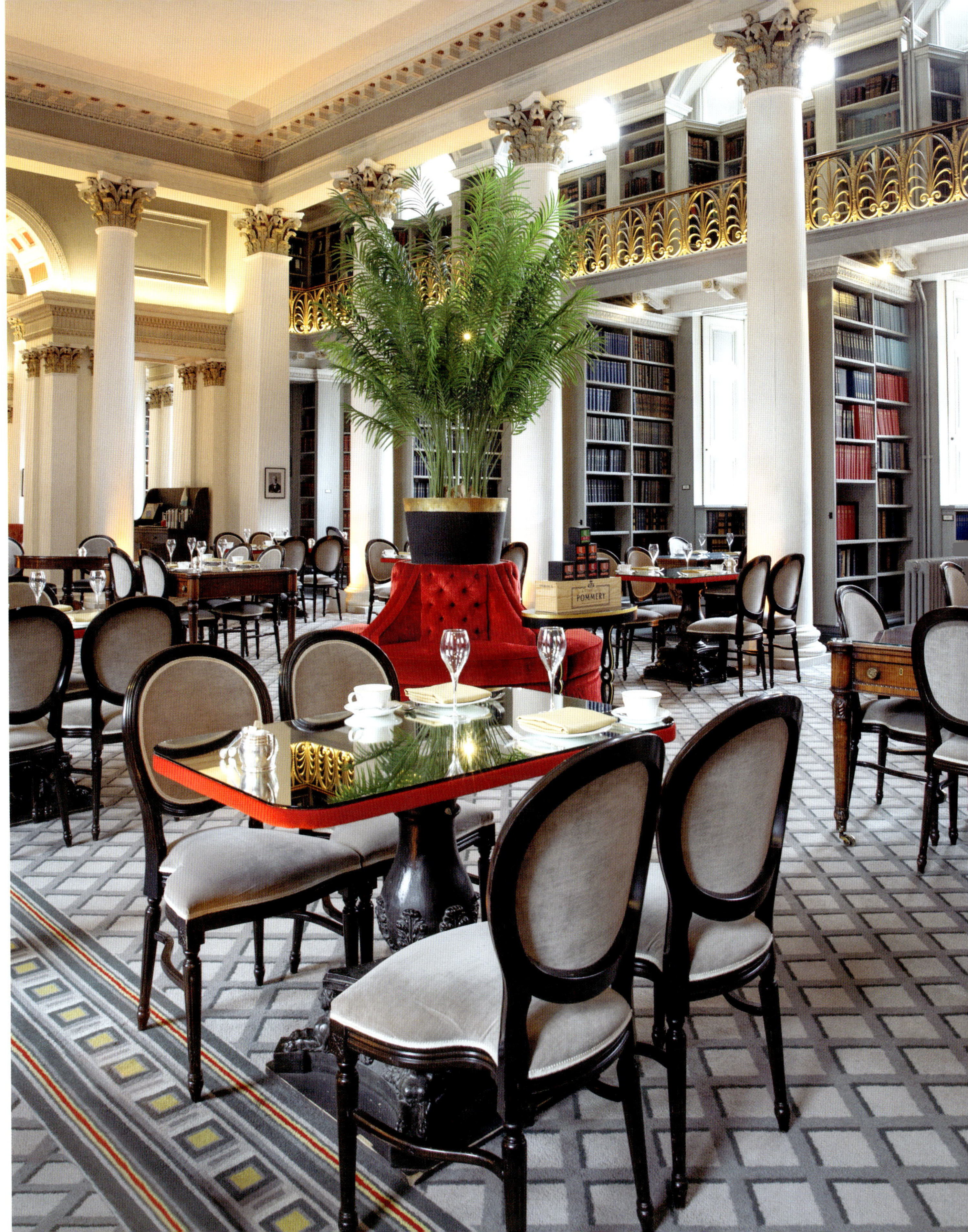

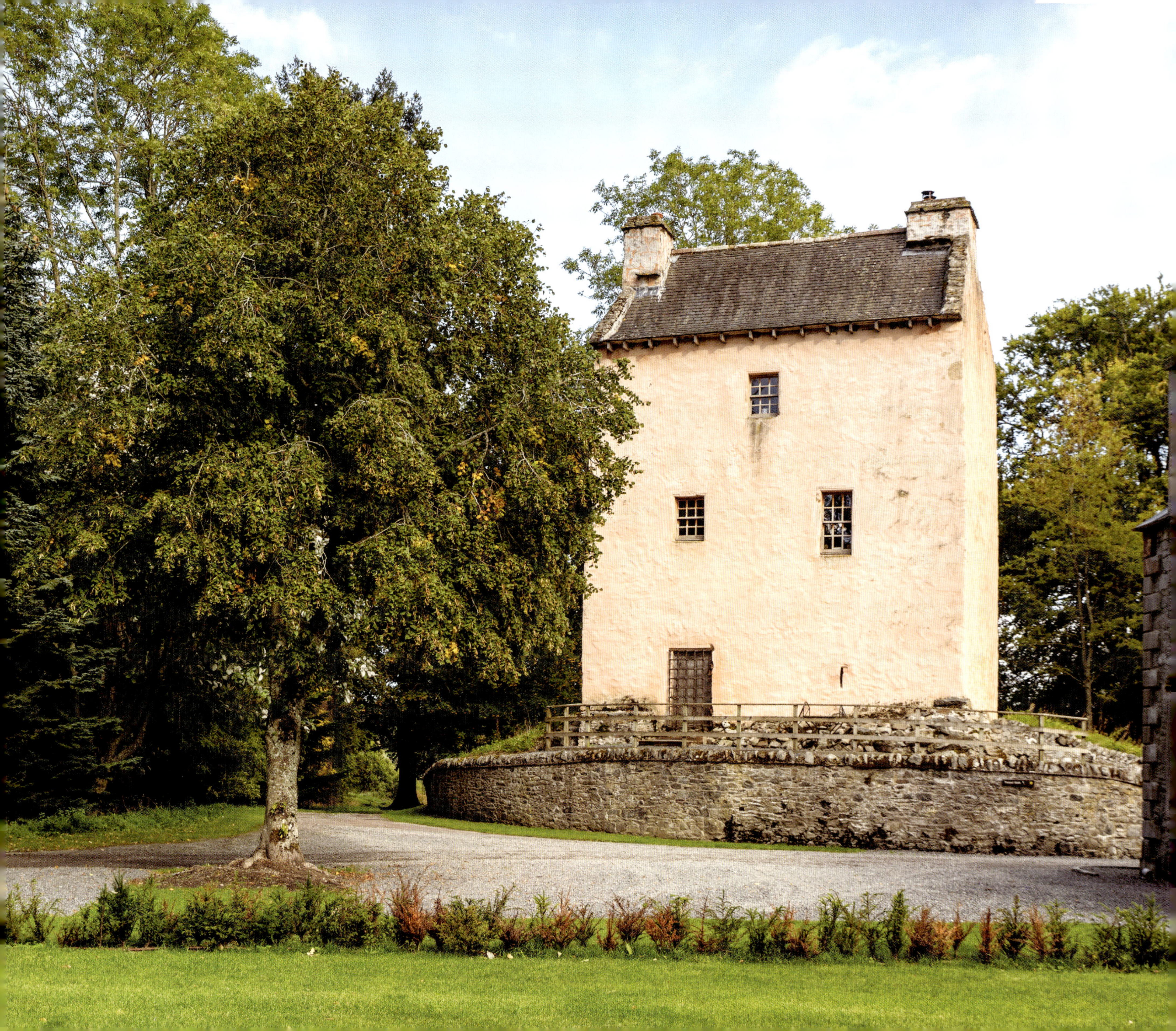

A TARRY IN THE HIGHLANDS

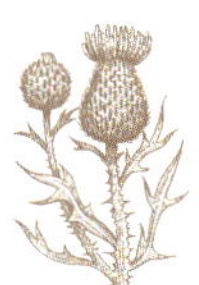

Built by the 4th Laird of Barns centuries ago, Barns Tower nestles into its pastoral setting near Neidpath Castle, just minutes from the enchanting burg of Peebles. This cozy getaway is set amid spectacular surrounds a stone's throw from the River Tweed. As September dances upon the rolling hills, late summer's faded green hues turn to burnished shades of gold, spreading an autumnal welcome mat for all who visit.

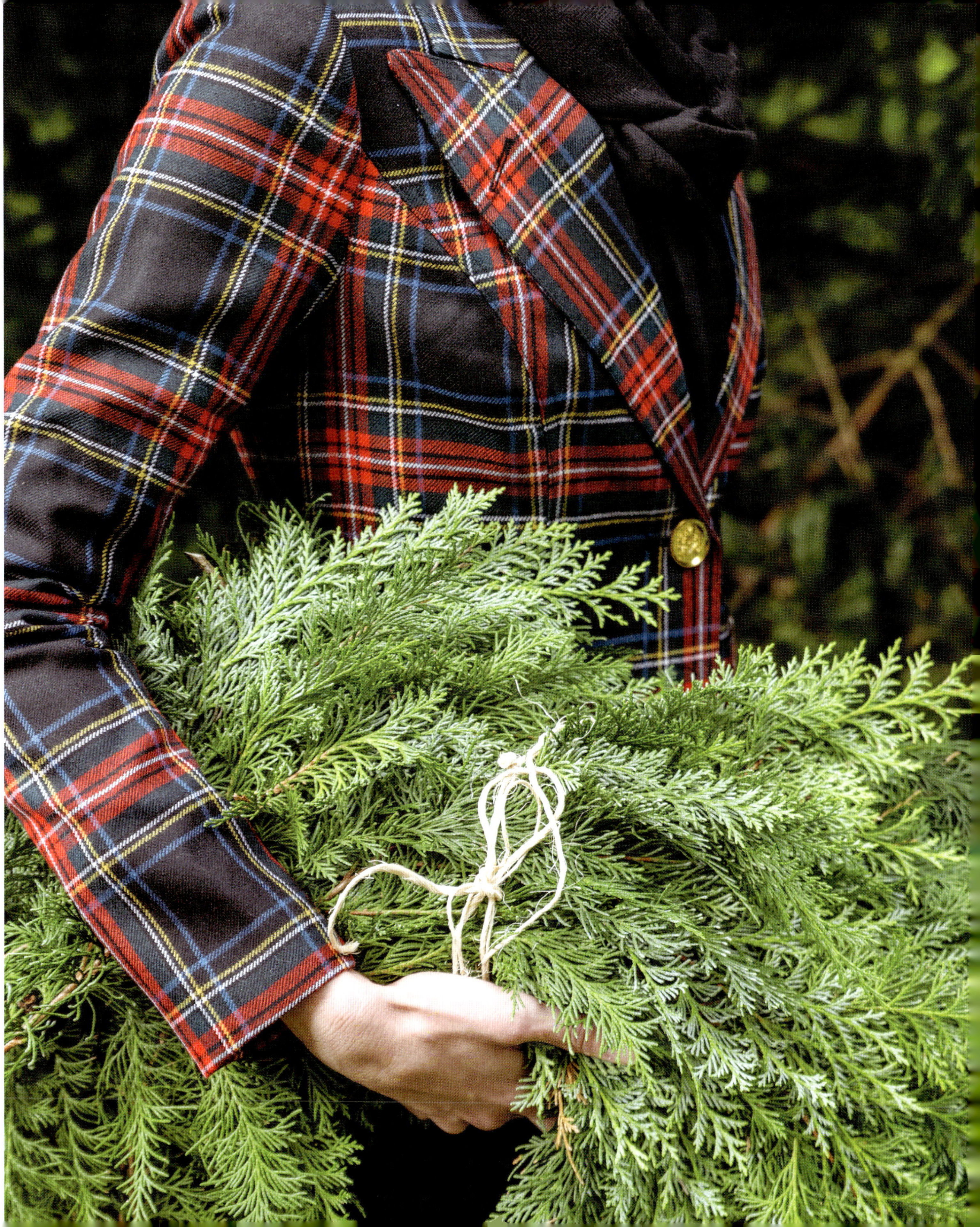

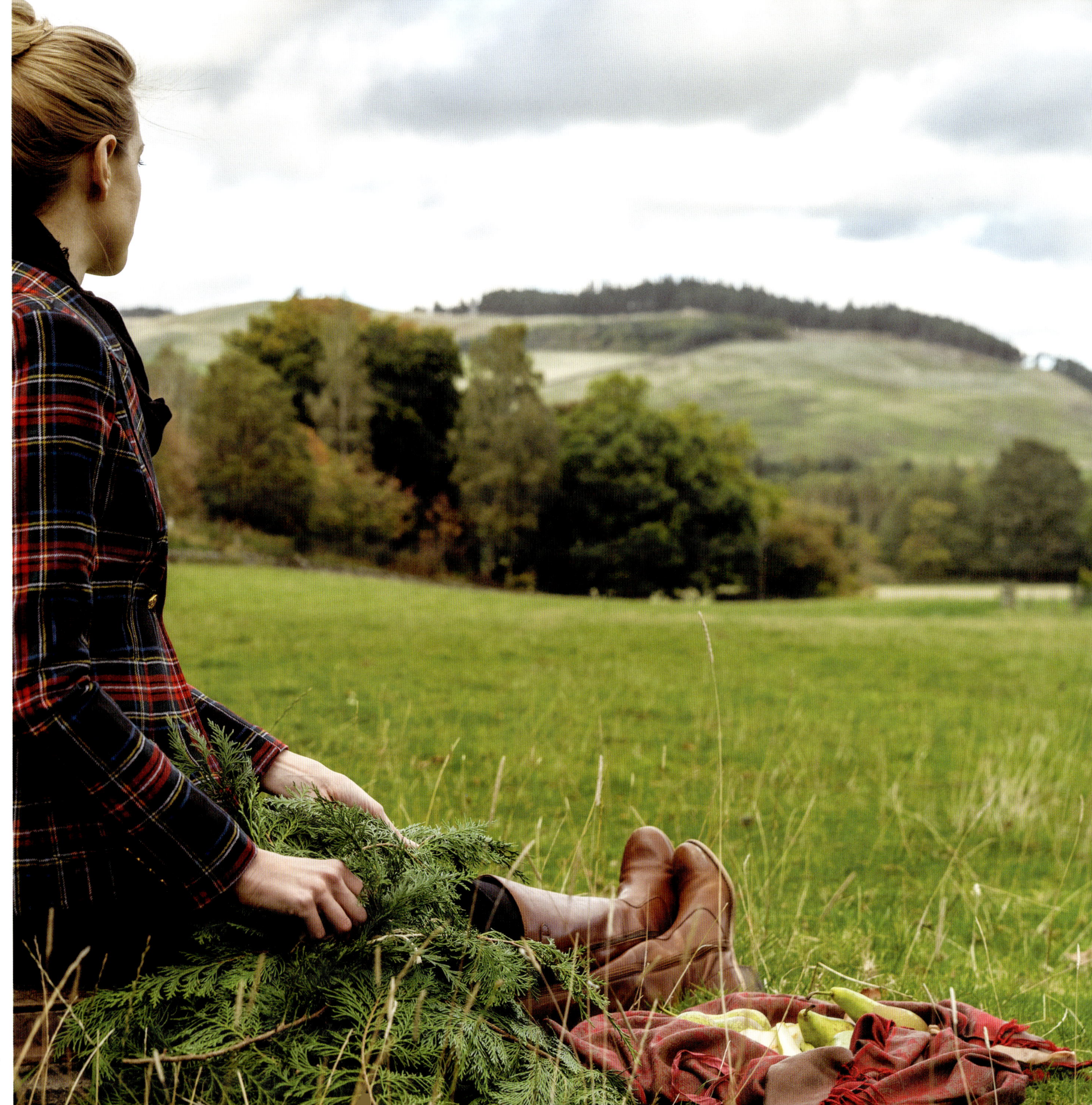

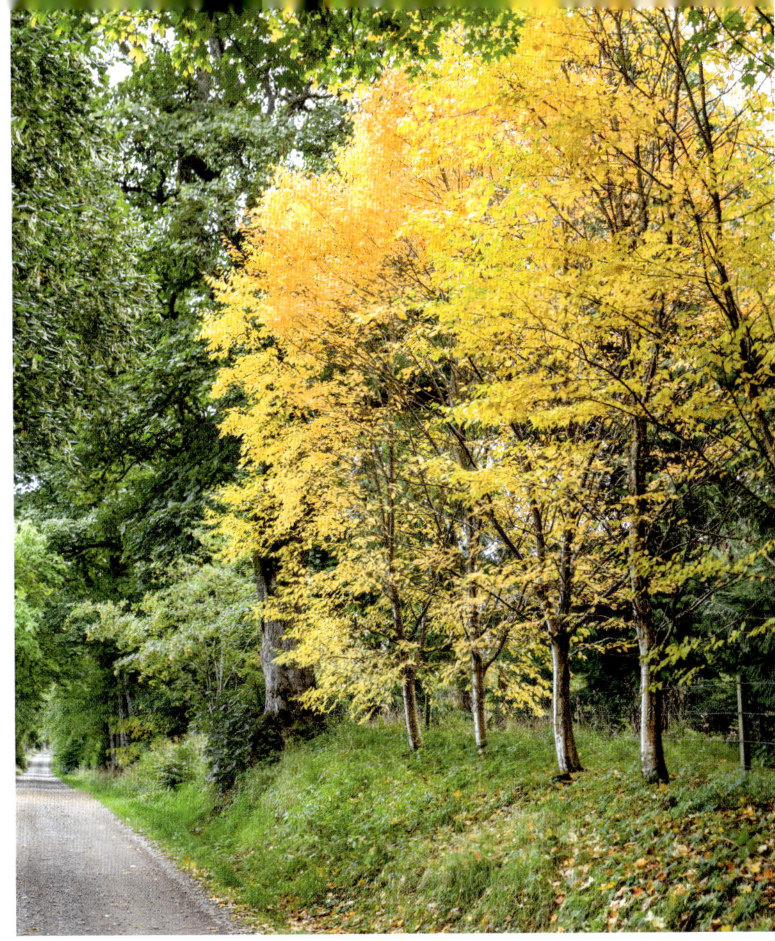

"Happiness flutters in the air whilst we rest among the breaths of nature."

—Kelly Sheaffer

Opposite and this page: Following an afternoon of gathering cedar boughs and other gleanings for fall arrangements, a lass dressed in a stylish Smithe tartan wool blazer pauses in her task to take in views of the Scottish countryside.

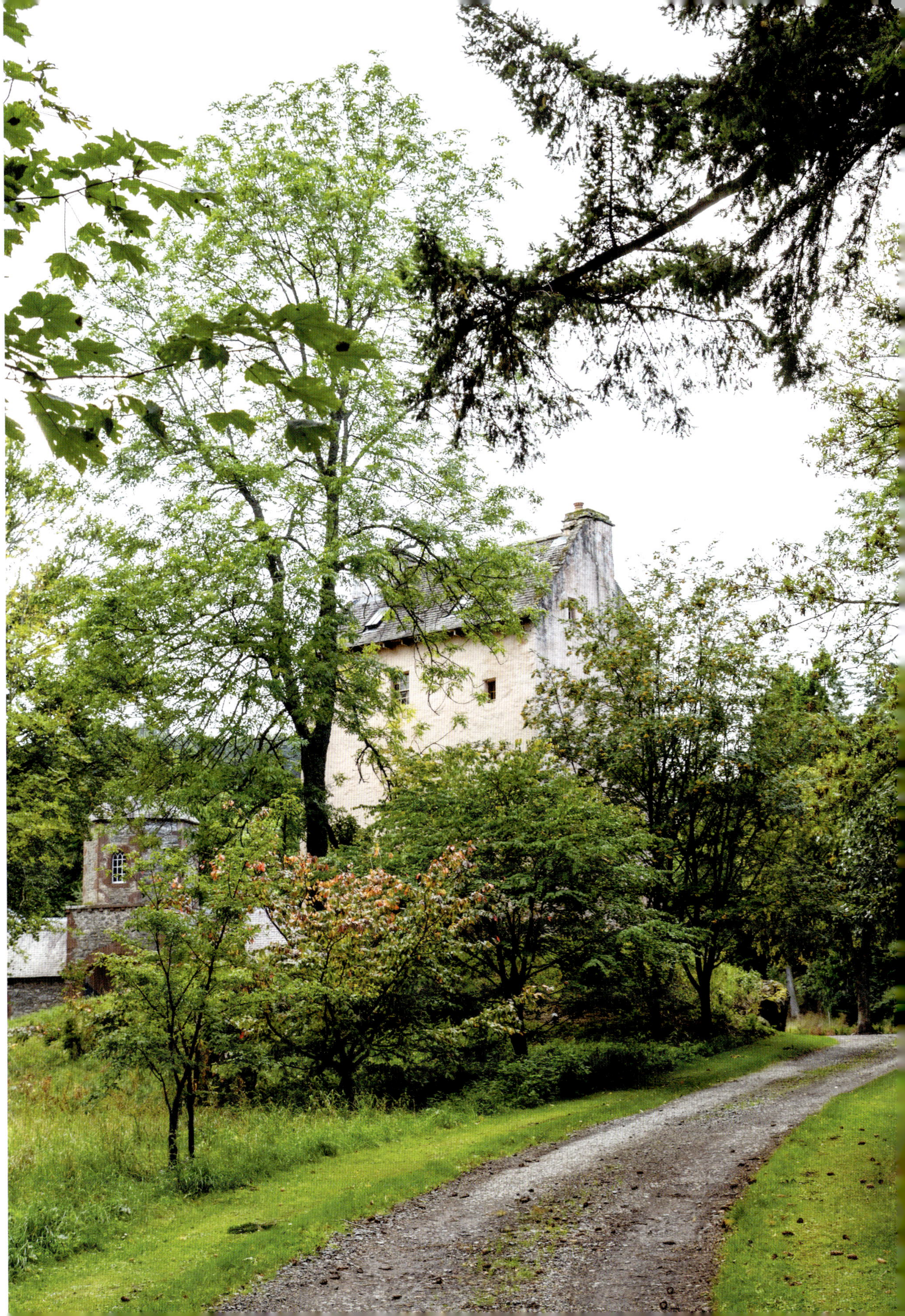

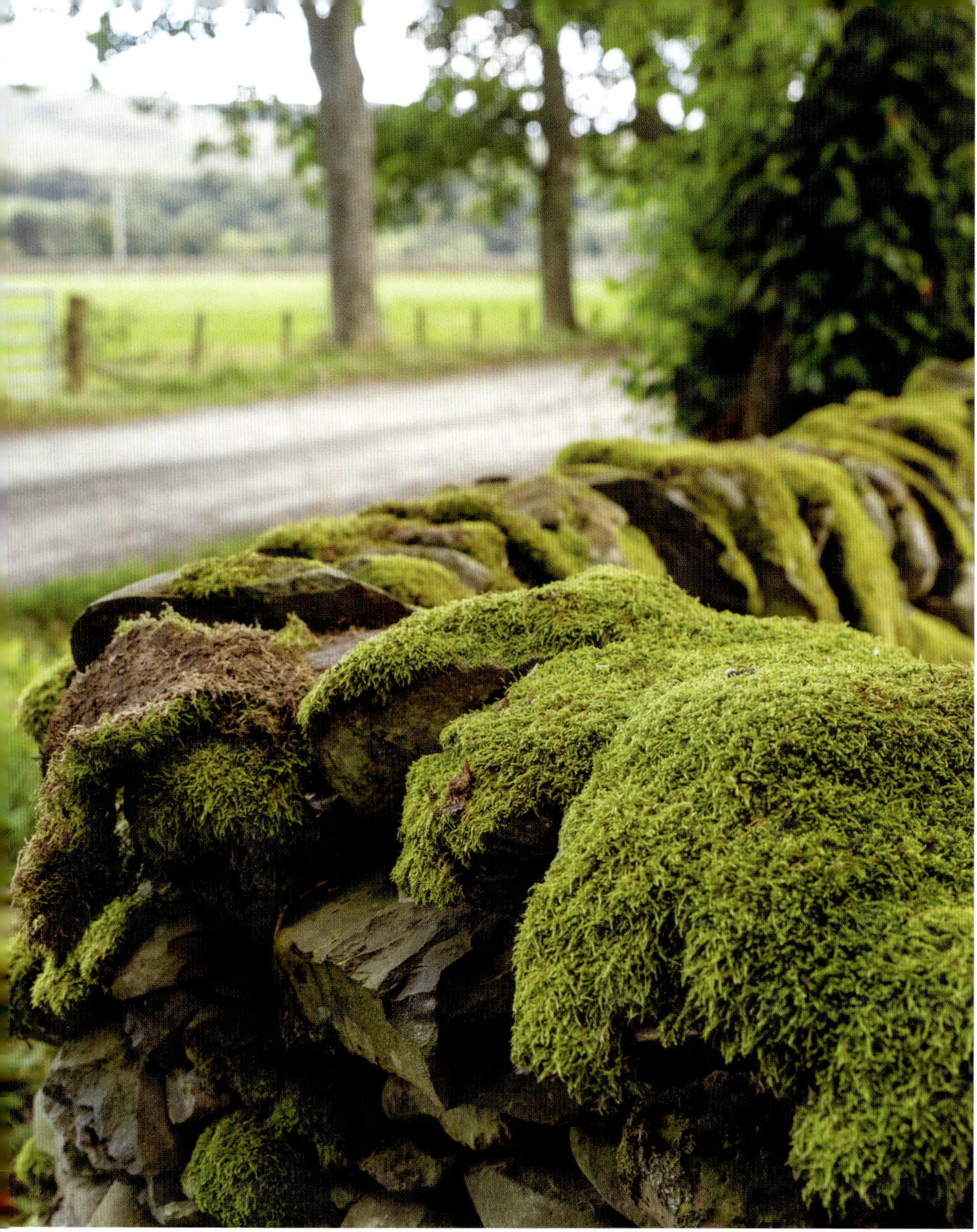

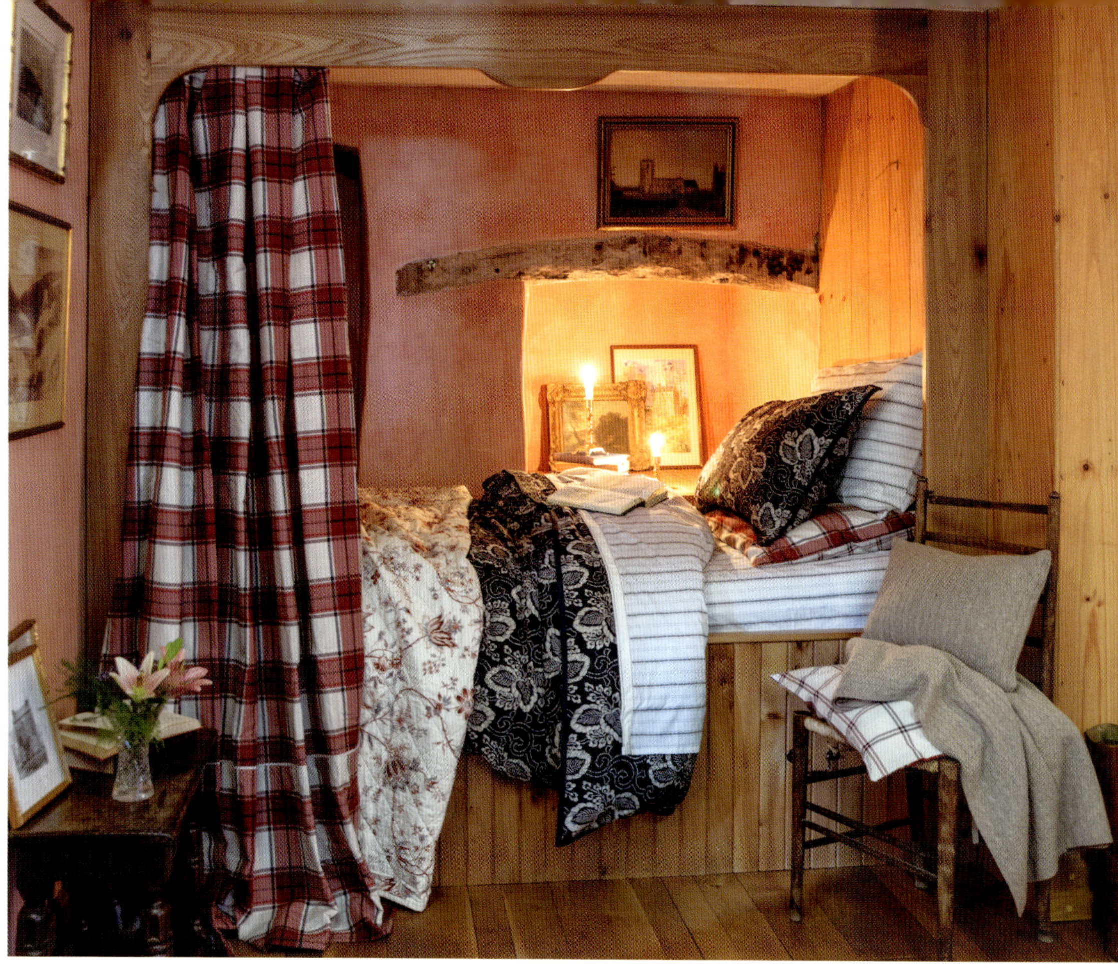

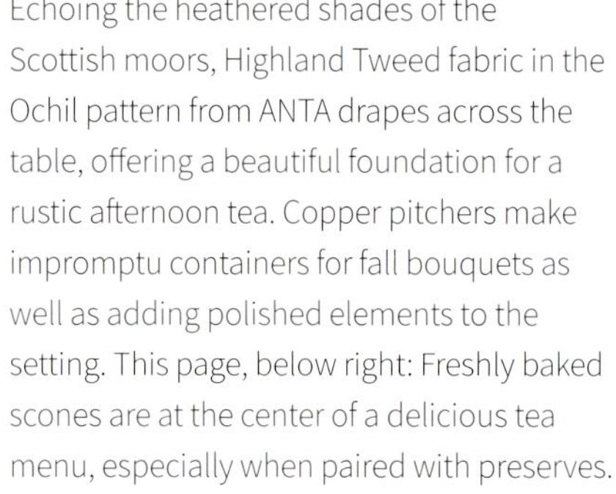

Echoing the heathered shades of the Scottish moors, Highland Tweed fabric in the Ochil pattern from ANTA drapes across the table, offering a beautiful foundation for a rustic afternoon tea. Copper pitchers make impromptu containers for fall bouquets as well as adding polished elements to the setting. This page, below right: Freshly baked scones are at the center of a delicious tea menu, especially when paired with preserves.

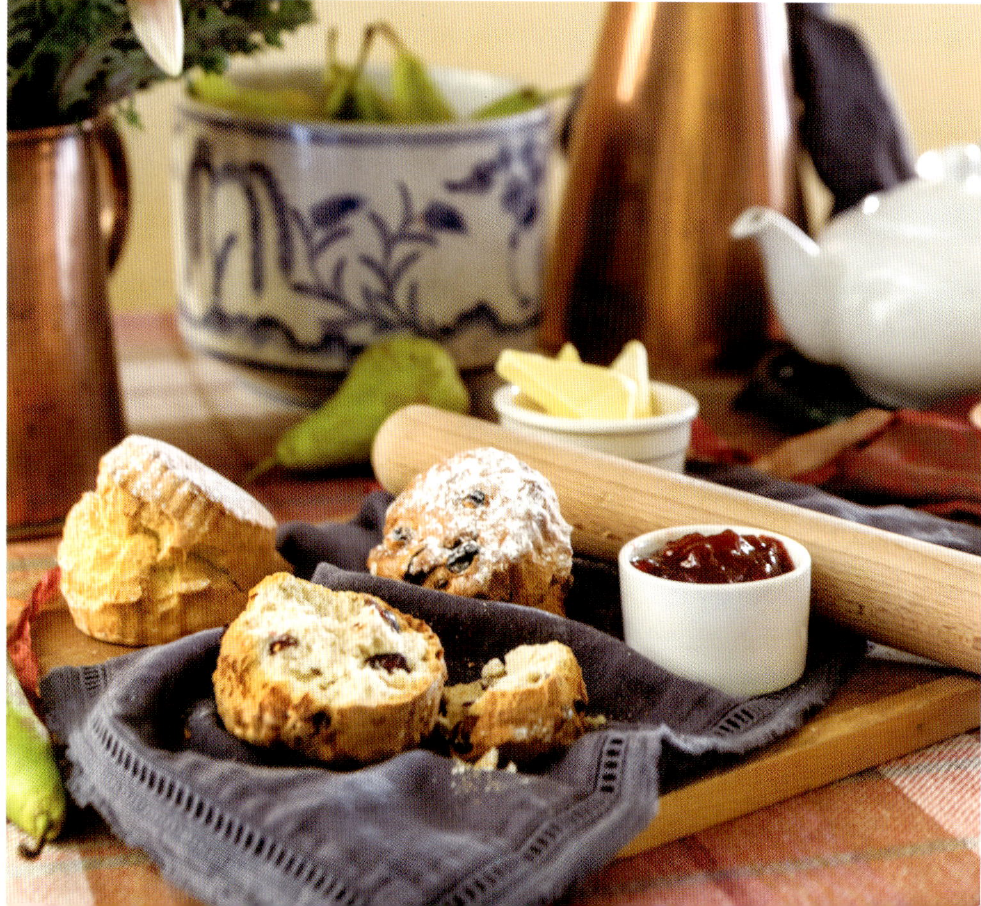

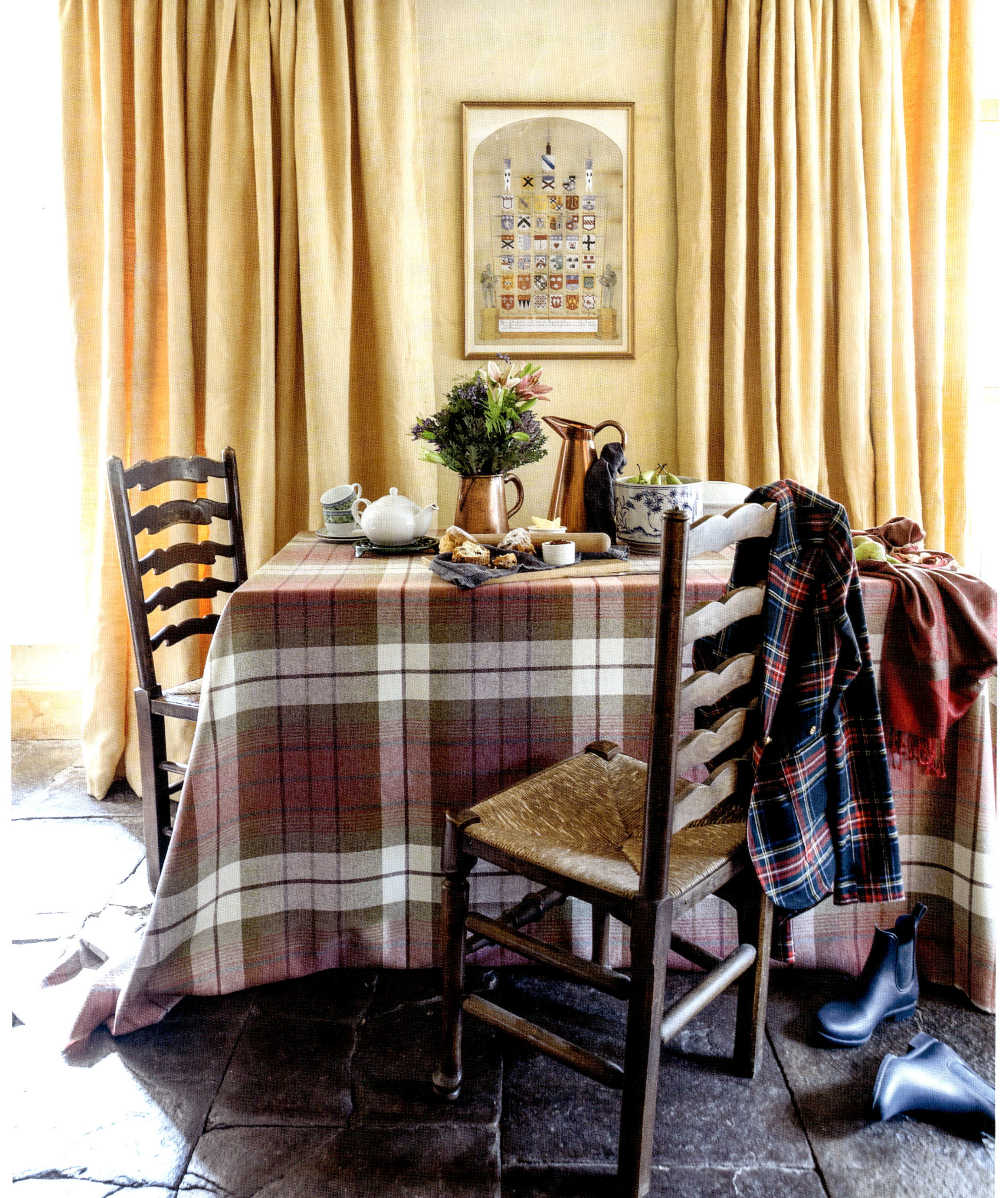

TAILORING A LEGACY

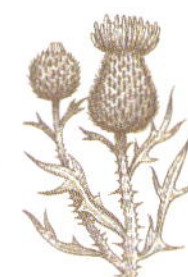

In a bucolic village ten miles west of Inverness, one finds a venerable establishment where a heritage of craftsmanship is preserved in every stitch. Since opening in 1858, Campbell's of Beauly has specialized in bespoke garments fit for royalty and has the honor of being awarded a Royal Warrant issued by King Charles III.

"We're a unique hidden gem," says John Sugden, who, along with his wife Nicola, took the reins of Campbell's from the previous owners in 2015. They strove to preserve character and charm, retaining original fixtures and fittings that endear the shop to loyal patrons.

While renowned for their Highland dress—it's likely that many of the kilts or tartan trews gracing dance floors when Highland reels are in full swing were sewn by the clothier's talented tailors and seamstresses—the business is perhaps even better known for sporting wear and has a long history of working with estates to design the perfect tweed pattern for each landscape. Taking cues from rocky glens, velvety moss, earthy bracken, or the golden glow of wild gorse, it's almost as if the land itself weaves through the fabric.

In addition to helping one blend with surroundings, tweed also exudes a timeless elegance and serves to keep the country's notorious chill at bay. Those seeking further sartorial Scottish options are sure to appreciate the array of woolen warmers that line the shelves of the emporium and offer a shopping experience that transcends trends to celebrate quintessential Caledonian style.

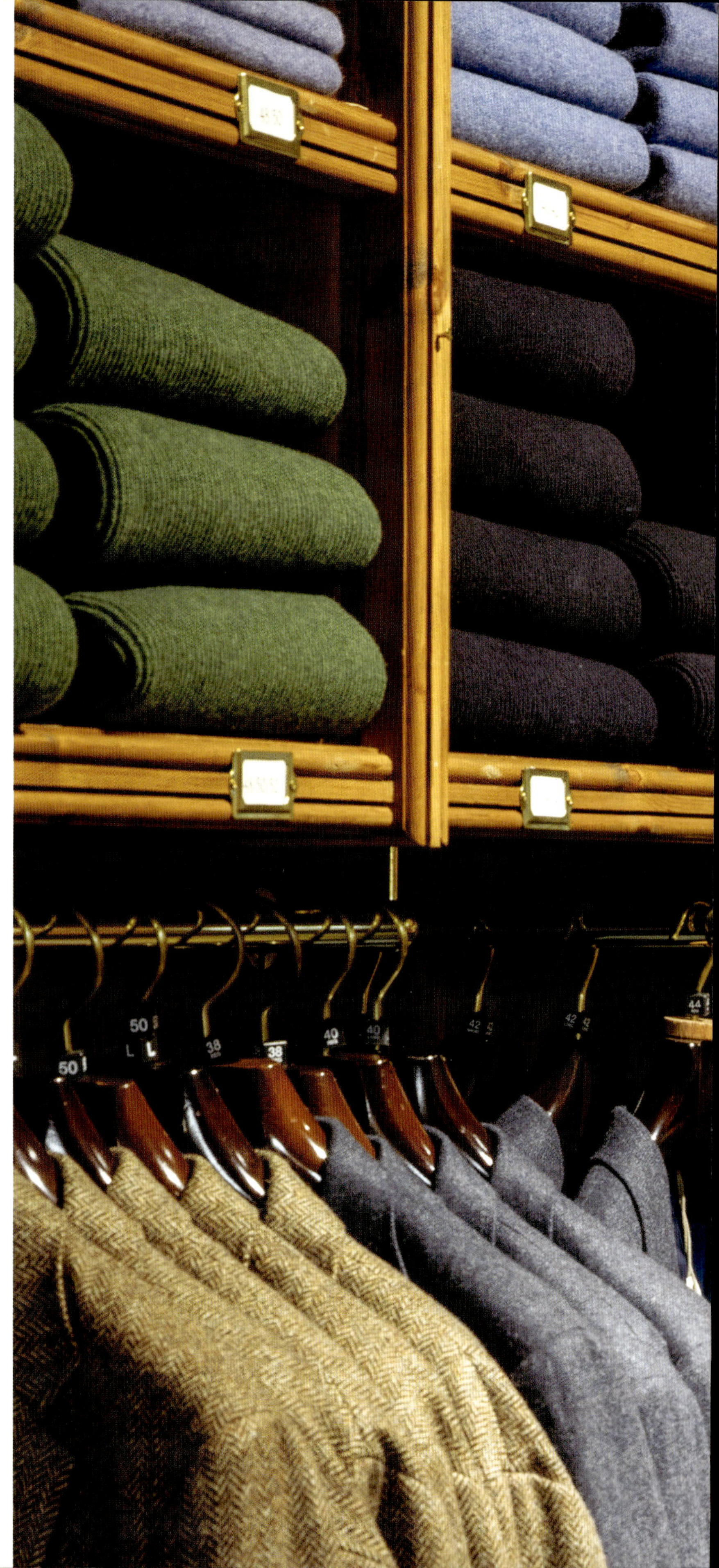

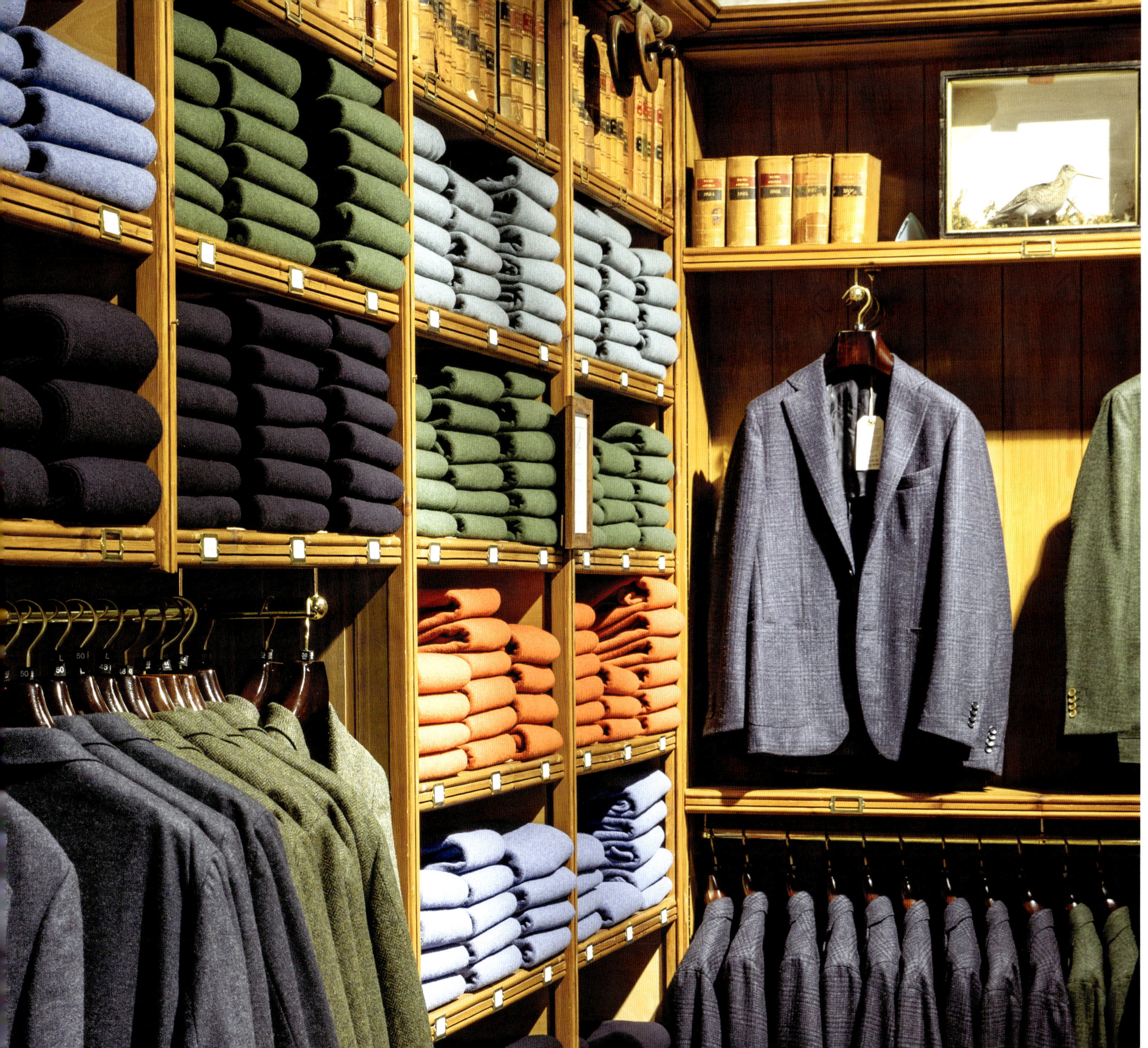

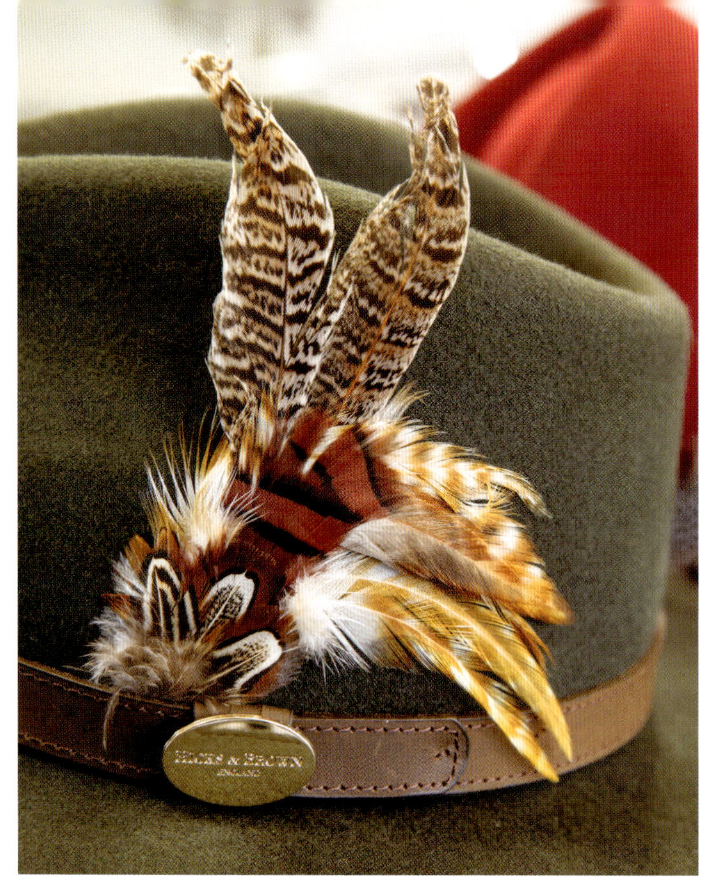
HICKS & BROWN

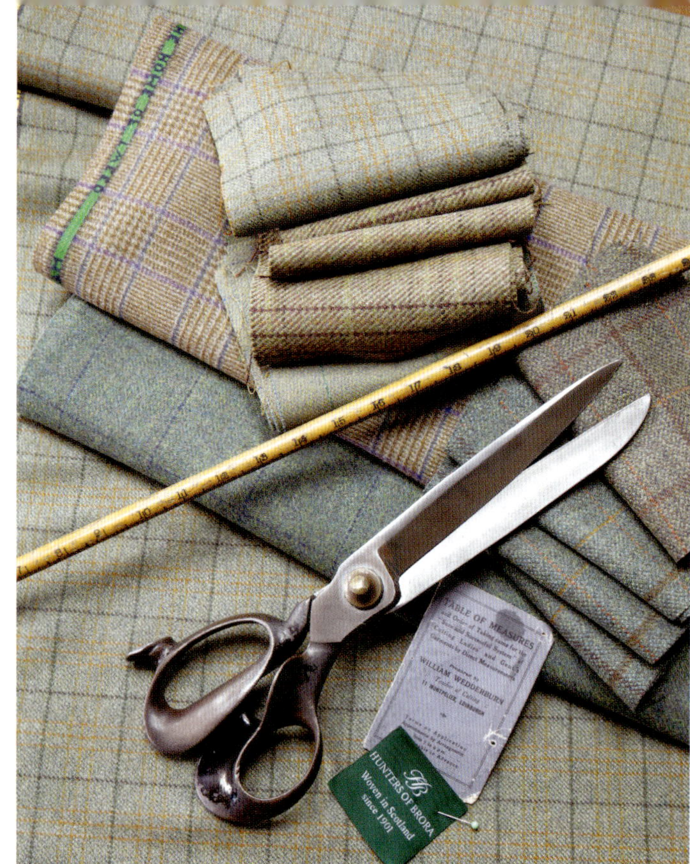

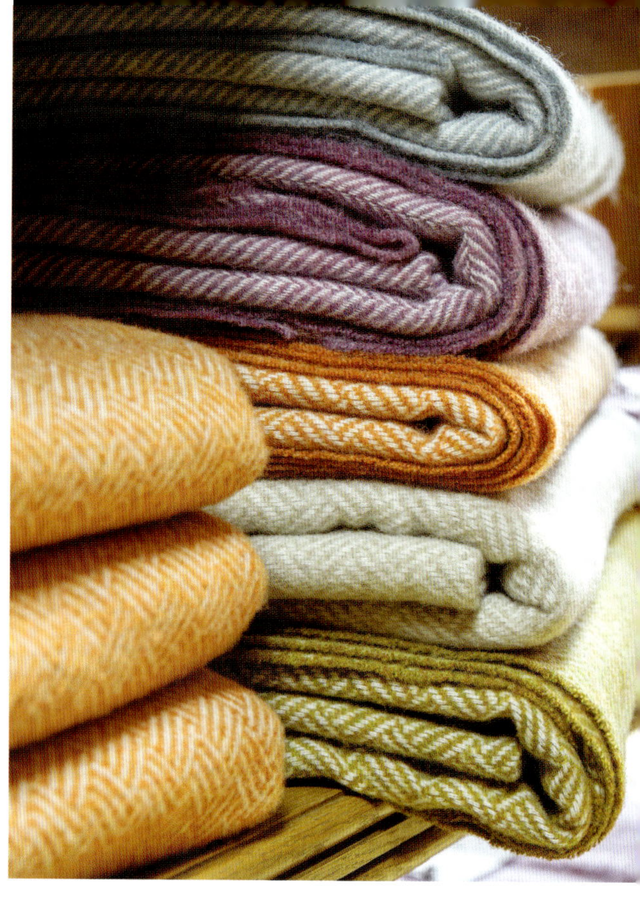

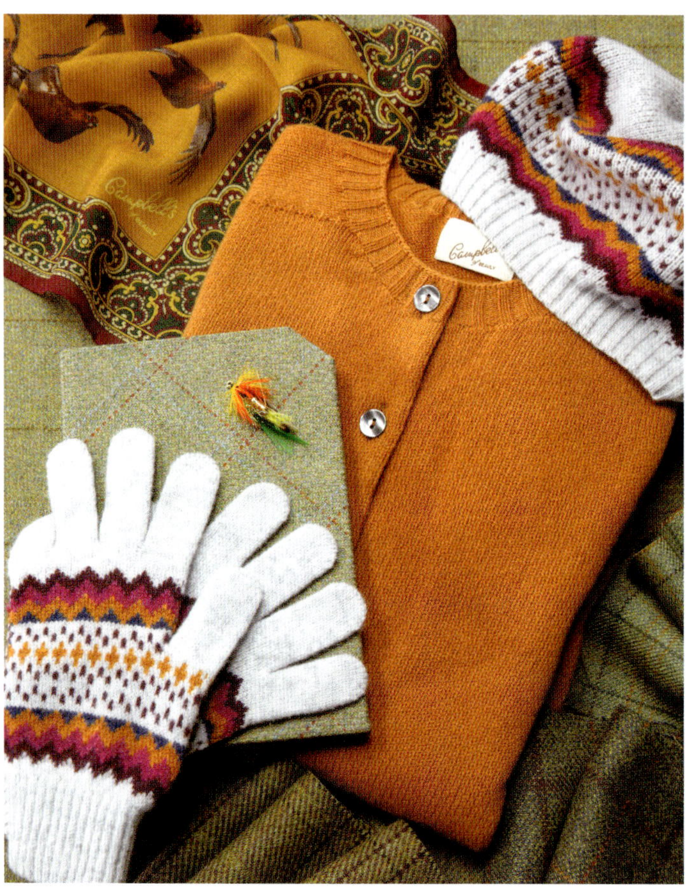

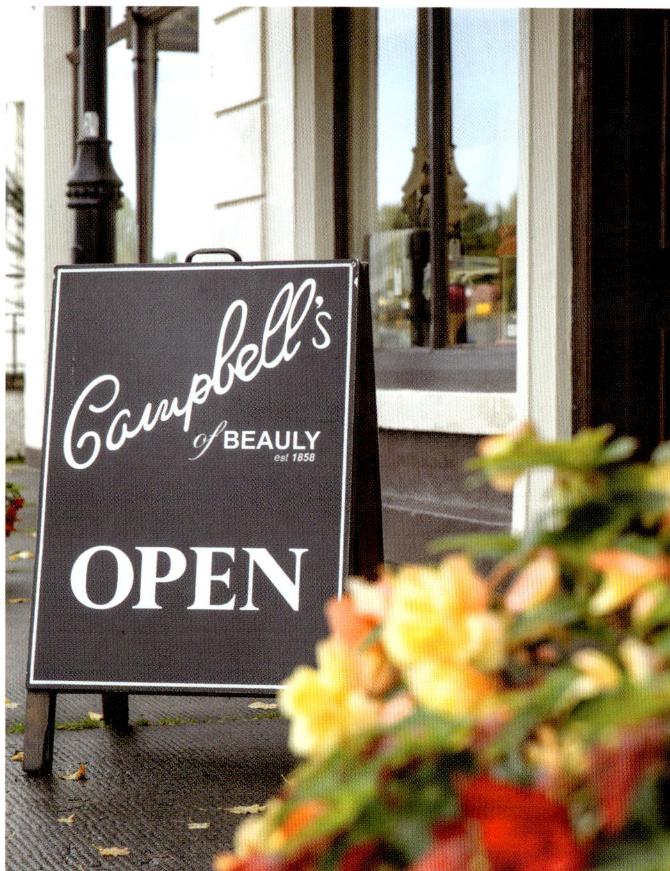
Campbell's
of BEAULY
est 1858
OPEN

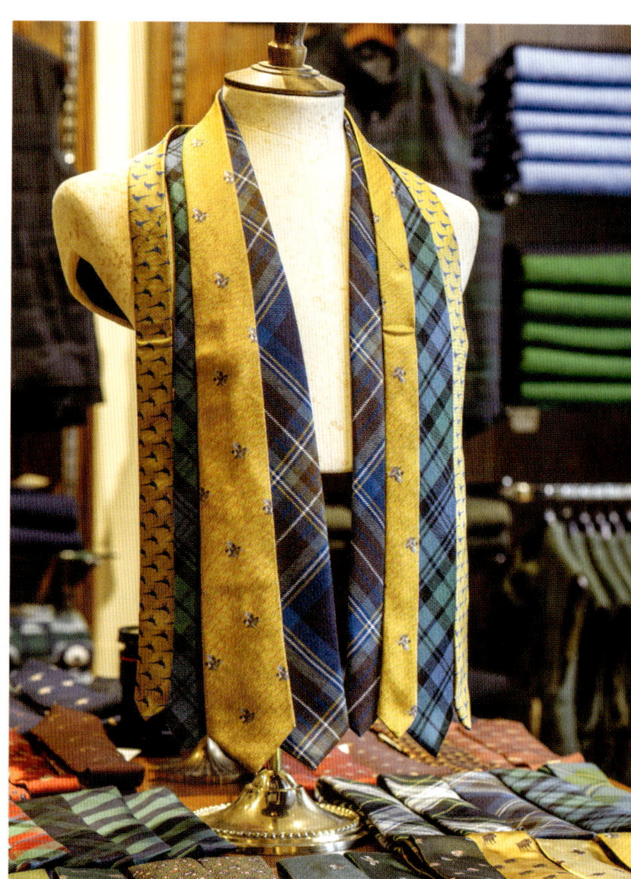

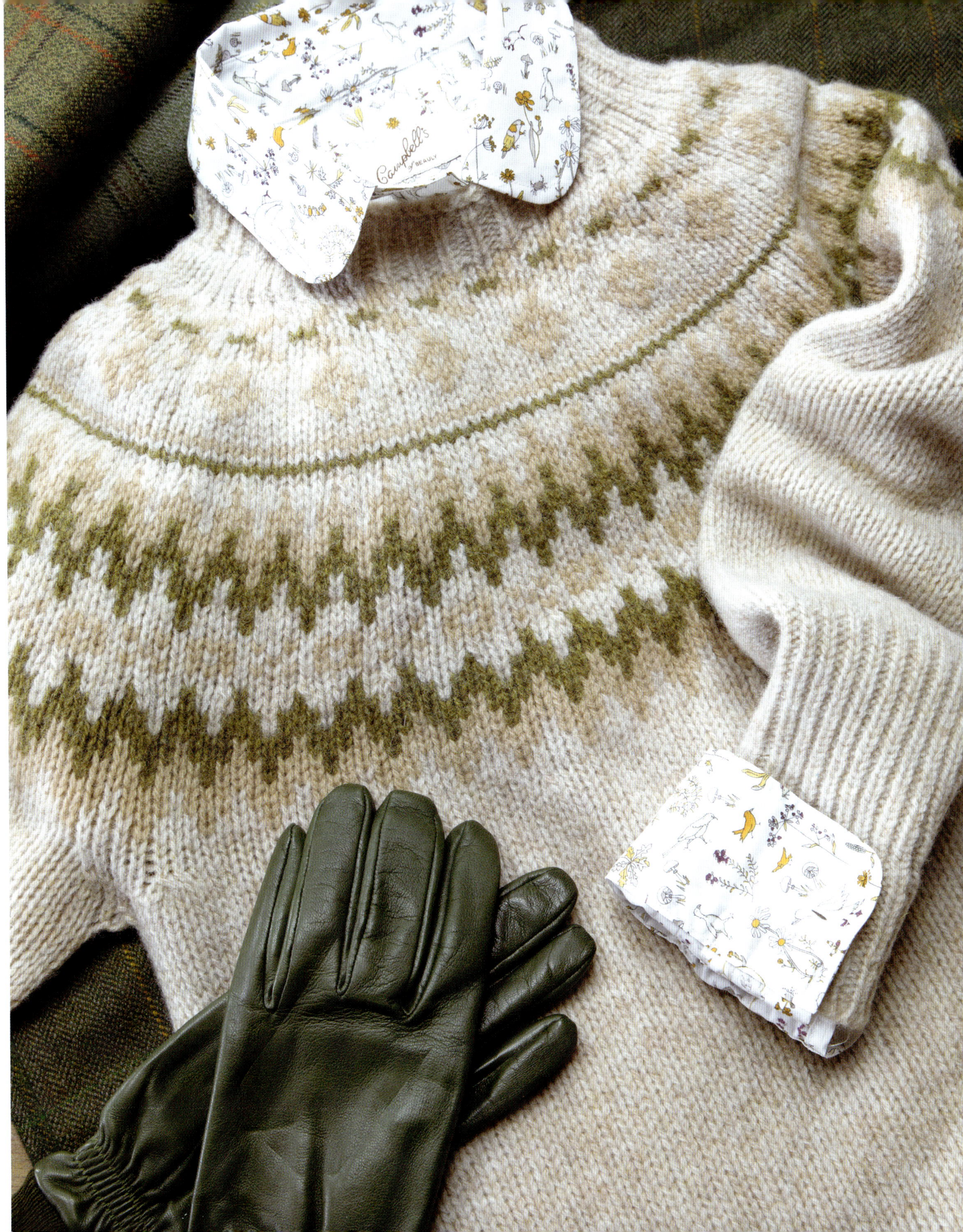

Right: Knit in Scotland with high-quality Shetland wool, a cozy Fair Isle jumper promises warmth for even the coldest of days. The sweetly curved collar of a Liberty-print blouse peeks out from the crew neck sweater, fashioning an effortlessly chic look. Opposite, clockwise from top left: The Suffolk Fedora from British brand Hicks & Brown is a classic topper embellished with a flourish of feathers. Bespoke offerings at Campbell's of Beauly include measuring clients in-house in order to create perfectly proportioned hand-sewn garments. Easy to tuck into a suitcase are cashmere scarves and wool or wool-silk neckties. Upon visiting for the first time, patrons will be amazed to peruse the shop's extensive array of wares, including garments, accessories, and more.

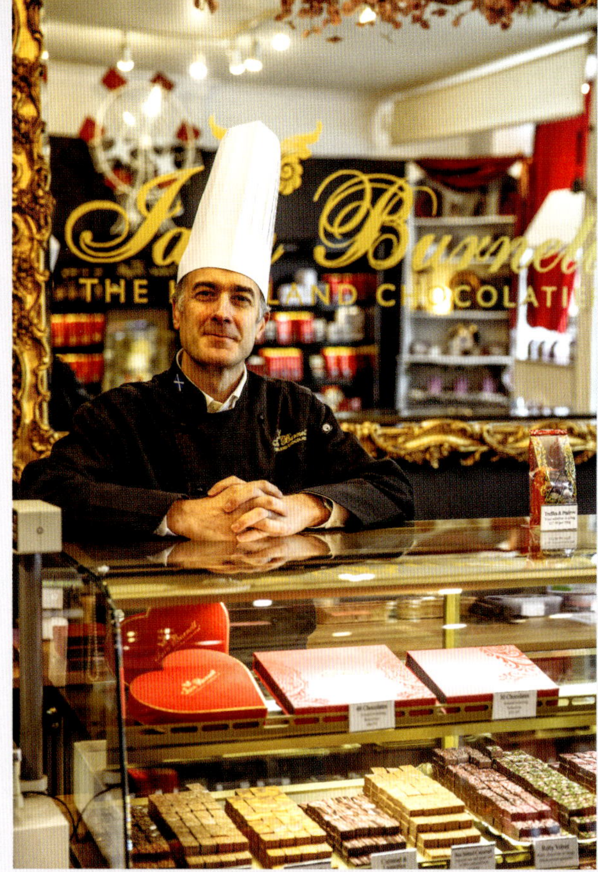

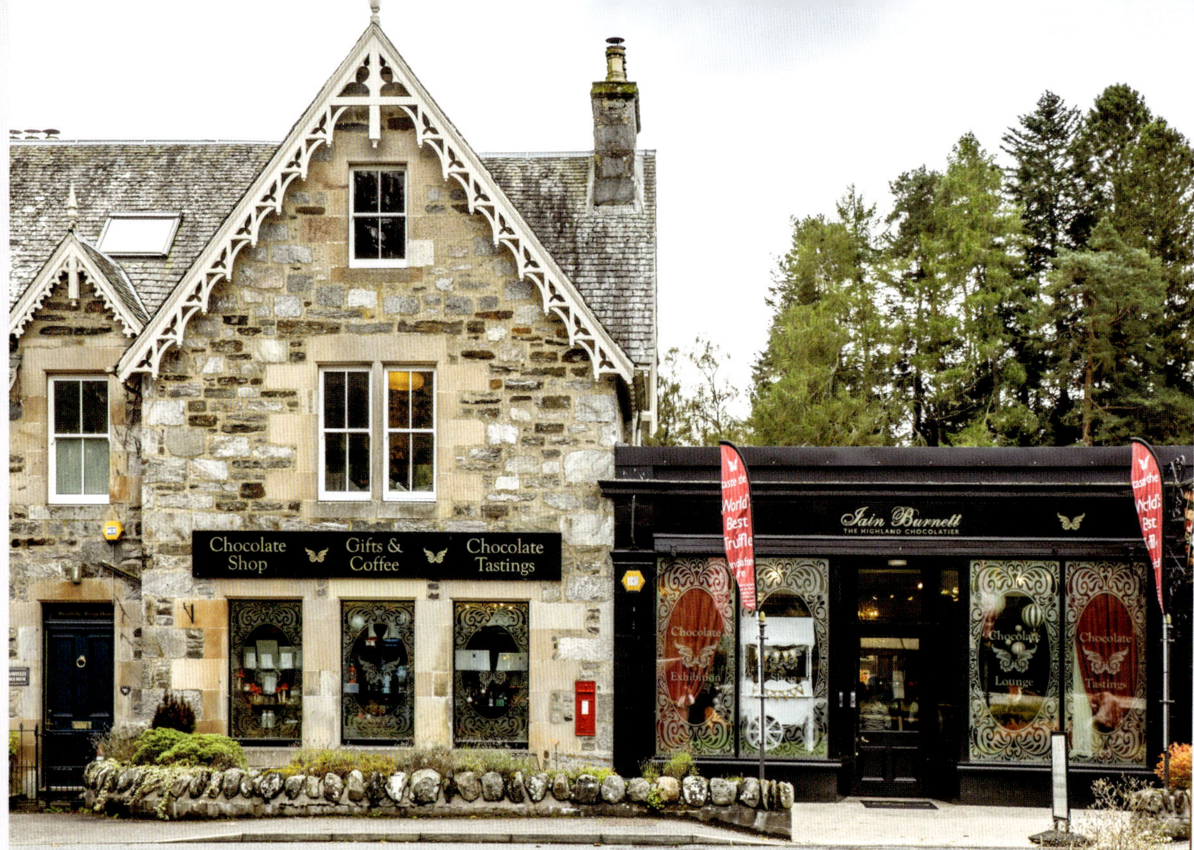

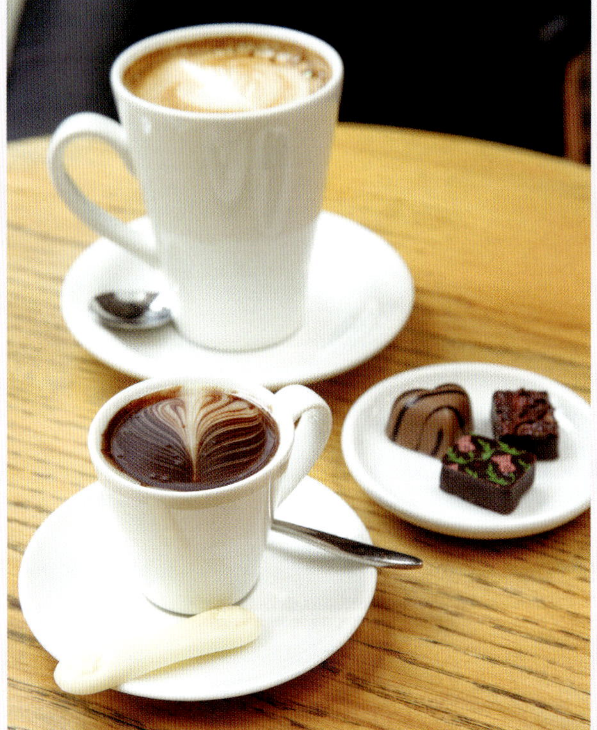

A Sweet Escape

Tucked in Perthshire amid heather-filled glens and crystalline waters a whimsical shop appears as if from a fairy tale, drawing patrons with the promise of decadent cocoa confections. Its menu of artisanal chocolates and pralines has graced the dessert course plates of Michelin Star restaurants, luxury hotels, and Queen Elizabeth II's table.

Ideally situated a stone's throw from dairies and apiaries, Highland Chocolatier selects the finest cream from herds of Scottish Friesian cows and local honey, blending these with the rich taste of cocoa from the volcanic island of São Tomé.

Trained by culinarily talented parents and later under experts of French, Belgian, and Swiss schools, Master Chocolatier Iain Burnett melds tutelage with a naturally gifted palate.

The velvet truffle stands out as a personal and customer favorite, with a soft ganache encircling sumptuous fillings. Iain maintains the three-day method of production is well worth the effort, as the end result nears magic, garnering dozens of industry awards as well as satisfied grins from sweet-toothed guests dining at the shop.

To experience the full array of offerings at Highland Chocolatier, a tasting flight showcases the artistry and flavor of each morsel. Iain may pair fresh fruits with silky chocolate, but perhaps the greatest ingredients he employs are an unyielding determination to constantly improve his craft and the desire to serve customers with graciousness. "It's not about telling them how to taste," he shares. "It's about their discovery."

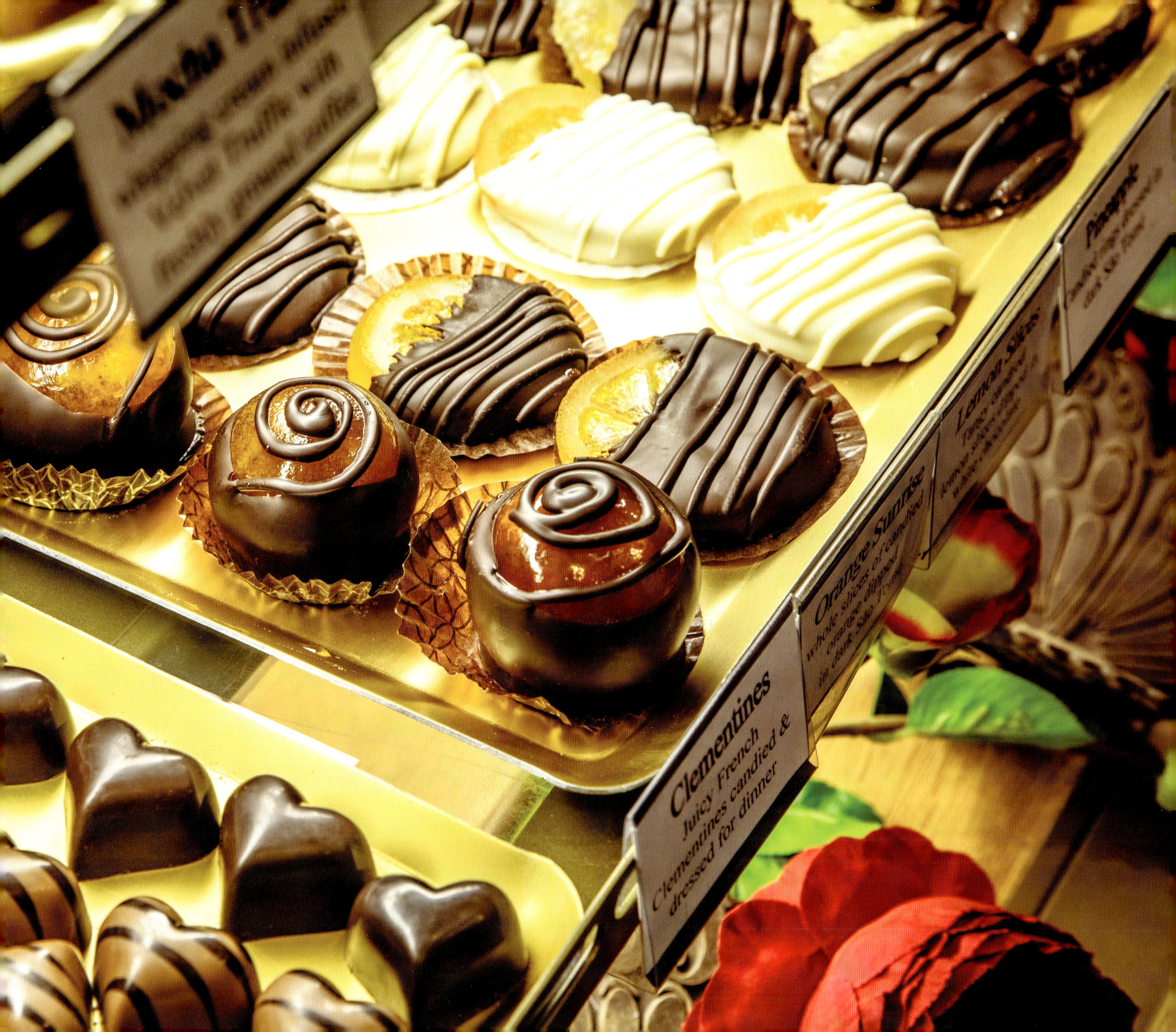
Clementines
Juicy French
Clementines candied &
dressed for dinner
Orange Sunrise
whole slices of candied
orange dipped
Lemon Slices
Pineapple

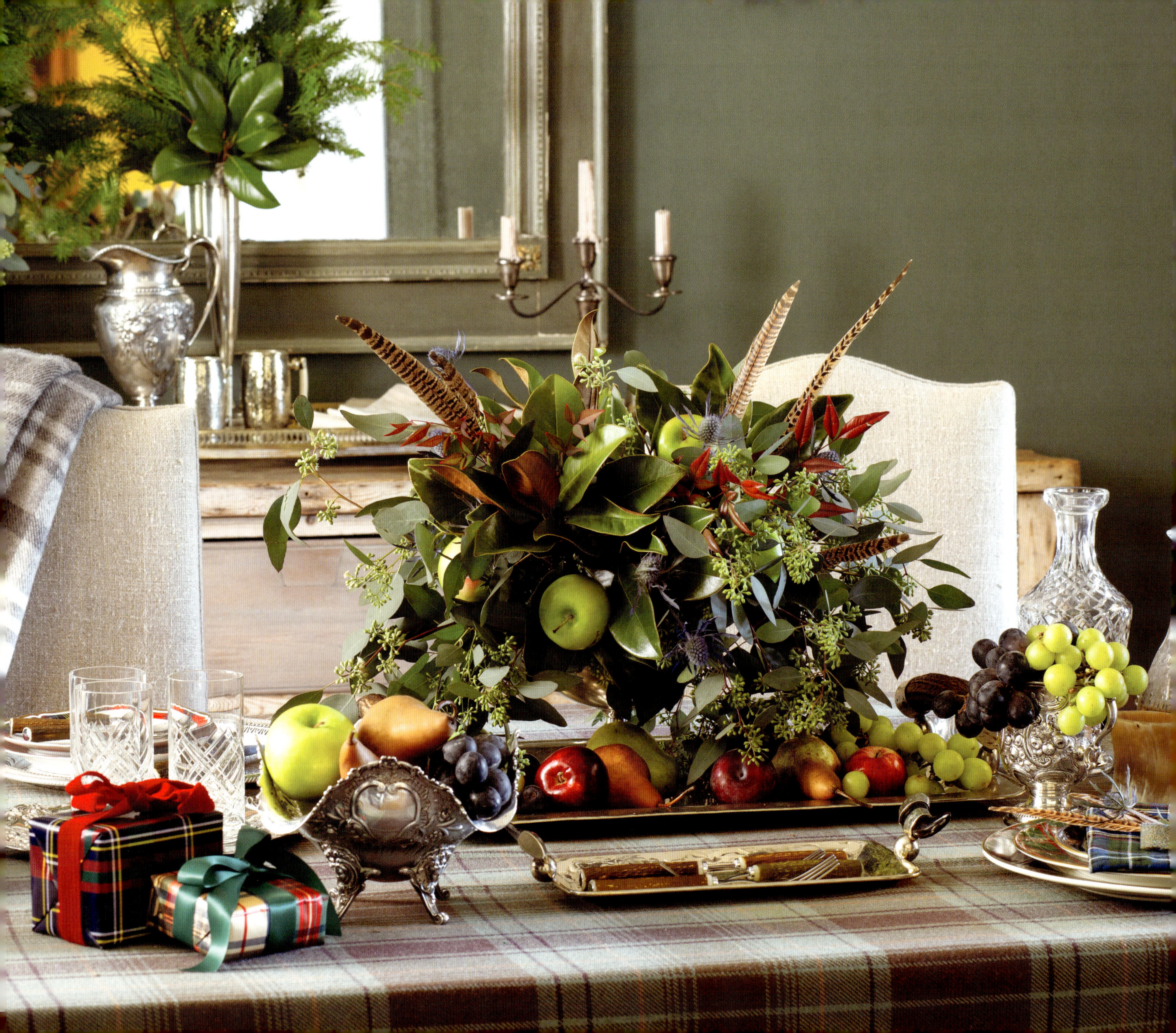

TARTAN TIDINGS

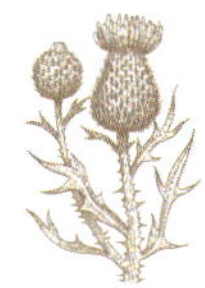

Through the annals of Scottish history, a classic pattern comprising interlocking lines weaves a thread of continuity. The appearance of tartans reaches back to the third century, features prominently in the wool kilts of Highlanders of the seventeenth and eighteenth centuries, and remains popular in modern adaptations from stylish frocks to elegant porcelain.

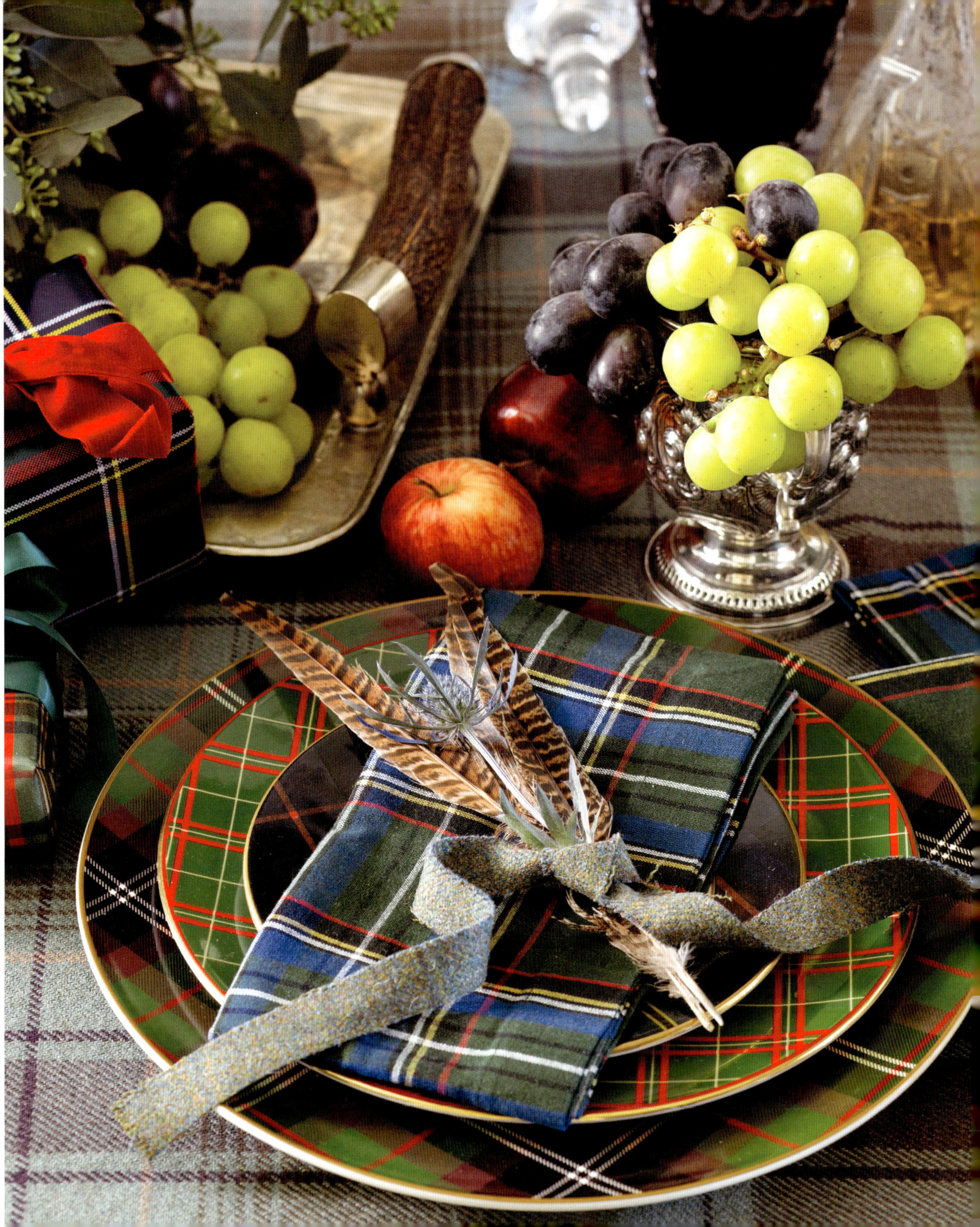

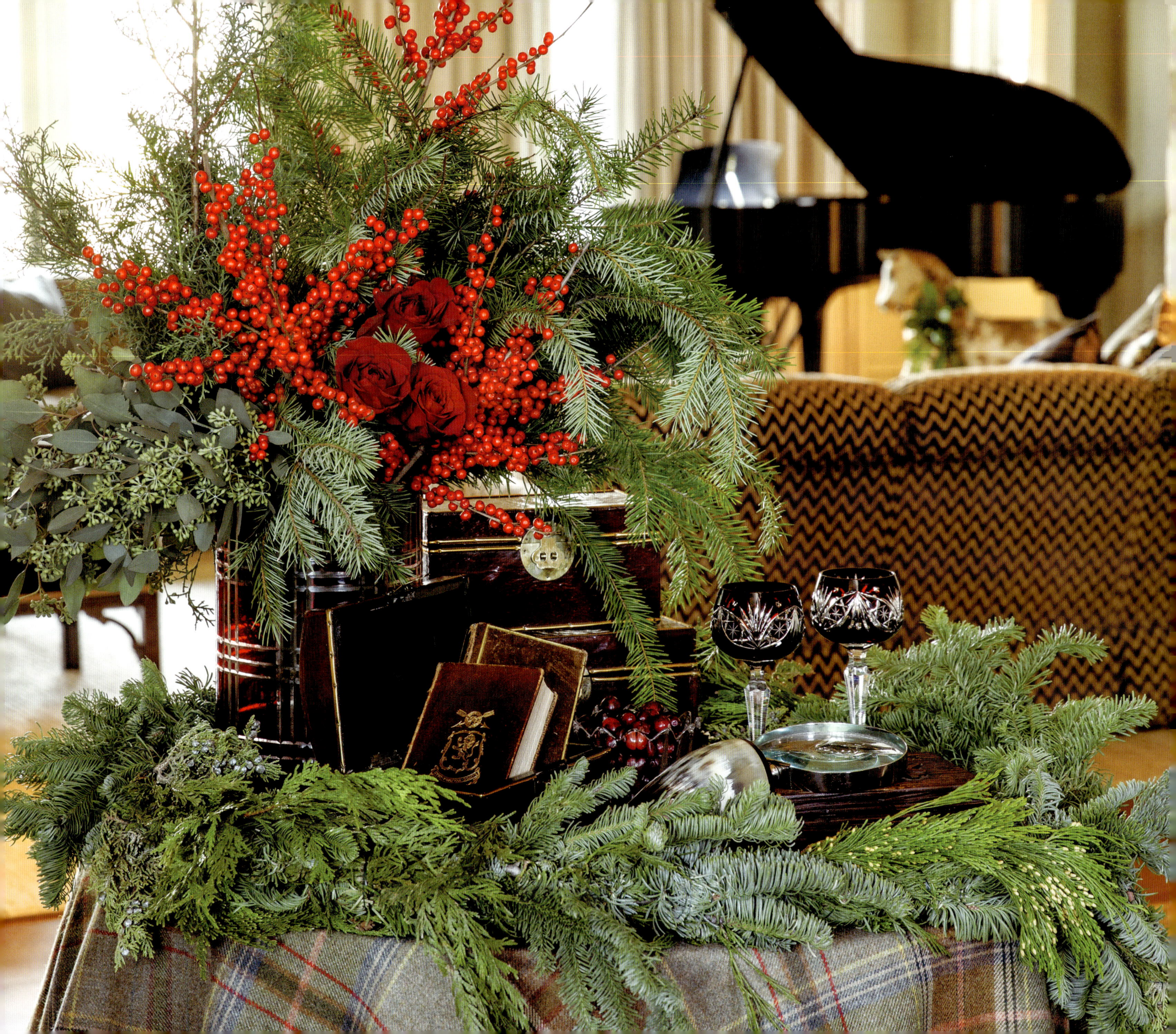

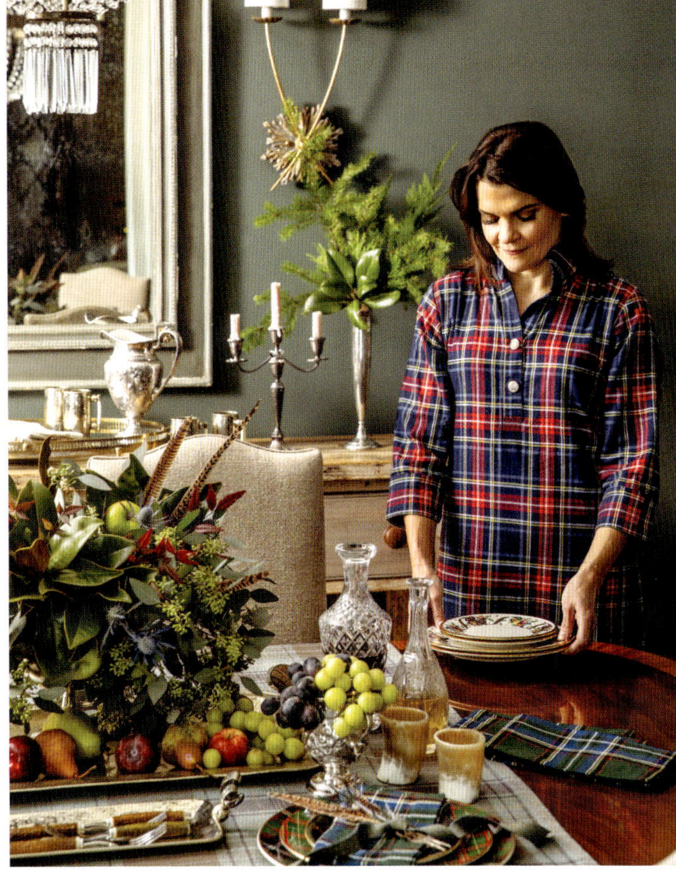

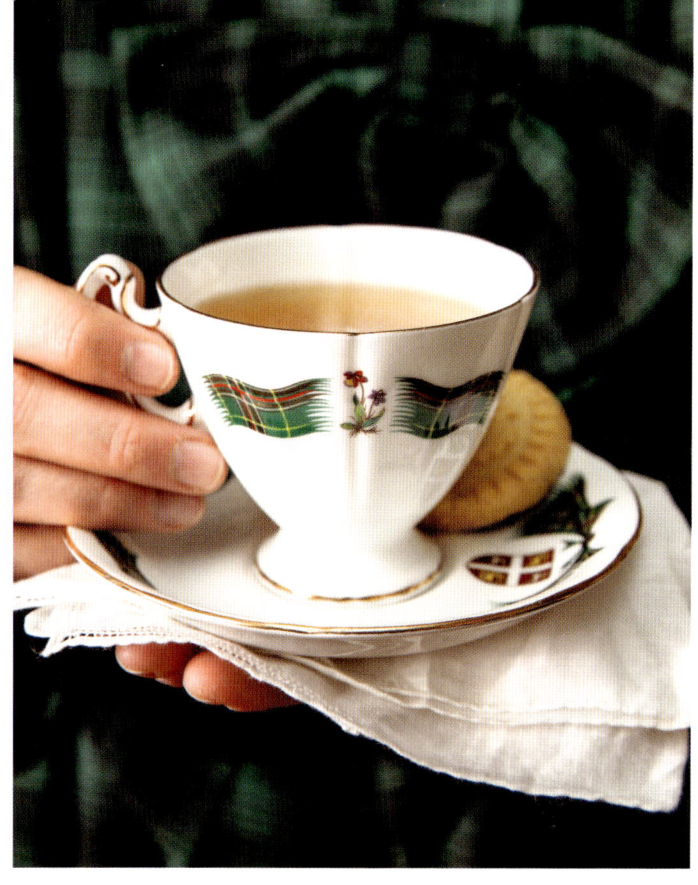

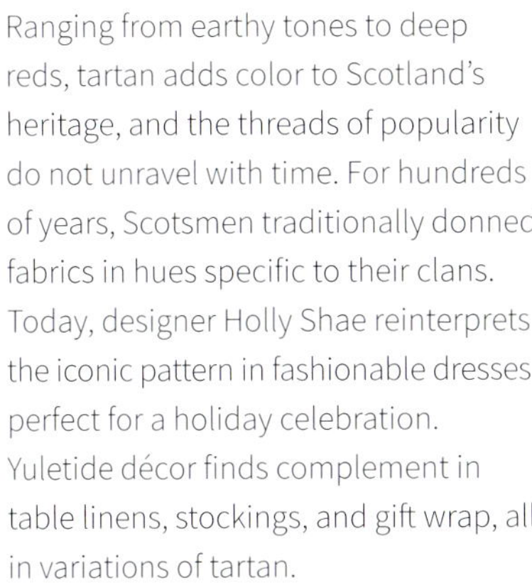

Ranging from earthy tones to deep reds, tartan adds color to Scotland's heritage, and the threads of popularity do not unravel with time. For hundreds of years, Scotsmen traditionally donned fabrics in hues specific to their clans. Today, designer Holly Shae reinterprets the iconic pattern in fashionable dresses perfect for a holiday celebration. Yuletide décor finds complement in table linens, stockings, and gift wrap, all in variations of tartan.

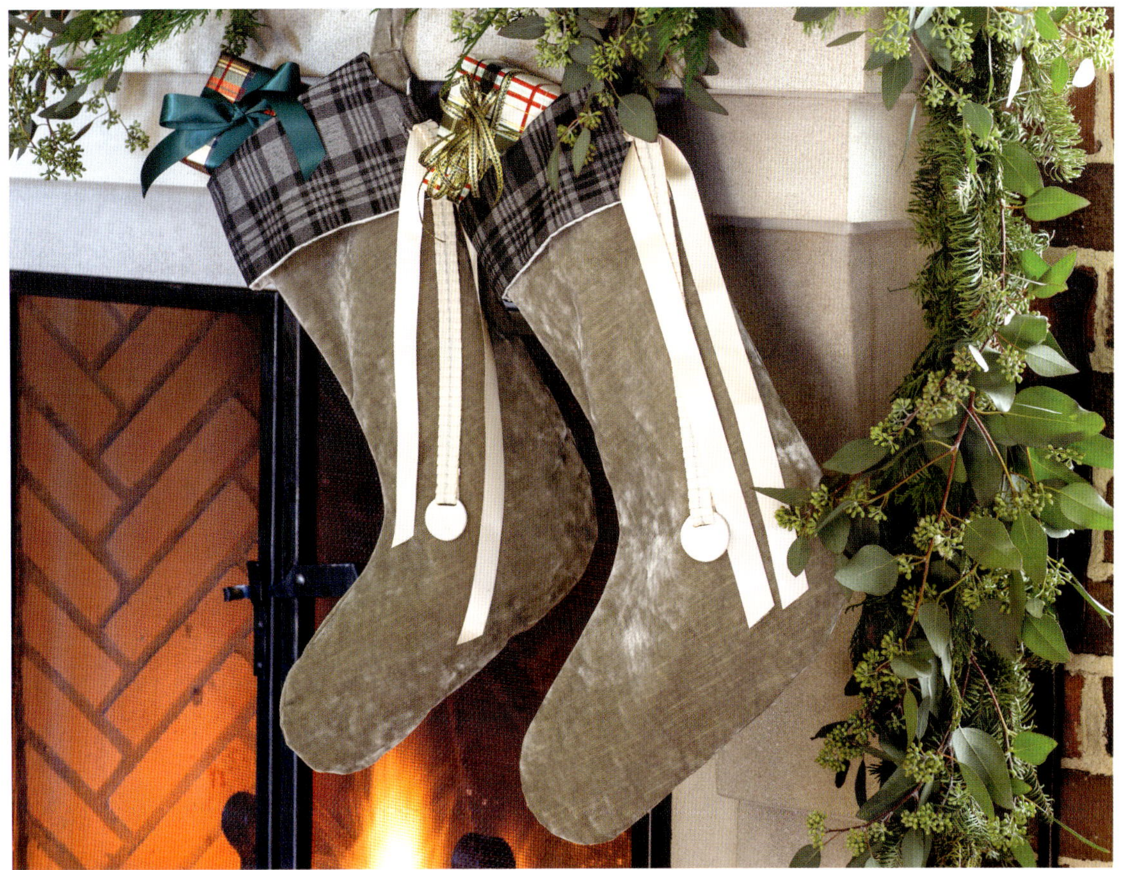

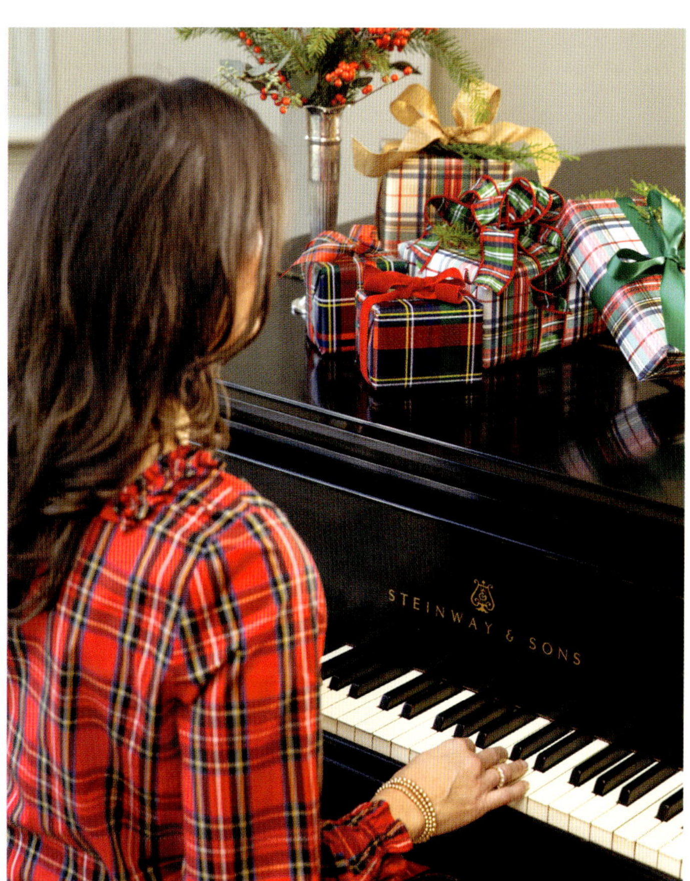

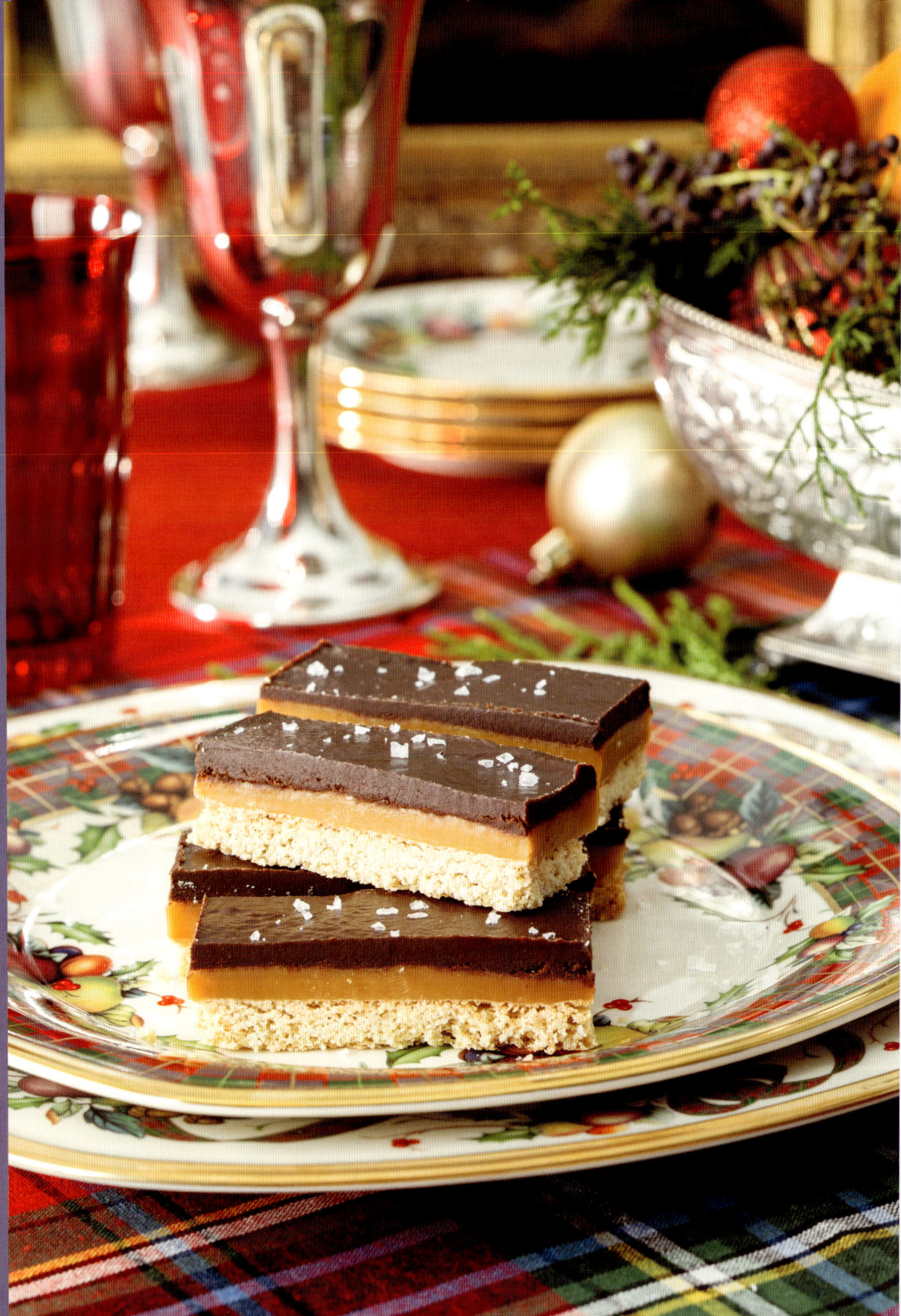

Millionaire Bars

Makes approximately 27

½ cup plus 6 tablespoons unsalted butter, softened, divided
¾ cup firmly packed light brown sugar, divided
1½ teaspoons vanilla extract, divided
¾ teaspoon kosher salt, divided
1 cup all-purpose flour
1 (14-ounce) can sweetened condensed milk
3 tablespoons light corn syrup
⅓ cup heavy whipping cream
1 (4-ounce) bar bittersweet chocolate, chopped
Garnish: flaky sea salt

1. Preheat oven to 350°. Line a 9-inch square pan with parchment paper.

2. In the bowl of a stand mixer fitted with the paddle attachment, beat ½ cup butter, ¼ cup brown sugar, ½ teaspoon vanilla extract, and ½ teaspoon salt at medium speed until creamy, 2 to 3 minutes, stopping to scrape down sides of bowl. With mixer at low speed, gradually add flour to butter mixture, beating just until combined, stopping to scrape down sides of bowl. Press dough into bottom of prepared pan.

3. Bake until top is dry and golden brown, 15 to 20 minutes. Let cool completely in pan on a wire rack.

4. In a medium saucepan, heat condensed milk, remaining 6 tablespoons butter, remaining ½ cup brown sugar, and corn syrup over medium heat. Cook, stirring frequently, until butter is melted and mixture is combined. Bring to a boil, stirring constantly; reduce heat to low and simmer, stirring constantly, until mixture is amber colored and thickened and a candy thermometer registers 235°, 10 to 15 minutes. The mixture should begin pulling away from sides of pan while stirring. Remove from heat and immediately stir in remaining 1 teaspoon vanilla extract and remaining ¼ teaspoon salt. Pour over shortbread, spreading into an even layer using a small offset spatula. Let cool completely.

5. In a medium saucepan, heat cream over medium-high heat until just hot but not boiling. Remove pan from heat and add chopped chocolate. Let stand for 1 minute, and then stir until chocolate melts completely and mixture is smooth. Pour over cooled caramel layer, using a small offset spatula to spread evenly. Garnish with sea salt, if desired.

6. Refrigerate until set, 20 minutes. Let come to room temperature before cutting into bars. Store in an airtight container at room temperature for up to 1 week.

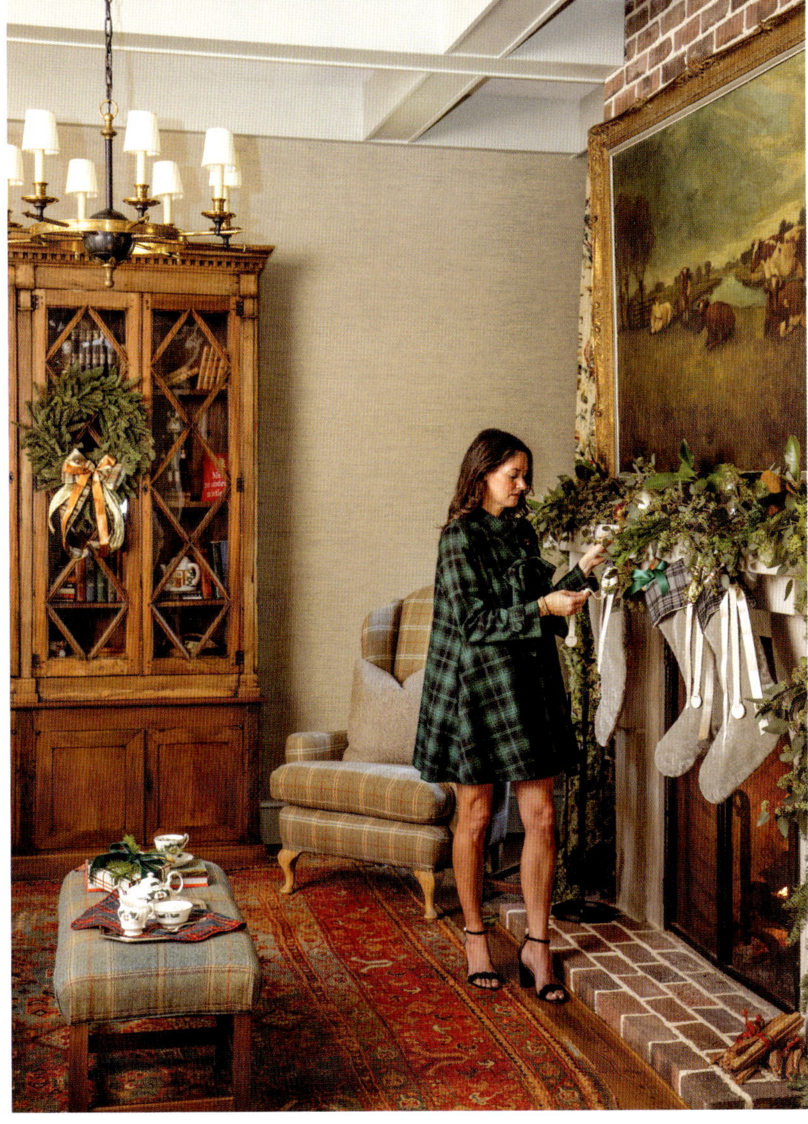

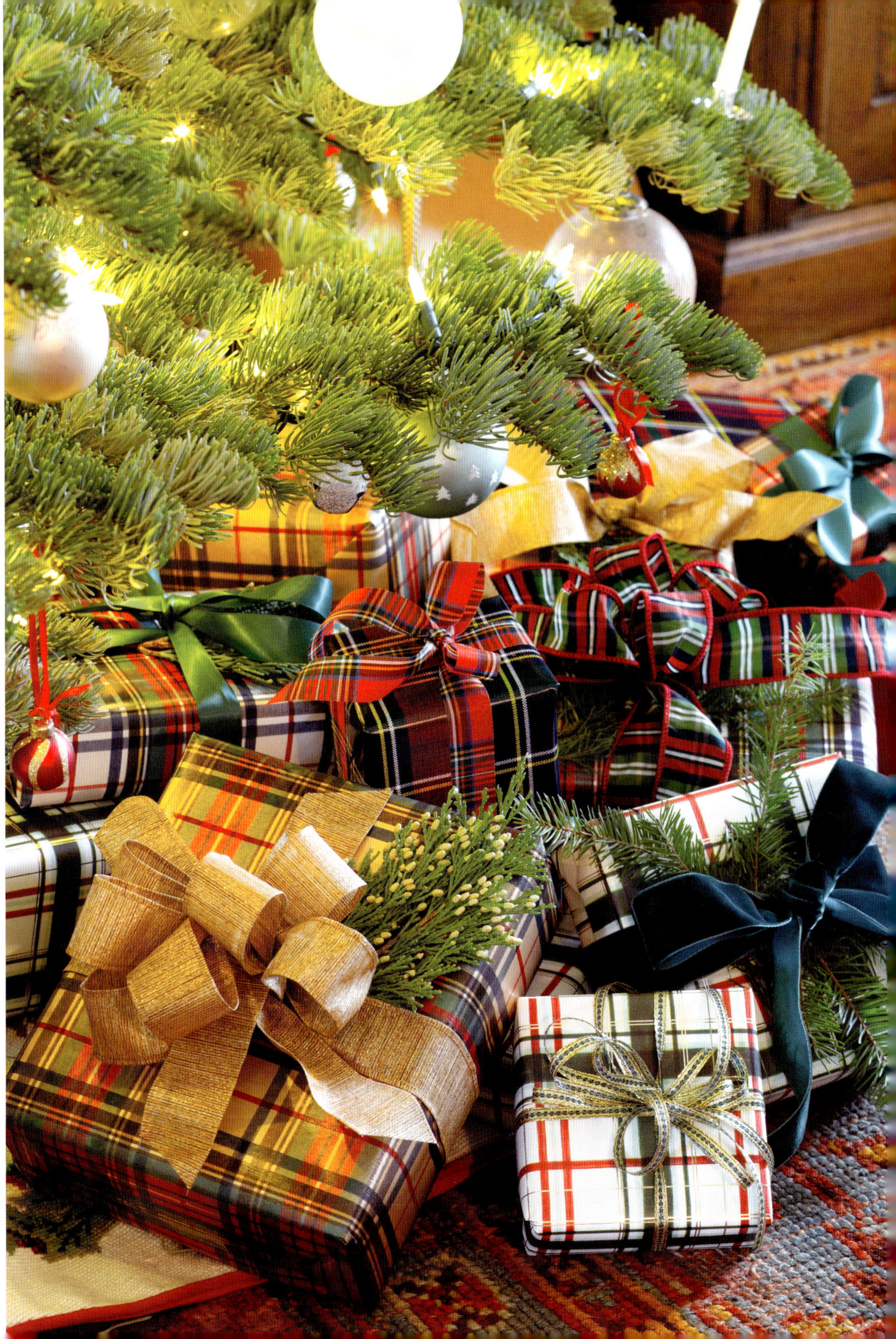

Opposite: Presented atop a pairing of Lenox Holiday Tartan china plates, Millionaire Bars offer a delectable taste of Christmas in Scotland. The nostalgic treat features layers of creamy caramel and rich chocolate over golden shortbread, with a sprinkle of flaky sea salt adding the final grace note. This page: Calling to mind the rugged expanse of rolling green hills and the misty coastline of Scotland's Highlands, tartan remains a classic choice. Whether used upon the table, in clothing, or as a decorative accent, the versatile print abounds with Scottish heritage and pride.

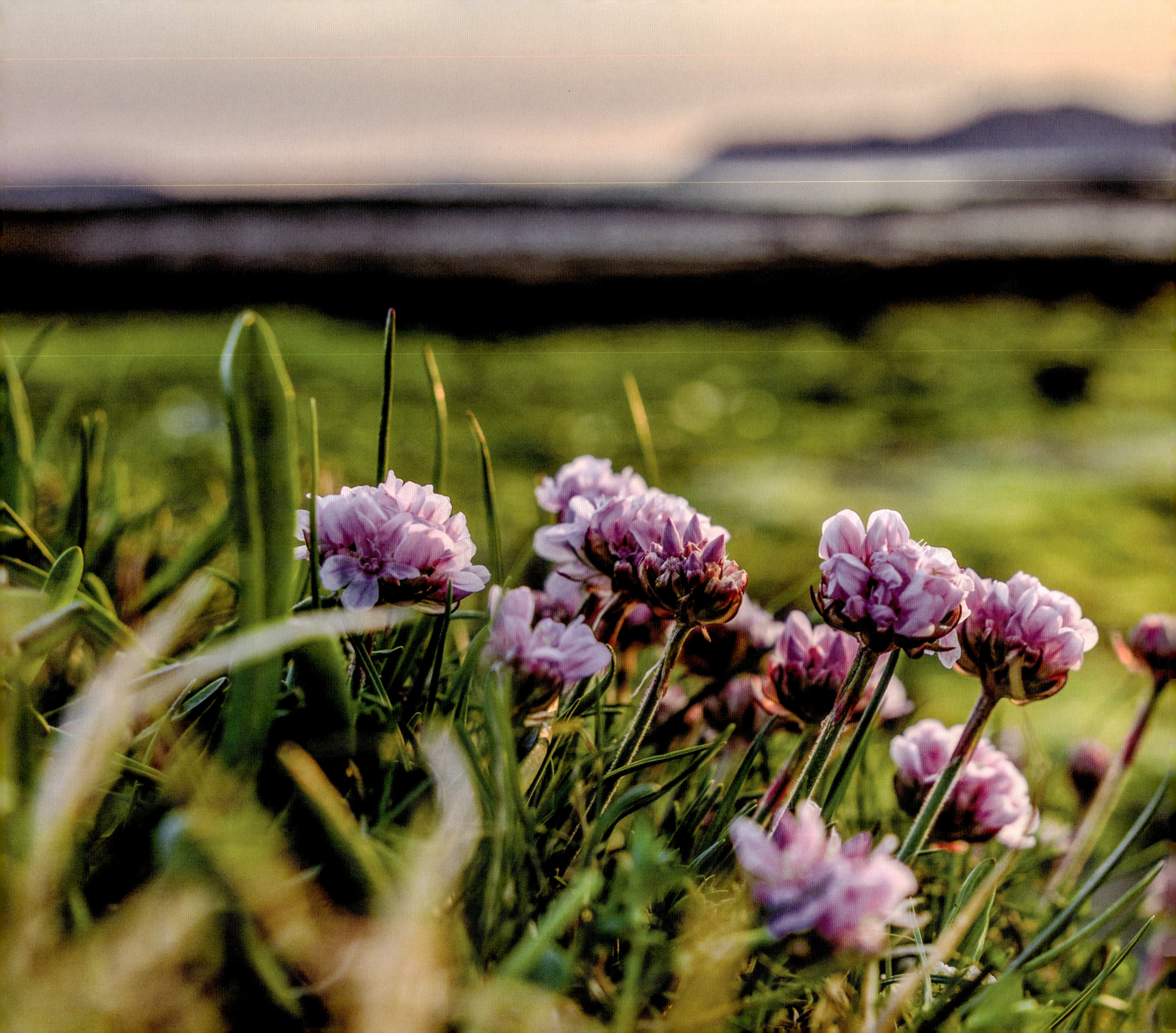

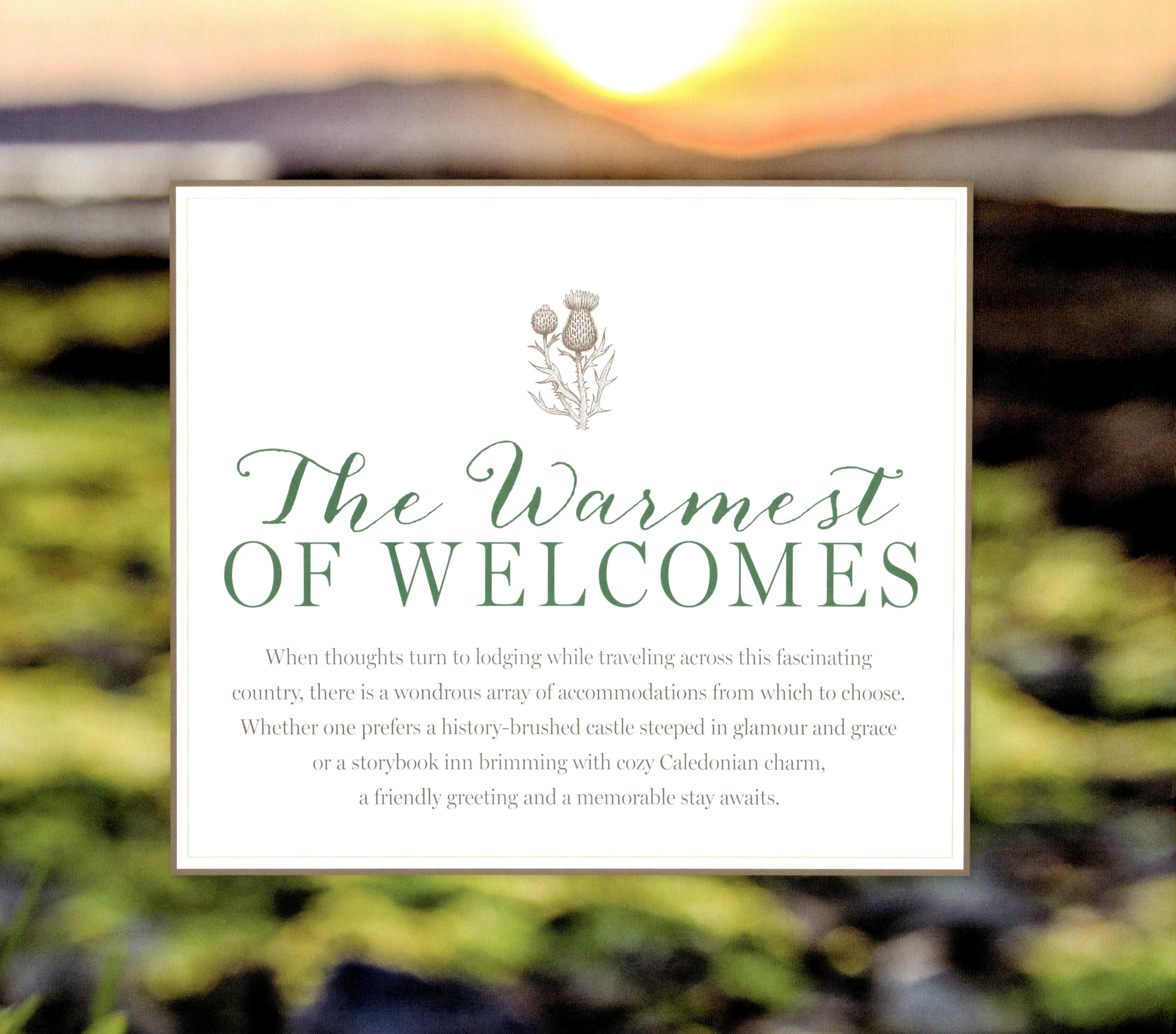

The Warmest OF WELCOMES

When thoughts turn to lodging while traveling across this fascinating country, there is a wondrous array of accommodations from which to choose. Whether one prefers a history-brushed castle steeped in glamour and grace or a storybook inn brimming with cozy Caledonian charm, a friendly greeting and a memorable stay awaits.

LUXURY ON THE HILLTOPS

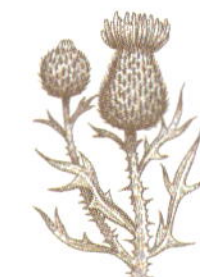

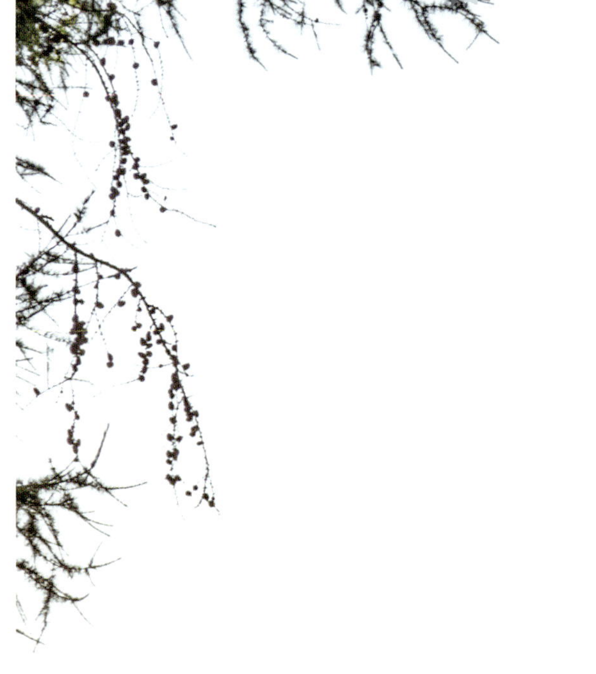

The historic Scottish Highlands are awash with mystery. Here, tucked amid the noble mountains, glistening waterways, and amber foliage, a five-star boutique hotel awaits in the mist. The Fife Arms, truly glorious in every way, welcomes sojourners to come experience the magic of Braemar.

This quaint village, situated approximately two-and-a-half hours north of Edinburgh, is famous for its annual Braemar Gathering, held in September as part of the Highland games. Though modest in size, the destination is rich with culture, being home to a castle, whiskey distillery, and countless outdoor excursions, due to its location in the heart of the vast Cairngorms National Park.

For those eager to discover these pleasures and more, the Fife Arms is a perfect place to begin. The hotel brims with history, having served as a Victorian coaching inn for ages before being transformed by its current stewards, a pair of distinguished gallery owners who have filled the place with an impressive collection of artworks. Within these finely adorned walls, guests will find hospitality in one of forty-six individually designed rooms, each decorated in honor of a notable figure, poet, or part of nature. Outside the hotel's doors, visitors can also find many memorable moments thanks to a staff of Ghillies, Highlands attendants who guide patrons to memorable experiences, such as plein air sketching, lunch on a remote moor with a private chef, or wilderness fishing, where one can even cook the day's catch. No matter what the stay holds, this much is certain: Here, there are treasures waiting to be discovered.

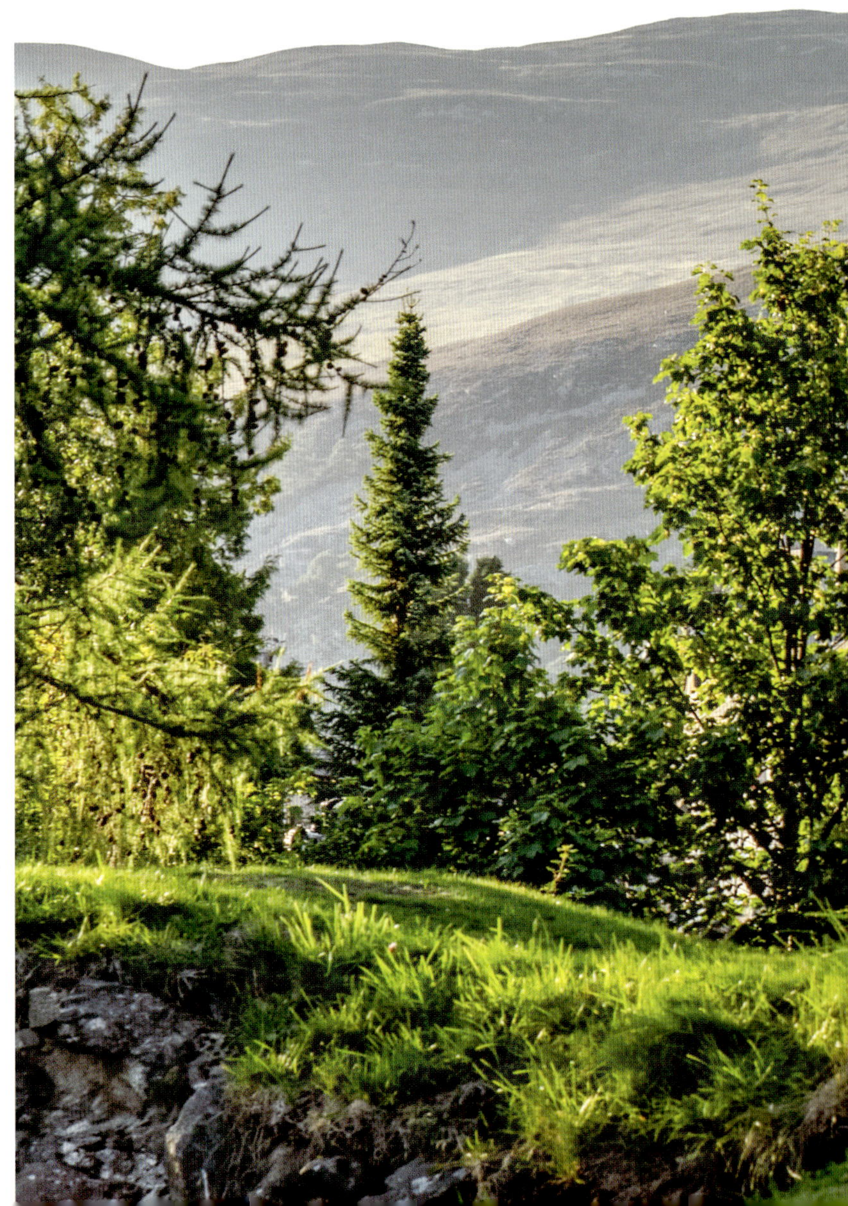

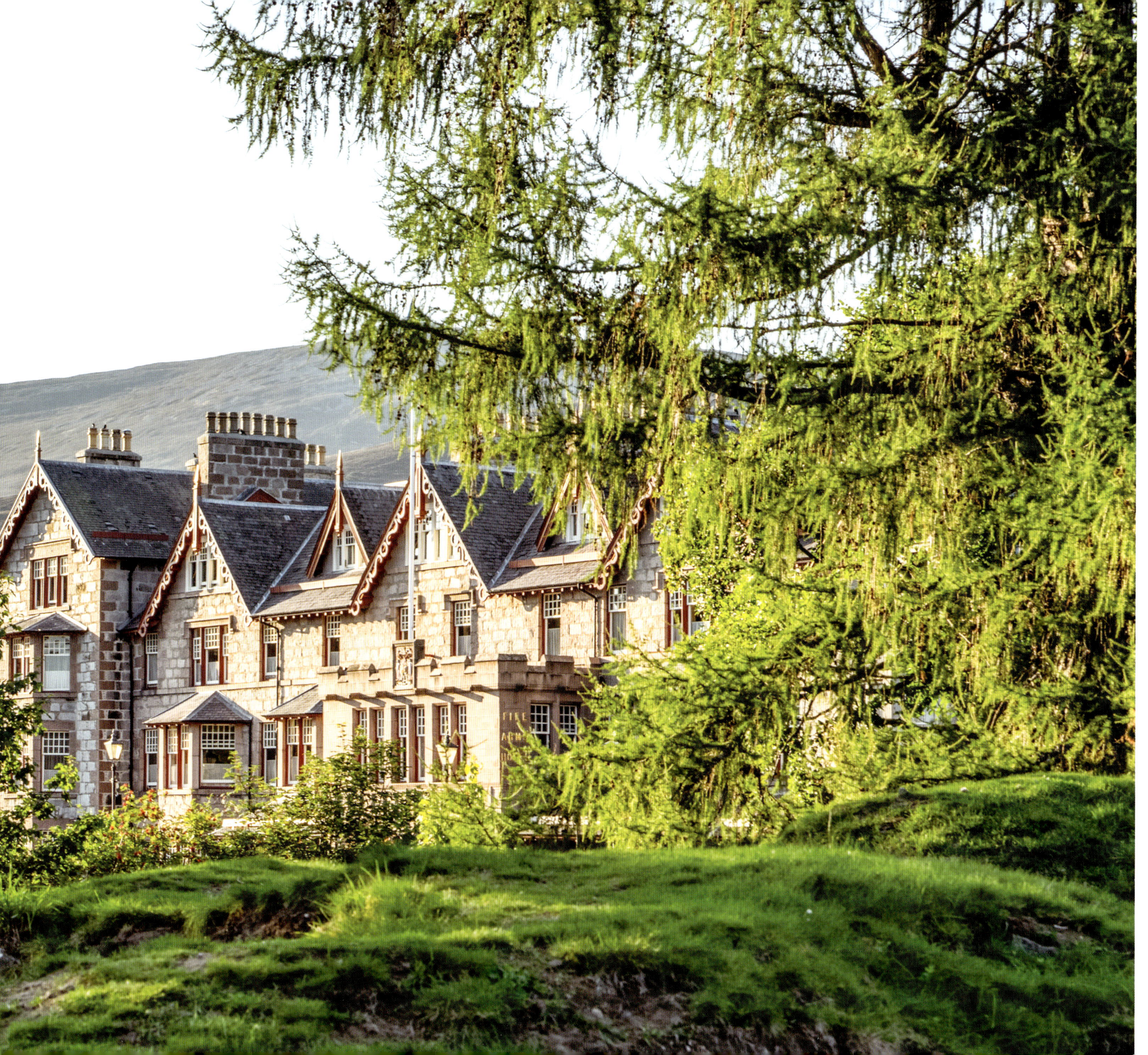

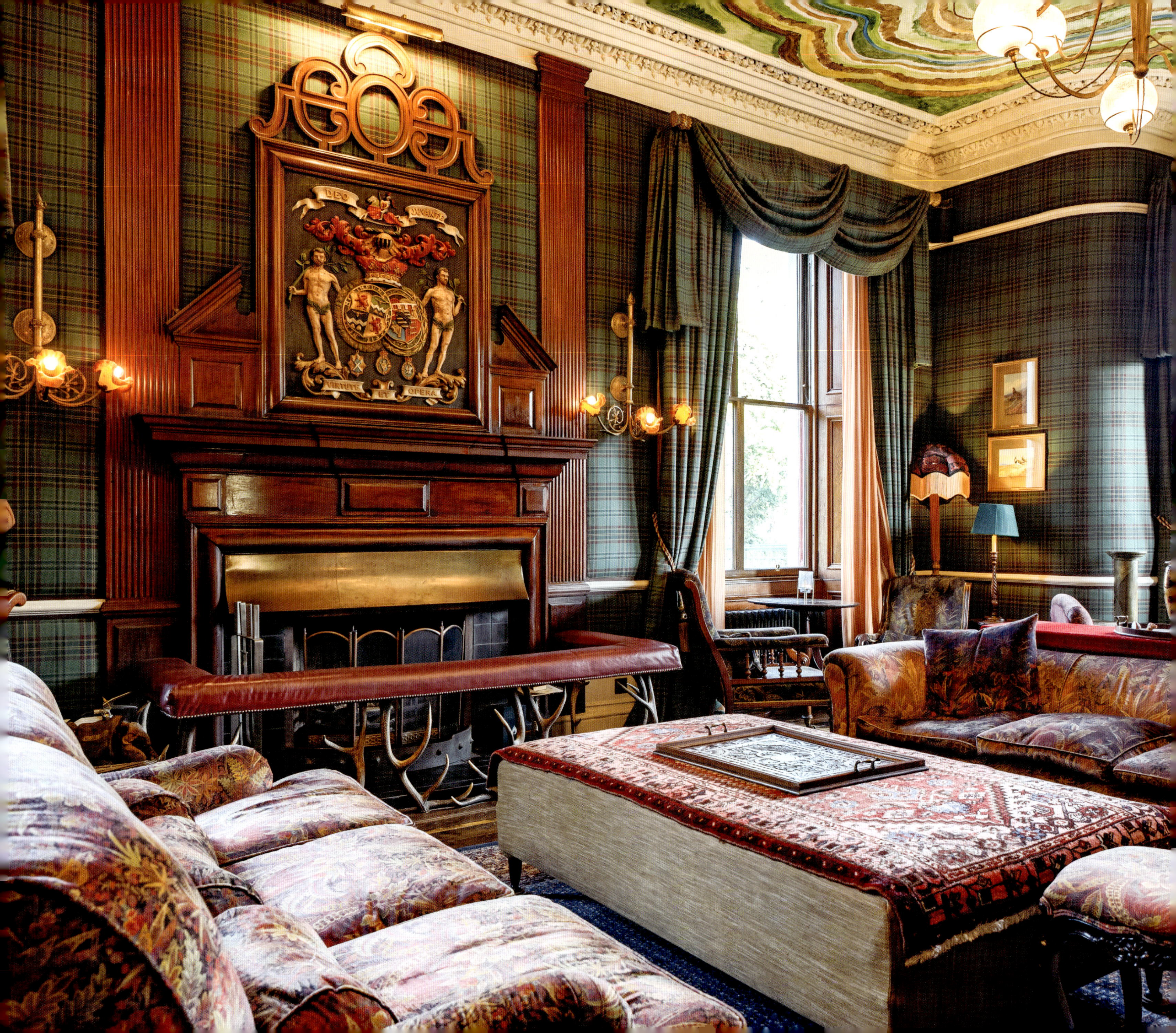
DEO
JUVANTE
VIRTUTE
ET
OPERA

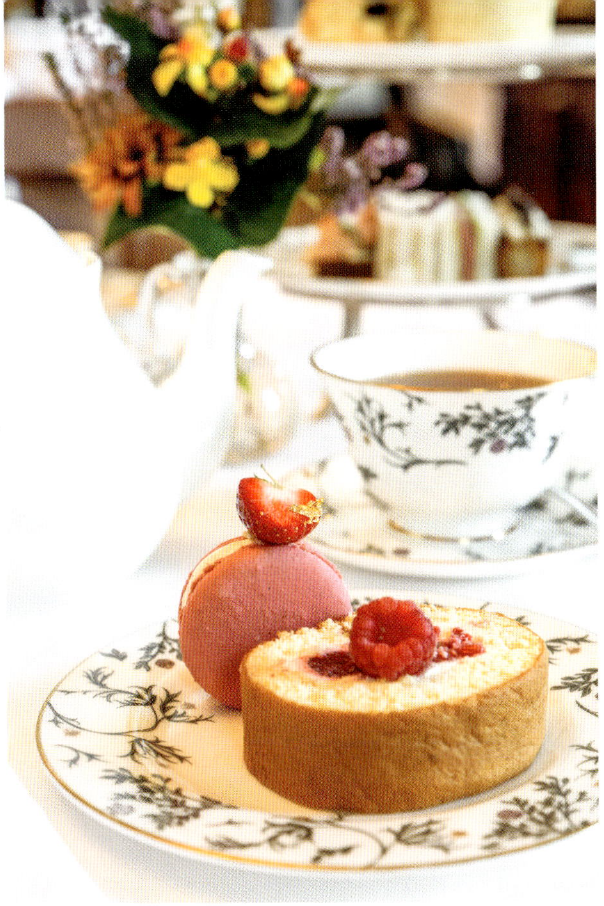

Opposite: Sumptuous furnishings, tartan walls, and collected treasures make the Drawing Room a cozy spot to linger over coffee or an evening beverage. Also served in this welcoming space is afternoon tea. Above: Teatime is a special tradition at The Fife Arms hotel, with a tempting array of sweets following a course of delicate savories. Right: The brimful desk in this guest room sits below a portrait of Lord Byron, the poet in honor of whom these lodgings were decorated.

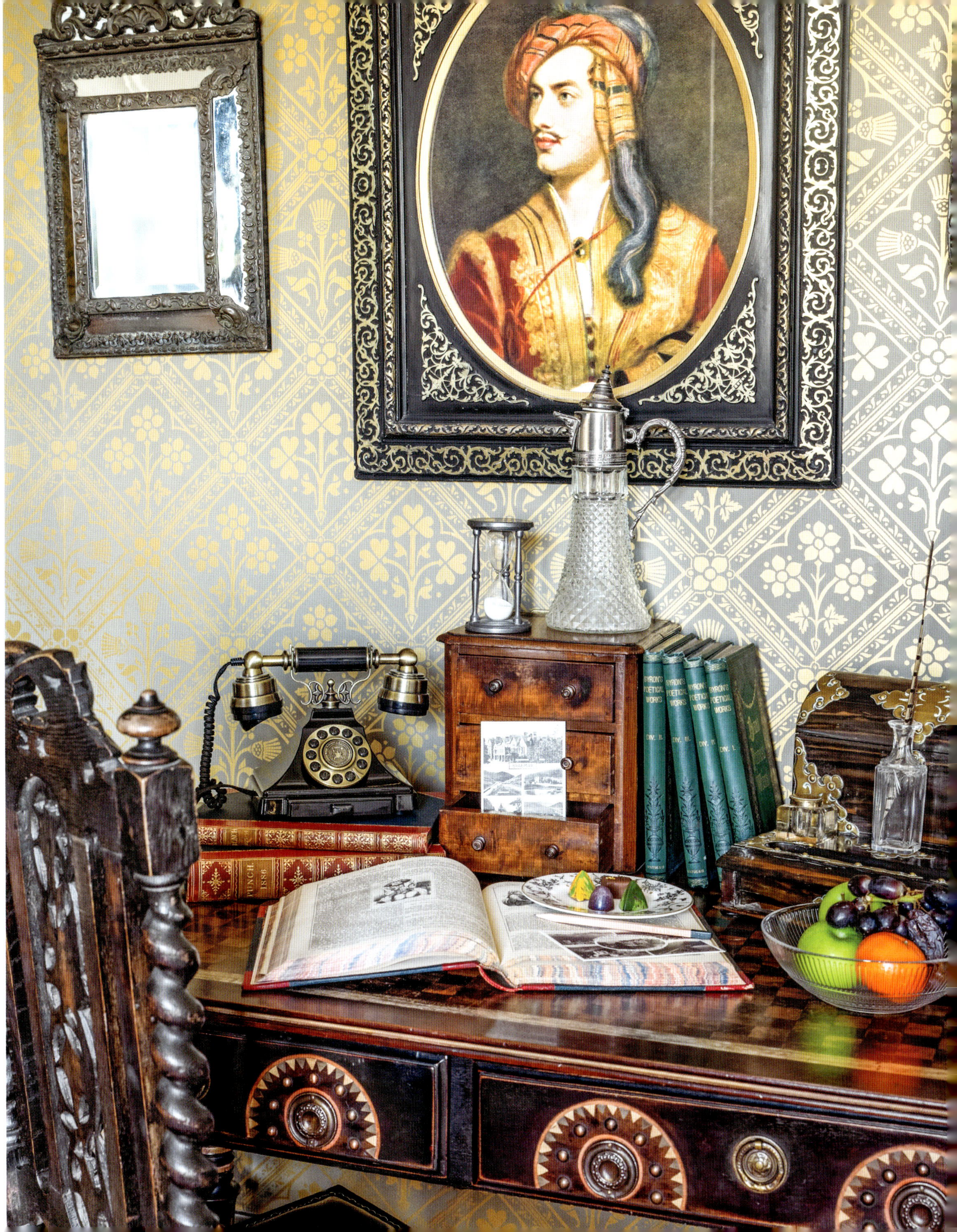

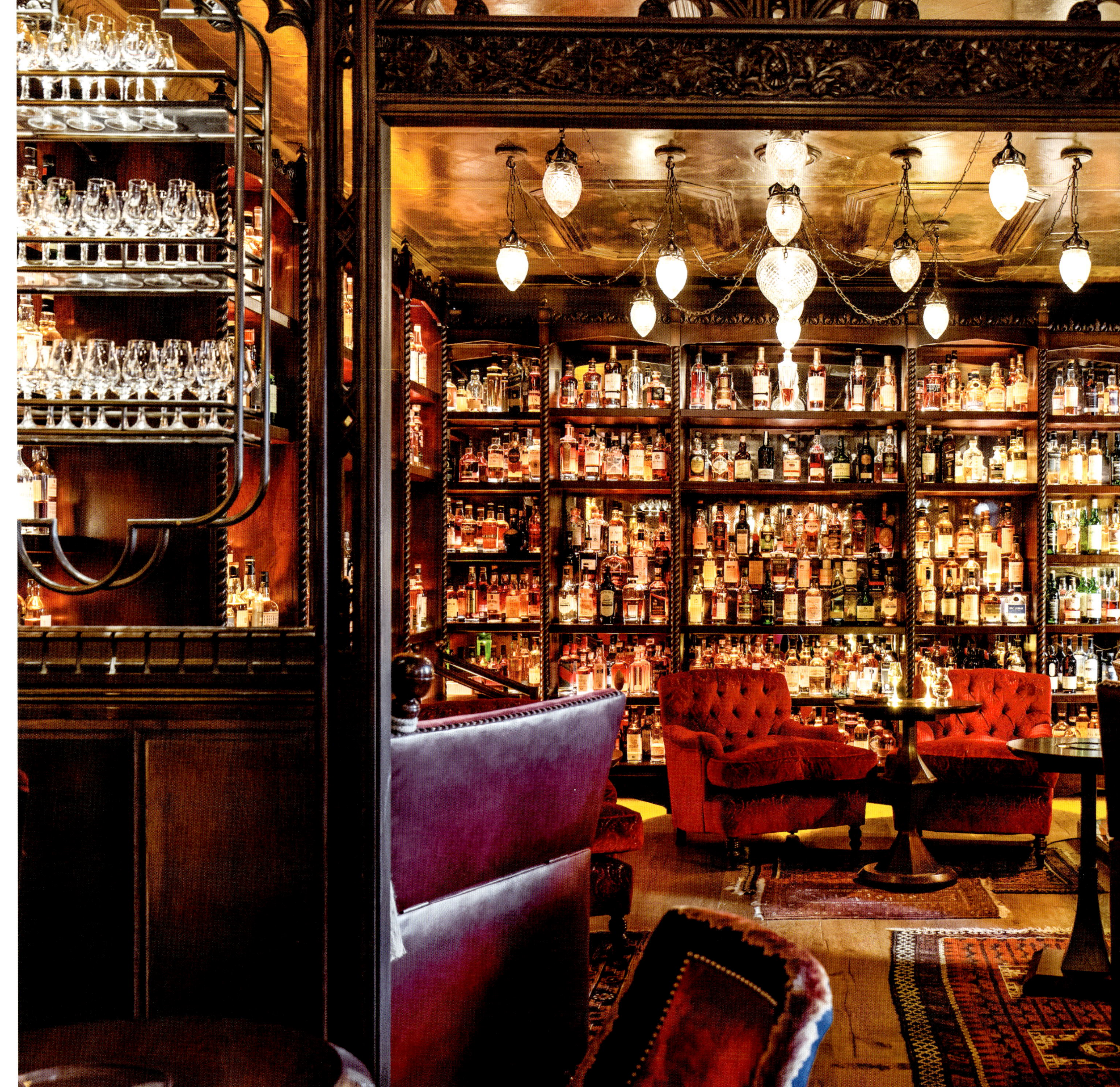

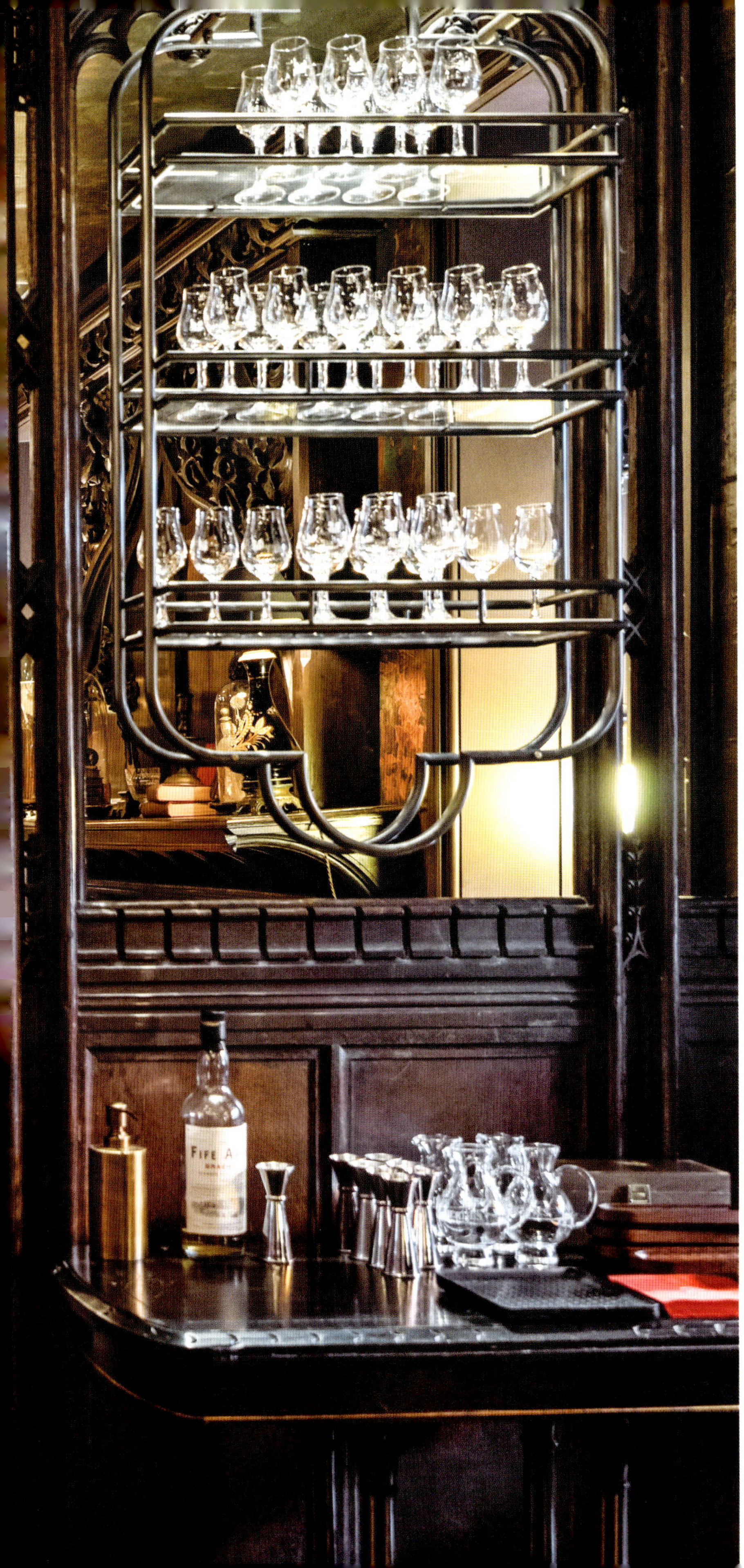

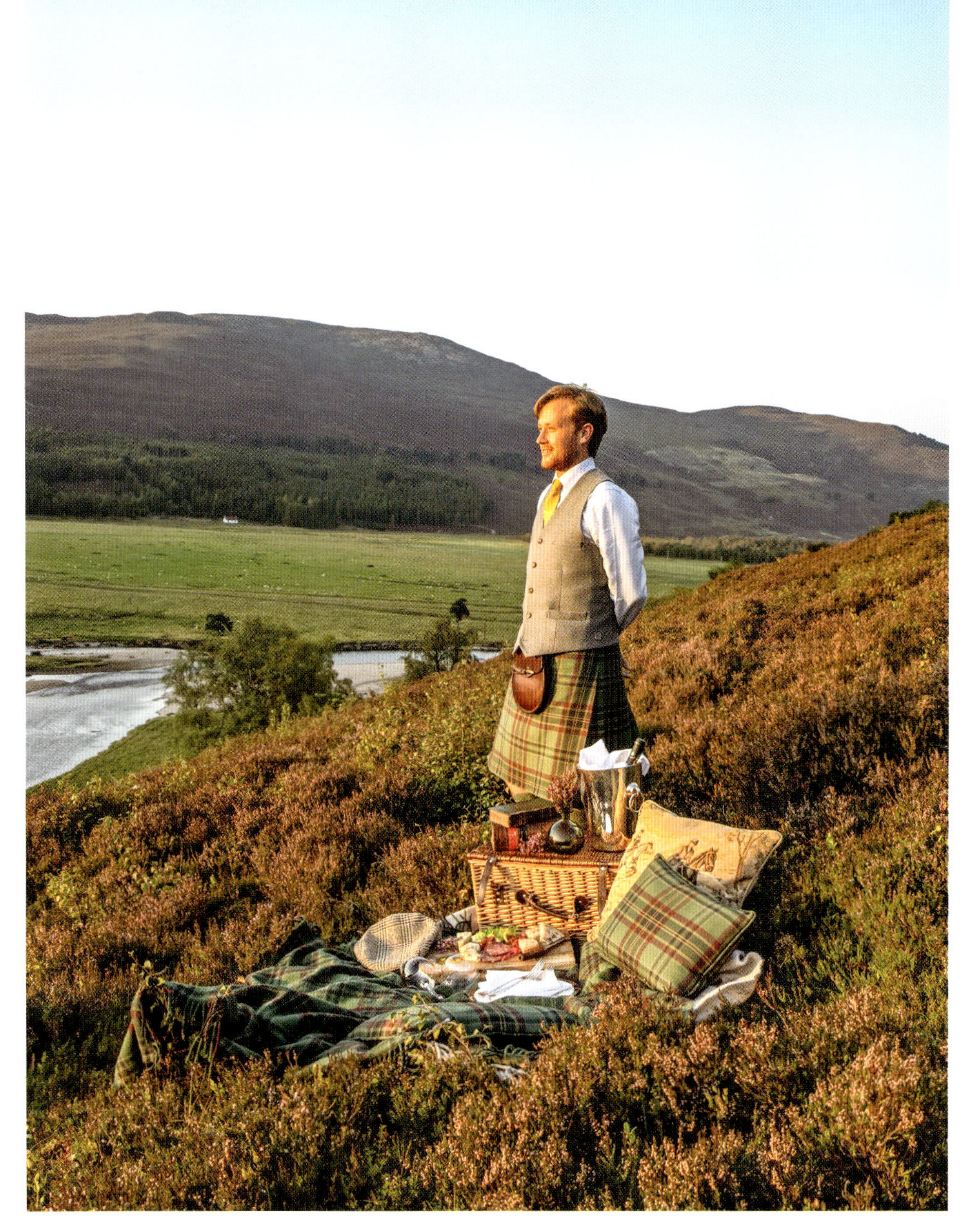

"Staring into a Scottish landscape, I have often asked myself why—in spite of all appearances—bracken, rocks, man, and sea are at some level one."

—Neal Ascherson

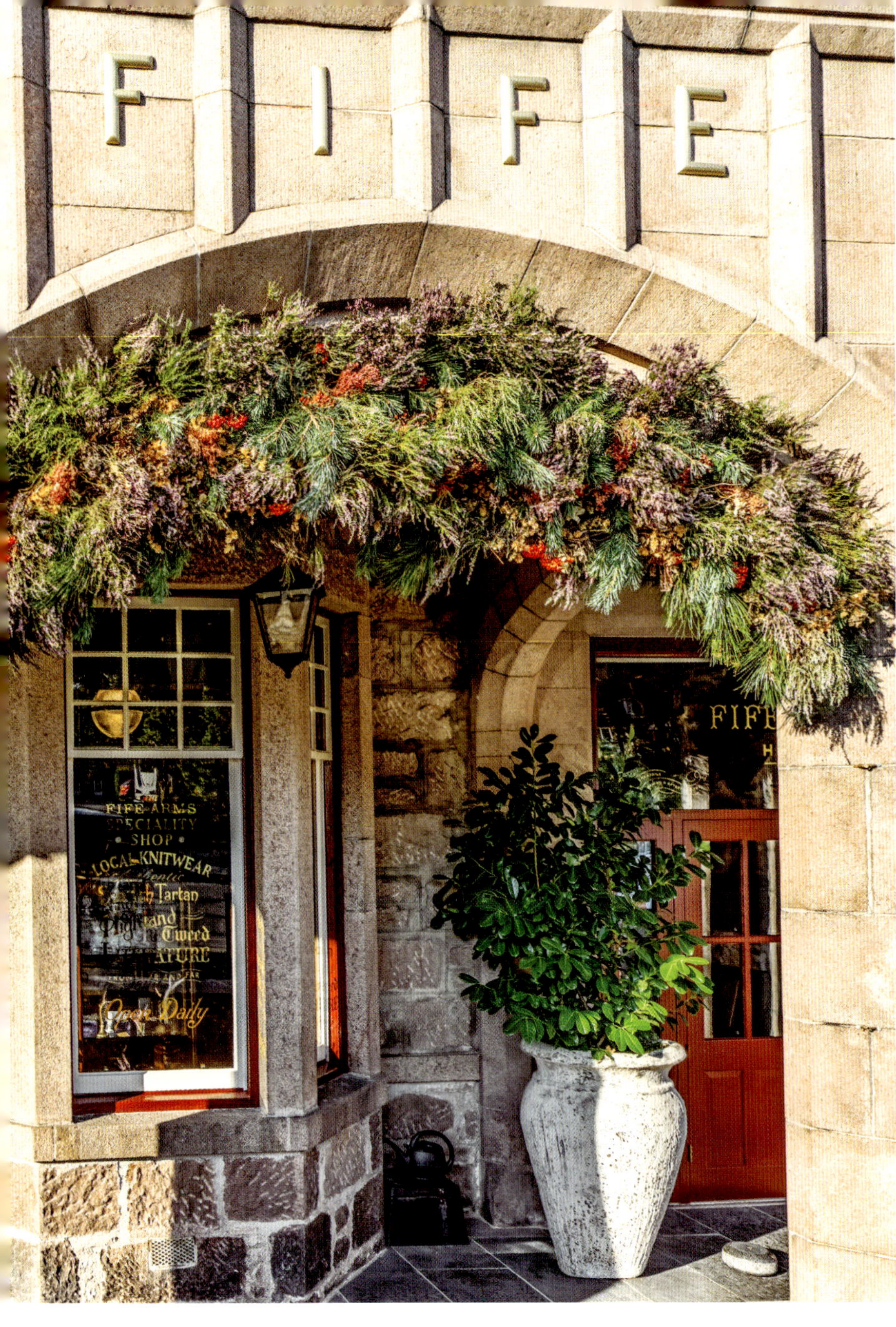

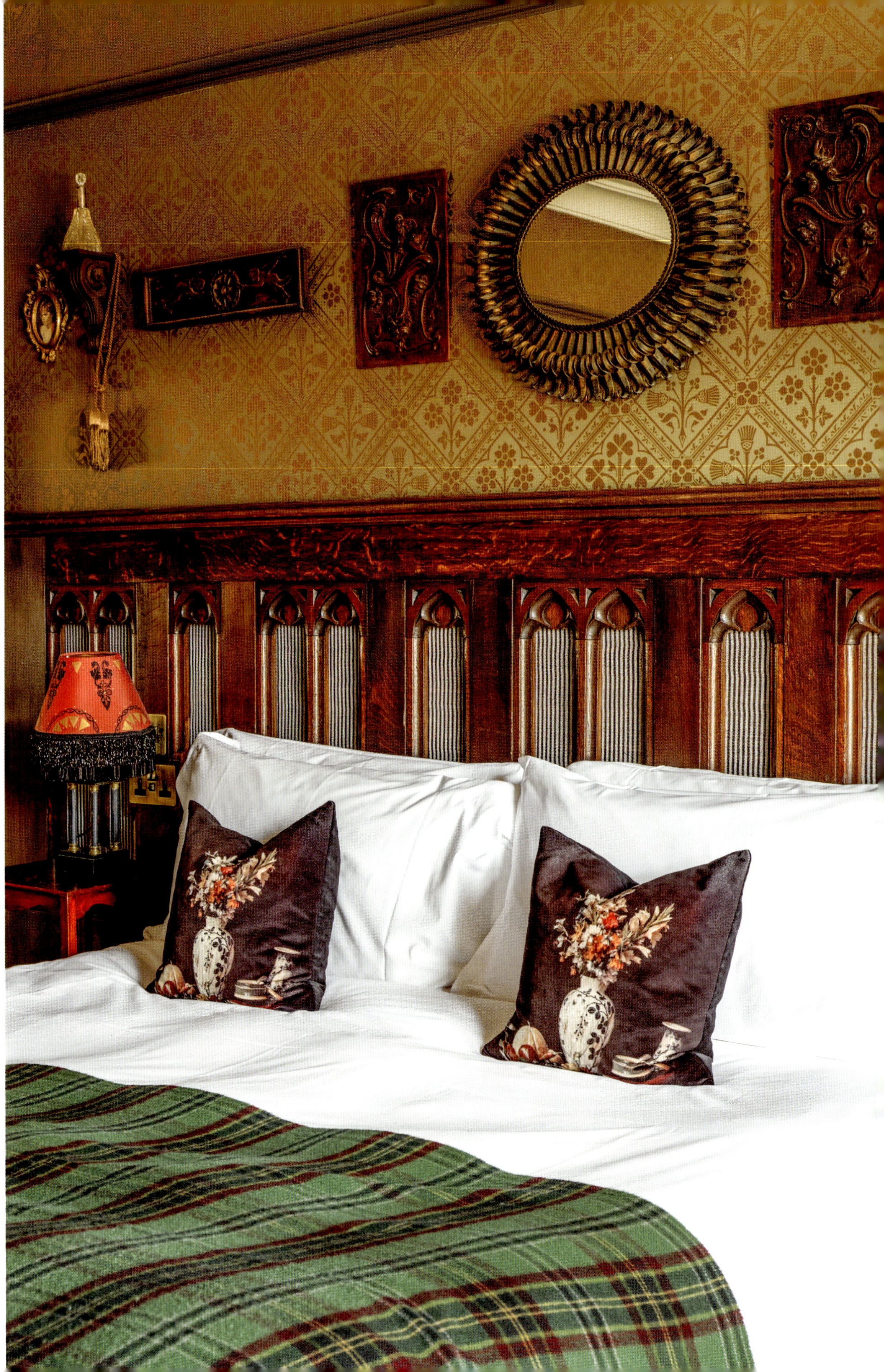

From snug Croft Rooms fitted with cabin beds to five-star Royal Suites richly appointed with antiques and artwork related to historical figures, there are accomodations to suit the needs of every guest.

Forests brimming with Scots pine and heather lie just a few minutes' walk from the hotel. The building, erected in the nineteenth century, has been a town landmark since the time of Queen Victoria, who often visited Braemar. Right: Clunie Water, an offshoot of the River Dee, runs behind the hotel, lending a tranquil presence to the scene.

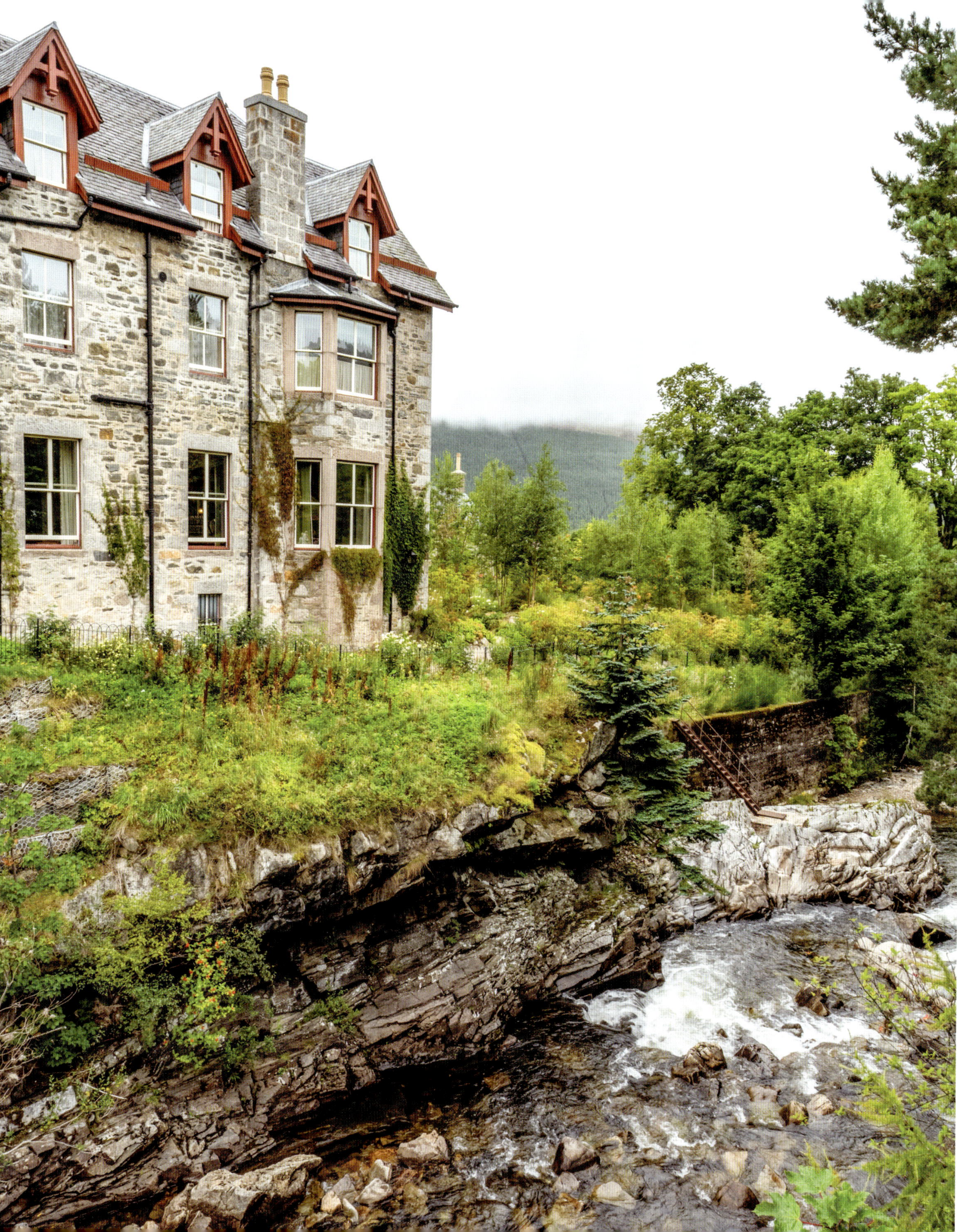

GETAWAY TO GLENTERNIE

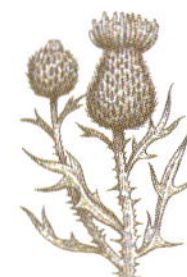

The journey to Glenternie House is much like approaching a secluded castle tucked in a hidden valley deep in rural Scotland. One must follow curving roads between the hills near Peebles, pass through the gate guarded by a quaint stone residence, and finally travel up the long driveway before arriving at the manor itself. Tall turrets point skyward, and curiosities fill the mind as a hand reaches up to knock—how the house might look inside, what characters may have occupied its rooms, and what the world must have been like at the time of its construction.

Today, visitors are welcomed by owners and hosts Lucy and Anthony Woodd. Over the course of two decades, the couple transformed this Victorian mansion into a comfortable bed-and-breakfast—a place for tourists to rest their heads and satisfy their hearts. "It seemed an interesting and fun way to meet new people, raise a bit of money, and utilize rooms that are not always occupied," says Lucy. She and her husband reared their two children here before opening the bed-and-breakfast in 2015.

Glenternie has had numerous owners. The first was David Kidd, a bachelor who built the house for himself and his elderly sisters in the 1860s, after making his fortune inventing the gummed envelope. Unfortunately, he died before its completion, but his sisters resided

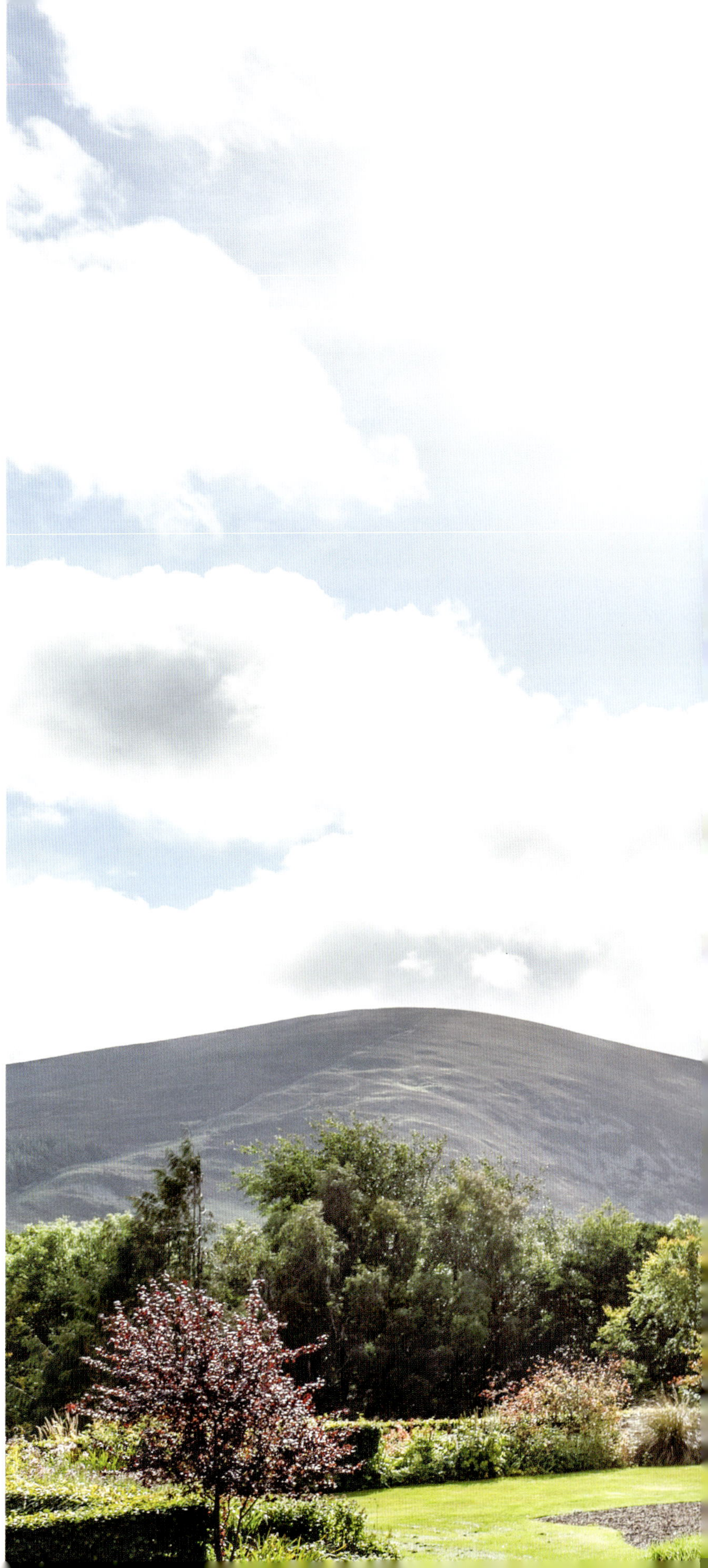

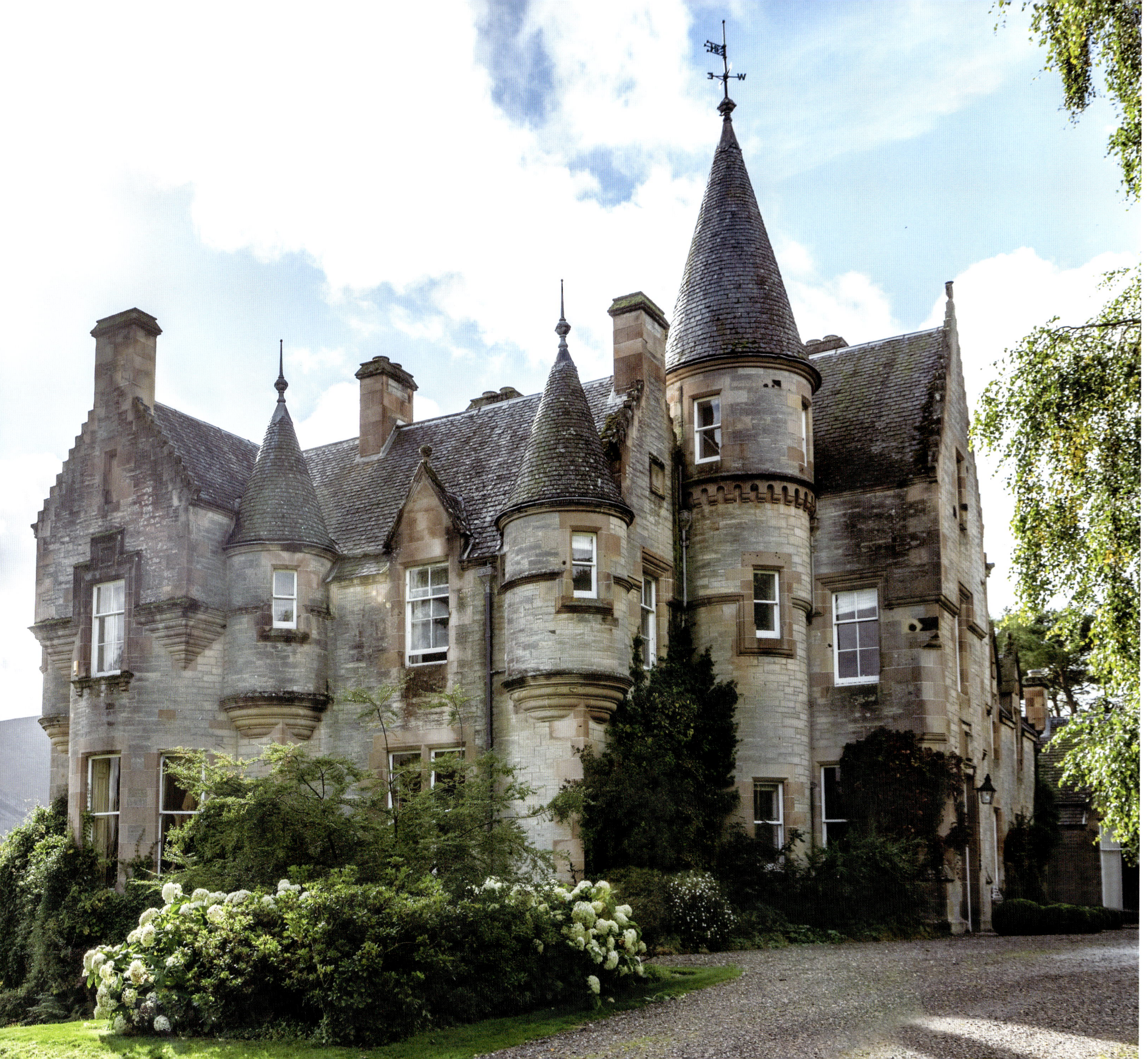

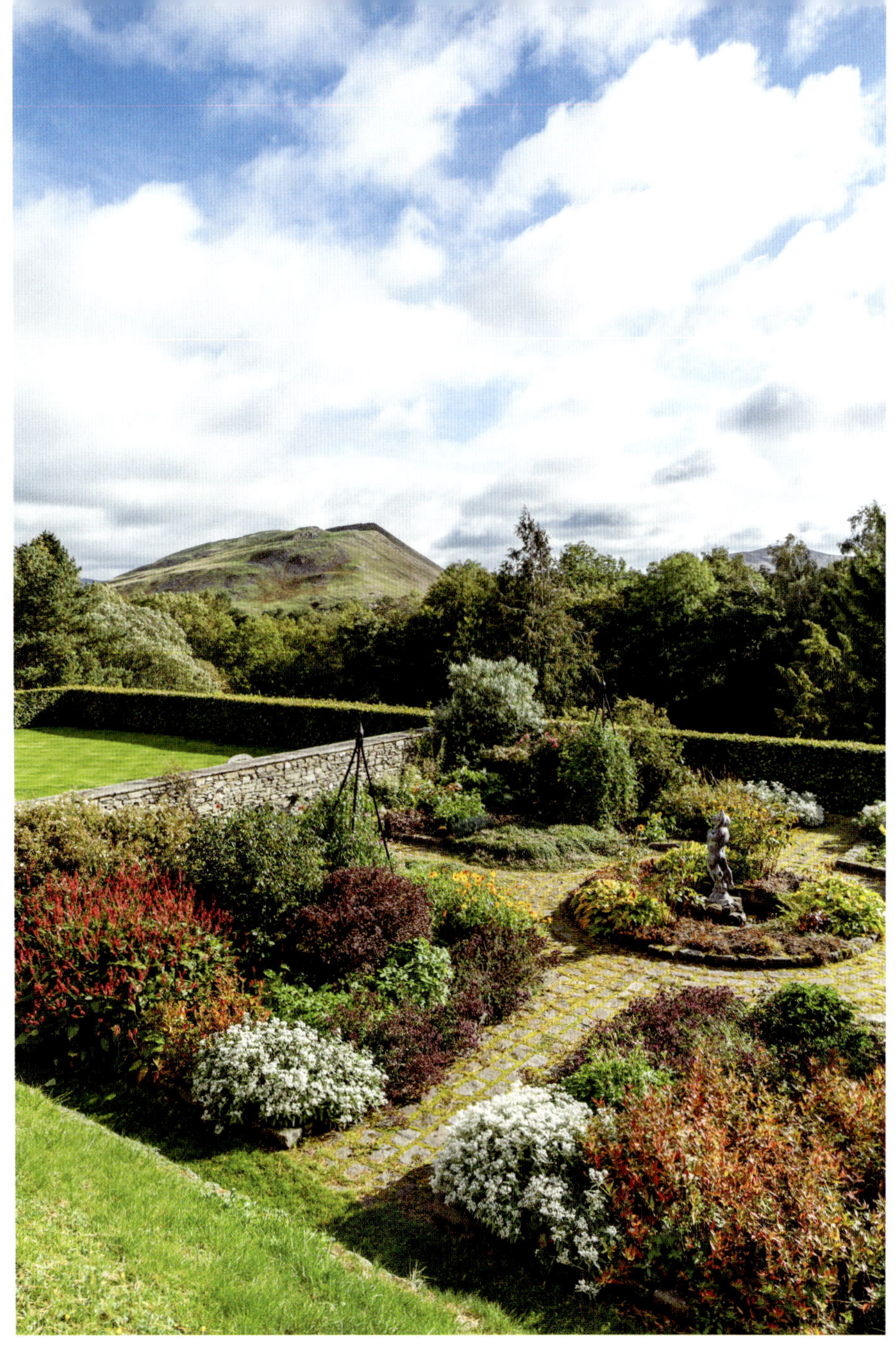

"To be kind to all, to like many and love a few, to be needed and wanted by those we love, is certainly the nearest we can come to happiness."

—Mary, Queen of Scots

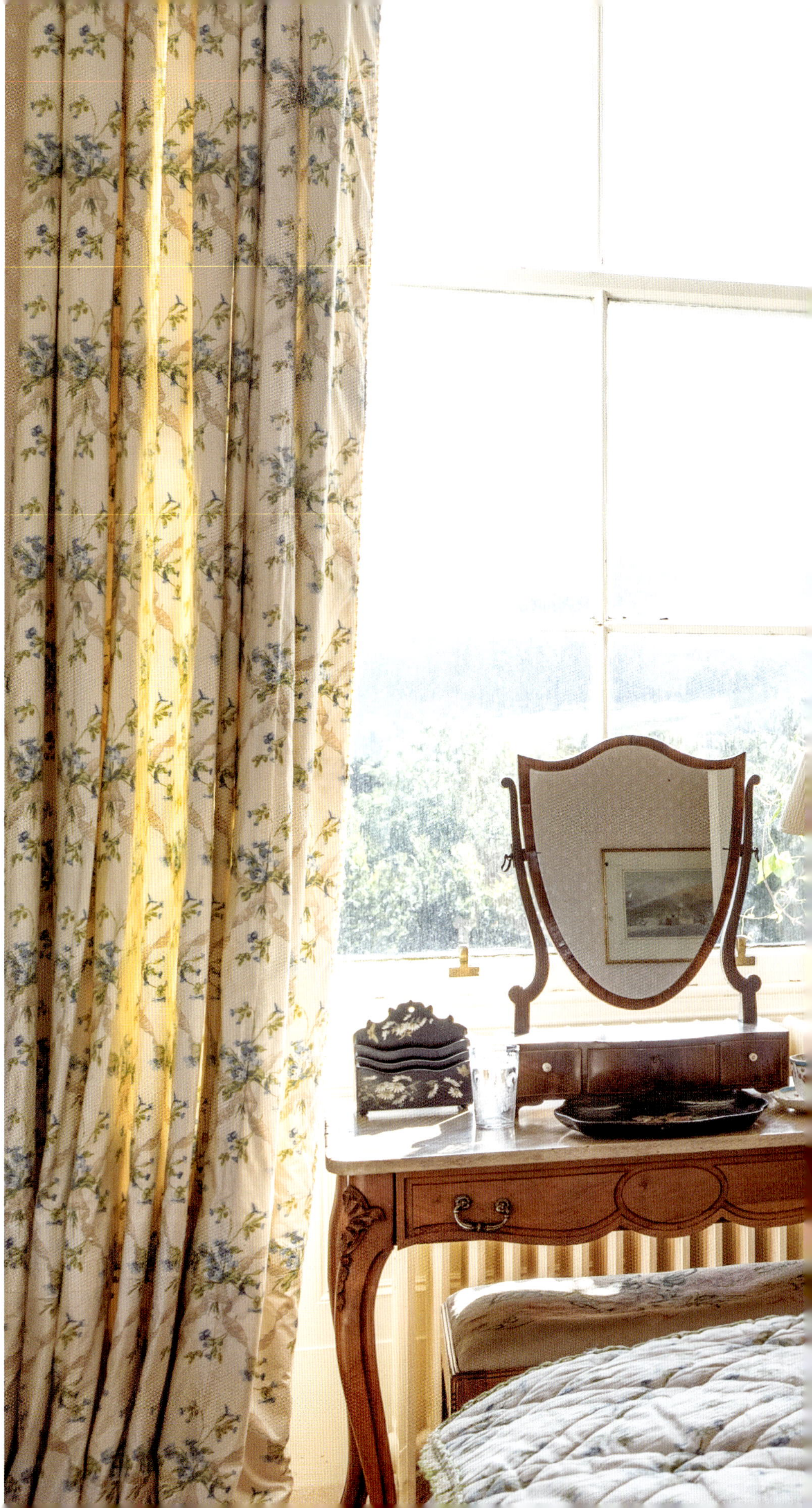

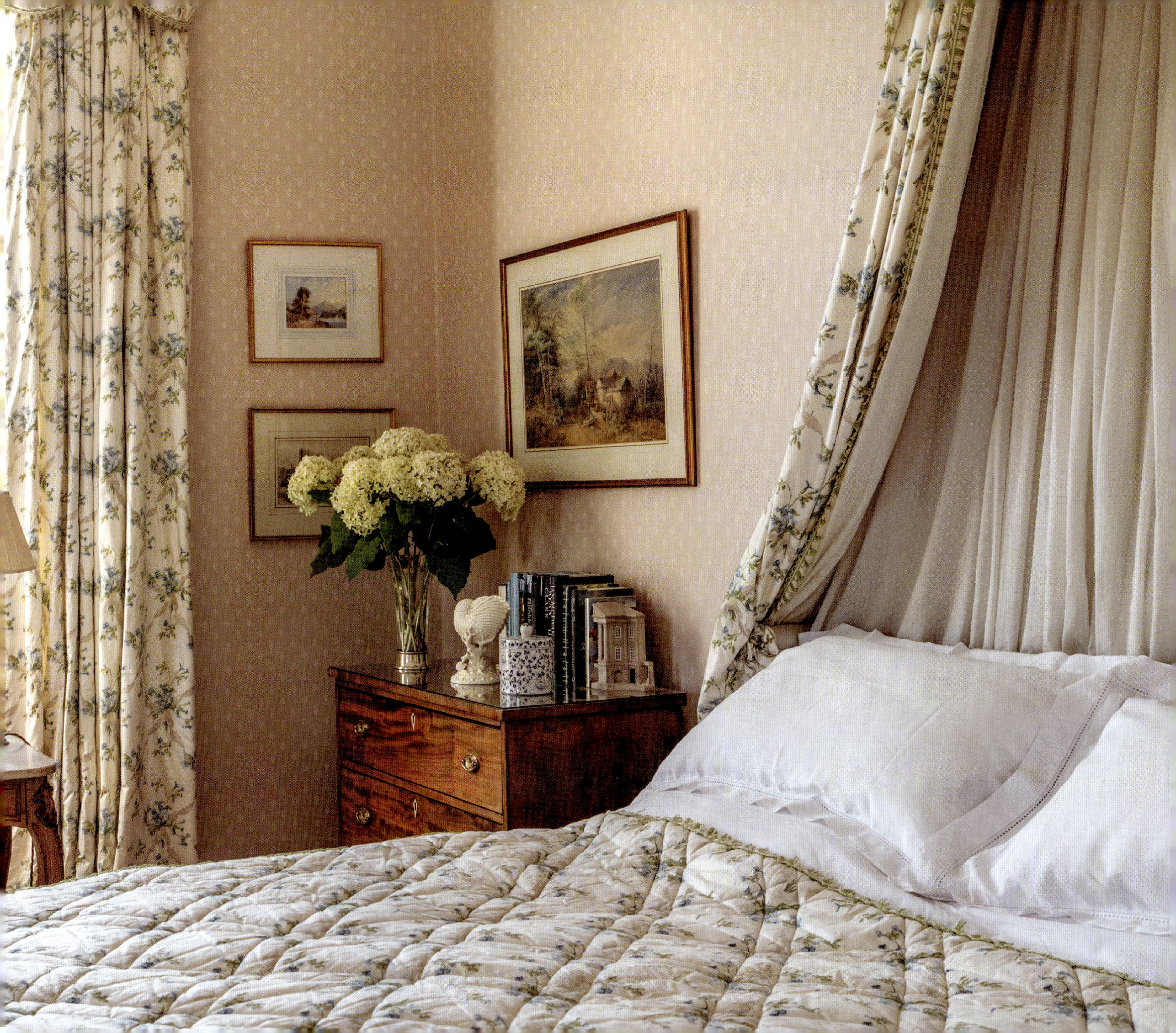
IAN McEWAN
ATTACK

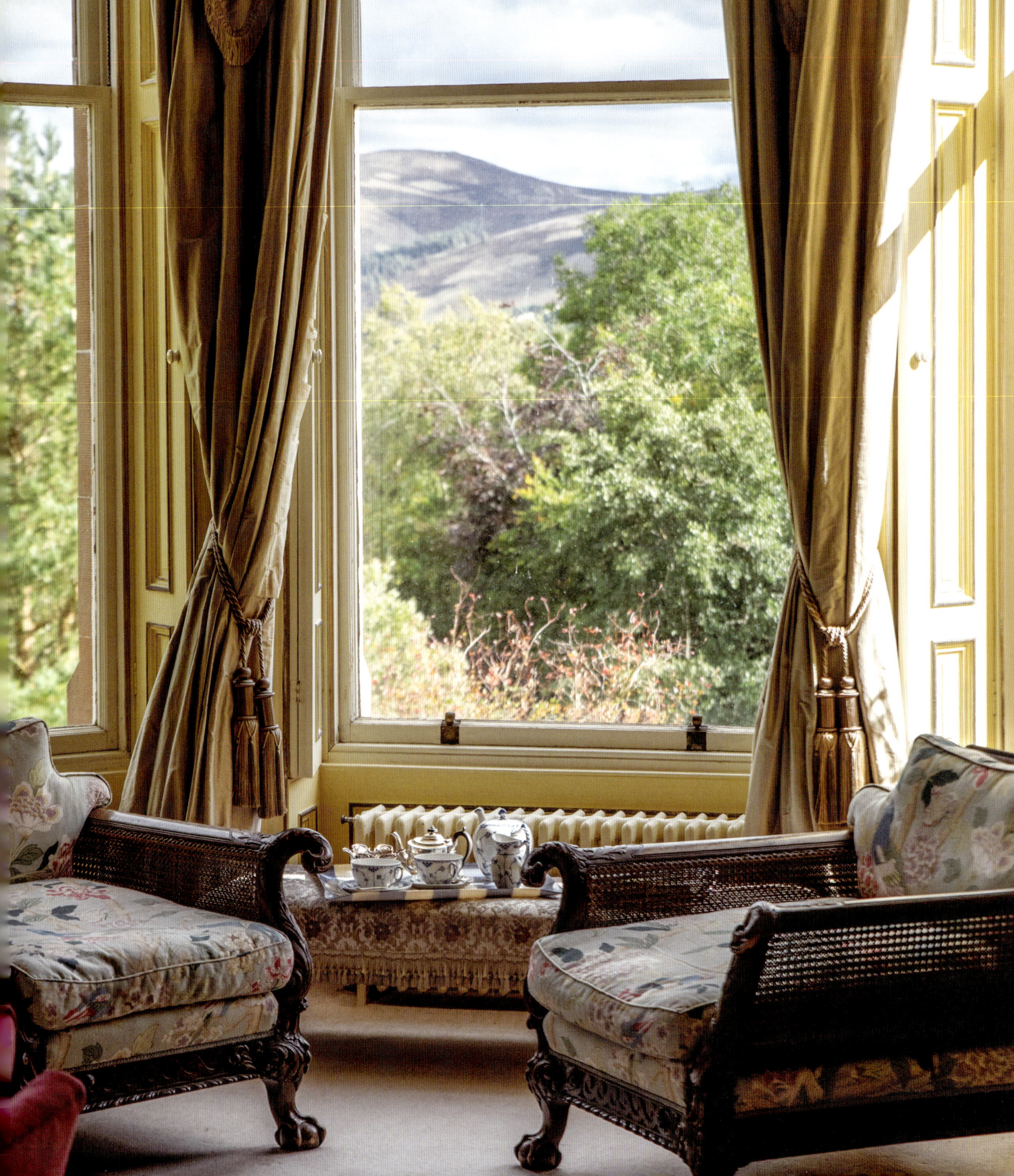

Glenternie can accommodate four sojourners between its two guest rooms. Welcoming them into her home with quintessential hospitality, innkeeper Lucy Wood serves a full Scottish breakfast in the dining room, where the travelers may also request an evening meal. Left and opposite, right: The drawing room, which looks out on the Southern Uplands, retains the original gilded cornice and paneling. Below left: A Georgian walnut bureau from Anthony's family is one of many antiques lending charm to the abode.

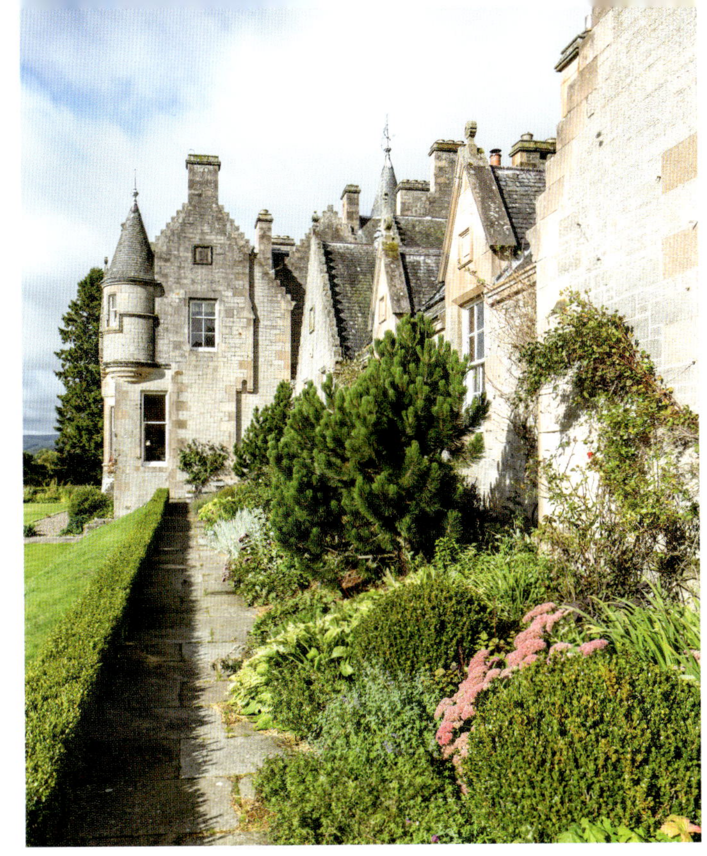

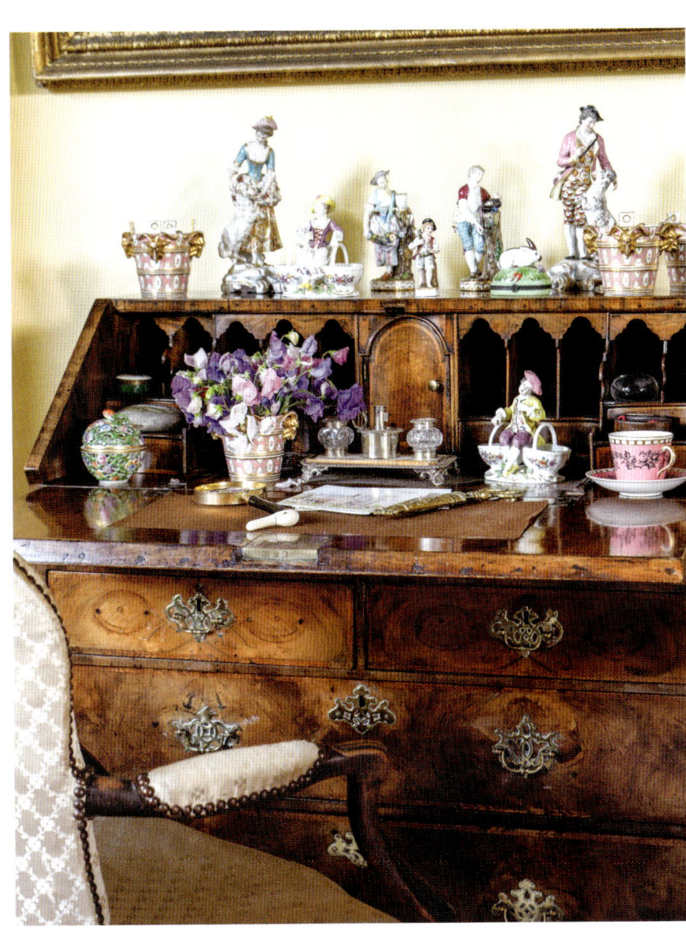

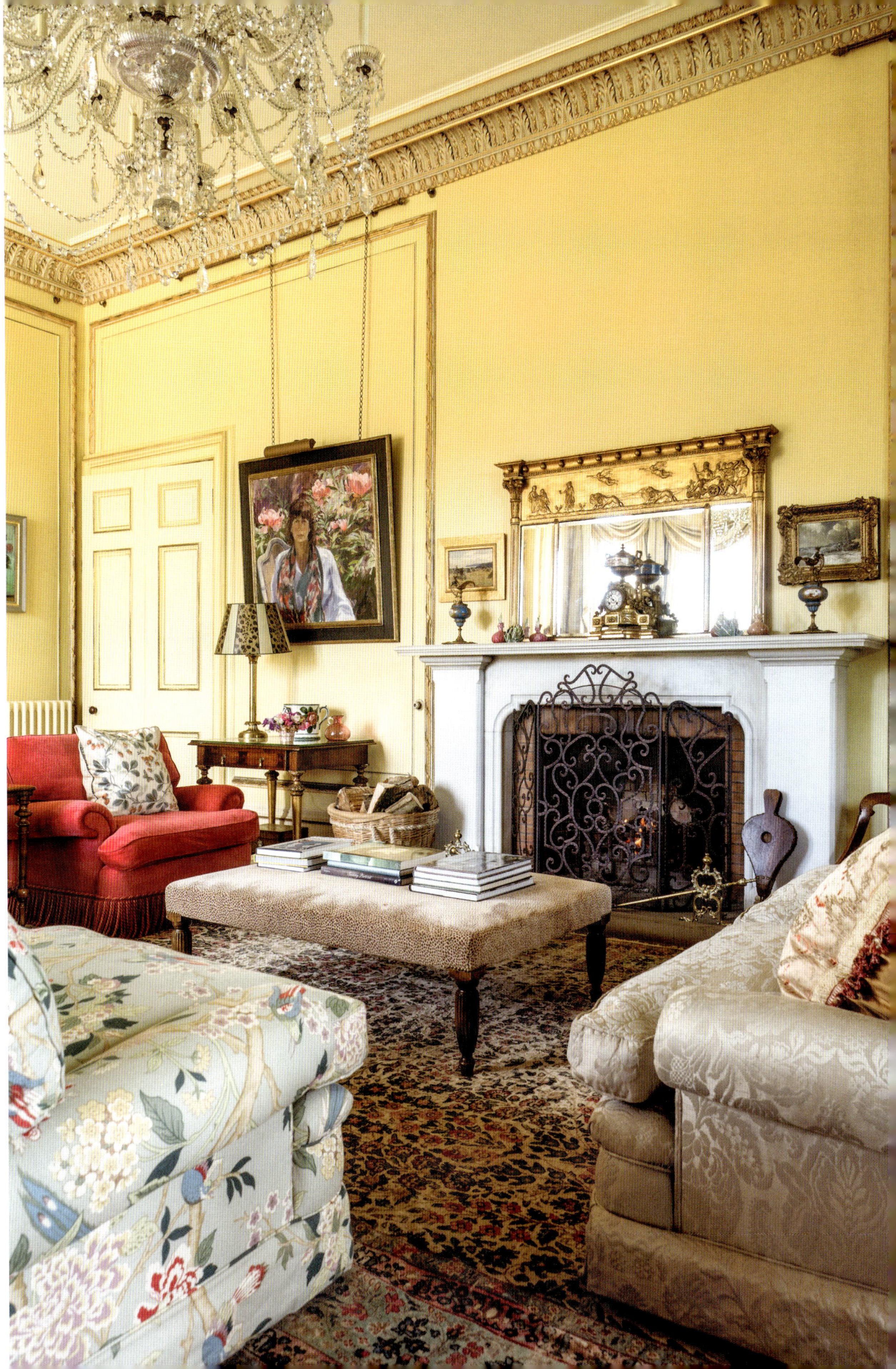

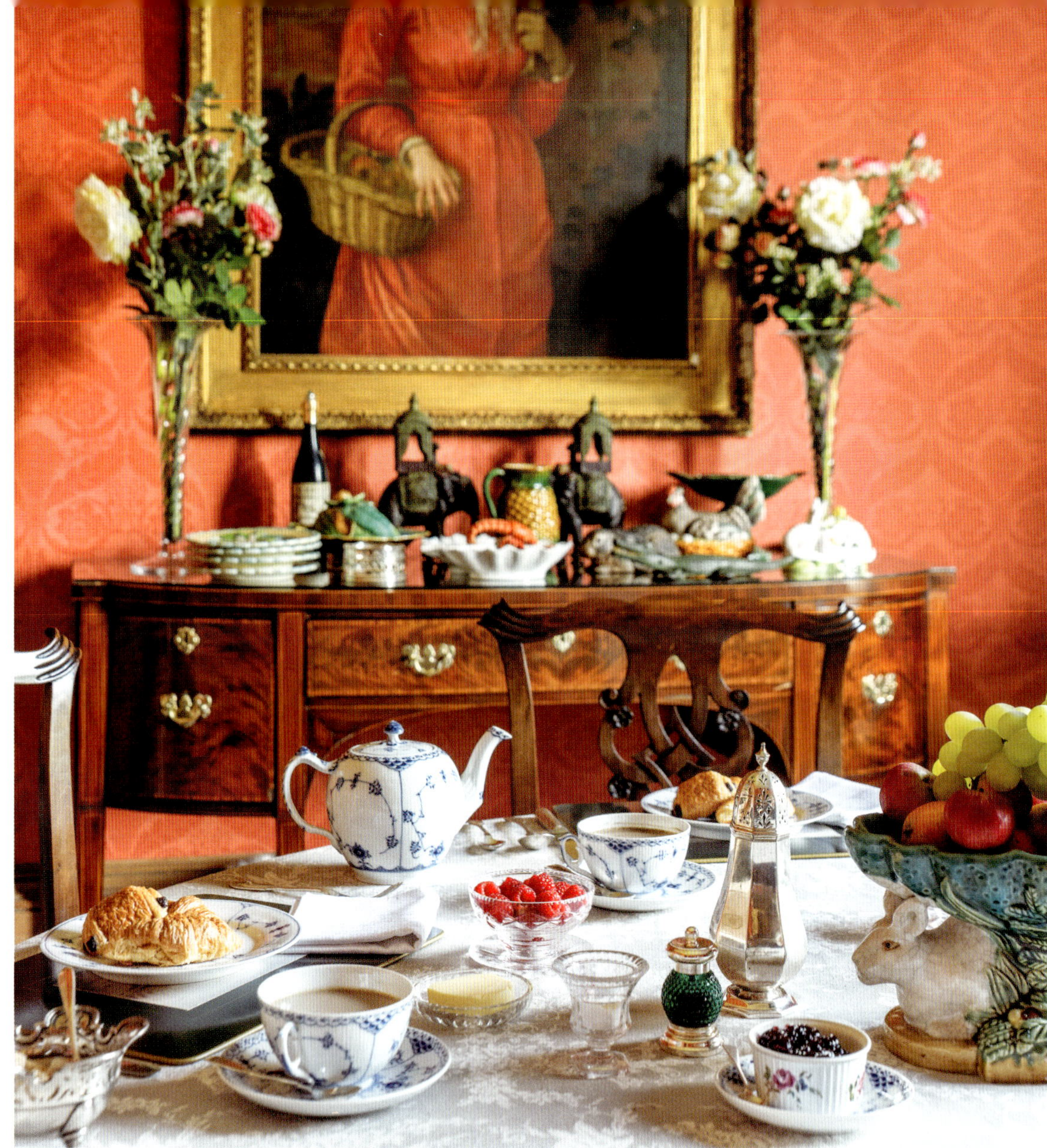

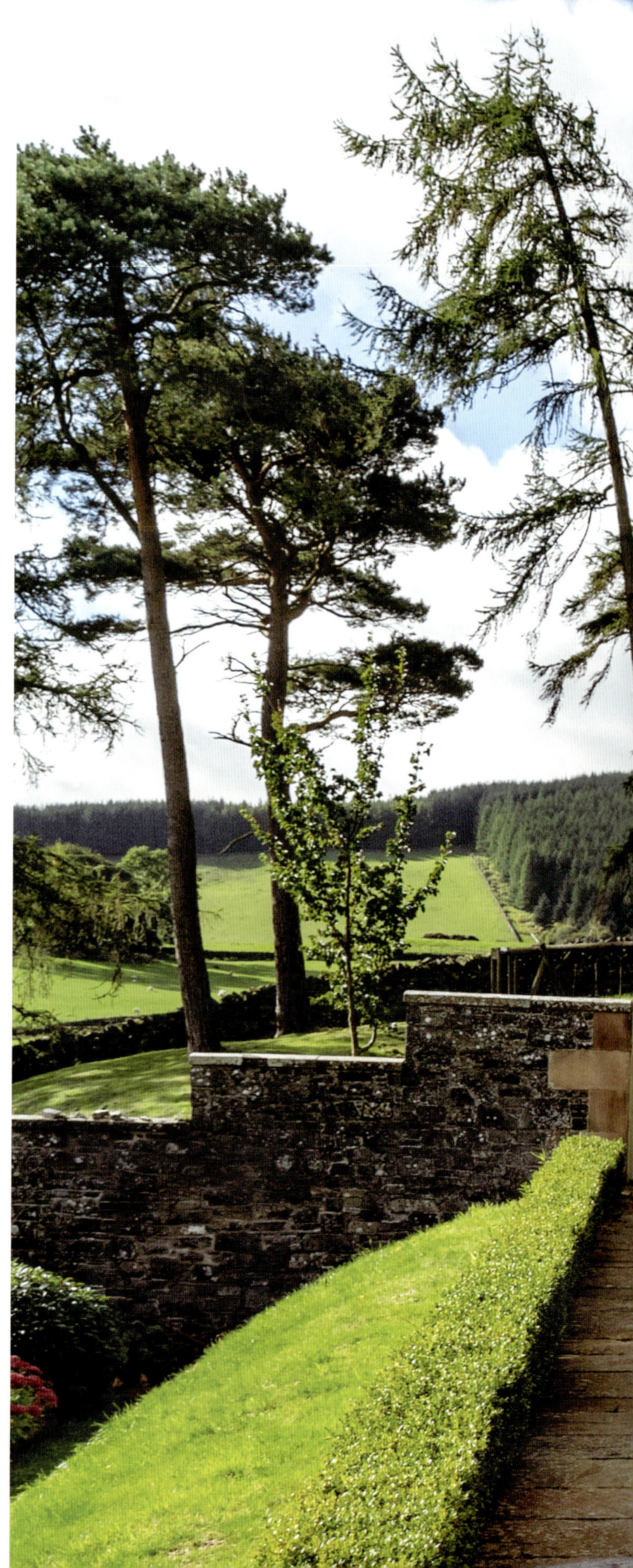

in the dwelling for many years. Later proprietors divided the mansion to accommodate two separate families—a change that the Woodds reversed. They also added central heating and other amenities, built the garden, and rearranged the rooms to suit today's living.

The interior is decorated with a historical atmosphere in mind, using mostly furniture inherited from family members. Lucy's interest in antiques has also helped find unique pieces over the years, some of which adorn Glenternie and others that are displayed in her antiques shop beneath Anthony's gallery in Edinburgh.

The bed-and-breakfast is not far from Scotland's capital but is remote enough that visitors can still enjoy a taste of rural life. Splendid views, winding roads, nearby castles, and small historic towns all invite exploration in this peaceful and uplifting destination.

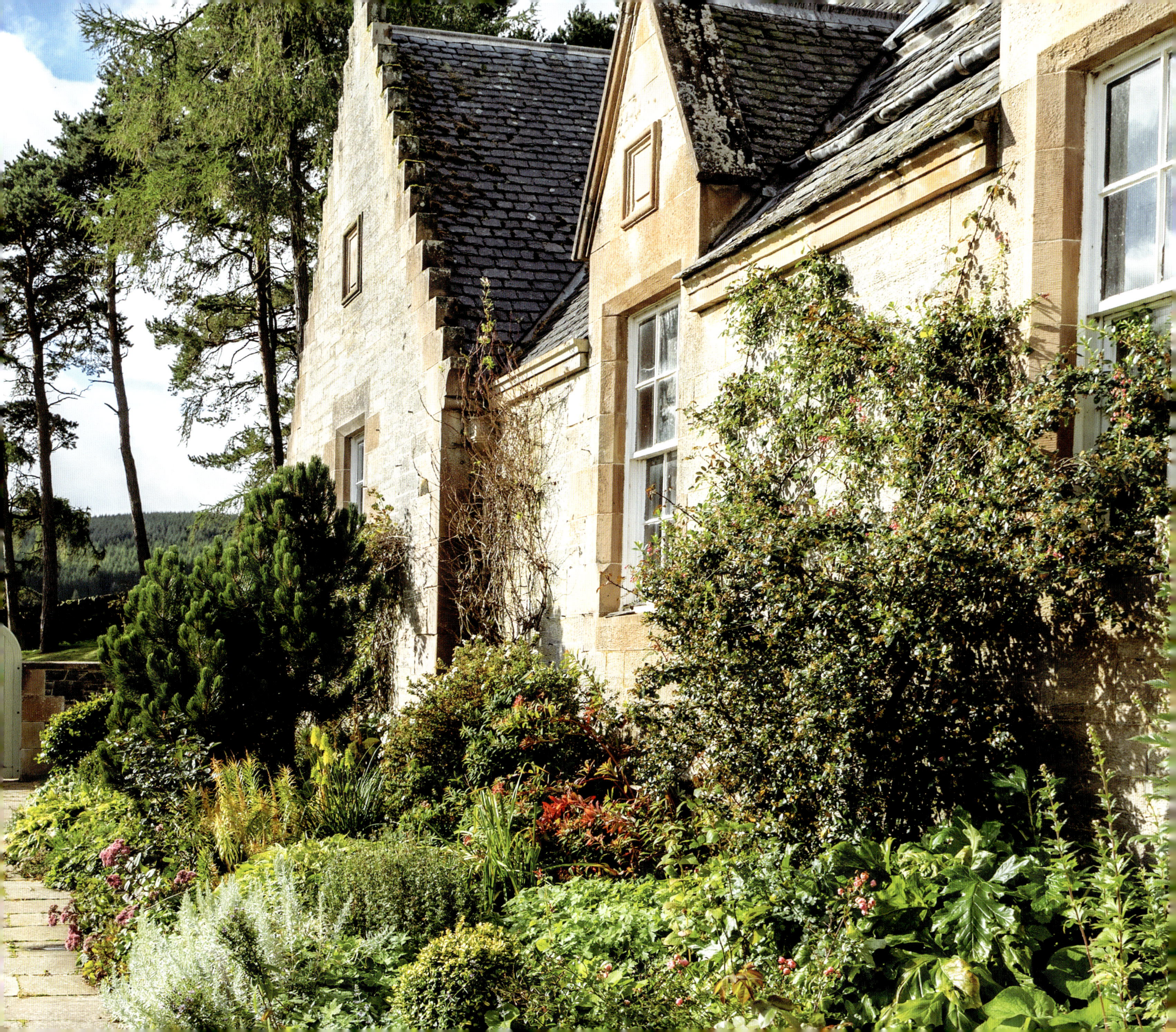

A SCOTTISH SANCTUARY

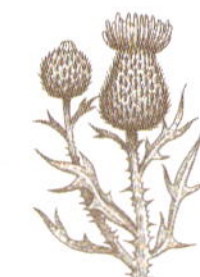

Edinburgh, Scotland, is often counted among Europe's most breathtaking destinations. Its eponymous stone castle is perched high upon a central promontory—a regal presence presiding over the city. Centuries of history unfold on streets that radiate from the majestic structure. Nearby, within secluded gardens on the fringe of the urban district, imposing gates frame a grand hotel.

Built in 1687 as the home of the Lord Provost, the Baroque-style house was restored early in the twenty-first century under the vision and artistic eye of owner James Thomson as the exclusive Prestonfield. The renovation focused on reviving the character of the ancient property and re-establishing its distinctive appeal. Wildly colorful and extravagant, the avant-garde surroundings retain the distinguished ambience of a gracious historic manor. Opulent décor, including many of the original fine furnishings, enhances the luxurious environs of this famed retreat.

As guests approach the main entrance through the porte cochere, an impeccable staff comes out to welcome and assist them. Beyond the carved-wood doors, a cornucopia of visual delights awaits. Center stage, artful arrangements of seasonal flowers and produce spill from baskets and tumble out of urns. Broad expanses of plush, patterned carpet and gleaming

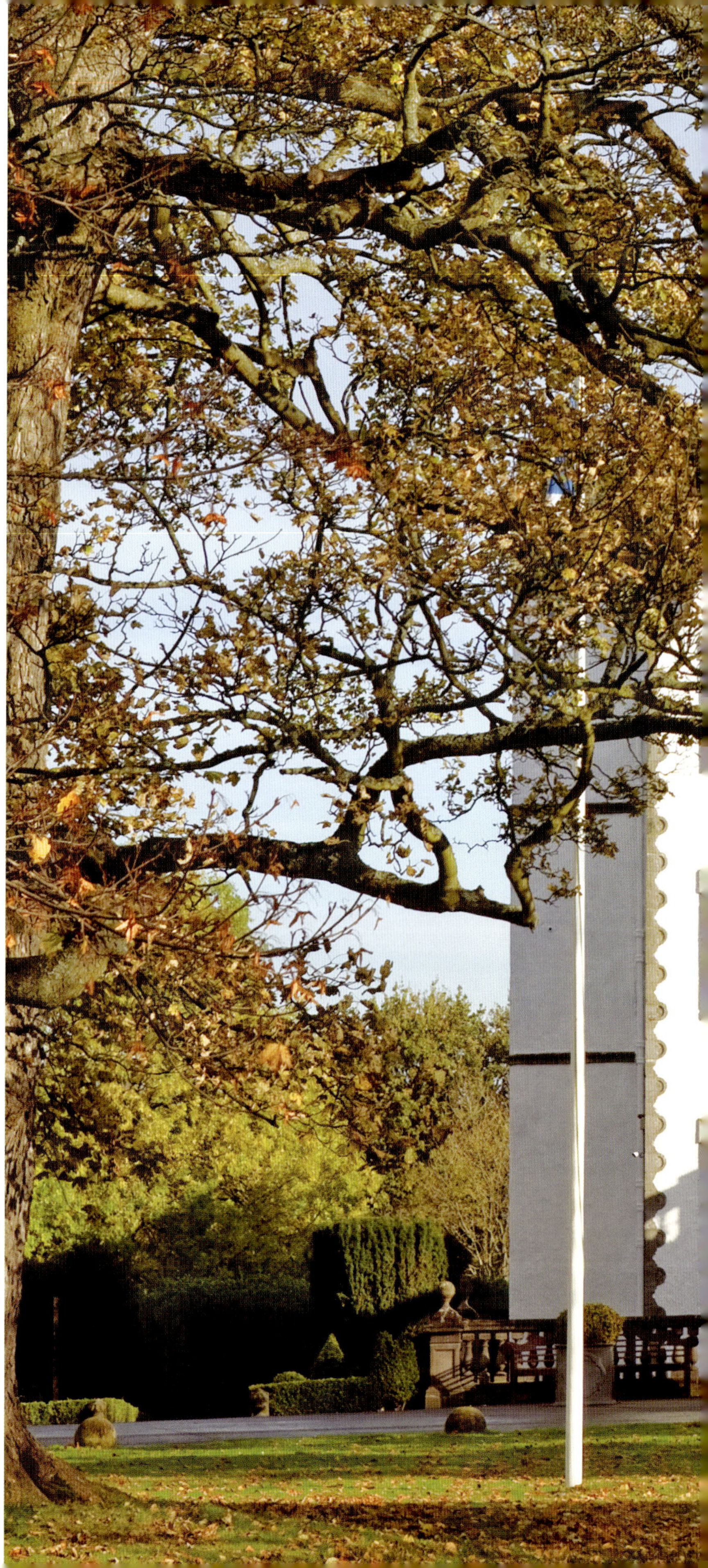

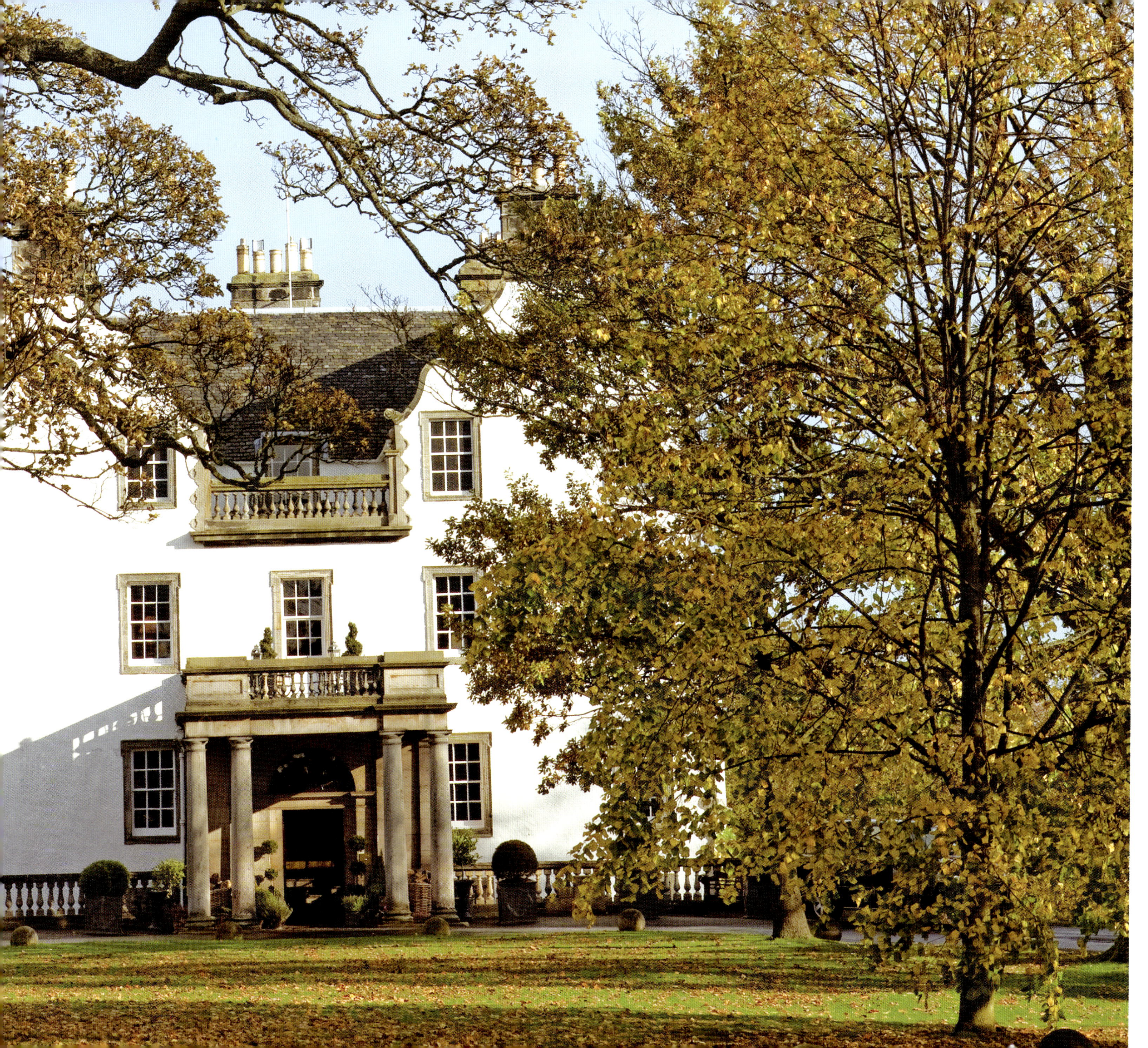

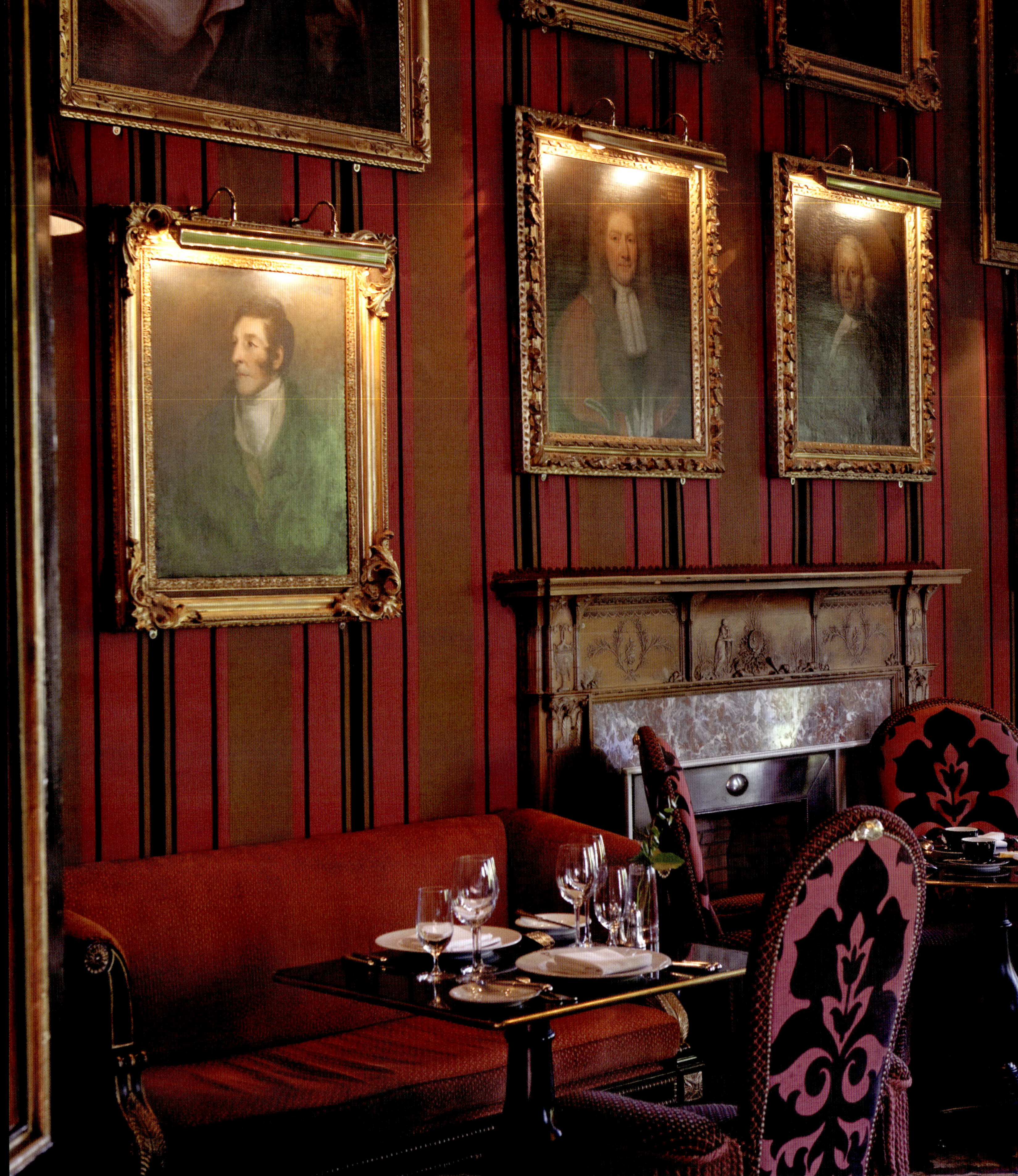

Left: The name of Prestonfield's fine-dining restaurant, Rhubarb, recalls the estate's culinary history as the first in Scotland to propagate the succulent Asian plant. Opposite, right: Panels of gilded seventeenth-century Córdoba leather line the walls of the Leather Room, adding a sense of richness to the splendid setting. Above left and below: Intricately woven textiles and tapestries fill the guest suites.

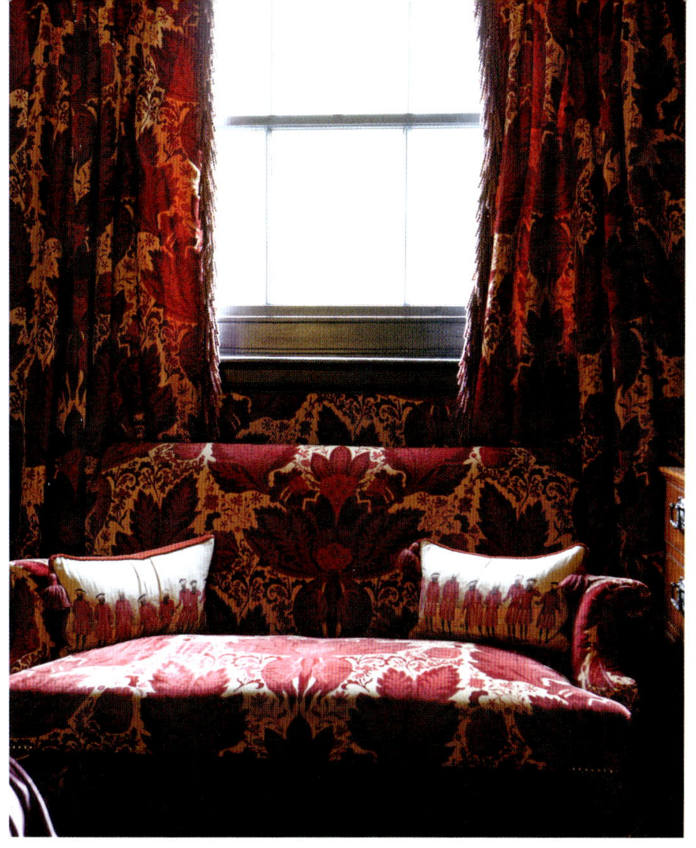

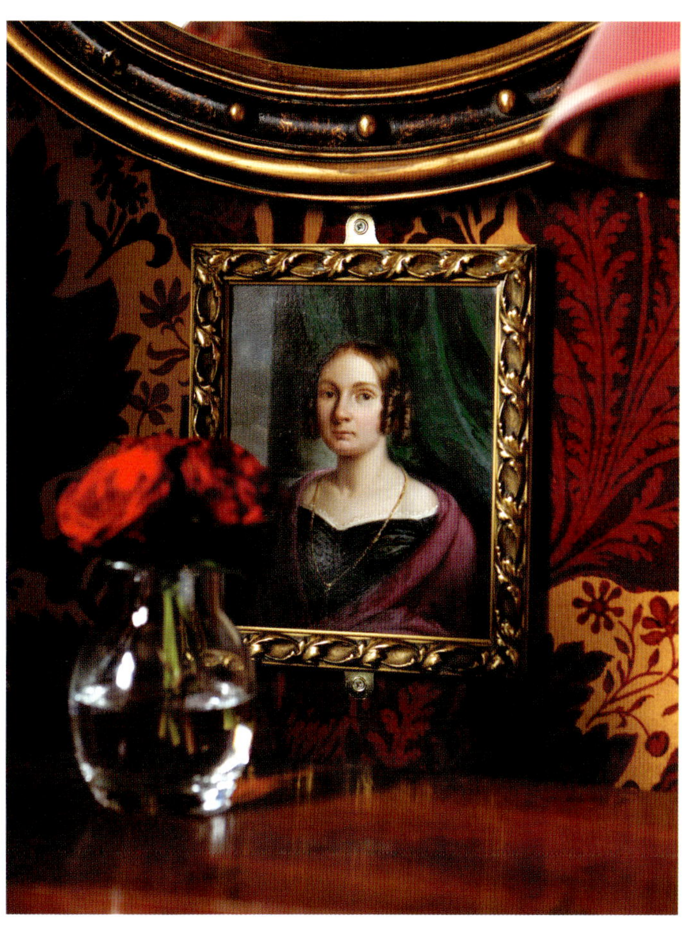

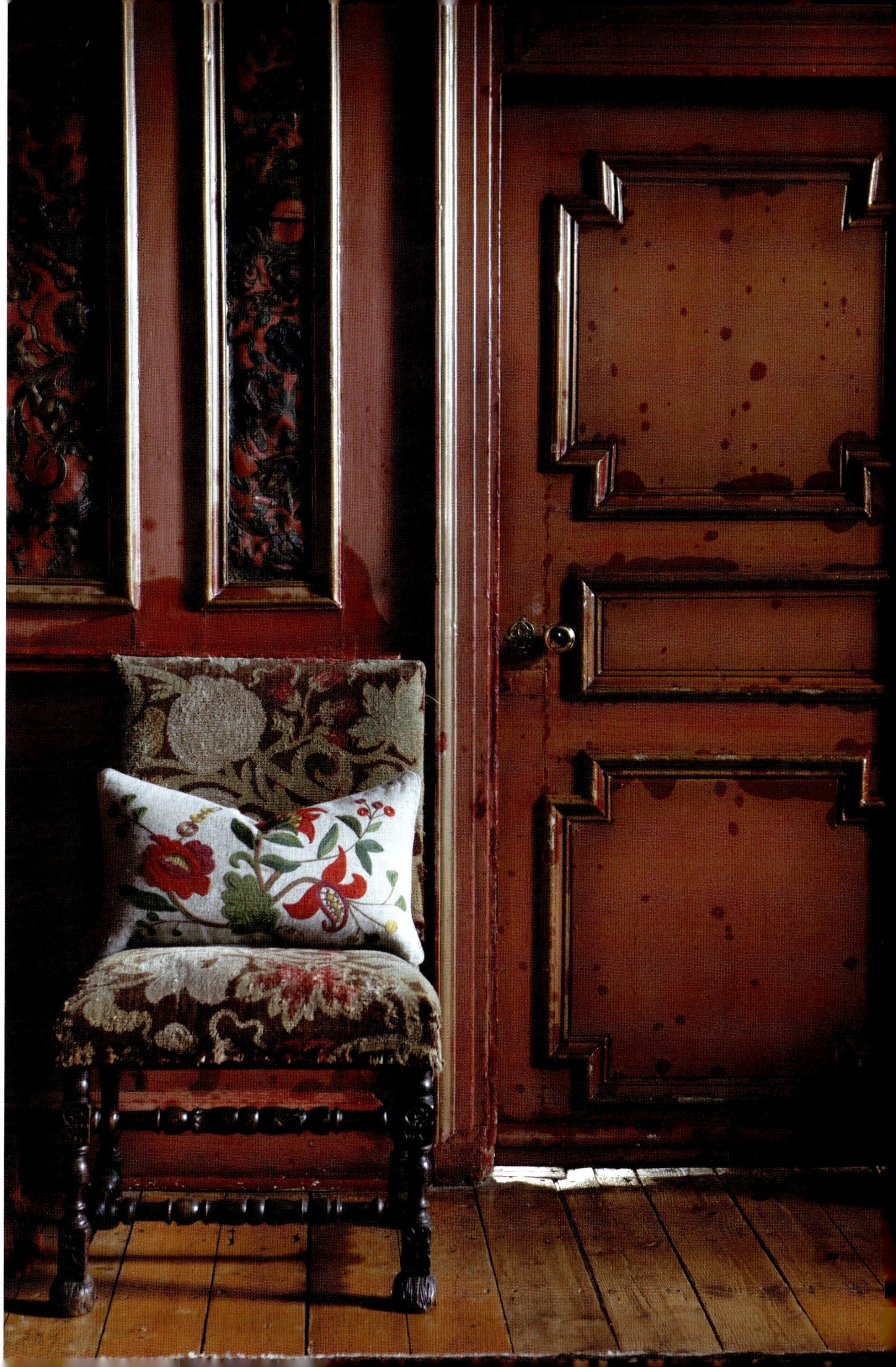

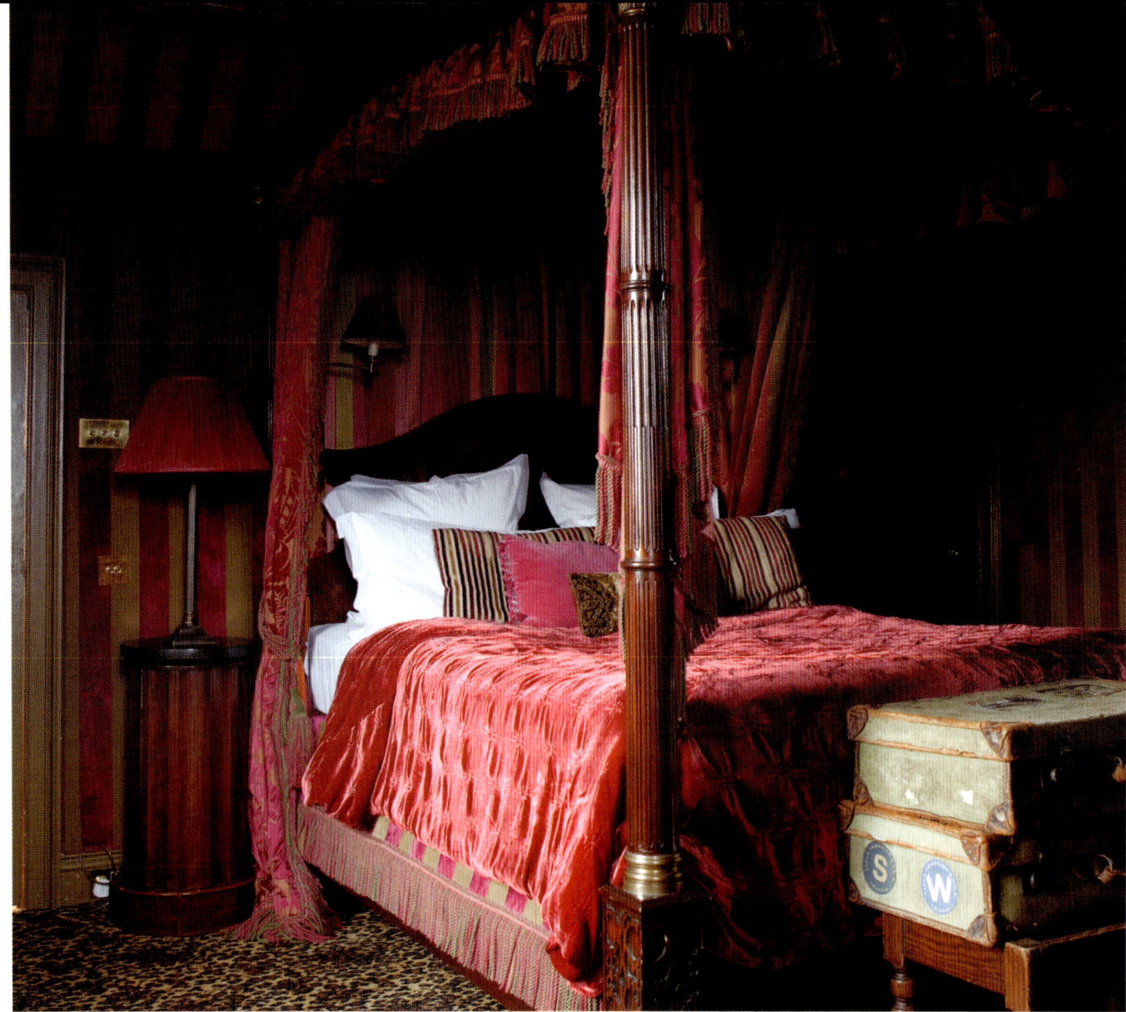

marble extend down a sweeping corridor to the reception area. Arched doorways offer tantalizing glimpses of richly arrayed public rooms, each one featuring its own stylized design scheme.

The five-star property boasts eighteen bedrooms and five suites that provide a level of personalized hospitality rivaling that experienced at a dear friend's country home. Just a few of the thoughtful touches include plumped pillows, freshly made sweets arranged upon the sitting-room table, a desk replete with writing accoutrements, and a deep bathtub ideal for soaking in after an invigorating day of taking in Edinburgh's finest sights.

Guests seeking relaxation, as well as those who prefer more active pursuits, will find plenty of entertaining diversions, such as croquet games on the manicured lawn, golfing on an adjacent course, bird-watching, strolling through parkland, or borrowing a bicycle for the day. Afternoon tea is served throughout the premises in grand salons and drawing rooms as well as in a diminutive Gothic teahouse nestled in the gardens. Dinner reservations are highly sought after in the hotel's chic restaurant, which serves innovative farm-to-table cuisine in a pair of elaborately decorated Regency-style dining rooms. Stunning interiors and superb level of service at Prestonfield contribute to an unforgettable experience for all who visit this charmingly eclectic boutique hotel.

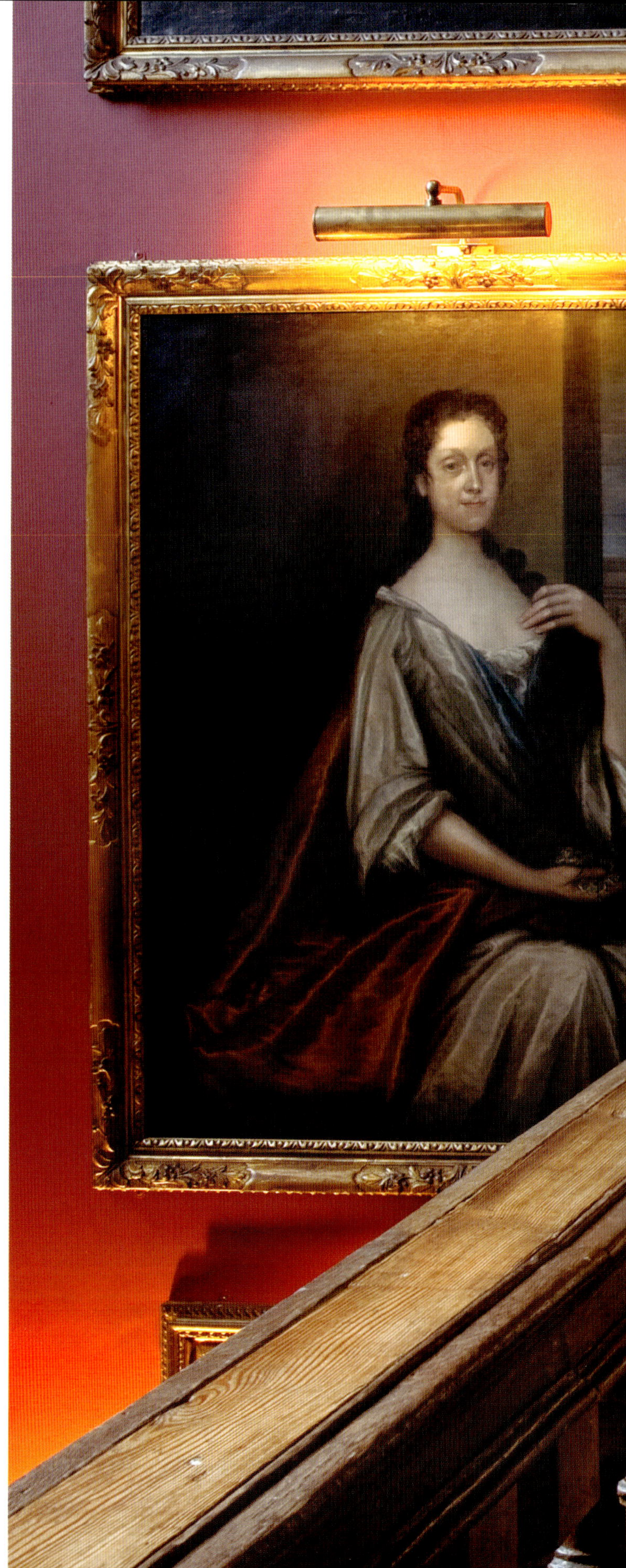

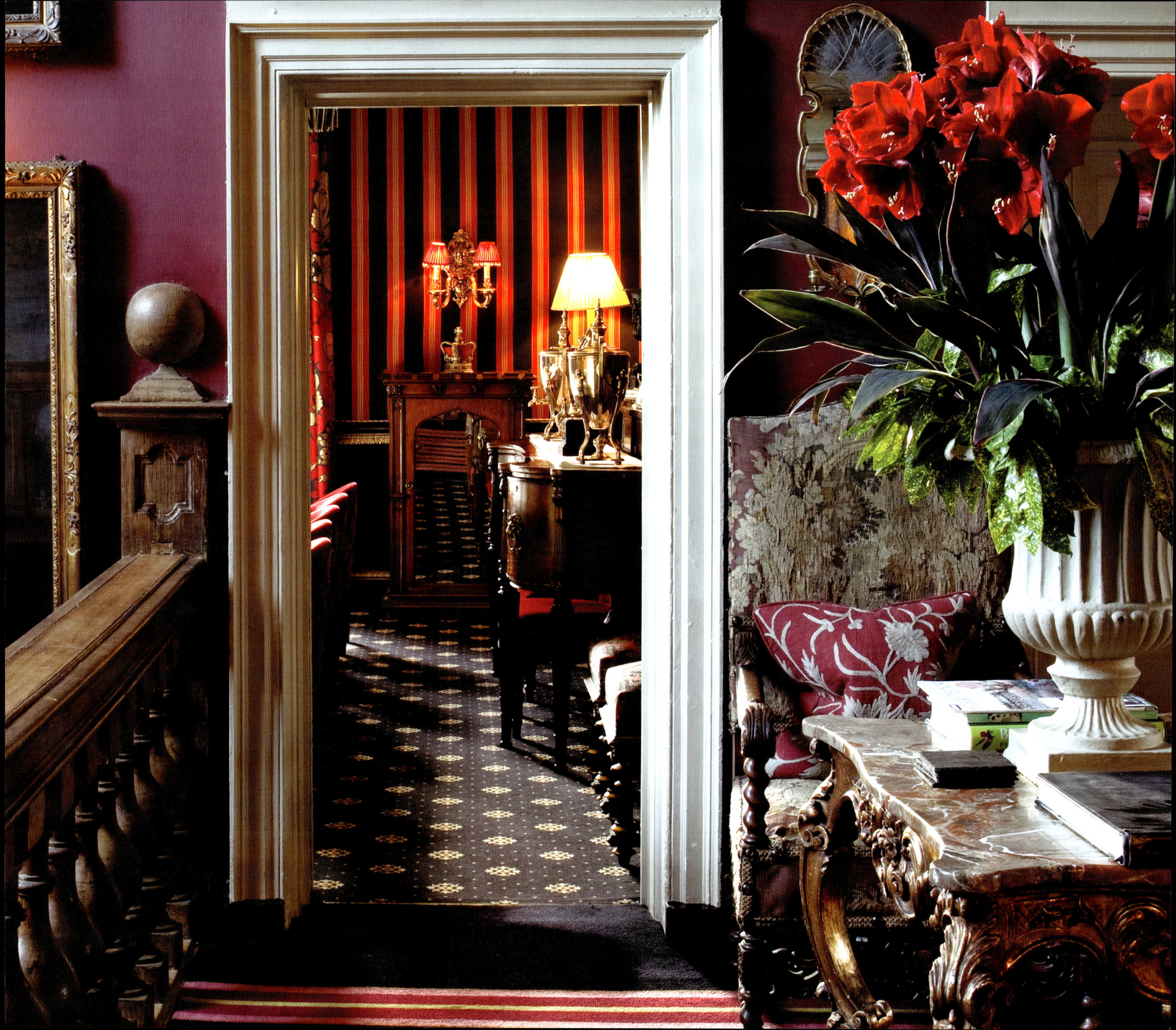

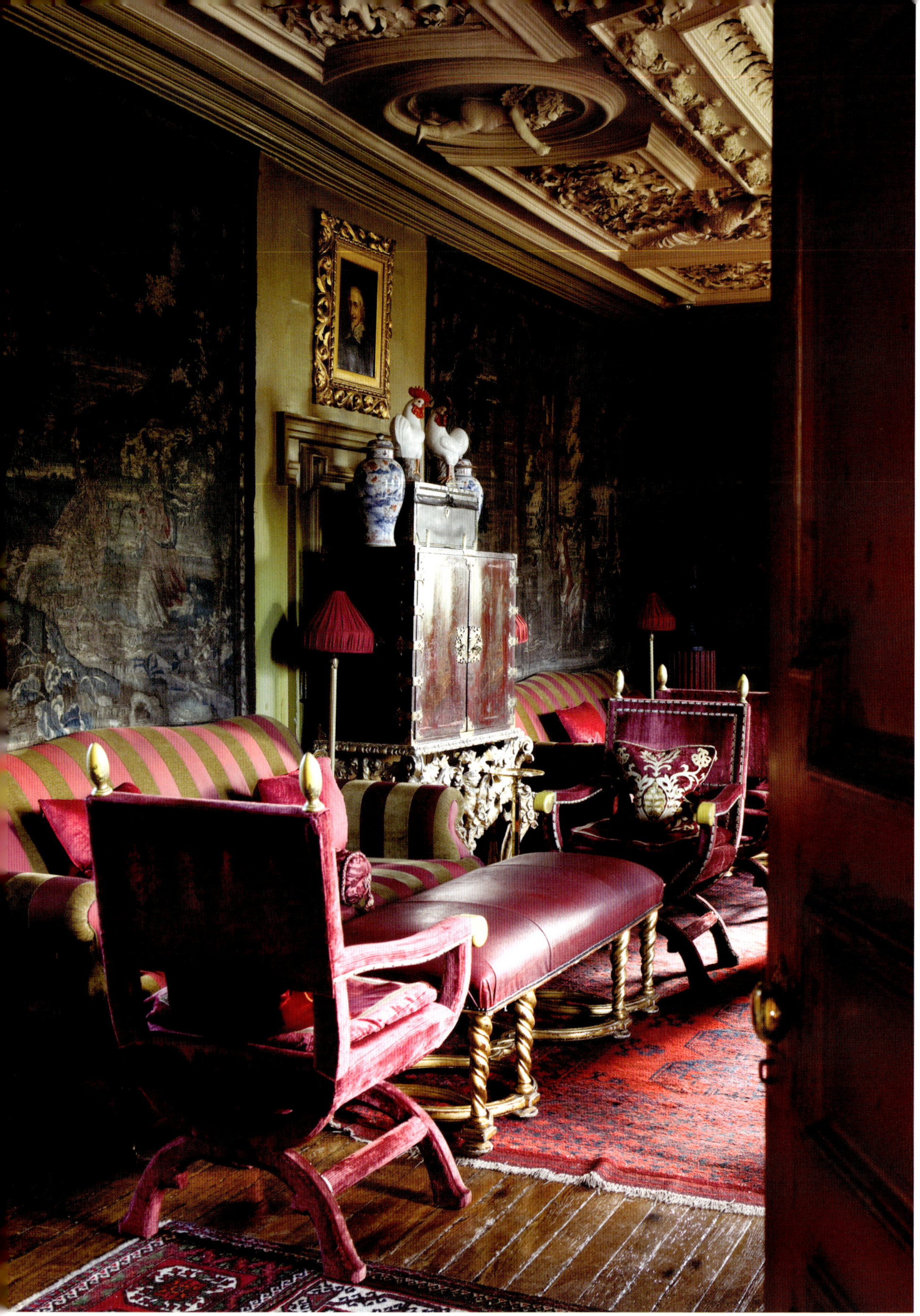

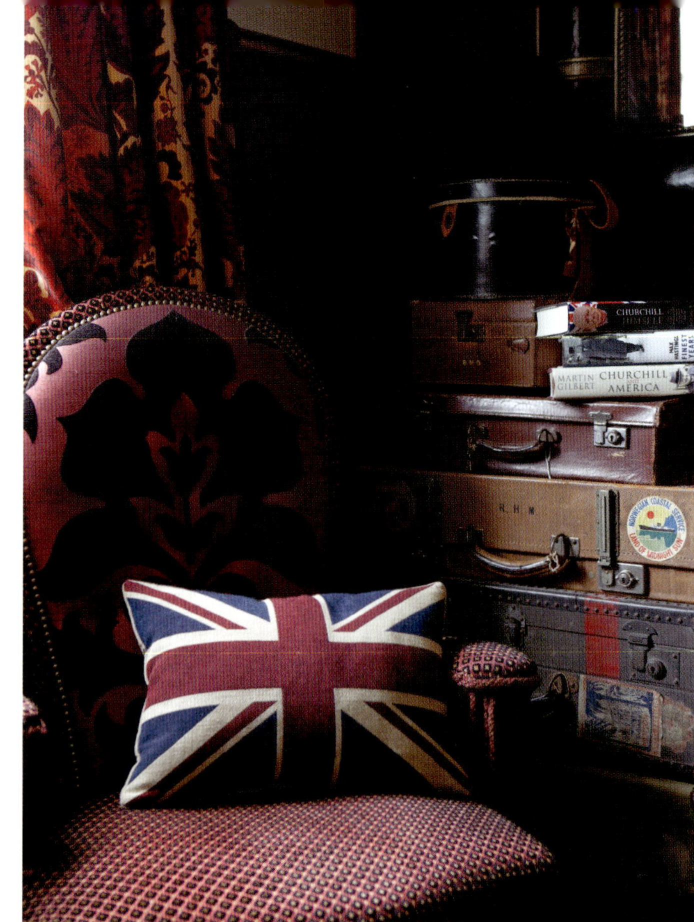
CHURCHILL
MARTIN GILBERT
CHURCHILL AMERICA

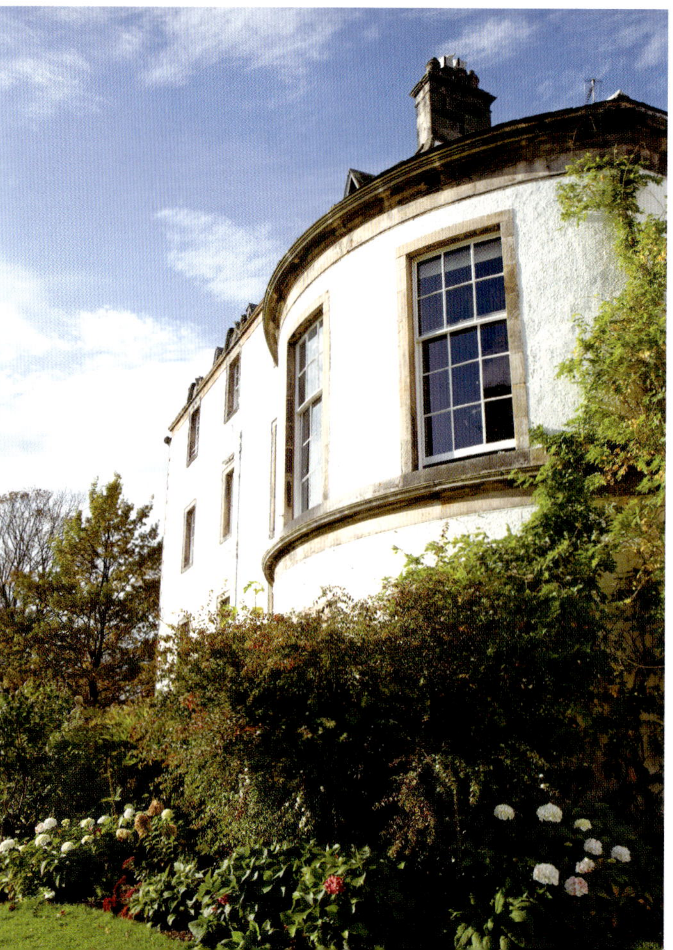

"When I looked out in the morning it is as if I had waked in Utopia."

—George Elliot

Deeply saturated hues and luscious textures adorn every surface of Prestonfield, creating a soothing, cocooned environment in which guests can retreat. Right: Friends meet for afternoon tea or an evening aperitif in the Yellow Room, a lavishly furnished petite salon on the main level. Opposite, below right: The gleaming white façade of the auberge stands in stately contrast to the vibrant palette of the interiors. The studied design extends to the grounds, with acres of landscaped gardens and lush lawns to explore.

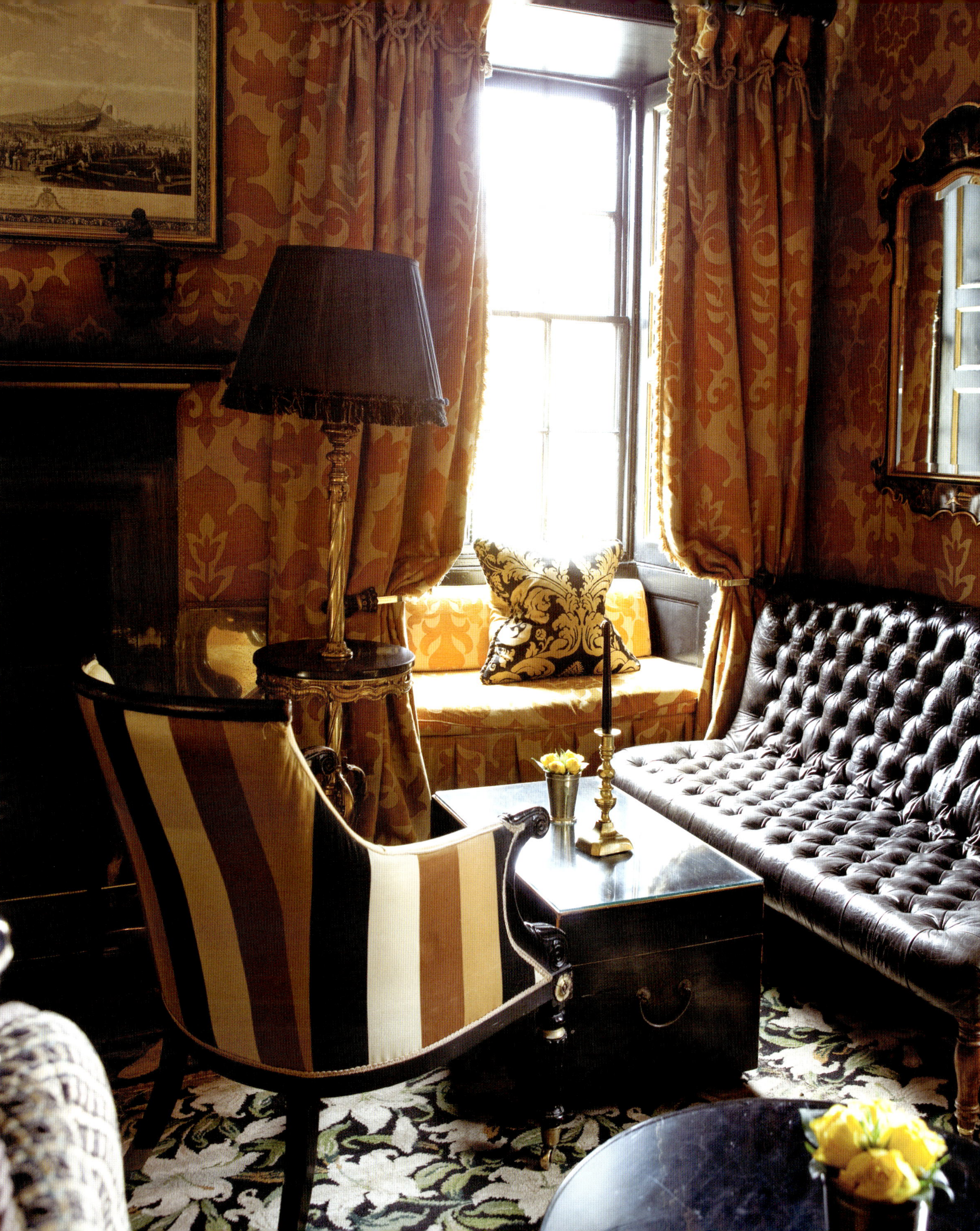

HIGHLAND HOSPITALITY

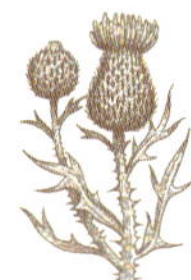

Kinloch Lodge stands gallantly against the enchanting light, mist, and mystique of Scotland's Isle of Skye. Overlooking the shores of Loch Na Dal on the Sound of Sleat, this former seventeenth-century ancestral dwelling and hunting lodge has become a harbor of Highland hospitality. The venerable property has remained in the original family for generations.

Current steward, Isabella Macdonald, grew up in the hotel and returned to take the reigns from its previous innkeepers, her parents. The critically acclaimed Scottish cook and food writer Claire Macdonald and her husband, Lord Macdonald, Godfrey Macdonald of Macdonald, High Chief of Clan Donald, opened Kinloch to the public decades ago. Throughout the years, the esteemed couple worked meticulously to bring to the inn a passionate and welcoming spirit they believe captures the essence of the region.

"I had a vision of sharing this wonderful location with others," says Claire, known internationally for self-taught culinary skills and enthusiasm for simple dishes featuring locally grown ingredients. "I believed we could offer visitors an exceptional Highland experience based on genuine hospitality, which is at the heart of everything we do."

Executed to perfection, the Macdonalds' warm generosity has been appreciated by the hundreds of guests who have visited—and often returned to—Kinloch Lodge. Upon arrival,

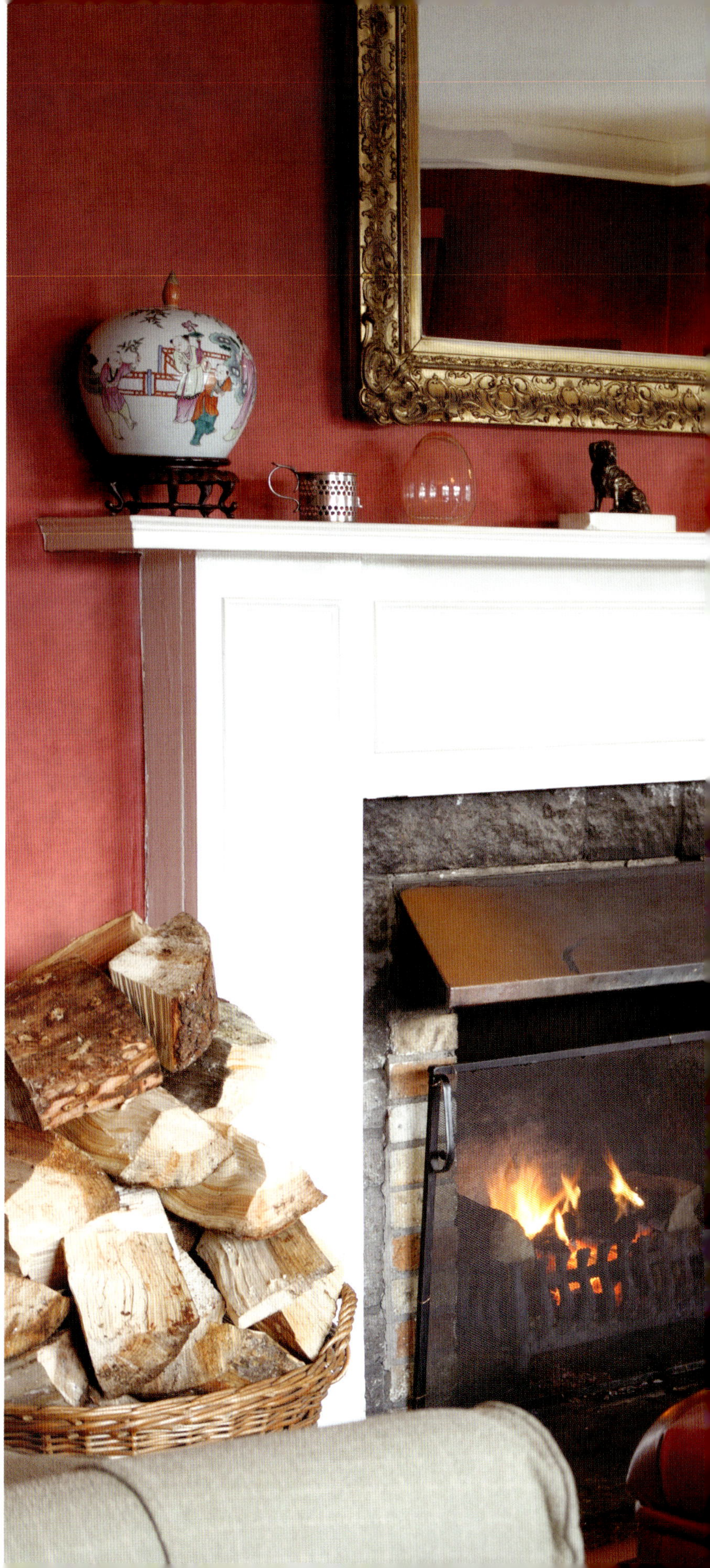

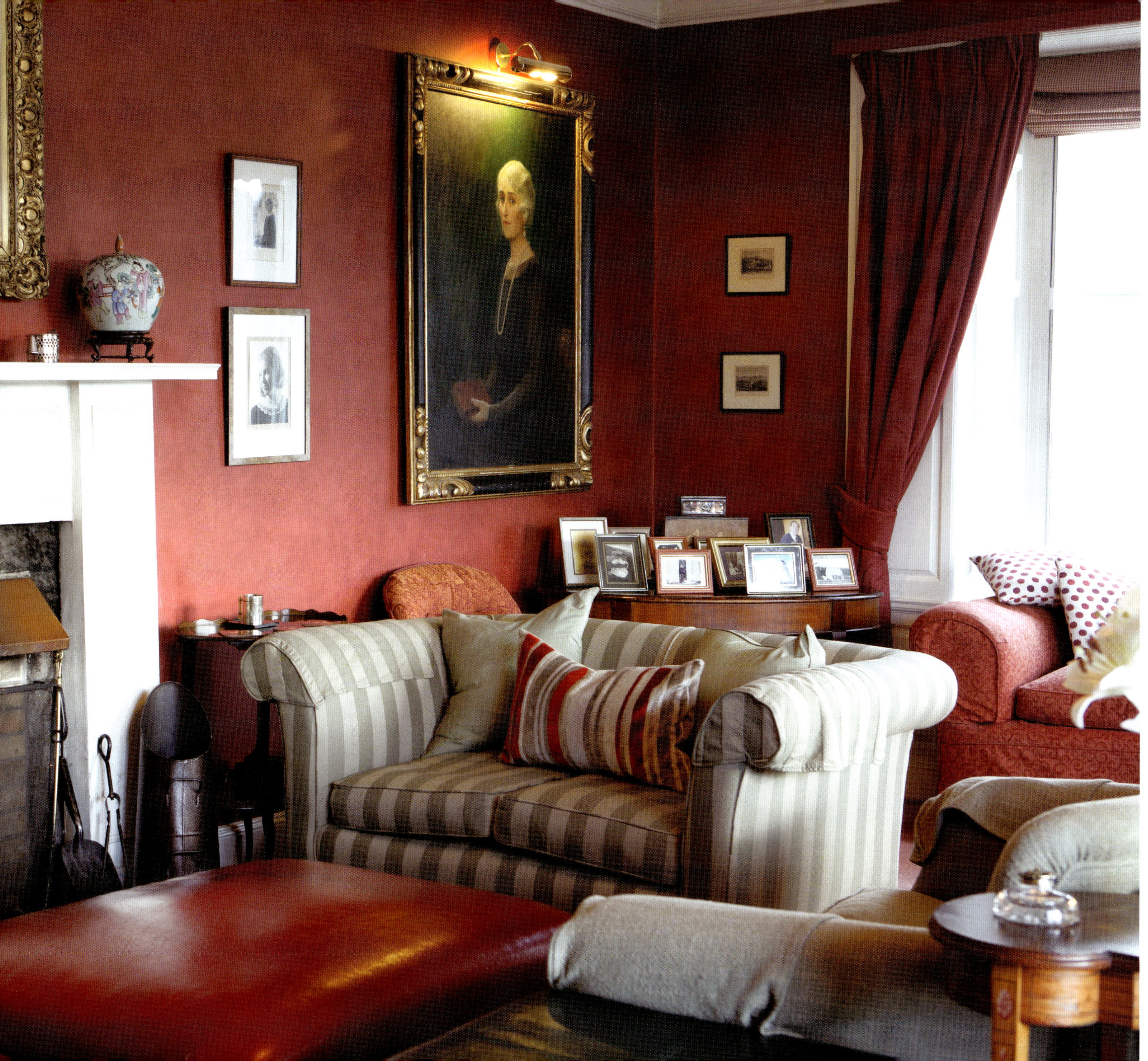

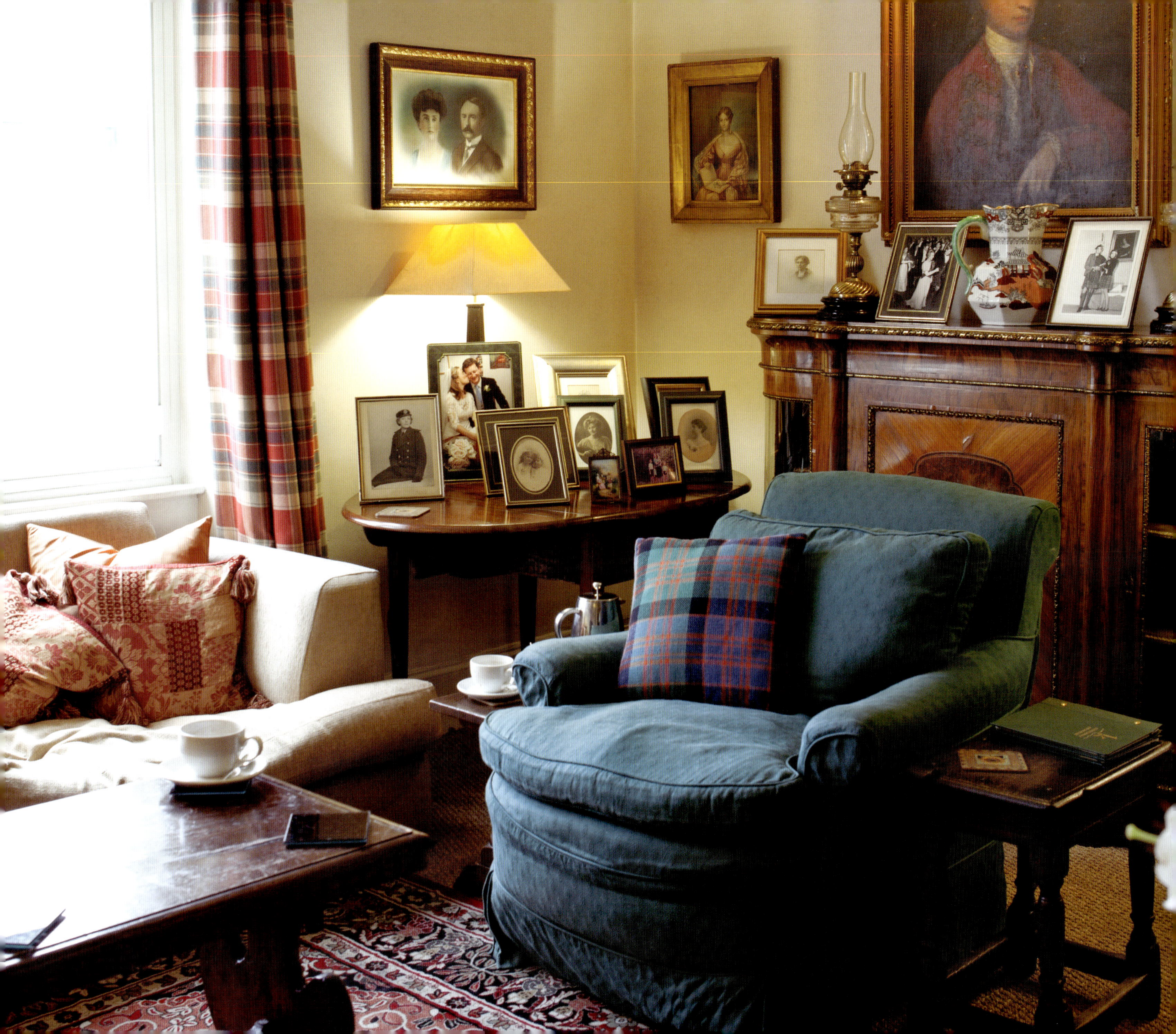

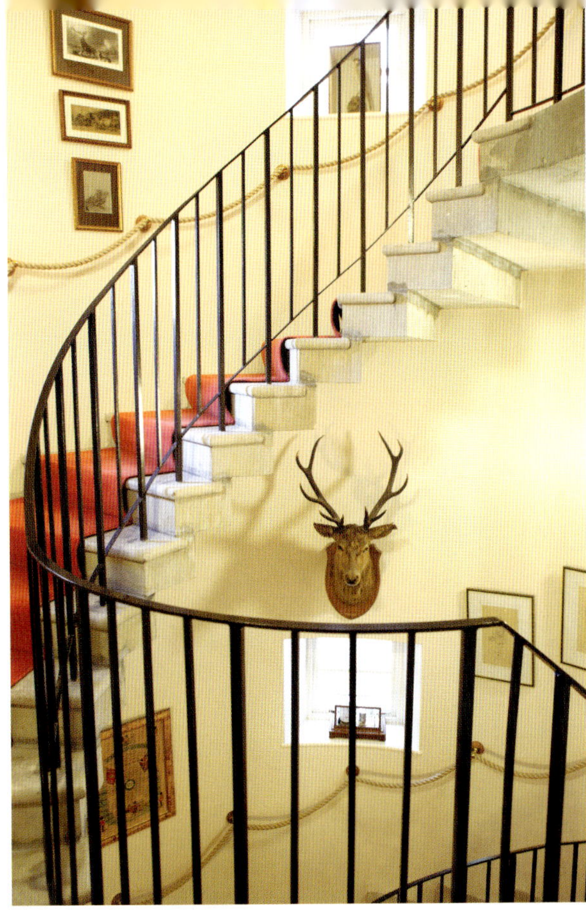

Amidst the arresting grandeur of Kinloch Lodge, guests are made to feel warmly welcomed and blissfully relaxed. The scenic surrounding property offers leisurely pursuits, including breathtaking coastal walks, sporting excursions, and tours of nearby Dunvegan Castle. Opposite: Supple seating invites one to pause to plan out a day of exploration. This page, right: The superb regional fare served in the dining room features Scotland's rich larder of produce, poultry, game, and shellfish.

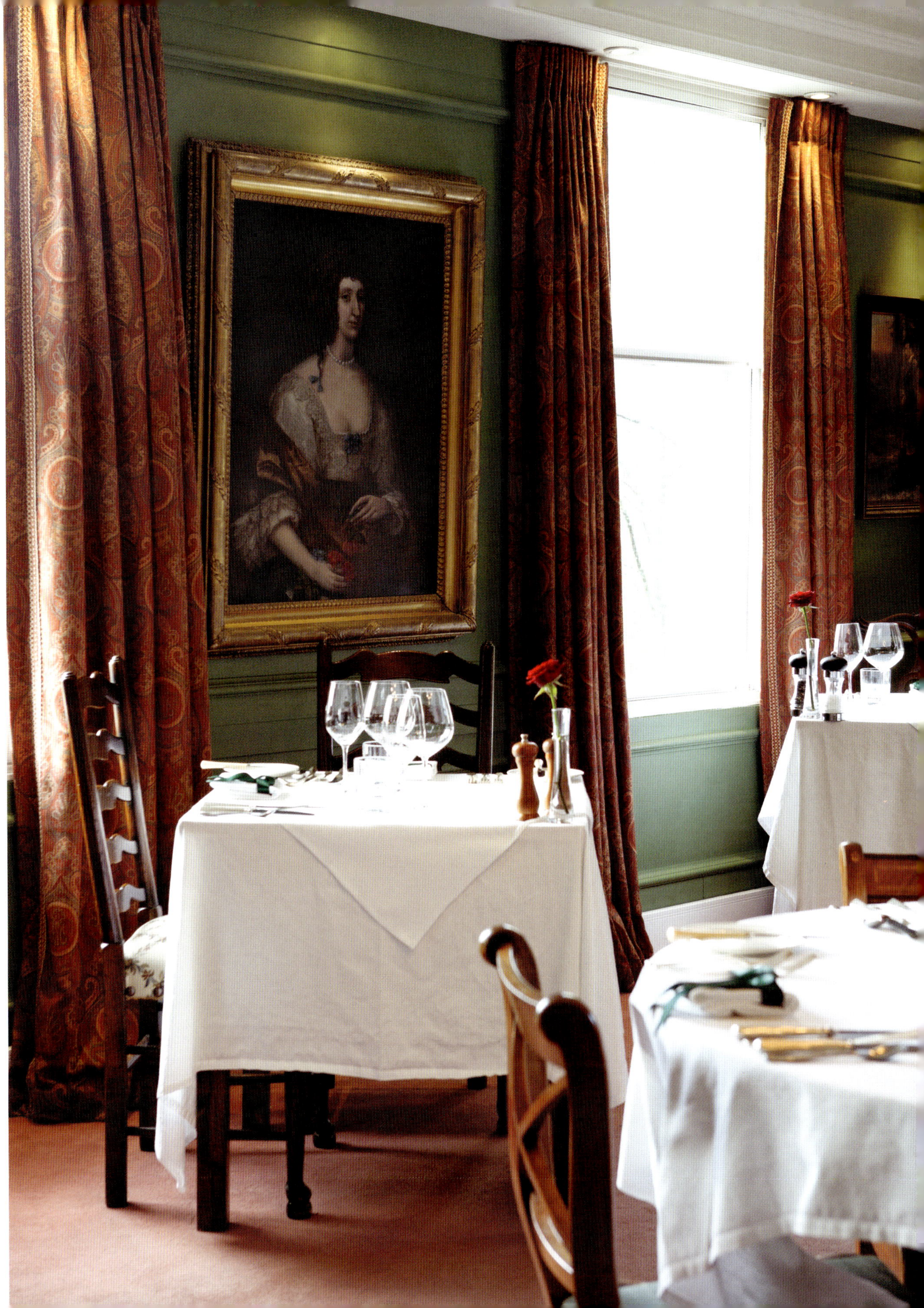

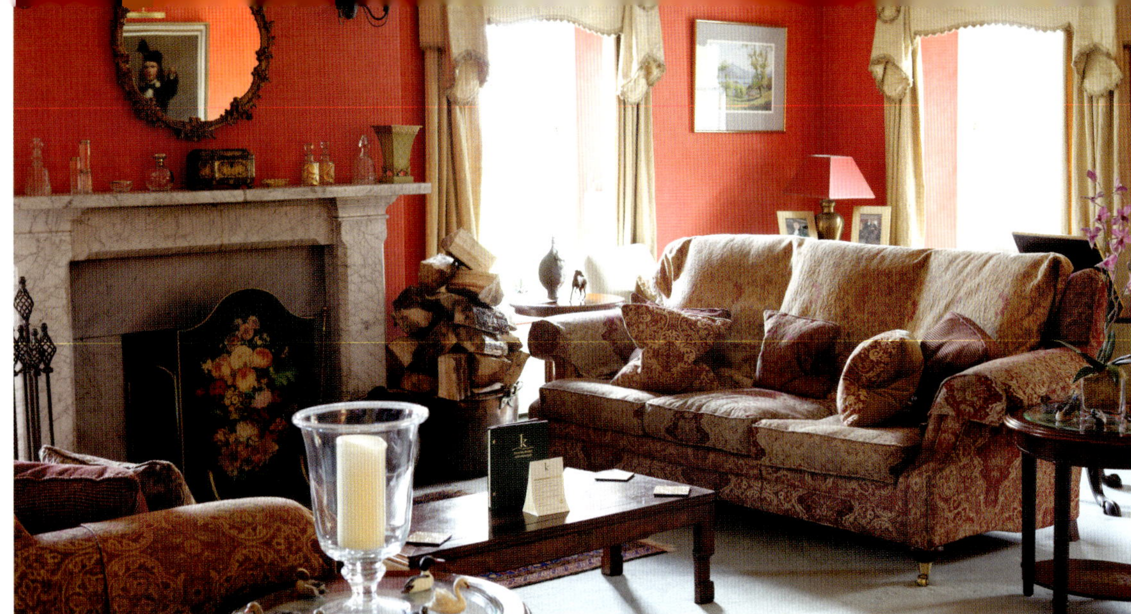

Left and below: Traditional afternoon tea served in front of the fire in each drawing room is perhaps one of the property's most iconic representations of Scottish bonhomie. Considered a Kinloch Classic are the lodge's flaky scones, served with whipped cream and strawberry jam. As a reminder of the delicious cuisine enjoyed during a stay, guests will likely want to collect a sampling of best-selling cookbooks by Claire Macdonald, whose approach to British home cooking informs the hotel's offerings of fresh and flavorful regional fare.

patrons are immediately engaged in a prepossessing family atmosphere within the informally relaxed interiors. Crackling log fires, comfy overstuffed sofas, and conversation-evoking ancestral portraits radiate an authentic Scottish charm. Of course, the stunning natural scenery dotted with meandering coastlines, towering black mountains, and commanding seaside castles is the icing on the cake.

"Like all islands, ours has a strong sense of identity and a genuine community spirit," Claire notes. "The people who live here work the land, fish the surrounding sea, and utilize the natural resources around them. We want our guests to feel that same attachment to our heritage and to the hotel." This deeply rooted commitment to the Isle of Skye is a bequest passed down to her children, along with a heart for hospitality. "My daughter Isabella and her husband are now at the helm," the former innkeeper adds, "and they have exciting plans to ensure Kinloch Lodge is here for many more generations."

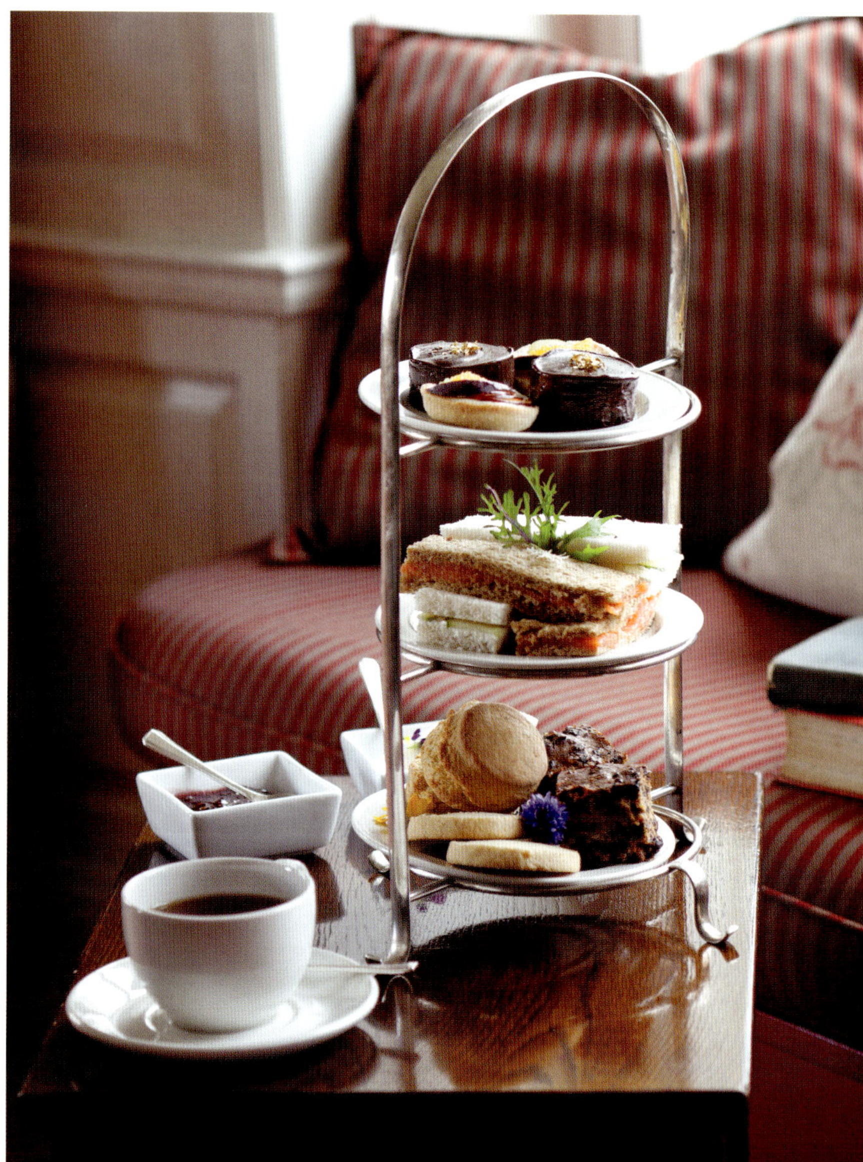

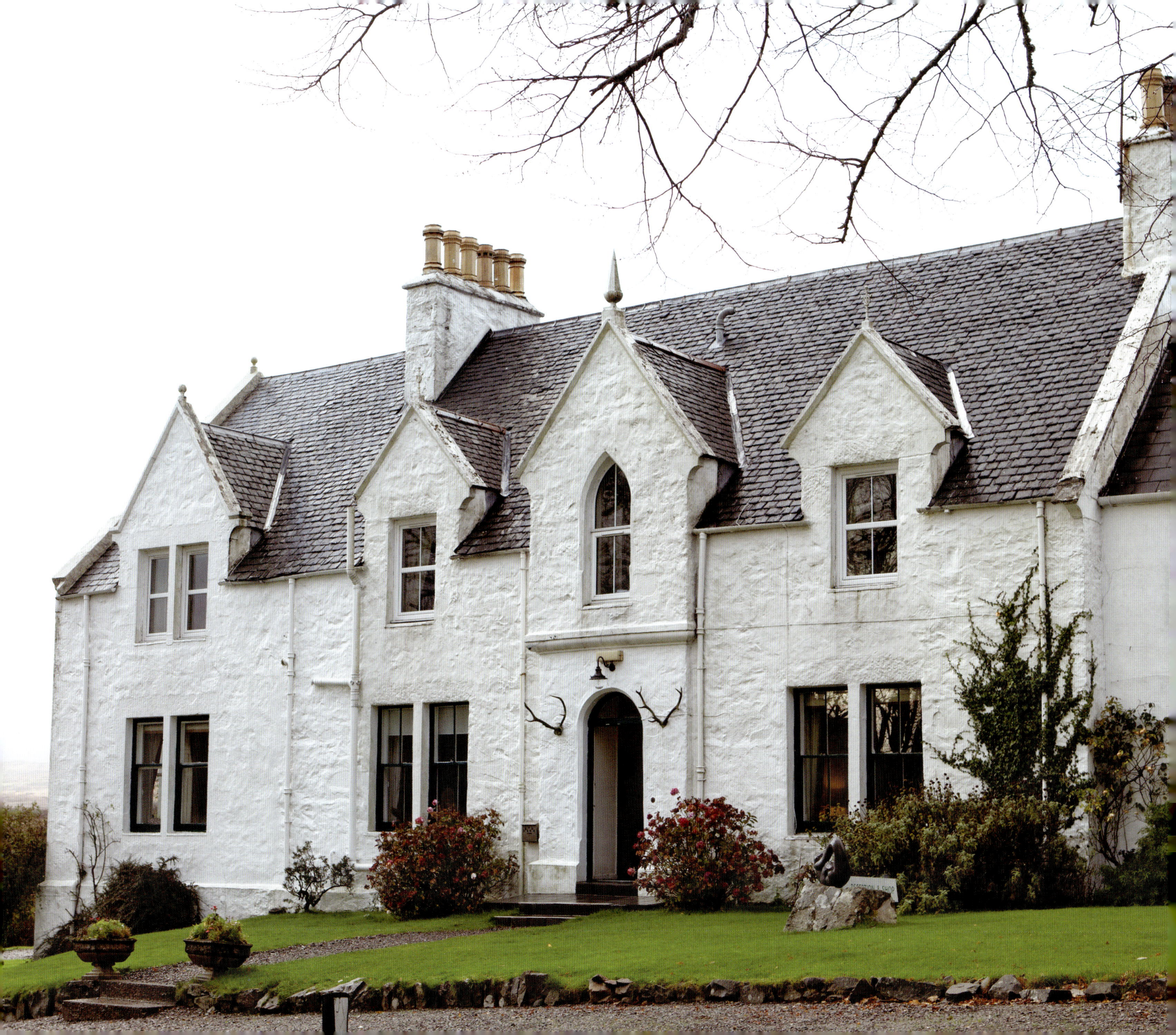

ON THE BANKS OF THE TAY

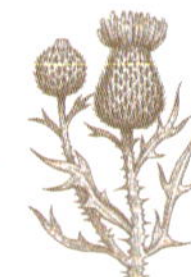

Author Sir Walter Scott once called Perthshire "the fairest portion of the northern kingdom," and seeing the countryside ablaze in autumn color surely confirms his opinion. The rich green of the native Scots pine contrasts with the bright golds and scarlets of deciduous trees, while the moors are swathed in the purple hues of fall-blooming heather. It is not surprising that visitors are drawn to the area to enjoy the splendor of the season.

This strikingly prismatic scenery forms the setting for one of the great country retreats in Scotland, the Ballathie Country House Hotel and Estate. Its location on the banks of the River Tay allows for the convenient exploration of both back roads and big cities. Edinburgh and Glasgow are just a short drive away, as is the famed Old Course at St Andrews Links.

But one need not leave the premises to enjoy the delights of Ballathie. Guests can stroll the property, which includes a working cattle farm, and partake in a variety of sporting activities, from fishing to cycling.

The hotel's primary structure was built in 1880, and though recently refurbished, it has retained the period features that bestow the establishment with its signature grandeur. In addition to the Main House, there are sixteen rooms in the Riverside building, accessible from a pathway leading through the garden, and twelve rooms in Sportsman's Lodge, all of which boast stellar accommodations.

Though fall is spectacular at Ballathie, one may rest assured that the beauty is on display all year long for those who dream of escaping to pastoral surrounds while still indulging in luxurious amenities.

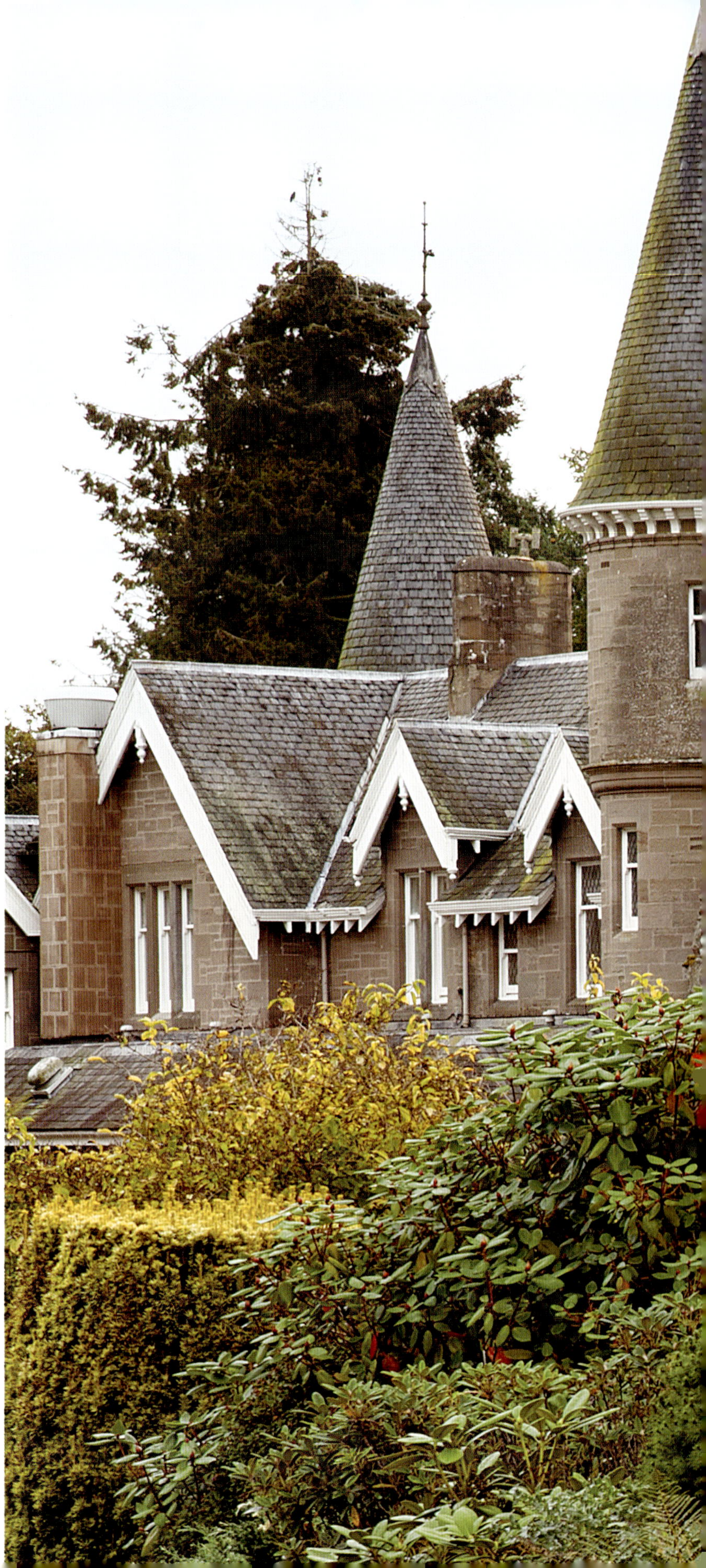

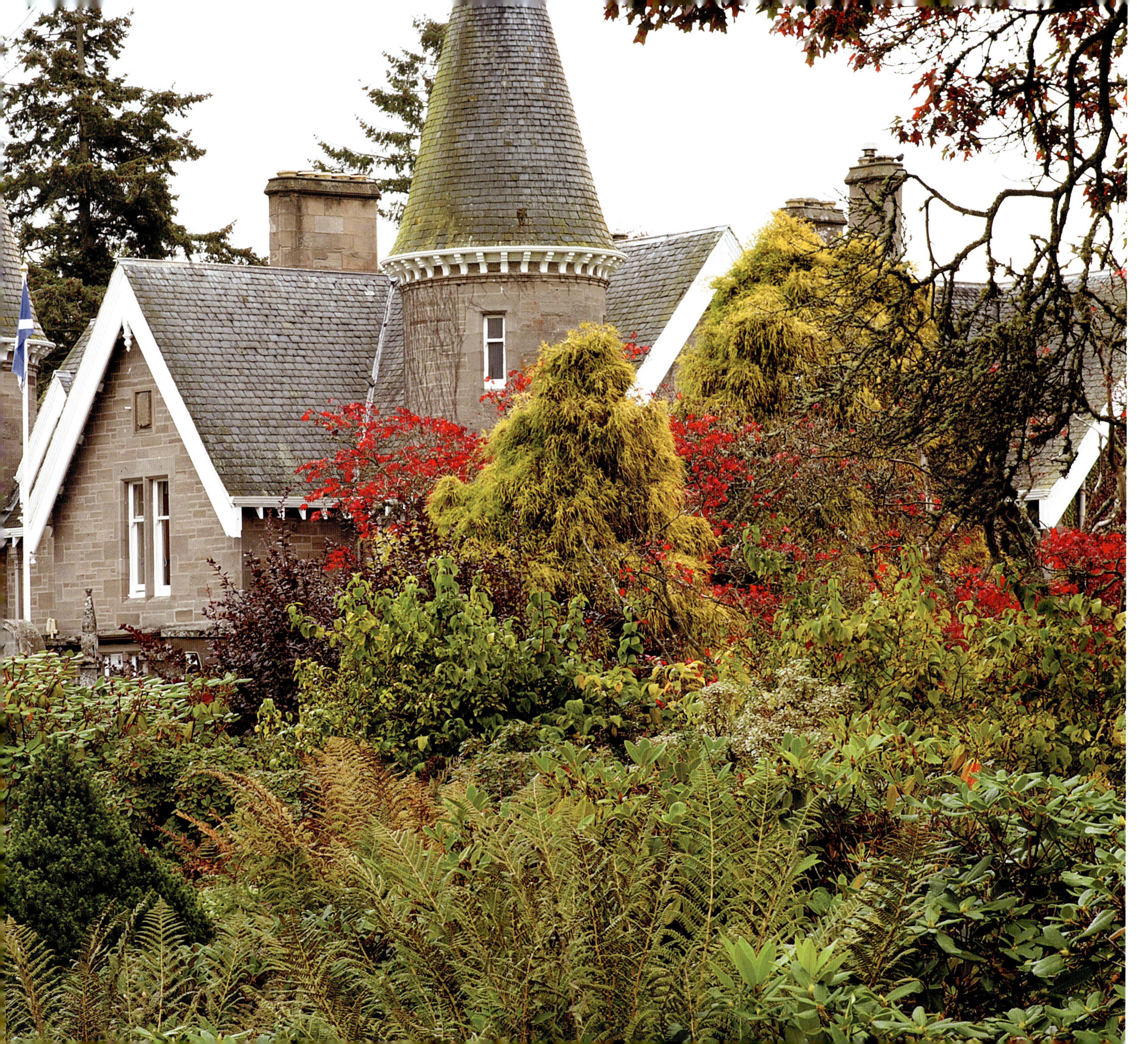

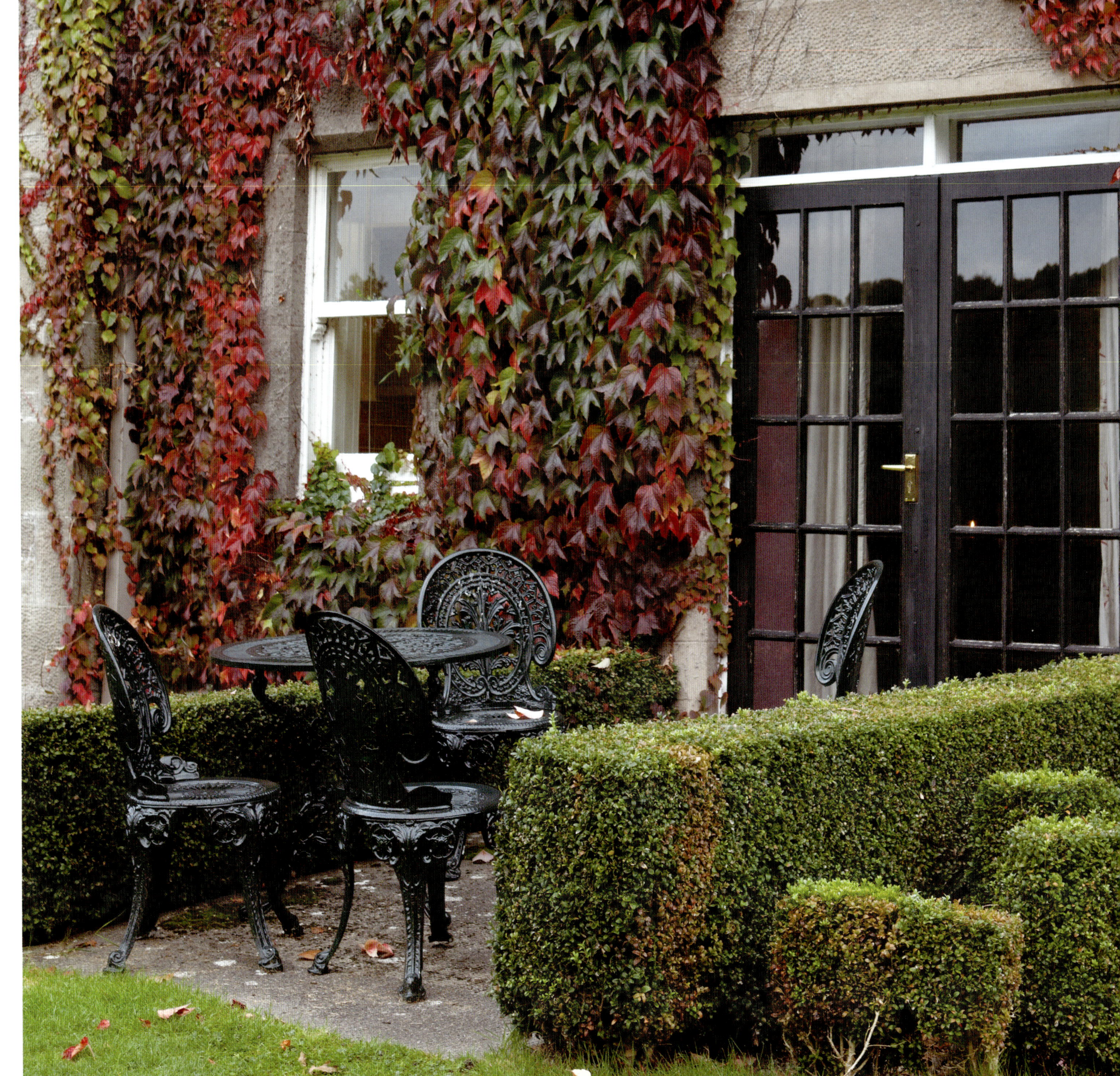

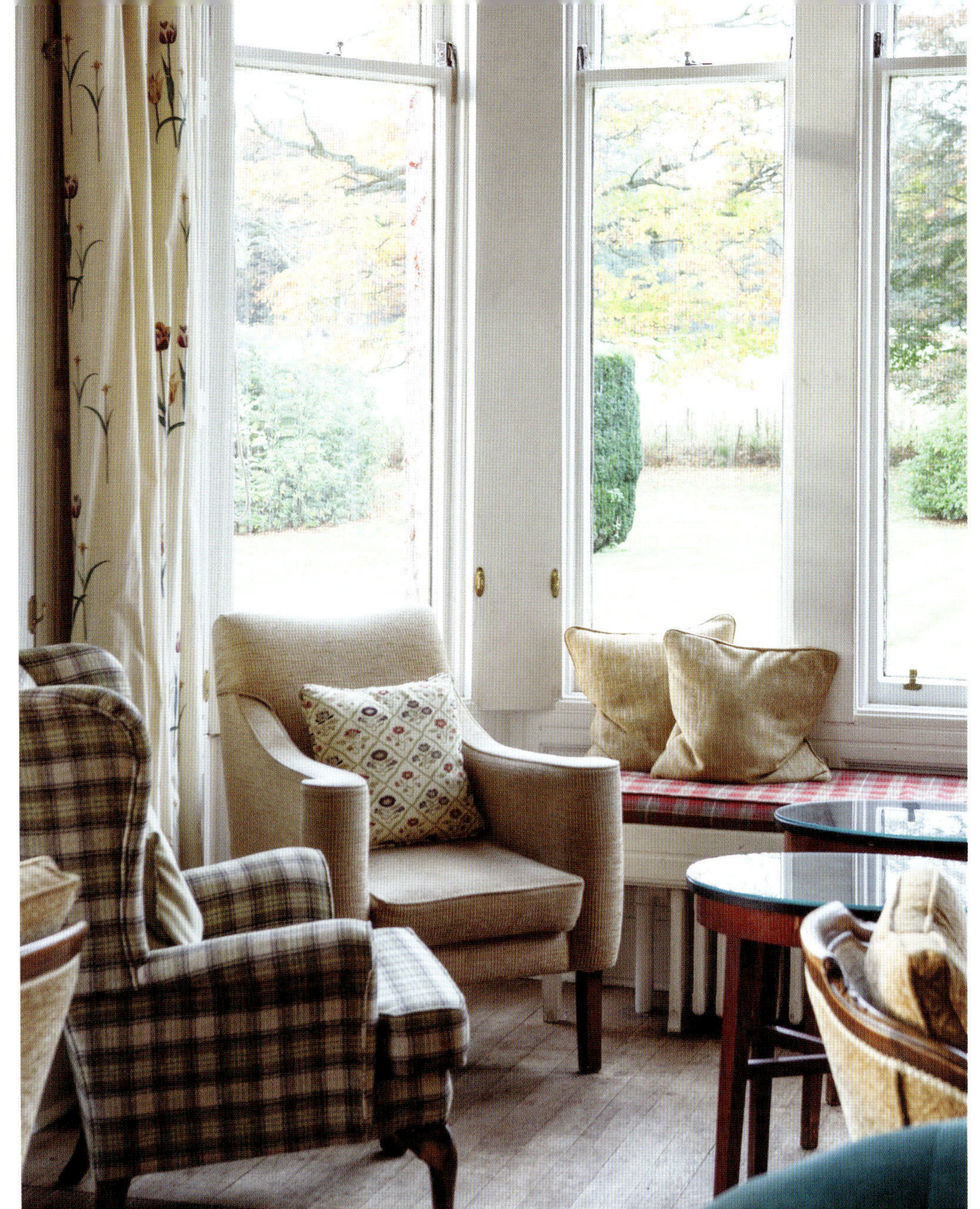

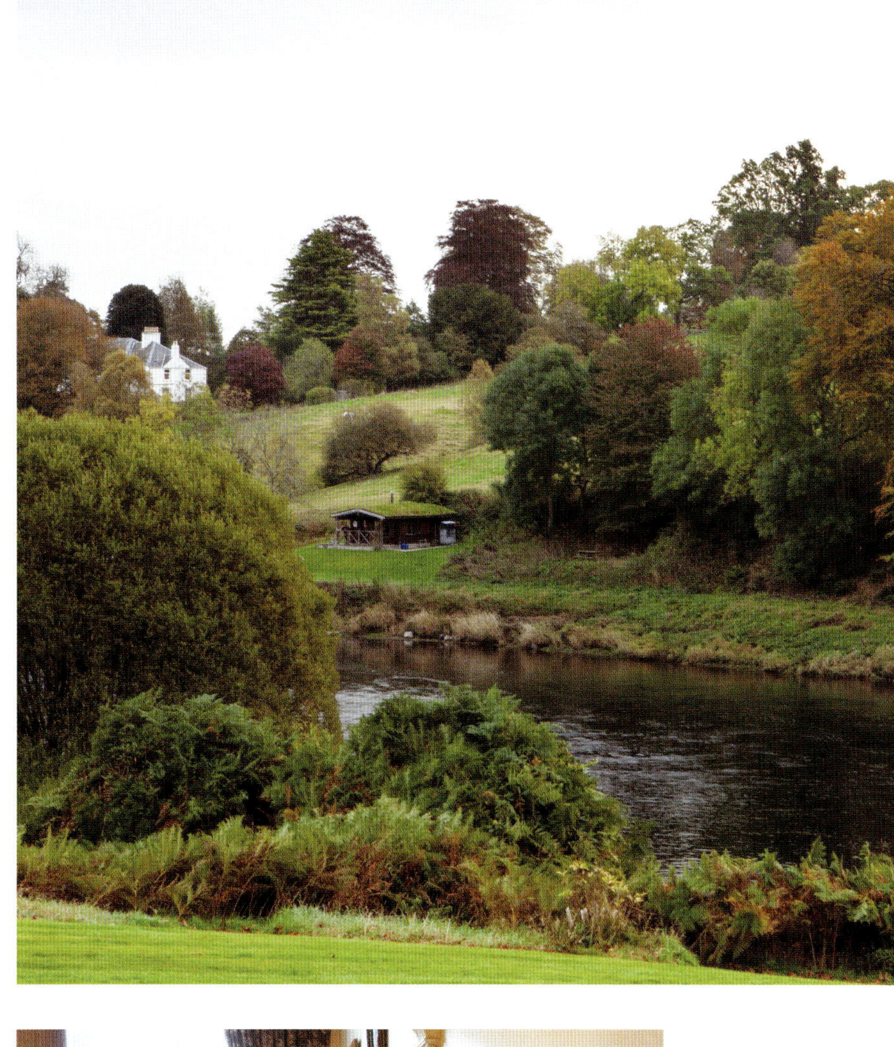

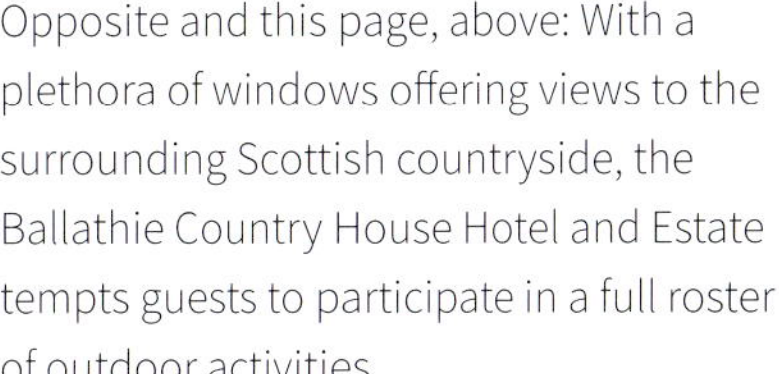

Opposite and this page, above: With a plethora of windows offering views to the surrounding Scottish countryside, the Ballathie Country House Hotel and Estate tempts guests to participate in a full roster of outdoor activities.

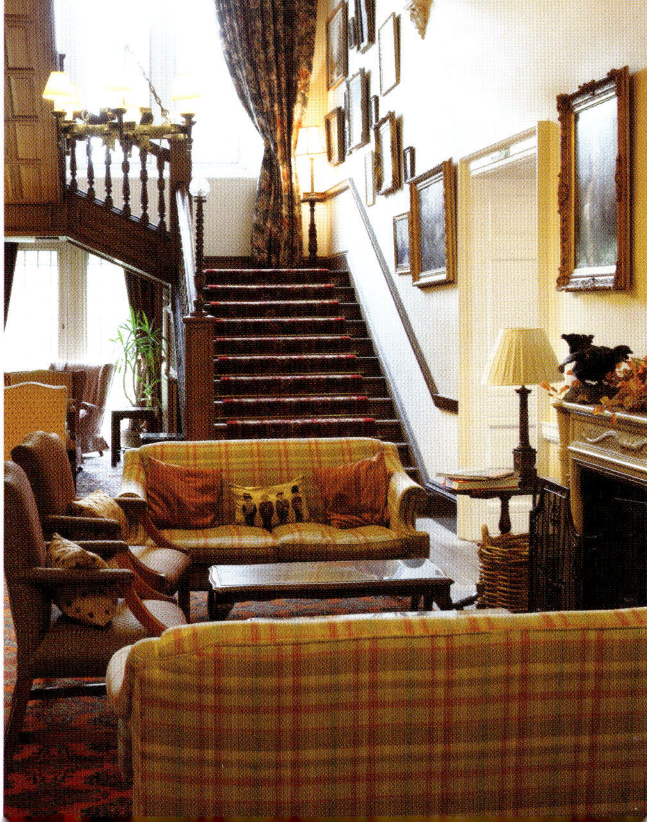

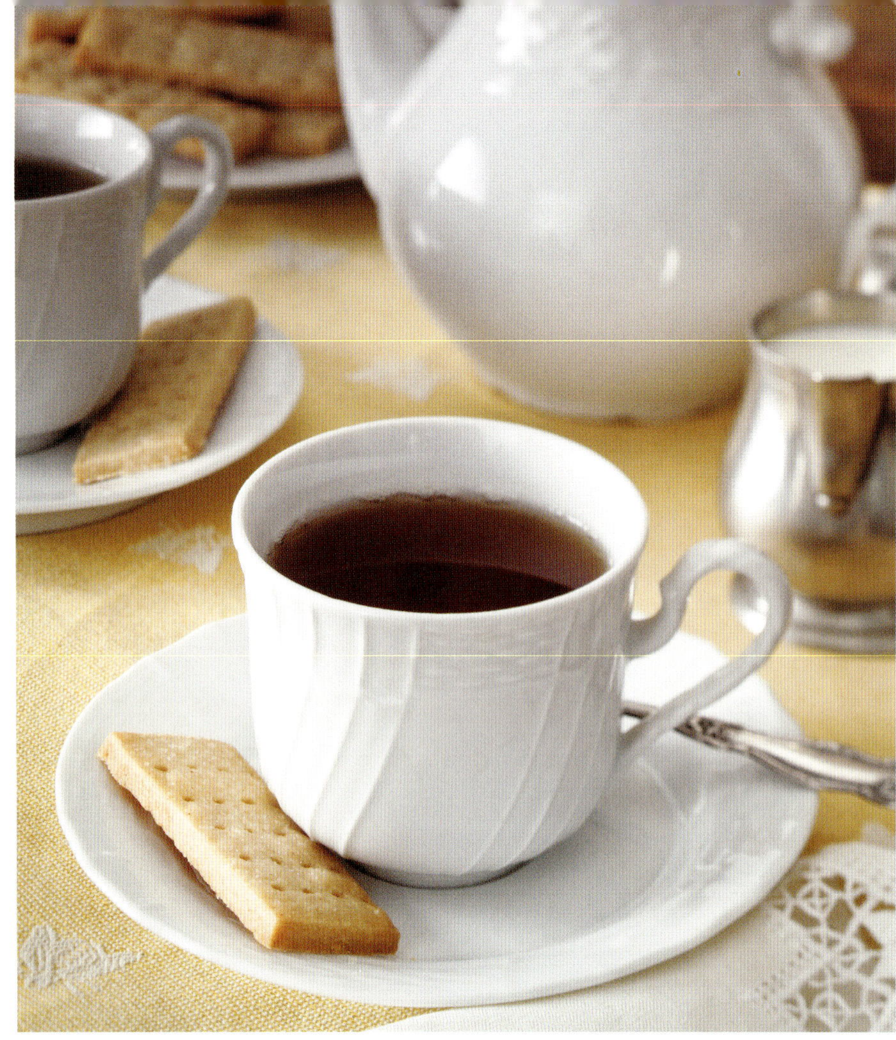

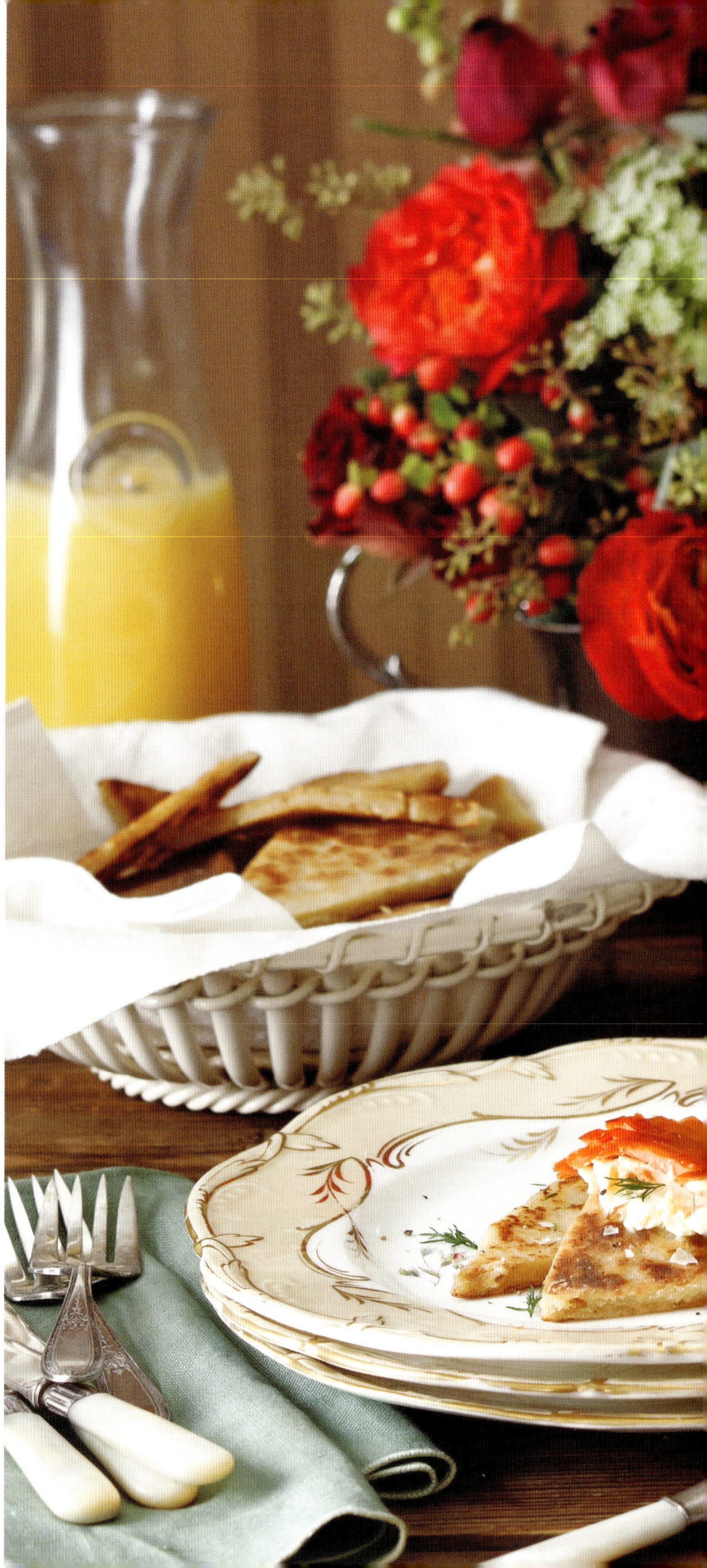

SUNRISE OVER SCOTLAND

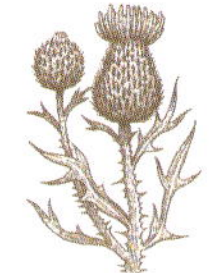

Recalling the hearty fare served in the dining rooms of some of our favorite boutique hotels, chefs in the *Victoria* test kitchens share a satisfying menu for a full Scottish breakfast. These classic recipes offer sustenance to carry sojourners through a morning of exploration in the Caledonian countryside.

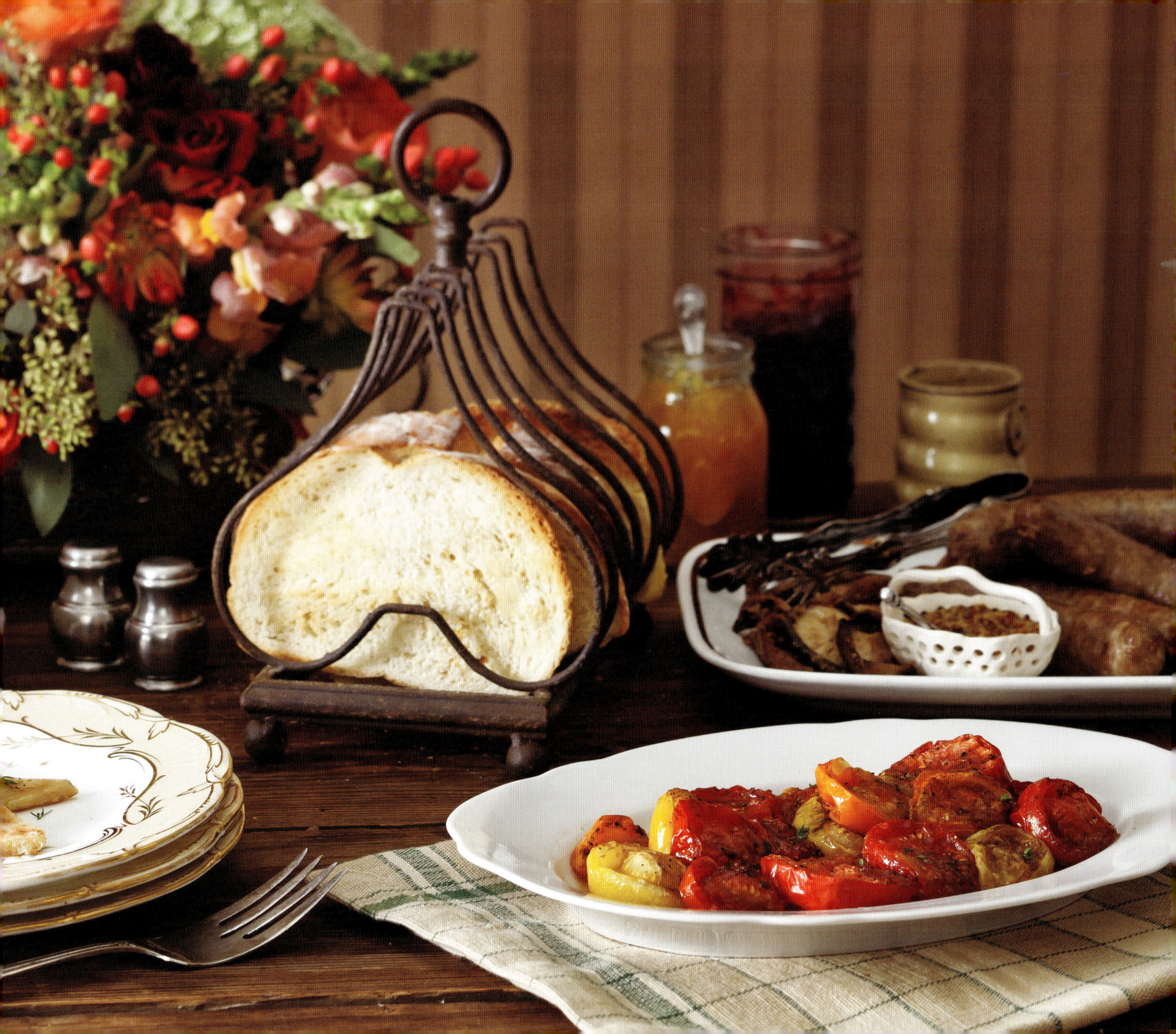

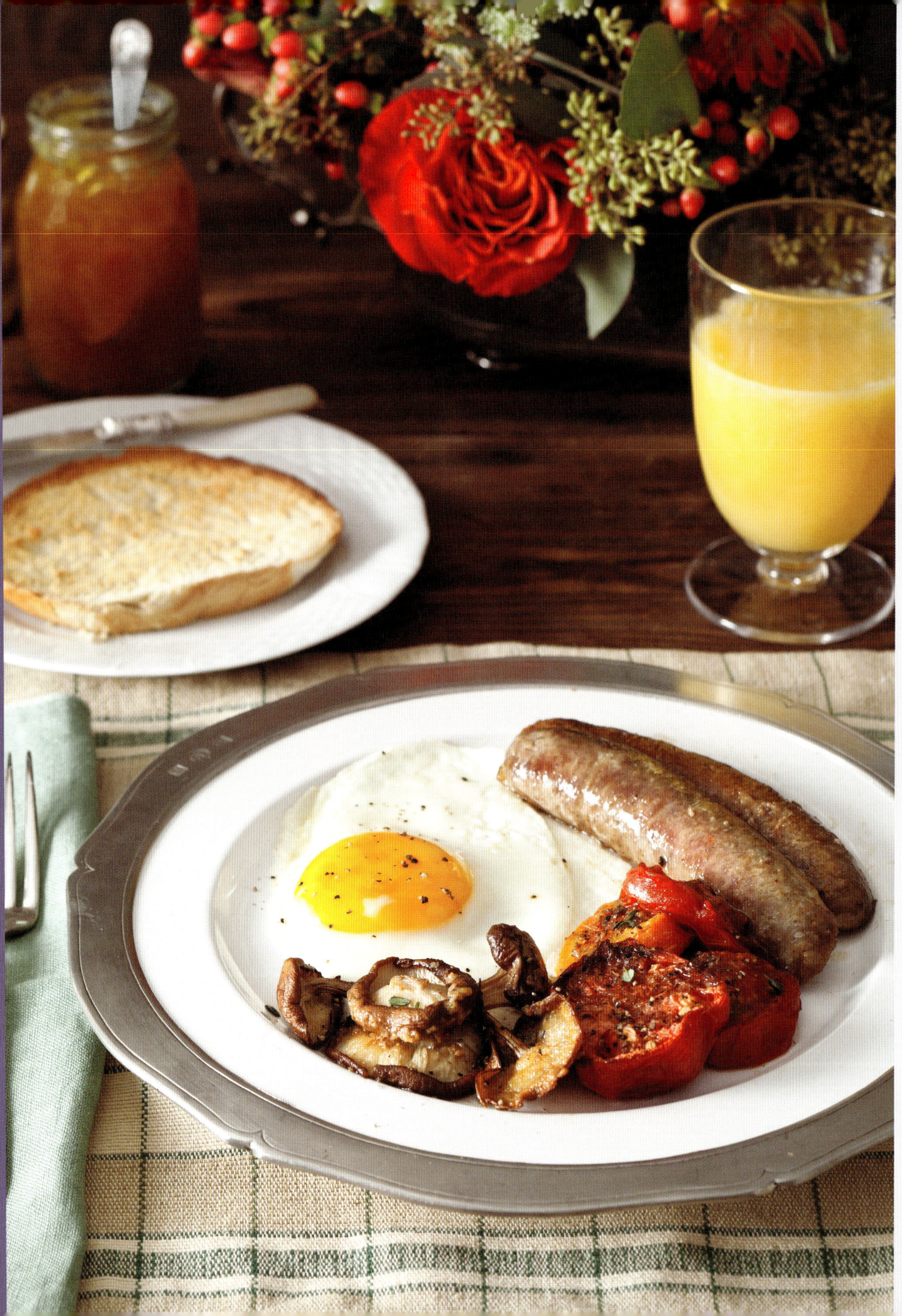

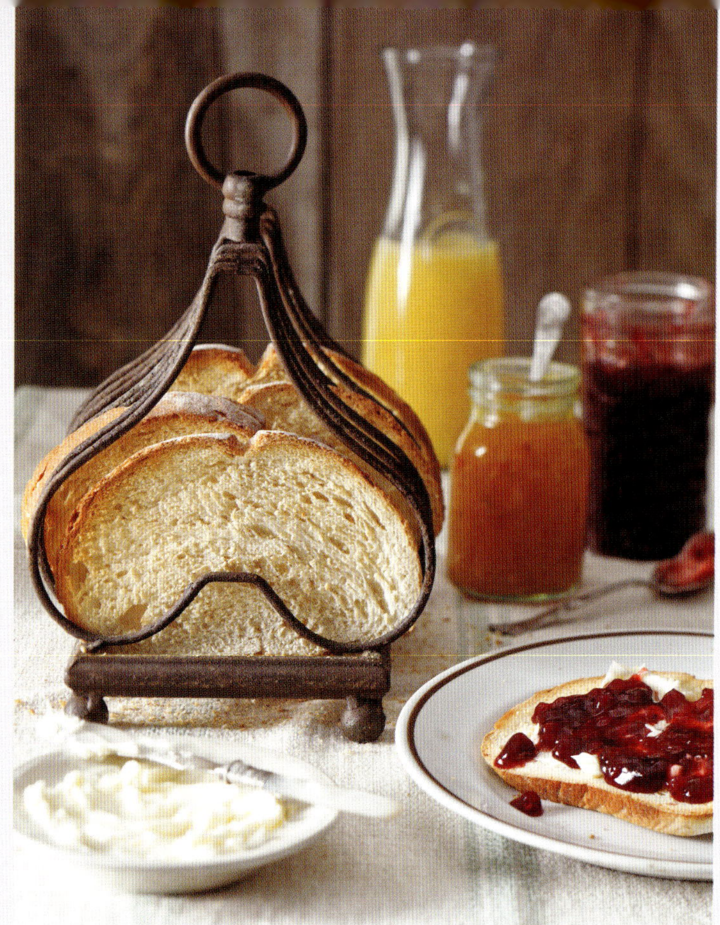

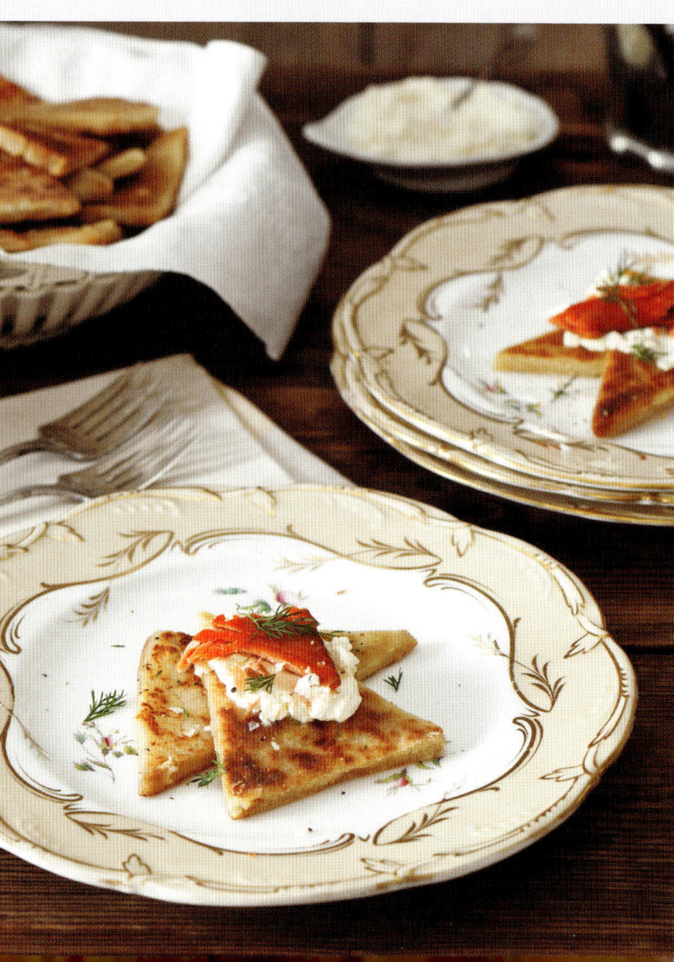

The Perfect Sunny-Side Up Fried Egg

Makes 1

1 large egg, room temperature
2 tablespoons butter
Salt
Pepper

1. In a small bowl, crack egg, making sure egg is fresh and there is no discoloration.
2. In a medium nonstick skillet, melt butter over medium-high heat. Once butter is melted, reduce heat to medium. Add egg to skillet, and season to taste with salt and pepper. Cook just until outer edge of white is set, 2 to 3 minutes. Continue cooking until entire white is completely set, about 1 minute. Remove from heat, and transfer to a plate; serve immediately.

Classic Tatties (Potato Scones)

Makes approximately 24

2 large russet potatoes, washed, peeled, and diced
½ cup butter, softened
1 cup potato flour
½ teaspoon baking powder
½ teaspoon sea salt
¼ teaspoon ground black pepper
½ (8-ounce) package English Cheddar, diced
Vegetable oil
Devonshire cream
Smoked salmon
Garnish: fresh dill

1. In a medium pan, place potatoes and cover with water. Bring to a boil over medium-high heat. Reduce heat and simmer until potatoes are tender, 10 to 15 minutes. Remove from heat and drain.
2. Using a potato masher, mash potatoes until smooth. Add butter and stir to combine.
3. In a small bowl, combine potato flour, baking powder, sea salt, and pepper. Add flour mixture to potato mixture, stirring until combined and mixture forms a dough.
4. On a lightly floured surface, knead dough into a ball. Cover with a moist towel and let cool for 15 to 20 minutes.
5. Using a rolling pin, roll dough to a 10x12-inch rectangle. Sprinkle half of rectangle with cheese, and fold to create a 5x6-inch rectangle; gently roll out to ¼-inch thickness. Cut dough into 4x2½-inch wedge-shaped scones. Reroll scraps as necessary.
6. Heat a large cast-iron skillet over medium heat. Add 1 teaspoon oil and continue to heat. Add scones, no more than 4 at a time, and cook for about 4 minutes; turn and continue cooking until golden brown and cheese is melted, about 4 minutes. Repeat with remaining scones, adding more oil as needed. Serve immediately with Devonshire cream and smoked salmon. Garnish scones with dill, if desired.

Bangers and Truffle-Scented Mushrooms

Makes 6 servings

3 tablespoons olive oil, divided
1 pound sausage links
2 tablespoons butter
2 tablespoons sliced shallots
1 (8-ounce) package baby bella mushrooms
1 (8-ounce) package cremini mushrooms
¾ cup chicken broth
1½ teaspoons Worcestershire sauce
1 teaspoon sea salt
½ teaspoon ground black pepper
1 tablespoon truffle oil
Garnish: fresh parsley

1. In a medium saucepan, heat 2 tablespoons olive oil over medium heat until hot. Add sausages and brown; remove sausages from pan, discarding drippings. Keep sausages warm in a 200° oven while cooking mushrooms.
2. In same pan, add remaining 1 tablespoon olive oil and butter; heat until butter is melted. Add shallots and cook, stirring occasionally, until tender, 3 to 5 minutes. Add mushrooms and cook, stirring occasionally until mushrooms are lightly browned, about 5 minutes. Add broth, Worcestershire sauce, sea salt, and pepper. Continue to cook over medium heat until liquid is almost evaporated, about 5 minutes. Remove pan from heat; drizzle with truffle oil and serve warm with sausages. Garnish with parsley, if desired.

Pan-Roasted Tomatoes

Makes 4 servings

1 (12-ounce) package heirloom cherry tomatoes, halved lengthwise
3 tablespoons lemon-infused olive oil
1 tablespoon Grenache vinegar
1 teaspoon sea salt
½ teaspoon ground black pepper

1. Preheat oven to 375°. Line a rimmed baking sheet with foil.
2. Place tomatoes, cut sides up, on prepared pan.
3. In a small bowl, whisk together olive oil and vinegar; drizzle over tomatoes. Season with sea salt and pepper.
4. Bake until tomatoes are slightly charred, about 45 minutes. Remove from oven and let cool slightly; serve warm.

Scottish Shortbread Cookies

Makes approximately 24 cookies

1 cup unsalted butter, softened
½ cup firmly packed light brown sugar
½ teaspoon vanilla extract
2¼ cups all-purpose flour
¼ teaspoon cinnamon
¼ teaspoon cardamom
¼ teaspoon salt

1. Preheat oven to 350°. Line 2 baking sheets with parchment paper; set aside.
2. In a large bowl, beat butter, brown sugar, and vanilla extract with a mixer at medium-high speed until fluffy, about 5 minutes.
3. In a small bowl, whisk together flour, cinnamon, cardamom, and salt. Reduce mixer speed to low; gradually add flour mixture until combined and mixture forms a dough.
4. On a lightly floured surface, knead dough for 5 minutes, adding enough flour to prevent dough from sticking. Roll dough to ½-inch thickness. Cut into 3x1-inch strips. Place cookies 1 inch apart on prepared pans. Using a fork, mark tops of cookies in desired pattern.
5. Bake until edges are golden, 15 to 20 minutes.

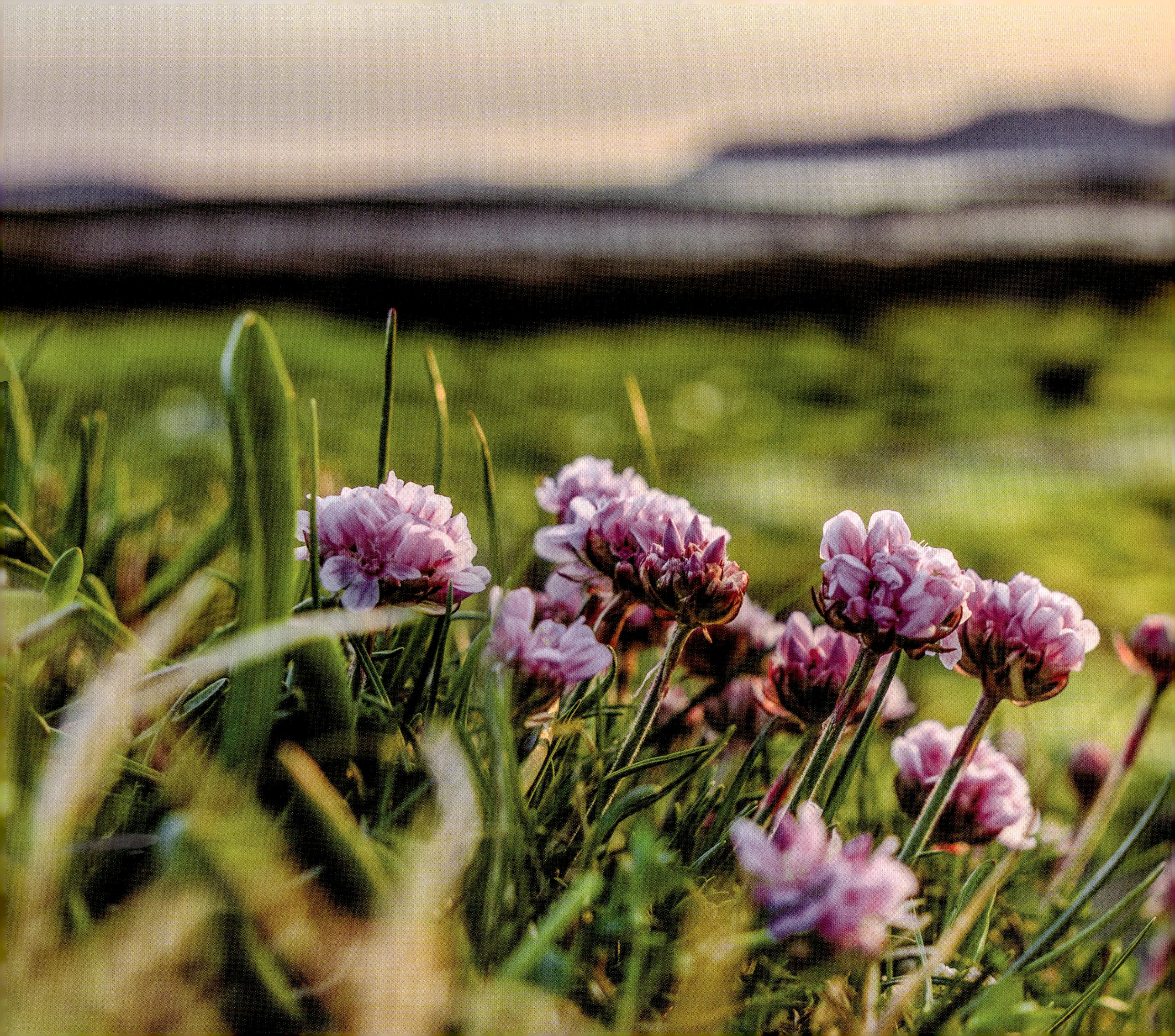

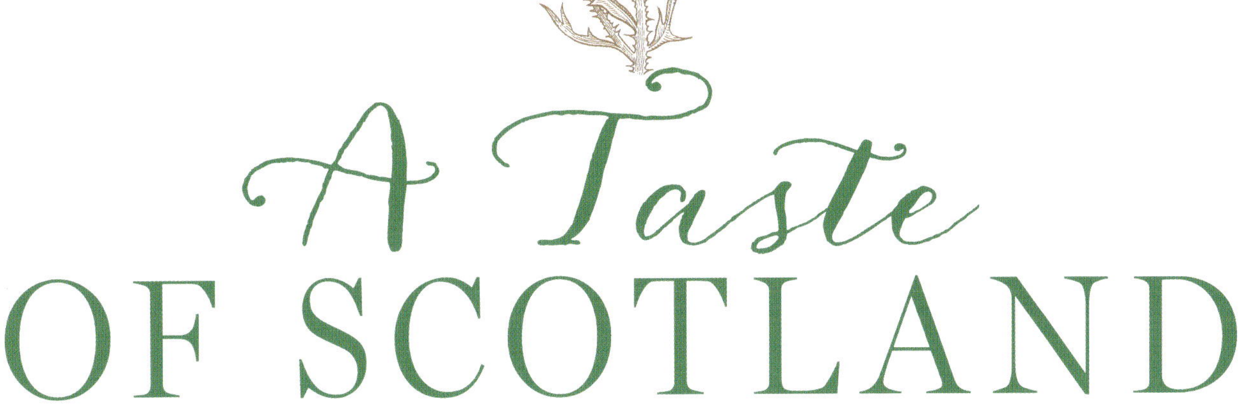

A Taste OF SCOTLAND

Whether gracing the landscape in the Scottish countryside or hidden among the ancient buildings in Edinburgh, a bounty of hidden gems awaits exploration, from King Charles III's prized project in Ayrshire to hallowed houses of worship and the home of beloved author and historian Sir Walter Scott.

THE SOUL OF AN AUTHOR

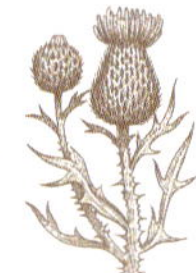

When venerated nineteenth-century author and historian Sir Walter Scott purchased the 110-acre Cartleyhole property "on a bare haugh and bleak bank by the side of the Tweed," he was eager to turn the forlorn landscape into the flourishing estate of his imagination. In fact, he began planting trees before he ever moved his family into the plot's humble farmhouse, which would also benefit from his grandiose plans. But before he began renovating the house, he was keen to obtain more land, and within just a few years' time, he had increased the demesne more than tenfold.

Scott renamed the expansive property Abbotsford after the nearby ford across the River Tweed once used by the monks of Melrose Abbey. The dwelling grew as his wealth and stature grew. Over the years, he added various rooms and wings, sometimes demolishing one extension to create a new one. He eventually razed the original farmhouse to make way for a key addition, which contained the entrance hall, the library, and more.

Scott often referred to his home as his "conundrum castle," and any visitor who walks through these magnificent halls—often rambling but filled with fascination and historical character—would certainly understand his affectionate sobriquet.

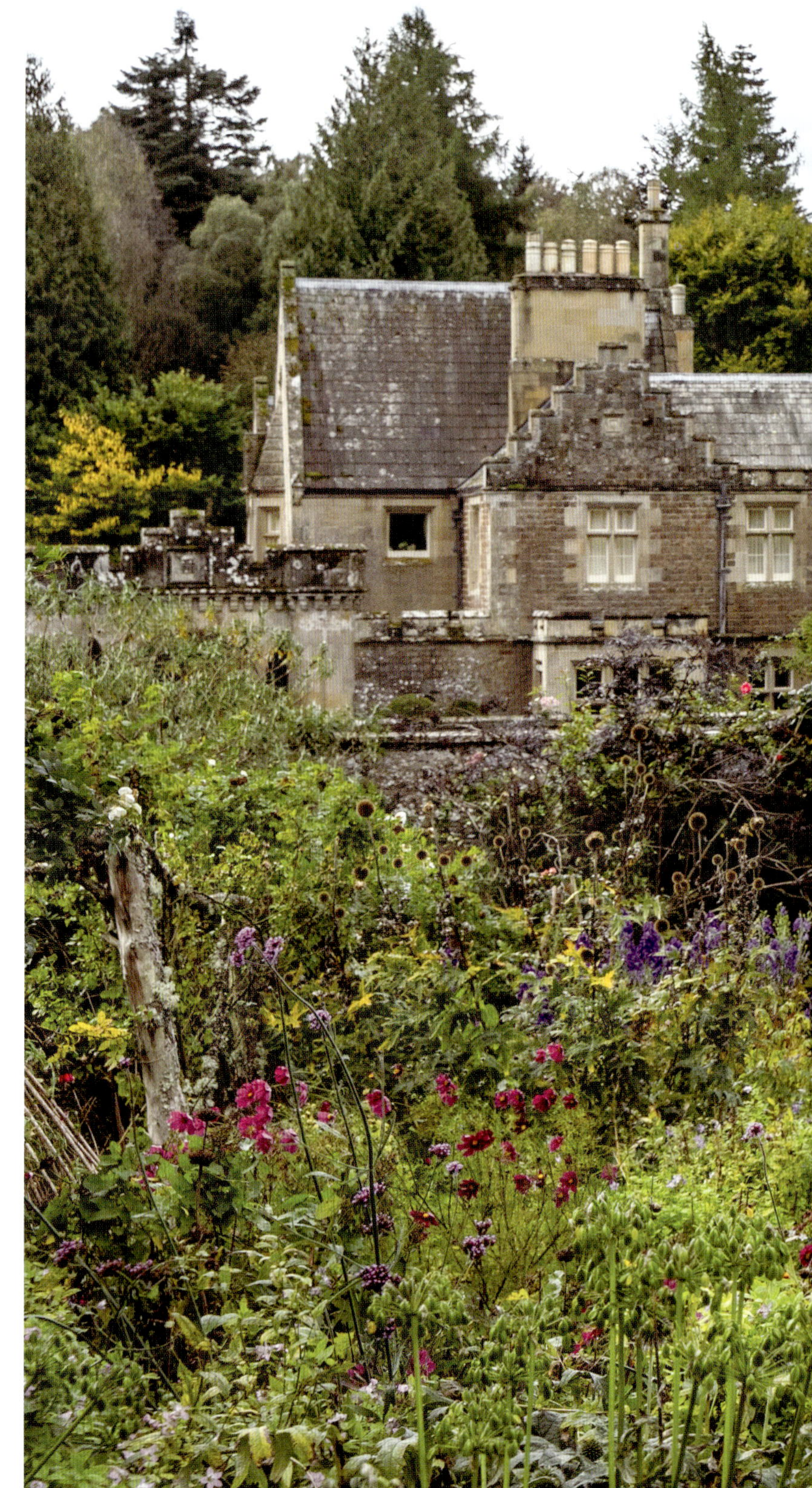

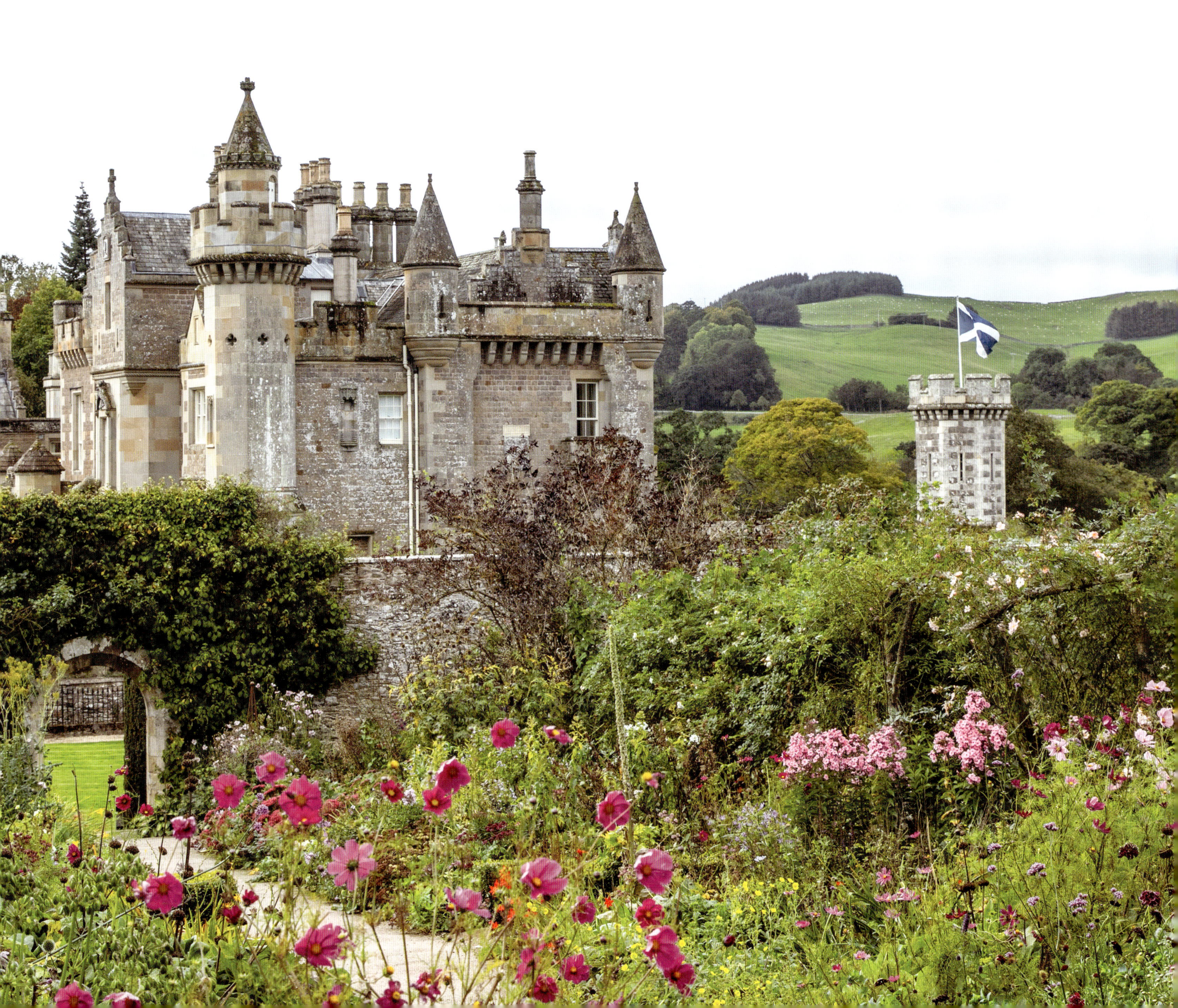

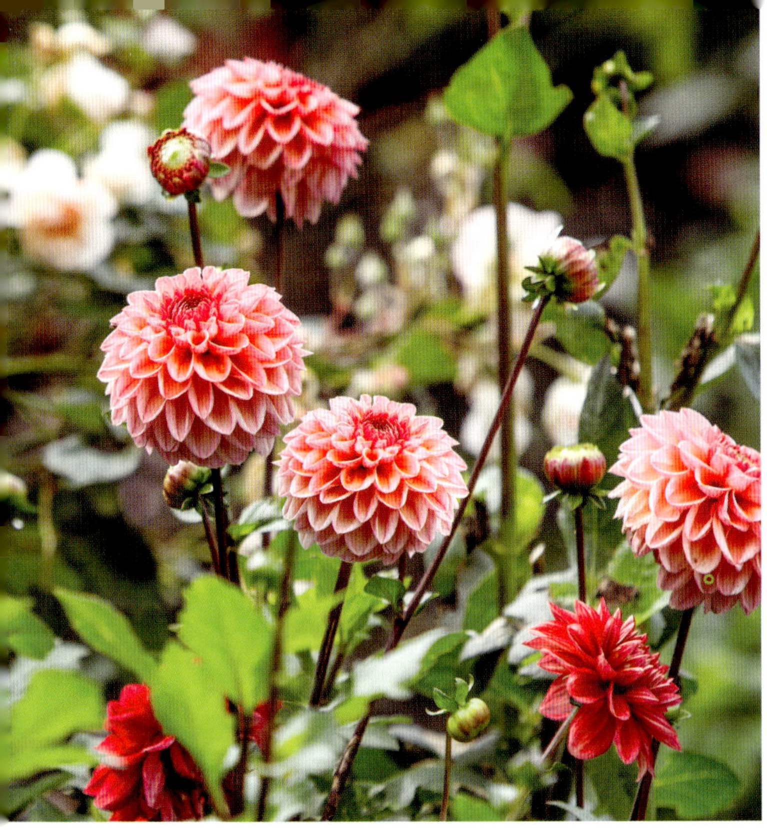

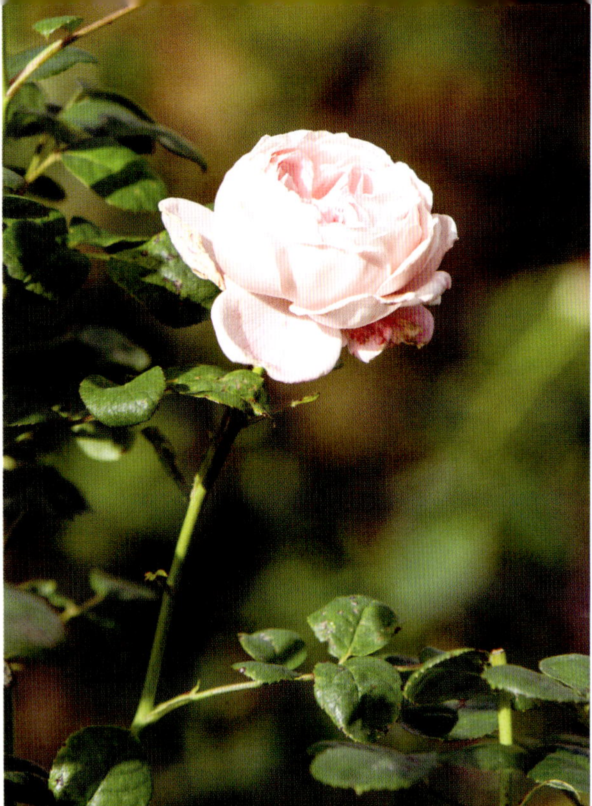

This page and opposite: When conceiving the design for Abbotsford's bountiful Regency-style garden, Sir Walter Scott consulted several artists and architects, as well as his circle of friends. The writer wished to create a synergy between the luxurious interiors and the natural world surrounding his home. To that end, the walled garden was divided into a series of outdoor rooms, brimming with a wondrous assortment of flowering plants, as well as fruits, vegetables, and herbs.

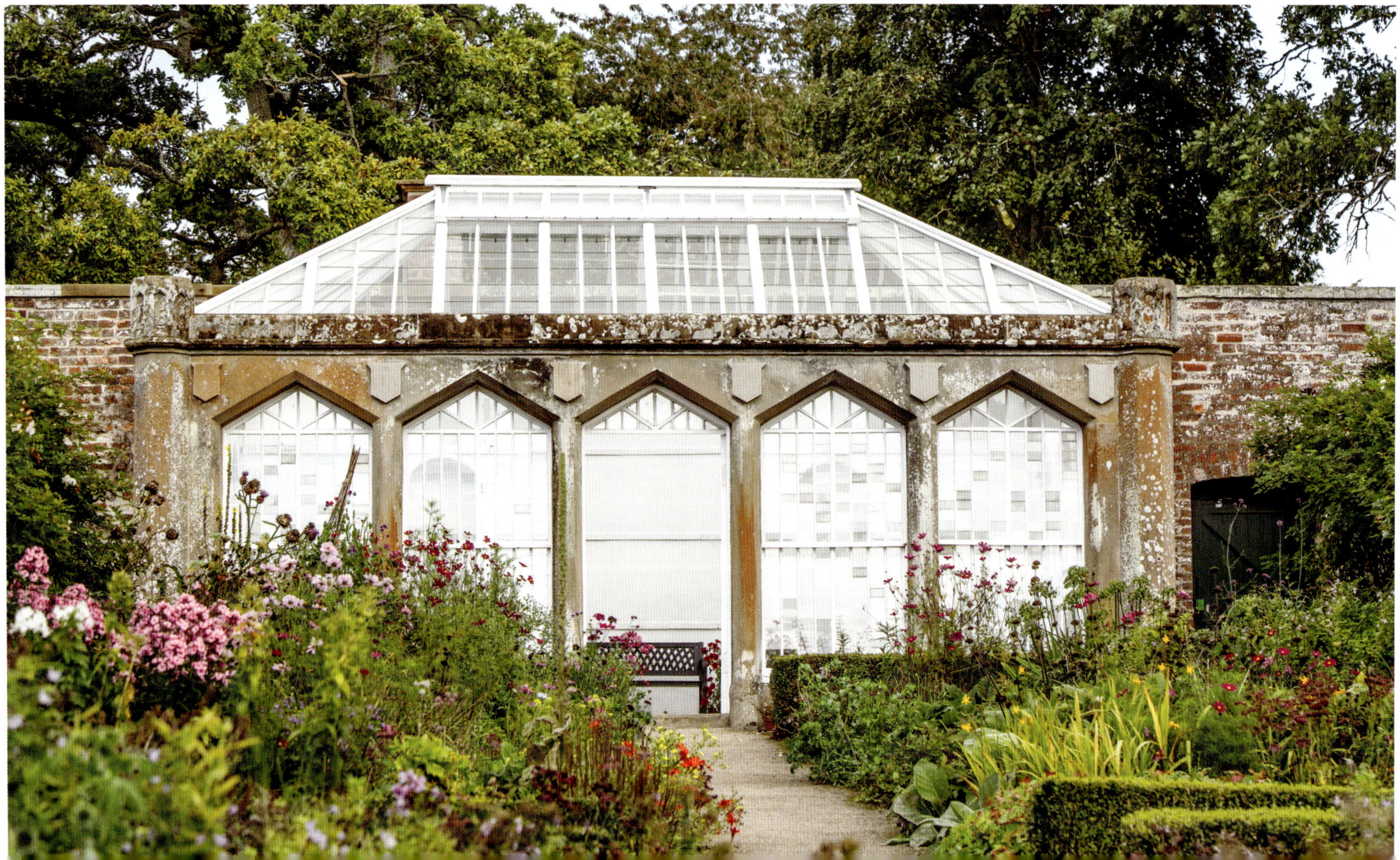

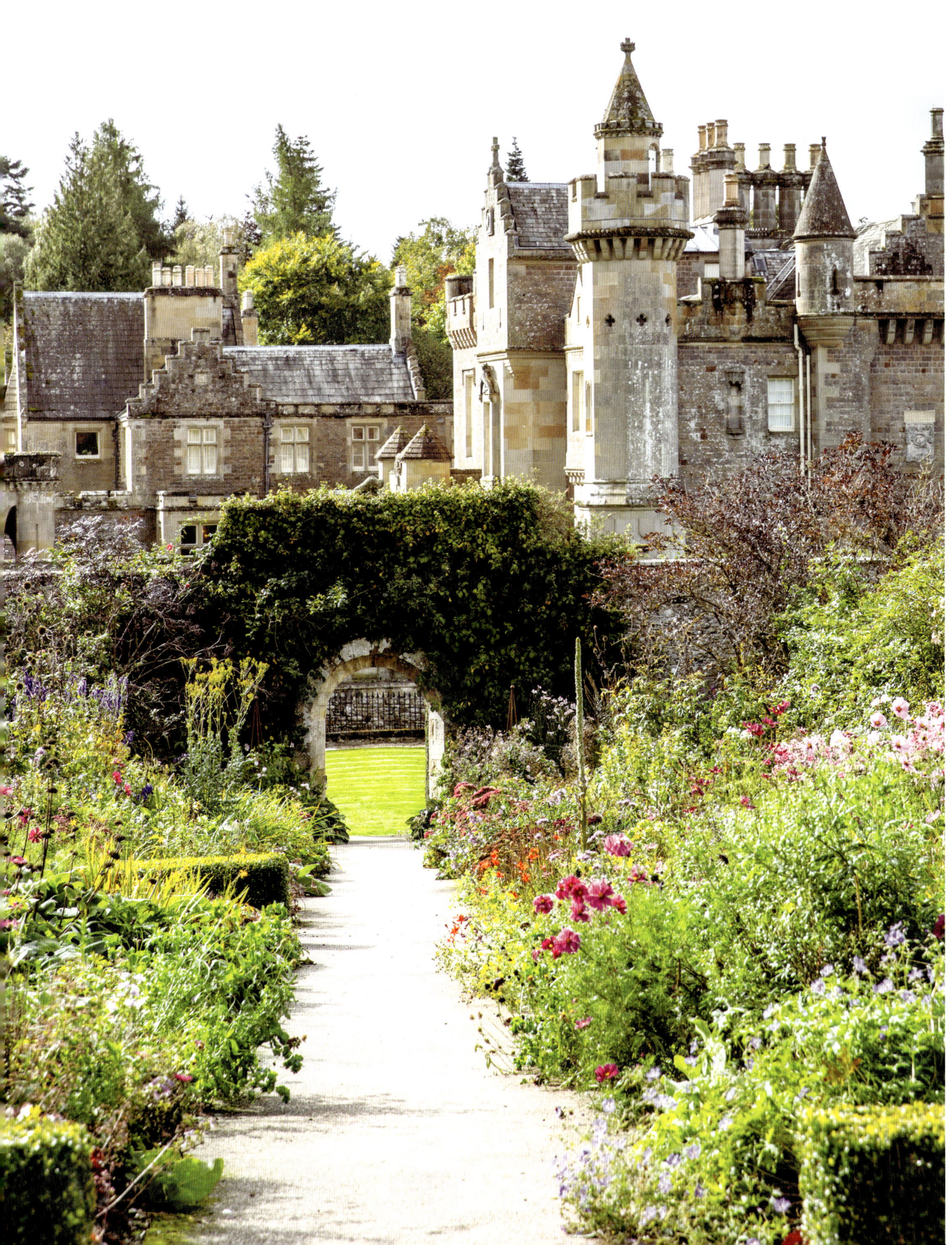

"Teach your children poetry; it opens the mind, lends grace to wisdom, and makes the heroic virtues hereditary."

—Sir Walter Scott

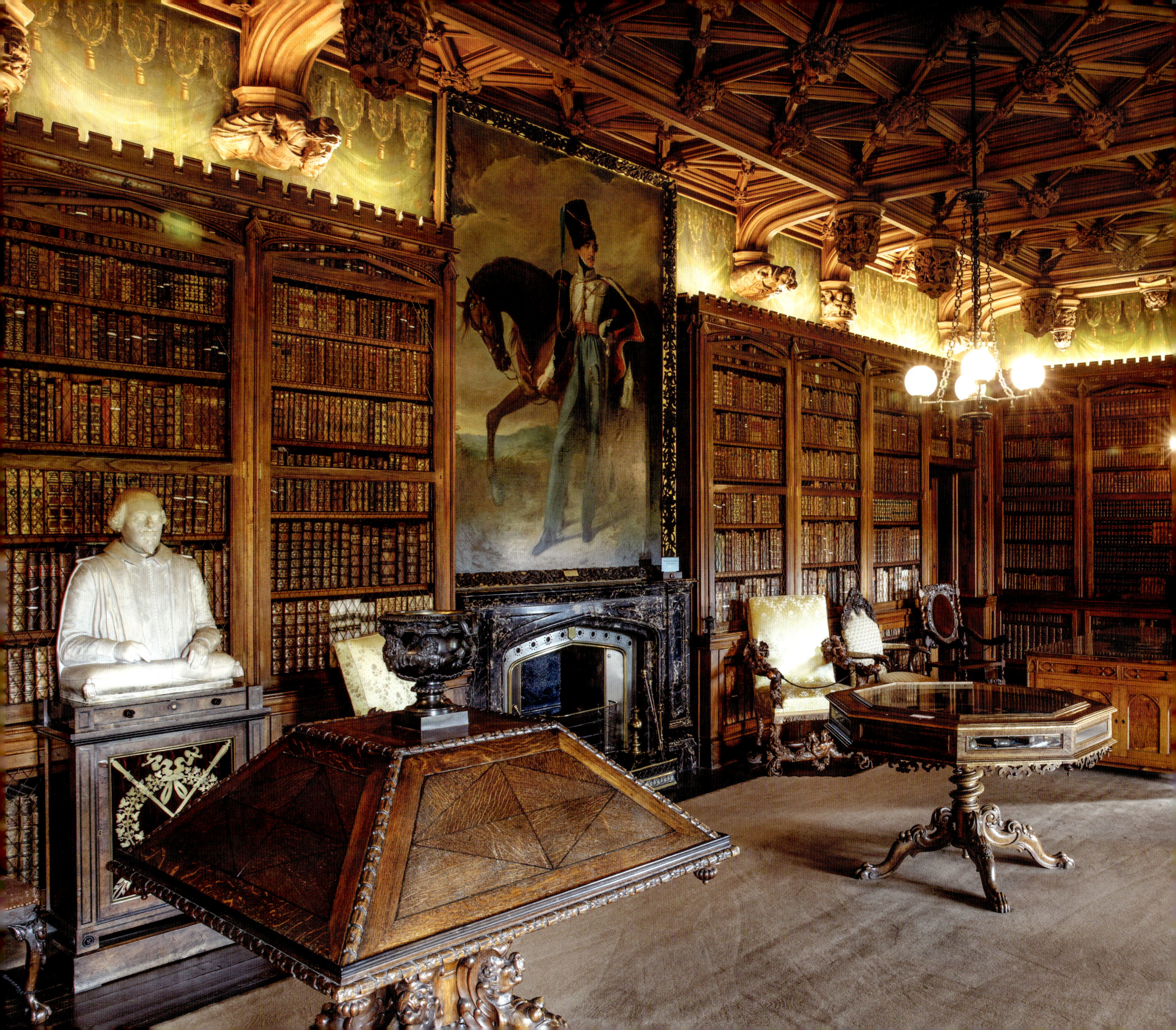

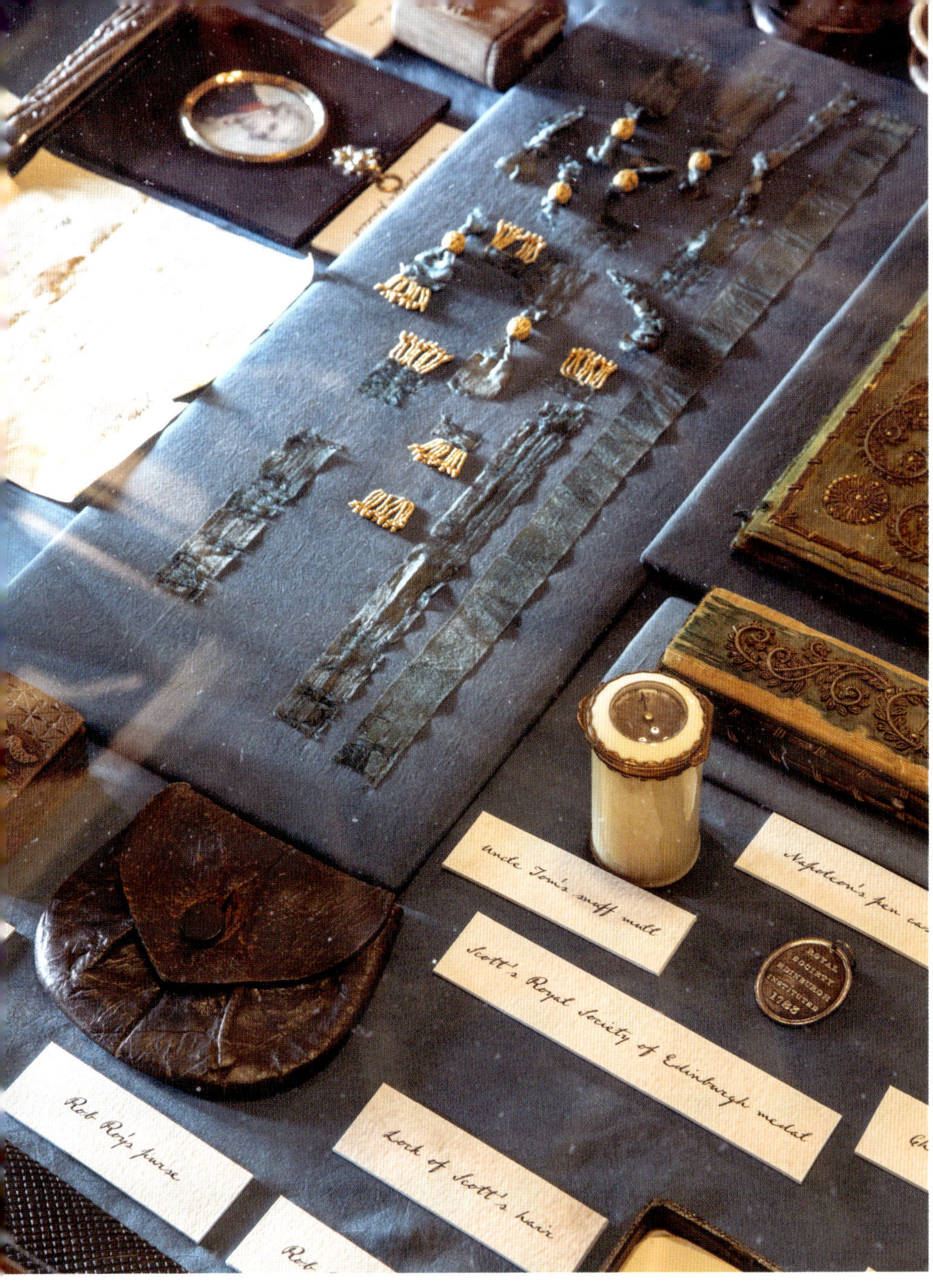

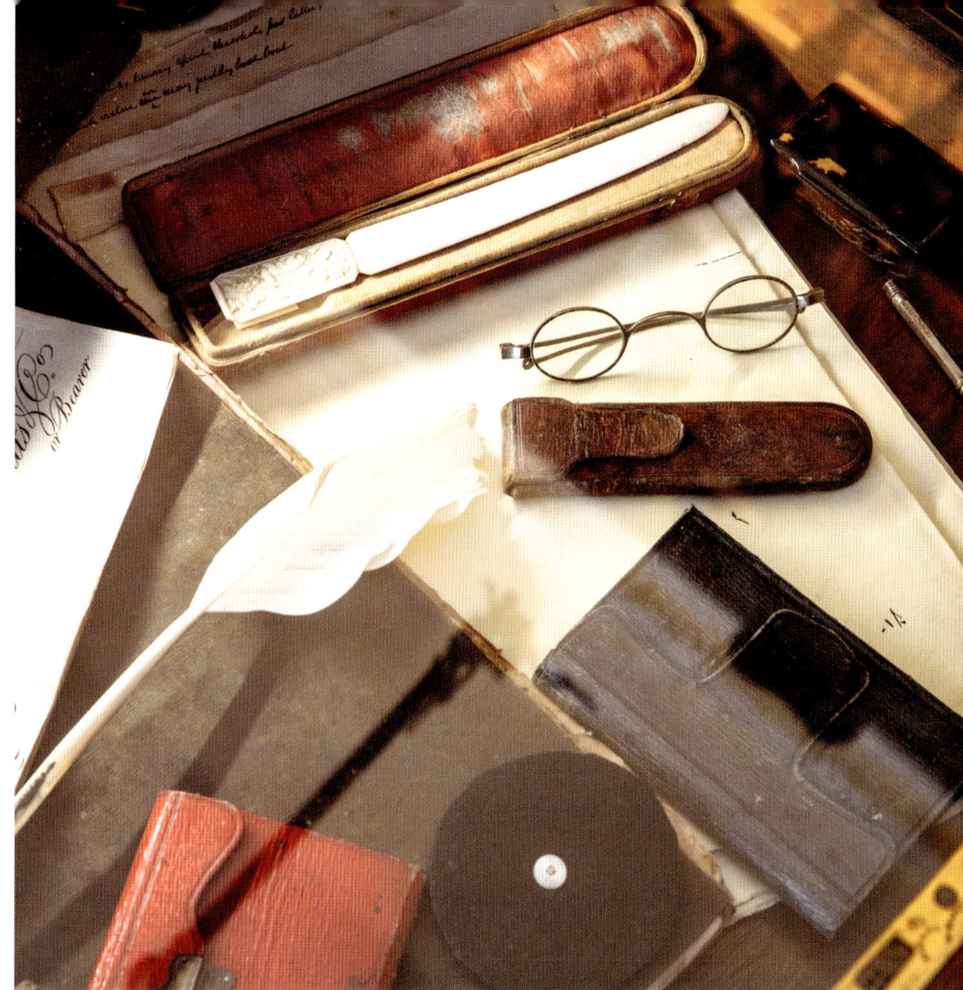

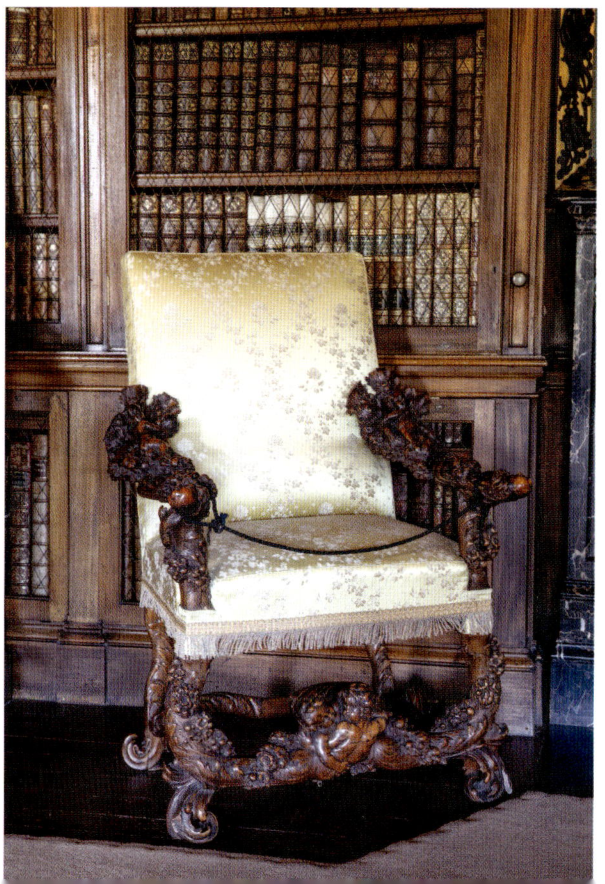

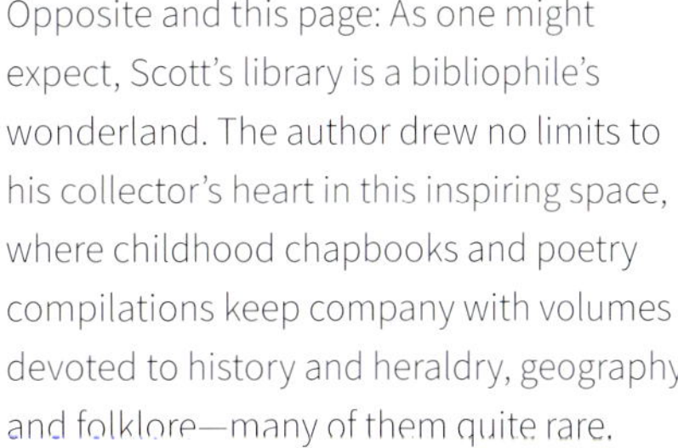

Opposite and this page: As one might expect, Scott's library is a bibliophile's wonderland. The author drew no limits to his collector's heart in this inspiring space, where childhood chapbooks and poetry compilations keep company with volumes devoted to history and heraldry, geography and folklore—many of them quite rare.

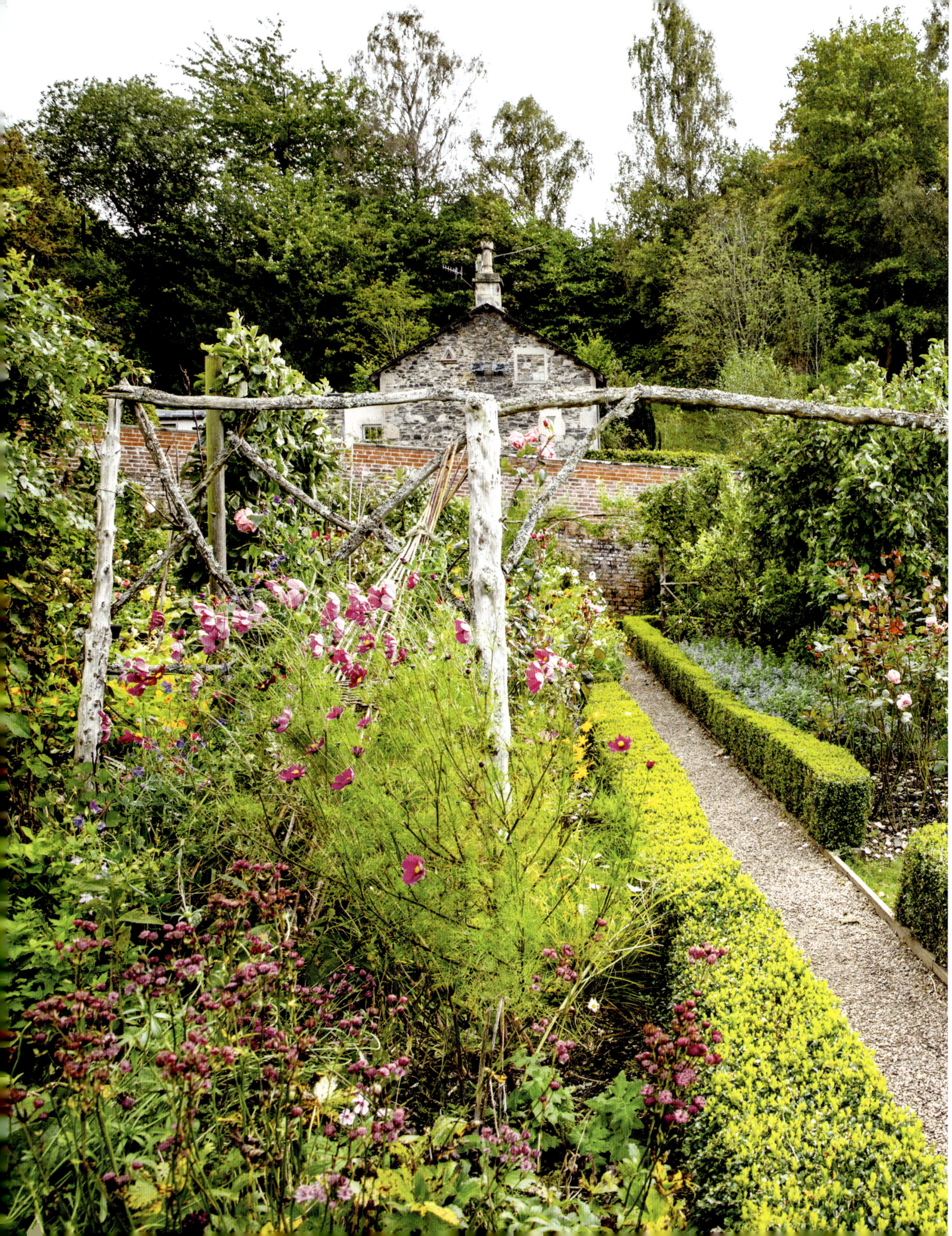

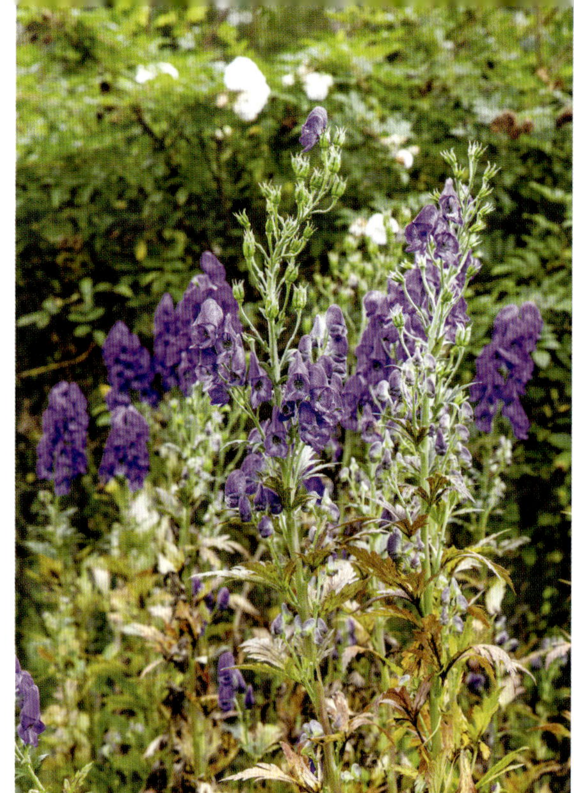

This page: Scott's hand guided every aspect of the 1,400-acre estate, from the gardens and woodlands to the riverside paths. Opposite: The owner's fascination with Scottish history and artifacts is on full display in the exquisite Entrance Hall, where the carved-stone fireplace takes its inspiration from the Abbot's Seat at nearby Melrose Abbey.

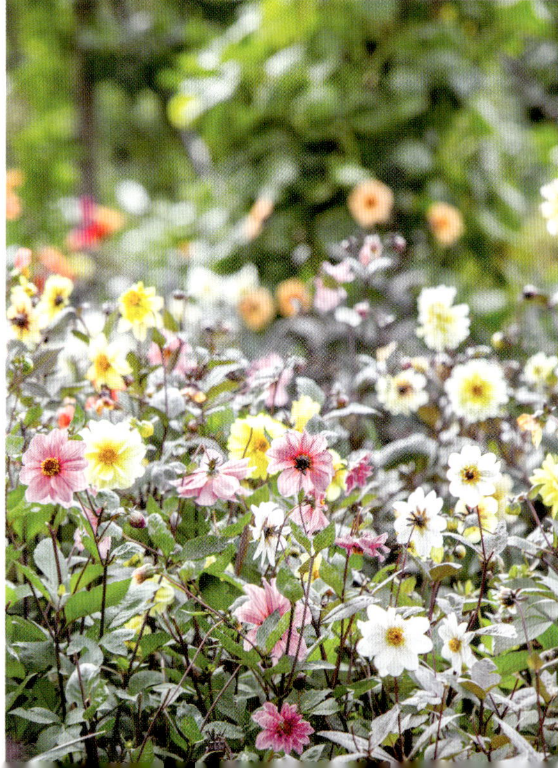

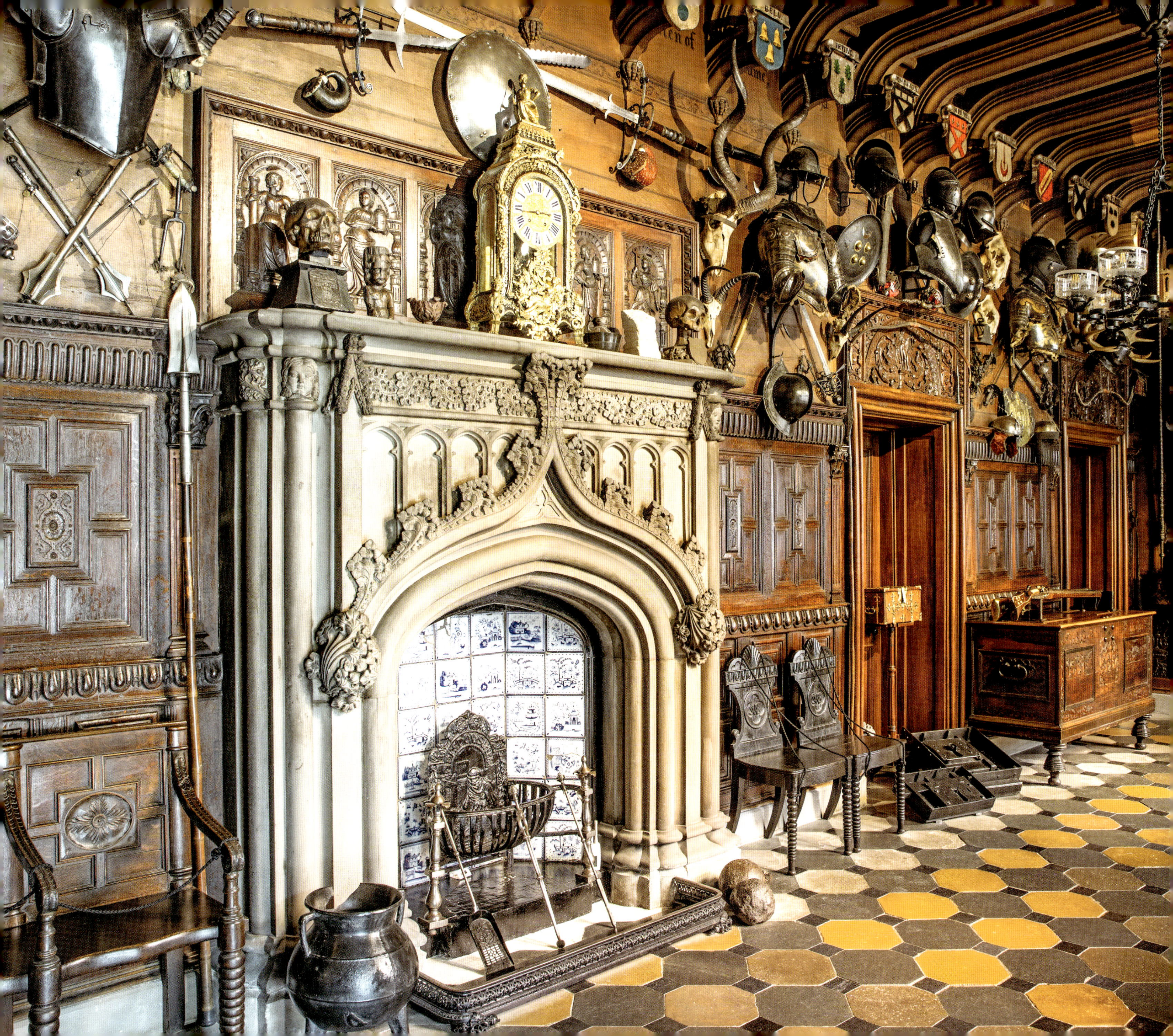

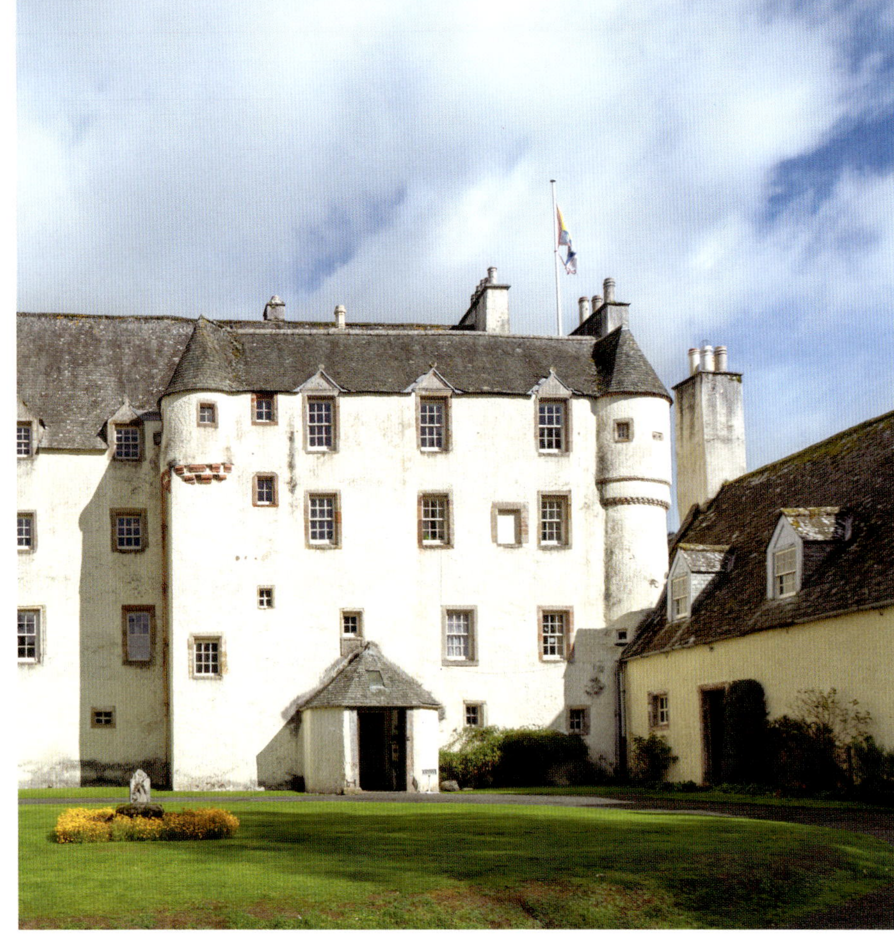

A PLACE TO CALL HOME

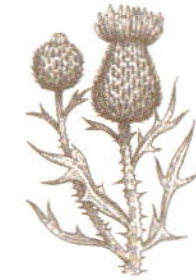

Scotland's oldest inhabited home, Traquair House, stands between the hamlets of Melrose and Peebles in the community of Innerleithen. With a history that spans more than nine centuries, the manor was originally built as a royal hunting lodge, hosting a number of Scottish monarchs through the years. The Stuart family has resided here continuously since 1491, with the current generation welcoming visitors to glimpse its greatness.

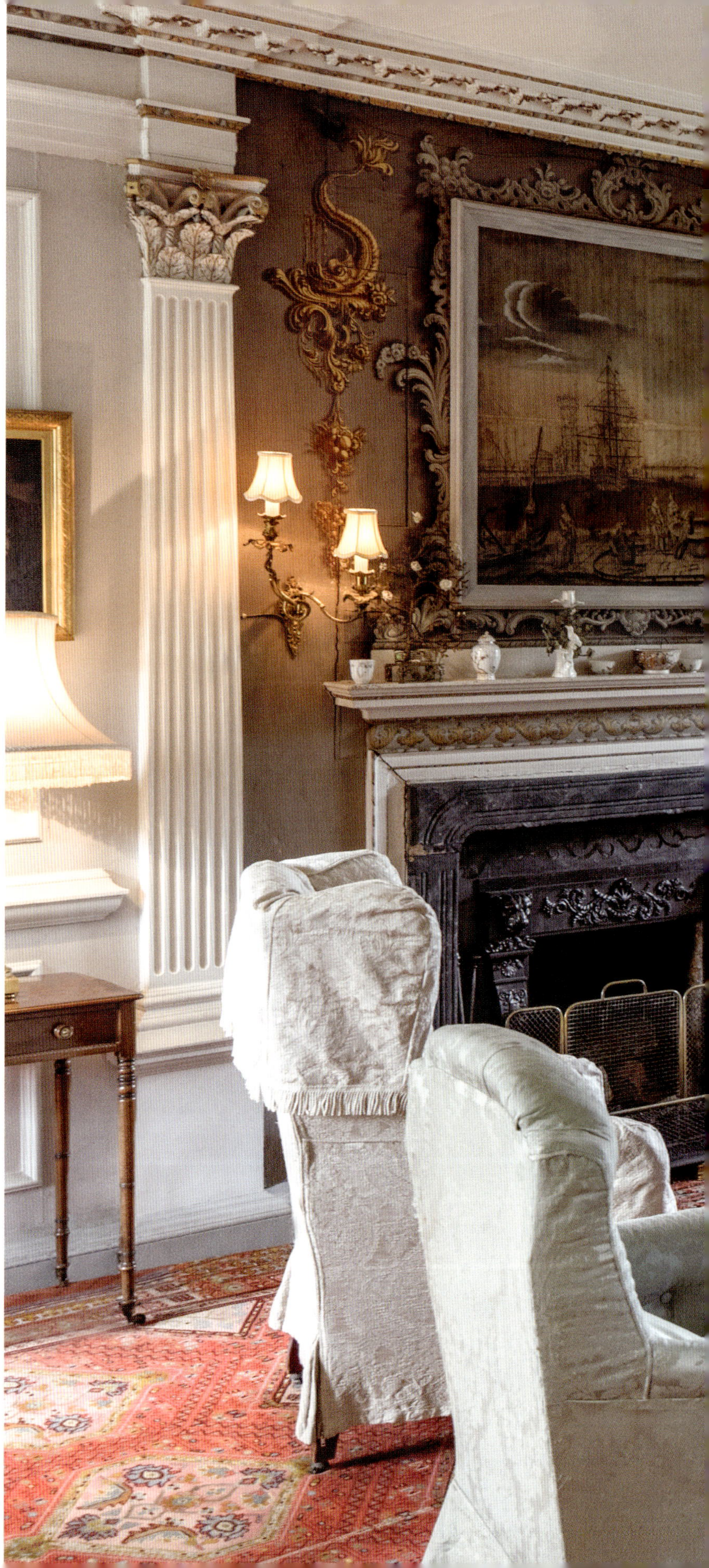

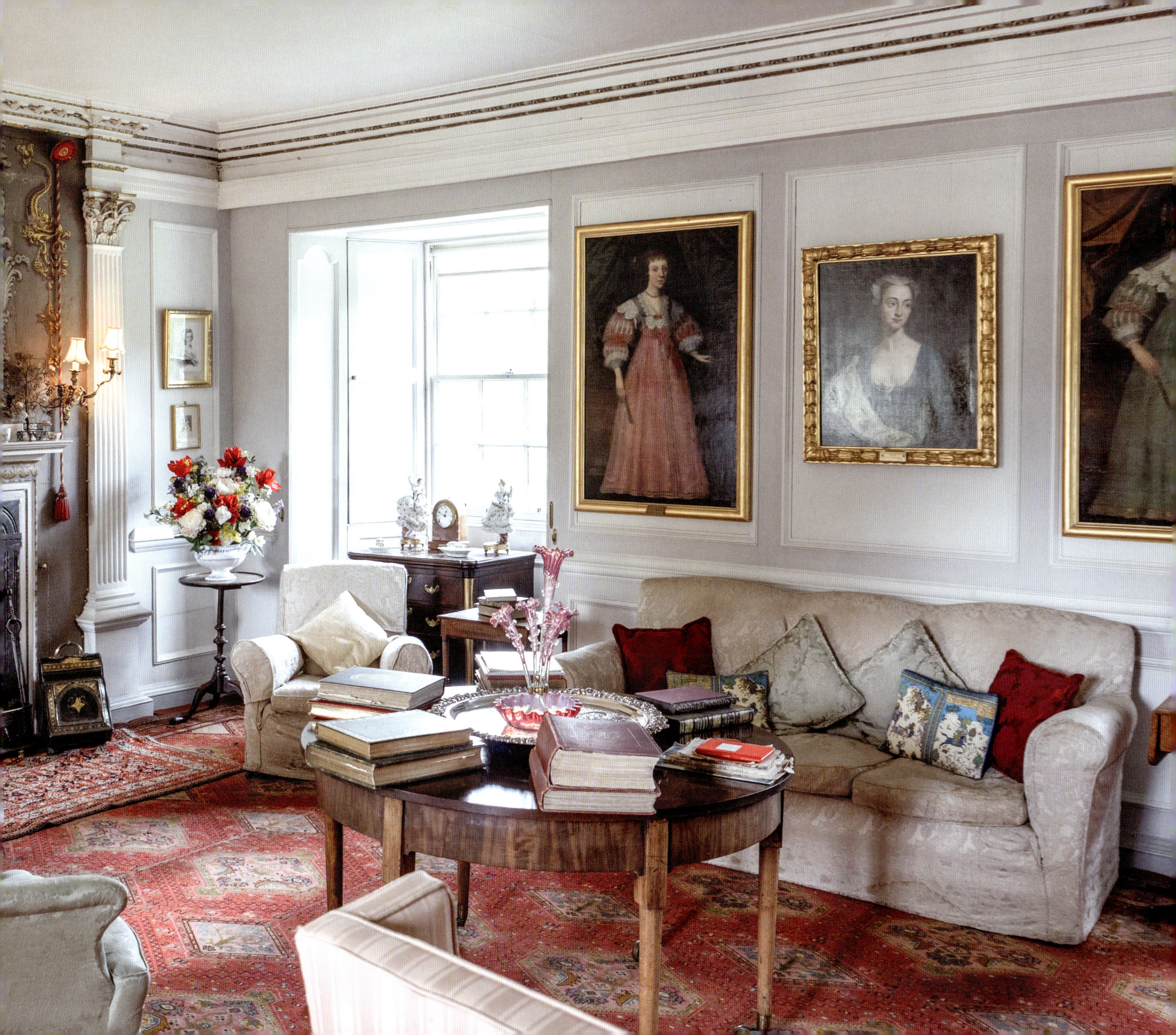

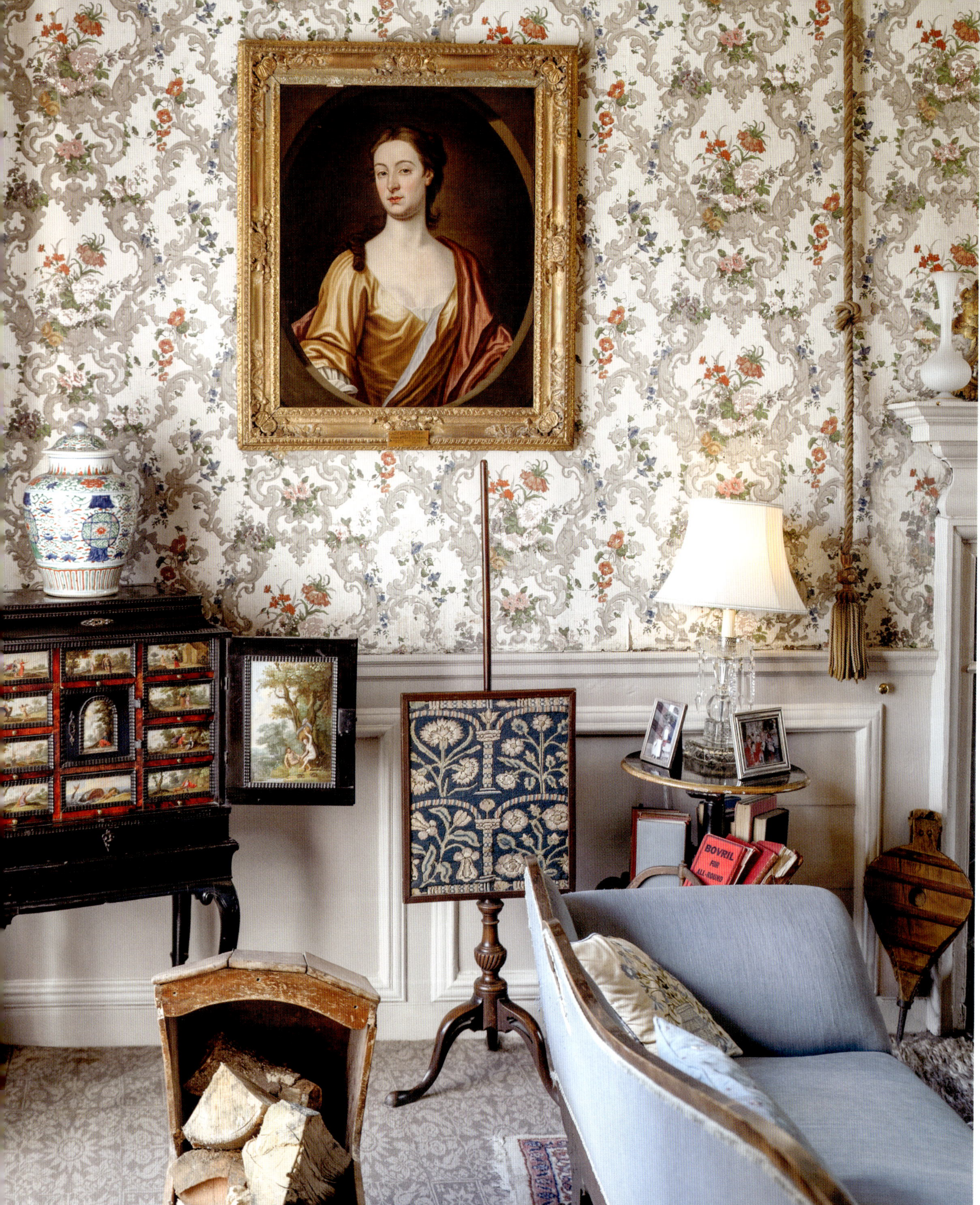

"All of my associations with coorie come from childhood—being invited to feel welcome, safe, and loved, close by the side of someone making just enough room."

—Neil Oliver

At Traquair House, a portrait of the Duchess of Perth, daughter of the 4th Earl of Traquair, hangs in the Lower Drawing Room, left, where ladies would have taken tea or retired after a meal in the Dining Room, opposite, right. Above left: The Still Room transitioned from a garden parlor to the housekeeper's quarters, where certain household items were held for safekeeping. Of particular note are the trompe l'oeil painting above the mantel and the collections of fine English and Chinese porcelain. Previous spread: The High Drawing Room, originally designed in medieval style, was remodeled in the mid-eighteenth century to incorporate classical elements, such as the Greek columns flanking the fireplace.

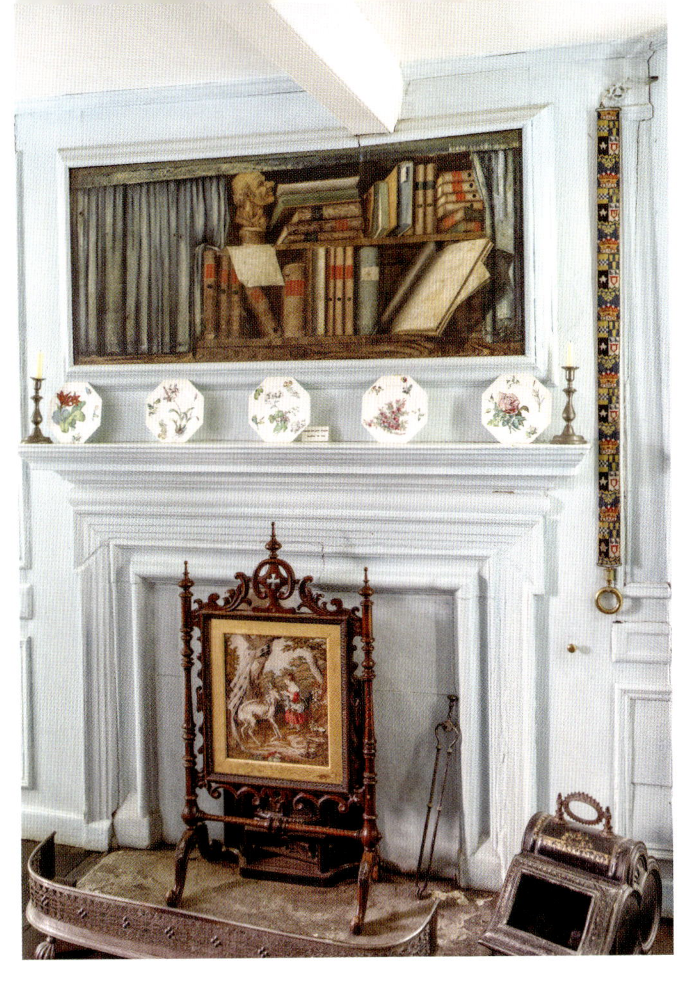

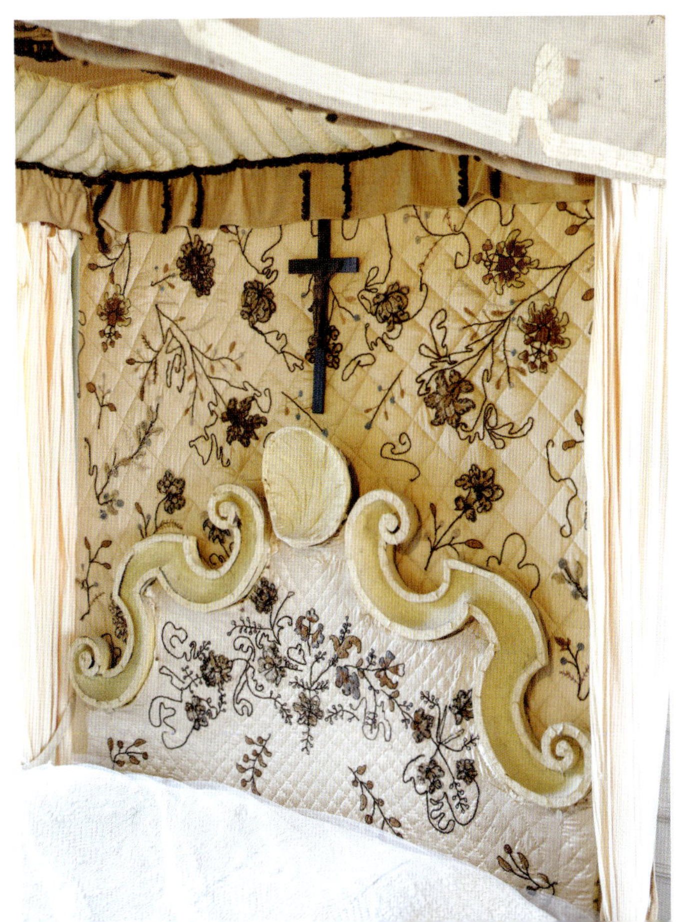

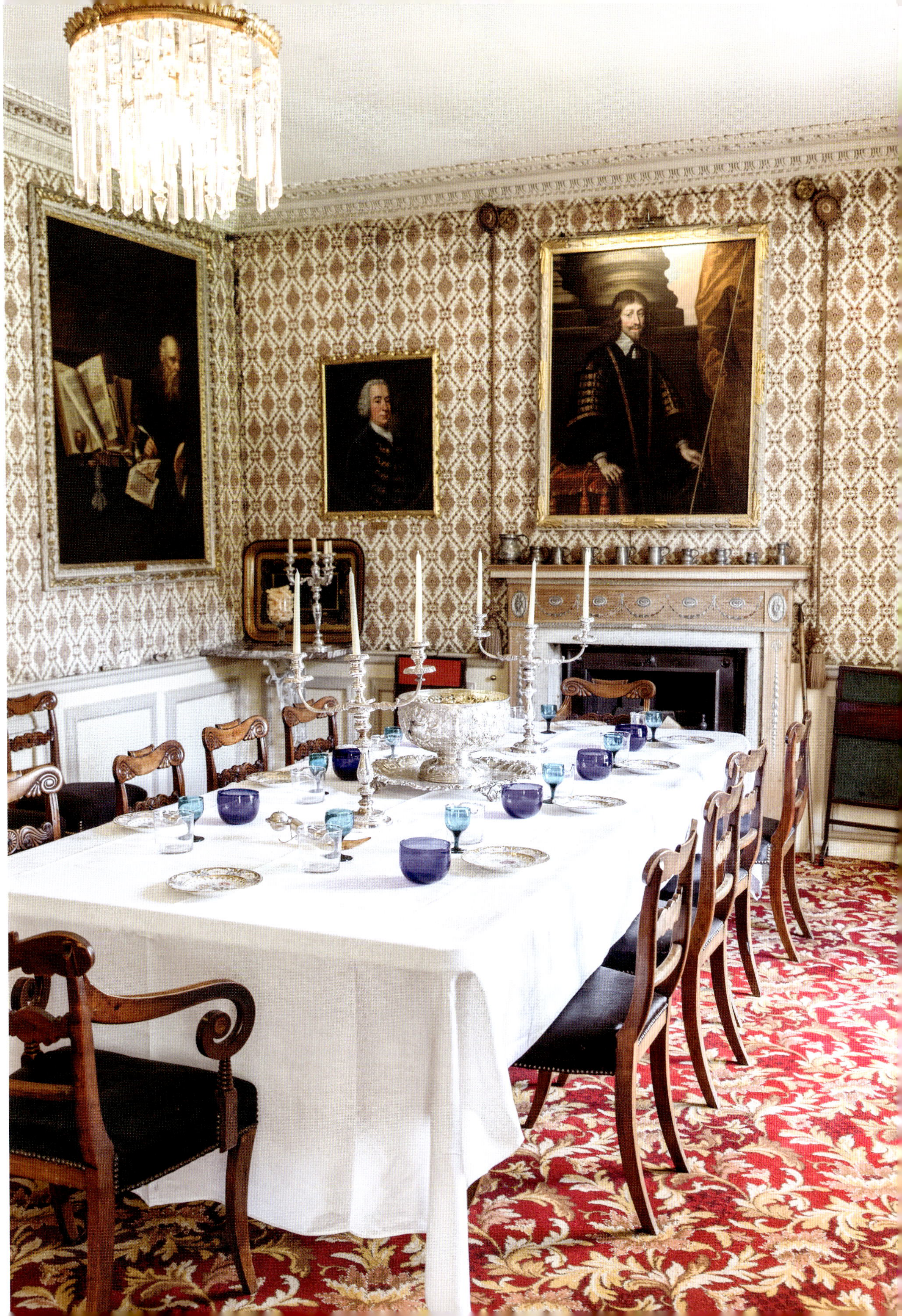

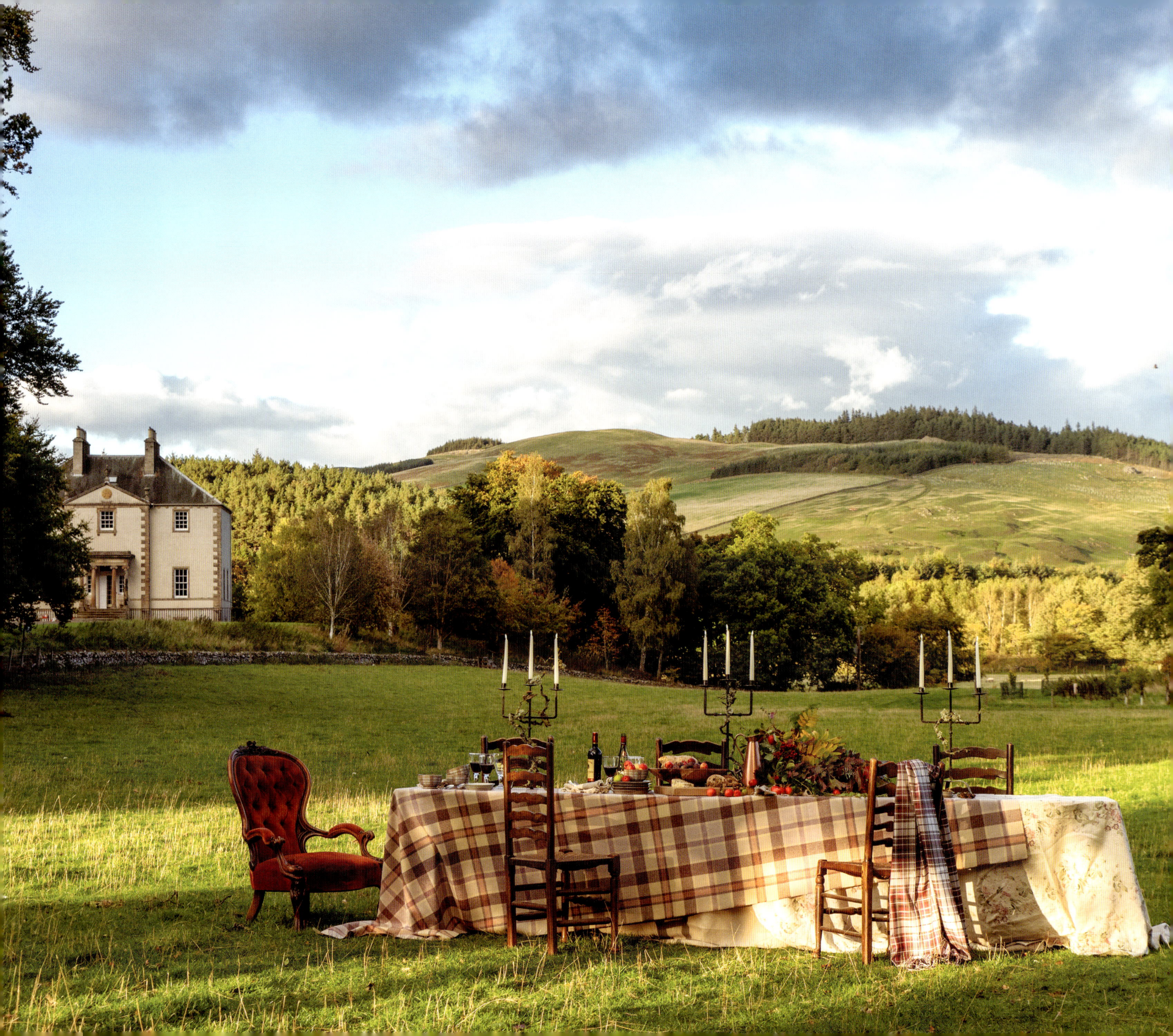

A FEAST OF SCOTTISH SPLENDOR

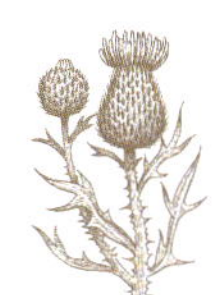

The quintessential cuisine of Scotland developed around the country's natural provender, including a bounty of indigenous game and the wealth of seafood to be found along the coasts. This menu, developed by chefs in the *Victoria* test kitchens, pays tribute to this heritage with two savory dishes, Venison Pies and Cullen Skink. Calling to mind the roots and herbs that historically served as menu staples, Mashed Turnips offer a creamy counterpoint seasoned with chives. The meal ends on the sweetest of notes with Cranachan Trifle, a brimful dessert that mingles cookie crumbles, granola, clouds of whisky cream, and fresh berries.

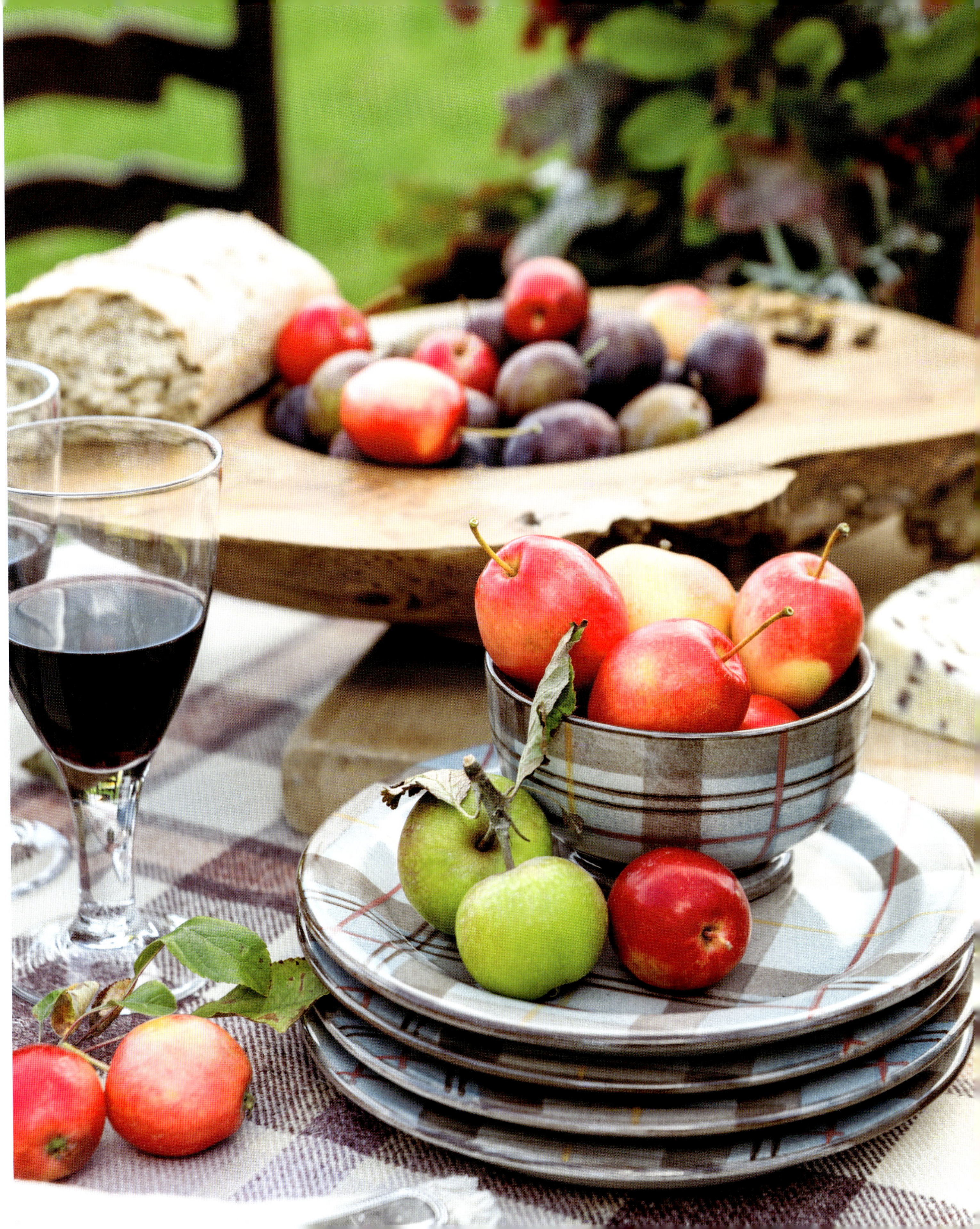

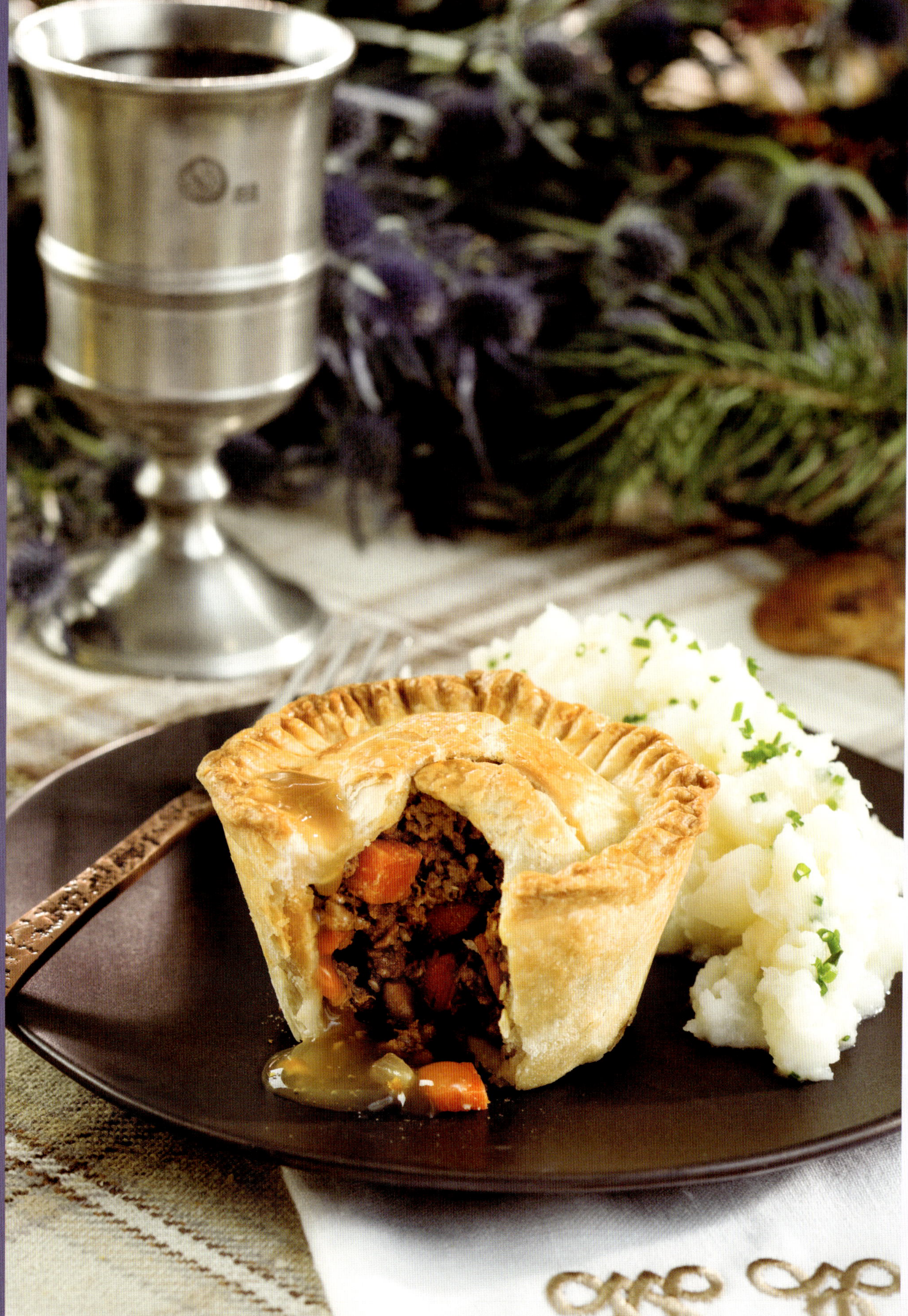

Venison Pies

Makes 6

For crust:
4¼ cups bread flour, divided
1 teaspoon kosher salt
1 cup plus 6 tablespoons cold unsalted butter, cubed
½ cup cold milk

For filling:
½ tablespoon olive oil
1 cup diced sweet onion
1 cup diced carrots
1 pound ground venison
¼ teaspoon ground cloves
2 tablespoons tomato paste
1 teaspoon kosher salt
¼ teaspoon ground pepper
1 large egg
1 tablespoon heavy whipping cream

1. For crust: In the work bowl of a food processor, pulse together 4 cups flour and salt. Add butter and pulse until mixture resembles coarse crumbs. With processor running, add milk in a slow, steady stream. Process until a smooth dough forms, about 1 minute.
2. Turn out dough and divide dough in half. Shape each half into a disk, and wrap in plastic wrap. Refrigerate for at least 2 hours or up to 3 days.
3. For filling: In a medium sauté pan, heat olive oil over medium heat. Add onion and cook until fragrant, about 2 minutes. Stir in carrots and cook until slightly tender, about 1 minute. Transfer mixture to a large heatproof bowl. Stir in venison, cloves, tomato paste, salt, and pepper until combined. Let cool on a wire rack.
4. Preheat oven to 375°. Spray a 6-cavity jumbo muffin pan* with baking spray with flour.
5. Let dough stand at room temperature until just softened, about 10 minutes. On a lightly floured surface, roll out dough to a ⅛-inch thickness. Using a 6-inch round cutter, cut 6 rounds from dough, rerolling scraps as needed. Press dough into wells and up sides. Spoon approximately ½ cup filling into each dough-filled well.
6. Using a 4-inch round cutter, cut 6 rounds of dough. Place dough over filling. For each well, trim edges, fold edges of both crusts under, and crimp, if desired.
7. In a small bowl, whisk together egg and cream. Brush tops of pies with egg wash. Cut several 1-inch slits in top of dough to release steam.
8. Bake until golden brown, about 30 minutes. Let cool slightly before serving.

We used a Williams Sonoma Goldtouch Nonstick Large Muffin Pan.

Cullen Skink

Makes 4 to 5 servings

8 cups water
2½ teaspoons kosher salt, divided
4 cups Yukon gold potatoes, diced
4 tablespoons unsalted butter, divided
1 pound boneless smoked haddock
1 clove garlic, minced
1 cup finely diced sweet onion,
½ cup thinly sliced leeks (white parts only)
2 bay leaves
1 tablespoon fresh parsley, finely chopped
1 teaspoon fresh thyme
½ teaspoon ground black pepper, divided
½ teaspoon ground mustard
3 cups heavy whipping cream, divided
Garnish: chopped fresh parsley, fresh thyme

1. In a large saucepan, bring 8 cups water to a boil over medium-high heat. Add 1 teaspoon salt and potatoes. Cook until tender, 8 to 10 minutes. Drain potatoes, discarding liquid.
2. In a large Dutch oven, melt 2 tablespoons butter over medium heat. Add haddock; cook for 1 minute on each side. Remove haddock. Use a fork to flake one-fourth of haddock.
3. Melt remaining 2 tablespoons butter in Dutch oven. Add garlic, onion, leeks, bay leaves, parsley, thyme, pepper, mustard, and remaining 1½ teaspoons salt; cook until fragrant, about 2 minutes. Add cream. Bring to a boil over medium-high heat; reduce heat and stir in potatoes. Use a potato masher to mash potatoes. Add three-fourths haddock, and simmer soup, stirring occasionally, for 15 minutes.
4. To serve, ladle into bowls. Top with flaked haddock, and garnish with chopped parsley and thyme, if desired.

Note: If smoked haddock is not available, any smoked white fish may be substituted.

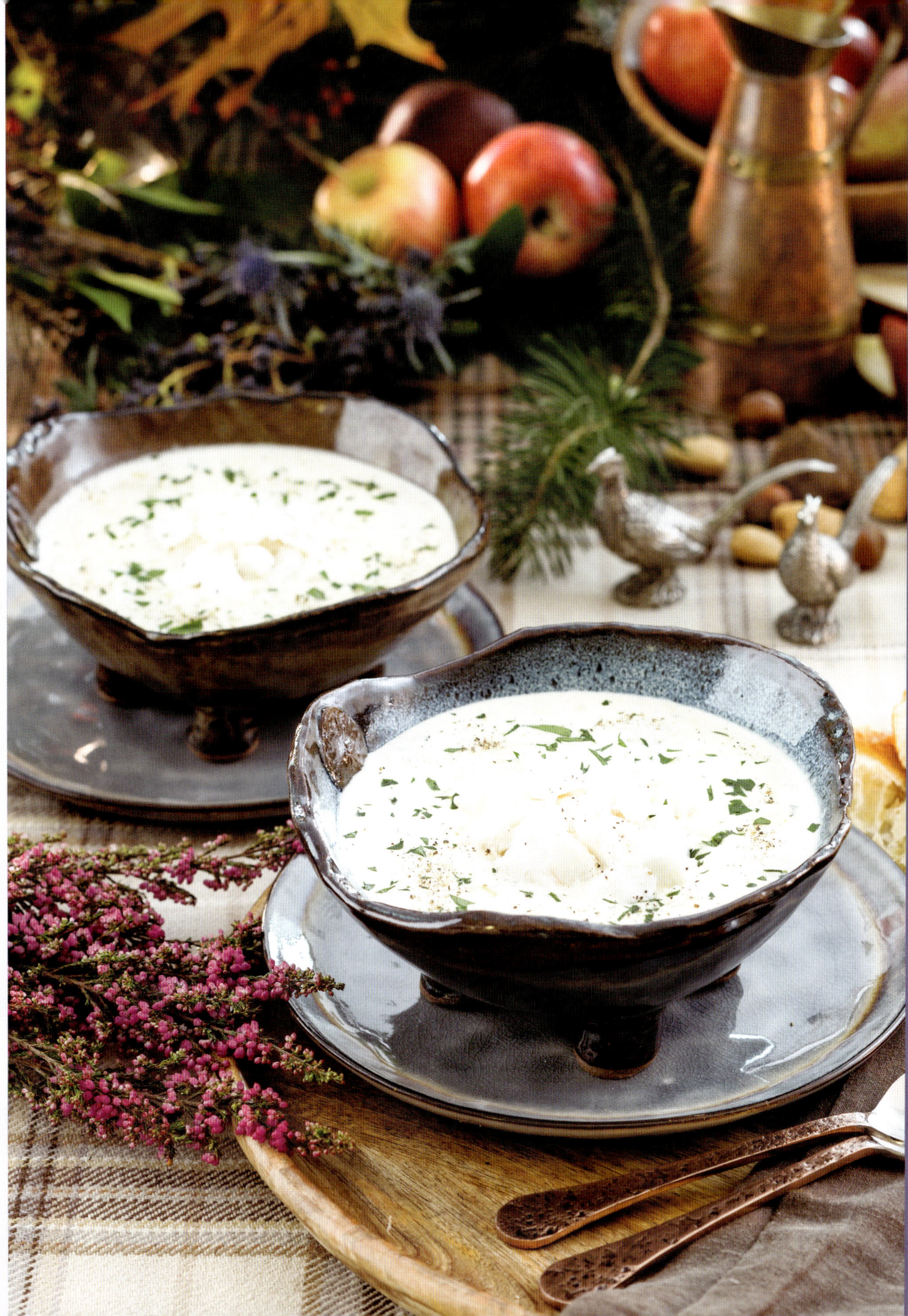

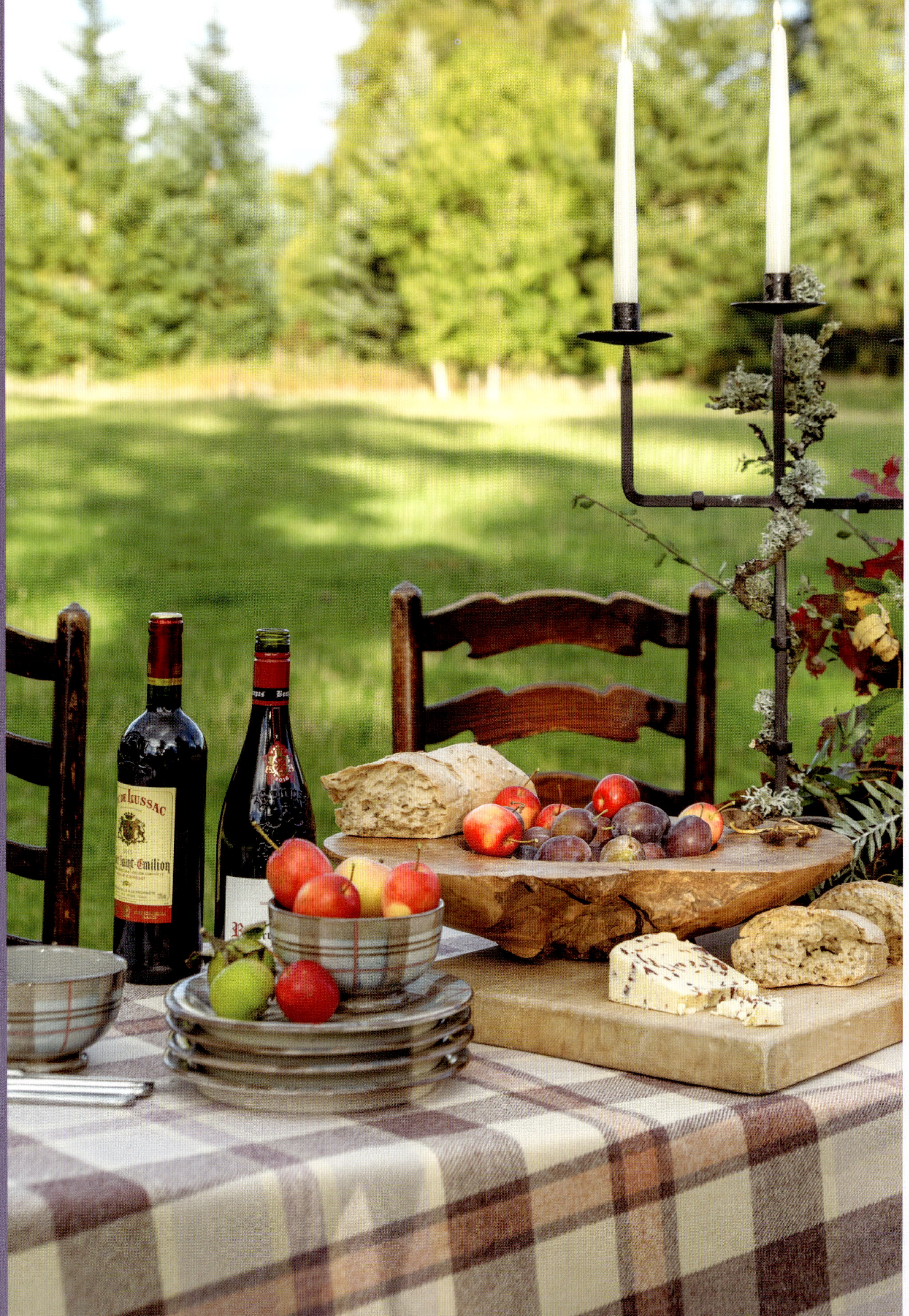

Mashed Turnips

Makes approximately 2 cups

6 cups water
2¼ teaspoons kosher salt, divided
4 cups turnips, washed, peeled, and diced
4 tablespoons unsalted butter, softened
1 tablespoon warm milk
1 tablespoon minced fresh chives
Garnish: chopped fresh chives

1. In a large saucepan, bring 6 cups water to a boil over medium-high heat. Add 1 teaspoon salt and turnips. Cook until tender, about 10 minutes.
2. Drain turnips, discarding liquid. Add butter and remaining 1¼ teaspoons salt. Using a potato masher, mash turnips to desired consistency. Stir in milk and fold in minced chives. Serve warm and garnish with chopped chives, if desired.

Cranachan Trifle

Makes 8 (6-ounce) servings

For granola:
1 cup old-fashioned oats
2 tablespoons firmly packed light brown sugar
1 tablespoon vegetable oil
1½ tablespoons honey
⅛ teaspoon kosher salt
1 tablespoon egg white

For shortbread:
3 tablespoons unsalted butter, softened
2 tablespoons confectioners' sugar
¼ teaspoon vanilla extract
⅓ cup plus 2 tablespoons all-purpose flour
⅛ teaspoon kosher salt

For whisky cream:
2 ounces cream cheese, softened
½ cup confectioners' sugar, sifted
1 cup heavy whipping cream
2 tablespoons honey
1 teaspoon Scotch whisky

1½ cups raspberries
Garnish: honey

1. Preheat oven to 250°. Line a rimmed baking sheet with a silicone baking mat.

2. For granola: In a large bowl, stir together oats, brown sugar, oil, honey, salt, and egg white. Spread mixture onto prepared pan. Bake until deep golden brown and crunchy, 50 minutes to 1 hour, stirring every 20 minutes. Let cool completely on a wire rack. Store in an airtight container in a cool, dry place for up to 2 weeks.

3. Preheat oven to 325°.

4. For shortbread: In a medium bowl, beat butter, confectioners' sugar, and vanilla extract with a mixer at medium speed until creamy, about 3 minutes. Scrape down sides of bowl with a rubber spatula.

5. In a medium bowl, stir together flour and salt. With mixer at low speed, gradually add flour mixture to butter mixture, beating until combined. Increase mixer speed to medium, and beat until very light and fluffy, about 3 minutes.

6. Turn out dough onto a sheet of parchment paper, and roll to ¼-inch thickness. Transfer dough and parchment paper to a rimmed baking sheet.

7. Bake until lightly browned, 12 to 15 minutes. Let cool completely on a wire rack. Crumble and store in an airtight container until ready to use.

8. For whisky cream: In the bowl of a stand mixer fitted with the paddle attachment, beat cream cheese and confectioners' sugar until smooth. Scrape down sides of bowl with a rubber spatula. Switch to a whip attachment. Add cream and beat at medium speed until soft peaks form. Add honey and Scotch, and beat until stiff peaks form. Refrigerate in an airtight container until ready to use.

9. To assemble: Spoon 2 tablespoons shortbread crumbles into the bottom of each trifle dish. Sprinkle with a single layer of raspberries. Spoon whisky cream into a piping bag fitted with a medium round tip; pipe a layer of cream over raspberries. Top each trifle with 2 tablespoons granola. Repeat layers. Garnish with a drizzle of honey, if desired.

**We used a Wilton #12 decorating tip.*

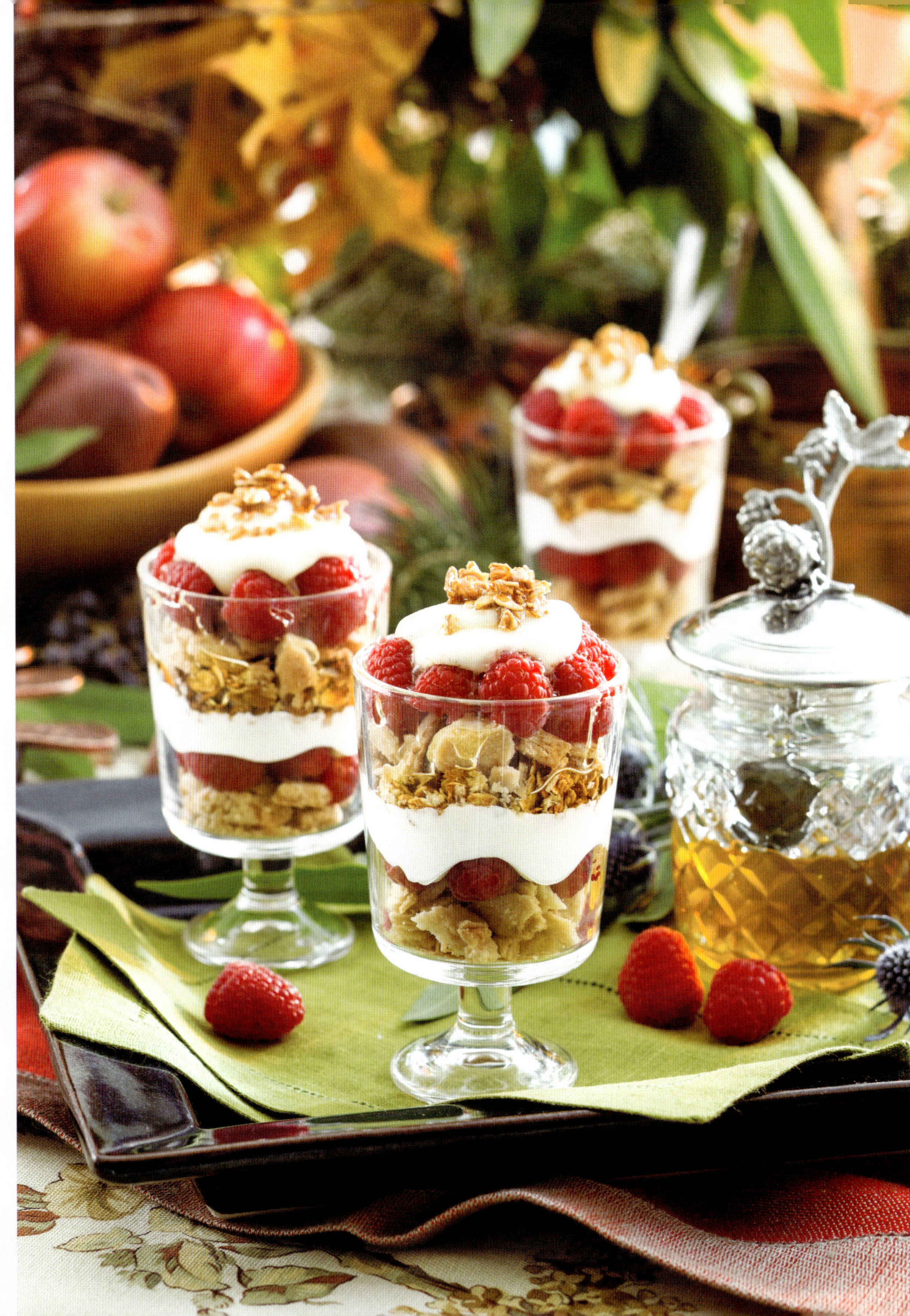

WITHIN THESE HOLY WALLS

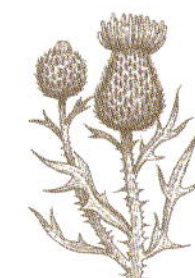

Though there are scores of ancient buildings rimming the capital city's Royal Mile, the St Giles' Cathedral truly stands out, due to its dramatic Gothic-style architecture, complete with flying buttresses and pointed arches, along with a grand crown tower dating to the fifteenth century. As the High Kirk of Edinburgh, St Giles traces its beginnings to 1124, named to honor the seventh-century Greek holy man who was later canonized. Theologian John Knox was appointed minister here in 1560.

The church's interiors are simply magnificent, with stunning tierceron vaulted ceilings and a profusion of stained glass windows lending both beauty and an awe-inspiring sense of sanctity. One nineteenth-century restoration corrected St Giles's precariously tilting walls; the solution involved encasing the entire building—save the stable crown tower—in ashlar sandstone. A second remodel, spearheaded by William Chambers, removed interior stone walls to return the kirk to its original medieval appearance.

Thistle Chapel, the vestry dedicated to the Order of the Thistle, Scotland's most prominent order of chivalry, lies at the southeast corner of St Giles. Chapel walls are lined with knights' stalls, crowned by carved canopies with coats of arms and heraldic helmets placed above. Designed by Sir Robert Lorimer, the small but exquisite space was completed in 1911.

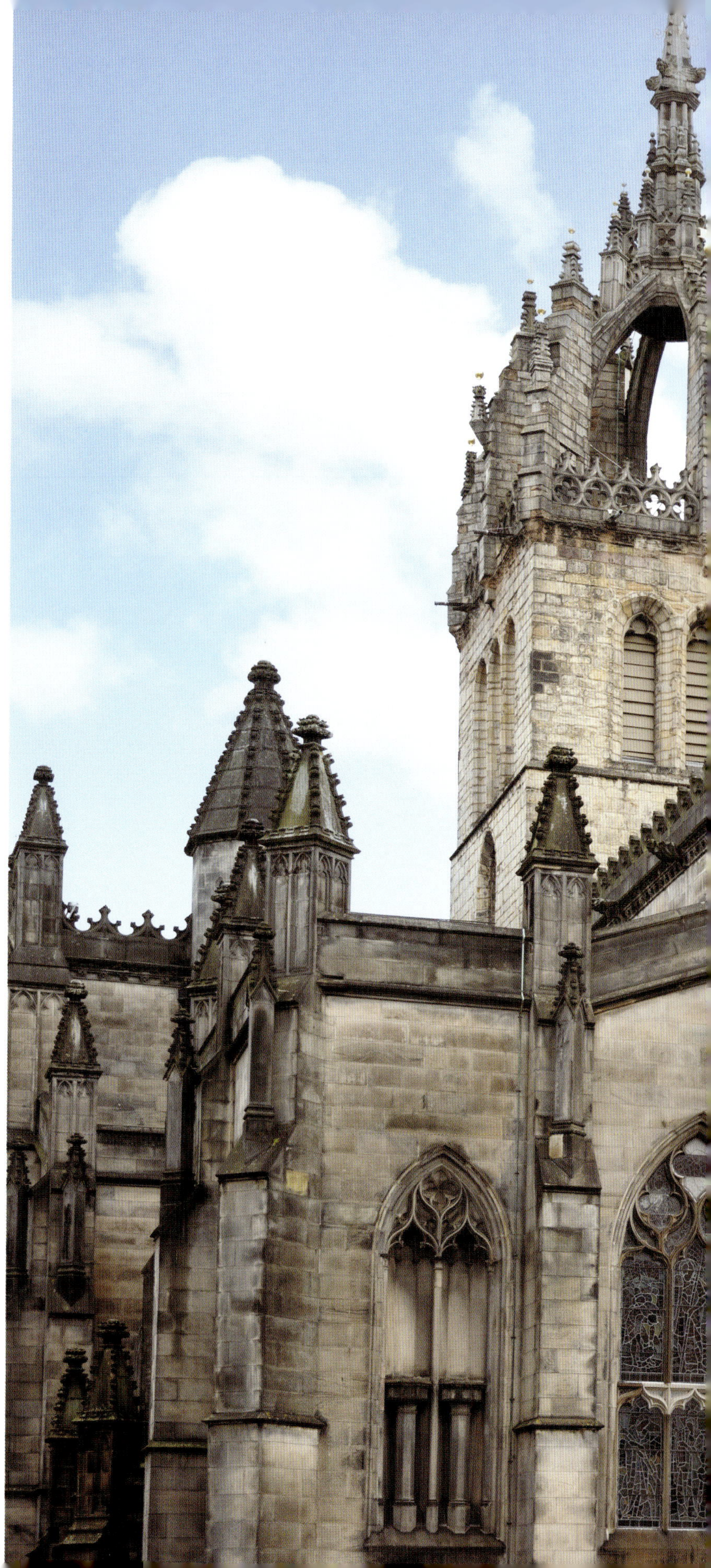

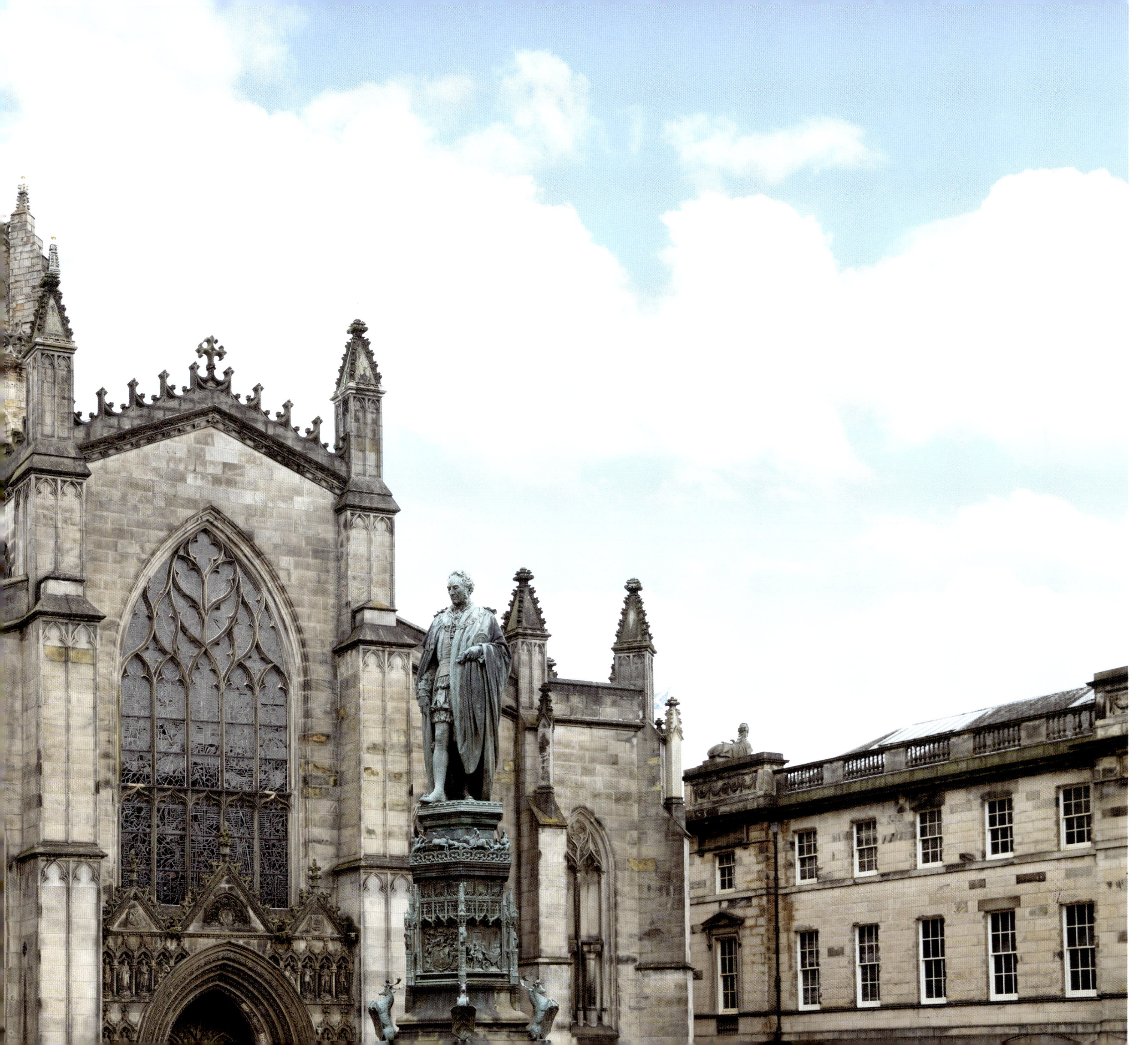

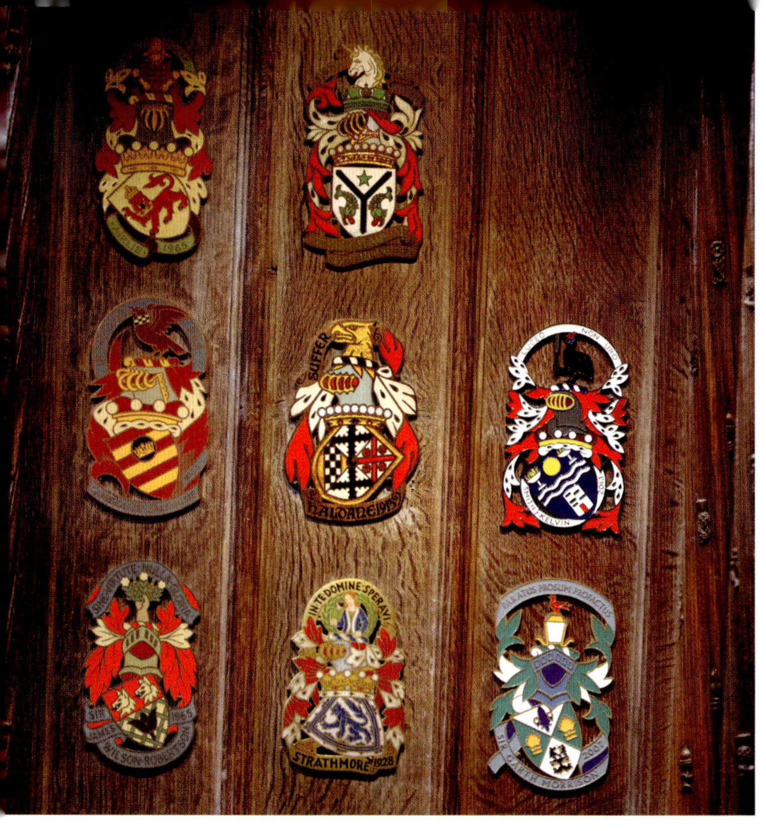

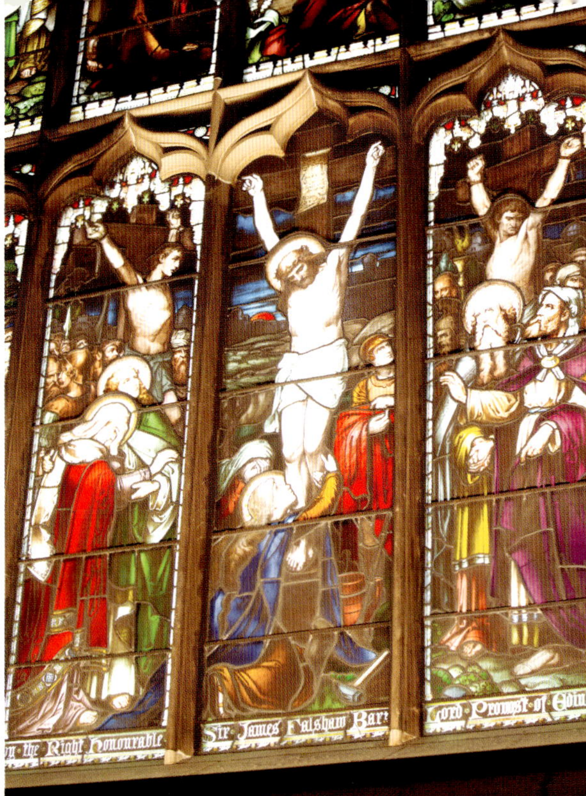

This page, above right: The colorful stained glass window on the back wall of St Giles depicts Christ's crucifixion in the lower portion and His resurrection in the upper panes. Below: Thistle Chapel comprises three bays, with the apse positioned in the eastern end. More than two hundred tons of sandstone were used to construct its remarkable ceiling, which is punctuated with nearly one hundred bosses evocative of Scottish medieval architecture. Opposite: An image of St. Paul graces the cathedral-style stained glass window overlooking St Giles's Preston Aisle section.

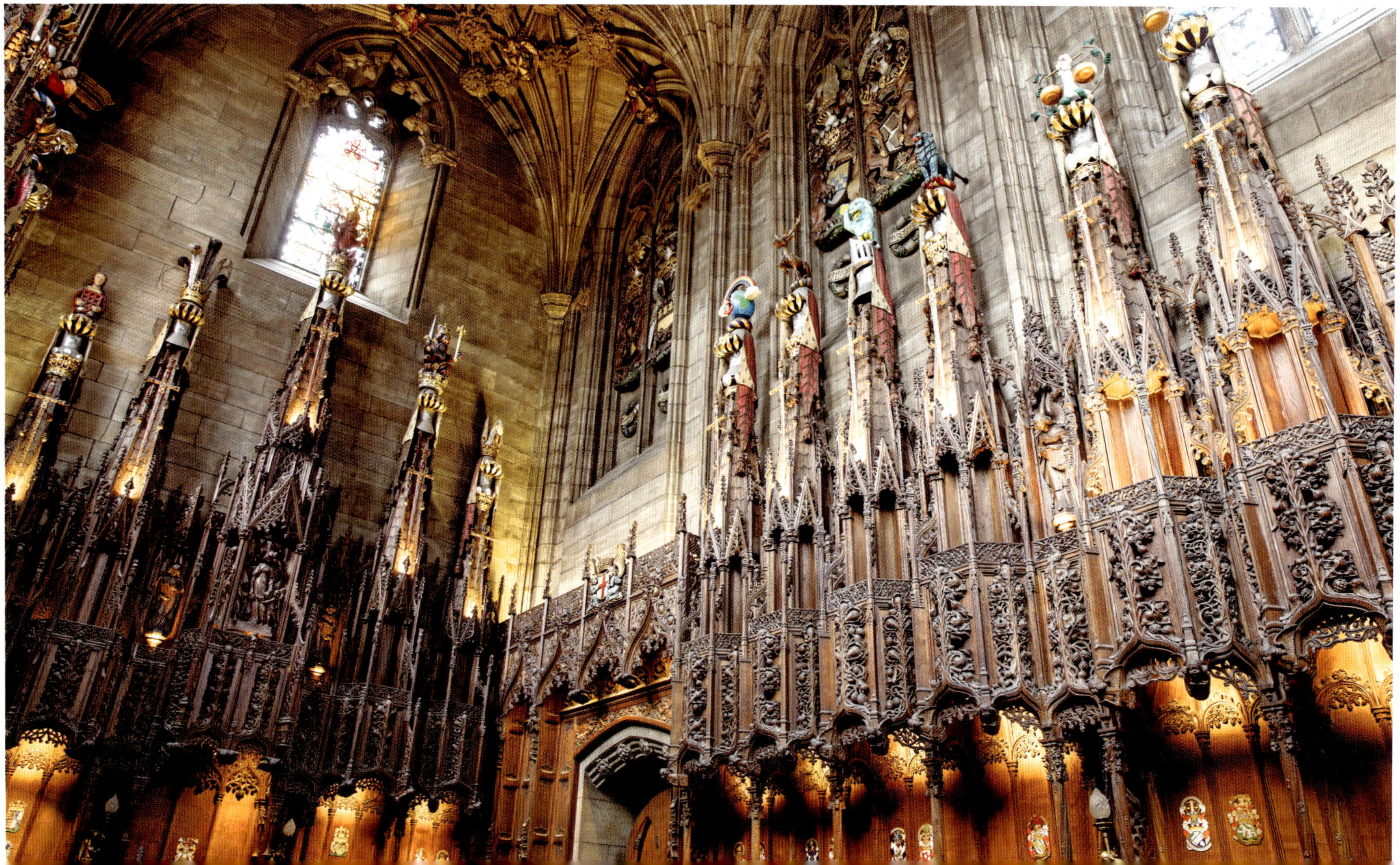

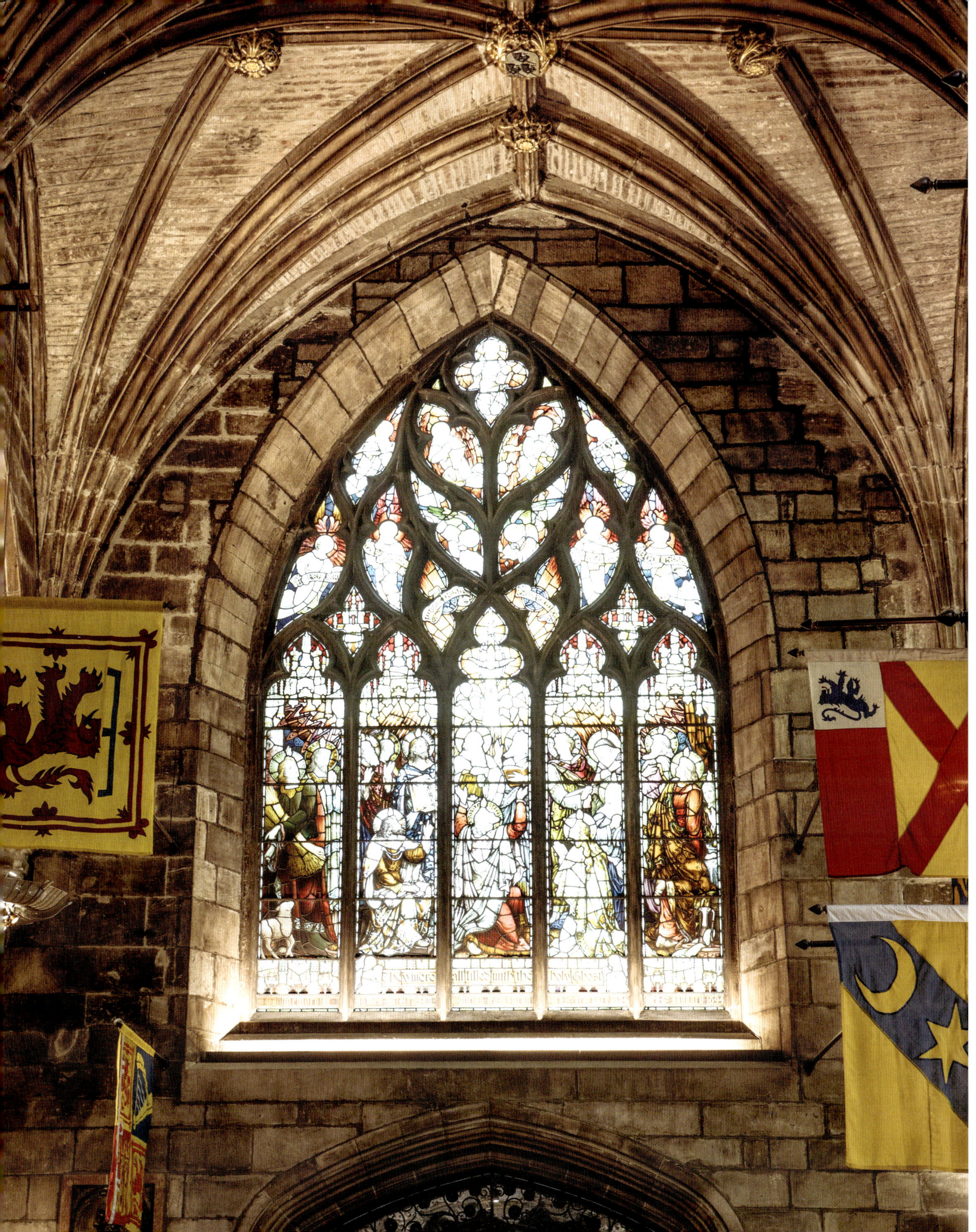

"Mankind was never so happily inspired as when it made a cathedral."

—Robert Louis Stevenson

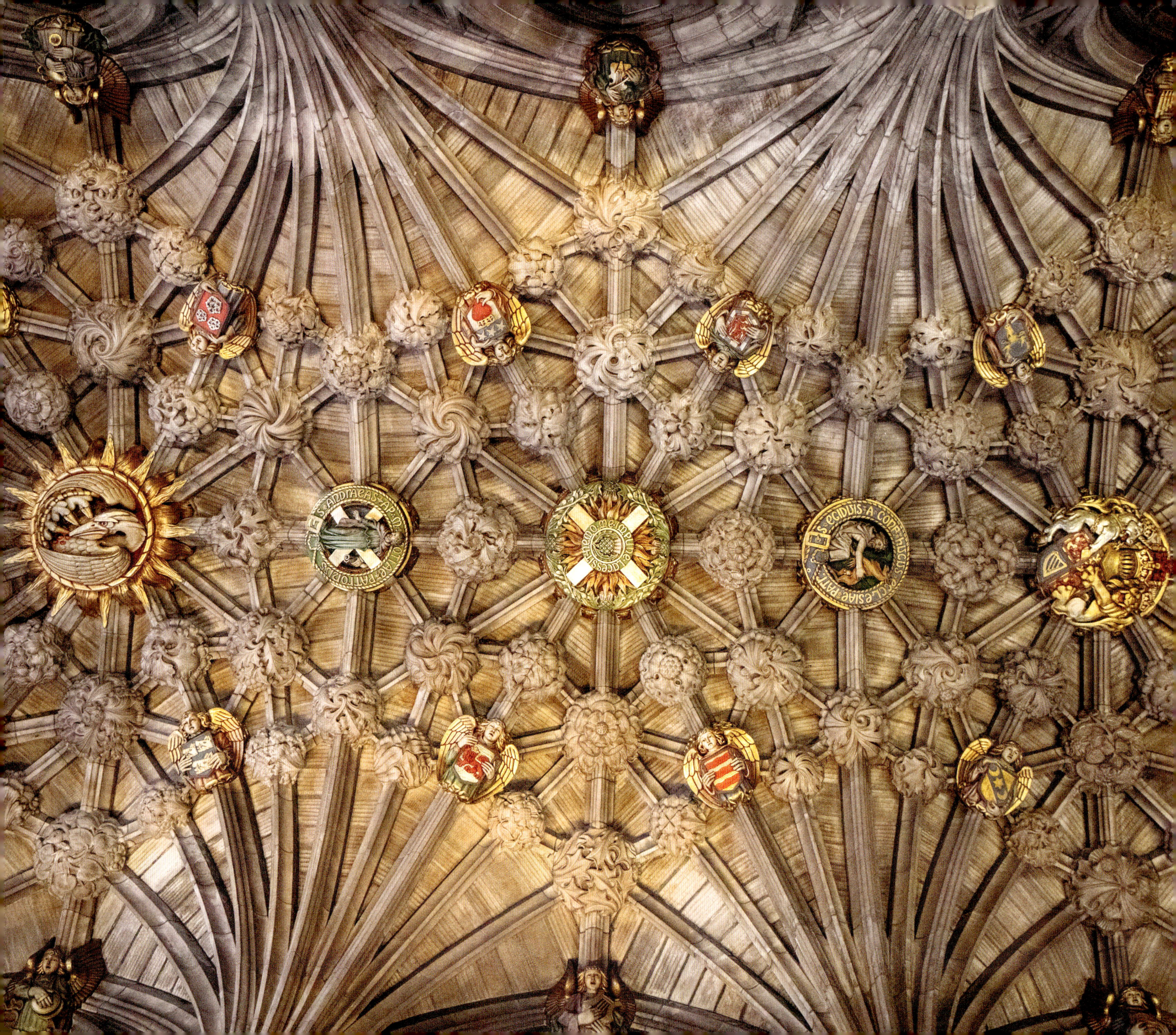
S. ANDRAEAS AP. SCOTIAE PATRONUS
S. EGIDIUS A CONF. HUIUS ECCLESIAE PATR.

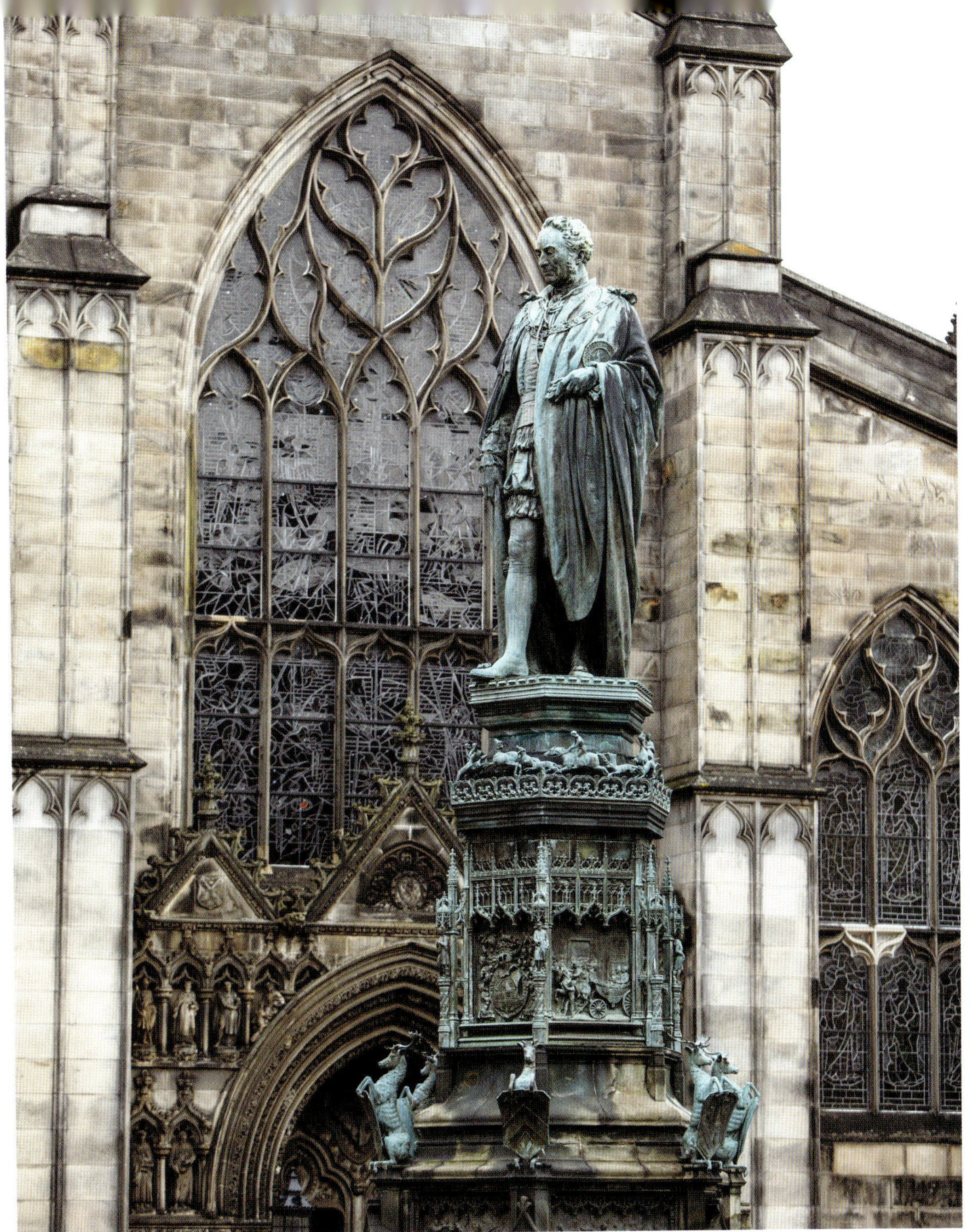

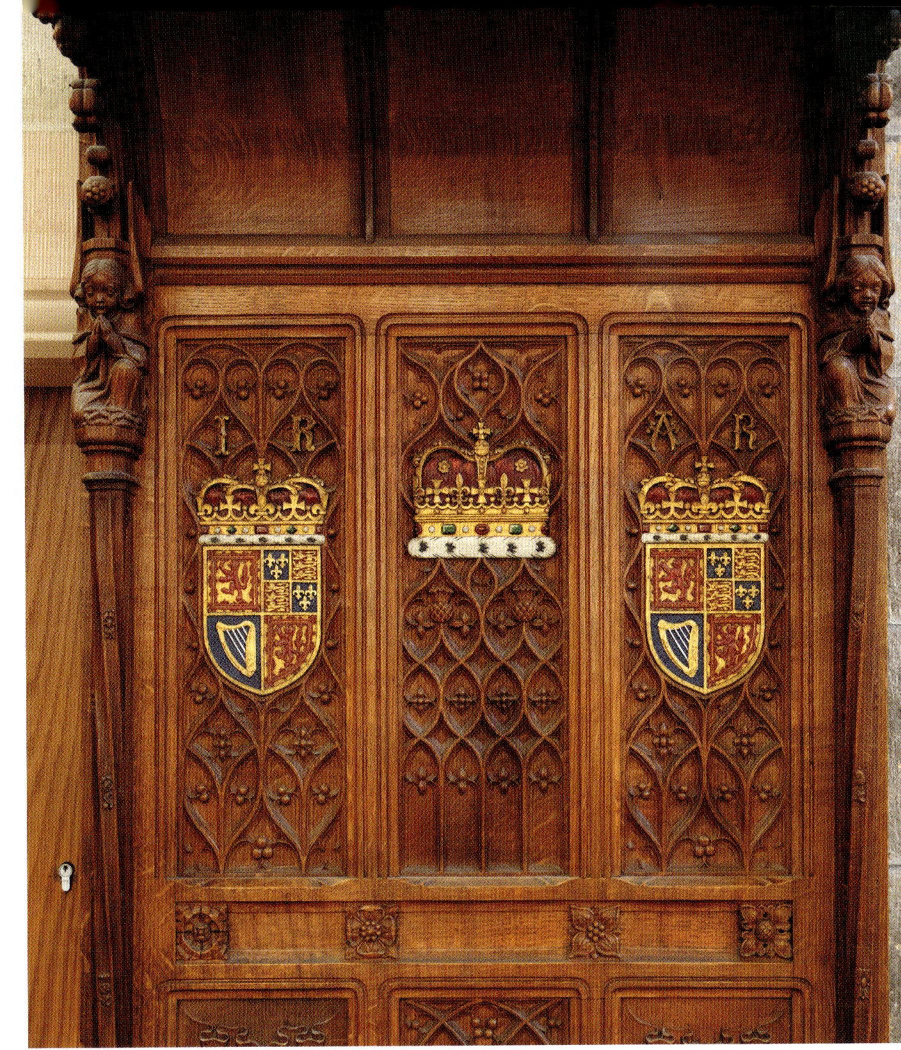

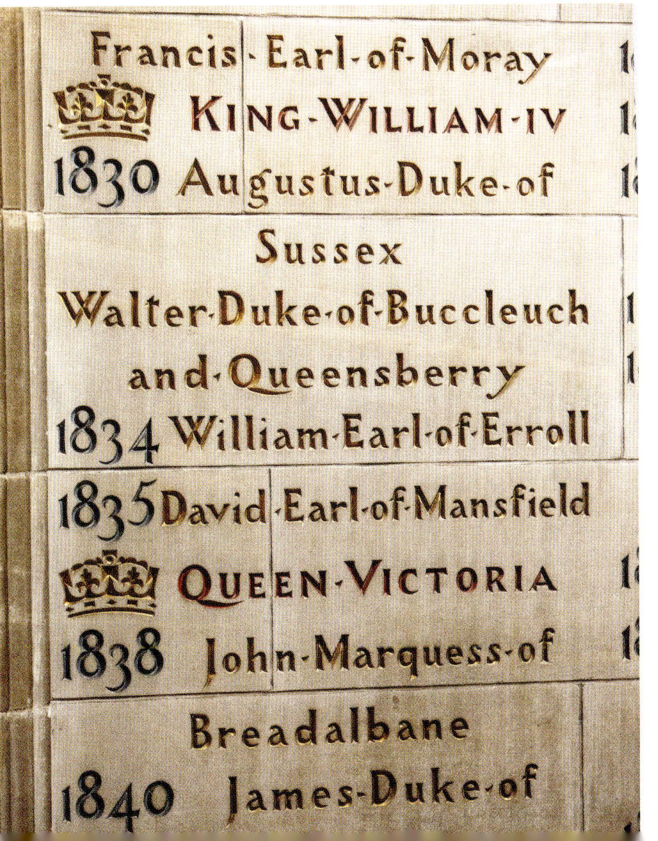

Opposite: Thistle Chapel's impressive lierne-vaulted ceiling is studded with a panoply of foliate bosses featuring the national flowers of the United Kingdom. This page, above left: Draped in the Victorian Gothic-style robes representing the Order of the Garter, nobleman Walter Francis Montagu Douglas Scott, 5th Duke of Buccleuch and 7th Duke of Queensbury, is honored with an imposing statue, which stands in the forecourt of St. Giles' Cathedral.

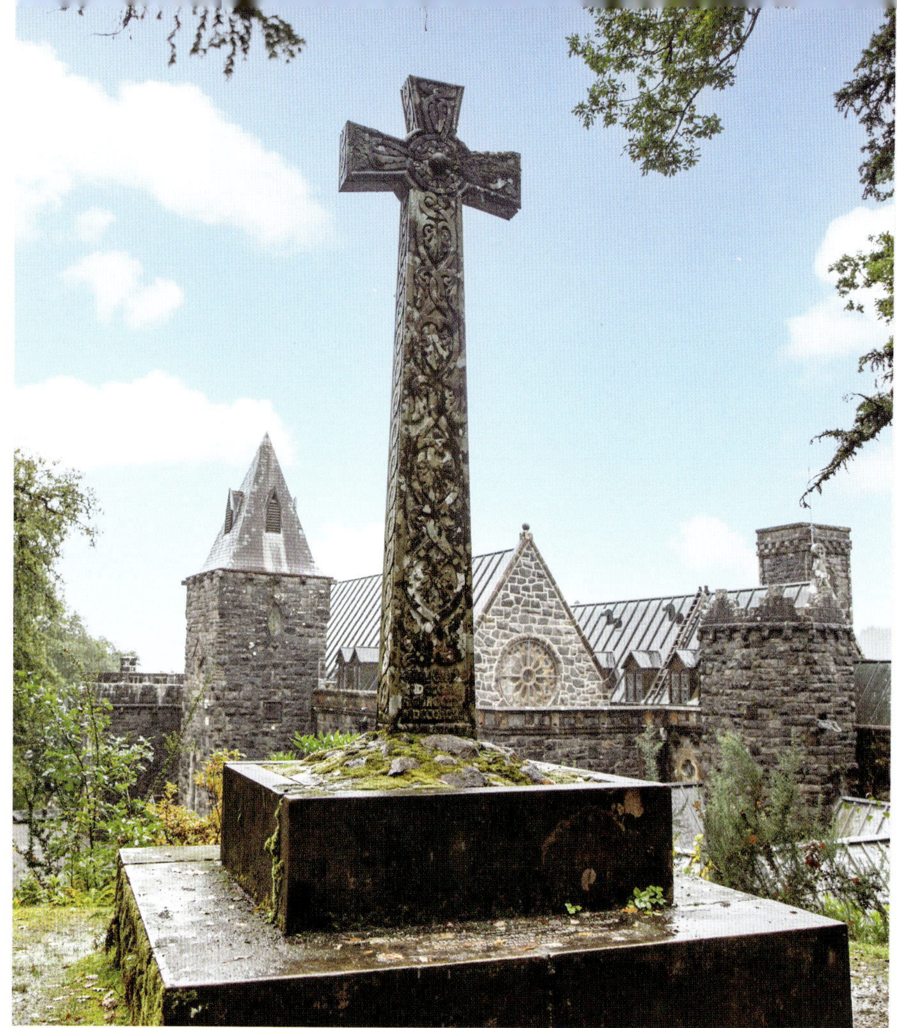

IN REVERENCE AND LOVE

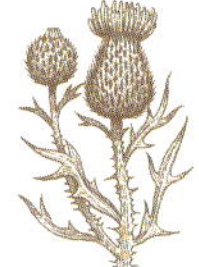

Though built in the late 1880s, Saint Conan's Kirk, with its weathered stone façade and medley of architecture styles, seems centuries old, which was the intent of architect Walter Douglas Campbell. Built on his Argyll property to save his mother the distant drive to the parish church, this masterpiece began as a labor of love but quickly became a poignant preoccupation.

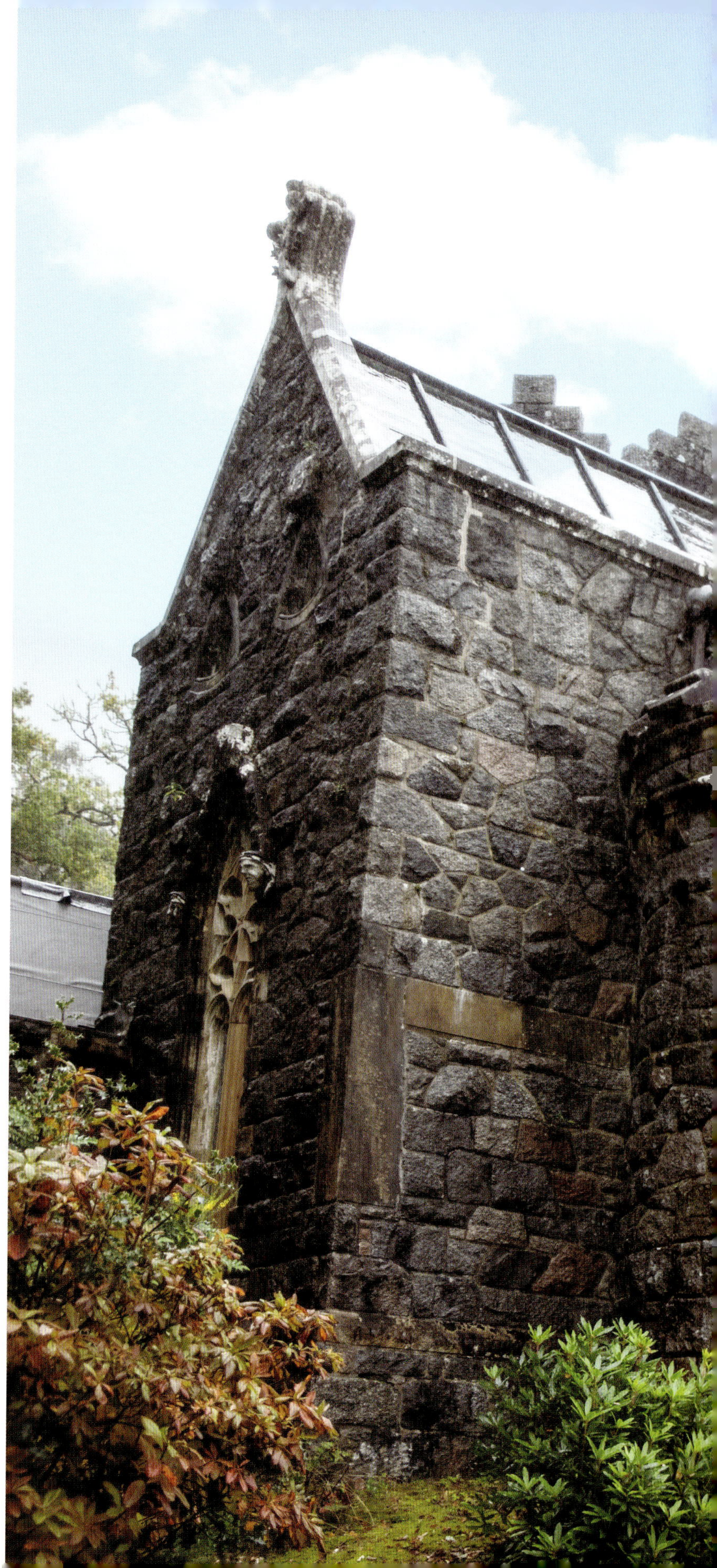

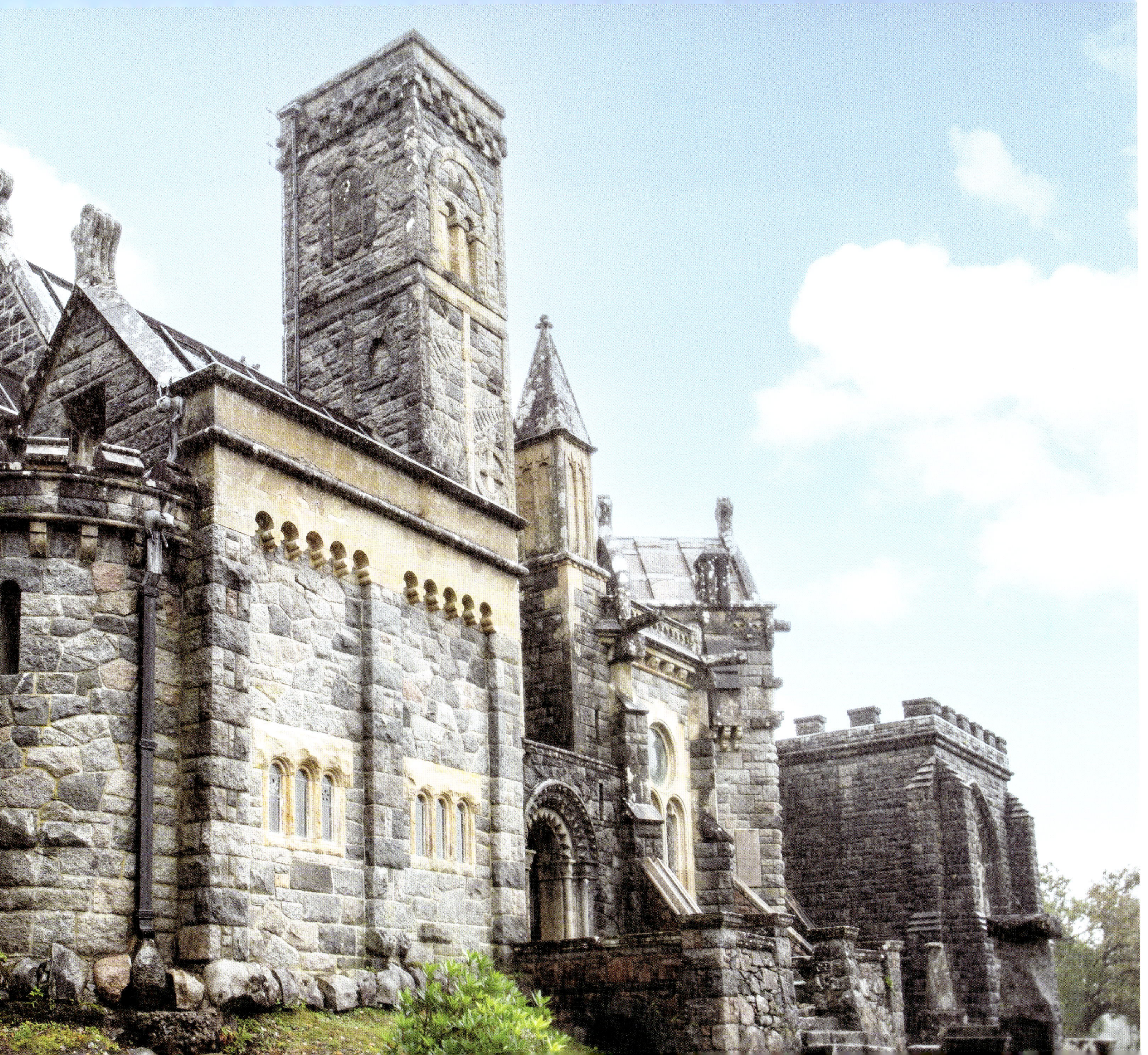

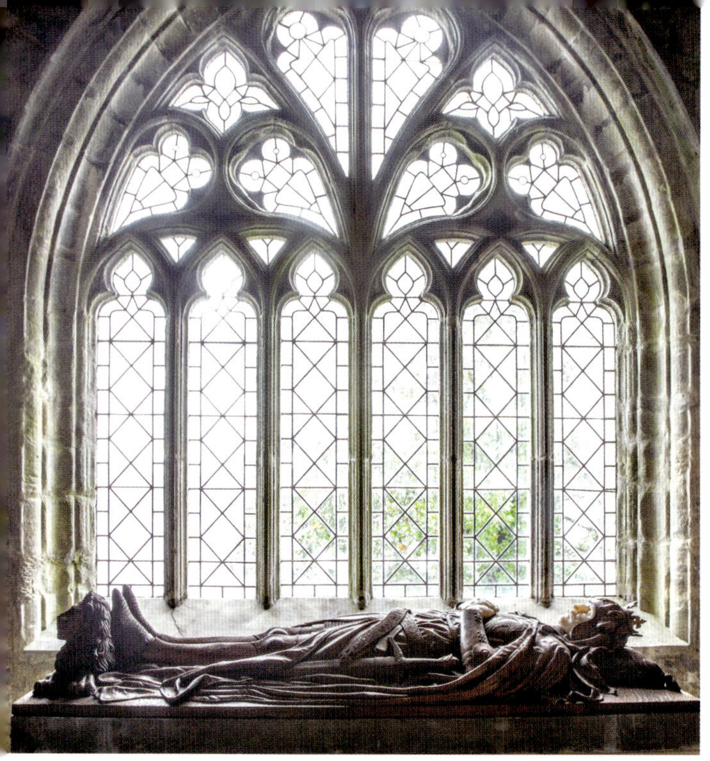

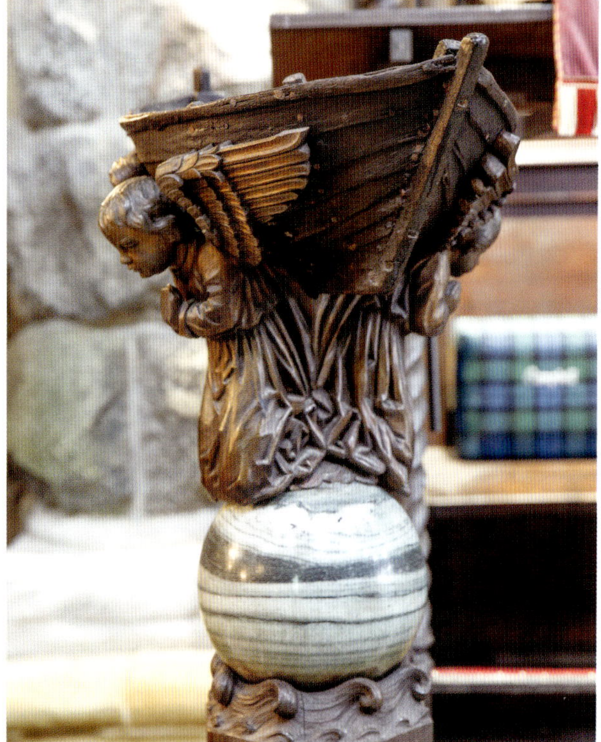

Above left: One of three bethels contained within the kirk, the Bruce Chapel honors Scottish King Robert I—commonly known as Robert the Bruce—with an effigy carved in alabaster and wood. Above right: Saint Conan's ornate baptismal font was fashioned in the likeness of a Breton fishing boat. Below: Carved from Spanish chestnut, the stalls in the chancel display the armorial shields of ancient clans.

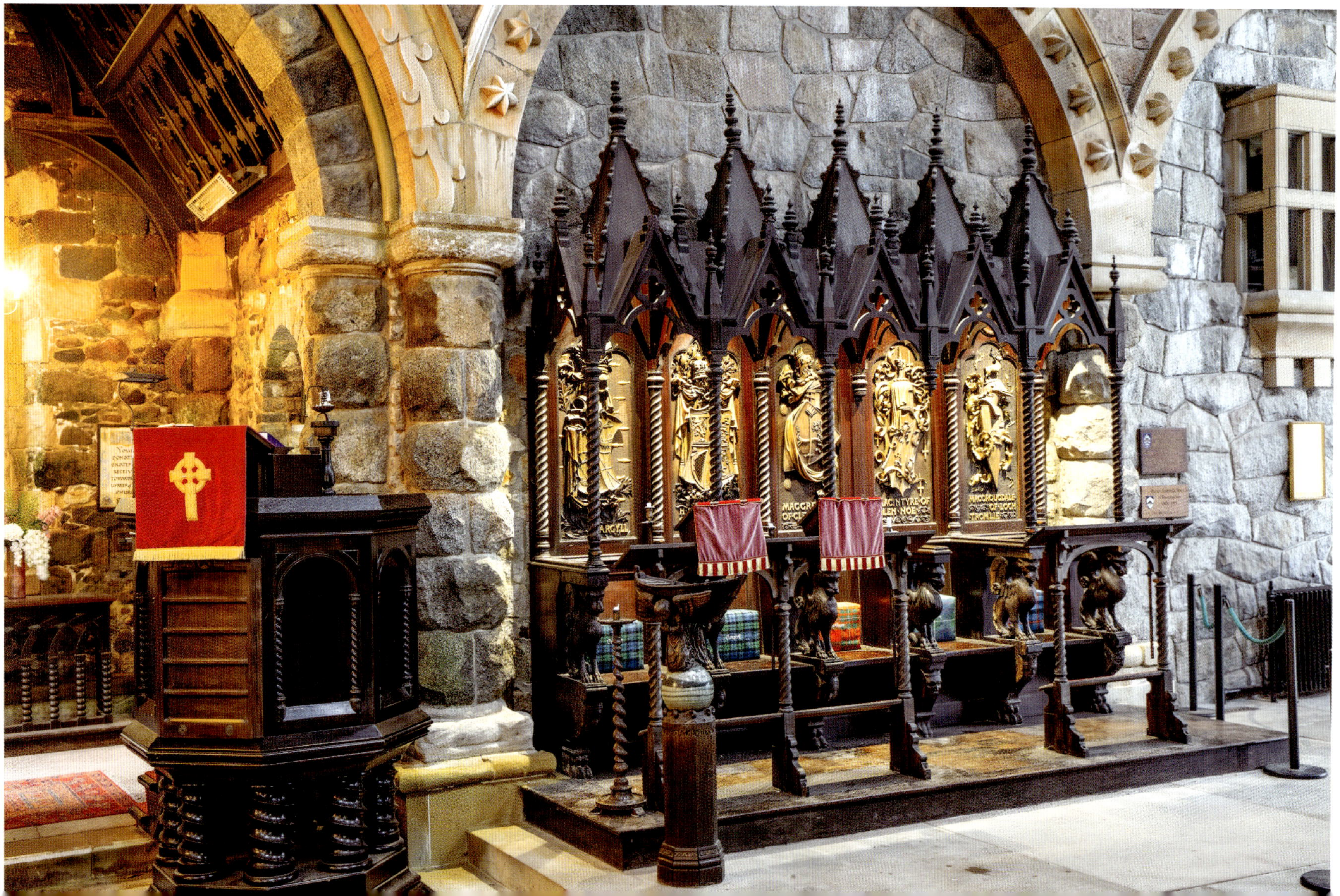

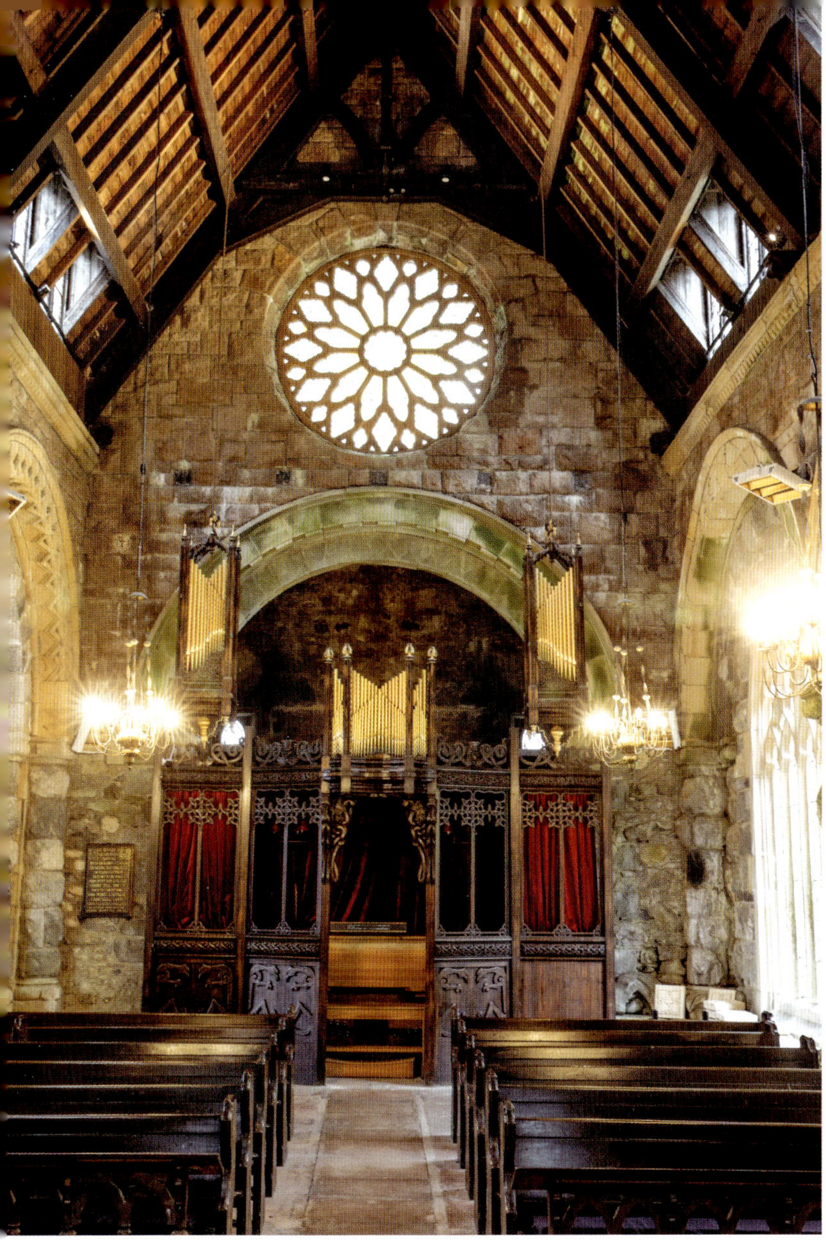

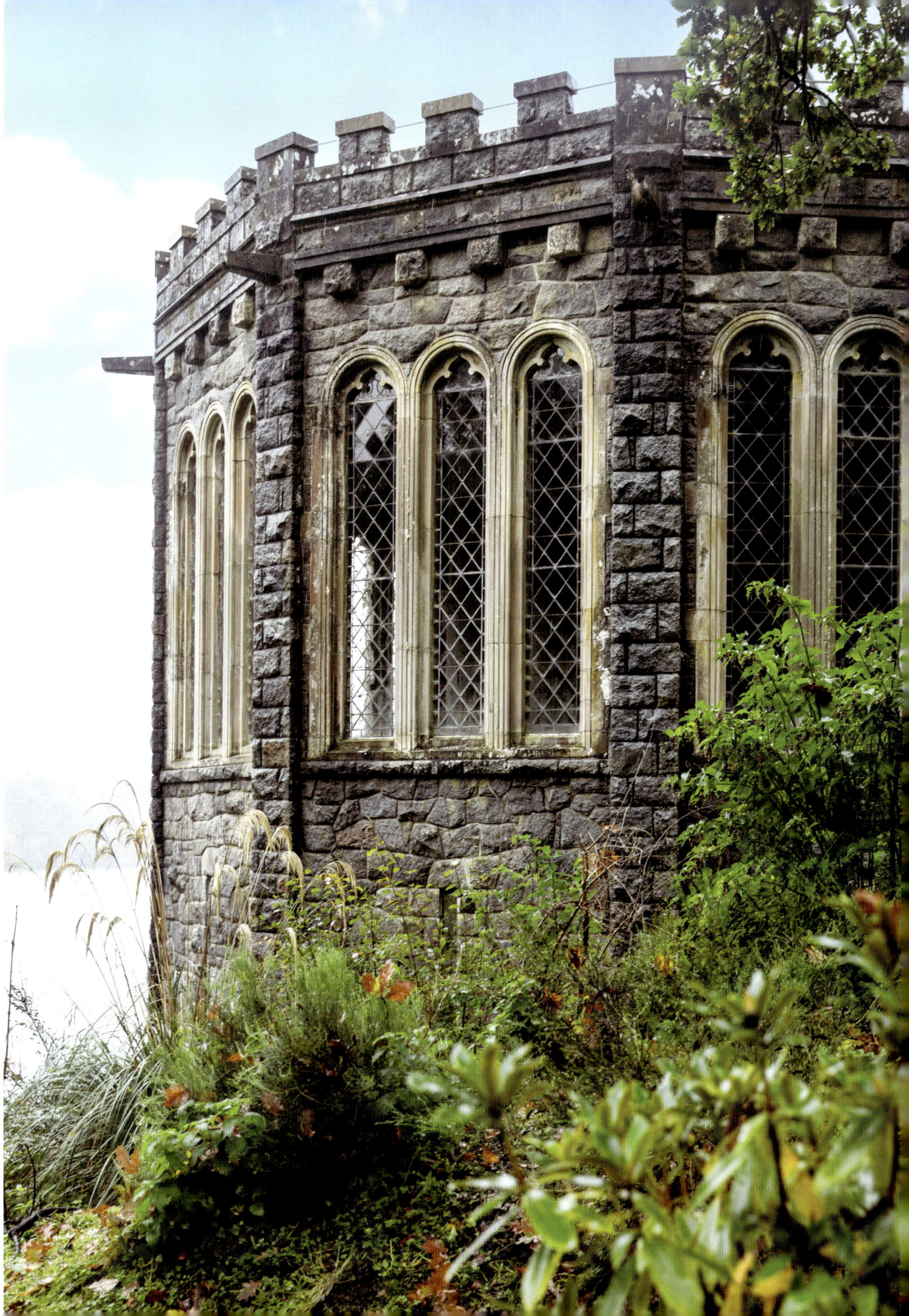

Above: A dramatic wood-beamed ceiling and Norman-style stone arches frame the view to the nave's iconic Rose Window, which was hand-painted in the Victorian custom by the architect's sister. Right: Named for a local saint with connections to Scotland's early Christian history, Saint Conan's Kirk, overlooking the picturesque Loch Awe, combines several ecclesiastical architectural styles, including Romanesque, Gothic, and Scottish Baronial.

A ROYAL INTERVENTION

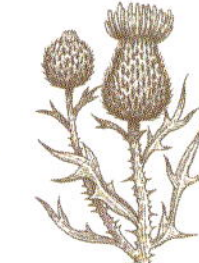

Set on 2,000 breathtaking acres amid the softly undulating hills of Ayrshire, the grand Palladian manor known as Dumfries House stands proudly against the early-autumn sky. The home was designed in 1754 by brothers John, Robert, and James Adam for William Crichton-Dalrymple, 5th Earl of Dumfries. When he lost his wife during the building process, the earl channeled his grief into turning his new residence into a showplace, spending great sums on Rococo-style furnishings to create vibrant interiors that exemplified the Scottish Enlightenment period.

The noble soon remarried, but when he died without an heir, the estate passed to his nephew. Dumfries remained in the family until John Bute inherited it in 1993. Weighed down by the death duties of his father and grandfather, John first offered the mansion, complete with the original Chippendale furniture, to the National Trust for Scotland, who declined to purchase it then and again in 2004.

A few years later, the house was put up for sale and the contents scheduled for auction. When a fund-raising campaign by preservationists fell short, King Charles III—then Prince Charles, known in Scotland as the Duke of Rothesay—learned of this irreplaceable property's plight and organized a consortium to buy Dumfries and developed it as a successful, self-sustaining venture.

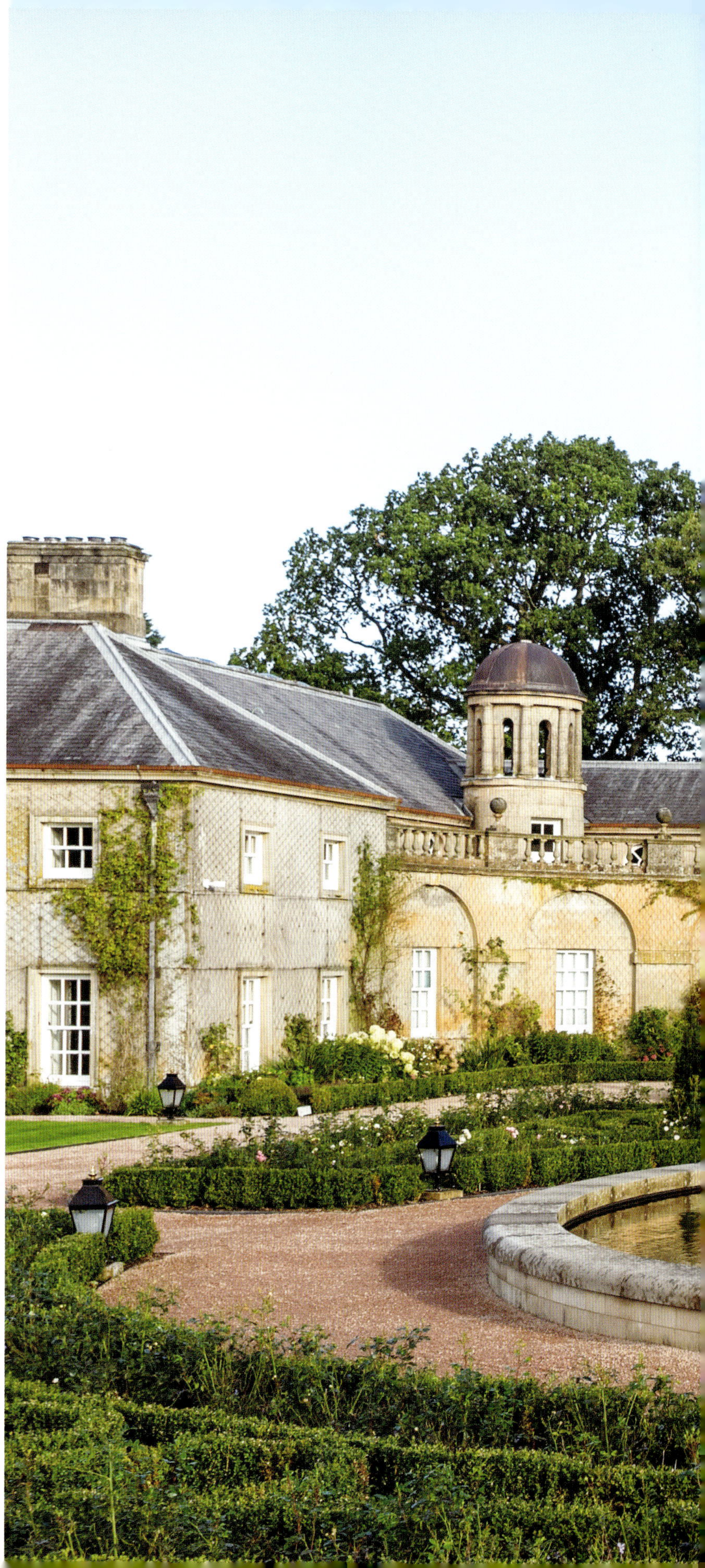

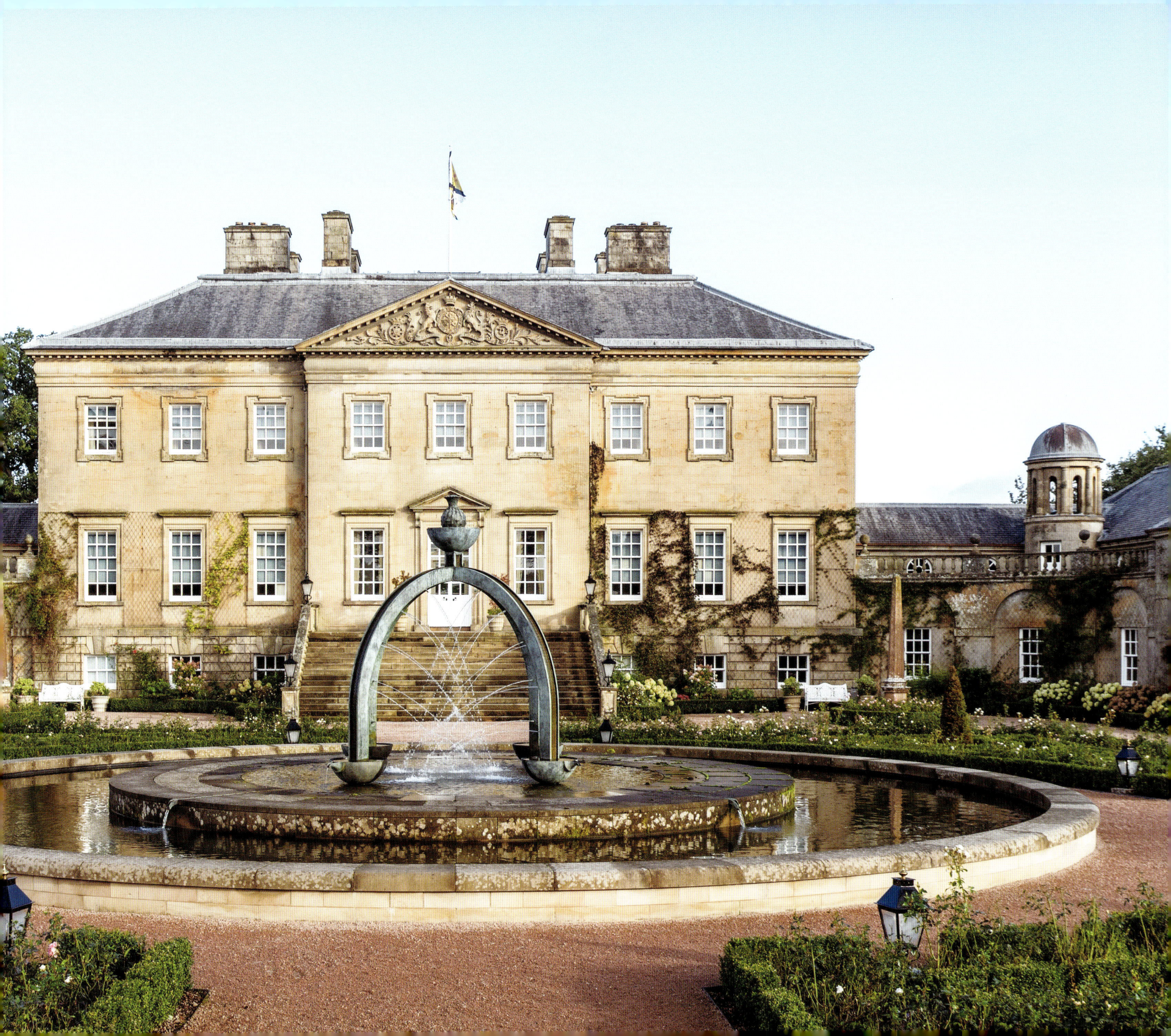

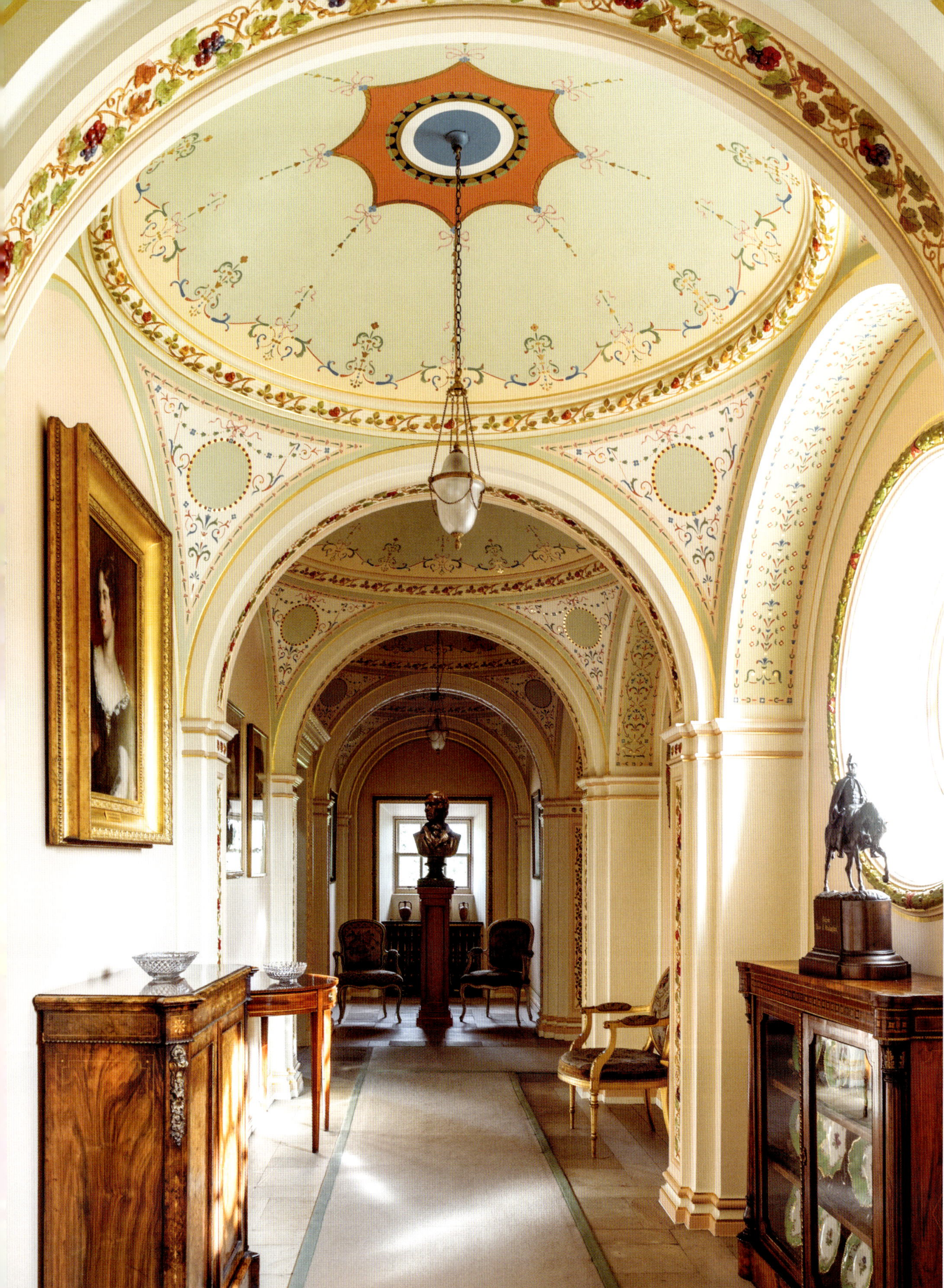

“The project has been as much about people as it has been about a physical place.”

—King Charles III

Left: The pewter Corridor, which takes its inspiration from Byzantine architecture, comprises eight square chambers crowned with domed ceilings and connected by semicircular arches. Enrobed in gray paint in the 1960s, the area was meticulously restored to its original prismatic designs.

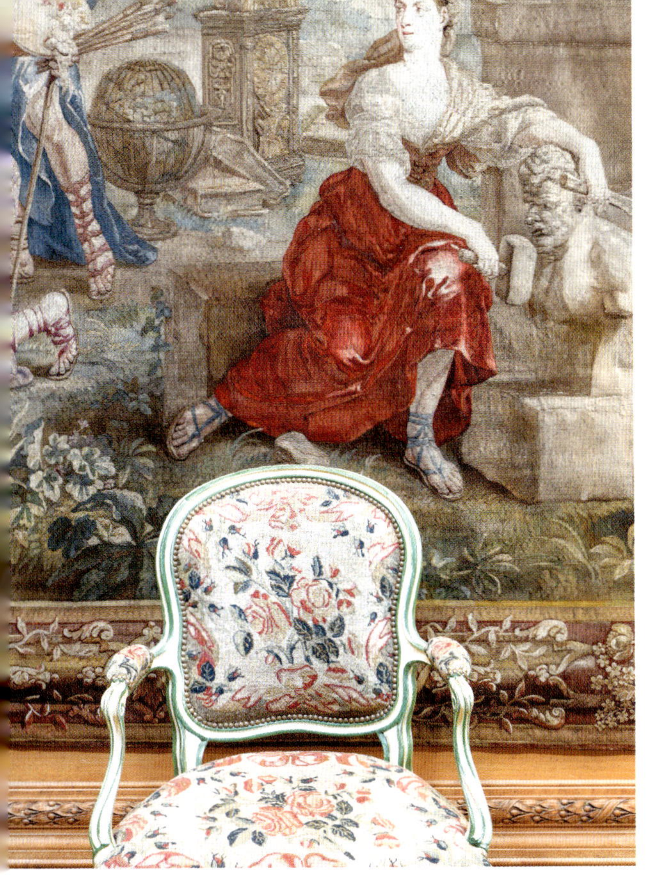

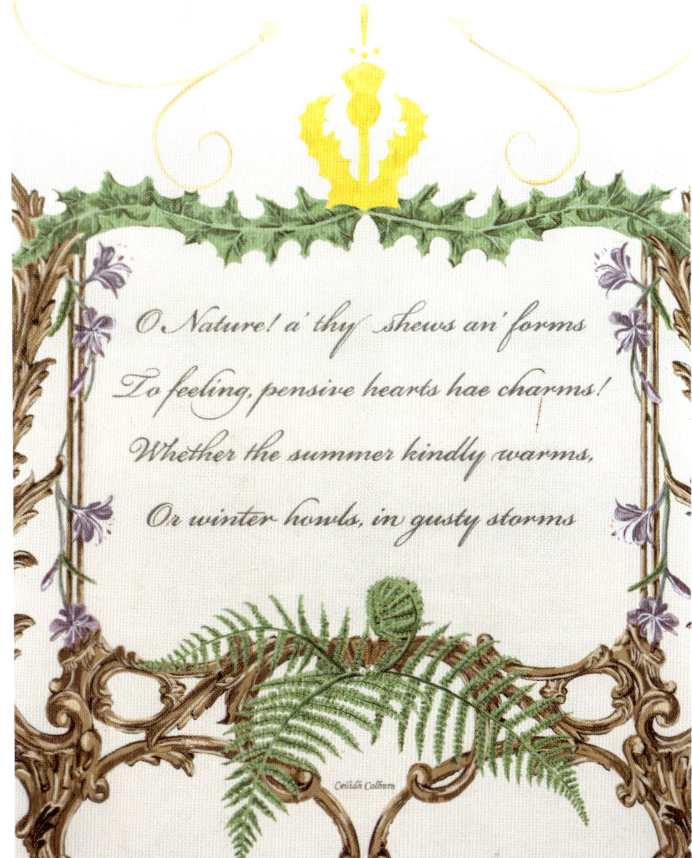
O Nature! a' thy shews an' forms
To feeling, pensive hearts hae charms!
Whether the summer kindly warms,
Or winter howls, in gusty storms

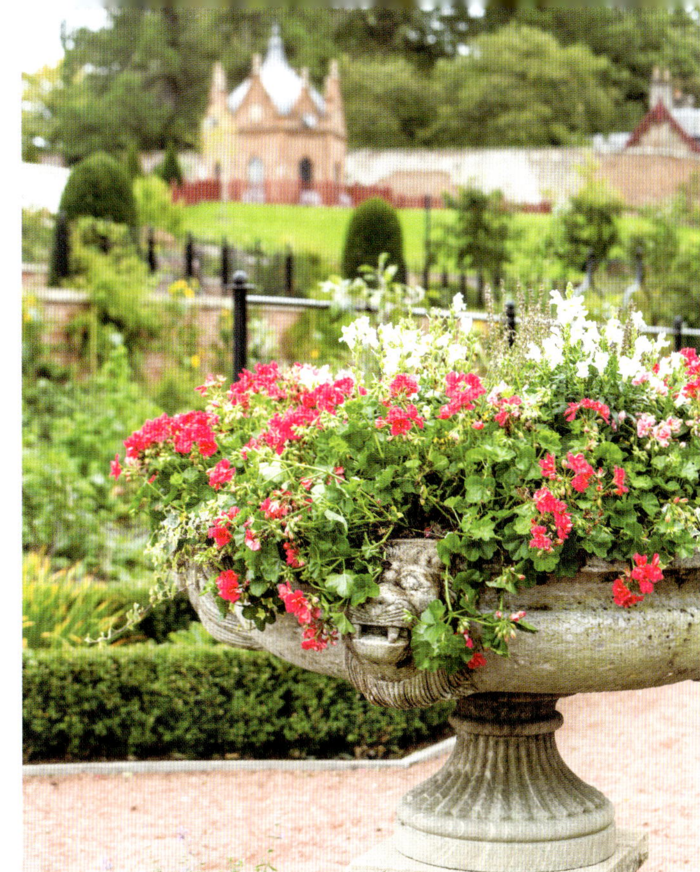

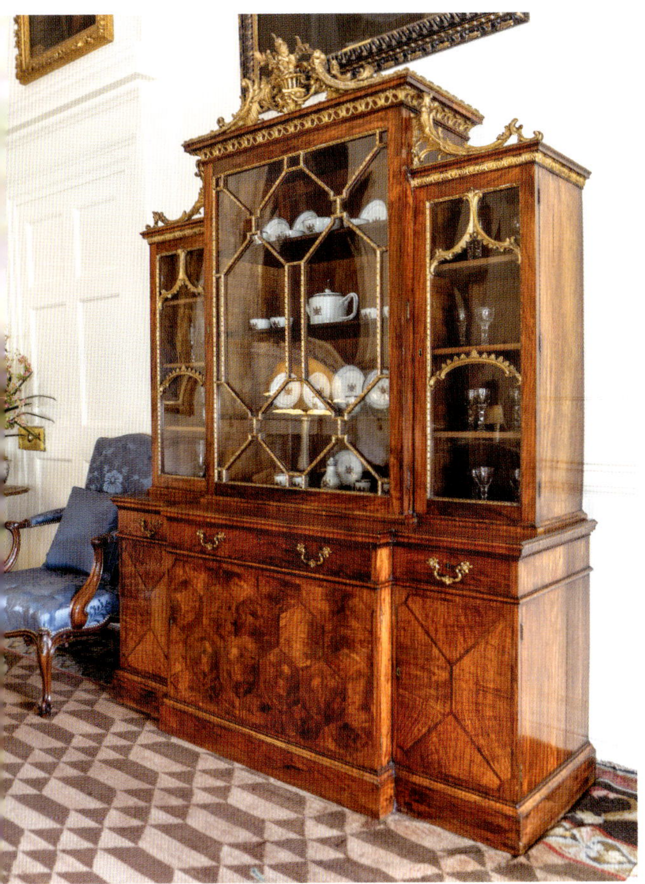

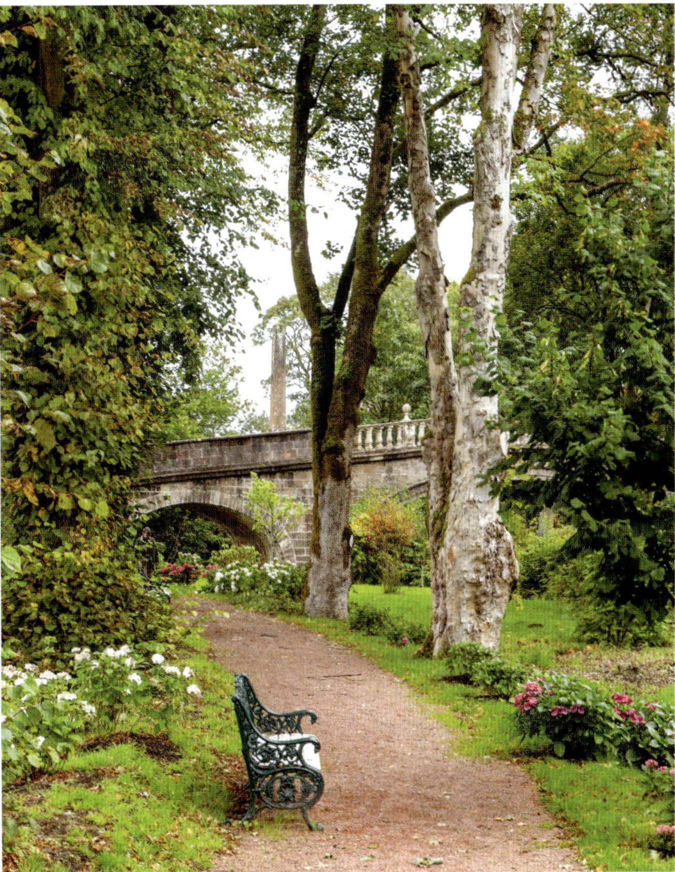

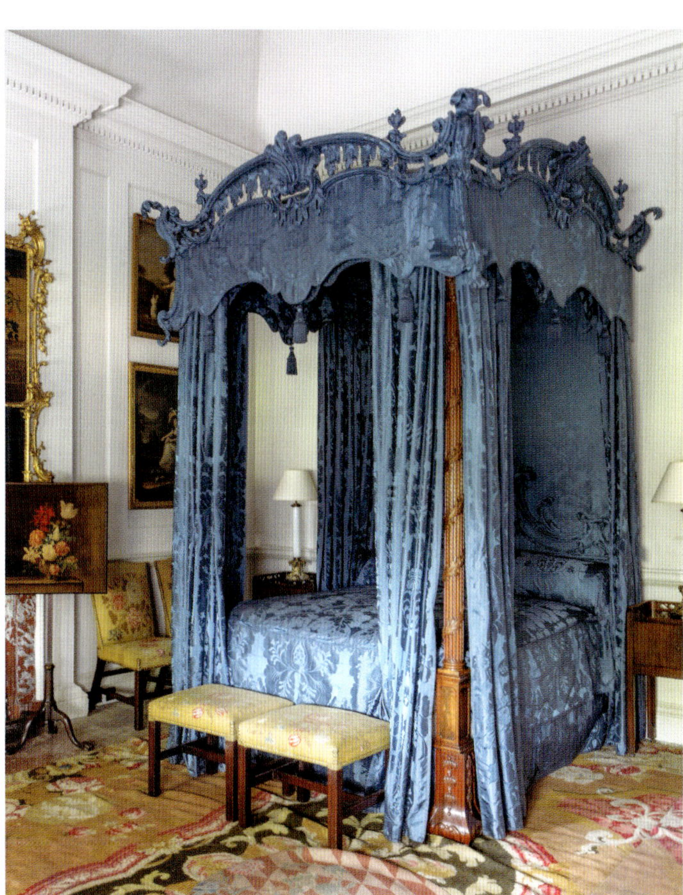

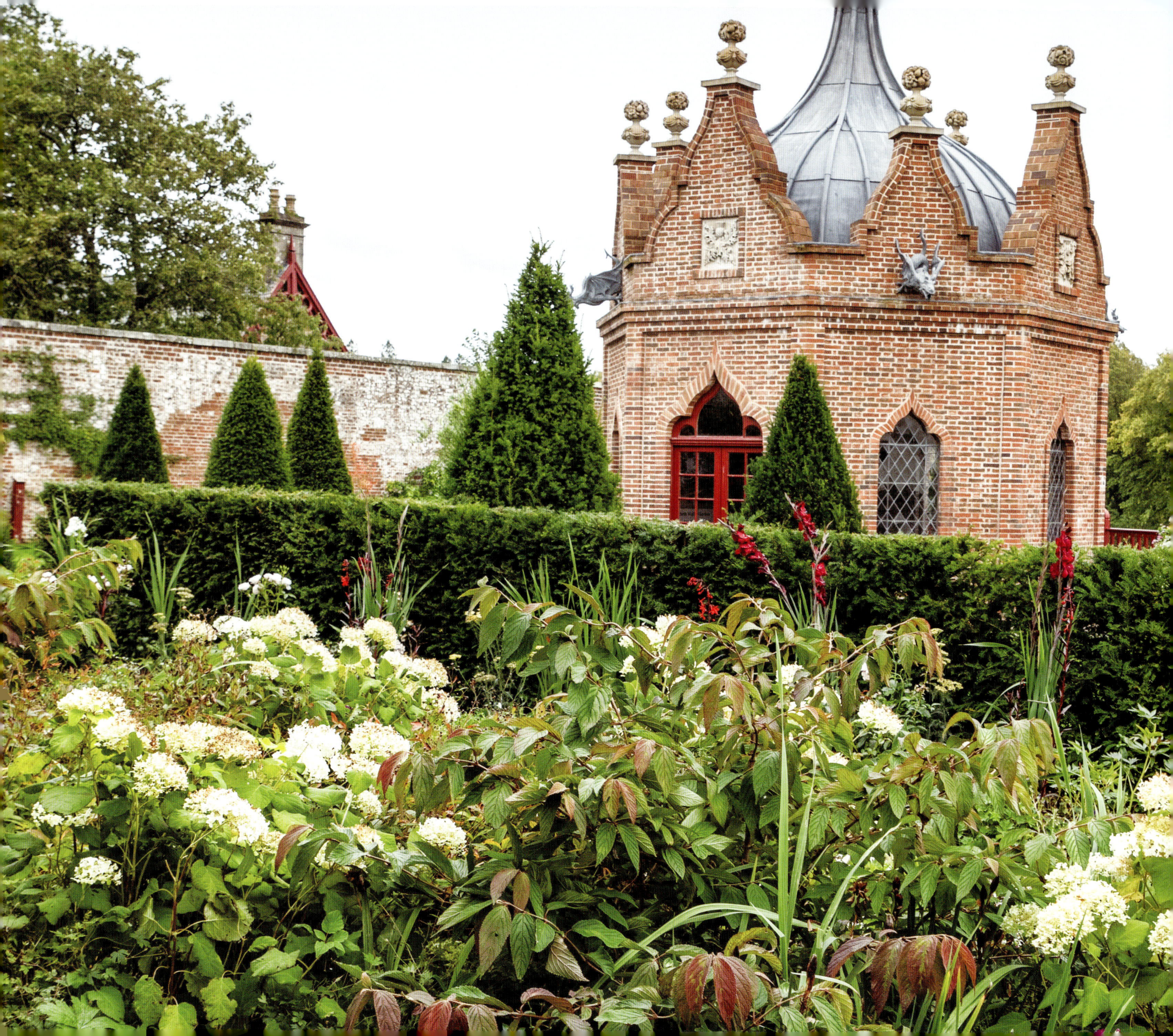

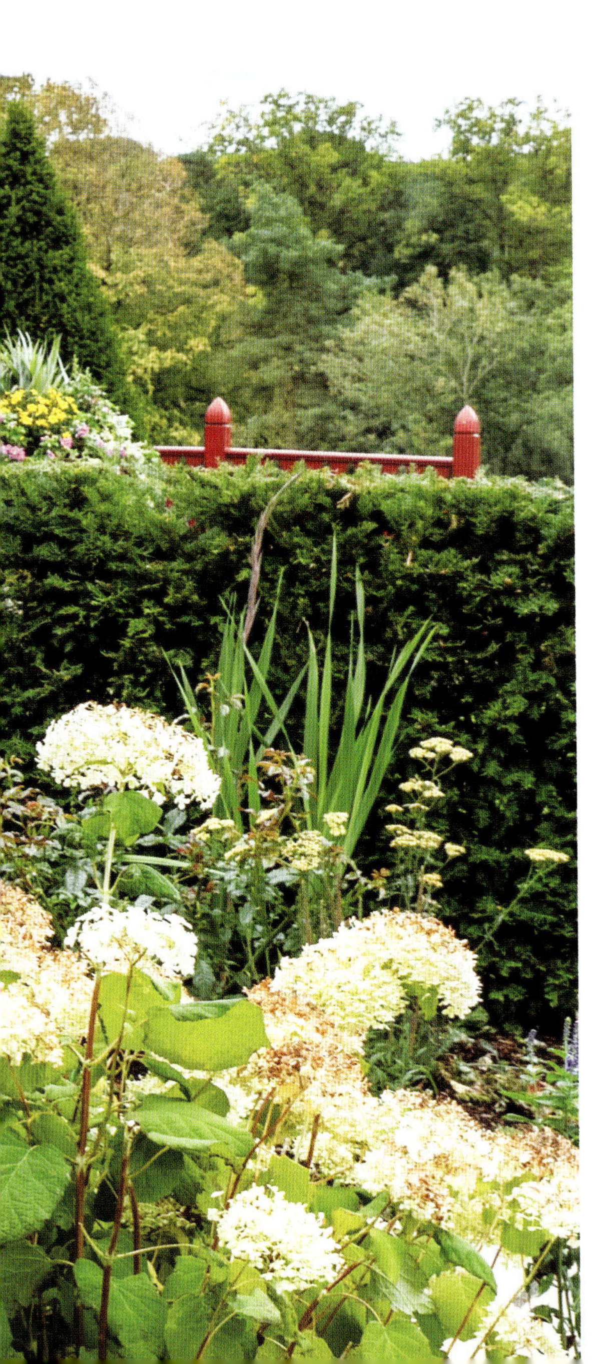

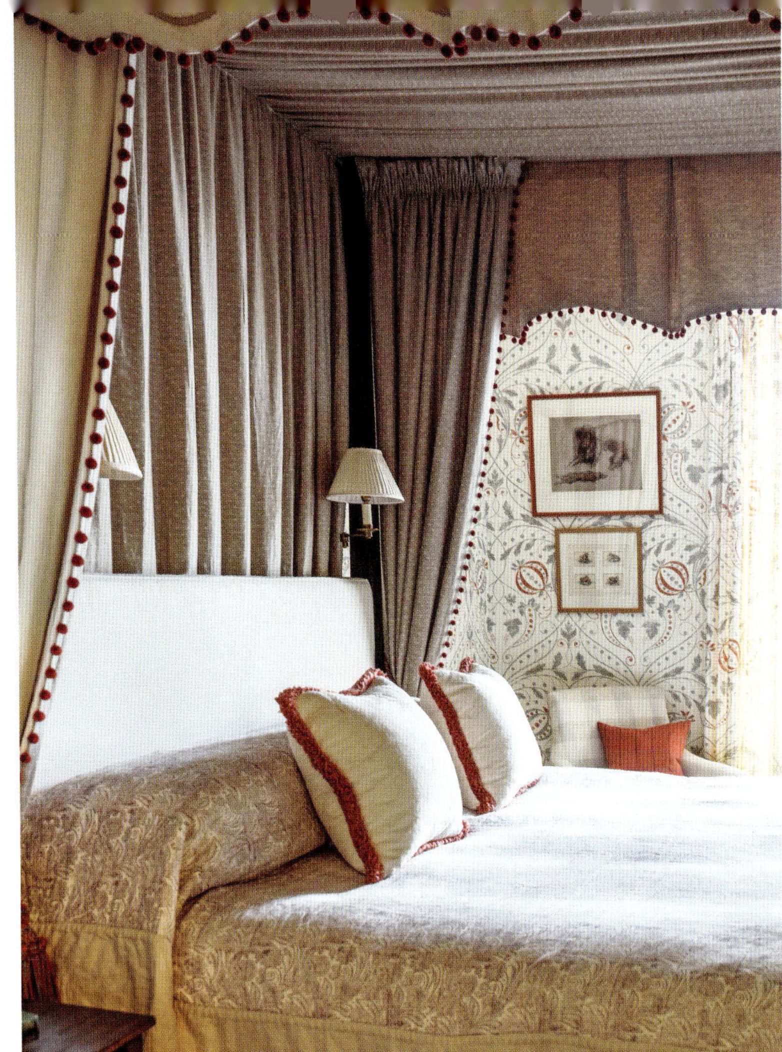

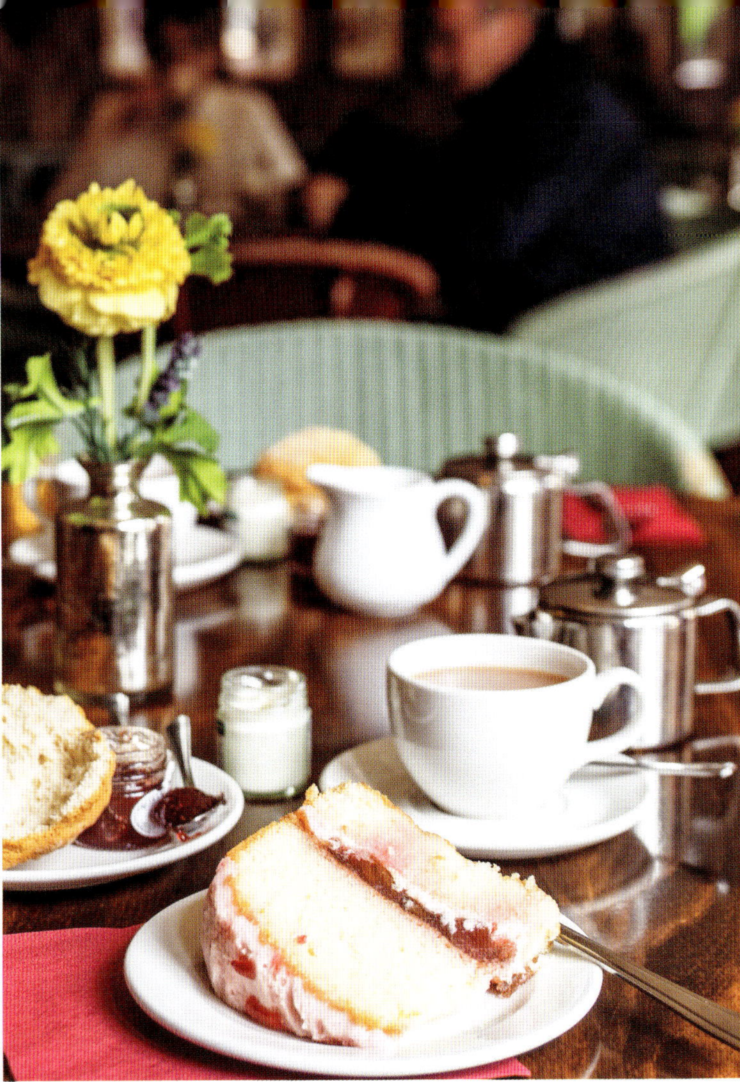

From exquisite Flemish arrases in the Tapestry Room and brilliant sapphire-hued damask silk Chippendale elbow chairs in the Blue Drawing Room to the dazzling splendor of the Pink Dining Room, the prismatic interiors are not only pure joy for the eyes, they also illustrate the ebullient empiricism of the time period. Italian architect Andrea Palladio's influence spills from the façade into the dramatic Entrance Hall, leaving no doubt that this is an affluent family. Brimming with coats of arms, crests, and cartouches of ancestral properties, the cavernous space also features a thistle motif—a nod to the 5th Earl's order of chivalry.

The lush surroundings are equally remarkable. Paths meander through the Arboretum, which connects the Avenue Bridge to the Queen Elizabeth Walled Garden. Once a bog, this 5-acre area, named for the British Empire's late monarch, boasts hundreds of trees and colorful herbaceous borders, along with a fruits-and-vegetables plot that serves as an educational tool for school-age children.

Located within the estate, the five-star Dumfries House Lodge offers twenty-two guest rooms, and there are several dining options as well, underscoring King Charles's mission to maintain this magnificent manor and its grounds for all to enjoy.

The Coach House Café serves light fare, above right, while the Lodge has twenty-two en suite guest rooms, above left. Opposite: A brick folly rises amid the gardens.

ALONG THE PEBBLED PATH

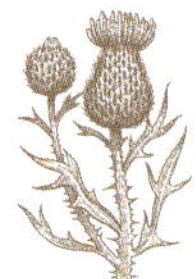

A comforting, low murmur echoes off the silver stream known as the Water of Leith as it winds through Scotland's capital. Eventually feeding into the Firth of Forth, the river, hedged in teeming rainforest-like foliage, was once the epicenter for twelfth-century grain-milling hamlets, including Dean Village and Stockbridge.

As Edinburgh grew in both prosperity and population after the last Jacobite Rebellion of 1745, the thriving metropolis developed outward, dubbing the additional territory New Town. The construction of Saint Bernard's Bridge and the four-arched Dean Bridge in the early 1800s unbarred the path for these industrial communities to transform into residential havens.

Dean Village's red sandstone housing, Well Court, was commissioned in 1883 by Sir John Findlay as affordable living quarters. The building rests, now fully restored, on the banks of the Water of Leith, and its prominent location is a hallmark for passersby. Surrounding structures mimic similar Victorian-style architecture, allowing the area to proudly maintain its whimsical and romantic patina.

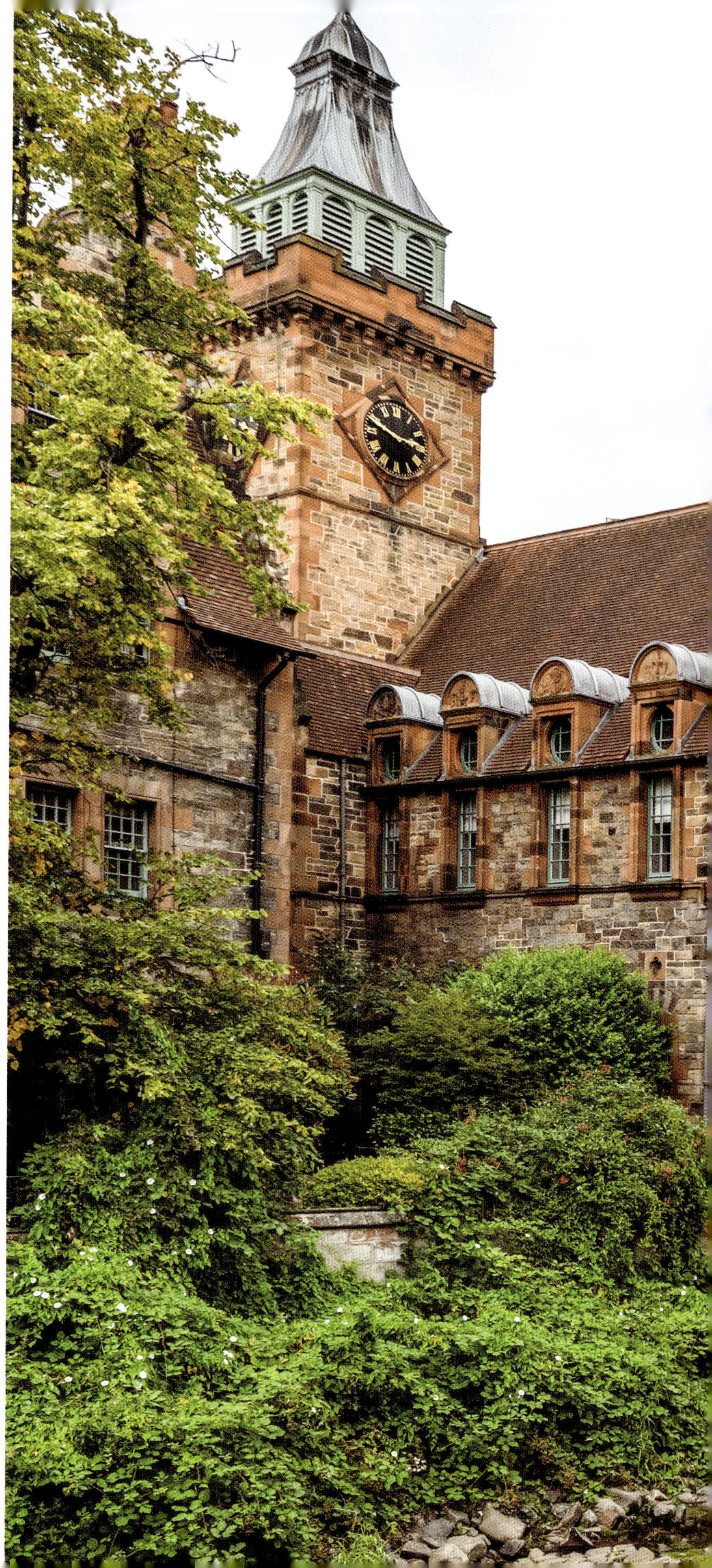

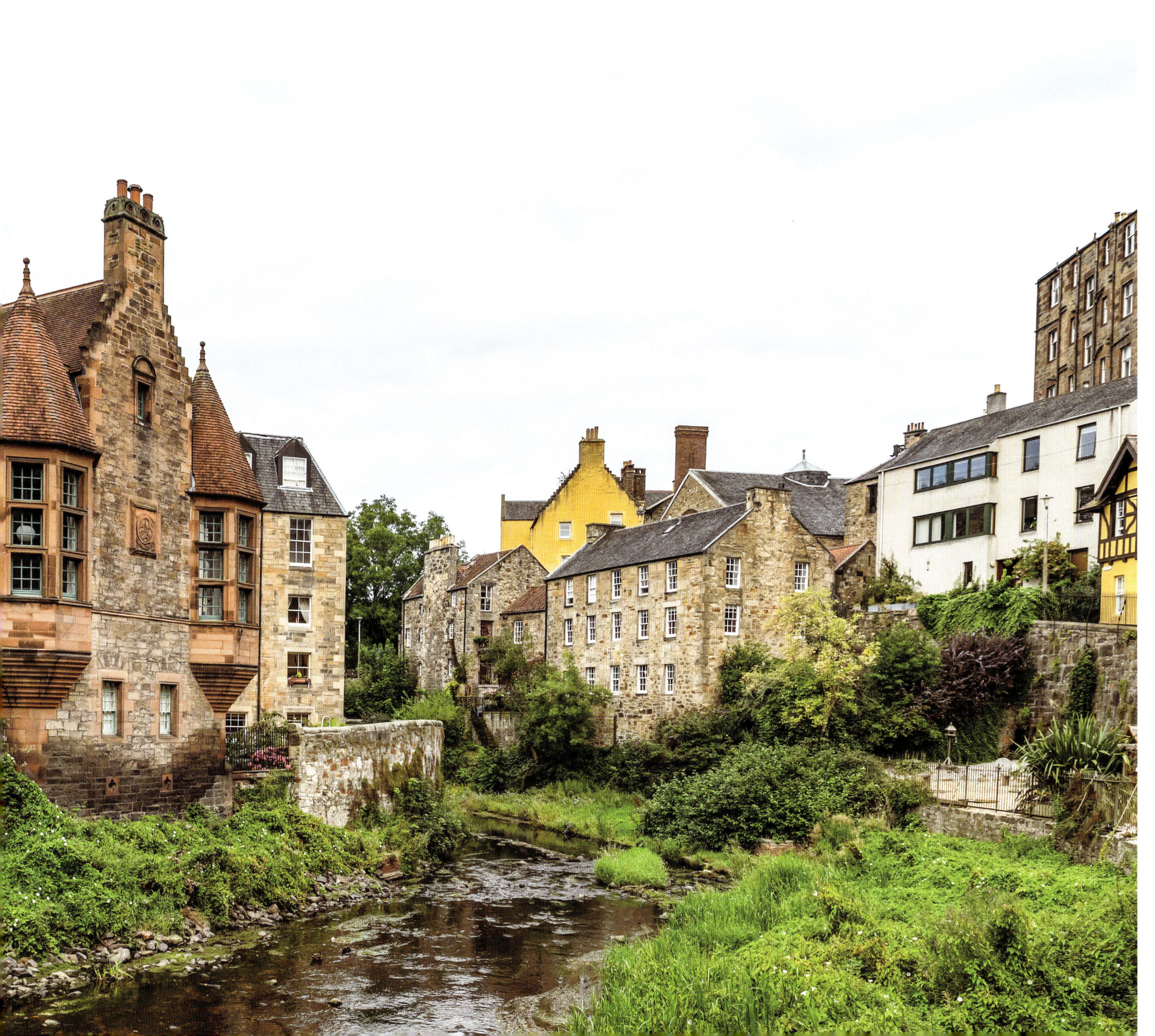

Below: A statue of Hygeia, the Greek goddess of health, was erected at St. Bernard's Well following eighteenth-century tales that circulated regarding the mineral water's medicinal properties. Right: Charming Stockbridge destinations include St Vincent's Chapel, with its cheery red door. Opposite: The area's colorful welcome continues with an exuberant display of plants along a stairway.

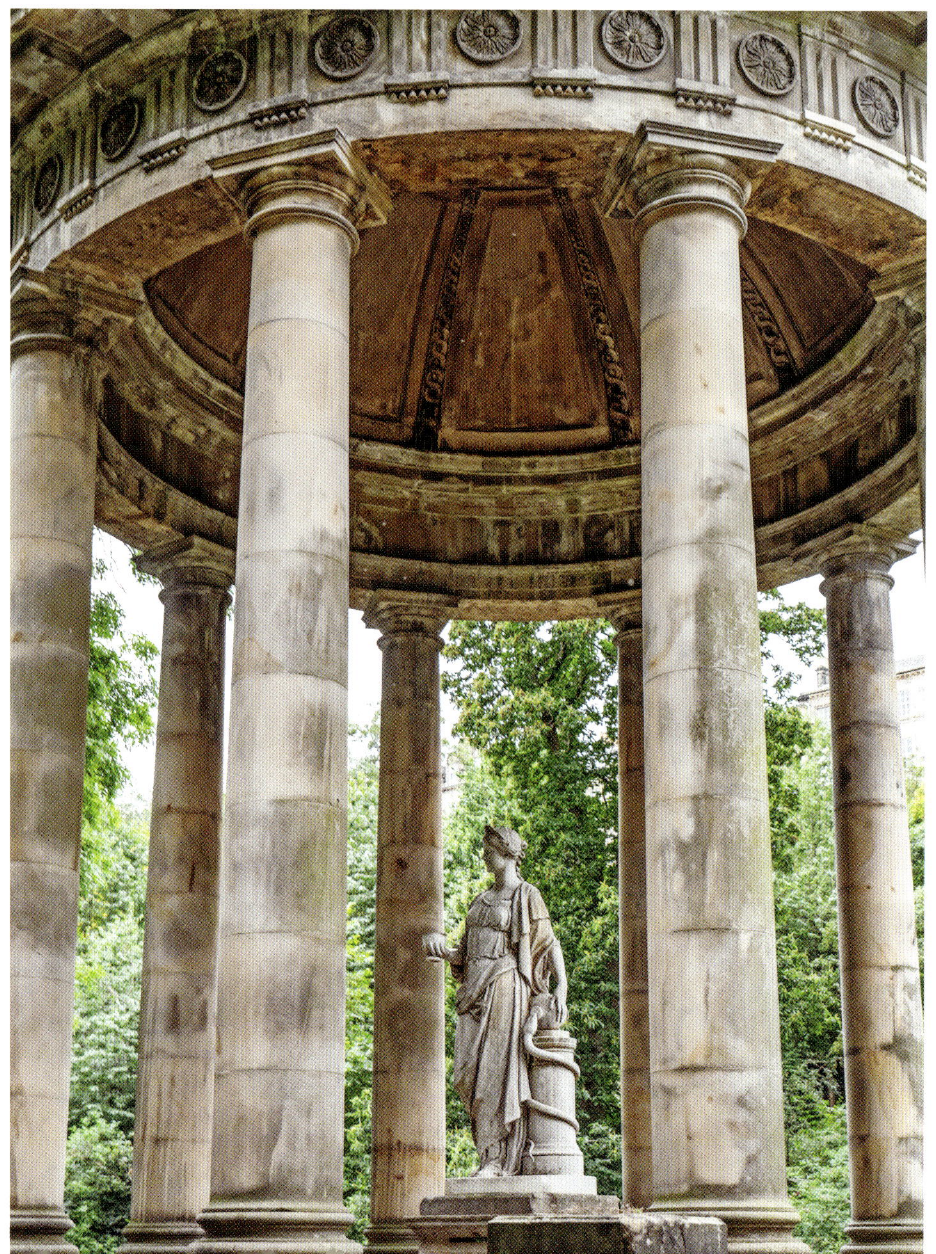

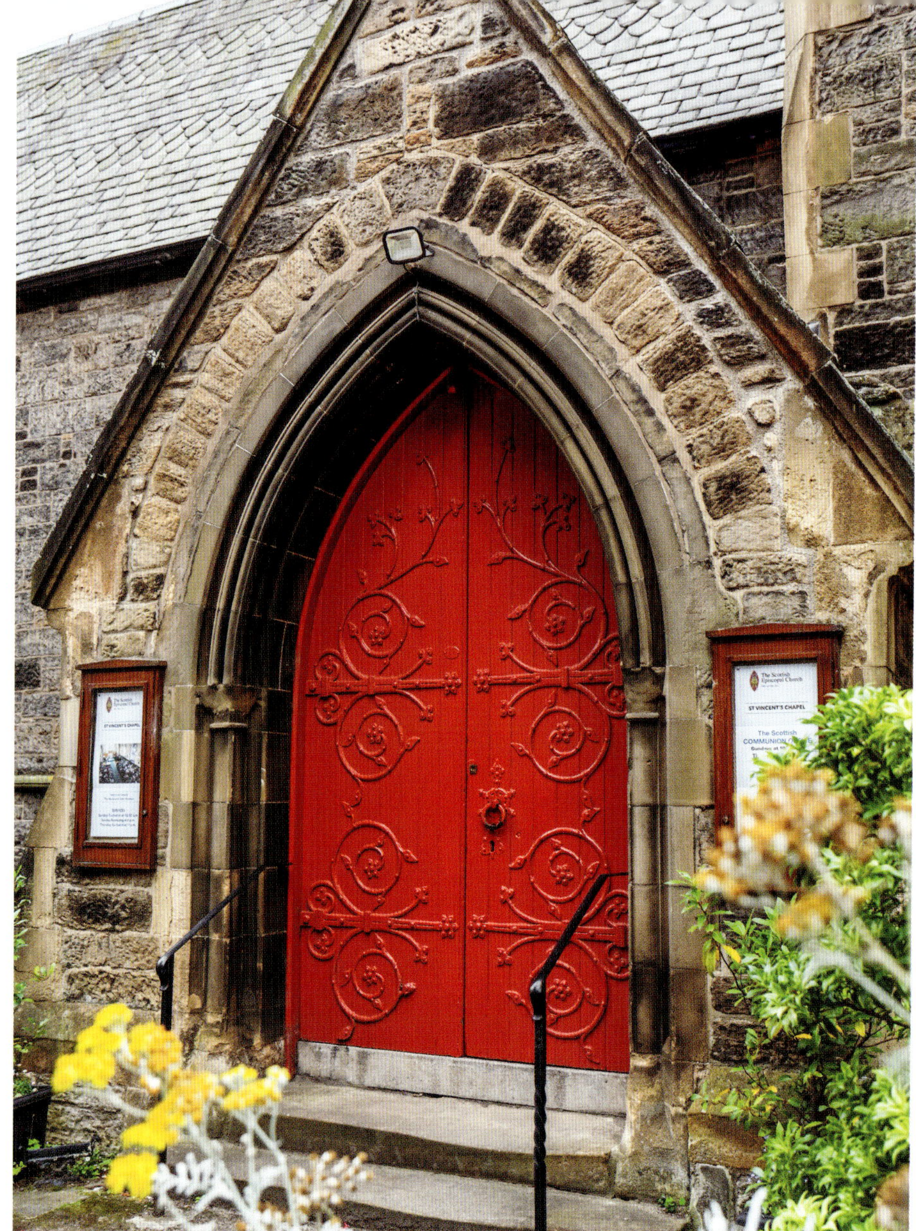

Following the footpath on the scenic Water of Leith Walkway, bustling Stockbridge greets those looking for a dose of Gaelic culture. Authentic cafés, eclectic emporiums, and notable landmarks, including Saint Stephen's Church, now a world-class theater, and the statue of Hygeia at Saint Bernard's Well, dot the area known for its unique bohemian ethos.

With age-old pebbled stones underfoot and endless Caledonian heritage around each corner, visitors to these old-world environs need only open their eyes—and hearts—to the magnificence that gently flows downstream.

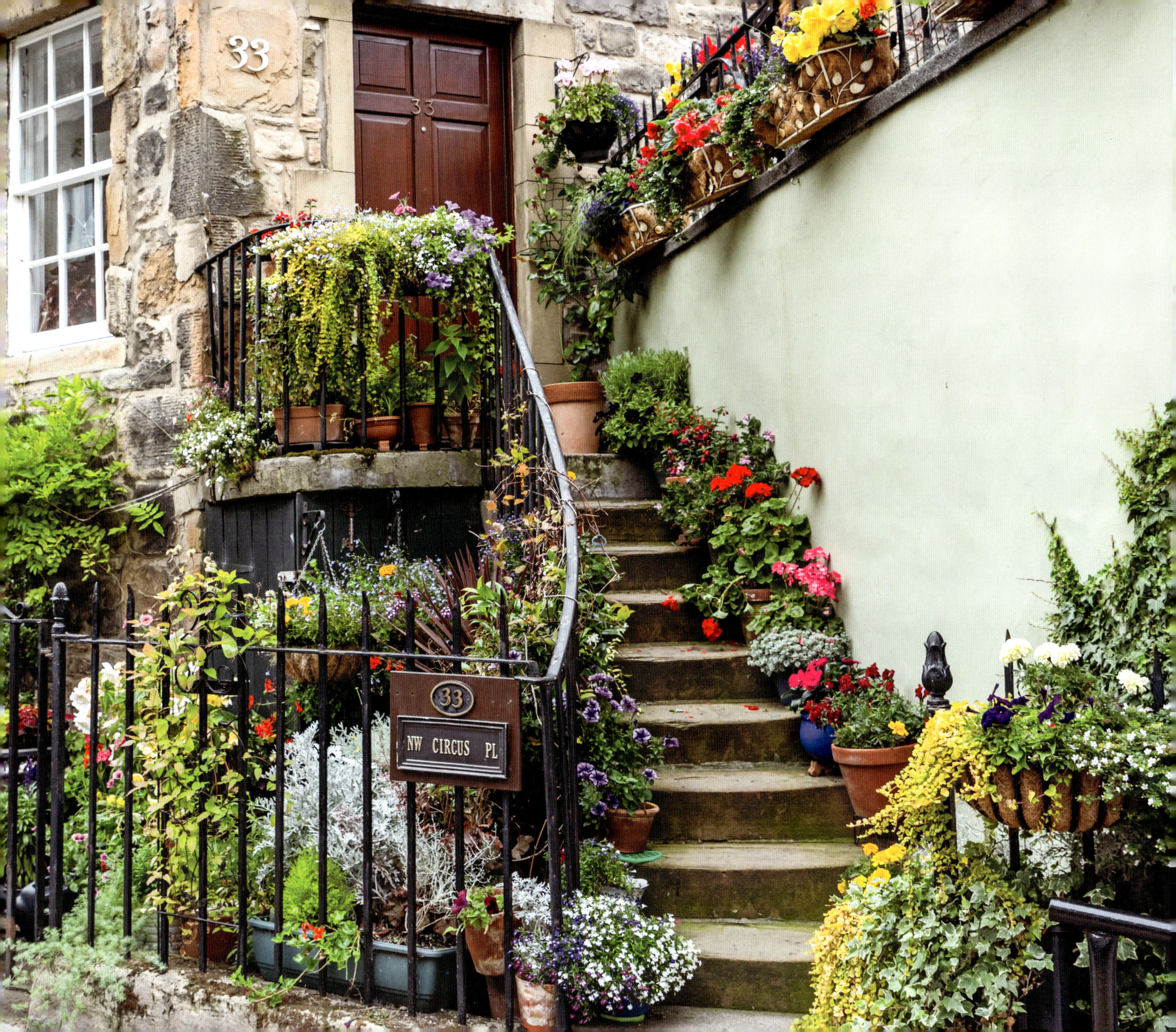
33
33
NW CIRCUS PL

CREDITS & RESOURCES

Our Hearts Are in Scotland
Editor: Melissa Lester
Creative Director: Melissa Sturdivant Smith
Senior Features Editor: Leslie Bennett Smith
Features Editor: Lydia McMullen
Administrative Senior Art Director: Tracy Wood Franklin
Editorial Assistant: Audra Shalles
Senior Copy Editor, Lifestyle: Rhonda Lee Lother
Senior Digital Imaging Specialist: Delisa McDaniel

CONTRIBUTING PHOTOGRAPHERS
JANE HOPE: pages 10, 14–41, 68–77, 88–95, 114–121, 132–137, 158–171, 200–204, 208, and 220–229
KATE SEARS: pages 7, 42–55, 106–111, 122–127, and 172–185
MARCY BLACK SIMPSON: pages 186–189
MELISSA STURDIVANT SMITH: pages 60, 63, and 232
STEPHANIE WELBOURNE STEELE: cover and pages 2, 4–8, 58–59, 61–67, 78–87, 96–105, 128–131, 138–143, 146, 192–199, 205–207, and 209–219

CONTRIBUTING STYLISTS
ANNE EMORY BANKSTON: pages 186–189
SIDNEY BRAGIEL: pages 144–149
MELISSA STURDIVANT SMITH: pages 58–67, 78–87, 96–105, 114–121, 128–131, 132–137, 142–143, 192–199, 205–207, and 209–219

CONTRIBUTING WRITERS:
KASSIDY ABERNATHY: pages 226–228
KAREN CALLAWAY: pages 11, 13–14, 20–35, 40, 44, 57–111, 113, 128–131, 132–137, 151, 182, 191–203, and 210–225
JEANNE DE LATHOUDER: pages 176, 178
BRITTANY WILLIAMS FLOWERS: pages 168, 172
LYDIA MCMULLEN: pages 142–147
AUDRA SHALLES: page 138
LESLIE BENNETT SMITH: pages 114–121, 152, 160, and 166

CONTIRBUTING RECIPE DEVELOPERS AND FOOD STYLISTS
BECCA CUMMINS: page 148
KATHLEEN KANEN: page 148
JADE SINACORI: pages 204–209
LOREN WOOD: pages 186–189

WHERE TO STAY & SHOP

Below is a listing of properties, products and companies featured in this book. Items not listed are privately owned and are not for sale. Styles and availability may vary.

Cover and pages 7 and 192–199: The Abbotsford Trust, Abbotsford, Melrose Roxburghshire TD6 9BQ, United Kingdom, scottsabbotsford.com.
Pages 2 and 78–87: Glamis Castle, Angus DD8 1QJ, United Kingdom, glamis-castle.co.uk.
Pages 4–5 and 58–67: Drummond Castle Gardens, Crieff PH7 4HN, United Kingdom, drummondcastlegardens.co.uk.
Pages 6 and 96–105: Inveraray Castle, Inveraray PA32 8XE, United Kingdom, inveraray-castle.com.
Pages 14–19: Melrose Abbey, Abbey Street, Melrose Roxburghshire TD6 9LG, United Kingdom, historicenvironment.scot/visit-a-place/places/melrose-abbey/. Burts Hotel, Market Square, Melrose, Scottish Borders TD6 9PN, United Kingdom, burtshotel.co.uk.
Pages 20–29: Balmoral Castle, Balmoral Estates, Ballater, Aberdeenshire AB35 5TB, United Kingdom, balmoralcastle.com. Castle Fraser, Sauchen, Inverurie, Aberdeenshire AB51 7LD, United Kingdom, nts.org.uk/visit/places/castle-fraser. Leith Hall, Huntly AB54 4NQ, United Kingdom, nts.org.uk/visit/places/leith-hall. Palace of Holyroodhouse, Canongate, Edinburgh EH8 8DX, United Kingdom, rct.uk/visit/palace-of-holyroodhouse. The Castle & Gardens of Mey, Thurso KW14 8XH, United Kingdom, castleofmey.org.uk.
Pages 30–39: West Coast Railways, Jesson Way, Crag Bank, Carnforth, Lancashire LA5 9UR, United Kingdom, westcoastrailways.co.uk/jacobite/jacobite-steam-train-details.cfm.
Pages 40–55: Special thanks to VisitScotland, visitscotland.com, and Tasting Scotland, tastingscotland.com. The Scotsman Hotel, 20 N. Bridge, Edinburgh EH1 1TR, United Kingdom, scotsmanhotel.co.uk. Deanston Distillery, Near Doune, Perthshire, Scotland FK16 6AG, deanstonmalt.com. Balmoral Hotel, 1 Princes Street, Edinburgh EH2 2EQ, United Kingdom, roccofortehotels.com. Princes Street Gardens, Princes Street, Edinburgh EH2 2HG, United Kingdom, edinburgh.gov.uk. The Hermitage, near Dunkeld, Perthshire PH8 0HX, United Kingdom, nts.org.uk/visit/places/the-hermitage. Murrayshall Country Estate, Scone, Perth PH2 7PH, United Kingdom, murrayshall.co.uk. The House of Bruar, Pitlochry, Perthshire PH18 5TW, United Kingdom, houseofbruar.com. Balgove Larder Farm Shop, Butchery & Café, Strathtyrum, St Andrews, Fife KY16 9SF, United Kingdom, balgove.com. St Andrews Castle, The Scores, St Andrews, Fife KY16 9AR, United Kingdom, historicenvironment.scot/visit-a-place/places/st-andrews-castle/.
Pages 68–77: Dunrobin Castle, Golspie, Sutherland KW10 6SF, United Kingdom, dunrobincastle.co.uk.
Pages 88–95: Fyvie Castle, Fyvie, Turriff, Aberdeenshire AB53 8JS, United Kingdom, nts.org.uk/visit/places/fyvie-castle.
Pages 106–111: Scone Palace, Perth PH2 6BD, United Kingdom, scone-palace.co.uk.
Pages 114–121: Neidpath Castle, Peebles EH45 8NW, United Kingdom, neidpathcastle.com. Walker Slater: Meredith Plus 2s in Navy Fine Herringbone Lambswool Tweed, Emma Jacket in Charcoal Donegal Style Green Windowpane; walkerslater.com. Burberry: wool cape and silk scarf; Coach: women's pumps; similar styles available, from Bloomingdale's, bloomingdales.com. Konstantino: assorted jewelry; Lafayette 148: pants and turtleneck sweater; Burberry: silk scarf; similar styles available from Saks Fifth Avenue, saksfifthavenue.com. Alfred Sung: Strapless High/Low Satin Twill Ballgown in Burgundy; similar

styles available from Nordstrom, shop.nordstrom.com. Remaining fashions, similar styles available at anthropologie.com, jcrew.com, and ralphlauren.com.
Pages 122–127: Edinburgh Castle, Castlehill, Edinburgh EH1 2NG, United Kingdom, edinburghcastle.scot. For more information on the Orkney Islands and Orkney Craft Trail, see orkney.com. Hoxa Tapestry Gallery, Hoxa, South Ronaldsay, Orkney KW17 2TW, United Kingdom, hoxatapestrygallery.co.uk. ANTA, West Bow, Edinburgh EH1 2JP, United Kingdom, anta.co.uk.
Pages 128–131: The Colonnades at the Signet Library, Parliament Square, Edinburgh EH1 1RF, United Kingdom, thesignetlibrary.co.uk.
Pages 132–137: Barns Tower, Peebles EH45 9JL, United Kingdom, neidpathcastle.com/barns-tower. Smythe: Tartan Wool Blazer; similar styles available from Nordstrom, shop.nordstrom.com. Ralph Lauren: Iconic Cabled Cashmere Travel Set in Natural, assorted bedding, similar styles available; ralphlauren.com.
Pages 138–141: Campbell's of Beauly, Highland Tweed House, High Street, Beauly IV4 7BU, United Kingdom, campbellsofbeauly.com.
Pages 142–143: Highland Chocolatier, Grandtully, Perthshire PH9 0PL, United Kingdom, highlandchocolatier.com.
Pages 144–147: Dresses from Holly Shae, hollyshae.com.
Pages 152–159: The Fife Arms, Mar Road, Braemar, Aberdeenshire AB35 5YN, United Kingdom, thefifearms.com.
Pages 160–167: Glenternie House, Kirkton Manor, Peebles EH45 9JN, United Kingdom, glenterniehouse.com.
Pages 168–175: Prestonfield, Prestonfield House, Priestfield Road, Edinburgh EH16 5UT, United Kingdom, prestonfield.com.
Pages 176–181: Kinloch Lodge, Sleat, Isle of Skye IV43 8QY, United Kingdom, kinloch-lodge.co.uk.
Pages 182–185: Ballathie Country House Hotel & Estate, Kinclaven, Stanley, Perthshire PH1 4QN, United Kingdom, ballathiehousehotel.com.
Pages 186–189: Henhouse Antiques: creamware breadbasket, ironstone platter, mother-of-pearl-handled flatware, creamware pierced plates, decorative salad plates; @henouseantiques on Instagram. Attic Antiques: plate rack, silverware, table linens, teapot, teacups and saucers; atticantiquesal.com. Match: Piccoli Salt & Pepper Set, Dinner Plate, creamer; and Simon Pearce Barre Goblet; Earthborn Studios, Inc. Espresso Cup; from Bromberg's, brombergs.com.
Pages 200–203: Traquair House, Innerleithen, Peeblesshire EH44 6PW, United Kingdom, traquair.co.uk.
Pages 204–209: ANTA: Fabric by the Metre, Isobel Anderson Salad Plate, Isobel Anderson Porridge Bowl; anta.co.uk.
Pages 210–215: St Giles' Cathedral and Thistle Chapel, High Street, Edinburgh EH1 1RE, United Kingdom, stgilescathedral.org.uk.
Pages 216–219: St Conan's Kirk, Lochawe, Argyll PA33 1AQ, United Kingdom, stconanskirk.org.uk.
Pages 220–225: Dumfries House, Cumnock, Ayrshire KA18 2NJ, United Kingdom, dumfries-house.org.uk.
Pages 226–229: The Water of Leith Conservation Trust, waterofleith.org.uk. Well Court, Dean Path, Edinburgh EH4 3BE, United Kingdom; ewh.org.uk/project/well-court. Golden Hare Books, 68 Saint Stephen Street, Stockbridge, Edinburgh EH3 5AQ, United Kingdom, goldenharebooks.com. St. Bernard's Well, 2 Clarendon Crescent, Edinburgh EH4 1PT, United Kingdom; visitscotland.com/info/see-do/st-bernards-well-p1420171. St. Vincent's Chapel, Scottish Episcopal Church, Saint Vincent Street, Edinburgh EH3 6SW, United Kingdom, stvincentschapel.org.uk.

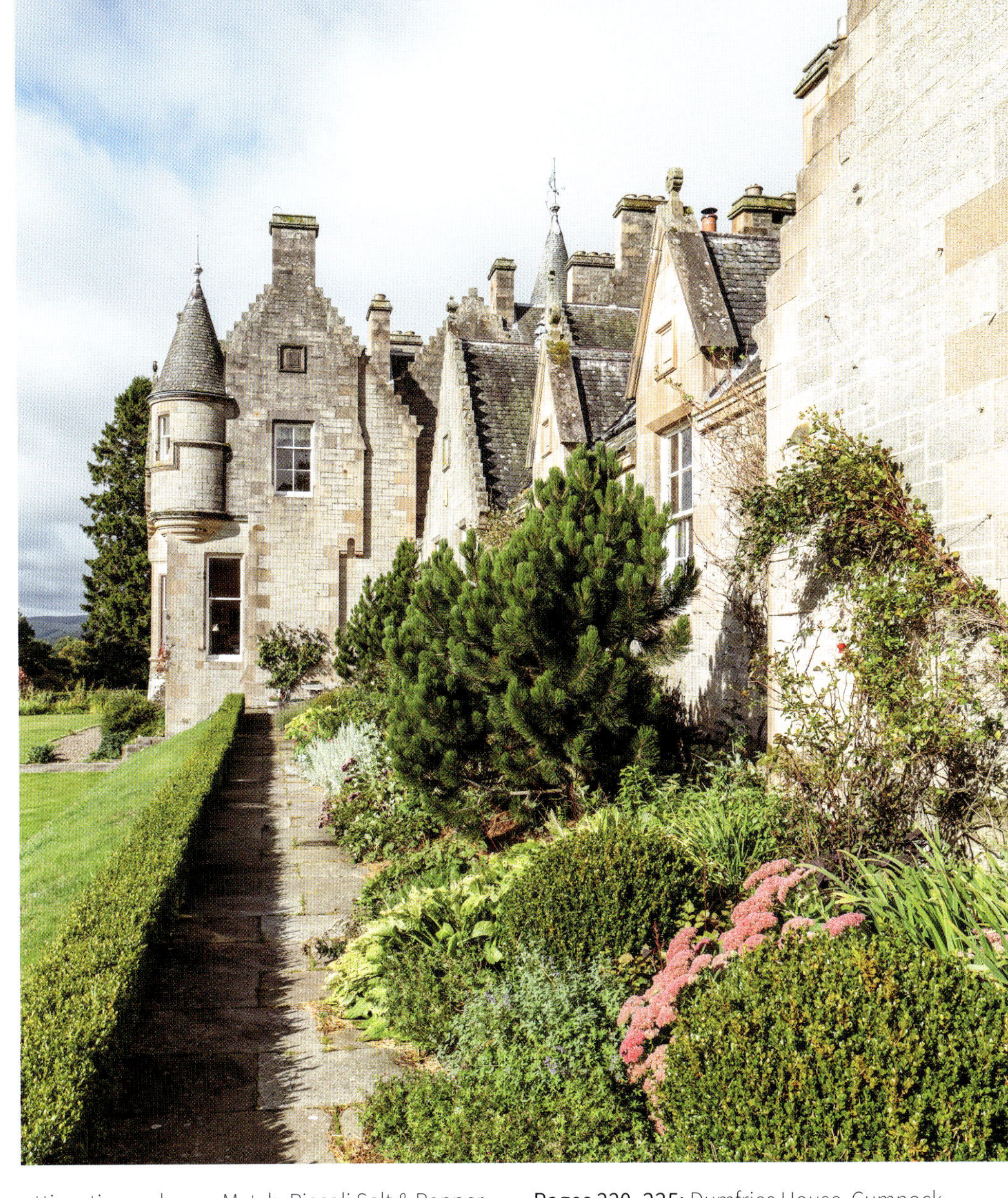

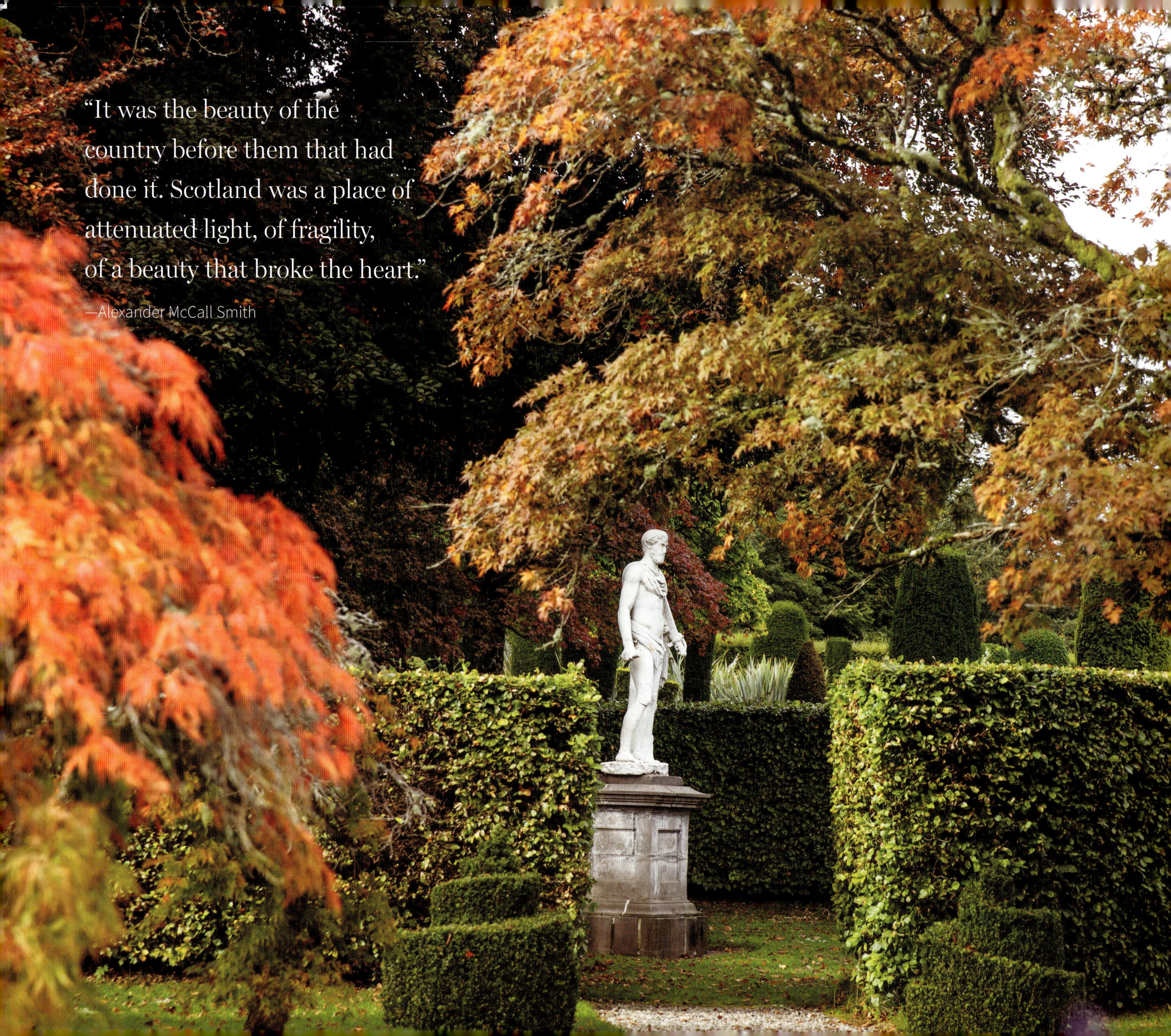

"It was the beauty of the country before them that had done it. Scotland was a place of attenuated light, of fragility, of a beauty that broke the heart."

—Alexander McCall Smith

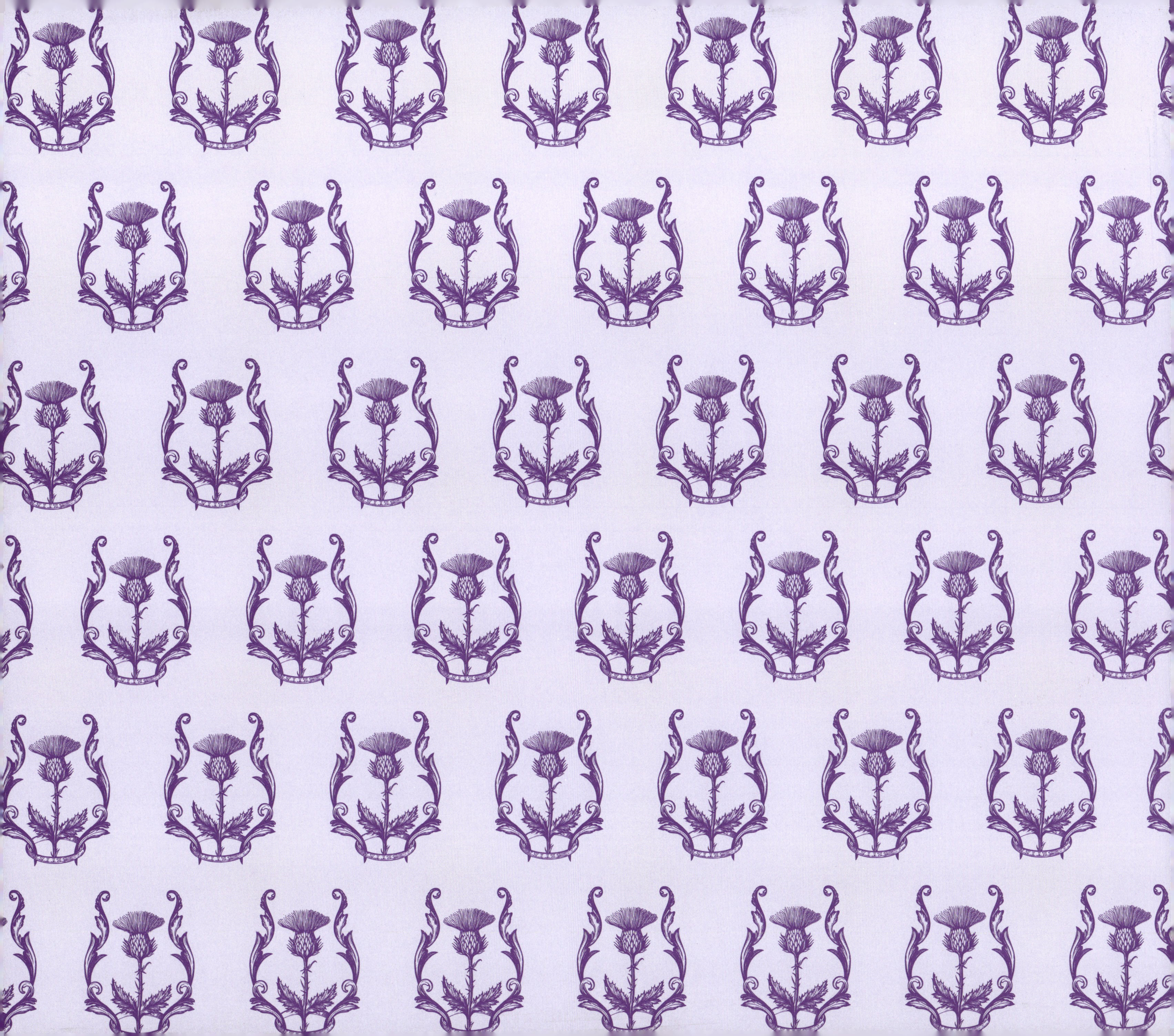

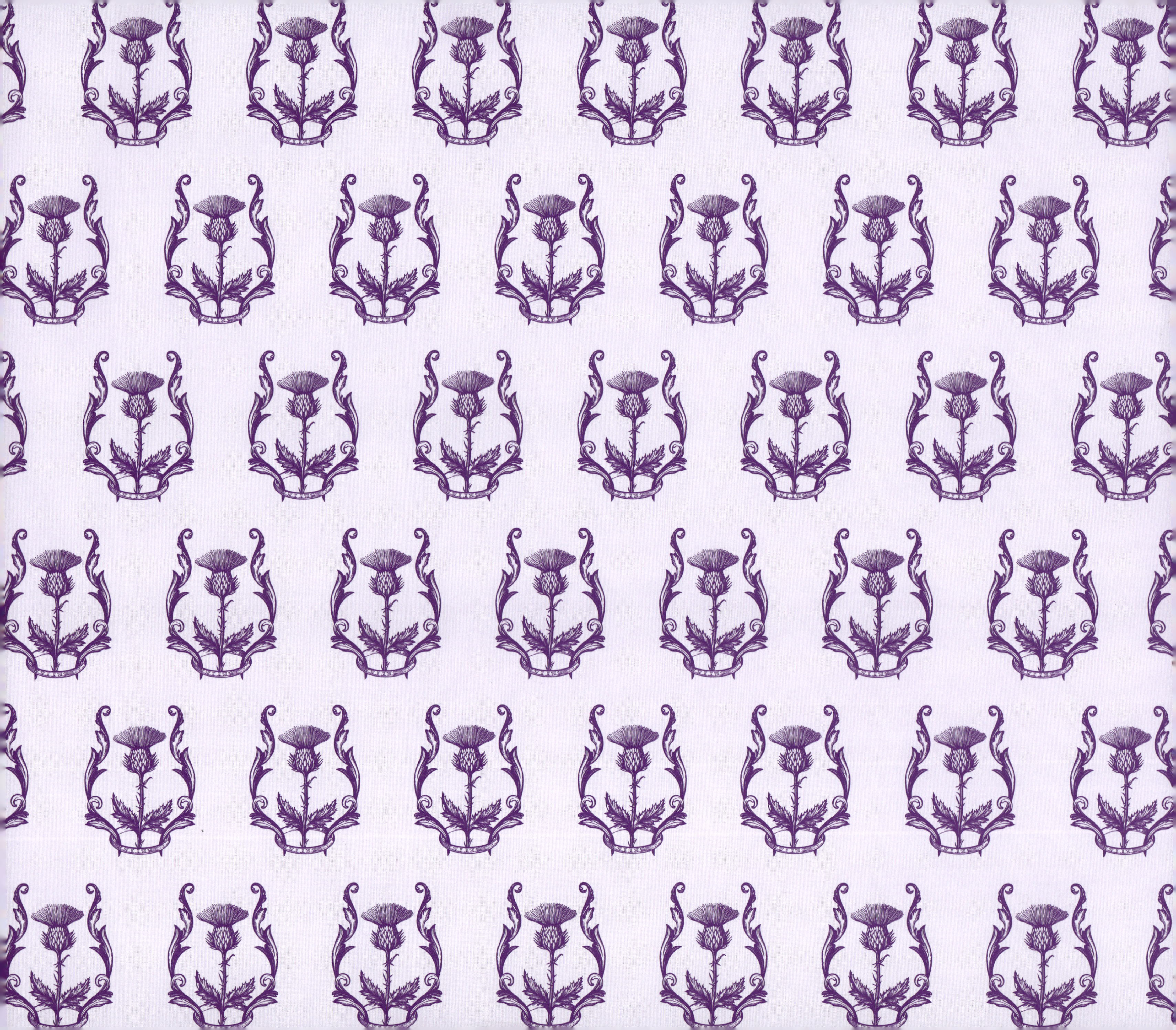